D0161856

AMERICAN EXPERIENCE

Poverty
in America

AMERICAN EXPERIENCE

Poverty in America

Catherine Reef

Facts On File

An imprint of Infobase Publishing

Images on pages 172, 193, 224, 227, and 234 are reproduced with the permission of
Milton Rogovin. For more information on Milton Rogovin, see www.miltonrogovin.com.

Poverty in America

Copyright © 2007 by Catherine Reef
Maps and graphs copyright © 2007 by Infobase Publishing

All rights reserved. No part of this book may be reproduced or utilized in any form
or by any means, electronic or mechanical, including photocopying, recording, or by any
information storage or retrieval systems, without permission in writing from the publisher.
For information contact:

Facts On File, Inc.
An imprint of Infobase Publishing
132 West 31st Street
New York NY 10001

ISBN-10: 0-8160-6062-2
ISBN-13: 978-0-8160-6062-7

Library of Congress Cataloging-in-Publication Data
Reef, Catherine.
Poverty in America / Catherine Reef.
p. cm.—(American experience)
Includes bibliographical references and index.
ISBN 0-8160-6062-2 (alk. paper) 1. Poor—Services for—United States—Case studies.
2. Volunteer workers in social service—United States—Case studies. 3. Public welfare—United
States—History. 4. Social service—United States—History. I. Title. II. American experience
(Facts on File, Inc.)
HV4045.R44 2006
362.50973—dc22   2006006896

Facts On File books are available at special discounts when purchased in bulk quantities for
businesses, associations, institutions, or sales promotions. Please call our Special Sales Department
in New York at (212) 967-8800 or (800) 322-8755.

You can find Facts On File on the World Wide Web at http://www.factsonfile.com

Text design by Joan M. McEvoy
Cover design by Dorothy Preston
Maps and graphs by Dale Williams

Printed in the United States of America

VB FOF 10 9 8 7 6 5 4 3 2 1

This book is printed on acid-free paper.

Note on Photos

Many of the illustrations and photographs used in this book are old, historical images. The quality of the prints is not always up to current standards, as in some cases the originals are from old or poor-quality negatives or are damaged. The content of the illustrations, however, made their inclusion important despite problems in reproduction.

To live miserable we know not why, to have the dread of hunger, to work sore and yet gain nothing,—this is the essence of poverty.

—*Robert Hunter,* Poverty, *1904*

Contents

Introduction

In 1888 a Massachusetts writer named Edward Bellamy published a phenomenally popular book entitled *Looking Backward: 2000–1887*. In this utopian novel, a 30-year-old American named Julian West falls asleep in 1887 and inexplicably wakes up in the United States of 2000. There, he discovers, class divisions have been done away with, workers in all occupations earn the same salary, and poverty no longer exists. "Every man, however solitary may seem his occupation, is a member of a vast industrial partnership, as large as the nation, as large as humanity," explains West's guide to life at the close of the 20th century, the chauvinistic Dr. Leete.[1] Criticizing 19th-century society, Leete says, "The necessity of mutual dependence should imply the duty and guarantee of mutual support; and that it did not in your day constituted the essential cruelty and unreason of your system."[2]

This image shows poverty in America at the start of the 20th century: a New York City tenement dweller and her possessions, ca. 1905–1910. *(Library of Congress, Prints and Photographs Division, LC-USZ62-12989)*

To Leete, the 19th-century belief that some people were more deserving than others of support amounts to robbery, and charity is an insult. He fails to comprehend how the workers of West's time "could have had any heart for their work, knowing that their children, or grand-children, if unfortunate, would be deprived of the comforts, and even necessities of life." He confesses, "How men dared leave children behind them, I have never been able to understand."[3]

The year 2000 has come and gone, but Bellamy's enlightened society has yet to evolve. The United States remains a nation where some people possess great wealth and some own very little.

If poverty, as it has existed throughout history and endures in all parts of the world, can be defined as absolute or relative, then most of the poverty in the United States today is relative. People living in absolute poverty lack the fundamental resources necessary to sustain life for an extended period, such as a diet providing sufficient calories and nutrients, shelter from the elements, protective clothing, and safe drinking water. Universally, people living at this level of deprivation are recognized as poor. Relative poverty, in contrast, is measured against the standard of living prevalent in a society, which changes over time. As a country's standard of living rises, so does the public's perception of what is required for minimal subsistence. In the United States of the 1960s, telephones, televisions, and automobiles were considered luxuries that were beyond the means of most of the poor. It outraged middle-class Americans of that decade to hear of a telephone or TV set in a welfare recipient's home. Yet today most Americans view those items as necessities that are appropriate to the affluent and poor alike, and people in the United States can even be considered poor while living in homes with air-conditioning and microwave ovens.

This does not mean that relative poverty is benign. Charles Lebeaux of the Wayne State University School of Social Work remarked in 1963 that "in our world lack of buying power, even when it is not so absolute as to lead to starvation or death, leads to a very real social starvation and social death."[4] Lebeaux's observation remains true in 21st-century America, because to participate fully in society—to attend school or church, to join organizations like the Girl Scouts or Boy Scouts, to benefit from computer technology—costs money. "Poverty settles like an impenetrable prison cell over the lives of the very poor, shutting them off from every social contact, killing the spirit, and isolating them from the community of human life," Lebeaux wrote.[5]

People lived in absolute poverty in the United States as late as the mid-20th century, and perhaps a small number do today. Certainly the Great Depression of the 1930s transformed many lives into a struggle for existence. American Indians on some rural reservations in the 1940s lived in poverty that could be called absolute, as did undocumented Mexicans inhabiting holes burrowed into farms in the Southwest in the 1950s and African Americans in the Mississippi Delta who regularly endured gnawing hunger in the 1960s.

Poverty persists in absolute or relative form, as do questions about how best to offer assistance. For this reason the history of poverty in America is an account, not just of the poor themselves and the conditions under which they have lived, but also of how government and private citizens have responded to their want. Both sides of the story have significance, as Billy G. Smith, Ph.D., professor of history at Montana State University, has noted, because, "The character of the indigent and the way in which they are treated reveals a great deal about their society."[6]

Lending a Helping Hand

The English colonists in North America were religious people, and the prosperous settlers among them aided those who met with misfortune, in a spirit of Christian charity. No one minded giving alms to a widowed neighbor or taking in an orphan as long as settlements remained small and people understood one another's circumstances. With the continuing arrival of immigrants and the growth of towns, however, colonists became less benevolent. Calvinism taught them that industry pleased God and indolence left the mind open to vice, so they distinguished between the idle and the deserving poor—those who brought pauperism upon themselves and those who were impoverished by circumstances beyond their control, perhaps illness, old age, or the death of a provider.

Beginning in 1642, the colonies enacted legislation based on an English law, the Elizabethan Poor Law of 1601. The colonial laws created a system of taxation and distribution of "outdoor relief," or aid given to the deserving poor in their homes, which might take the form of money, food, clothing, firewood, or services. Additionally, settlement laws were put in place to discourage the transient poor from claiming a right to aid as residents of a city or colony. Most recipients of outdoor aid were women who had been widowed or abandoned by their husbands while they still had children to raise. These women clearly deserved assistance because it was almost impossible for them to find employment that would support their families. The rest of the able-bodied poor were expected to work, but as available farmland and town properties grew harder to find or afford, it became increasingly difficult for them to take their place as self-supporting members of society.

Prosperity proved especially elusive for the men and women who immigrated to North America as indentured servants. Most of these individuals, who contracted to labor for a colonial master for three to five years in exchange for their passage, were fleeing poverty in Europe. They reached North America without assets, accumulated nothing during their period of indenture, and thus began life as free Americans without capital and possibly without a trade. An estimated 500,000 people entered indentured servitude in the British colonies voluntarily, and one-tenth that number served sentences as colonial indentured servants for crimes committed in Great Britain.

The colonists' values and goals conflicted with those of the Native population. To the Pequot and Narragansett of New England, and to Native people throughout North America, private ownership of resources and commodities, including land and food, was an alien concept. Indians depended on communal ownership of land and the sharing of resources to promote the survival of the group. As a rising European population desired land for settlement, the colonists engaged in conflicts aimed at uprooting or wiping out the Native peoples. These largely successful wars claimed casualties among the colonists as well and left many people in need.

Among the European settlers, churches and charities took up collections for the poor and eased society's burden. They were an invaluable source of help at times when the weight was heaviest—during a severe winter or after a fire that left many people homeless, such as the 1760 blaze that consumed nearly 350 buildings in Boston and plunged 214 families into poverty.

As the poor became more numerous in colonial America, the growing demand for assistance caused many people to question the wisdom of providing outdoor relief. Helping the poor in their homes was costly and possibly unwise: Such benevolence might destroy recipients' incentive to work and thus contribute to the destitution it was intended to curb. A money-saving measure that began to gain favor was "indoor," or institutional, aid provided in a poorhouse, or almshouse. There the indigent were sheltered and the able-bodied among them required to work in order to help pay for their upkeep. Mandatory work was also intended to achieve two seemingly contradictory objectives, to instill the habit of industriousness and to punish.

By the second half of the century, almshouses were firmly established in New York City, Philadelphia, and other colonial cities, yet the debate about how best to aid the poor would continue. Should society supply its neediest members with money, provisions, and shelter, or should the poor be required to earn their support? More than 200 years later this question remains unresolved.

States Enact Poor Laws

After winning its independence from Great Britain, the United States was a federation of states that retained many rights, including the right to look after their own poor. Individual states and territories enacted poor laws that resembled those of the colonial era.

Ratification of the U.S. Constitution in 1788 preceded by just two years the start of the Industrial Revolution in the United States. After an English immigrant named Samuel Slater built the first American textile mill in Pawtucket, Rhode Island, mills and factories sprang up in eastern cities and riverside New England

A Christian woman and her children, some of the "deserving poor," endure homelessness and starvation in a prosperous U.S. city in this illustration from 1856. *(Library of Congress, General Collection)*

towns and drew workers from outlying farms. European immigrants were arriving at the same time, and the newcomers—native and foreign-born alike—worked for low wages and lived under the threat of layoffs during slack times. They crowded into working-class neighborhoods that quickly deteriorated into slums. The contrast between fashionable residential streets and the teeming slums just blocks away was too startling to ignore. Neighborhoods such as New York City's Five Points, which was reputedly overrun with criminals and prostitutes and constantly erupting in drunken brawls, held a lurid fascination for a nation that was being forced to recognize poverty as a problem. Urban slums nurtured cholera, typhus, and other diseases that spread to the larger community, often reaching epidemic status. Far too many children born into urban poverty died of intestinal maladies, contagious diseases, or trauma in the first year of life.

Life became even grimmer for slum dwellers during the periods of economic downturn known as panics. The first of these, the Panic of 1819, put an estimated 500,000 people out of work. As hunger and homelessness reached emergency proportions, charities, churches, and private citizens coped by dishing out soup and taking up collections. Still, few people acknowledged that economic forces contributed to most of the poverty they witnessed.

Seeking to understand the size and scope of the problem, several states surveyed poverty and relief in the early 19th century. The 1824 survey conducted in New York State found nearly 7,000 people who were permanently poor and more than twice as many who moved in and out of poverty, often because they did seasonal work. State residents were paying close to $500,000 a year to support their poor and remove transients from their communities, yet the poor were not learning to live independently. The author of the New York report, Secretary of State J. V. N. Yates, recommended a statewide system of county poorhouses to cut costs and instill habits such as diligence and thrift that would lead inmates out of poverty. New York rapidly implemented Yates's plan, and by 1835 there were poorhouses in all but four counties in the state. Massachusetts, Maryland, and other states also built networks of county poorhouses.

Some people entered institutions for the poor of their own free will, but most went by court order. The destitute regarded the poorhouse as a refuge of last resort. Upon entering, inmates surrendered their possessions, their privacy, and their freedom, and once inside they followed a strict routine, eating, sleeping, and working at designated times. Inmates were employed at manufacturing, farming, road repair, or household chores, but if productive work was not to be had, they were giving busywork, such as stacking wood, because it was believed any task was better than idleness.

Efforts to cut costs led to crowding in institutions, famous for their filth and odors, that became warehouses for the old, the sick, prostitutes, alcoholics, and petty criminals. Children in this environment were exposed to the vices thought to contribute to poverty and kept in contact with their parents, whom society considered incompetent and irresponsible. An alternative solution in many places was the orphan asylum, an institution that housed the children dependent on society for care until they could be apprenticed. Some orphanages were public institutions, but many were founded and operated by charitable or religious groups.

Orphanages were far from a perfect solution to the problem of caring for poor and dependent children. They met basic material needs (shelter, food, and clothing) and offered some schooling and religious training, but they neglected children's emotional and psychological well-being—or so critics insisted. It was pointed out that children raised in the regimentation of the asylum never learned to think for themselves and that the matron and staff of a crowded orphanage lacked the time and energy to give each child the love and attention he or she required. The critics insisted that children thrived best in a home with a family, and if not with their flesh-and-blood family, then with some other. The fact that orphanages could only house a fraction of the children needing care was another concern. Many children still languished in poorhouses or fended for themselves on crowded city streets, where they were exposed to any number of harmful influences.

"The very *condensing* of their number within a small space, seems to stimulate their bad tendencies," said the Reverend Charles Loring Brace, first chief officer of the Children's Aid Society of New York City.[7] In 1854 Brace's organization began "placing out" the city's street youth on farms, principally in the Midwest. The trains that carried the children west stopped in rural towns where farm families chose a boy to do chores or a girl to help in the kitchen, but whether a child went to a loving home or an abusive situation was determined literally by the luck of the draw. In 1884 Brace and his associates claimed to have resettled more than 60,000 children, most of them successfully, but this assertion is impossible to verify because of sloppy record keeping and scanty follow-up by the Children's Aid Society. Organizations in Boston, Baltimore, and other cities also placed poor city children with rural families.

Henry Robinson, a former slave, was photographed in 1938 or 1939 by an employee of the Federal Writers' Project. *(Library of Congress, Prints and Photographs Division, LC-USZ62-125158)*

An Enforced Poverty in the South

In July 1863 the tightly condensed poor population of New York City rioted in response to the Conscription Act, a federal law that instituted a military draft. The act permitted conscripted recruits to pay $300 in lieu of service, thus placing the responsibility for winning the Civil War unfairly on the poor, who could never afford such a sum. Also fueling resentment was President Abraham Lincoln's Emancipation Proclamation, which on January 1, 1863, granted freedom—on paper—to the largest group of North Americans living in poverty, the enslaved African Americans in Confederate-held territory. By fighting to win the war, poor Northerners would be liberating people who might migrate to their cities and compete with them for jobs.

When the Civil War began, in April 1861, 4 million enslaved African Americans lived and toiled in the South. Because they survived on too little food, wore inadequate clothing, and lived in substandard shelter, slaves endured enforced poverty. Not only were they compelled to labor without reward, but they were also denied rights that other Americans took for granted, including the right to marry legally and raise their children to adulthood, to worship as they chose, to seek an education, or to have their grievances heard in court. The great majority lived and worked on large plantations, raising cotton, tobacco, sugar, and other crops. They labored for their masters from sunrise to sunset, then cooked their own food, tended their own children, sewed, and washed in the last few hours before sleep.

As businessmen concerned with profits, plantation owners kept expenses as low as possible when feeding and caring for their slaves, with the result that the lives of slaves were no more comfortable than those of the poor whites who inhabited the surrounding countryside. Slaveholders issued weekly rations that were deficient in calories and nutrients, consisting of cornmeal, salt pork, and little else. Many men and women rounded out their family's diet by raising vegetables and chickens, fishing, hunting, and stealing, but commonly enslaved African Americans showed signs of rickets and other deficiency diseases. Home for most of the slaves was a drafty, minimally furnished one-room cabin, where they cooked over an open hearth and slept on a straw mattress or pile of rags. Clothing, as was food, was rationed; made from cheap, rough cloth, slaves' garments irritated the skin and frequently wore out before new ones were issued.

Along with deprivation, many slaves endured whipping, shackling, and other forms of cruel and merciless punishment at the hands of their master and his paid overseer. The fact that slaves could be sold at any time made it an all-too-real possibility that parents and children or husbands and wives could be separated permanently and without warning. Therefore, it is no surprise to learn that slaves rebelled, in ways formidable and small. Uprisings such as the Stono Rebellion of 1739, which left more than 60 people, black and white, dead in North Carolina, or the armed rebellion led by two Virginia slaves, Gabriel Prosser and Jack Bowler, in 1800, spread fear among white Southerners, but they failed as efforts to liberate the enslaved. Escapes carried out by slaves alone or in small groups proved to be a more effective way of delivering people to freedom, although after the Civil War began and Union forces moved into the South, African Americans abandoned the plantations and appealed to the army for care and protection.

Peacetime Challenges

Union victory in the Civil War, occurring in April 1865, presented the United States with a massive social problem: how to help millions of former slaves adjust to life as free Americans. The Freedmen's Bureau, a federal agency formed for this purpose, operated schools in the South for African Americans, tried to find them work and places to live, and distributed food and supplies. Blacks and whites alike were hungry in the war-torn South, so the bureau issued about one-third of its rations to whites.

The Freedmen's Bureau and black Americans faced a formidable obstacle in the majority of southern whites, who were determined to keep the former slaves in an impoverished, second-class status through means legal and illegal. Within months of the war's end, Mississippi became the first southern state to enact a Black Code, which was a set of laws limiting the rights and activities of African Americans. Restricted mobility and harsh consequences for vagrancy kept many former slaves working on plantations for poverty wages. Some white southerners, unwilling to rely on laws alone, formed hate groups such as the Ku Klux Klan, which targeted blacks, immigrants, Jews, and Catholics. These organizations sought to keep African Americans at the bottom level of society through intimidation.

Many poor southerners, black and white, were tenant farmers. If they rented the land that they worked with a fraction of the harvest, they were known as sharecroppers. The sharecropping system was designed to enrich landlords and keep tenants impoverished, so as industry moved into the agricultural South, factories attracted poor farmers to cities such as Birmingham, Alabama.

By 1880 farmers earning a meager living from the rocky, depleted soil of the Appalachian Mountains commonly supplemented their income through seasonal work in the timber and mining industries. Bypassed by many passenger and freight lines and put at a disadvantage by bad roads, the people of Appalachia would be increasingly isolated as the nation moved into the 20th century. Before 1930 most Appalachian miners lacked union representation and were, therefore, at the mercy of mining

Freedmen's Bureau agents distribute rations to hungry people in the defeated South, regardless of race. (*Library of Congress, General Collection*)

Male residents sit outside the carpenter's shop, Onondaga County, New York, poorhouse, ca. 1900. *(Photo courtesy of the Town of Onondaga Historical Society)*

companies that paid low wages and took back a substantial fraction of employees' earnings for rent, fuel, and other living expenses associated with company-owned housing. Isolation bred ignorance of preventive health measures, with the result that hookworm, trachoma, and other maladies were common throughout the region.

Scattered over the countryside, the rural poor were unseen by much of the population as they toiled and went without material comforts. More visible—and therefore more alarming—were the urban poor, whose numbers were growing every day as immigrants arrived unskilled and without resources. The white, Protestant, native-born majority mistrusted these new arrivals, who after 1880 tended to be from southern and eastern Europe and to be Catholic or Jewish. These immigrants spoke little or no English, and there was worry that their foreign ways might alter American culture for the worse.

Reexamining Charity

Local governments continued to move away from outdoor aid and toward institutionalization as the preferred way to care for the dependent population: the poor, drifters, problem drinkers, and the insane. Beginning in 1875, concern that children still resided in poorhouses led to state laws barring their placement in institutions for the adult poor. As a result of the laws some youngsters were indentured or moved to orphanages, but laws were poorly enforced, and children remained part of the poorhouse population.

Private charities met people's immediate needs for money, food, clothing, and other supplies, but after 1869 almsgiving came under attack by the charity organization movement, which taught that alms given freely and carelessly encouraged dependency, increased poverty, and hindered social progress. Charity organization societies attempted to impose order as they investigated applicants for aid, assessed their needs, and referred the worthy poor to the most suitable agencies. Their volunteers also called on the poor in their homes to encourage self-reliance. The first such group in the United States, the Charity Organization Society of Buffalo, New York, was founded in 1877 by an Episcopal minister, the Reverend Stephen Humphreys Gurteen.

The settlement-house movement arose roughly at the same time. Settlement houses served as community centers that helped poor, urban, largely immigrant neighborhoods from within. Settlement-house workers lived among the people; they assisted and encouraged local residents to participate more fully in American life. Settlement houses offered a range of services, from English classes to job training, from child care to clinics. The first settlement house in the United States, the Neighborhood Guild, was founded in New York City in 1886.

Some settlement houses, such as the Lincoln Settlement in Brooklyn, New York, and the Frederick Douglass Center in Chicago, were established in the early 20th century to aid African Americans who had moved north. The number of African Americans leaving the South remained relatively small until 1890, when an infestation of boll weevils devastated the cotton crop and took away people's livelihood. In northern cities, blacks competing for employment against native-born and immigrant whites faced enormous prejudice, and although they had moved beyond the reach of Black Codes, they were usually forced to take dead-end jobs at low wages and to pay high rents for substandard housing in predominantly black neighborhoods.

The northward movement of African Americans intensified in 1916, when World War I temporarily halted European immigration—an important source of cheap factory labor—as it placed a demand for military vehicles and weaponry on U.S. manufacturers. This population shift, known as the Great Migration, would send an estimated 1 million people to the North from the early 20th century through 1940. The changing demographics spawned riots in East St. Louis, Illinois, and other cities where white residents reacted to their new black neighbors with fear and violence. Rioting intensified throughout the United States in the summer of 1919, when soldiers returning from the war reacted against perceived competition for jobs and housing from African Americans. In July 1919 four days of attacks on black citizens by white veterans in Washington, D.C., left 30 known dead; in the same month 13 days of rioting in Chicago left 38 dead and 537 injured.

American Indians also faced obstacles to economic and social equality. Indians received a mixed message from white America: They were encouraged to assimilate, to adopt the language, faith, and way of life of the dominant culture, but at the same time they were made to understand that their ethnicity would forever set them apart.

By 1890 the Indians had been defeated and forced onto reservations, and the government was finding ways to decrease their holdings. One federal law, the General Allotment Act of 1887, divided many reservations into individual allotments that Indians were to cultivate in the manner of U.S. farmers. The act also empowered the government to sell "surplus" reservation land to white settlers, with the result that by 1900 Indians' holdings had declined by nearly 50 percent from what they were in 1881, decreasing from more than 155 million acres to about 78 million. Much of the allotted land was dry, rocky, and infertile, and most of the Indians who farmed it lacked the capital and training necessary for success.

In the early 20th century Indians also provided labor for railroad and other construction projects, but they worked for meager wages that kept their families in want. A survey published in 1928 by the Institute for Government Research cast light on the depth and breadth of poverty on reservations. Tuberculosis and other

American Indians line up to receive government rations at Blackfeet Agency, Montana, ca. 1926. *(Denver Public Library. Western History Collection, X-31107)*

contagious diseases were rampant, and more than one-fourth of babies born on reservations died in the first year of life. As the formal title of the report, *The Problem of Indian Administration,* implied, the researchers blamed federal Indian policy for much of the poverty they observed. Their conclusions led to the appointment in 1933 of an innovative commissioner of Indian affairs, John Collier, who persuaded Congress to end the allotment system, which had cost the Indians so much reservation land and ran counter to the Indian tradition of holding land communally, and to permit the establishment of tribal governments with passage of the Indian Reorganization Act of 1934. Another federal law passed in 1934, the Johnson-O'Malley Act, funded schools and medical and social services at the state level for Indians living off reservations.

At this time unemployment and hardship were being experienced nationwide as a result of the Great Depression. The causes of the depression, the most severe period of economic decline in U.S. history, included reduced consumer demand for manufactured goods and unregulated speculation in the stock market, and they had been building for some time. The stock-market crash of October 1929, however, occurring during the presidency of Herbert Hoover, was the dramatic event that marked the start of the crisis in the minds of many. Banks and businesses closed in the wake of the crash, and thousands of people lost their savings and their livelihood and experienced poverty for the first time.

As unemployment reached 4.5 million in 1930 and 8 million in 1931, and homes and farms succumbed to foreclosure, churches and private charities stretched their resources to cope. Meanwhile, Hoover counseled the nation to have faith in the economy and its ability to correct itself soon. Hoover, a Republican, was philosophically opposed to federal intervention in matters he considered properly left to the states and citizens, but in January 1932 he established the Reconstruction Finance Corporation, a government agency that made loans to banks and businesses in an effort to jump-start the economy. The public perceived this move as evidence that Hoover favored the interests of corporate America over those of ordinary people, however.

War veterans expressed their dissatisfaction with government inaction in June 1932 by gathering in Washington, D.C., to demand passage of a bill that would have given them immediate payment of a cash bonus they were scheduled to receive in 1945. After the bill's defeat on June 15, the so-called Bonus Army conducted a three-day "Death March" on Pennsylvania Avenue. Many veterans lingered in Washington into July, when Hoover ordered the military to evict them.

The Bonus Army protests on the U.S. Capitol grounds, July 13, 1932. *(Library of Congress, Prints and Photographs Division, LC-USZ6-525)*

Voters registered their disapproval the following November by rejecting Hoover's bid for reelection and choosing Franklin D. Roosevelt as their president. The Democrat Roosevelt saw his victory as an endorsement of active leadership in this crisis. After his inauguration in March 1933, he signed the Emergency Banking Act to boost the money supply, and the laws constituting the New Deal followed in quick succession. These included legislation that put people to work by creating programs such as the Civilian Conservation Corps (CCC), which gave jobs to young men from families on relief, and the Works Progress Administration (later Work Projects Administration [WPA]), which employed millions on a broad range of projects to benefit the public, from building bridges and hospitals to painting murals in post offices. The Federal Emergency Relief Administration (FERA), established in 1933, helped states meet the demand for public assistance; the Agricultural Adjustment Act, also passed in 1933, attempted to boost the prices paid for farm products by restricting production; and the Social Security Act of 1935 funded retirement pensions and aided groups traditionally considered worthy: the aged, the disabled, and dependent women and children. The New Deal improved morale and put money into millions of pockets, but it was a temporary fix, at best. In 1938 between 10 million and 11 million Americans were still unemployed.

Compounding the hardship was a severe drought that afflicted a large portion of the Southwest in the 1930s. In Oklahoma, Arkansas, New Mexico, Colorado, and neighboring states, dry topsoil lay exposed to winds that lifted it high above the Earth, carried it for hundreds of miles, and then let it fall to the ground in choking dust storms. No crop could grow, and no livestock could thrive. Thousands of families gave up trying to make a living from the farms of the dust bowl and tried their luck in other regions, including the agricultural valleys of California. Yet living conditions in California proved worse for most of the uprooted people of the

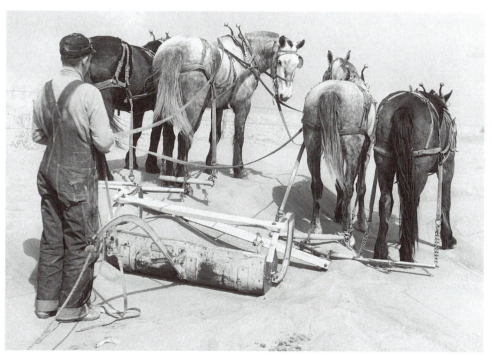

A farmer and his team clear drifts of dusty soil from a highway near Guymon, Oklahoma, March 1926. *(Library of Congress, Prints and Photographs Division, LC-USF34-2490D)*

Southwest than those they left behind. Families camped beside roads, unwanted. They slept under cardboard or tree branches or crawled into railroad boxcars for shelter, and they faced hunger and even starvation.

Prosperity—But Not for All

The federal government opened camps to shelter migrant laborers and through them helped thousands of families weather the rough years of the depression, but these were a stopgap that failed to produce economic stability for the wandering poor of the 1930s. It was the need to equip the United States and its allies to fight World War II that finally began factory wheels turning and put people to work. Military conscription also reduced the ranks of the unemployed.

The nation's attention shifted from troubles at home to events occurring overseas, and people pushed images of breadlines and ragged children to the backs of their minds. As historian J. Wayne Flynt has noted, "When times are generally good, the poor become less visible and more easily dismissed."[8] Yet although poverty might have been harder to spot, it still existed. As did earlier wars, World War II created hardship for some families by removing a breadwinner. Also, as in the past, some disabled veterans had trouble finding a place in the workforce.

In the rural Southwest, thousands of Mexican-American and Mexican agricultural workers labored for very low wages and lived in extreme want. Many were undocumented workers living in the United States illegally. In 1942 the United States and Mexico instituted the Labor Importation Program, known popularly as the bracero program, to import temporary Mexican laborers legally and afford them such protections as a minimum wage and guaranteed term of work. After the war, in the 1950s, about 300,000 Mexicans were employed each year on U.S. farms through this program. A large number remained in the United States illegally after their contracted term of work expired and became part of the impoverished undocumented population.

In 1954 the U.S. government launched an effort known as Operation Wetback to track down Mexicans living in the United States illegally and return them to Mexico. This initiative resulted in the forced or voluntary removal of hundreds of thousands of people from the United States, predominantly from the Southwest and California, but some who were repatriated lived as far north as Chicago. Nevertheless, Mexicans continued to sneak across the border to seek work in the United States despite the ill will generated by Operation Wetback.

Appalachia remained one of the poorest regions in the United States in the 1950s. At a time when positions were opening in a variety of industries throughout the nation, Appalachia was losing jobs in its two principal industries, agriculture and mining. Appalachia had an average per capita income in 1959 that was 25 percent lower than that of the rest of the nation, and its population was less educated and more likely to be unemployed. Living conditions had improved for many residents since the 1930s, but nearly 40 percent of housing in Appalachia was substandard in 1960.

Poverty still plagued Native Americans during and after World War II. Indian farmers continued to lack the resources and knowledge necessary to compete successfully with white farmers, with the result that in 1949 the average Indian farmer earned $500 from agriculture, and the average white farmer earned five times that amount. In the postwar years the government rejected the goals of the Indian Reorganization

Act of 1934, and in 1953 Congress began terminating Indians' status as wards of the government and reducing federal responsibility for the Native population.

The government was not completely uninterested in the poor. At the start of the 1950s a congressional subcommittee surveyed low-income Americans and determined that one-fourth of low-income nonfarm households were headed by persons age 65 or older. Also overrepresented in the low-income population were unskilled workers, a group that was vulnerable in a time of rapidly changing technology; minorities; members of female-headed households; and adults with low educational attainment.

In 1955 economists working for the Social Security Administration determined that poor Americans spent one-third of their income on food. For the purpose of measuring the poor population the government established a poverty line determined by tripling the cost of a nutritionally adequate diet and adjusted it annually for inflation. Any family or individual with an income at or below this line was considered poor. The poverty line was—and is—an arbitrary and probably inadequate measure. "Poverty is a discrepancy between needs and resources—or between needed and actual consumption," observed economist Robert J. Lampman in 1966, "and it remains at bottom a matter for judgment as to where to set the line separating the poor from the nonpoor."[9]

Reawakening to Need

In 1962 the writer Michael Harrington published *The Other America*, a book that was to have an enormous impact. As spreading slums had a century earlier, Harrington's book confronted the nation with the reality of poverty. In it Harrington described

The Congress of Racial Equality (CORE) protests conditions in slum housing in New York City, 1964. *(Library of Congress, Prints and Photographs Division, LC-USZ62-115077)*

life in America as experienced by the marginalized people of inner-city ghettos and depressed rural pockets and identified the groups overrepresented among the poor: the very old and the very young; African Americans, Native Americans, and Hispanics; and the unemployed and underemployed.

Harrington called on his country to take action, and the federal government responded. In 1964 President Lyndon B. Johnson launched the "War on Poverty," an ambitious legislative attack on poverty in this wealthy nation. Johnson's key weapon was the Economic Opportunity Act of 1964. Among the programs established under this act were Job Corps, which offered training and work experience to high school dropouts, and Operation Head Start, which prepared preschoolers for kindergarten. The Economic Opportunity Act empowered the poor at the community level through day care centers, clinics, loans, and Volunteers in Service to America (VISTA), a program that assigned unpaid workers from other parts of the country to depressed areas. Other federal laws enacted during Johnson's presidency that were intended to benefit low-income Americans included the Food Stamp Act of 1964, which enabled qualifying families to buy food at reduced cost, and the Higher Education Act of 1965, which funded college loans and adult education. In 1965 Congress also created Medicare and Medicaid, health insurance programs for the aged and the poor.

The renewed interest in poverty inspired a great amount of social research, both public and private. The newly created National Advisory Commission on Rural Poverty reported in 1967 that the rural poor were increasingly isolated from mainstream American life. Some had incomes so low that their children were chronically hungry. Rural poverty fueled urban poverty, the commission concluded, because many of the rural poor migrated to cities in search of opportunity. The commissioners defined poverty as something deeper than inadequate income. Poverty, they wrote, "is a lack of access to respected positions in society, and lack of power to do anything about it. It is insecurity and unstable homes. It is a wretched existence that tends to perpetuate itself from one generation to the next."[10]

Oscar Lewis, an anthropologist who advised the government during the War on Poverty, defined a "culture of poverty" based on his research in the United States and other countries. According to Lewis, this culture arose in places that were geographically distant from one another if certain conditions were present. The culture of poverty flourished in New York City; Mexico City; San Juan, Puerto Rico; and other places, but always in capitalist societies that had a high population of unemployed, unskilled laborers without access to social, economic, or political resources. Members of this culture had little education and lived in crowded slums.

In 1965 the Department of Labor, under Secretary of Labor Daniel P. Moynihan, published a controversial report on the social and economic status of African Americans, titled *The Negro Family*. This document claimed that slavery had left African Americans with weak family ties and was ultimately to blame for the fact that one-fourth of African-American families were headed by women. The apparent breakdown in the two-parent family structure in turn had led to low educational attainment, unemployment, and poverty.

Two years later Senator Robert F. Kennedy made headlines when he toured the Mississippi Delta, a region of deep poverty, and interviewed chronically hungry adults and children in front of news cameras. Also in 1967 a group of physicians conducting a more thorough investigation of poverty and hunger in Mississippi for the Southern Regional Council encountered people so removed from any social services, community resources, or source of income that they might as well have been living in a third world country.

The Reverend Martin Luther King, Jr., was concerning himself with poverty in the final months of his life. King was assassinated on April 4, 1968. In May, his successor as head of the Southern Christian Leadership Conference, the Reverend Ralph Abernathy, led a Poor People's Campaign in Washington, D.C. Abernathy took poor Americans of all races and ethnicities to the nation's capital to live in a model settlement called Resurrection City. The campaign culminated in a day of speeches at the Lincoln Memorial, on June 19. Abernathy promised on that day to stay in Washington and fight nonviolently until the nation demanded assurance that the needs of the poor would be met, but police shut down Resurrection City on the morning of June 24, and the poor left Washington, having achieved very little.

In 1968, with 7.5 million people receiving public assistance, many Americans had become disenchanted with the War on Poverty and government programs to aid the poor. The federal government and individual states enacted restrictive or punitive measures to curb the number of single women and minors supported by Aid to Families with Dependent Children (AFDC), a welfare program funded through the Social Security Administration and administered at the state level. In 1967 the federal government began requiring some adult welfare recipients to seek employment or enter job training through the Work Incentive Program. Measures such as these matched the political philosophy of Richard M. Nixon, who was elected president in 1968, and Ronald Reagan, who was elected in 1980.

Nixon dismantled a number of social programs established during the Johnson administration, but Reagan, who entered office in a period of high unemployment and double-digit inflation, went further. Believing that government support had helped create an "underclass" of poor Americans alienated from the rest of society, and favoring minimal government interference in people's lives, Reagan signed the Omnibus Budget Reconciliation Act of 1981, which redirected government spending away from social programs and toward defense. He was confident that if corporate American prospered, so would people at every economic level.

Reagan's approach put unemployment and inflation under control, but it failed to address poverty. Between 1980 and 1988 the unemployment rate dropped from 7 percent to 5.4 percent, and the inflation rate declined from 10.4 percent to 4.2 percent. In 1983, however, the poverty rate was 15.3 percent, and the number of working poor was growing. Without a safety net of social programs, the homeless population became increasingly visible and included families with young children.

Robert J. Lampman explained in 1962 that over time, "the number and composition of the poor population changes as a result of births and deaths, differential growth of groups having different susceptibility to poverty, migration and shifting among groups, and differential change in the incidence of poverty within the several demographic groups."[11] In the 1980s, as manufacturers moved from northern industrial centers to the South and Southwest, unemployed factory workers emerged as a new impoverished group. The population of poor, undocumented immigrants was also growing and serving as a source of cheap labor for agriculture and illegal sweatshops.

Poverty remained disproportionately high among American Indians, although the Termination policy had long been abandoned. In 1981, 60 percent of Indians lived below the official poverty line; 10 years later the rate was virtually unchanged on some reservations, and nearly one-third of Indian households received public assistance. African Americans also experienced poverty at a higher-than-average rate, as the number of poor African Americans living in U.S. cities grew from 5.6 million in 1980 to 10.4 million in 1990. Children as well were overrepresented among the poor; in 1989, 40 percent of the poor in the United States were under 18 years of age, and children of minority groups were especially at risk. Many poor children lived in families headed by women who were single either because they were divorced or because they had never married. A large number of these women depended on public assistance, but others worked at jobs paying wages that kept their families poor. Poverty remained high in rural locations such as central Appalachia, which had a poverty rate approaching 24 percent in 1989 and 1995, and among migrant farm laborers and their families, who still consumed a deficient diet, lived in substandard housing, and suffered high rates of disease at the close of the 20th century.

From Welfare to Workfare

The U.S. government launched the War on Poverty of the 1960s with high hopes that were never realized. Since that time Americans and their leaders have opposed addressing poverty through government "handouts" and social programs that cost taxpayers' money. For the past two decades the trend has been toward finding ways to move people from welfare rolls to the workforce. The work ethic, a legacy of the Calvinist settlers, remains strong in the United States, and most Americans think it is better for people to work than be supported by welfare, even if their earnings fail

This photograph shows Seventh Street, N.W., Washington, D.C., 1988. *(John Reef)*

to lift them out of poverty. Full employment is a worthier goal than elimination of poverty, according to the American value system.

By 1987, 40 states had instituted various types of welfare-to-work, or workfare, programs. In 1988 welfare-to-work became a national policy when Reagan signed the Family Support Act. This federal law made it mandatory for most single parents on welfare to find employment or enroll in school or training at government expense through the Job Opportunities and Basic Skills Training Program (JOBS).

President Bill Clinton went further, transforming welfare from a permanent source of financial support for the indigent to a form of temporary assistance for people down on their luck, with the Personal Responsibility and Work Opportunity Reconciliation Act (PRWORA) of 1996. This law required states to terminate benefits after two years and imposed a lifetime limit of five years of public support for every recipient.

It will be some time before any long-term consequences of PRWORA become evident, but some short-term effects have been observed. In 1999 welfare supported 7.3 million people, or less than 4 percent of the population, which was the lowest level of welfare dependence since the 1970s. The poverty rate in 2000, 11.3 percent, was the lowest it had been since 1979. Most of the people who made the transition from welfare to work were single mothers who found jobs as custodians, cashiers, or food-service workers and earned wages that kept their families in poverty. Also, an estimated 700,000 families removed from the welfare rolls by PRWORA were suffering financially because the head of household could not maintain steady employment as a result of disability, addiction, or logistical obstacles, such as lack of transportation or child care.

Some critics of the program cautioned that an economic recession would create a crisis for thousands of families no longer eligible to collect welfare. Also, children's advocates questioned the value of the program for young people. They asked, even if it was acceptable for adults to remain impoverished while working, was it right and proper for their children to be poor? Poor children were more likely than other youngsters to have health and developmental problems. They grew up in neighborhoods that confronted them with crime, gangs, and drug use. They attended schools that were underfunded and understaffed, and they lived in houses that exposed them to lead paint, faulty wiring, and other hazards.

"[T]he United States stands in ignominious isolation," concluded a 1991 study by the Joint Center for Political and Economic Studies. "Among industrialized countries, the United States has the highest incidence of poverty among the nonelderly and the widest distribution of poverty across all age and family groups. It is also the only western democracy that has failed to give a significant portion of its poor a measure of income security."[12]

Dr. Leete, the fictional enlightened guide to the year 2000, might say that poverty persists in the United States because Americans are applying a material standard to a moral question.

CHAPTER ONE

The Deserving Poor in Colonial America
1601–1775

The Pilgrims who sailed to North America in the 1620s anticipated a lean and hungry life. Not only were they founding tiny settlements along a vast, wooded coastline thousands of miles from their homeland, but also their faith taught them to live simply and plainly, to work hard and shun vice. According to Calvinist teaching, human beings were by nature depraved, and it was the task of every man, woman, and child to seek salvation through prayer, introspection, and self-discipline. As Christians in duty bound to help the less fortunate, people in the first English settlements extended their hands in neighborly assistance to the poor and disabled living among them.

For a time it was enough to take in an old or widowed relation, give food and firewood to a needy neighbor, or bind an orphaned child as an apprentice. As towns grew, though, they acquired a complex social structure, and by the middle of the 17th century, people who had begun to encounter strangers in the street felt the need for a written, formalized policy for aiding the poor.

Colonial Poor Laws

The model for colonial legislation was the Elizabethan Poor Law of 1601, which had established a system in England for public support of the poor through compulsory taxation. In towns throughout England, overseers of the poor were charged with collecting taxes and distributing aid. Similar legislation was enacted in Plymouth Colony in 1642, in Virginia in 1646, in Pennsylvania in 1705, and in the other colonies during this period as well.

Most of the aid provided under these laws was "outdoor relief," or assistance given to the poor in their own homes, which took varied forms. In 1691 New York City granted three shillings sixpence per week to the landlord of a Captain Collier, to cover the cost of the captain's maintenance. In 1727 St. Paul's Parish in Chowan County, North Carolina, reimbursed the Reverend Daniel Earl for meeting the immediate expenses of a woman named Judith Mainer and her two children. Aid often took the form of food, firewood, water, blankets, clothing, or shoes, or even funeral expenses or medical care. New York City, for example, appointed an official doctor of the poor. Alternatively, a simple and popular way to aid the destitute was to board them in the homes of private citizens of sufficient means, usually in households headed by men. The children of the poor might also be indentured, either by their desperate parents or by local magistrates who arranged indentures privately or through public auctions. By contractual arrangement, these children worked in the home or fields of a master until they came of age. The master, in turn, was required to furnish room and board and was expected to be of good character. Overseers of the poor determined who was eligible for relief and the form that relief would take, and they supervised the distribution of money, provisions, and services.

Because Calvinism taught that idleness was a sin, colonists provided aid only to the deserving poor, those whose destitution resulted from age, illness, physical or mental disability, widowhood, abandonment, or other unpreventable circumstances and no fault of their own. Although life expectancy was shorter in the 18th century than it is today, some people survived into their 70s, 80s, or 90s. Many of the "very old," "ancient," and "stricken in years" whose names appeared on colonial relief rolls lived with diminished vision, chronic illness, or other infirmities and were unable to earn their support.[1]

Most recipients of outdoor relief, though, were widowed or abandoned women and their children. Whereas today widowhood almost always occurs late in life, a widow in the colonial period was likely to be in her 30s and have young children to raise. Colonial officials held men and women to different standards when determining eligibility for relief. A healthy man was expected to seek employment, but any woman who was able to find work received only half a man's wages; as a result, the typical widow could not support herself even without the burden of child care.

The able-bodied who, by all appearances, lived immoral lives and chose not to work frequently were indentured, run out of town, whipped, or thrown into jail. "For those who indulge themselves in idleness, the express command of God unto us is, that we should let them starve," said the influential Puritan minister Cotton Mather.[2] Relief was also limited to the white population. Throughout the colonies, enslaved African Americans were by law the property of their masters and therefore denied any rights, including the right to public assistance. Free blacks were not treated equally with whites either, however, and of necessity formed their own support networks. When it is remembered that three-fourths of the people who crossed the Atlantic Ocean to reach the colonies were Africans taken by force, it becomes evident that a large portion of the population lived in want and without access to assistance.

Immigrants Arrived Poor

Settlers continued to be drawn to the New World throughout the colonial period, many fleeing widespread poverty in Europe. Between one-half and two-thirds of Europeans immigrating to the North American colonies—as many as 500,000 people between 1580 and 1775—arrived as indentured servants. So eager were they to escape economic misery that they had agreed in writing to spend three to five years, on average, working off the cost of their passage for an unknown master who would purchase their indenture when the ship reached a colonial port. Indentured servitude was like slavery in that contracts could be sold and servants transferred from benevolent masters to cruel or even sadistic ones. Yet unlike slaves, servants who survived their period of indenture were free.

The hazards of ocean crossings, including rough weather and inadequate provisions, contributed to immigrants' misery and dependency. The records of the Boston selectmen show that on October 31, 1741, the *Seaflower* arrived from Belfast after 16 weeks at sea, carrying 106 passengers who had been bound for Philadelphia. Forty-six people had died on the voyage, and the starving survivors

Poverty was widespread in Europe at the time Britain established colonies in North America. This London beggar and her children were sketched in 1711. *(Library of Congress, Rare Books and Special Collections Division)*

had consumed the bodies of six. Sixty-five immigrants required hospitalization, to be paid for by the ship's owner or the patients' indentured servitude. Four months later, though, the selectmen judged some of these immigrants "proper Objects of Publick Charity."[3]

As the 18th century progressed, it became more and more difficult for freed indentured servants and new immigrants to move up from the lowest economic level of colonial society. Many lacked the necessary capital to acquire land for farming, and city property fell increasingly into the hands of a wealthy minority. It is estimated that a mere tenth of indentured servants went on to become independent farmers and that another tenth set up shop as artisans. The rest, if they did not die before gaining their freedom, worked as common laborers or took to the road, wandering from one town or city to the next in search of food, work, or a change of fortune.

Also, from 1718 through 1775, Britain deported between 45,000 and 50,000 convicts to the American colonies to serve their sentences as indentured laborers. These workers endured longer periods of servitude, typically seven years, with some sentenced to labor for 14 years or even for life. These indentured workers were the most likely to be abused, because masters often considered beatings and other mistreatment part of their punishment.

The Native Population

The Europeans who settled North America encountered an indigenous population with values and beliefs far different from their own. The Native people belonged to distinct tribal nations that had adapted to the geographical regions they inhabited. For example, the Iroquois of the eastern woodland were hunter-gatherers. The Pueblo of the Southwest farmed the soil, and the Plains peoples were nomads who followed the herds of bison. As diverse as they were, the Indians had in common concepts of property ownership and the individual's role in society that were directly opposed to those of Europeans.

Among American Indians it was essential to live in harmony with the environment. The community managed hunting grounds with concern for preserving animal resources. A successful hunter shared his bounty with the community because the welfare of the group was essential to survival and because status was measured not by acquisition but by giving. In farming communities chiefs collected a share of the maize, beans, and squash harvested and distributed it to the needy. They also apportioned goods received in trade with Europeans.

As early as the 1500s contact with Europeans exposed Native Americans to Old World pathogens to which they had no natural immunity. Smallpox, typhus, measles, and other contagious diseases that crossed the Atlantic on European ships swept away large numbers of Indians. One way people coped was through emigration and resettlement. That is, a community that had lost many members abandoned its environs and joined another established settlement. At times Indians welcomed emigrants from other societies and intermarried with the newcomers. After a smallpox outbreak of 1699, the Natchez, who inhabited what is now southwest Mississippi, integrated survivors of the Tioux, Grigra, and other tribal nations. Not only did their generosity help the needy refugees survive, but it also aided the Natchez by increasing their numbers and therefore their ability to defend themselves against enemies.

The English settlers considered themselves culturally superior to the American Indians, so when their attempts to impose Christianity and European customs on the "savages" failed, they began armed conflicts aimed at exterminating the Native people or driving them off their land. In the first of these contests, the Pequot War of the 1630s, English Pilgrims engaged in a series of skirmishes with the Pequot of the Connecticut River valley. The Pequot were a powerful people who had been weakened by fighting with other Indians and by smallpox imported from Europe. In 1637 the colonists and their Indian allies burned a Pequot village near Mystic, Connecticut, and in the space of an hour killed between 400 and 700 people living there. Most surviving Pequot were soon killed or captured and enslaved. Campaigns against the Indians were overwhelmingly successful, and by the time of the American Revolution, the Pequot, Narragansett, and most other eastern Indians had been largely wiped out. Yet the fighting took a heavy toll among the colonists, too, leaving a significant number disabled, widowed, or orphaned and in need of support.

Settlement Laws

As immigrants arrived from Europe in need of assistance, frontier families uprooted by Indian wars sought safety in large coastal towns such as Boston. For a variety of reasons, therefore, transients were part of the population of early American towns and cities. Because colonists willing to help their relatives and fellow townspeople remained wary of newcomers, provincial assemblies instituted residency requirements for those receiving public aid or even desiring to remain within a jurisdiction. These stipulations, too, were based on an English law, the Settlement Act of 1662, which limited eligibility to those who had established residency by being born in the parish (the unit of local English government), owning land there, paying taxes to the parish, or serving there as an apprentice. Colonial residency requirements differed somewhat from the British model and from one colony to another. Individuals in Pennsylvania, for example, met residency requirements if they had been a servant or apprentice in a township or district for a year, had held public office and paid taxes for a year, or had leased a tenement or plantation within the jurisdiction for at least five pounds per year.

New York City required the constable of each city ward to search for strangers and report his findings to the mayor. The mayor also demanded a report from private citizens entertaining out-of-towners beyond seven days and ship captains taking newcomers into the city. In addition, innkeepers were to report to the constable the names, professions, dwelling places, and reasons for visiting the city of any strangers lodging with them longer than two days. In general, solid citizens looked down on vagrants as a potential source of trouble and considered them a rude, dirty, disorderly lot. Female transients were of particular concern, because they might add illegitimate children to the relief list. In most places, though, transients commonly lived among settled inhabitants for months or years and usually drew the attention of authorities only if a neighbor lodged a complaint against them for disturbing of the peace, belligerence, or pauperism.

Vagrant paupers who failed to meet colonial residency requirements risked being "warned out," or ordered to return to the town or parish that they had left. The subject of a complaint was required to appear before the town or city council to answer questions and plead his or her case. The council then determined whether the individual would remain in the community or be warned out. To transients, being warned out could mean leaving a home, job, and connections, so people commonly responded to a complaint by hiding or leaving town temporarily until interest in their case diminished. Some obeyed a warning-out order only to return later, but the punishment for repeat offenders was often a steep fine or public whipping. In North Carolina, some vagabonds were whipped by one county constable and transported to the next until they reached their county of origin. Settlement laws were a mixed blessing for local governments: They helped control costs of maintaining the poor, but they also prevented the unemployed from leaving depressed areas to seek work elsewhere.

Poverty increased in the colonies for reasons other than immigration and Indian wars. Fires and epidemics also left people in need. The most damaging fire in colonial America burned through Boston on March 23, 1760. The fire began in the center of town and quickly swept south and east through some of the most densely populated wards, destroying nearly 350 buildings and leaving more than 200 people homeless. Many tradesmen lost their places of business. Of the 365 households that claimed losses, 214 had been reduced to poverty by the fire. The blaze was so catastrophic that people throughout Britain and its colonies contributed to a relief fund.

Smallpox, scarlet fever, yellow fever, and other contagious diseases struck periodically in early America. The poor suffered disproportionately in epidemics, because they often were already weakened from hunger and lacked the resources to leave town, as more affluent citizens frequently did. A smallpox epidemic hit Boston especially hard in 1721 and 1722, claiming an estimated 840 lives in the city and surrounding area. In 1772, between 800 and 900 people died in a measles epidemic in Charleston, South Carolina, among them heads of households. Men also died or were left permanently disabled as a result of work-related accidents, especially if they were construction workers, fishermen, or longshoremen.

Churches and Charitable Groups

Private charity eased the burden on public coffers. Churches took up collections to aid needy congregants, and groups of like-minded citizens founded charitable, or "friendly," societies for the purpose of helping the poor of a particular faith or ethnic background. In Boston these groups included the Scots Charitable Society, founded in 1657, which helped poverty-stricken people of Scottish descent, and the Episcopal Charitable Society, which was founded in 1754 to aid destitute Anglicans. During the unusually harsh winter of 1740–41, when food and firewood grew dangerously scarce in Boston, the merchants and artisans of the Scots Charitable Society handed out money to desperate people—whether they were individuals known to the society or nameless transients. The crisis prompted the overseers of the poor to appeal to the city's churches, and congregations responded by donating the proceeds of two collections to an emergency fund.

Historians know that the proportion of colonists who were poor grew over the course of the 18th century because city and town records show increases in both poor taxes and the numbers of people asking for and receiving public assistance. The demand for help from private informal sources, churches, and charitable groups also rose. The "respectable," or "deserving," poor preferred to seek aid from private groups because being a public charge carried a stigma. In fact, beginning in 1705, paupers in New York City wore as a mark of shame a cloth badge emblazoned with the symbol N:Y in red or blue. Philadelphia and Charleston followed the example of New York and adopted similar systems.

Of course, not every needy person sought aid. Numerous colonists lived on the verge of poverty, frequently going hungry, enduring bitter cold, and doing without basic necessities. Domestic servants, tailors, shoemakers, longshoremen, and mariners were among the working people who typically lived at a level approaching poverty. Many of the poor and near poor had been weakened by a lifetime of too little food, relentless hard work, and tuberculosis and other infectious diseases. They suffered from protein and vitamin deficiencies and all too often produced low–birth weight babies, who were more prone to disease and death than average–birth weight babies.

In the countryside, where most people lived, many settlers exhausted themselves farming land of marginal value in places lacking access to urban markets and the benefits of provincial government. Tenant farmers in Maryland and elsewhere lived in huts and dressed in rags. They owned almost nothing, at most a pot and a few cooking utensils, some clothing, and one or two crude mattresses. They ate with their fingers and squatted on dirt floors. Because most poor farming families had six or more children, living conditions were crowded and unsanitary, and privacy was nonexistent. A fire, severe winter, dry summer, illness, or accident could be enough to push such a family into dire need.

In cities, the poor clustered in neighborhoods such as the Out Ward, one of the bleakest spots in New York City. The people of the Out Ward lived on the far side of a fortification bisecting Manhattan that was built in 1745 to protect inhabitants from attack during the French and Indian War. From their wooden shacks they had a fine view of activities more prosperous colonists preferred not to see: executions at the gallows, burials in potter's field, and butchering at the public slaughterhouse. New York's poor also frequented the fetid East River waterfront, where, after heavy rains, paupers could be seen picking through debris that had been washed toward the docks. Sailors, prostitutes, and gamblers gathered in taverns alongside the river that carried the city's refuse toward the sea. The waterfront was notorious as the frequent scene of violence and crime.

The Trend toward Indoor Relief

By the early 18th century, some people had begun to question whether outdoor relief was worth the expense, and even whether it was in the best interest of the poor. They asked whether there was a more economical way to help those in need, one that did not encourage idleness. It also seemed to many that outdoor relief destroyed the incentive to work when the laboring poor saw others receive handouts in return for doing nothing.

For towns and cities, outdoor relief was becoming a costly burden. Boston, which with a population of 8,500 was the largest colonial city in 1700, spent 500 pounds on the poor in that year. By 1735, the population had passed 15,000, and the city spent more than 4,000 pounds on poor relief. In 1753, Boston's population was greater than 18,000 and public expenditures on the poor reached 10,000 pounds. Philadelphia experienced a similar increase. In 1709, Philadelphia had a population of 2,500 and provided economic relief to 13 people. In 1765, Philadelphia was home to 18,100 people, 590 of them on relief. Public expenditures on the poor had increased from 158 pounds in 1709 to 3,681 pounds in 1765, and in that year city leaders increased the poor tax 66 percent. In 1766, the Philadelphia grand jury concluded that many in the city who were willing to work "cannot obtain sufficient Employment."[4] At the same time, private groups continued to supplement public spending. During the winter of 1759–60, a citizens' group, the Committee to Alleviate the Miseries of the Poor, went door to door in Philadelphia collecting money to buy firewood for impoverished city residents.

The end of the French and Indian War in 1763 contributed to an economic downturn in the colonies. British soldiers no longer spent their wages in colonial shops and taverns, and the British army no longer turned to colonial craftsmen for supplies. Beginning in 1765, colonists resentfully paid taxes to Great Britain for the first time, to help meet Britain's huge war debt. Colonial assemblies also awarded pensions to disabled veterans of this war and veterans' widows at a time when both unemployment and immigration were on the rise.

Institutionalization, or "indoor relief," became increasingly attractive. Sheltering paupers collectively at public expense seemed to be a way to reduce the visibility of the poor and cut costs both immediately and in the long run, by fostering good work habits and transforming inmates into productive members of society. For this reason, major cities began to open poorhouses, or almshouses, in the late colonial period.

Municipal authorities in New York City contemplated building a poorhouse as early as March 24, 1714, when they established a committee to consult the mayor about such a project. Although a temporary poorhouse may have soon been in use, it was not until 1736 that the city completed construction of a permanent structure, the Poor House, Work House, and House of Correction, a building whose name defined its purpose. This structure gave shelter to the aged, ill, and disabled poor, and a home and work to the able-bodied. Its staff also dispensed correction in the form of whippings to insubordinate slaves and servants sent there by their masters for this purpose. Some of the staff also prepared poor youngsters to qualify as apprentices. Within the brick walls were an infirmary, separate wards for inmates with lice, and cellar space for the uncooperative. When this institution opened in spring 1736, it housed at least 19 paupers. By March 1772, the inmates numbered 425. The residents subsisted on a diet of bread, cheese, broth, and pease porridge, or cooked, mashed peas combined with seasonings and sometimes milk. The person in charge, called the keeper, made sure that everyone living under his roof obeyed the rules and worked as required.

Also aptly named, Philadelphia's Bettering House was the largest building ever constructed in the colonies when it was completed in 1769. Its Quaker managers endeavored to teach skills and habits calculated to promote physical health, moral rectitude, and financial independence. They also maintained a wing of the institution as an almshouse for the indigent who were unable to work.

To the impoverished, the poorhouse, or almshouse, was a last resort, a place to go when reduced to an emaciated, nearly naked state, or numb and blue with winter's cold. Some who were carried to the almshouse on the verge of death were too far gone and failed to pull through. Indigent women also went to the almshouse to give birth if they had nowhere else to go. Some of the poor spent the frigid months behind almshouse walls, isolated physically and socially from the rest of the population, and fended for themselves during the rest of the year.

Poverty and the Revolution

Poverty increased alarmingly in the years preceding the American Revolution. Some historians now theorize that because living in want ate away at people's loyalty to the British Crown and the colonial social system, poverty was an indirect cause of the war. The wandering poor became a common sight in colonial cities, and the standard of living declined among the laboring classes. Pennsylvania responded to the rise in transients by passing stricter residency laws in 1767 and 1771, yet in 1772, one of every four free residents of Philadelphia was poor or nearly poor, including 60 percent of mariners, 25 percent of weavers, and 20 percent of carters, porters, bricklayers, and cordwainers (shoemakers), according to public records.

Boston's population suffered great economic hardship in 1774, when Parliament closed the port in retaliation for the Tea Party of December 16, 1773, in which colonists boarded three British ships and threw their cargoes of tea overboard to protest a tax on imported tea. People throughout the colonies responded to the crisis in Boston and in doing so gained a sense of national unity that would help them win the coming war. Relief took the form of farm produce at harvest, livestock, and clothing and cash in winter. Colonists contributed through church collections, charitable organizations, and individual gifts. "Every part of this extensive Continent appears to be deeply interested in the fate of this *unhappy Town*," noted one Boston resident.[5] In Boston and the surrounding towns, warehouse owners, carters, and merchants waived their usual fees and commissions to help their fellow citizens.

Once fighting began in 1775, colonists fleeing regions threatened by British invasion or ruined in battle sought refuge in towns and cities. The order imposed by poor laws broke down, and communities deemed it difficult or impossible to satisfy the needs of all the poor and uprooted. New York found it necessary to form a committee to administer relief to displaced residents throughout the state. When smallpox broke out in occupied Boston, the British general, William Howe, had 300 of the city's poor sent to the town of Chelsea. After an appeal for help from Chelsea's town leaders to General George Washington, the General Court of Massachusetts sent a committee to investigate. The committee ordered the poor "smoked and cleansed" as a disinfecting measure and then divided them among surrounding towns.[6] The General Court reimbursed Chelsea for the care of any who were too weak or ill to be moved.

Military service offered a respite to impoverished men, just as it would in later wars. Transients, poor laborers, free African Americans, and slaves joined militia companies, helped to win important battles, and even became heroes. One such soldier was Salem Poor, a former slave who enlisted in the 5th Massachusetts Regiment on April 24, 1775. On June 17, 1775, the regiment defended fortifications on Breed's Hill and Bunker Hill, overlooking Boston Harbor. With their third assault the British captured the positions, but not before Poor had shot and killed British lieutenant colonel James Abercrombie.

Salem Poor and his compatriots fought to achieve an independent nation, one in which poverty would endure and the public-welfare system would remain essentially unchanged.

Chronicle of Events

1601

• The Elizabethan Poor Law establishes a system in England for public support of the indigent.

1637

• English Pilgrims destroy a large Pequot settlement near Mystic, Connecticut, and kill as many as 700 people.

1642

• Plymouth Colony enacts the first poor law in colonial America, based on the Elizabethan Poor Law.

1646

• Virginia enacts its first poor law.

1657

• The Scots Charitable Society is founded in Boston to help the poor of Scottish descent.

1662

• England's Settlement Act establishes residency requirements for recipients of public assistance; it serves as a model for colonial residency laws.

1699

• The Natchez incorporate survivors from the Tioux, Grigra, and other Indian nations after a smallpox epidemic.

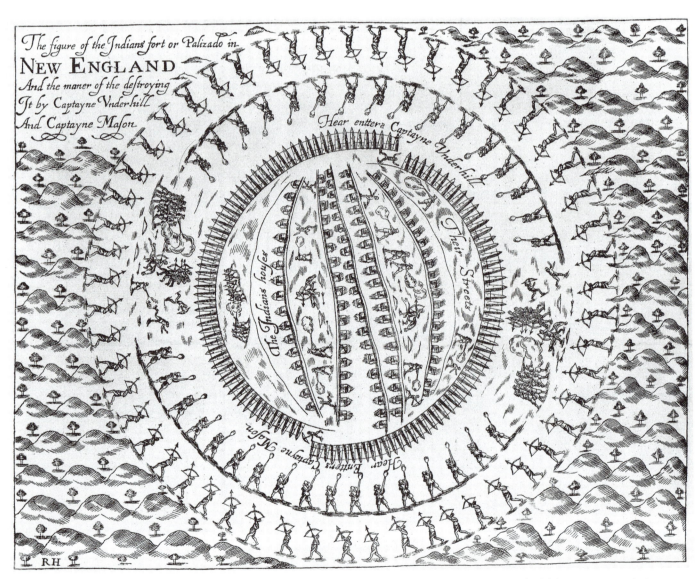

A campaign against the Pequot is depicted in a British book of 1638. The illustration shows how a colonial force commanded by Captains John Mason and John Underhill destroyed the Pequot village near Mystic, Connecticut, on May 26, 1637. *(Library of Congress, Prints and Photographs Division, LC-USZ62-32055)*

1700

• Boston has a population of 8,500 and spends £500 on the poor.

1701

• Pennsylvania enacts a poor law.

1705

• New York City becomes the first colonial municipality to require paupers to wear identifying badges.

1709

• Philadelphia has a population of 2,500 and provides relief to 13 people at a cost of £158.

1714

• *March 24:* New York City forms a committee to make plans for a poorhouse.

1718–1775

• Britain sentences 45,000 to 50,000 convicts to indentured servitude in the American colonies.

1721–1722

• A smallpox epidemic kills approximately 840 people in Boston.

1735

• Boston's population is greater than 15,000; the city spends more than £4,000 on poor relief.

1736

• New York City completes construction of the Poor House, Work House, and House of Correction, which initially houses approximately 19 inmates.

1740–1741

• The Scots Charitable Society provides for resident and transient poor during an unusually harsh winter; churches contribute to an emergency fund.

1753

• Boston is a city of more than 18,000 spending £10,000 on poor relief.

1754

• The Episcopal Charitable Society of Boston is formed to aid needy Anglicans.

1759–1760

• The Committee to Alleviate the Miseries of the Poor buys firewood for the poor of Philadelphia using donated funds.

1760

• *March 23:* A large, rapidly moving fire destroys a significant section of Boston, reducing 214 families to poverty.

1763

• The end of the French and Indian War leads to an economic depression.

1765

• Philadelphia's population has reached 18,100, and 590 people are on relief at a cost of £3,681; Philadelphia increases its poor tax 66 percent.
• Britain taxes the colonists for the first time.

1767

• Philadelphia tightens residency requirements.

1769

• Philadelphia's Bettering House reaches completion.

1771

• Philadelphia again passes stricter residency requirements.

1772

• Between 800 and 900 people die of measles in Charleston, South Carolina.
• One in four Philadelphians is poor or nearly poor.
• *March:* New York City's Poor House, Work House, and House of Correction shelters 425 inmates.

1774

• Britain responds to the Boston Tea Party by closing the port of Boston and causing economic hardship in that city. People throughout the colonies go to Boston's aid.

1775

• As many as 500,000 Europeans have entered North America as indentured servants.
• The first fighting of the American Revolution takes place; poor men join militia companies and help to win the war.

Eyewitness Testimony

[F]rom this time forward, no assistance shall be given by the Deacons of this City New Amsterdam, to any persons residing outside the jurisdiction of this City, unless they bring with them from the Deacons or Overseers of the Poor at the place of their residence a certificate of their character and poverty in manner as follows:

N.N. residing under the jurisdiction of N.N. hath applied to us for some assistance and support, and, as his character and poverty are well known to us, we would willingly have provided him therewith, but the low state of our Treasury hath not allowed us to do so. We have, therefore, to request, on his behalf, the Deacons of the City of *Amsterdam* in *New Netherland* to lend him a helping hand according to their usual discretion.

Peter Stuyvesant, governor of New Netherland, and the Colonial Council, 1661, in David M. Schneider, The History of Public Welfare in New York State, *1609–1866, p. 24.*

This vestry takeing Notice of Mary Hutson servant of Mrs. Frances Sheppard, who hath brought Thre Severall bastard Children which have been nursed at the Charge of this Parrish, and hath never yet been presented for ye Same as the Law Directs, and there being further Information now made that Joseph Smith a Taylor, and Servt to the said Mrs. Sheppard peremptorily owns himself Father of the latter of the Said Thre Bastard Children. To the End the same may by Duly Inquired into Doe order that Joseph Harvie doe deliver a Coppie hereof to ye next Court held for this County that they may Call before them ye said Mary and Joseph, and proceed against them as the Law Directs &c.

Entry in the vestry book of Christ Church Parish, Middlesex County, Virginia, January 5, 1685, in Howard Mackey, "Social Welfare in Colonial Virginia: The Importance of the Old Poor Law," p. 360.

At a meeting of ye Trustees 14 of June did then order that according to ye directions of ye Justices to take care of the poore and orphans within our parish, and the children of Thomas Reeves and Ben Davis deceased being both fatherless and motherless, that Isaac William and Aaron Burnatt do bond out said orphans, According on ye 15th day were five of the said orphans bound out.

Records of the town of Southampton, New York, 1694, in David M. Schneider, "The Patchwork of Relief in Provincial New York, 1664–1775," p. 479.

IT *is the Duty of the Poor to adore God's Providence in it, and study how they may submit to Him Patiently under it.* They ought not to Murmur at God's Providence, as if He Injured them, nor seek by any Indirect Means to ease themselves of it; but to Trust in God who cares for such; and be the more sollicitous to secure for themselves, the *Riches* which cannot be taken away; remembring, that as *Riches* are not Evidence of God's *Love,* so neither is *Poverty* of His *Anger* or *Hatred;* being such things as in themselves make Men neither *better* nor *worse;* and are equally improvable for Eternal Salvation.

Samuel Willard, pastor of the South Church of Boston and vice president of Harvard College, in a sermon delivered 24 July 1705, A Compleat Body of Divinity, *p. 708.*

I have often taken some Care of the Poor, that have not a Character of Godliness upon them. So I found out ten or a dozen such People and I carried them some Relief of money and I gave them the best Council I could, and I left also a good Book in their Hands to direct and excite the Practice of serious Religion in them. Who can tell but in this Way of Treating with such poor Creatures, they may be some of them won over to the Wayes of Piety.

Cotton Mather, influential Puritan minister, writing in his diary, January 1707, in Elizabeth Wisner, "The Puritan Background of the New England Poor Laws," p. 382.

We are told that "pure religion and undefiled (a jewel not counterfeited, and without a flaw,) is to visit the fatherless and widows in their affliction." The orphans and the widows, and all the children of affliction in the neighborhood, must be visited and relieved with all suitable kindness.

Neighbors! Be concerned that the orphans and the widows may be well provided for. They meet with grievous difficulties, with unknown temptations. When their nearest relatives were living, they were perhaps, but meanly provided for: what then must be their present solitary condition? That condition should be well considered; and the result of the consideration should be, "I delivered the orphan who had no helper, and I caused the widow's heart to sing for joy."

By the same rule, all the afflicted in the neighborhood are to be considered. Would it be too much for you once in a week, at least, to think "What neighbor is reduced to pinching and painful poverty, or impoverished with heavy losses? What neighbor is languishing with sickness, especially with severe disease, and of long continuance? What neighbor is broken-hearted with the loss of a dear and desirable relative? What neighbor has a soul violently as-

Cotton Mather was a leading colonial theologian. *(Library of Congress, Prints and Photographs Division, LC-USZ62-92308)*

saulted by the enemy of souls?" and then consider, "What can be done for such neighbors?"

Cotton Mather, influential Puritan minister, 1710, Essays to Do Good, *pp. 71–72.*

Were a man able to write in seven languages; could he daily converse with the sweets of all the liberal sciences to which the most accomplished men make pretensions; were he to entertain himself with all ancient and modern history; and could he feast continually on the curiosities which the different branches of learning may discover to him:—All this would not afford the ravishing satisfaction which he might find in relieving the distress of a poor, miserable neighbor; nor would it bear any comparison with the heartfelt delight which he might obtain by doing an extensive service to the kingdom of our great Savior in the world, or by exerting his efforts to redress the miseries under which mankind is generally languishing.

Cotton Mather, influential Puritan minister, 1710, Essays to Do Good, *p. 178.*

That this Province is in a deplorable Situation, none can justly deny. How it came to be in such dreadful Circumstances, is an important Inquiry; and how to Remedy the Evils we now suffer, is Matter of the highest Concernment, of the utmost Consequence. Poverty and Discontent appear in every Face, (except the Countenances of the Rich,) and dwell upon every Tongue. Trade and Business, (as Birds leave an inclement Climate) are flying away.—Children leave their aged Parents, and go off among Strangers, Provision is dear, Money scarce, few Inhabitants, Taxes high, House Rent high, Clothing dear, Fuel dear, Creditors oppressive.—Such is our Condition that the Hand cannot feed the Mouth, and what is so Rebellious as the Belly!

Vincent Centinel (pseudonym), Boston pamphleteer, 1750, Massachusetts in Agony, *p. 3.*

As for disabled Persons, it was never the Design of the Apostle to command, that, *if any would not work, neither should they eat:* No; tho' their Incapacity for Labour was brought upon them by their own Folloes and Vices. It is very unhappy indeed when this is the Case, as, God knows, it too often is. And such Persons have infinite Reason to look back upon their past mad and sinful Conduct with Grief and Shame: But yet, if they are really unable to do any Thing, in a way of Labour, towards their own Support, they are by no means to be neglected. They are, in common, with other disabled Persons, the proper Objects of Charity, the Poor of this World, concerning whom it is the will of God, that they should be pitied and help'd. And the Rich should look upon themselves obliged to shew Compassion towards them. If any should *see a Brother or Sister,* of this Character, *naked, and destitute of daily Food,* they should not only say to them, depart in Peace, be ye warmed and *filled, but give them these Things which are needful to the Body;* suiting their Charities to their particular Wants and Circumstances.

But we are under no such Obligations with respect to the other Sort of poor People, those who *can* work, but *won't;* who may have Work to do, and have Activity of Body to do it, but no Will to employ themselves in Labour. Concerning these Poor, it is the Command of an inspired Apostle, *that they shall not eat,* i.e. shall not be maintained as the Charge of others; shall not live upon the Charities of their Christian Friends and Brethren.

Charles Chauncy, minister of the First Church, Boston, 1752, The Idle-Poor Secluded from the Bread of Charity by the Christian Law, *pp. 7–8.*

Now if Labour is thus necessary for the Support of Life, it is contrary to all Reason, that those should eat the Bread of Charity who won't work, while yet they have ability therefor. What Right have the lazy and indolent, who are both healthy and strong, to live on the Fruits of other Men's Labour? Wherein lies the Fitness of this? If without Labour the World can't subsist, for any to sit idle, depending upon a Supply from other Men's Industry, is certainly incongruous to a high Degree. Why should some Men labour and toil to get Bread for those who spend their Time in doing nothing? The Supposition is absurd. It is not fair; it favours neither of Reason nor Justice, that the diligent and laborious should, by their Bounties, relieve the Wants of those, who are poor and needy, not thro' Incapacity for Bodily Exertions, but because they are sluggish and idle.

Charles Chauncy, minister of the First Church, Boston, 1752,
The Idle-Poor Secluded from the Bread of Charity
by the Christian Law, *p. 9.*

[The charitable man] ministers to the bodily Infirmities and Wants of men, and comforts the Heart oppressed with the Sorrow of the World,—by sympathizing Looks; by soothing Words; by prudent Advice; by readily performing a Variety of friendly Offices; and chearfully distributing a proper Portion of that Estate with which God blessed Him. As for Riches—he has learned their just Value and true Improvement: he knows that there is *no Good in them, but for a Man to rejoice and to do Good in his Life.* And that for which he chiefly values them, and blesses God the Giver of them, is, that they furnish him with many Opportunities of tasting the divine Pleasure, that flows from annihilating the Misery, and augmenting the Happiness of his fellow Men; that they capacitate him to emulate a Character, that appears with distinguished Advantage in holy Writ; the Character of one who was the best, as well as the greatest Man in all the East.

Samuel Cooper, pastor of the Brattle Street Church, Boston,
August 8, 1753, A Sermon Preached in Boston,
New-England, before the Society for Encouraging
Industry, and Employing the Poor, *pp. 4–5.*

[T]hat Charity that *seeketh not her own,* forms the large-hearted and disinterested Patriot—his Bosom glows with Love to his Country—he prefers it's Peace and Prosperity *to his chief Joy*—his clear and active Head, his eloquent and persuasive Tongue employed in it's Service—he is concerned that Religion and Vertue may be protected

and flourish in it—he promotes wise and salutary Laws—he provides a sure Sanctuary to injured Innocence, and that just Vengeance may be dealt to the injurious—He forms Designs of Enlarging the Wealth and Power of his Country, by enlarging it's Commerce; by removing what obstructs it's old Channels, and pointing out new ones; and by introducing and encouraging the most useful Arts and Manufactures. Such Designs, he is sensible, when carried into Effect, produce an unknown Deal of Good, the Fruits of them are reaped by vast Numbers at once; and they tend to keep alive Industry and Vertue among a People. And therefore, tho' his private Bounties do often visit helpless Poverty, in here retired Abodes; yet he takes Care, that these Bounties do not become the Wages of Idleness; being well aware, that *then* they would be worse than lost; and that nothing but Industry, and a full employment of such as have Ability for Work, and make Plenty and Happiness circulate thro' a whole Community.

Samuel Cooper, pastor of the Brattle Street Church, Boston,
August 8, 1753, A Sermon Preached in Boston,
New-England, before the Society for Encouraging
Industry, and Employing the Poor, *pp. 7–8.*

That altho' She is thankful that herself & Daughter are so well provided for, with all the necessarys of Life, & in so plentiful a manner, Yet as they were both brought up in a delicate way, begs leave to assure us, that the Provisions of the Almshouse are generally too gross for their nice Stomachs, & especially at Breakfast, & Supper Times, neither is there care taken to provide anything pretty for them, to Sup, in the Afternoons; they therefore beg the favour of us to desire you to take this Important affair into your most serious Consideration & if you find the case fairly Represented, You may allow them Tea, Coffee, Chocolate or any thing else that you verily belief will be more agreeable to their palates.

Letter to the Overseers of the Poor regarding Philadelphia
Almshouse inmate Mary Marriot, March 29, 1757, in Lisa
Wilson, Life after Death, *p. 62.*

HELP! HELP! HELP!

WOOD at *Three Pounds Ten shillings* a Cord, a Price never before heard of! The countryman says, *We have wood enough:* The Boatman says, *I could fetch two Loads while I am bringing and unloading one;* The Merchants employ the Carman in carrying their——Sugars, &c. The Widow hears a noise in her Yard, rises from her Bed at Midnight, from her Window sees a Thief, and asks him what he is doing, he answers, *I must have Wood;* in the Morning views her small Pile, and laments the Loss of half a Cord. The Rich engross—when perhaps two Hundred Families have not a Stick to burn. And (it is said) thus it is, in one House, where two Persons now lie dead of the Small Pox.

Should not the Fathers of the City do something in this Extremity?

Cannot our Magistrates appoint an Officer or Officers to inspect every Boat, to agree on the Price of the While, distribute their Wood in small Quantities at the Price agreed on, command the Carmen, from every other Service, to attend the Boat till unloaded. If this or something to the same purpose be not done, what may be the Condition of this City before the beginning of February next.

Pennsylvania Gazette, January 10, 1760, p. 2.

I think the best way of doing good to the poor, is, not making them easy *in* poverty, but leading or driving them out of it. In my youth, I travelled much, and I observed in different countries, that the more public provisions were made for the poor, the less they provided for themselves, and of course became poorer. And, on the contrary, the less was done for them, the more they did for themselves, and became richer. There is no country in the world where so many provisions are established for them; so many hospitals to receive them when they are sick or lame, founded and maintained by voluntary charities; so many almshouses for the aged of both sexes, together with a solemn general law made by the rich to subject their estates to a heavy tax for the support of the poor. Under all these obligations, are our poor modest, humble, and thankful? And do they use their best endeavours to maintain themselves, and lighten our shoulders of this burthen? On the contrary, I affirm that there is no country in the world in which the poor are more idle, dissolute, drunken, and insolent.

Inventor Benjamin Franklin, 1766, "On the Price of Corn and Management of the Poor," p. 230.

From the lower part of Lynch's Creek I proceeded to the upper—and from the Greater to the Lesser; The Weather was exceeding Cold and piercing—And as these People live in open Logg Cabbins with hardly a Blanket to cover them, or Cloathing to cover their Nakedness, I endur'd Great hardships and my Horse more than his Rider—they having no fodder, nor a Grain of Corn to spare.

Charles Woodmason, a traveling minister on the South Carolina frontier, 1767, in Richard J. Hooker, ed., The Carolina Backcountry on the Eve of the Revolution, *p. 16.*

In this Circuit of a fortnight I've eaten Meat but thrice, and drank nought but Water—Subsisting on my Bisket and Rice Water and Musk Melons, Cucumbers, Green Apples and Peaches and such Trash. By which am reduc'd very thin. It is impossible that any Gentleman not season'd to the Clime, could sustain this—It would kill 99 out of 100—Nor is this a Country, or place where I would wish any Gentleman to travel, or settle, altho' Religion and the State requires a Number of Ministers—Their Ignorance and Impudence is so very high, as to be past bearing—Very few can read—fewer write—Out of 5000 that have attended Sermon this last Month, I have not got 50 to sign a Petition to the Assembly. They are very Poor—owing to their extreme Indolence for they possess the finest Country in America, and could raise but ev'ry thing. They delight in their present low, lazy, sluttish, heathenish, hellish Life, and seem not desirous of changing it. Both Men and Women will do any thing to come at Liquor, Cloaths, furniture, &c. &c. rather than work for it—Hence their many Vices—their gross Licentiousness Wantonness, Lasciviousness, Rudeness, Lewdness, and Profligacy they will commit the grossest Enormities, before my face, and laugh at all Admonition.

Charles Woodmason, a traveling minister on the South Carolina frontier, 1767, in Richard J. Hooker, ed., The Carolina Backcountry on the Eve of the Revolution, *p. 52.*

I might here add many affecting instances of their extreme poverty—that multitudes of children are obliged to go barefoot through the whole winter, with hardly clothes to cover their nakedness,—that half the houses are without any chimneys,—that many people had no other beds than a heap of straw,—and whole families had scarce anything to subsist upon, for months together except potatoes, roasted in the ashes.

The Reverend Jacob Bailey of Pownalborough, Maine, writing about his congregation, 1771, in William S. Bartlett, The Frontier Missionary, *p. 88.*

In the forenoon went out of town a little way to see the Alms house or House of employment for the poor community called the bettering house. It lies just by the Hospital, & is one of the principal Ornaments of this place, being a very pretty building, large & in good taste. It is built of Brick, & consists of a Main Body & two wings, & in the two corners are two square buildings, higher than the other parts, which are two stories high, besides a ground & Garret story. It has Piazzas round on the Inside It is allotted for the employment of the poor, & the entertainment of the poor, old & infirm.—The men & women who were able were employed in spinning wool & Flax; in twisting thread & yarn upon twist mills, in picking Oakhum, & other things. Though most of the women in it are old & infirm, yet there are some young ones in it, who bear no modest character, & by what I saw of them, the general character of them appeared to be just. Some of them, begged me to try to get them out, but I did not know how.

Robert Honyman, Scottish immigrant, describing the Philadelphia Bettering House, March 8, 1775, in Philip Padelford, ed., Colonial Panorama, 1775, *pp. 17–18.*

CHAPTER TWO

Industrialization, Immigration, and Urban Poverty
1790–1864

In 1820, in Poughkeepsie, New York, a young man named John Daely pleaded guilty to a charge of horse theft and was grateful to be sentenced to eight years in the state prison. According to an account of the case in the *Carolina Sentinel,* "The Times were so hard he could get no work, and could hit upon no other plan so ready and certain to provide him with a home and steady employment."[1] The United States was struggling through an economic depression known as the Panic of 1819, and for many citizens, steady work was hard to find and a place to live was impossible to afford. For the first time, there was large-scale unemployment in U.S. cities. In a nation of 9,638,000 people, an estimated 500,000 were out of work. Some of the hungry went from house to house, begging for money and food.

As in the colonial period, private charity supplemented public aid. The citizens of Baltimore opened 12 soup stations to feed the hungry of their city, and in Philadelphia the needy lined up for a pint of soup per day. In New York City church congregations ladled out soup and took up collections for the poor. In 1819 a new organization, the New York Society for the Prevention of Pauperism, had estimated that 8,000 paupers were living in their city of 120,000. A year later, between 12,000 and 13,000 New Yorkers were receiving some kind of charitable relief. "A deeper gloom hangs over us than was ever witnessed by the oldest man," wrote one newspaper correspondent.[2]

States Regulate Poor Relief

After national independence, states had retained their colonial poor laws with very little modification. European countries may have had national policies for relieving poverty, but the U.S. Constitution made no provision for the care of the poor. In a nation that valued limited central government, it seemed appropriate for each state to see to the welfare of its residents.

In 1797 the political philosopher Thomas Paine conceived a plan to eliminate poverty. He proposed that every nation create a fund to give the equivalent of £15 British to every free person upon reaching the age of 21, "to enable *him*, or *her* to begin the world," and the equivalent of £10 to free adults turning 50 "to enable them to live in old age without Wretchedness, and go decently out of the World." Paine thought that poverty was the product of Western civilization and that it did not exist among people living close to nature, such as American Indians. Civilization, wrote Paine, "has operated two ways, to make one part of society more affluent, and the other part more wretched than would have been the lot of either in a natural state." Compared with that of the poor, Paine observed, "The life of an Indian is a continual holiday."[3]

Neither the United States nor any other nation established a fund like the one Paine advocated. Congress did, however, create relief programs for three population groups: merchant seamen, destitute veterans, and Native Americans. Sick and disabled merchant seamen received treatment at federal marine hospitals, in order to relieve port cities of the burden of their care, through the Marine Hospital Fund, established by Congress in 1798. The Revolutionary War Pension Act of 1818 provided support to indigent veterans of the Revolution, but by 1833, when the U.S. Bureau of Pensions was formed, cash benefits had been extended to needy veterans of all wars. In 1800, Congress appropriated funds for food, tools, medical care, and cash allowances for Indians, thus protecting many Native people from starvation. In addition, several times in the antebellum period the government responded to appeals to help specific groups of American Indians on a one-time basis. For example, in 1860 the Indian Department (later the Bureau of Indian Affairs) gave financial assistance to impoverished Indians who had been forced by local whites to leave a Texas reservation they had occupied for 15 years.

Because the federal programs benefited only a small minority of Americans in need, most of the poor seeking help turned to local resources. New poor laws went on the books as states and territories were formed west of the Appalachian Mountains. The first of the new laws, enacted in the Northwest Territory in 1790, was modeled on the laws in northern states and provided for appointed overseers to implement relief measures at the township level. Kentucky, which entered the Union in 1792, had a poor law modeled on those of the southern states, where freeholders in each county elected an overseer of the poor.

The Panic of 1819 had complex causes, including lax banking practices and poor governmental control of the monetary system. What most affected urban workers, though, were fluctuations in the demand for manufactured goods. The Industrial Revolution, which began in British textile manufacturing in the first half of the 18th century, had reached the United States in 1790, when the first American textile mill was built at Pawtucket, Rhode Island. Before long, U.S. factories were producing farm machinery, clocks, firearms, and other items. When the War of 1812 curtailed foreign trade, domestic manufacturing had expanded to meet the need for machine-made products, especially cloth. Factories went up in cities and towns, primarily in New England, New York, and Pennsylvania, and manufacturers made a tidy profit on a variety of goods, from textiles to glass, soap, dyes, and refined sugar.

The influx of imported goods that came with the return of peace in 1815, coupled with a contraction of the money supply, caused prices to fall. Manufacturers—who had large amounts of capital at stake—responded by cutting wages and laying off workers. The number of workers employed in Philadelphia dropped from 9,672 in 1816 to 2,137 in 1819, and other cities experienced similar decreases in employment.

The Creation of Slums

Industrialization generated a demand for unskilled and semiskilled labor that drew men, women, and children away from agriculture and led to unplanned urban growth and the creation of city slums. The most infamous American slum was the Five Points section of Manhattan, which centered on the intersections of Orange, Cross, and Anthony Streets (now Baxter, Park, and Worth Streets). The brothels and saloons of Five Points were reputed to be the gathering places of criminals. Prostitutes as young as 13 worked the streets of Five Points; sometimes mothers and daughters solicited men together. "Every house was a brothel, and every brothel a hell," said the Reverend Lewis Pease, who in 1851 founded the Five Points House of Industry, a workshop and school sponsored by the National Temperance Society.[4] Pease hoped to combat poverty by offering work and education to neighborhood residents.

Many people who wandered the city by day spent the night in one of the cheap, dirty, windowless basement boardinghouses in Five Points, where a few cents bought them one of the two-tiered bunks that were nothing more than canvas stretched between two wooden rails. Latecomers slept on the floor. Archaeological research conducted in the 1990s revealed, however, that many of the community's overcrowded shanties and subdivided houses were home to hardworking poor families who took in boarders, collected rags, peddled fruit, and did whatever else they could to generate income.

The most notorious spot in this most notorious American slum was the Old Brewery. In the 18th century this massive structure had kept the city's tankards full of beer, but around 1837 it was converted to a tenement house. Only out of desperation did the poorest of the poor grope their way through its unlit hallways and seek shelter in its filthy, windowless apartments. It was not uncommon for two, three, or four families to share a foul basement room. The Old Brewery appealed to the public's taste for sensationalism. It was rumored that murderers hid their victims' bones within the building's walls, and that in its rooms thievery and debauchery were rampant. The days of the Old Brewery came to an end when the Ladies' Home Missionary Society purchased it and had it demolished in 1853. On its site they erected a mission building from which to spread their gospel of prayer and virtue.

The unsavory reputation of Five Points stemmed in part from the fact that many of its residents were immigrants, from Ireland, Germany, and other northern European countries. Immigration contributed significantly to the extraordinary population growth that New York and other cities experienced in the early national period. In the 1790s about 3,000 immigrants came to New York City each year. The city's population increased by more than 80 percent between 1790 and 1800, rising from 33,131 to 60,515, according to the U.S. Census Bureau. By 1810 it had grown again by almost 60 percent, to 96,373. A state census conducted in 1825 determined that New York City had a population of 166,086.

Not only did immigrants' customs and dress appear exotic and threatening to the traditional American way of life, but in addition a large number of immigrants were Catholics. The United States in the 19th century was a largely Protestant country with many citizens who were biased against Roman Catholicism. Americans also frequently complained that immigrants brought disease and that they had been criminals and paupers in their own countries. The assertion that immigrants

Prostitutes smoked in doorways and commotion spilled into the streets in the Five Points section of New York City, as these scenes from 1859 reveal. *(Emmet Collection, Miriam and Ira D. Wallach Division of Art, Prints and Photographs, The New York Public Library, Astor, Lenox and Tilden Foundations)*

had been poor in their homelands was often true, especially after 1840, when large numbers of Irish immigrated to the United States to escape starvation after potato-crop failures. Immigrants who survived the ocean crossing—and in some years one in six died aboard ship—were likely to step ashore malnourished and weak, and those who arrived newly widowed or orphaned were in need of immediate financial help. Immigrants' names therefore lengthened relief rolls and lists of almshouse residents. As early as 1795, 44 percent of the inmates in New York City's poorhouse were immigrants or their children.

It was the crowded, unsanitary condition of slums, however, and not the ethnicity of their inhabitants, that made them breeding grounds for typhus, cholera, yellow fever, and other diseases. As in the colonial period, epidemics put people in need. Yellow fever attacked Philadelphia with ferocity in late August 1793. Of 1,000 people admitted to a temporary hospital, nearly 500 died. It was "dreadfully destructive" to the poor, said the writer and publisher Mathew Carey. "It is very probable, that at least seven-eighths of the number of the dead, were of that class."[5]

Fear of contagion was deadly in some cases, too. It proved fatal, for example, to a woman who went into labor after her husband died of the fever, when no one dared to assist her. Fear caused men to stop shaking hands when they met in public and pedestrians to travel in the center of the street, at a safe distance from houses where people had died. Fear closed businesses and put people out of work, creating enormous hardship. At the height of the epidemic, Philadelphia provided emergency relief in the form of money, food, and firewood to 1,200 households each week. The city ended the emergency relief program on November 23, when the epidemic was easing and business was picking up again.

Urban poverty took a heavy toll among the very young. No U.S. infant-mortality statistics from the early 19th century exist, but researchers who have reconstructed family records from Philadelphia and other cities have determined that infant mortality was highest among the poorest Americans. Babies most often succumbed to intestinal disease transmitted from polluted water, spoiled milk, or faulty hygiene. Contagious diseases such as whooping cough and measles also claimed many young lives, as did burns and other trauma resulting from abuse or neglect. Poor infants were more likely to have low birth weights, to be born to tubercular mothers, or to be born to women who died giving them birth.

Meanwhile, charitable groups continued to ease the public's burden by helping targeted groups. In New York City, for example, the Female Assistance Society gave aid to 1,500 poor women in 1814, and the Association for the Relief of Respectable, Aged, Indigent Females assisted 150 women age 60 and older to spare them the shame of accepting public assistance. In November 1821, the Society for the Relief of Poor Widows, another New York–based group, had 254 widows and 667 children younger than 10 on its pension list.

Americans Open Their Eyes to Poverty

By the early 1820s, as the economy began to recover, Americans were acknowledging that poverty was a widespread social problem. The link between economic conditions and living in need was less evident, however. The financially comfortable remained critical of the poor, blaming crowded relief rolls and high unemployment on alcohol abuse and poor laws that encouraged idleness. Poor laws were also coming under scrutiny because they were increasingly difficult and expensive to implement in growing cities. In 1800, approximately 60,000 people lived in Philadelphia and the neighboring districts, an area of a few square miles. Twenty years later, the guardians of the poor distributed relief to the needy among 100,000 people living in the Philadelphia region, which by then encompassed a much larger area. Residents of Philadelphia proper paid the bulk of the region's poor tax and protested that most of the money went outside the city limits, where the majority of recipients of outdoor relief lived. The city-dwelling poor were likely to be sent to the Bettering House, a less costly alternative. Unsure of the course to take, the legislatures of Pennsylvania, New York, Massachusetts, and New Hampshire surveyed poverty and relief measures in their own and neighboring states.

J. V. N. Yates, secretary of state in New York, conducted the survey in his state in 1824. Yates classified the poor on New York relief rolls as permanent and occasional—those supported at public expense year round and those who sought aid only in the autumn and winter. The latter group included people who worked outdoors and were unemployed in cold weather, such as fishermen, oystermen, bargemen, some building tradesmen, and many day laborers. Also counted with the occasional poor were agricultural workers who drifted to cities in winter in order to collect relief. Yates counted 6,896 permanent and 15,215 occasional paupers in his state. He blamed intemperance for two-thirds of the permanent and one-half of the occasional pauperism and pointed out that 5,883 relief recipients were foreign born. In his report he also raised a concern that would be voiced increasingly in years to come, that children raised in poverty were being schooled in crime.

The expense of maintaining the poor in New York, based on tax revenues, had risen distressingly: from $245,000 in 1815 to $368,645 in 1819 and $470,000 in 1822. Yates estimated the cost of maintaining one person on outdoor relief to be between $33 and $65 per year; for someone old or infirm, the expense could reach $100 or more. In contrast, a county might spend $20 to $35 a year to support one pauper in an almshouse attached to a farm, where the able-bodied could work and help supply their own food. There were other expenditures to consider as well. For example, in 1822, the counties and cities of New York had spent more than $25,000 removing 1,796 transients to different parts of the state. Yates calculated that the same amount could have maintained 833 people in almshouses for one year, noting as well that removal of the poor also ran counter to the principles of benevolence and humanitarianism on which the United States had been founded. Too much was being spent unwisely, Yates said, explaining that poverty and distress only seemed to grow in proportion to the amount paid out to correct them. He pointed out other problems with the poor law, including its neglect of the education and moral training of poor children and its failure to provide employment to impoverished adults.

Clearly, something had to be done. One alternative was to stop spending public funds on the poor altogether and let them be taken care of through voluntary contributions, a step that many citizens favored. To Yates and others, though, a better plan was to rely more on indoor care and deemphasize outdoor relief. In 1824, when Yates conducted his survey, there were 18 poorhouses in New York State and several more being constructed or planned. Yates concluded his report by recommending that poorhouses be built in every county throughout the state, because even with the cost of constructing new shelters or converting existing structures into poorhouses, money would be saved. Further, because poorhouses were intended to impart habits of work and thrift, Yates optimistically predicted that the savings would become greater every year as a result of the diminution of poverty that institutionalization was bound to produce.

The Rise of the Poorhouse

Before the end of the year, the New York State legislature incorporated Yates's proposals into a new poor law that radically changed the way relief was dispensed in New York. By 1835, 51 of the state's 55 counties had poorhouses. In 1840, 8,225 people in New York were living on indoor relief; in 1850, the poorhouse population was nearly 10,000.

New York set a trend: Massachusetts, which had 83 almshouses in 1824, would have 180 in 1840 and 219 in 1860. By 1860, Maryland had almshouses in nearly every county, and other states had made similar progress in the move toward indoor relief. In 1827, Philadelphia took the extreme step of outlawing outdoor relief

The Chester County, Pennsylvania, poorhouse looked this way in 1800 (artist unknown). *(Chester County Historical Society, West Chester, Pennsylvania)*

altogether, but this measure proved harsh and controversial, especially during the next of the economic depressions that occurred at roughly 20-year intervals in the 19th century, the Panic of 1837. In 1839 the city again provided outdoor aid along with institutionalization. Cook County, Illinois, also ended outdoor relief in 1848 and reinstated it during the next depression, in 1858, as a result of such severe overcrowding at the poorhouse that needy people were turned away.

Some inmates entered poorhouses voluntarily, but others were committed against their will; as a result, impoverished Americans now lived with the constant threat of institutionalization. Men and women entering poorhouses gave up their belongings, any money they had, and much of their freedom. Counties confiscated inmates' possessions and used them in the institution or sold them to offset costs, although more than one unscrupulous manager helped himself to the meager belongings surrendered by the poor. People entering the poorhouse in Salem County, Pennsylvania, were required to take with them everything they owned—all their clothing, household furnishings, and any jewelry or other valuable items—when they entered the poorhouse. There and elsewhere, husbands and wives slept apart, because men and women were quartered separately. The second almshouse built in Baltimore was typical of big-city institutions. Construction began on this three-story brick structure in 1820. Two wings extended from the central structure, one to house men and the other to house women. The African Americans who slept in the basement were also segregated by sex. A wall divided the courtyard to keep

The Workmen's Home was a model tenement constructed by the New York Association for Improving the Condition of the Poor in 1855. *(Library of Congress, General Collection)*

male and female inmates apart outdoors. The institution's outbuildings included a bakery, a smokehouse, a stable, and a building "in which corpses are deposited until interment."[7]

Typical of rural facilities was the poor farm of Seneca County, New York. Over a two-year period, from 1830 to 1832, the county acquired a farmhouse, barn, and 126 surrounding acres that included arable land, peach and apple orchards, and two quarries. The farmhouse was expanded to meet demand, and by 1838 it consisted of a main building measuring 42 by 46 feet with a wing 26 feet long and 22 feet wide. Inside were kitchens, quarters for the poor and the staff, and rooms set aside for women who were confined for childbirth or were breast-feeding babies.

Poorhouse inmates lived under constant watch: Institution managers granted or withheld permission for them to have visitors or leave the grounds, and if a poorhouse was attached to a workhouse or working farm, staff kept the inmates under constant surveillance to prevent them from slacking off. Work was mandatory for able-bodied inmates in most places. At the House of Industry constructed in South Boston in 1821, inmates grew produce for consumption and sale. They also made palm-leaf hats and raised silkworms to generate income. Women in poorhouses were commonly expected to spin and weave, and men were frequently assigned the odious task of picking oakum, which entailed shredding old ropes by hand. The resulting fiber, or oakum, was an ingredient in caulking for ships. Life within an almshouse followed a strict schedule. In Boston and other cities, bells announced the time for rising, eating, working, and sleeping.

Inmates who broke the rules were punished as if they were prisoners. In New Castle County, Delaware, residents were locked in a dark room for 48 hours and given only bread and water for pretending to be ill, refusing to work, drinking or possessing alcohol, or committing other infractions. The almshouse steward had to prove an inmate's guilt to three overseers of the poor, however, before punishment could be administered. At other institutions, rule breakers might be placed in leg irons or be assigned extra work. Of course, an almshouse was not a prison, and inmates who had committed themselves were free to leave.

Local dignitaries speaking at the openings of poorhouses throughout the United States boasted that their institutions would offer respite to those who were desperately in need and stand as a deterrent to the idle, intemperate poor. Almshouses were going to remove people from the lure of vice and opportunities for crime and teach them to resist future temptation.

The severe destitution of the Panic of 1837, a crisis in which one-third of laborers were without work and the rest saw their wages fall 30 percent to 50 percent, led to the creation in 1843 of the New York Association for Improving the Condition of the Poor (AICP). This influential organization endeavored to raise the moral character of the poor. Its "friendly visitors"—almost exclusively middle-class Protestant men—carried messages of temperance, thrift, and self-discipline up tenement staircases to the homes of the poor. Claiming that cash relief was an invitation to vice, the association dispensed such necessary articles as food, firewood, and clothing, but only in small quantities to meet immediate needs. Its volunteers also worked to improve slum living conditions by advocating sanitation and housing reform.

In 1855, under the direction of its founder and executive secretary, Robert M. Hartley, the AICP opened a model tenement intended for African Americans, the Workmen's Home. "The reason for selecting this class of tenants is that they are usually forced into the worst kind of dwellings, and are deprived of most social privileges,

"Mag Davis" was one of the many poor who supported themselves in warm weather by begging, stealing, and occasionally working and who wintered in the poorhouse. *(Library of Congress, General Collection)*

and consequently were specially deserving commiseration," according to the association's 1856 annual report.[6] The six-story brick building covered six city lots and remained the largest multifamily dwelling in New York City until the 1880s. Each of its 87 apartments consisted of three rooms and a large closet that could serve as a second bedroom. The Workmen's Home offered little improvement on existing slum tenements, however. Most of its rooms were dark, and ventilation was poor. Plumbing problems were chronic, and the halls became gathering places for loiterers.

Disappointing Results

There were a number of reasons shelters for the poor failed to achieve the desired results. For one thing, the men hired as stewards were untrained and uneducated. They were often skilled at farming, tailoring, or other work the inmates performed, but they were ignorant about the management of an institution. Typical was Zephania Lewis, who was appointed keeper of the Seneca County Poor Farm in 1830. A local farmer, Lewis supervised the men at work in the fields and quarries. For an annual salary of $325 the county hired Lewis; his wife, who managed the house and the female inmates; and his son and daughter, aged 14 and 11. The inmates showed little inclination to work, so despite having an experienced farmer in charge, production fell far short of projections, and the county had to buy a significant amount of food to supplement what was raised.

For another thing, despite the lofty statements about refuge and reform, the principal purpose of an almshouse was to save the community money. Thus, while some poorhouses were clean, efficient, and peaceable, most were dirty, pest-ridden, foul-smelling, and badly run. Old men and women, prostitutes, unmarried pregnant women, abandoned children, the terminally ill, and the insane lived crowded together. At the almshouse near Bellevue Hospital in New York City, overlooking the East River, crowding became so severe that attic lofts and basement rooms were converted into dormitories. The problems were not limited to cities. Rural Oswego, New York, for example, housed 75 paupers in a nine-room house. In the late 1840s a committee inspecting the poor farm in Seneca County wrote that "such is the dilapidated, pathetic and rickety state of the building—its rooms so low, so confined, badly lighted and worse ventilated and withal so wretchedly arranged . . . it must entirely fail in its main objective that of preserving the health and comfort of the ill fated beings reduced to the hard necessity of becoming its suffering inmates."[8]

Conditions were worst for the mentally ill. Although hospitals for the insane existed in 19th-century America, they were few in number and the care they provided was far from adequate. Most people who exhibited psychotic behavior presented a problem to their communities. When families were unable to care for them at home, these men and women became the county's responsibility. The popular belief that the insane were incurable, insensitive to pain or extremes in temperature, and unaware of their surroundings led to horrific abuse. The mentally ill were isolated in closets or dark rooms, sometimes without clothing, blankets, furniture, or anything to do. They were chained to walls and floors, kept in pens as if they were animals, and surrounded by their own waste.

In fall 1842, the reformer Dorothea Dix began a thorough inspection of conditions for the mentally ill in the almshouses and prisons of her home state, Massachusetts. She compiled a 30-page report based on her research to the state legislature. *"I tell what I have seen,"* she wrote.[9] Dix went on to travel the United States to document abuse of the mentally ill and lobby for change. Her efforts were directly responsible for the establishment of state mental hospitals in New Jersey, North Carolina, and other states. In 1854, Congress passed a bill allocating 10 million acres of public land for the construction of institutions for the mentally ill, the blind, and the deaf, but President Franklin Pierce vetoed the bill, stating, "I can not find any authority in the Constitution for making the Federal Government the great almoner of public charity throughout the United States."[10] Caring for people in need would remain the responsibility of the states.

Another segment of the almshouse population—children—elicited greater concern. An 1853 grand-jury inspection of the Chicago Almshouse revealed that the home was "entirely inadequate," but that "the section devoted to women and children is so crowded as to be very offensive."[11] Although poorhouses indentured many young residents, many others remained institutionalized and exposed to disease, dirt, and adults addicted to alcohol or hardened to prostitution or crime. Poorhouses bound many young residents as apprentices or indentured servants—with or without the children's consent. Other youngsters remained to grow up in county homes for the poor and seemed destined to acquire the habits such as laziness and intemperance that would condemn them to a life of poverty. To separate children from evil influences and provide them with shelter and care, therefore, communities increasingly turned to another type of institution, the orphan asylum.

A small number of orphanages had existed in North America since the 18th century, founded to house children orphaned in Indian attacks, epidemics, and wars. Most were run by religious or charitable groups and accepted either boys or girls, although some took children of both sexes. Most were for white children only; however, a few, including New York City's Colored Orphan Asylum, a Quaker institution, were established for African Americans. Orphanages increased in number in the 19th century, especially after the cholera epidemic of 1849, which left large numbers of poor children in need of substitute care. The Chicago Orphan Asylum opened September 11, 1849, partly to ease the burden on the county poorhouse caused by this epidemic. By 1860 there were 124 orphan asylums operating in the United States.

Alternatives for Children

The orphanage became the repository for youngsters removed from almshouses as well as for those whose impoverished families could no longer afford to keep them at home. Some asylum residents were full orphans, but most were half-orphans, or children who had one living parent. As the century progressed, asylums accepted a greater percentage of needy children who had two living parents.

Asylum managers endeavored to separate their charges permanently from the harmful influences of the poor community, including their own families. For this reason, many institutions required parents to surrender all rights to their children upon committing them. Therefore, upon making a crude mark on a printed form, thousands of men and women who had never learned to read or write severed all ties to their children. Orphanages that permitted parents to retain their rights strictly limited visiting.

The orphan asylum was to be a haven, but a temporary one. Most residents were indentured after a stay of about four years. According to their 1841 Annual Report, the women who managed the Washington City Orphan Asylum worked to place children "in a situation where every effort will be made so to inform their minds, and mould their characters that they may be useful members of society while they remain on Earth."[12] Other managers had similar goals. Children whose parents retained rights went home if and when the family's economic situation improved. In 1841, the managers of the Washington asylum also noted that within the past year two children had been "returned to their friends."[13]

Orphanages were cleaner and safer than poorhouses, but they were denounced for another reason: the regimentation of asylum life. Following a strict daily schedule for meals, study, worship, chores, and sleep robbed children's lives of spontaneity, critics said. Young people who dressed in uniforms, responded to bells, and marched silently from one activity to the next never learned to think for themselves. What is more, asylums served only a fraction of the poor population. In cities, thousands of abandoned, orphaned, and runaway children slept on the streets and begged, picked pockets, peddled, or engaged in prostitution during their waking hours. Estimates of the number of homeless children in New York City in 1849 ranged from 3,000 to 30,000.

In 1853, a group of New York ministers founded the Children's Aid Society, with the Reverend Charles Loring Brace as chief officer. Brace, who had spent two years as a missionary to the urban poor, saw the armies of street youth as a serious social problem in the making. If society failed to intervene, these young people were likely to mature into criminals or, more ominously, rise up in revolt. Brace and his colleagues held the opinion that orphaned and homeless children belonged with families and not in institutions. For that reason, they began placing city children with foster families in agricultural communities, where, it was hoped, they would escape the lure of vice and gain the love, attention, and guidance that family life provided. Brace wrote that "every child of bad habits who can secure a place in a Christian home, is in the best possible place for his improvement."[14]

By 1860, the society has "placed out" more than 5,000 children, mostly in the Midwest. Its agents collected children from city streets—including many who had homes and families of their own—and took them west by train. As the "orphan train" stopped in midwestern towns, farm families selected children to take in. The Children's Aid Society did no background checks, kept careless records, and rarely followed up on the children placed, so although Brace boasted of a high success rate, the number of children who were mistreated or ran away is unknown. Similar societies were formed in other cities and states, including Baltimore, Boston, and Pennsylvania.

The Draft Riot of 1863

The urban violence predicted by Charles Loring Brace erupted in his own city in summer 1863, when the Union and Confederacy had been at war for more than two years. Two events ignited New York City's poor, unskilled, largely Irish-immigrant working population. The first was President Abraham Lincoln's issuing of the Emancipation Proclamation, which granted freedom to slaves in Confederate-held territory, effective January 1, 1863. New York's poor feared a resulting influx of African Americans eager to work for low wages and take away their jobs. The second inflammatory event occurred on March 3, 1863, when Congress passed the Conscription Act, making all men between the ages of 20 and 35, and unmarried men age 35 to 45, eligible for military service. The draft was to be conducted by lottery in each congressional district, but drafted men could escape military duty by providing a substitute to serve in their place or by paying $300. The law was therefore perceived as one that favored men of means; the burden of military service was bound to be greater for the poor.

The protest began nonviolently, with a work stoppage on the morning of Monday, July 13. Sometime after 10:00, antidraft demonstrators demolished the headquarters of the provost marshal of the Ninth District, where the lottery was to be drawn. The ranks of the rioters swelled rapidly. "Their numbers soon became so vast, that the police force, unaided by the military, were found incapable of resisting their progress," said Mayor George Opdyke. "Before night they had swept over a large portion of the city, arresting the progress of industry wherever they went, cutting telegraph wires, tearing up railroads, stopping carriages, omnibuses, and rail-cars, sacking and applying the torch to numerous buildings, and barbarously murdering every colored man that fell into their hands."[15] Among the victims was 23-year-old Abraham Franklin, who was disabled but nevertheless worked as a coachman. Franklin was sitting at the bedside of his ill mother when the mob broke into the apartment, beat him, and hanged him before his mother's eyes. Also murdered was Jeremiah Robinson, who attempted to flee the city in his wife's hooded cloak. Some boys spotted his beard, and immediately the rioters tortured and murdered him and threw his body in the East River. The mob also looted the homes of the wealthy and burned the Colored Orphan Asylum.

Army units—survivors of the Battle of Gettysburg—arrived on Thursday, July 16, and began to restore order. Despite the mob's promises to wipe out the city's black population, only 11 African Americans were among the approximately 120 people who died in the riot. Eight soldiers, two police officers, and two volunteers aiding the police were also killed. The rest of the dead were protesters. Hundreds of people were injured, including Police Superintendent John A. Kennedy, who was severely beaten, and property damage was extensive. Some New Yorkers provided the African Americans left homeless with shelter, food, and cash.

It was widely accepted that rioting was the natural outcome when people were raised in tenement conditions. In 1864 the *New York Tribune* editor Horace Greeley reported that 700 families, or 3,500 men, women, and children, lived in a single, crowded Manhattan tenement block. The tenement poor "are with us always," he wrote. "At present they curse New-York, and through her the country and all humanity."[16]

Chronicle of Events

1790

• A poor law is enacted in the Northwest Territory, calling for appointed overseers to administer relief in each township.
• The first American textile mill opens in Pawtucket, Rhode Island.
• The population of New York City is 33,131.

1792

• Kentucky enters the Union; according to the Kentucky poor law, counties elect overseers of the poor.

1793

• An epidemic of yellow fever devastates Philadelphia; the city provides emergency relief to 1,200 households each week.

1797

• Thomas Paine proposes a national fund for the elimination of poverty.

1798

• Congress establishes the Marine Hospital Fund to provide medical care to sick and disabled merchant seamen.

1800

• Congress appropriates funds to aid indigent Native Americans.
• The population of New York City is 60,515.
• Approximately 60,000 people live in the Philadelphia area.

1810

• The population of New York City reaches 96,373.

1812

• War with England reduces foreign trade; domestic manufacturing expands.

1814

• In New York City the Female Assistance Society aids 1,500 poor women, and the Association for the Relief of Respectable, Aged, Indigent Females provides relief to 150 women age 60 and older.

Strong drink leads to poverty and ruin in this cautionary illustration from 1846. *(Library of Congress, Prints and Photographs Division, LC-USZ62-14627)*

1815

• The resumption of peace results in an influx of imported goods and domestic wage cuts and layoffs.
• New York State spends $245,000 on poor relief.

1816

• In Philadelphia, 9,672 workers are employed.

1818

• The Revolutionary War Pension Act gives financial support to needy veterans.

1819

• The United States enters an economic depression known as the Panic of 1819; 500,000 workers are unemployed.
• In Philadelphia, 2,137 workers are employed.
• The New York Society for the Prevention of Pauperism estimates that 8,000 paupers live in New York City.
• Poor relief costs New York State $368,645.

1820
- Between 12,000 and 13,000 New Yorkers receive charitable relief.
- The population of the Philadelphia region is about 100,000.
- Construction of the second almshouse in Baltimore begins.

1821
- *November:* The pension list of New York's Society for the Relief of Poor Widows contains the names of 254 women and 667 children younger than 10.

1822
- New York State spends $470,000 on poor relief and another $25,000 removing 1,796 transients to their counties of residence.

1824
- J. V. N. Yates, secretary of state in New York, surveys poverty in his state.
- Eighteen poorhouses are operating in New York.
- Massachusetts has 83 operating almshouses.

1825
- The population of New York City is 166,086.

1827
- Philadelphia makes outdoor relief illegal.

The neighborhood turns out to see a funeral procession leave a Baxter Street tenement, Five Points, New York City, in 1865. *(Library of Congress, Prints and Photographs Division, LC-USZ62-121734)*

1830–1832
- Seneca County, New York, acquires a farmhouse, barn, and acreage for its poor farm.

1833
- The U.S. Bureau of Pensions is formed; impoverished veterans of all U.S. wars receive government relief.

1835
- Fifty-one of New York's 55 counties have poorhouses.

1837
- The United States enters a severe depression known as the Panic of 1837.

1838
- The house on the Seneca County poor farm has been enlarged into a structure measuring 42 by 46 feet with a wing measuring 26 by 22 feet.

1839
- Philadelphia reinstates outdoor relief.

1840
- In New York, 8,225 people receive indoor relief.
- There are 180 almshouses in Massachusetts.

1842
- Dorothea Dix inspects treatment of the mentally ill at Massachusetts almshouses.

1843
- The New York Association for Improving the Condition of the Poor is established.

1848
- Cook County, Illinois, outlaws outdoor relief.

1849
- A cholera epidemic leaves many poor children in need of care.
- Estimates of the number of homeless children in New York City range from 3,000 to 30,000.
- *September 11:* The Chicago Orphan Asylum opens.

1850
- Almost 10,000 New Yorkers receive indoor relief.

1851

• The Reverend Lewis Pease founds the Five Points House of Industry.

1853

• A grand-jury inspection of the Chicago Almshouse reveals inadequate conditions, especially for women and children.
• The Children's Aid Society is formed and begins placing New York City street children with rural families.
• The Ladies Home Missionary Society has the Old Brewery torn down and constructs a mission on its site in the Five Points section of Manhattan.

1854

• President Franklin Pierce vetoes the Ten Million Acre Bill.

1855

• The New York Association for Improving the Condition of the Poor opens a model tenement, the Workmen's Home.

1858

• Another economic depression begins.
• Cook County reinstates outdoor relief.

1860

• The U.S. Indian Department provides emergency aid to poor Native Americans in Texas.
• Massachusetts now has 219 almshouses; there are almshouses in all Maryland counties but one.
• There are 124 orphan asylums in the United States.
• The Children's Aid Society has placed more than 5,000 children with farm families.

1863

• *January 1:* The Emancipation Proclamation, the document freeing slaves in Confederate-held territory, becomes effective.
• *March 3:* The Federal Conscription Act becomes law, making men age 20 to 35 and single men age 35 to 45 eligible for the draft; men may pay $300 to the government in lieu of service.
• *July 13–15:* A mob consisting largely of the working poor riots in New York City.
• *July 16:* Union forces restore order to New York City.

Eyewitness Testimony

What is the chief end of Man?
To gather up riches—to cheat all he can,
To flatter the rich—the poor to despise,
To pamper the fool—to humble the wise.

The rich to assist—to do all in his power
To kick the unfortunate still a peg lower.

To deal fair with all men, where riches attend
them,
To grind down the poor, where there's none to
defend them.

Independent Gazetteer, *Philadelphia, 1797, in Ronald
Schultz,* The Republic of Labor, *p. 103.*

The contrast of affluence and wretchedness continually
meeting and offending the eye, is like dead and living
bodies chained together. Though I care as little about
riches as any man, I am a friend to riches, because they
are capable of good. I care not how affluent some may
be, provided that none be miserable in consequence of
it.—But it is impossible to enjoy affluence with the felicity
it is capable of being enjoyed, whilst so much misery is
mingled in the scene.

Thomas Paine, political philosopher, 1797, Agrarian
Justice, *p. 10.*

It is the practice of what has unjustly obtained the name
of civilization (and the practice merits not to be called
either charity or policy) to make some provision for persons becoming poor and wretched, only at the time they
become so.—Would it not, even as a matter of economy,
be far better, to devise means to prevent their becoming
poor? This can be done by making every person, when
arrived at the age of twenty-one years, an inheritor of
something to begin with. The rugged face of society,
checquered with the extremes of affluence and want,
proves that some extraordinary violence has been committed upon it, and calls on justice for redress. The great
mass of the poor, in all countries, are become an heredi-
tary race, and it is next to impossible for them to get out
of that state themselves. It ought also to be observed,
that this mass increases in all the countries that are called
civilized. More persons fall annually into it, than get out
of it.

Thomas Paine, political philosopher, 1797, Agrarian
Justice, *p. 11.*

June 29: Admitted Mary McNeal an Irish Woman, and
hath legal residence, this poor creature had the Misfortune of breaking one of her thighs, last Wednesday, by
falling down a pair of Stairs; her Husband John McNeal
is a poor labouring man and not being able to support
himself and her in the situation she is in, he obtained
an Order of Admission from James Coffings and Henry
Molier to bring her in here. Debit Southwark.

June 30: Materials issued to be Manufactured: Twelve
pounds flax, sixteen pounds Tow, and two pounds Wool
to be spun, and about four hundred weight of Junk to be
picked into Oakum.

July 1: Admitted Joseph and Christiana, alias Harriet,
Arriet. Joseph is Three years and seven months old, Harriet
One year and seven months old. These Children were discharged the 1st last April with their Father and Mother, the
latter of whom is now dead, and the Father not being able
to support them, has obtained an Order of Admission from
Mr. Thomas Hockley and brought them here. Debit City.

Discharged Oliver Lynch, and notwithstanding his
nonresidency; has been a very troublesome to and fro
Customer, too lazy to work out doors, or in doors, although he can eat two mens allowance and was punished
with two days confinement for his idleness, but all to no
purpose. Admitted the 15th May last. Credit Southwark.

July 3: Eloped Matthew Richards, and notwithstanding
his being seventy years of age, scaled the fence this Morning, by break of day. He had been out but a short time, when
he was brought back in a Cart, and he has now jumped it
again; said old man is much addicted to liquor for which
reason and the disturbance he makes in the streets when in
that condition, has been often out into prison; he has been
here often, and always took this method of getting out; his
Wife who is a striving industrious body, but cannot live with
him on account of his frequent intoxications and abuse—
but rather than he should expose himself, and his family too,
in the manner he does, she obtained an Order of Admission for him the 31st last May from James McGlathery and
James Collings on promising them at the same time, that
she would call at this house every week and pay One dollar
for his board, which she has done. Credit Southwark.

Eloped Aaron Larkin a Mulatto Man who was admitted the 7th Ultimo [of last month] with a very highly
venereal complaint, and for being made sound again has
taken this ungratefull method of acknowledging Thanks
to his benefactors.

*Entries from the daily occurrence docket, Philadelphia
Almshouse, 1800, in Billy G. Smith, ed.,* Life in Early
Philadelphia, *pp. 39–40.*

After preaching this evening to the poor in the alms-house, I went by request to pray with two females, who have attended on my ministry, and are now confined to their beds. One is an aged widow, who is pious, and who, I believe, will recover, to limp along through life, on two crutches, to everlasting glory. She will recover, to suffer more pain, and peddle pin-cushions to procure some of the conveniences of life, which cannot be distributed in public alms-houses. . . .

The other person is a younger widow, whose hands and feet, having been frozen, are now in a state of pro-gressive putrefaction. She sent me a message, requesting me to visit her; but it was apparently in vain. Her agony was unutterable. Her eyes were swollen, and horribly wild, as if ready to burst from their sockets. I asked if I should pray with her, and she shrieked out, "O yes! yes! yes!" but while I spake, her agony and groans must have excluded both hearing and reflection. Such an hour of human misery as this, I have never before witnessed.

Ezra Styles Ely, preacher to the hospital and almshouse, New York City, January 10, 1811, Visits of Mercy, *pp. 28–29.*

On the 24th of the last month, the writer preached in the ward of the alms-house in which he held public wor-ship this morning: but the room was almost cleared of its late inhabitants. He was then surrounded by many, who have since gone to the state of the dead, and others are stretched on the same beds, to die in their turn, in the same manner. It may be necessary, here, to observe, that those persons who are unable to support themselves in sickness, are carried to the hospital, where there is a probability of their being restored to health; but when they have chronical complaints, or when the hospital is full, they are brought to the alms-house, to die and be buried at the public expense. Servants and labourers, who have not been sufficiently prudent or successful, to make provision for a lingering disease, find this institution their last home—but one. From the hospital, those who are pronounced incurable are also removed to this place, that their removal may make room for new patients, who may be assisted by the medical and surgical attendance.

Ezra Styles Ely, preacher to the hospital and almshouse, New York City, March 10, 1812, Visits of Mercy, *pp. 77–78.*

Last week, a child was found, in the evening, at the gate of the alms-house, which was deaf, dumb, and lame. It was sewed up in a blanket; and since no one acknowl-edged it, the institution humanely received it. It is one of the effects of Christianity, that such asylums are provided

by the community. The child appears to be about twelve years of age. But who were the parents? Had they been so poor as to be unable to support the child, they would have brought him openly, and claimed support. If they were able to protect the child, and yet deserted it, they have souls, which "were made of sterner stuff."

Ezra Styles Ely, preacher to the hospital and almshouse, New York City, March 10, 1812, Visits of Mercy, *pp. 79–80.*

It is not an opinion hastily formed, nor is it altogether sin-gular, that many charitable institutions, or institutions for affording pecuniary or other equivalent aid to the indigent, exert, on the whole, an unhappy influence on society. Is it not true, that, by these institutions, designed for the best of purposes, provision is in fact made for idleness and other vices? If people believe, that they shall be relieved when in distress, they will not generally make exertions, will not labour when they are able and have the opportunity. Ac-cording to their views of things, they have no inducement to labour, or make provision for a time of need. This in-duces idleness, and idleness is the parent of vice.

Ward Stafford, missionary to the poor of New York City, March 1817, New Missionary Field, *p. 43.*

A pauper [in England] means a man that is *able and willing to work,* and who *does work like a horse;* and who is *so taxed,* has so much of his earnings taken from him *by them* to pay the interest of *their* Debt and the pensions of themselves and their wives, children, and dependents, that he is actu-ally starving and fainting at *his work.* This is what is meant by a *pauper in England.* But, at New York, a pauper is, *gen-erally,* a man who is unable, or, which is more frequently the case, unwilling to work; who is become debilitated from a vicious life; or, who, like boroughmongers and Priests, finds it more pleasant to live upon the labour of others than upon his own labour. A pauper in England is fed upon bones, garbage, refuse meat, and *"substitutes for bread."* A pauper here expects, and has, as much flesh, fish and bread and cake as he can devour. How gladly would many a little tradesman, or even little farmer, in England, exchange his diet for that of a New York pauper!

William Cobbett, English traveler, 1818, A Year's Residence in the United States of America, *pp. 378–79.*

I have read much of what has been written respecting the establishment of poor-houses, and have paid attention to various plans which have been proposed for dispensing with them; but I never yet met with the suggestion of any plan which appeared to me to be practicable, or which I thought would be endured in this country.

In our own alms-house there were, when I last visited it, about 1600 paupers. I have often heard it said that *many found shelter there who did not require or deserve an asylum of that description.* I endeavoured to satisfy myself how far this suggestion was founded in fact. After having seen every individual under the poor-house roof, and conversed with a great proportion of them, *I left the establishment with a conviction that none were there as paupers who could with any humanity be turned out. We have been frequently told that the poor and indigent should be left to rely on the charity of individuals.* Let us suppose that the 1600 unfortunate people I have mentioned, were cast out, and told they must beg. *I fear death would as often relieve them from misery, as charity.* But suppose it were otherwise: would we, in the community, *endure the sight of the aged, the infirm, and the cripple, asking alms of every passenger? Would we endure to see our fellow-creatures perishing in the streets?* . . . Here, I am certain. Such scenes would not be tolerated, though the expense of our public charities should be tenfold. But if we have not these establishments, how are the poor to obtain relief, but by becoming mendicants? and when their physical powers are prostrated by age, sickness, or accident, what shall be done with them? Humanity forbids us to answer—*let them linger and die like beasts upon our pavements.* An asylum must be provided for them; and our charitable institutions are no more than a compliance with this moral obligation.

Cadwallader D. Colden, mayor of New York City, 1819, in Mathew Carey, Appeal to the Wealthy of the Land, *p. 35.*

1. That of all modes of providing for the poor, the most wasteful, the most expensive, and most injurious to their morals and destructive of their industrious habits is that of supply in their own families.

2. That the most economical mode is that of Alms Houses; having the character of Work Houses, or Houses of Industry, in which work is provided for every degree of ability in the pauper; and thus the able poor made to provide, partially, at least for their own support; and also to the support, or at least the comfort of the impotent poor.

3. That of all modes of employing the labor of the pauper, agriculture affords the best, the most healthy, and the most certainly profitable; the poor being thus enabled, to raise, always, at least their own provisions.

4. That the success of these establishments depends upon their being placed under the superintendance of a Board of Overseers, constituted of the most substantial and intelligent inhabitants of the vicinity.

5. That of all causes of pauperism, intemperance, in the use of spirituous liquors, is the most powerful and universal.

Five principles of pauper relief, Massachusetts General Court, Committee on Pauper Laws, 1821, Report, *p. 9.*

We have a poor house, with about 80 acres of land attached to the same, The males, who are able to labour, are employed on the farm, and in curing turf for their fuel, which, for a few years past, *has made a great saving for the town.* The females are employed in spinning, weaving, making clothes for the family, taking care of the sick, &c.

It is found by experience, that *the poor can be better taken care of, and supported cheaper, in the alms-house than at large.*

Public overseer of the poor, Andover, Massachusetts, 1827, in Joseph Dewey Fay, Pauperism, *Part 3, p. 1.*

All the world in that busy land [the United States] is more or less on the move, and as the whole community is made up of units, amongst which there is little of the principle of cohesion, they are perpetually dropping out of one another's sight, in the wide field over which they are scattered. Even the connexions of the same family are soon lost sight of—the children glide away from their parents, long before their manhood ripens;—brothers and sisters stream off to the right and left, mutually forgetting one another, and being forgotten by their families. Thus, it often happens, that the heads of a household die off, or wander away, no one knows where, and leave children, if not quite destitute, at least dependent on persons whose connexion and interest in them are so small, that the public eventually is obliged to take care of them, from the impossibility of discovering any one whose duty it is to give them a home. At Charleston, Savannah, and other parts of the country where the yellow fever occurs frequently, and where that still more dreadful curse of America—spirit-drinking—prevails, to at least as great an excess as in the other States, it very often happens that children are left, at the end of the sickly season, without any relations, or natural protectors at all. Of course, I speak now of the poorer inhabitants, part of whom are made up of emigrants, either from foreign countries, or from other parts of America. It seems, indeed, to be the propensity of needy persons in all countries to flock to great cities, where they generally aggravate to a great degree their own evils and those of the city.

The wealthier inhabitants of these towns, though they cannot interfere to prevent such things, are universally ready, not only with their money, but with their personal exertions, to relieve the distress of their less fortunate fellow creatures; and I must say, for the honour of the Americans, that nothing can be more energetic than the way in which they set about the establishment and maintenance of their public charities. Some of these institutions may possibly be questionable in their good effects on society, but there is never any deficiency of zeal or liberality in their support.

Basil Hall, English traveler, 1829, Travels in North America, in the Years 1827 and 1828, Vol. 3, pp. 165–67.

She worked 6 months for Wm. Adams who lived on an adjacent farm, she next lived with Joshua Hasty 5 months same neighborhood, next lived with her aunt, Nancy Taylor, living 2 miles from her Uncle, for 2 months, next came to this City & lived with James Cletchen, Tavernkeeper, Spruce Street near the Delaware, for 3 months, next lived with George Lee Sadler in Spruce Street for 3 months, next went to housekeeping in Water Street, above Spruce Street in a Cellar, for 9 months, next in Fitzwater street for a year, paid 50 cents a Week, next in a house in Spruce Street belonging to George Lee for 5 months, broke up house keeping, & has been *knocking about.*

Recent history of Mary Ann Hasty, a widow, recorded upon her admittance to the Philadelphia Almshouse, December 11, 1828, in Lisa Wilson, Life after Death, p. 61.

In the year 1825, I met with a family who had been reduced from a respectable life to the greatest poverty and distress. It consisted of Mrs. C—, who was left *a widow with four children, and an aged mother dependent upon her for support.* I was introduced to them under circumstances which excited in my breast feelings of the deepest interest. Mrs. C. was extremely ill, as was also one of her children, and her poor old mother almost work out with fatigue and anxiety of mind: in addition to which she had become nearly blind from too close application to her needle, and was utterly unable to supply their necessary wants. I think I *never witnessed a scene of greater distress, or one which presented more urgent claims upon the bounty of your Society.* The timely relief thus afforded, was doubtless a mean, in the hand of Providence, of saving them when they were ready to perish. Every winter since they have received a little assistance from the Society, and by persevering industry have been enabled to support themselves with credit and respectability. Last winter Mrs. C. and her eldest daughter were both well settled in marriage, and the aged mother lives with them alternately, and upon this society descends the blessings of the widow and the fatherless.

Letter from a member of the New York Society for the Relief of Poor Widows with Small Children, 1829, in Mathew Carey, Essays on the Public Charities of Philadelphia, pp. 29–30.

It may be said—it is frequently said—that among the poor there are depraved and worthless characters, whose intemperance and vices have been the causes of their sufferings, and who therefore are unworthy of sympathy or relief. The first part of the position is true, but the inference is unwarranted, and unworthy of human nature. At all events, the accusation is unjust, as regards the mass of the poor; but suppose it were correct, does it follow, that it is justifiable to turn a deaf ear or to harden the heart to the sufferings of poor fellow mortals, in want of food to satisfy the cravings of hunger, or of clothing to screen their shivering limbs from the inclemency of the weather, because their distress may have resulted from imprudence, or even from vice? I believe not.

Mathew Carey, writer and publisher, 1829, Essays on the Public Charities of Philadelphia, pp. iv–v.

I visited a room in Shippen street . . . which contained no furniture, but a miserable bed, covered with a pair of ragged blankets. Three small chunks lay on the hearth. The day was intensely cold. The occupant, a woman, far too slenderly clad, had two children, one about five years old, the other about fifteen months. Both were inadequately dressed for the season, and were *destitute of shoes and stockings. The younger child had had its hands and feet severely frost-bitten, and the inside of the fingers were so much cracked with the frost, that a small blade of straw might lie in the fissures!*—What a hideous case in such a city as Philadelphia!

Mathew Carey, writer and publisher, 1829, Essays on the Public Charities of Philadelphia, p. v.

The industry and virtue of the laboring poor appear undeniable, from the fact, that there is no occupation, however deleterious or disgraceful, at which there is any difficulty in procuring labourers, even at the most inadequate wages. The labour on canals in marshy situations, in atmospheres replete with pestilential miasmata, is full proof on this point. Although the almost certain consequence of labouring in such situations is prostration of health, and danger of life; and that no small proportion of the labourers . . . return to their families in the fall or winter with health and vigor destroyed, and labouring under protracted fevers and agues, which in many cases undermine their constitutions, and return in after-years, and too often hurry them prematurely into eternity: their places are readily supplied by other victims who offer themselves up on the altars of industry.

Mathew Carey, writer and publisher, 1833, Appeal to the Wealthy of the Land, p. 13.

[A]mong the most prominent causes of pauperism, we must indisputably class intemperance. This is the frightful monster of wretchedness and wo, that, besides all his other countless and indescribable ills, would blast our people and our very soil with the curse of poverty. Let us only contemplate the moral features of the inmates of this establishment, and ascertain the peculiar circumstances, that brought here the largest number of them; and we shall scarcely need to search elsewhere for the truth of our declaration, relative to the pauperizing fatality of ardent spirits. Of the hundred and thirteen persons, being the whole number of the poor, now in this house, forty-two have been reduced to penury by their own intemperance; and twenty-one have been brought here, through the intemperance of others. So that sixty-three persons, being three-fifths of the whole number of the inmates, have become paupers, from the tremendous poison of strong drink. Of the hundred and thirteen persons, that have been brought to this house, during the present year, and have either died or been dismissed, sixty-six have been drunkards. When moreover you consider, that, of the hundred and thirteen persons, now the inmates of this house, twenty-four are children, and twenty-three are idiotic or insane, and that about two thirds of the remainder are personally the victims of intemperance, you must be convinced that this awful vice is probably the cause of nearly two thirds of the whole pauperism of our country.

Charles Burroughs, rector of St. John's Church, Portsmouth, New Hampshire, December 15, 1834, A Discourse Delivered in the Chapel of the New Almshouse, in Portsmouth, N.H., pp. 63–64.

That some of the indigent among us die of scanty food, is undoubtedly true; but vastly more in this community die from eating too much, than from eating too little; vastly more from excess, than starvation. So as to clothing, many shiver from want of defences against the cold; but there is vastly more suffering among the rich from absurd and criminal modes of dress, which fashion has sanctioned, than among the poor for deficiency of raiment. Our daughters are oftener brought to the grave by their rich attire, than our beggars by their nakedness. So the poor are often over-worked, but they suffer less than many among the rich who have no work to do, no interesting object to fill up life, to satisfy the infinite cravings of man for action. According to our present modes of education, how many of our daughters are victims of ennui, a misery unknown to the poor, and more intolerable than the weariness of excessive toil. The idle young man, spending the day in exhibiting his person in the street, ought not to excite the envy of the over-tasked poor, and this cumberer of the ground is found exclusively among the rich.

William Ellery Channing, Unitarian minister and writer, April 9, 1835, A Discourse Delivered before the Benevolent Fraternity of Churches in Boston, on Their First Anniversary, p. 3.

A family, crowded into a single and often narrow apartment, which must answer at once the ends of parlor, kitchen, bed-room, nursery, and hospital, must, without great energy and self-respect, want neatness, order, and comfort. Its members are perpetually exposed to annoying, petty interference. The decencies of life can be with difficulty observed. Woman, a drudge, and in dirt, loses her attractions. The young grow up without the modest reserve and delicacy of feeling, in which purity finds so much of its defence. Coarseness of manners and language, too sure a consequence of a mode of life which allows no seclusion, becomes the habit almost of childhood, and hardens the mind for vicious intercourse in future years. The want of a neat, orderly home, is among the chief ills of the poor. Crowded in filth, they cease to respect one another. The social affections wither amidst perpetual noise, confusion, and clashing interests. In these respects, the poor often fare worse than the uncivilized man.

William Ellery Channing, Unitarian minister and writer, April 9, 1835, A Discourse Delivered before the Benevolent Fraternity of Churches in Boston, on Their First Anniversary, pp. 9–10.

From their cheerless rooms, [the poor] look out on the abodes of luxury. At their cold, coarse meal, they hear the equipage conveying others to tables groaning under plenty, crowned with sparkling wines, and fragrant with the delicacies of every clime. Fainting with toil, they meet others, unburdened, as they think, with a labor or a care. They feel, that all life's prizes have fallen to others. Hence burning desire. Hence brooding discontent. Hence envy and hatred. Hence crime, justified in a measure to their own minds by what seem to them the unjust and cruel inequalities of social life.

William Ellery Channing, Unitarian minister and writer, April 9, 1835, A Discourse Delivered before the Benevolent Fraternity of Churches in Boston, on Their First Anniversary, p. 11.

From the denunciations of street beggars, which appear sometimes in our papers, a stranger might be tempted to suppose that they are almost as numerous and as great a nuisance as they are in Paris or Naples. But I am strongly inclined to believe, that except in very severe winters, and since the lamentable prostration of business, and destitution of employment that have prevailed of late, there never have been at any one time, in this city [Philadelphia], 50 or 60 street beggars,—and never one-fifth part of the number of the male sex, except the maimed, the wounded, and the blind.

There are, it is true, numbers of industrious females whose wages are so miserably inadequate for their support, that they are sometimes compelled by dire necessity to apply to charitable individuals to help them to pay their rent, to prevent their being turned out of doors, or to redeem their clothes from pawnbrokers. Society, thus by its crying injustice forces them to beg, and then denounces and abuses them for yielding to necessity! Nothing can be more unjust. But these ill-fated women cannot be styled street beggars, in the proper acceptation of the term.

Mathew Carey, writer and publisher, December 20, 1837,
A Plea for the Poor, p. 14.

The winter of 1837–38, though happily mild and open till far into January, was one of pervading destitution and suffering in our city [New York], from paralysis of business and consequent dearth of employment. The liberality of those who could and would give was heavily taxed to save from famishing the tens of thousands who, being needy and unable to find employment, first ran into debt so far as they could, and thenceforth must be helped or starve. . . .

I lived that winter in the Sixth Ward,—then, as now, eminent for filth, squalor, rags, dissipation, want, and misery. A public meeting of its citizens was duly held early in December, and an organization formed thereat, by which committees were appointed to canvass the Ward from house to house, collect funds from those who could and would spare anything, ascertain the nature and extent of the existing destitution, and devise ways and means for its systematic relief. Very poor myself, I could give no money, or but a mite; so I gave time instead, and served, through several days, on one of the visiting committees. I thus saw extreme destitution more closely than I had ever before observed it, and was enabled to scan its repulsive features intelligently. I saw two families, including six or eight children, burrowing in one cellar under a stable,—a prey to famine on the one hand, and to vermin and cutaneous

maladies on the other, with sickness adding its horrors to those of a polluted atmosphere and a wintry temperature. I saw men who each, somehow, supported his family on an income of $5 per week or less, yet who cheerfully gave something to mitigate the sufferings of those who were really poor. I saw three widows, with as many children, living in an attic on the profits of an apple-stand which yielded less than $3 per week, and the landlord came in for a full third of that. But worst to bear of all was the pitiful plea of stout, resolute, single young men and young women: "We do not want alms; we are not beggars; we hate to sit here day by day idle and useless; help us to work,—we want no other help: why is it that we can have nothing to do?"

Horace Greeley, founder and editor of the New York Tribune,
recalling the winter of 1837–38,
Recollections of a Busy Life, *pp. 144–45.*

I once heard a physician of a high family, and of great respectability in his profession, say, that when he sent his slaves to the work-house to be flogged, he always went to *see* it done, that he might be sure they were properly, i.e. *severely* whipped. He also related the following circumstance in my presence. He had sent a youth of about eighteen to this horrible place to be whipped and *afterwards* to be worked upon the treadmill. From not keeping the step, which probably he COULD NOT do, in consequence of the lacerated state of his body; his arm got terribly torn, from the shoulder to the wrist. This physician said, he went every day to attend to it himself, in order that he might use those restoratives, which *would inflict the greatest possible pain.* This poor boy, after being imprisoned there for some weeks, was then brought home, and compelled to wear iron clogs on his ankles for one or two months. I saw him with those irons on one day when I was at the house. This man was, when young, remarkable in the fashionable world for his elegant and fascinating manners, but the exercise of the slaveholder's power has thrown the fierce air of tyranny even over these.

Angelina Grimke Weld, abolitionist, 1839, in Theodore
Dwight Weld, American Slavery as It Is, *p. 55.*

Let us go . . . and passing this wilderness of an hotel with stores about its base, like some continental theatre, or the London Opera House shorn of its colonnade, plunge into the Five Points. But it is needful, first, that we take as our escort these two heads of the police, whom you would know for sharp and well-trained officers if you met them in the Great Desert. . . .

This is the place: these narrow ways, diverging to the right and left, and reeking everywhere with dirt and filth. Such lives as are led here, bear the same fruits here as elsewhere. The coarse and bloated faces at the doors, have counterparts at home, and all the wide world over. . . .

What place is this, to which the squalid street conducts us? A kind of square of leprous houses, some of which are attainable only by crazy wooden stairs without. What lies beyond this tottering flight of steps, that creak beneath our tread? a miserable room, lighted by one dim candle, and destitute of all comfort, save that which may be hidden in a wretched bed. Beside it, sits a man: his elbows on his knees: his forehead hidden in his hands. "What ails that man!" asks the foremost officer. "Fever," he sullenly replies, without looking up. Conceive the fancies of a fevered brain, in such a place as this!

Ascend these pitch-dark stairs, heedful of a false footing on the trembling boards, and grope your way with me into this wolfish den, where neither ray of light nor breath of air, appears to come. A negro lad, startled from his sleep by the officer's voice—he knows it well—but comforted by the assurance that he has not come on business, officiously bestirs himself to light a candle. The match flickers for a moment, and shows great mounds of dusky rags upon the ground, then dies away and leaves a denser darkness than before, if there can be degrees in such extremes. He stumbles down the stairs and presently comes back, shading a flaring taper with his hand. Then the mounds of rags are seen to be astir, and slowly rise up, and the floor is covered with heaps of negro women, waking from their sleep; their white teeth chattering, and their bright eyes glistening and winking on all sides with surprise and fear.

Charles Dickens, British novelist, 1842, American Notes for General Circulation, *pp. 108–10.*

December 24; thermometer below zero; drove to the poorhouse; was conducted to the master's family-room by himself; walls garnished with handcuffs and chains, not less than five pair of the former; did not inquire how or on whom applied; thirteen pauper inmates; one insane man; one woman insane; one idiotic man; asked to see them; the two men were shortly led in; appeared pretty decent and comfortable. Requested to see the other insane subject; was denied decidedly; urged the request, and finally secured a reluctant assent. Was led through an outer passage into a lower room, occupied by the paupers; crowded; not neat; ascended a rather low flight of stairs upon an open entry, through the floor of which was introduced a stove pipe, carried along a *few feet,* about six inches above the floor,

through which it was reconveyed below. From this entry opens a room of moderate size, having a sashed-window; floor, I think, painted; apartment ENTIRELY unfurnished; no chair, table, nor bed; neither, what is seldom missing, a bundle of straw or lock of hay; cold, very cold; the first movement of my conductor was to throw open a window,

Dorothea Dix is at the top left in this cover illustration from an 1861 ladies' magazine depicting women who do good. The others are Mary Du Bois, founder of the New York Nursery and Child Hospital (top right); Elizabeth Gurney Fry, Quaker prison reformer (center); Grace Darling, who rescued survivors of a wrecked steamship off England's Northumberland coast (lower left); and Florence Nightingale, British nurse and hospital reformer (lower right). *(By permission of the Houghton Library, Harvard University)*

a measure imperatively necessary for those who entered. *On the floor* sat a woman, her limbs immovably contracted, so that the knees were brought upward to the chin; the face was concealed; the head rested on the folded arms; for clothing she appeared to have been furnished with *fragments* of many discharged garments; these were folded about her, yet they little benefitted her, if one might judge by the constant shuddering which almost convulsed the poor crippled frame. Woful was this scene; language is feeble to record the misery she was suffering and had suffered! . . . Poor wretch! she, like many others, was an example of what humanity becomes when the temple of reason falls in ruins, leaving the mortal part to injury and neglect, and showing how much can be endured of privation, exposure, and disease, without extinguishing the lamp of life.

Dorothea L. Dix, reformer, 1843, describing a woman in Saugus, Memorial: To the Legislature of Massachusetts, *pp. 9–10.*

The master of one of the best regulated almshouses, viz. that of Plymouth, where every arrangement shows that the comfort of the sick, the aged, and the infirm, is suitably cared for, and the amendment of the unworthy is studied and advanced, said, as we stood opposite a latticed stall, where was confined a madman, that the hours of the day were few, when the whole household was not distracted from employment by screams, and turbulent stampings, and every form of violence, which the voice or muscular force could produce. This unfortunate being was one of the "returned incurables," since whose last admission to the almshouse, they were no longer secure of peace for the aged, or decency for the young; it was morally impossible to do justice to the sane and insane in such improper vicinity to each other. . . . Poorhouses, converted into madhouses, cease to effect the purposes for which they were established and instead of being asylums for the aged, the homeless, and the friendless, and places of refuge for orphaned or neglected childhood, are transformed into perpetual bedlams.

Dorothea L. Dix, reformer, 1843, Memorial: To the Legislature of Massachusetts, *pp. 25–26.*

We might consider the poor under three divisions.

First—Those who are supported from day to day by their honest industry. Not able to accumulate property, but yet, with diligence and a wise economy, able to meet their small expenses, and thus are happy and independent.

Second—Those who are willing to work, but from old age and feebleness, or disease, are not able, by their labor, to

meet their necessary expenses;—those who have sought for employment and have sought in vain, or if they have found it, have received such small compensation, as to make it necessary for them to receive the aid of charity. And,

Third—Those who might work, but who prefer IDLENESS; who have no self-respect or desire to be useful; who obtain from others all that they possibly can, and yield nothing in return; and those who are not only slothful, but vicious; who are impostors and vagrants; who neither practise nor wish to practise, either forethought, economy or sobriety.

R. C. Waterston, clergyman and author, 1844, An Address on Pauperism, Its Extent, Causes, and the Best Means of Prevention, *p. 5.*

There are many who love sloth; they would rather live upon the toil of others, than toil themselves. Their greatest anxiety is, how they may supply their wants without labor. And hence comes beggary; but beggary does not always succeed so well with an honest story, as a false one, and hence comes fraud. But at times even fraud does not succeed, and the impostor becomes a thief. Idleness, when indulged, becomes a habit and the habit becomes inveterate, and this inveterate habit makes a pauper, and that pauperism may soon lead to crime. There is something purifying in the glow of labor, but the idler's very mind seems to moulder; his faculties shrink, or they become diseased and unbalanced, and those who have not the energy for work will be active in vice. One great cause of pauperism is sloth.

R. C. Waterston, clergyman and author, 1844, An Address on Pauperism, Its Extent, Causes, and the Best Means of Prevention, *pp. 16–17.*

But even the lot of these should be *considered* as well as *condemned.* Their very baseness demands our pity. Even the most reckless and abandoned, with the marks of humanity well nigh worn out of them; are they not objects for our commiseration? Perhaps circumstances beyond their control, have made them what they are. For how many human wrecks is society answerable! And let not society spurn the object its own neglect has made! Born in penury, and educated in vice; unfortunate in physical organization, and still more unfortunate in the low excitements to which that organization has been exposed. Every thing within and around them has tended to degrade. No smile to cheer, no voice to encourage, they have become reckless, and deem man and society alike their foe. Looked upon with no confidence, they cherish no faith; and distrusted by others, they distrust all in return, and hope to gain nothing except by fraud. Even such, low as they are, we should labor to reclaim. Let us not meet them with ridicule and oppression, but with justice and mercy, which, while it condemns, seeks to save.

R. C. Waterston, clergyman and author, 1844, An Address on Pauperism, Its Extent, Causes, and the Best Means of Prevention, *p. 7.*

The snow drifts through the city. And the streets are nearly deserted. The watchman, with slow pace, walks his dreary rounds. At times a carriage passes in the distance, bearing some one from the gay assembly. From one small window struggles a feeble gleam of light. Is it some lonely watcher who keeps vigils by the sick bed, or in the chamber of death? No. It is the poor woman, bending with fatigue, still plying her needle; and in the morning, when she seeks her employer, perhaps she has earned hardly enough to purchase bread for her children. She may return once more almost heart-broken to her toil; but toil, alas! how little is it sweetened with pleasure.

R. C. Waterston, clergyman and author, 1844, An Address on Pauperism, Its Extent, Causes, and the Best Means of Prevention, *p. 19.*

Some time during the Autumn of last year I attended at No. 249 Stanton-street, Charles Peterson, aged about forty-five years, of intemperate habits. He had Pneumonia, followed by Typhus symptoms, and lived but two or three days after my first visiting him. He had been sick for several days previously, and without medical attendance. At No. 96 Sheriff-street, and in the immediate neighborhood of this case, and at nearly the same time, I had another of like character, of about the same age, and of similar habits. This case likewise terminated fatally in the course of a few days. . . .

Both of these men, with their families, were wretchedly poor, living in cellar rooms, some six feet below the street, dark and damp, with very scanty ventilation, and ceilings, or rather beams so low, that I could not stand erect between them. The apartments at my first visit were filthy and offensive in the extreme; yet some improvement became evident afterwards, as I generally in this class of patients, find it necessary in the first place, to lecture them on the importance of cleanliness, ventilation, temperance, &c.

I attribute the rest of these cases, mainly to the situation, manner of living, and habits of the subjects. This at least was the conclusion I recollect I came to at the time;

my attention having been arrested at the fatality of cases which at first appeared likely to have a successful issue, as I had often had others of a like nature, terminate well under more favorable circumstances.

The widow of the patient, at 96 Sheriff-street, died last spring, with fever of a low form in the same miserable house. *Subsequently at this house a quantity of water was found under the flooring.*

Stephen Wood, M.D., physician to the Eastern Dispensary, August 17, 1844, in John H. Griscom, The Sanitary Condition of the Laboring Class of New York, *1845, p. 17.*

[T]he most offensive of all places for residence are the *cellars.* It is almost impossible, when contemplating the circumstances and conditions of the poor beings who inhabit these holes, to maintain the proper degree of calmness requisite for a thorough inspection, and the exercise of a sound judgment, respecting them. You must descend to them; you must feel the blast of foul air as it meets your face on opening the door; you must grope in the dark, or hesitate until your eye becomes accustomed to the gloomy place, to enable you to find your way through the entry, over a broken floor, the boards of which are protected from your tread by a half inch of hard dirt; you must inhale the suffocating vapor of the sitting and sleeping rooms; and in the dark, damp recess, endeavor to find the inmates by the sound of their voices, or chance to see their figures moving between you and the flickering blaze of a shaving burning on the hearth, or the misty light of a window coated with dirt and festooned with cobwebs—or if in search of an invalid, take care that you do not fall full length upon the bed with her, by stumbling against the bundle of rags and straw, dignified by that name, lying on the floor, under the window, if window there is.

John H. Griscom, New York City public health inspector, 1845, The Sanitary Condition of the Laboring Class of New York, *p. 8.*

We followed through a dirty passage, so narrow, a stout man would have found it tight work to have threaded it. Looking before us, the yard seemed unusually dark. This we found was occasioned by a long range of two story pens, with a projecting boarded walk above the lower tier, for the inhabitants of the second story to get to the doors of their apartments. This covered nearly all the narrow yard, and served to exclude light from the dwellings below. We looked in every one of these dismal abodes of human wretchedness. Here were dark, damp holes, six feet square, without a bed in any of them, and generally without furniture, occupied by one or two families: apartments where privacy of any kind was unknown—where comfort never appeared. We endeavoured with the aid of as much light as at mid-day could find access through the open door, to see into the dark corners of these contracted abodes; and as we became impressed with their utter desolateness, the absence of bedding, and of ought to rest on but a bit of old matting on a wet floor, we felt sick and oppressed. Disagreeable odours of many kinds were ever arising; and with no ventilation but the open door, and the foot square hole in the front of the pen, we could scarcely think it possible that life could be supported, when winter compelled them to have fire in charcoal furnaces. . . . It is not in the power of language to convey an adequate impression of the scene of this property.

Quaker inspectors of an African-American slum in Philadelphia, 1849, A Statistical Inquiry into the Condition of the People of Colour of the City and Districts of Philadelphia, *pp. 37–38.*

[W]e are standing at midnight in the center of the Five Points. Over our heads is a large gas-lamp, which throws a strong light for some distance around, over the scene where once complete darkness furnished almost absolute security and escape to the pursued thief and felon, familiar with every step and knowing the exits and entrances to every house. . . .

Opposite the lamp, eastwardly, is the "Old Brewery." . . . The building was originally, previous to the city being built up so far, used as a brewery. But when the population increased and buildings, streets and squares grew up and spread all around it, the owner—shrewd man, and very respectable church deacon—found that he might make a much larger income from his brewery than by retaining it for the manufacture of malt liquor. It was accordingly floored and partitioned off into small apartments, and rented to persons of disreputable character and vile habits. . . . Every room in every story had its separate family or occupant, renting by the week or month and paying in advance. In this one room, the cooking, eating and sleeping of the whole family, and their visitors, are performed. Yes—and *their visitors;* for it is no unusual thing for a mother and her two or three daughters—all of course prostitutes—to receive their "men" at the same time and in the same room—passing in and out and going through all the transactions of their hellish intercourse, with a sang froid at which devils would stand aghast and struck with horror.

All the houses in this vicinity, and for some considerable distance around—yes, every one—are of the same character, and are filled in precisely the same manner.

George G. Foster, reporter for the New York Tribune, *1850,* New York by Gas-Light and Other Urban Sketches, *pp. 121–22.*

An alley extends all around the building; on the north side it is of irregular width, wide at the entrance; and gradually tapering to a point. On the opposite side the passage-way is known by the name of "Murderer's Alley," a filthy, narrow path, scarcely three feet in width. There are double rows of rooms throughout the building, entered by the alleyways on either side. Some of these rooms are just passably decent; the majority are dirty, dark, and totally unfit for occupation. The dark and winding passage-ways, which extend throughout the whole building, must have afforded a convenient means of escape to thieves and criminals of all kinds; there are also various hiding-places recently discovered, which have also, no doubt, afforded the means of escape to offenders against the laws. In the floor in one of the upper rooms, a place was found where the boards had been sawed; upon tearing them up, human bones were found, the remains, no doubt, of a victim of some diabolical murder. The whole of the building above-ground is rickety and dilapidated—some of the stairs even creak when trodden upon. Our way was explored by the aid of a single lamp, in company with two gentlemen and a guide; beside these there were a number of rather rough-looking customers, who appeared as much interested as anyone else. But it was not until one of the gentlemen complained, in one of the dark passage-ways, of a strange hand in his pocket, that these three characters were suspected. Then our guide informed us, in an under-tone, that we were surrounded by a gang of the most notorious pickpockets and thieves of that section, and that we must take good care of our watches, or we would lose them before we were aware. . . .

The above-ground part of the premises cannot be better imagined than by supposing it just as bad as it can be,—once plastered, but now half the wall off, in some places mended by pasting newspapers over it, but often revealing unsightly holes. The under part, or basement of the building, is even still worse on the south-west corner; in a lower room, not more than fifteen feet square, *twenty-six* human beings reside. A man could scarcely stand erect in it; two men were sitting by the blaze of a few sticks when our company entered; women lay on a mass of filthy, unsightly rags in the corner—sick, feeble, and emaciated; six or seven children were in various attitudes about the corner; an old table covered with a few broken dishes; two women were peeling potatoes, and actually pulling off the skins with their finger nails; the smoke and stench of the room was so suffocating that it could not be long endured, and the announcement that, in addition to the misfortune of poverty, they had the measles to boot, started most of our party in a precipitate retreat from the premises.

On the front side of the building the basement is deeper, but if possible worse. Here were seen only a few miserable-looking women—one was drunk and stupid, and lay upon the bare floor in the corner; in a side room, in front of a fire-place, and before a full blaze, sat two women, who looked as low and debased as any human beings could. No furniture was in the room, with only the floor for their bed, and the scant dresses they wore for their only covering.

But it may be asked: What do these wretched people do for a living? We answer: The men are street-sweepers and thieves, the women beg and steal what they can, the children sweep crossings in wet weather, and cut up the kindling-wood which we all see them carry about the streets. A great deal of this last business, we observed, was carried on in the "Old Brewery." What more they do who can tell? Miserable beings! life is at best but an unpleasant necessity, but to them it must be an awful punishment.

A description of the Old Brewery, 1850, in "The Five Points," National Magazine, *March 1853, p. 268.*

[T]he debased poor . . . unhappily, are too numerous and dangerous a class to be allowed to increase, without special efforts to reduce their number. Their indolent and vicious habits are so firmly established, that they are not likely to be changed, except under a course of powerful and effective treatment. They generally have not only an insuperable aversion to labor, but also to the Alms-House, because of its salutary privations and restraints. They love to clan together in some out-of-the-way place, are content to live in filth and disorder with a bare subsistence, provided they can drink, and smoke, and gossip, and enjoy their balls, and wakes, and frolics, without molestation. Instead of putting their children to school, or to some useful trade, they are driven out to beg, pick up fuel, sweep the street crossings, peddle petty wares, &c., that they may themselves live lazily on the means thus secured.

New-York Association for Improving the Condition of the Poor, 1851, Eighth Annual Report, *p. 18.*

Miserable-looking buildings, liquor-stores innumerable, neglected children by scores, playing in rags and dirt, squalid-looking women, brutal men with black eyes and disfigured faces, proclaiming drunken brawls and fearful violence, complete the general picture,

Gaze on it mentally, fair reader, and realize, if you can, while sauntering down Broadway, rejoicing in all the refinements and luxuries of life, that *one minute's* walk would place you in a scene like this. Gaze on it, men of thought, when treading the steps of the City Hall or the Hall of Justice, where laws are framed, and our city's interests discussed and cared for—*one minute's* walk would place you in this central point of misery and sin. Gaze on it, ye men of business and of wealth, and calculate anew the amount of taxation for police restraints and support, made necessary by the existence of a place like this. And gaze on it, Christian men, with tearful eyes—tears of regret and shame—that long ere now the Christian Church has not combined its moral influences, and tested their utmost strength to purge a place so foul; for this, reader, is the "Five Points!"—a name known throughout the Union, in England, and on the continent of Europe. The "Five Points!" a name which has hitherto been banished from the vocabulary of the refined and sensitive, or whispered with a blush, because of its painful and degrading associations. The "Five Points!" What does that name import? It is the synonym for ignorance the most entire, for misery the most abject, for crime of the darkest dye, for degradation so deep that human nature cannot sink below it.

"The Five Points," National Magazine, *February 1853, p. 169.*

The Poor House is entirely inadequate to the wants of this county for the healthful and convenient accommodation of so large a number as our county agent finds it necessary to lodge and feed here. We find from 130 to 140 inmates—some 40 sick, and a large number quite infirm. From the number of inmates, and the limited space in the buildings, we find the rooms literally filled with beds, and badly ventilated; the sick and the well necessarily thrown to-gether, making it extremely unpleasant for both. The want of more room is more particularly apparent in the apartment appropriated to the women with children, which, although kept quite neat and clean, is so crowded as to be very offensive to one going to and from the open air.

Chicago Weekly Democrat, *February 19, 1853, in* James Brown, The History of Public Assistance in Chicago, 1833 to 1893, *p. 20.*

The ill-ventilation in winter of the rooms of the poor—a thing, too, so stubbornly persisted in—is usually charged upon them as their disgraceful neglect of the most simple means to health. But the instinct of the poor is wiser than we think. The air which ventilates, likewise *cools*. And to any shiverer, ill-ventilated warmth is better than well-ventilated cold. Of all the preposterous assumptions of humanity over humanity, nothing exceeds most of the criticisms made on the habits of the poor by the well-housed, well-warmed, and well-fed.

Herman Melville, American novelist, 1854, "Poor Man's Pudding and Rich Man's Crumbs," in The Complete Shorter Fiction, *p. 293.*

[T]he *paupers* and the *beggars* do not constitute the sum total of the POOR. Would to God they did. The great mass of the poor are those who are struggling by toil, privation, and even in destitution, to get bread and clothing for themselves and children, and a place to shelter them from the cold and the storm, *without begging, or calling upon the public authorities for aid.* Oh, my God! . . . I see them living—suffering in garrets and cellars—and pent-up rooms—with no ventilation; damp, filthy, destructive to health and happiness. I see the widow and the orphan—and the honest poor man, with a large family—weak and sickly himself from long and constant toil to furnish bread and clothing for his dear ones. I behold them all in poverty; at times positively suffering for want of bread and fuel; and yet toiling on and on, from week to week, year in and year out, perhaps without a murmur, and yet with no hope of relief.

G. W. Quinby, Universalist minister in Yarmouth, Maine, 1856, The Gallows, the Prison, and the Poor-House, *p. 295.*

[I]n twenty districts there are over one thousand two hundred tenement houses of the lowest description, occupied by not less than ten families in each. In some of these not less than seventy families reside, and into a few, more than one hundred families are crowded. . . . In one building, one hundred and ten families are gathered, some of them numbering eight or ten members, occupying one close apartment, and huddled indiscriminately in damp, foul cellars, to breathe the air of which is to inhale disease. Here, in their very worst aspect, are to be seen the horrors of such a mode of living. Here are to be found drunken and diseased adults, of both sexes, lying in the midst of their filth; idiotic and crippled children, suffering from neglect and ill-treatment; girls just springing into womanhood, living indiscriminately in the same apartment with men of all ages and all colors; babes left so destitute of care and nourishment, as to be only fitted for a jail or hospital in after years, if they escape the blessing of an early grave.

New York Association for Improving the Condition of the Poor, 1856, Thirteenth Annual Report, *p. 43.*

Mary was . . . born to an inheritance of poverty and vice. She was brought by her father as a temporary boarder; but when we saw him, time after time, under the influence of the intoxicating cup, we determined, if possible, to save his daughter from the misery that must follow a return to such a home. Her father's absence from the city favored our design, and we soon secured a home for Mary with a kind lady, who engaged to train her up for usefulness. She seemed so spirit-broken by her early home influences, that we had little expectation she would ever rise above them, or make any thing in life much above an ordinary Irish servant. It was with much pleasure that we lately received the following letter from her guardian: "Mary came to live with me in March, 1854. She has attended school most of the time since. The teacher says she is a good scholar, and fond of study. She has an active mind, and will, I hope, make a useful person. Her health is good, and she enjoys life as much as any child I ever saw."

Mary herself writes, in a good, childish hand: "I go to school, and study geography, arithmetic, spelling, and other studies. We are to have an exhibition this week, and I am to assist. I go to Sunday-school."

L. M. Pease, ed., New York Five Points House of Industry Monthly Record, *May 1857, pp. 17–18.*

On the dirty floor . . . with legs extended, and almost naked, feet bare, and his whole body shaking with the cold, sat one of the objects of my visit, a boy five years old. He was holding in his lap a half-rotten head of cabbage, from which he kept picking, and greedily eating the frozen leaves. So intent was he on satisfying his appetite, that he scarcely noticed my entrance. Scattered around him were the contents of an old basket from which he had made his selection. These were decayed potatoes, frozen apples, and turnips, pigs' ears and calves' feet; and among a variety of other things, a sheep's head, with its eyes staring right at me. These things were collected by the mother, either by begging or stealing them from the gutters of Washington Market. Here was not all the fruits of her day's labor, for on her way home she had stopped, as was her custom, at a vile penny soup-house, and parted with the choicest bits for rum.

A few feet removed from the boy, and nearly behind the door, sat the mother, in an old rickety chair, her head fallen back, her eyes closed, her mouth wide open, her hair dishevelled about her face and neck, her arms hanging by her side, and her breath labored. . . .

Leaning against her, bare-footed, half-clad, dirty, and ragged, folding to her shivering bosom a dry loaf of bread, stood a wan, sunken-eyed girl only three years old. She cast on me a look of recognition, took the bread in her skeleton fingers, extended it towards me, a smile lighting up her sad and sickly features, and exclaimed: "I've got bread!" That smile was meteor-like; it lingered but a moment, then vanished, leaving her face darker than before. She dropped her head, pressed the bread back to her bosom again, drew a long breath, and sighing, said: "Mother's drunk." . . .

These little innocents were taken to the House of Industry, and carefully cared for; but neglect and want had so weakened their hold on life, that they were soon added to the number of the little ones above.

L. M. Pease, ed., New York Five Points House of Industry Monthly Record, *May 1857, pp. 25–26.*

The children of the poor are not essentially different from the children of the rich; the same principles which influence the good or evil development of every child in comfortable circumstances, will affect, in greater or less degree, the child of poverty. Sympathy and hope are as inspiring to the ignorant girl, as to the educated; steady occupation is as necessary for the street-boy, as the boy of a wealthy house; indifference is as chilling to the one class, as to the other; the prospect of success is as stimulating to the young vagrant, as to the student in the college.

The great mistake we make in regard to the children of the poor, is our too rigid *classification.* It is true there is a certain similarity among them, but the grand truth more and more forces itself upon us, that each poor, deserted, unfortunate little creature in the streets is an *individual,* like no other being whom God has created. He has his own tastes—his own habits—his peculiar temptations—his especial weaknesses, and his own virtues. We may class him, from certain external resemblances, with a hundred or a thousand other lads, and yet he is still distinct and individual. . . .

Nature seems especially to indicate small groups of parents and children, or old and young, as the best forming-institution for young minds. Children in large numbers together, in constant intercourse, appear never to exert a healthful influence on each other: in the higher classes, habits of deceit, and unnatural vices are spread among them; and in the lower, all the seeds of vice which might otherwise lie dormant, spring up and grow noxiously.

Charles Loring Brace, founder of the Children's Aid Society, 1859, The Best Method of Disposing of Our Pauper and Vagrant Children, *pp. 4–5.*

The high brick blocks of the closely packed houses where the mobs originated seemed to be literally hives of sickness and vice. It was wonderful to see and difficult to believe that so much misery, disease, and wretchedness could be huddled together and hidden by high walls, unvisited and unthought of so near our own abodes. Lewd but pale and sickly young women, scarcely decent in their ragged attire, were impudent, and scattered everywhere in the courts. What numbers of these poorer classes are deformed, what numbers are made hideous by self-neglect and infirmity! Alas, human faces look so hideous with hope and self-respect all gone, and familiar forms and features are made so frightful by sin, squalor, and debasement! To walk the streets as we walked them in those hours of conflagration and riot was like witnessing the day of judgment, with every wicked thing revealed, every sin and sorrow blazingly glared upon, every hidden abomination laid before hell's expectant fire.

N. P. Willis, journalist, describing the tenements of New York in the wake of the 1863 draft riots, in Robert W. De Forest and Lawrence Veiller, The Tenement House Problem, *Vol. 1, p. 92.*

I am a whitewasher by trade, and I have worked, boy and man, in this city for sixty-three years. On Tuesday afternoon I was standing on the corner of Thirtieth street and Second avenue, when a crowd of young men came running along and shouting, "Here's a nigger, here's a nigger." Almost before I knew of their intention, I was knocked down, kicked here and there, badgered and battered without mercy, until a cry of "the Peelers are coming" was raised; and I was left almost senseless, with a broken arm and a face covered with blood, on the railroad track. I was helped home on a cart by the officers, who were very kind to me, and gave me some brandy before I got home. *I entertain no malice and have no desire for revenge* against these people. Why should they hurt me or my colored brethren? We are poor men like them; we work hard and get but little for it. I was born in this State and have lived here all my life, and it seems hard, very hard, that we should be knocked down and kept out of work just to oblige folks who won't work themselves and don't want others to work.

"An old man in Sullivan street," 1863, in Report of the Committee of Merchants for the Relief of Colored People, Suffering from the Late Riots in the City of New York, *p. 22.*

On the Monday succeeding the riot, we visited Weeksville, a settlement of colored people, situated some three miles from the ferries, where we found a large number of refugees from the city of New York, and many that had been driven out from their homes in Brooklyn, the inhabitants having furnished them such shelter as they were able, with their limited means and small facilities for accommodating several hundred strangers thrown upon them. We found not only Weeksville, but Carsville, New Brooklyn, and the whole vicinity extending to Flatbush and Flatlands, had more or less refugees scattered in the woods and in such places as they could find safety and shelter. All being thrown out of employment and means of support, your committee immediately made arrangements for furnishing them daily supplies of food. With the assistance of Mr. Edgar McMullen, who had for a few days previous been assisting them, we had food (as we think prudently and judiciously) distributed daily from July 20th, to August 14th. The amount so given out in Bread, Hams, Flour, Rice, Sugar, and Tea, and in some few cases of great need small sums of money, amounted to eight hundred and fifty 27-100 Dollars ($850. 27).

Your committee found so many cases of distress in the city, arising from injuries received during the riot, from losses, and from want of employment, that we found it necessary to have someplace where they could apply for relief. We engaged with the approval of your committee, Rev. Henry Belden, to dispense our charities. He opened the rooms of the Poor Association and engaged four colored Ministers of Brooklyn, to assist in visiting the families of those applying for assistance.

The number of applicants relieved were 752, whose families numbered 2,250; amount donated them, sixteen hundred and ninety dollars ($1,690).

We gave out in small sums at various times, thirty-nine 50-100 dollars ($39.50) making the whole amount disbursed in Brooklyn, twenty-five hundred and seventy-nine 80-100 Dollars ($2,579) which leaves in our hands for special cases that may arise, seventy-five 47-100 Dollars ($75.47). . . .

The majority of the colored people are now at work at their accustomed places of business.

William W. Wickes and R. P. Buck, committee members, September 11, 1863, Report of the Committee of Merchants for the Relief of Colored People, Suffering from the Late Riots in the City of New York, *p. 30.*

[A] few of the worst specimens of tenements have passed away, and few people think much about the rest, though everybody suffers from them. It necessarily follows that they are perfect fiery furnaces in case of fire, with only one or two narrow wooden staircases, with weak walls and lofty windows, from which women and children can jump to the pavement or burn. Of course, simple cleanliness, to say nothing of ideas of decency, is impossible; of necessity, every element of pleasure in life, beyond the most sensual sort, is utterly unknown. Everybody knows this; knows that these places are noisome, dirt-soaked, vile, debasing; everybody should know that life to be spent under such conditions is not a gift, being a weight in itself, and affording small glimpses of a better to come. In those places garbage steams its poison in the sun; there thieves and prostitutes congregate and are made . . . there are the deaths that swell our mortality reports; from there come our enormous taxes in good part; there disease lurks, and there is the daily food of pestilence awaiting its coming.

Horace Greeley, November 23, 1864, "Tenement Houses— Their Wrongs," p. 4.

CHAPTER THREE

"Who Can Describe Their Misery?": Poverty and American Slavery
1619-1865

No survey of poverty in U.S. history can be complete without a discussion of slavery. If being poor is defined as living hand to mouth; having to cope with undernourishment, inferior housing, and scanty, inadequate clothing; enduring chronic or frequent ill health; and holding tenuously to one's means of survival, then the enslaved African Americans qualified as poor. The slave population lived at a minimal subsistence level and struggled continually against hunger, cold, illness, and pain, as did all impoverished Americans. Additionally, the slaves were denied basic freedom, kept in ignorance, forced to labor, and subjected to corporal punishment that was often severe and administered according to whim.

Between August 20, 1619, when a Dutch ship delivered 20 Africans to the Jamestown settlement in Virginia, and January 1, 1808, when the importation of slaves became illegal in the United States, traders took an estimated 400,000 Africans to the English colonies in North America and the independent nation they became. Initially Africans in the colonies labored as indentured servants, but established planters and tradesmen feared potential competition for land and markets from indentured servants who had joined the ranks of the free, and within a short time blacks' length of servitude became indefinite. The first colony to sanction black slavery by law was Massachusetts, which did so in 1641; by 1750, every colony had a law permitting the enslavement of people of African descent. The industrial northern states began the gradual manumission of their slaves in 1804, and for the next 60 years, slavery was an institution of the middle and southern states, which needed abundant cheap labor for large-scale agricultural development. There were more than 1 million African Americans living in slavery in the South by 1810 and 4 million by 1860.

Some slaves belonged to small farmers who owned fewer than five, but most lived on large plantations employing 20 or more. By 1840 there were 46,000 plantations throughout the South. The majority of plantation slaves did agricultural

Scenes of 19th-century plantation life: Slaves harvest cotton as the overseer patrols on horseback (top); daily activity occurs in the slave quarter (bottom). *(Library of Congress, Prints and Photographs Division, LC-USZ62-12848)*

work, raising cotton, rice, sugar, tobacco, and other crops. There were also slaves who were domestic servants or skilled artisans such as blacksmiths and carpenters, working on plantations or in southern cities. Roughly 500,000 enslaved African Americans lived in southern towns and cities in 1860.

Slaves were considered property and valued strictly for their labor. This meant that working for their master took up nearly all their time and energy. They attended to everything and everyone else—from personal needs to family and children—only as time permitted.

Plantation Labor

The principal southern crop was cotton, which thrived in the warm temperatures of the Deep South and was grown to supply textile mills in the North and abroad. By 1860 the South was producing 5,387,000 bales of cotton annually, more than half of it from the four states in which most of the largest plantations were located: Georgia, Alabama, Mississippi, and Louisiana. Throughout the long southern growing season, enslaved farmhands were in the cotton fields by 4:30 A.M. to till the soil, sow seed, hoe, weed, pick off insects, or harvest the mature cotton bolls as the time of year demanded. They worked until dusk Monday through Friday and for half a day on Saturday, for most of their lives, from the time they were big enough to put in a day's labor until they were too old to bend and lift heavy bales. They worked in rain or sunshine, in blistering heat or in cold so bitter that it drove them to warm themselves over bonfires.

The number of hours worked in a day varied according to the times of sunrise and sunset, seasonal demands, and the master's inclination. The slaves on the sugar plantations of Louisiana, who were mostly men, labored 18 hours a day at harvest, seven days a week. Sugarcane had to be cut and processed quickly because once it had ripened, it would soon spoil. Workdays tended to be shorter in the coastal low country of South Carolina and Georgia, which was better suited to growing rice. The periodic flooding of the fields that was necessary for rice culture promoted the breeding of mosquitoes, though, and this meant that slaves who grew rice were continually exposed to malaria.

Many masters feared their slaves might revolt if driven too hard, and with good reason. Slave uprisings did occur, although they were infrequent; the largest in the colonial period began in the predawn hours of September 9, 1739, when about 20 slaves assembled near the Stono River, less than 20 miles from Charlestown (now Charleston), South Carolina. They entered a gun shop in St. Paul's Parish, armed themselves, and murdered the two white shopkeepers who were present. They then traveled south, killing whites and adding slaves to their rebellion. By the time slave owners caught up with them and put down the revolt, they numbered between 60 and 100. At day's end, at least 20 whites and more than twice as many blacks had been killed.

After the Stono Rebellion, South Carolina lawmakers passed a strict Slave Code, which was a set of laws limiting slaves' activities. Slaves were now forbidden to assemble, for example, or to learn to read. The laws also restricted their workday to no more than 14 hours from September 25 through March 25, and no more than 15 hours for the rest of the year.

Plantation slaves worked under the supervision of an overseer who patrolled the grounds on horseback, armed with a pistol or knife to maintain order and discourage runaways. The overseer was charged with keeping the slaves on task and producing a bountiful crop and had authority to administer whippings. He usually was drawn from the local population of poor whites.

Materially, life was no better for poor southern whites than it was for enslaved blacks. Both groups lived lives of hunger, deprivation, and hard labor. Some growers hired poor whites to do the worst jobs on their plantations rather than risk the well-being of their slaves, who represented an investment. Irish immigrants, for

Slaves march under the threat of the overseer's whip. *(Library of Congress, Prints and Photographs Division, LC-USZ62-117931)*

example, dug the trenches needed to drain water from sugarcane fields. Many slaves looked down on the poor whites, having learned from their masters that these were lazy and immoral people. Others befriended their poor white neighbors and even shared food with them in times of urgency. Yet however mean their existence may have been, the poor whites had their freedom.

The free population of the United States included blacks as well as whites, but the races did not enjoy freedom equally. About half the free black population, which numbered nearly 500,000 in 1860, lived in slaveholding states, predominantly in the Southeast and in Louisiana. Most free blacks earned their living as craftsmen or hired laborers. They were denied the right to vote throughout the South and barred from testifying against whites in every slave state but Delaware and Louisiana. It was also against the law throughout the South for blacks and whites to marry. Life was somewhat better for African Americans in northern states, such as New York. The New York State Census of 1855 counted 11,840 African Americans living in Manhattan. The majority were employed as domestic workers. Other common occupations included laborer, dressmaker, cook, waiter, laundry worker, porter, and coachman. There were six black physicians and one lawyer. Between 1825 and 1865 just 2 percent of the city's African Americans owned property worth $250 and were therefore qualified to vote.

Food, Clothing, and Shelter

For plantation owners, providing slaves with the necessities of life was a business expense, and they rationed food, issued clothing, and provided housing with an eye on the bottom line. The master determined the quantity, quality, and variety of provisions, usually deciding that what was adequate for the average slave was good enough for all. Many masters justified to themselves the poverty they forced upon their slaves by stating that enslaved African Americans generally lived more comfortably than millions of European peasants, an assertion that was accurate.

To maximize cotton production, planters of the Deep South commonly reduced the amount of land devoted to raising livestock by purchasing hogs, cattle, and mules from southern Appalachia. Between 1840 and 1860, the demand for these animals exceeded Appalachian production, so Southerners turned to suppliers farther north, in Kentucky and Ohio.

Other factors were working against Appalachia's farmers and would contribute to later poverty in the region. For instance, crop production was failing to keep pace with a growing population, which meant that per capita wealth in the region was in decline. Also, families long settled in Appalachia traditionally had large numbers of children and partitioned farms for purposes of inheritance, causing individual holdings to decrease in acreage from one generation to the next. Perhaps more ominously for Appalachian farmers, though, technology was passing them by. Farmers in the newly settled Midwest were employing threshers and other recent innovations in agricultural machinery to boost production, but these were impractical to use on the rocky, hilly Appalachian terrain. Increasingly, too, railroads improved access to eastern markets for farmers in the Midwest. Ohio, Indiana, Illinois, Michigan, and Wisconsin gained 8,341 miles of railroad track in the 1850s, but trunk lines would come later to the Appalachian states.

On plantations food typically was distributed on the weekend, and people had to make it last through the long week ahead. The amount and quality of food slaves received varied from one plantation to the next, but a typical week's ration for an adult field hand consisted of a peck of cornmeal and two to four pounds of bacon or salt pork, occasionally supplemented with coffee, molasses, or sugar. Slaves in the low country were likely to receive rice and chickpeas rather than corn. Slaveholders generally kept the choicest cuts of pork for themselves, but it was widely thought that fatty meat was more nutritious and what the slaves preferred.

The basic diet was deficient in calories and nutrients, so many slaves supplemented their rations by growing yams, greens, and other vegetables; raising chickens; fishing; and hunting squirrels, opossums, raccoons, and other small game. Some also resorted to stealing food. Nevertheless, many slaves lacked the energy for heavy work and showed reduced resistance to disease. In addition, the bent legs of rickets, the swollen bellies of kwashiorkor, and signs of other vitamin deficiency diseases were not uncommon among plantation slaves.

A number of masters observed their slaves eating dirt, which indicates that some enslaved African Americans acquired the eating disorder pica, which is defined as a craving for nonnutritive substances. Pica can be a cultural practice or a means of

An African-American family poses outside a boarded-up slave cabin on the Hermitage Plantation near Savannah, Georgia. *(Library of Congress, Prints and Photographs Division, LC-D4-70118)*

easing hunger pangs, but it may also be triggered by dietary deficiencies. Ironically, in pica the substance consumed does not alleviate nutritional shortcomings.

On some large plantations field hands contributed part of their rations for a communal midday meal that was prepared by a cook who was also enslaved. Generally, though, slaves cooked their own food over the fireplaces in their cabins, which were clustered at a distance from the master's home (the "big house" or "great house"), in a section of the plantation known as the slave quarters. Some 18th-century slaves slept in haylofts, military-style barracks, or makeshift shelters, and many of the earliest slave cabins were built of mud and thatch, according to West African design. As the slave population became increasingly American-born, however, and southern whites suppressed any expression of African folkways, the cabins conformed to the construction methods of the prevailing culture.

Shelters for slaves became larger and sturdier as the 19th century progressed. The typical one-room slave cabin of the 1850s measured 16 by 20 feet. It was constructed of wood and had a raised plank floor and unglazed windows with wooden shutters. Some cabins were built of brick or tabby, which was a mixture of oyster shells, lime, and sand. A cabin housed one or occasionally two families, but often a family had taken in an orphaned child or an ill or aged person needing care. According to the U.S. census of 1860, an average of 5.2 people lived in each slave cabin, but anecdotal evidence reveals frequent overcrowding. Louis Hughes, a former slave who wrote an autobiography, recalled that on the Virginia plantation where he grew up, it was usual for eight or nine people to share a cabin. Other former slaves reported as many as 12 people to a cabin. Privacy was rare in such circumstances.

Chinks in the walls caused the cabins to be drafty in winter, yet poor ventilation made them stifling in summer. Residents tried to keep their homes clean, but crowding and time limitations made housework difficult. Slave cabins were commonly described as dirty and thought to promote the spread of disease. Some overseers were charged with enforcing standards of personal and household cleanliness among the slaves in their charge. On other plantations owners required cabins to be emptied and thoroughly cleaned twice a year or whitewashed annually, inside and out.

The cabins of enslaved African Americans were sparsely furnished with tables, stools, and chairs that were either handmade or purchased with the small earnings slaves received from the sale of their own crops or livestock or from skilled services rendered. Slaves made their own candles and fashioned bowls, jugs, and ladles from hollow gourds. In coastal areas they collected mussel and oyster shells to use as spoons and knives. A bed could have been a straw-filled mattress, a pile of rags, or even a wooden plank. Slaveholders gave out light cotton blankets about once every three years, and enslaved women stitched quilts from scraps of cloth. Nevertheless, many residents of slave cabins slept with their feet toward the fire for warmth on cold nights.

Plantation owners issued clothing to their slaves twice a year. In the late antebellum period, most planters spent between seven and 10 dollars a year to clothe an adult slave, although some spent 15 dollars or more. On many plantations, however, enslaved women wove cloth and sewed garments to produce all of the hands' clothing. As a rule men received two suits of clothing, each consisting of a shirt and pair of pants, one for summer and one for winter, and a jacket for the cold months. Women were given two dresses or the necessary cloth and sewing supplies to make them. Slaves' clothing was fashioned from inexpensive, sturdy fabric such as osnaburg, a coarse linen. These rough clothes scratched the skin unmercifully when new and softened only with wear. "Even to this day I can recall accurately the tortures that I underwent when putting on one of these garments," wrote Booker T. Washington, who spent his first years in slavery, in 1901. "It is almost equal to the feeling that one would experience if he had a dozen or more chestnut burrs, or a hundred small pin-points, in contact with his flesh."[1] Slaves' garments frequently wore out before new ones were issued, with the result that many field hands worked in tattered clothing that afforded almost no protection from the winter cold or the summer sun. Every laborer was issued a pair of shoes annually, but these were cheaply made and stiff. They fit poorly and readily fell apart. Some people rubbed their shoes with grease to soften them, but many men and women preferred to work barefoot on all but the coldest days.

Children, who rarely wore shoes, dressed in simple smocks that hardly covered their bodies. It was not uncommon for young children to be completely naked in summer. Domestic servants, who had frequent contact with the master's family and guests, were generally dressed somewhat better than field hands, in either purchased clothes or hand-me-downs from the big house. Still, a slave's wardrobe was never adequate, regardless of his or her age, especially when the weather turned cold.

Slavery Affects Family Life

Women did their sewing, mending, and washing in the evening, after a long day in the fields. Evening was also the time for cooking and for attending to the young. It was often midnight before an exhausted field hand settled down to sleep, "[w]ith a prayer that he might be on his feet and wide awake at the first sound of the horn," said Solomon Northup, who spent the years 1841 through 1853 enslaved on a Louisiana cotton plantation.[2]

The demands of slavery forced most parents to neglect their children. Youngsters typically spent the day in the care of older siblings or aging women who could no longer do agricultural work. On large plantations children ate from communal troughs, using their hands or a seashell to scoop up crumbled corn bread and vegetables that may have been soaked in buttermilk. The children were called to their meals "like so many pigs, and like so many pigs they would come and devour the mush," said Frederick Douglass, who grew up in slavery on a Maryland plantation. "He that ate fastest got most; he that was strongest secured the best place; and few left the trough satisfied."[3] Not all enslaved children had milk to drink, and many who did enjoyed it only in spring and summer, the seasons of peak dairy production.

Mothers of infants carried their babies to the fields and placed them in a shady spot while they worked or left them with an older sister or brother who provided care that was haphazard at best. Pregnant women did a full day's work until a month before their expected delivery, at which time their workload was lightened and perhaps cut in half. They were given three weeks to a month off after giving birth and then required to return to their labors.

A woman typically began bearing children at age 16 and gave birth to eight, 10, or more over the course of her reproductive years. Poor nutrition and overwork contributed to low birth weights, and in some regions half the children born to enslaved women died in the first year of life. Slave children of all ages were four times as likely to die of all causes as were white children. They suffered disproportionately from diarrhea, intestinal worms, and tetanus, which was contracted when cuts had contact with bacteria in the soil. Some masters lowered the death rate on their plantations by keeping the quarters clean, teaching proper handling of the water supply, and giving people more time to rest.

Marriage among the enslaved received no legal sanction in the South. It represented a commitment between a man and a woman and recognition of the pair as husband and wife by the plantation community. It was not unheard of for a slaveholder to decide which of his slaves would marry, but most often enslaved women and men selected their own spouses after courtship. In a traditional slave wedding ritual, a couple jumped over a broomstick. Often, however, a white minister or the planter himself conducted a Christian wedding ceremony. If a man married a woman living on a different plantation, he needed a pass to visit on weekends and on Wednesday nights, if midweek visits were permitted.

Marriage vows and family ties offered no protection against permanent separation. One or more family members might be sold at any time. Most of those sold were in their teens or early 20s and were transferred from the Chesapeake Bay region to points west and south to raise cotton. In the 1820s and 1830s between 350,000 and 400,000 African Americans made this sorrowful journey. A person could be sold at any age, though. Some callous slaveholders rid themselves of the aged by resting and feeding them to make them appear younger and fitter and then putting them up for sale; they also took small children from their mothers' arms and placed them on the auction block. Children born from forced sexual relations between enslaved women and their white masters frequently were sold.

Just as anyone could be sold, anyone could be brutally and sadistically punished. Men, women, and young people were beaten and whipped for any number of transgressions, including getting to work late, working too slowly, walking about after dark, or displeasing a member of the master's family. Some masters and overseers administered whipping severe enough to cause significant blood loss and leave masses of scar tissue. Slaves were also mutilated, branded, placed in chains, or locked in stocks and pillories.

Abused but Unbroken

Slavery battered the human spirit but rarely destroyed it. Imaginations remained active, and people expressed themselves through music and storytelling. Slaves fashioned drums and banjos similar to the instruments their forebears played in Africa. They sang songs that united English lyrics with the flattened blue notes of their ancestral home. By telling tales, slaves kept another African practice alive in the New World: Africans traditionally passed along by word of mouth fables that explained humanity's place in nature. Tales of animals with human traits illuminated character and motivation, but in plantation stories bears, rabbits, and other North American creatures replaced the crocodiles and monkeys of Africa.

Slaves also protected their individuality by revolting or running away. Slave rebellions were planned and sometimes carried out all through the antebellum period. One of the largest was masterminded by two Henrico County, Virginia, slaves, Gabriel Prosser and Jack Bowler, in 1800. In secrecy, following instructions from the two men, slaves throughout the region spent months making clubs, bayonets, and bullets. Meanwhile, on Sundays Prosser surveyed Richmond, target of the planned uprising, to learn the layout of the city and the storage places of arms and ammunition. On August 30, 1800, more than 1,000 slaves assembled with their weapons six miles outside Richmond and prepared to march on the city. Two forces prevented their progress: the weather and armed white resistance. A violent rainstorm rendered impassible a bridge they would have needed to cross. Also, because two slaves had informed their owner of the upcoming rebellion, a warning had reached Governor James Monroe. Monroe called up more than 650 soldiers and alerted militia companies throughout the state. Although the army of slaves disassembled, authorities arrested many African Americans and executed approximately 35 rebels. Gabriel Prosser attempted to escape by sea, but he was captured and hanged.

In 1831, state and federal troops put down a violent slave rebellion in Southampton County, Virginia, that was led by Nat Turner, a slave and religious mystic, who believed he was destined to guide his people to freedom. On August 21, Turner and six accomplices murdered his master, Joseph Travis, and the entire Travis family. They then moved from one house to another, shooting, stabbing, and beating whites to death and recruiting black followers. By midday, August 22, when they decided to march toward the town of Jerusalem, Turner's force numbered more than 40 and was still growing. By the time military action halted the march, as many as 60 whites were dead. The state of Virginia executed 55 blacks, including Nat Turner, but nearly four times as many African Americans, most of them innocent, were murdered by whites in retaliation.

The great majority of slaves who rebelled against slavery did so singly, in pairs, or in small groups. They were people like Henry Bibb, who was born in Shelby, Kentucky, in 1815. "Among other trades I learned the art of running away to perfection," Bibb said. "I made a regular business of it, and never gave it up, until I had broken the bands of slavery."[4] The exact number of successful escapes is unknown, but thousands of people made the perilous journey from slavery to freedom. In the colonial era southern slaves sought refuge among the Seminole people of Spanish Florida. In

Free African Americans risked being kidnapped and sold into slavery. *(Library of Congress, General Collection)*

the 19th century refugees headed north. Escaping meant traveling stealthily through woods and swamps and along rivers, often by night. It carried numerous risks, including the possibility of recapture and punishment. Many people, fully aware of the chance they were taking, repeatedly attempted escape until they reached freedom.

In 1850 Congress passed the stringent Fugitive Slave Act, empowering federal commissioners to seize suspected escapees in northern states and return them to their owners. Those captured were denied a trial by jury or the chance to testify in their own defense, and private citizens who refused to aid in the recapture of suspected escaped slaves were subject to a fine and imprisonment. The Fugitive Slave Act of 1850 invigorated operation of the Underground Railroad, the network of more than 3,000 homes and other safe stations through which refugees were transported to freedom in the North and Canada.

The Civil War Brought Hope

With the outbreak of the Civil War, many slaves understood that their years of bondage were nearing their end. Despite white efforts to keep the slaves ignorant of outside events, news of the war traveled from one plantation to the next, and domestic servants overheard talk of battles and losses while waiting on the family in the big house.

From the war's start, any observant person could see that the southern way of life had been disrupted. Men were being called away and leaving agriculture in the hands of women and children. In some counties of Alabama and other states, these inexperienced farmers faced drought conditions in the summers of 1862, 1863, and 1864. As a result of these changes, there were sections of the South that failed to produce enough corn to feed their population. It was all but impossible to transport food to those in need because of poor roads and a lack of rail lines. Bands of starving widows and abandoned wives known as "corn women" roamed the countryside, begging for food and combing the earth for discarded ears of corn. Salt, essential for preserving meat, also grew scarce. A sack of salt that sold in the South for two dollars in 1861 cost 80 dollars a year later.

Throughout the Civil War, the Confederate government exempted one white man from service for every 20 slaves on a plantation. This was done for practical reasons, to help maintain agricultural production and control over the slaves, but the poor viewed it as discriminatory. The South lacked the resources to provision its troops, and tens of thousands of resentful Confederate soldiers walked away from an army that was unable to feed and clothe them and expected them to go into battle barefoot. Thus poverty would contribute significantly to the breakdown of the Confederacy.

Despite the military exemptions for slave owners, discipline and control grew lax on plantations as many masters and overseers joined the Confederate cause, and slaves escaped in ever-increasing numbers. On April 16, 1862, President Abraham Lincoln abolished slavery in the District of Columbia. Immediately, Washington's population of refugees from slavery—people called contrabands—exploded, rising from 400 in April to 4,200 in October. By 1865 there would be 40,000 former slaves in a city struggling to absorb them. Impoverished contrabands clustered in shacks, tents, and lean-tos along the C&O Canal and near military forts and hospitals or sought shelter in alleyways.

As the Union army moved into the South, needy African Americans appealed to the northern forces for help and support. Union generals put many of the able-bodied men to work as servants or laborers, who dug ditches, repaired roads, and carried

This contraband camp was near Richmond, Virginia. *(National Archives)*

water and supplies. They hired some of the women as hospital cooks and laundry workers. Contrabands also did the army's dirtiest work: disposing of hospital waste, cleaning latrines, and burying dead horses, mules, and soldiers. The army established camps for the women, children, and old men at Arlington, the former estate of Robert E. Lee in Virginia; at Grand Junction, Tennessee; and elsewhere throughout the South. In the contraband camps, people who had arrived homeless, hungry, and dressed in the rags they had worn to toil in the fields lived in abandoned shacks or tents pitched on muddy ground with never enough to eat. African-American youngsters in rags begged food from the soldiers and succumbed to smallpox, dysentery, and typhoid. Union officers were often at a loss about what to do with the former slaves; in Louisiana they leased contrabands to loyal planters for 10 dollars a month.

In the North private citizens formed organizations to aid the newly free and destitute African Americans. These groups included the Port Royal Relief Committee, established in Philadelphia on March 5, 1862. This group furnished food, blankets, shoes, hospital supplies, and women's and children's clothing to African Americans in Port Royal, South Carolina, who had been left to fend for themselves when whites abandoned plantations in advance of approaching Union forces. In 1864 this organization changed its name to the Pennsylvania Freedmen's Relief Association and enlarged its service area to include parts of Tennessee, Alabama, and Georgia. In 1862 Elizabeth Keckley, who was a former slave and the dressmaker and friend of Mary Todd Lincoln, founded the Contraband Relief Organization. The African-American women who belonged to this group collected funds and clothing for the many former slaves who sought refuge in Washington, D.C.

Effective January 1, 1863, all African Americans in Confederate-held territory were free in the eyes of the Union, according to President Lincoln's Emancipation Proclamation. The proclamation also permitted African-American men to enlist as soldiers in the Union army. Yet it was not until March 3, 1865, that Congress established the Bureau of Refugees, Freedmen and Abandoned Lands, better known as the Freedmen's Bureau, the federal agency that supervised relief efforts directed toward African Americans who had recently left slavery.

Chronicle of Events

1619

• *August 20:* A Dutch ship arrives at Jamestown, Virginia, carrying the first 20 Africans to the English colonies in North America.

1641

• Massachusetts becomes the first colony to sanction slavery by law.

1739

• *September 9:* Slaves stage a rebellion near the Stono River in South Carolina. The uprising leaves 20 whites and more than 40 blacks dead.

1750

• Laws permitting slavery are in effect in all 13 British colonies.

1800

• *August 30:* More than 1,000 slaves, led by Gabriel Prosser and Jack Bowler, assemble and prepare to march on Richmond. Federal troops and state militia halt the rebellion. Approximately 35 rebels are later executed.

1804

• The northern states begin gradual manumission of their slaves.

1808

• *January 1:* The importation of slaves becomes illegal in the United States.

Slaves and whites processed tobacco. On small plantations slaves lived and worked alongside their masters. *(Library of Congress, Prints and Photographs Division, LC-USZ62-29058)*

Contrabands aided the Union army by building a levee on the Mississippi River. *(Library of Congress, Prints and Photographs Division, LC-USZ62-106352)*

1810
- More than 1 million slaves live in the South.

1820–1840
- Between 350,000 and 400,000 enslaved African Americans are moved from the Chesapeake Bay region to the Deep South to raise cotton.

1825–1865
- Two percent of African Americans in New York City own $250 in property and are eligible to vote.

1831
- *August 21:* Nat Turner and his followers travel through the countryside in Southampton County, Virginia, murdering whites.
- *August 22:* Military force ends Nat Turner's rebellion. About 60 whites have been killed. The state of Virginia later executes 55 blacks, including Nat Turner.

1840
- Slaves raise cotton and other crops on 46,000 plantations throughout the South.

1840–1860
- Appalachian farmers cannot meet the demand from the Deep South for livestock.

1850
- Congress passes the Fugitive Slave Act. All citizens are now required to assist in the capture of runaway slaves.

1850s
- The typical slave cabin measures 16 by 20 feet.
- Railroad mileage in the states of Ohio, Indiana, Illinois, Michigan, and Wisconsin increases from 1,275 to 9,616.

1860
- The number of enslaved African Americans has reached 4 million.
- In large part because of its reliance on slave labor, the South produces 5,387,000 bales of cotton per year.
- On average 5.2 people occupy a slave cabin, according to U.S. census figures.
- Some 500,000 slaves live in Southern towns and cities.
- The free black population is approaching 500,000.

1861

• Salt sells for two dollars a sack in the South.

1862

• Elizabeth Keckley establishes the Contraband Relief Organization to aid former slaves in Washington, D.C.
• A sack of salt sells for 80 dollars in the South.
• *March 5:* The Port Royal Relief Committee is founded in Philadelphia.
• *April 16:* President Abraham Lincoln abolishes slavery in the District of Columbia; 400 refugees from slavery live in Washington.
• *October:* Some 4,200 contrabands live in the nation's capital.

1862–1864

• Drought harms agricultural production in some parts of the South.

1863

• *January 1:* The Emancipation Proclamation takes effect. It is the policy of the U.S. government that all slaves in Confederate territory are now free. Also, African Americans may now serve in the Union army.

1864

• The Port Royal Relief Committee changes its name to the Pennsylvania Freedmen's Relief Association and extends its service area.

1865

• Washington, D.C., has a contraband population of 40,000.
• *March 3:* The federal government establishes the Freedmen's Bureau.

Eyewitness Testimony

[S]o raw, so unexperienced am I in this mode of life, that were I to be possessed of a plantation, and my slaves treated in general as they are here, never could I rest in peace; my sleep would be perpetually disturbed by a retrospect of the frauds committed in Africa, in order to entrap them; frauds surpassing in enormity everything which a common mind can possibly conceive. I should be thinking of the barbarous treatment they meet with on ship-board; of their anguish, of the despair necessarily inspired by their situation, when torn from their friends and relations; when delivered into the hands of a people differently coloured, whom they cannot understand; carried in a strange machine over an ever agitated element, which they had never seen before; and finally delivered over to the severities of the whippers, and the excessive labours of the field. Can it be possible that the force of custom should ever make me deaf to all these reflections, and as insensible to the injustice of that trade, and to their miseries, as the rich inhabitants of this town seem to be?

J. Hector St. John de Crevecoeur, a visitor to Charlestown (now Charleston), South Carolina, 1782, Letters from an American Farmer, *pp. 162–63.*

In looking over the farms, you do not see the land divided into a number of fields, some of which are covered with grass and others with corn; but rather a kind of extensive garden, which is principally occupied by the Indian corn, an elegant and luxuriant plant which grows to the height of eight or ten feet. Here you will see rows of apple trees and there rows of peach trees bending under their burthen. On one side of the house you may find a garden of cucumbers, on the other one of melons. Such were the two farms which we visited when we went on shore. The dwelling houses were made of planks nailed to a wooden frame. The floor was of plank. There were no rooms above stairs, and no glass in the windows. Adjoining the house of the master was a hut for his blacks, formed of small pine trees, laid one upon another and fastened at the end by a notch; but they were not plaistered, either on the inside or the outside.

Harry Toulmin, Unitarian minister from Chowbent, Lancashire, England, describing farms in southeast Virginia, July 19, 1793, The Western Country in 1793, *p. 17.*

The masters [in Georgia] make a practice of getting two suits of clothes for each slave per year, a thick suit for winter, and a thin one for summer. They provide also one pair of Northern made sale shoes for each slave in *winter.* These shoes usually begin to rip in a few weeks. The negroes' mode of mending them is, to *wire* them together, in many instances. Do our northern shoemakers know that they are augmenting the sufferings of the poor slaves with their almost good for nothing sale shoes? . . . The above practice of clothing the slave is customary to some extent. How many, however, fail in this, God only knows. The children and old slaves are, I should think, *exceptions* to the above rule. The males and females have their suits from the same cloth for their winter dresses. These winter garments appear to be made of a mixture of cotton and wool, very coarse and *sleazy.* The whole suit for the men consists of a pair of pantaloons and a short sailor-jacket, *without shirt, vest, hat, stockings, or any kind of loose garments!* These, if worn steadily when at work, would not probably last more than one or two months; therefore, for the sake of saving them, many of them work, especially in the summer, with no clothing on them except a cloth tied round their waist, and *almost all* with nothing more on them than pantaloons, and these frequently so torn that they do not serve the purposes of common decency. The women have for clothing a short petticoat, and a short loose gown, something like the male's sailor-jacket, *without any under garment, stockings, bonnets, hoods, caps, or any kind of over-clothes.* When at work in warm weather, they usually strip off the loose gown, and have nothing on but a short petticoat with some kind of covering over their breasts. Many children may be seen in the summer months *as naked as they came into the world.* I think, as a whole, they suffer more for the want of comfortable bed-clothes, than they do for wearing apparel. It is true, that some by begging or buying, have more clothes than above described, but the *masters provide them with no more.* They are miserable objects of pity. It may be said of many of them, "I was *naked* and ye clothed me not." It is enough to melt the hardest heart to see the ragged mothers nursing their almost naked children, with but a morsel of the coarsest food to eat. The Southern horses and dogs have enough to eat and good care taken of them, but Southern negroes, who can describe their misery?

The Reverend Horace Moulton of Marlborough, Massachusetts, who spent the years 1817 through 1824 near Savannah, Georgia, in Theodore Dwight Weld, American Slavery as It Is, *p. 19.*

The men and women slaves received, as their monthly allowance of food, eight pounds of pork, or its equivalent in fish, and one bushel of corn meal. Their yearly clothing consisted of two coarse linen shirts, one pair of linen trousers, like the shirts, one jacket, one pair of trousers for winter, made of coarse negro cloth, one pair of stockings, and one pair of shoes; the whole of which could not have cost more than seven dollars. The allowance of the slave children was given to their mothers, or the old women having the care of them. The children unable to work in the field had neither shoes, stockings, jackets, nor trousers, given to them; their clothing consisted of two coarse linen shirts per year. When these failed them, they went naked until the next allowance-day. Children from seven to ten years old, of both sexes, almost naked, might be seen at all seasons of the year.

Frederick Douglass, who spent his boyhood in slavery in the 1820s, Narrative of the Life of Frederick Douglass, *p. 26.*

There were no beds given the slaves, unless one coarse blanket be considered such, and none but the men and women had these. This, however, is not considered a very great privation. They find less difficulty from the want of beds, than from the want of time to sleep; for when their day's work in the field is done, the most of them have their washing, mending, and cooking to do, and having few or none of the ordinary facilities for doing either of these, very many of their sleeping hours are consumed in preparing for the field the coming day; and when this is done, old and young, male and female, married and single, drop down side by side, on one common bed,—the cold, damp floor,—each covering himself or herself with their miserable blankets, and here they sleep till they are summoned to the fields by the driver's horn. At the sound of this, all must rise, and be off to the field. There must be no halting; every one must be at his or her post; and woe betides them who hear not this morning summons to the field; for if they are not awakened by the sense of hearing, they are by the sense of feeling; no age nor sex finds any favor. Mr. Severe, the overseer, used to stand by the door of the quarter, armed with a large hickory stick and heavy cowskin, ready to whip any one who was so unfortunate as not to hear, or, from any other cause, was prevented from being ready to start for the field at the sound of the horn.

Frederick Douglass, who spent his boyhood in slavery in the 1820s, Narrative of the Life of Frederick Douglass, *pp. 26–27.*

To the hideous moral evils that pervade this dismal subject [slavery], must be added a long catalogue of diseases and death, which thin the ranks of the unhappy sufferers, and drain the profits of their owners, A medical gentle-

man at Savannah told me, that pulmonary complaints are those which prove most fatal to the negroes, especially to such as cultivate the rice-grounds. The Blacks, he said, are not nearly so liable to intermittents as the Whites are, but pleurisy is more frequent amongst them, and generally proves fatal. On the cotton plantations, according to his account, the negroes are generally healthy—all the work being of a dry kind; but on rice estates, the hospitals are often quite crowded in autumn. He told me of a friend of his who had lost 40 out of 300 slaves last year.

This sickness is brought on chiefly by circumstances inevitably connected with the cultivation of rice, the negroes being almost constantly working in the water, or ankle deep in mud, ditching, drawing, or weeding, or turning over wet ground. They are sometimes overworked, in order to "meet the season," as it is called, and upon these occasions, they sink rapidly under their complicated hardships. The slaves, I was told, are so well aware of the amount of work which they are competent

A former slave photographed in 1939 near Marshall, Texas, holds a horn that was used to call slaves to the field. *(Library of Congress, Prints and Photographs Division, LC-USF33-012186-M1)*

to perform, that the imposition of a greater task seldom produces a greater final result. If additional labour, beyond the ordinary measure, be assigned them, they first become sulky, then sick, often droop and die, or if not, they are seized with despair, and run away, only to be caught again and punished.

Basil Hall, English traveler, 1829, Travels in North America, in the Years 1827 and 1828, *Vol. 2, pp. 222–23.*

The [free] black man, in the United States, said [Tennessee Supreme Court Judge John] Catron, is degraded by his color, and sinks into vice and worthlessness from want of motive to virtuous and elevated conduct. The black man in these states may have the power of volition. He may go and come when it pleases him, without a domestic master to control the actions of his person; but to be politically free, to be the peer and equal to the white man, to enjoy the offices, trusts, and privileges our institutions confer on the white men, is hopeless now and ever. The slave who receives the protection and care of a tolerable master holds a condition here superior to the negro who is freed from domestic slavery. He is a reproach and a by-word with the slave himself, who taunts his fellow slave by telling him "he is as worthless as a free negro." The consequence is inevitable. The free black man lives amongst us without motive and without hope. He seeks no avocation; is surrounded with necessities, is sunk in degradation; crime can sink him no deeper, and he commits it, of course. This is not only true of the free negro residing in the slaveholding states of the Union. In non-slaveholding states of this Union the people are less accustomed to the squalid and disgusting wretchedness of the negro, have less sympathy for him, earn their means of subsistence with their own hands, and are more economical in parting with them than he for whom the slave labors, for which he is entitled to the proceeds and of which the free negro is generally the participant, and but too often in the character of the receiver of stolen goods. Nothing can be more untrue than that the free negro is more respectable as a member of society in the non-slaveholding states than in the slaveholding states. In each he is a degraded outcast, and his fancied freedom a delusion. With us the slave ranks him in character and comfort, nor is there a fair motive to absolve him from his duties incident to domestic slavery if he is to continue amongst us. Generally, and almost universally, society suffers and the negro suffers by manumission.

George S. Yerger, 1834, in Caleb Perry Patterson, The Negro in Tennessee, 1790–1865, *pp. 174–75.*

Every Saturday night the slaves receive their allowance of provisions, which must last them till the next Saturday night. "Potatoe time," as it is called, begins about the middle of July. The slave may measure for himself, the overseer being present, half a bushel of sweet potatoes, and heap the measure as long as they will lie on; I have, however, seen the overseer, if he think the negro is getting too many, kick the measure; and if any fall off, tell him he has got his measure. No salt is furnished them to eat with their potatoes. When rice or corn is given, they give them a little salt; sometimes half a pint of molasses is given, but not often. The quantity of rice, which is of the small, broken, unsaleable kind, is one peck. When corn is given them, their allowance is the same, and if they get it ground . . . they must give one quart for grinding, thus reducing their weekly allowance to seven quarts. When fish (mullet) were plenty, they were allowed, in addition, one fish. As to meat, they seldom had any. I do not think they had an allowance of meat oftener than once in two or three months, and then the quantity was very small. When they went into the field to work, they took some of the meal or rice with them; the pots were given to an old woman, who placed two poles parallel, set the pots on them, and kindled a fire underneath for cooking; she took salt with her and seasoned the messes as she thought proper. When their breakfast was ready, which was generally about ten or eleven o'clock, they were called from labor, ate, and returned to work; in the afternoon, dinner was prepared in the same way. They had but two meals a day while in the field; if they wanted more, they cooked for themselves after they returned to their quarters at night. At the time of killing hogs on the plantation, the pluck, entrails, and blood were given to the slaves.

Nehemiah Caulkins of Waterford, Connecticut, who lived from 1824 through 1835 near Wilmington, North Carolina, in Theodore Dwight Weld, American Slavery as It Is, *p. 13.*

Follow them next to their huts; some with and some without floors:—Go at night, view the means of lodging, see them lying on benches, some on the ground, some sitting on stools, dozing away the night;—others, of younger age, with a bare blanket wrapped about them; and one or two lying in the ashes. These things *I have often seen with my own eyes.*

Examine their means of subsistence, which consists generally of seven quarts of meal or eight quarts of small rice for one week; then follow them to their work, with driver and overseer pushing them to the utmost of their strength, by threatening and whipping.

If they are sick from fatigue and exposure, go to their huts, as I have often been, and see them groaning under a burning fever or pleurisy, lying on some straw, their feet to the fire with barely a blanket to cover them; or on some boards nailed together in form of a bedstead.

Nehemiah Caulkins of Waterford, Connecticut, who lived from 1824 through 1835 near Wilmington, North Carolina, in Theodore Dwight Weld, American Slavery as It Is, pp. 16–17.

No free labor can compete with [slaves], for free labor must have wages that will bear the irregularities incident to all labor, such as occasional relaxation, illness, whims, changes, and dissipations. The free laborers are in families, and useless mouths are to be fed, houses, rents, furniture, taxes, doctors' bills, all amounting to some style and a considerable amount, have to be sustained. The slaves live without beds or houses so worth calling, or family cares, or luxuries, or parade, or show; have no relaxations, or whims, or frol-ics, or dissipations; instead of sun to sun in their hours, are worked from daylight till nine o'clock at night. Where the free man or laborer would require one hundred dollars a year for food and clothing alone, the slave can be supported for twenty dollars a year, and often is.

Nathaniel A. Ware, 1844, Notes on Political Economy as Applicable to the United States by a Southern Planter, *p. 201.*

Generally we had enough in quantity of food. We had however but two meals a day, of corn meal bread, and soup, or meat of the poorest kind. Very often so little care had been taken to cure and preserve the bacon, that when it came to us, though it had been fairly killed once, it was more alive than dead. Occasionally we had some refreshment over and above the two meals, but this was extra, beyond the rules of the plantation. And to balance this gratuity, we were also frequently deprived of our food as a punishment. We suffered greatly, too, for want of

This Currier & Ives print from 1872 presents an idealized image of slavery. *(Library of Congress, Prints and Photographs Division, LC-USZ62-23797)*

water. The slave drivers had the notion that slaves are more healthy if allowed to drink but little, than they are if freely allowed nature's beverage. The slaves quite as confidently cherish the opinion, that if the master would drink less peach brandy and whisky, and give the slaves more water, it would be better all round. As it is, the more the master and overseer drink, the less they seem to think the slave needs.

In the winter we took our meals before day in the morning and after work at night. In the summer at about nine o'clock in the morning and at two in the afternoon. When we were cheated out of our two meals a day, either by the cruelty or caprice of the overseer, we always felt it a kind of special duty and privilege to make up in some way the deficiency. To accomplish this we had many devices. And we sometimes resorted to our peculiar methods, when incited only by a desire to taste greater variety than our ordinary bill of fare afforded.

Lewis Clarke, 1845, Narrative of the Sufferings of Lewis Clarke, *p. 25.*

I have often been utterly astonished, since I came to the north, to find persons who could speak of the singing, among slaves, as evidence of their contentment and happiness. It is impossible to conceive of a greater mistake. Slaves sing most when they are most unhappy. The songs of the slave represent the sorrows of his heart; and he is relieved by them, only as an aching heart is relieved by its tears. At least, such is my experience. I have often sung to drown my sorrow, but seldom to express my happiness. Crying for joy, and singing for joy, were alike uncommon to me while in the jaws of slavery. The singing of a man cast away upon a desolate island might be as appropriately considered as evidence of contentment and happiness, as the singing of a slave; the song of the one and of the other are prompted by the same emotion.

Frederick Douglass, 1845, Narrative of the Life of Frederick Douglass, *p. 30.*

The negroes have been very much effected with Diarroahs & Dysentery which I before mentioned, but none have died & the grown negroes have not been attacked with it for some time, (though old Harry is noe labouring under its effects. . . .) The children (those at home) are at present considerably effected with it & I fear Nancy's child will die. . . .

With regard to the crop I must say is doing very well.

James Haynes, Georgia plantation overseer, July 1, 1846, in James M. Clifton, Life and Labor on Argyle Island, *p. 36.*

The first time I was separated from my mother, I was young and small. I knew nothing of my condition then as a slave. I was living with Mr. White whose wife died and left him a widower with one little girl, who was said to be the legitimate owner of my mother, and all her children. This girl was also my playmate when we were children.

I was taken away from my mother, and hired out to labor for various persons, eight or ten years in succession; and all my wages were expended for the education of Harriet White, my playmate. It was then my sorrows and sufferings commenced. It was then I first commenced seeing and feeling that I was a wretched slave, compelled to work under the lash without wages, and often without clothes enough to hide my nakedness. I have often worked without half enough to eat, both late and early, by day and by night. I have often laid my wearied limbs down at night to rest upon a dirt floor, or a bench, without any covering at all, because I had no where else to rest my wearied body, after having worked hard all the day. I have also been compelled early in life, to go at the bidding of a tyrant, through all kinds of weather, hot or cold, wet or dry, and without shoes frequently, until the month of December, with my bare feet on the cold frosty ground, cracked open and bleeding as I walked.

Henry Bibb, 1850, Narrative of the Life and Adventures of Henry Bibb, an American Slave, *pp. 14–15.*

Badly-cooked food, wherever permitted, an insufficiency of vegetables, and a want of cleanliness, are all causes of sickness. Much injury is frequently occasioned by the hands carrying their baskets full of cotton, during picking, for any great distance, on their heads. A load of 100 to 150 pounds pressing upon the skull, neck and back-bone, when the muscles are relaxed by fatigue, cannot but be injurious, and is a decided cause of sickness and accidents, such as sprains, ruptures, etc. In every instance, additional care in food, clothing, and household comforts; a ready supply of fuel in cold weather; an avoidance of exposure to rain and night air and dews; strict discipline; reasonable hours and moderate punishments, are followed by a corresponding degree of health and strength, and increase in the numbers of negroes.

Thomas Affleck, a Washington, Mississippi, planter, 1850, "On the Hygiene of Cotton Plantations and the Management of Negro Slaves," *pp. 433–34.*

The mortality of negro children is as two to one when compared with the whites, depending solely upon locality and care. Quarters are often badly located; children allowed to be filthy; are suckled hurriedly, whilst the mother is over-heated; are laid on their backs when mere infants, on a hard mattrass, or a blanket only, and rocked and bumped in badly-made cradles; not a few are over-laid by the wearied mother, who sleeps so dead a sleep as not to be aware of the injury to her infant; a vast proportion die under nine or ten days, from the most unskilful management of negro midwives, who do not know how to take care of the navel, and dose the infant with nasty nostrums from the moment of its birth; from having access to green fruit, eating acorns, etc., and from dirt eating. Of those born, one half die under one year; of the other half, say one-tenth die under five years; and of the remainder, a large proportion are raised. Dirt-eating is frequent amongst young negroes, and always kills them, if not cured. The constant use of molasses is said to induce it, but I cannot say how correctly. Those under the best care are liable to it. Seems to be occasioned by a morbid state of the stomach, and should be so treated. One dirt-eater upon a plantation, will infect the whole. Mostly infected at from two to ten years. Say one child in forty eats dirt. Children should have no sweet milk; none but sour, or buttermilk. They are very liable to worms, which kill a good many, or stunt them.

Thomas Affleck, a Washington, Mississippi, planter, 1850, "On the Hygiene of Cotton Plantations and the Management of Negro Slaves," pp. 435–36.

The woman Jane is yet sick. I fear she will never get well. Hector turned in the Sick House on Monday last, with Diarrhrea or Looseness, which has truly carried him extremely low. I have never had such a desperate case of Diarrhrea. He is now somewhat better, & will recover, provided Inflamation of the Stomach does not take place. Cudjue died very suddenly on Tuesday night of last week. He lay up one day & died the same night. No person knows what time he died, being dead next morning. The cows &cs. will be carried off next week. Only three of them has calves, the two youngest & one of the Middle aged ones. I will endeavour to sell the mule as early as convenient.

K. Washington Skinner, Georgia plantation overseer, May 30, 1851, in James M. Clifton, Life and Labor on Argyle Island, p. 80.

[M]y principal occupation was to nurse my little brother whilst my mother worked in the field. Almost all slave children have to do the nursing; the big taking care of the small, who often come poorly off in consequence. I know this was my little brother's case. I used to lay him in the shade, under a tree, sometimes, and go to play, or curl myself up under a hedge, and take a sleep. He would wake me by his screaming, when I would find him covered with ants, or musquitos, or blistered from the heat of the sun, which having moved round whilst I was asleep, would throw the shadow of the branches in another direction, leaving the poor child quite exposed.

The children of both sexes usually run about quite naked, until they are from ten to twelve years of age. I have seen them as old as twelve, going about in this state, or with only an old shirt, which they would put on when they had to go anywhere very particular for their mistress, or up to the great house.

The clothing of the men consists of a pair of thin cotton pantaloons, and a shirt of the same material, two of each being allowed them every year. The women wear a shirt similar to the men's, and a cotton petticoat, which is kept on by means of braces passing over their shoulders. But when they are in the field, the shirt is thrown aside. They also have two suits allowed them every year. These, however, are not enough. They are made of the lowest quality of material, and get torn in the bush, so that the garments soon become useless, even for purposes of the barest decency. We slaves feel that this is not right, and we grow up with very little sense of shame; but immorality amongst ourselves is not common, for all that.

John Brown, 1855, Slave Life in Georgia: A Narrative of the Life, Sufferings, and Escape of John Brown, a Fugitive Slave, pp. 7–8.

Our allowance of food was one peck of corn a week to each full-grown slave. We never had meat of any kind, and our usual drink was water. Sometimes, however, we got a drink of sour milk or a little hard cider. We used to make our corn into hominy, hoe and Johnny-cake, and sometimes parch it, and eat it without any other preparation. The corn was always of inferior quality, and weevil-eaten, so that though we got a peck, it did not yield in meal what it would have done had it been sound.

John Brown, 1855, Slave Life in Georgia: A Narrative of the Life, Sufferings, and Escape of John Brown, a Fugitive Slave, p. 14.

When the [rice] plant is about half leg high, the land is flooded to the depth of from six to eight inches. The growing crop remains under water three or four days, during which time the slaves are obliged to go into these swamps, grubbing up the grass between the rows. It is awful work. Men, women, and children are all employed incessantly, for it is a busy time. They work naked, or nearly so, and contract all sorts of maladies. There is the muddy soil into which you sink knee-deep, and which sends up the foulest smell and vapour, causing fever and sickness. The heat, too, from the sun over-head, reflected back into your face from the water, is intolerably painful, frequently bringing on giddiness and sun-stroke. Then the feet get water-poisoned, or you take the tow or ground-itch, when the flesh cracks and cankers. You also catch the "chiggers," a small insect that punctures the skin under the tow, where it deposits an egg. This soon turns into a live, but very minute, maggot, which breeds in the flesh very fast, causing a great lump to swell up, and an unendurable irritation. You have also to run the risk of getting bitten by all kinds of water-reptiles, and are sure to have some sickness or other. Fevers, agues, rheumatism, pleurisies, asthmas, and consumptions, are amongst the maladies the slaves contract in the rice-swamps, and numerous deaths result. It is very much more trying than either cotton or tobacco cultivation.

John Brown, 1855, Slave Life in Georgia: A Narrative of the Life, Sufferings, and Escape of John Brown, a Fugitive Slave, *pp. 154–55.*

It is a general custom, wherever I have been, for the masters to give each of their slaves, male and female, *one peck of corn per week* for their food. This, at fifty cents per bushel, which was all it was worth when I was there, would amount to twelve and a half cents a week for board per hand. It cost me at least eight dollars per week upon an average, while I was south, for board. A peck of corn per week is all that masters, good, bad or indifferent, allow their slaves, round about Savannah, on the plantations.

One peck of gourd-seed corn is to be measured out to each slave once every week. With this they make a soup in a large iron kettle, around which the hands come at mealtime, and dipping out the soup, mix it with their hominy, and eat it as though it were a feast. In all other places where I visited, the slaves had *nothing from their masters but the corn,* or its equivalent in potatoes or rice, and to this they were not permitted to come but *once a day.* The custom was to blow the horn early in the morning, as a signal for the hands to rise and go to work. When commenced, they continue to work until about eleven o'clock, A.M., when, at the signal, all hands left off, and went into their huts, built their fires, made their corn meal into hominy or cake, ate it, and went to their work again at the signal of the horn,

and worked until night, or until their tasks were done. Some cooked their breakfasts in the field while at work. Each slave must grind his own corn in a hand-mill after he has done his work at night. There is generally one hand-mill on every plantation for the use of the slaves. Some plantations have no corn; others often get out. The substitute for it is the equivalent of one peck of corn either in rice or sweet potatoes, neither of which is so good for the slave as corn. They complain more of being faint, when fed on rice or potatoes, than when fed on corn.

Philo Tower, northern minister, 1856, Slavery Unmasked, *pp. 190–91.*

The hovels or huts in which these poor beings spend the few hours of release from the toils of the field, and the lash of the driver, are for the most part of the poorest kind. They are nothing near so good as the Irish shanties on our northern public works. Not so good as the most of northern farmers would furnish to their dumb beasts. The following is the style of architecture:

Four crotched posts are driven into the ground, say ten by fourteen or fourteen by eighteen, poles stretched across these from post to post, then sided up with rough boards, and partially roofed in the same way. All of which are minus stoves and chimneys; some, however, have a very rude apology for a fire-place in one end, and a board or two off at that side, or on the roof, to let out the smoke. Others, for the want of something in the shape of a fire-place, make their fire up in the center of the hovel. None of these buildings have more than one apartment in them, and the only opening through which a human being may pass in and out, serves for both window and door.

Philo Tower, northern minister, 1856, Slavery Unmasked, *p. 193.*

As for wearing apparel, their masters make it a practice of getting two suits of clothes for each slave per year—a thick suit for winter, and a thin one for summer. They also provide one pair of northern-made sale shoes for each adult slave every winter, which lasts them but a few weeks before they rip to pieces and give out. The males and females have their suits from the same cloth for winter dresses, which appear to be made of a mixture of the coarsest kind of cotton and wool, mostly uncolored, and of a *sleazy, spongy texture.* The entire suit for the men consists of a pair of pantaloons and a short sailor jacket, *without vest, hat, stockings, shirt, or any kind of loose garments!* These, if worn all the while when at work, would not probably last to exceed two months; therefore, for the sake of saving them, many of them, especially in the spring and summer months, work almost naked, male and female.

Philo Tower, northern minister, 1856, Slavery Unmasked, *p. 195.*

All the wide-spread United States, infrangibly welded together by the product of slave labor, impart to their vast commerce an extent and freedom not anticipated when commerce and slavery compromised for more perfect union by a constitution, whose wisest framers could not anticipate such prodigious and early prosperity. Northeastern and southwestern commonwealths, without armed compulsion, held together in natural conjunction by reciprocal dependence: sovereign States rapidly filling with sovereign people, as peaceably as irresistibly realize the whole American experiment of self-government, by agriculture, and commerce, navigation and manufactures, all useful arts in unequalled progress, with the fine and elegant also in rapid introduction. States and cities multiplying, beyond example, the annual harvests of combined liberty and slavery, with scarce an effort, repel and annul speculative, far-distant, theoretical philanthropy in vain decrying such national greatness. Five millions added to two millions of slave owners, four millions the increase of seven hundred thousand slaves, eight more prosperous States, all the offspring of American union since independence. . . . Four millions of slaves living contented with eight millions of masters, enjoy habitations, food, and raiment such as no peasantry is allowed, and tranquility unknown wherever rampant abolition rails at their condition. Such is the history, such the growth of the United States, since Great Britain surrendered to them all their negro slaves as national property.

C. J. Ingersoll, 1856, African Slavery in America, *pp. 36–37.*

The amount of provision given out on the plantation per week, was invariably one peck of corn or meal for each slave. This allowance was given in meal when it could be obtained; when it could not, they received corn, which they pounded in mortars after they returned from their labor in the field. The slaves on our plantation were provided with very little meat. In addition to the peck of corn or meal, they were allowed a little salt and a few herrings. If they wished for more, they were obliged to earn it by over-work. They were permitted to cultivate small gardens, and were thereby enabled to provide themselves with many trifling conveniences. But these gardens were only allowed to some of the more industrious. Capt.

Helm allowed his slaves a small quantity of meat during harvest time, but when the harvest was over they were obliged to fall back on the old allowance.

Austin Steward, 1856, Twenty-two Years a Slave, and Forty Years a Freeman, *p. 14.*

On our plantation, it was the usual practice to have one of the old slaves set apart to do the cooking. All the field hands were required to give into the hands of the cook a certain portion of their weekly allowance, either in dough or meal, which was prepared in the following manner. The cook made a hot fire and rolled up each person's portion in some cabbage leaves, when they could be obtained, and placed it in a hole in the ashes, carefully covered with the same, where it remained until done. Bread baked in this way is very sweet and good. But cabbage leaves could not always be obtained. When this was the case, the bread was little better than a mixture of dough and ashes, which was not very palatable. The time allowed for breakfast, was one hour. At the signal, all hands were obliged to resume their toil. The overseer was always on hand to attend to all delinquents, who never failed to feel the blows of his heavy whip.

Austin Steward, 1856, Twenty-Two Years a Slave, and Forty Years a Freeman, *p. 16.*

Slavery is that system of labor which exchanges subsistence for work, which secures a life-maintenance from the master to the slave, and gives a life-labor from the slave to the master. The slave is an apprentice for life, and owes his labor to his master; the master owes support, during life, to the slave. Slavery is the Negro system of labor. He is lazy and improvident. Slavery makes all work, and it insures homes, food, and clothing for all. It permits no idleness, and it provides for sickness, infancy, and old age. It allows no tramping or skulking, and it knows no pauperism.

William J. Grayson, 1856, Preface, The Hireling and the Slave, Chicora, and Other Poems, *p. vii.*

Along the Yazoo river one meets with some of the richest soil in the world, and some of the largest crops of cotton in the Union. My first night in that region was passed at the house of a planter who worked but few hands, was a fast friend of slavery, and yet drew for my benefit one of the most mournful pictures of a slave's life I have ever met with. He said, and I believe truly, that the negroes of small planters are, on the whole, well treated, or at least as well as the owners can afford to treat them. Their master not

unfrequently works side by side with them in the fields. *
** But on the large plantations, where the business is carried on by an overseer, and everything is conducted with military strictness and discipline, he described matters as being widely different. *The future of the overseer depends altogether on the quantity of cotton he is able to make up for the market.* Whether the owner be resident or non-resident, if the plantation be large, and a great number of hands be employed upon it, the overseer gets credit for a large crop, and blame for a small one. His professional reputation depends in a great measure upon the number of bales or hogsheads he is able to produce, and neither his education nor his habits are such as to render it likely that he would allow any consideration for the negroes to stand in the way of his advancing it. His interest is to get as much work out of them as they can possibly perform. His skill consists in knowing exactly how hard they may be driven without incapacitating them for future exertion. The larger the plantation the less chance there is, of course, of the owner's softening the rigor of the overseer, or the sternness of discipline by personal interference. So, as Mr. H—— said, a cast mass of the slaves pass their lives, from the moment they are able to go afield in the picking season till they drop worn out into the grave, in incessant labor, in all sorts of weather, at all seasons of the year, without any other change or relaxation than is furnished by sickness, without the smallest hope of any improvement either in their condition, in their food, or in their clothing, which are of the plainest and coarsest kind, and indebted solely to the forbearance or good temper of the overseer for exemption from terrible physical suffering. They are rung to bed at nine o'clock, almost immediately after bolting the food which they often have to cook after coming home from their day's labor, and are rung out of bed at four or five in the morning. The interval is one long round of toil. Life has no sunny spots for them.

An English traveler in Mississippi writing to the London Daily News, *1857, in Frederick Law Olmsted,* A Journey in the Back Country in the Winter of 1853–4, *pp. 59–60.*

In the selection of his farm, he (the master) should have an eye to health, convenience of water, and a soil with such a substratum as to retain manures. His home should be neat but not costly—erected on an elevated situation—with a sufficient number of shade trees to impart health and comfort to its inmates. His negro quarters should be placed a convenient distance from his dwelling on a dry, airy ridge—raised two feet from the ground—so they

can be thoroughly ventilated underneath, and placed at distances apart of at least fifty yards to ensure health. In this construction, they should be sufficiently spacious so as not to crowd the family intended to occupy them—with brick chimneys and large fire-places to impart warmth to every part of the room. More diseases and loss of time on plantations are engendered from crowded negro cabins than from almost any other cause. The successful planter should therefore have an especial eye to the comfort of his negroes, in not permitting them to be overcrowded in their sleeping quarters.

Practical Farmer and Mechanic, October 6, 1857, in Caleb Perry Patterson, The Negro in Tennessee, *1790–1865, p. 65.*

It is the custom in Louisiana, as I presume it is in other slave States, to allow the slave to retain whatever compensation he may obtain for services performed on Sundays. In this way, only, are they able to provide themselves with any luxury or convenience whatever. When a slave, purchased, or kidnapped in the North, is transported to a cabin on Bayou Boeuf, he is furnished with neither knife, nor fork, nor dish, nor kettle, nor any other thing in the shape of crockery, or furniture of any nature or description. He is furnished with a blanket before he reaches there, and wrapping that around him, he can either stand up, or lie down upon the ground, or on a board, if his master has no use for it. He is at liberty to find a gourd in which to keep his meal, or he can eat his corn from the cob, just as he pleases. To ask the master for a knife, or skillet, or any small convenience of the kind, would be answered with a kick, or laughed at as a joke. Whatever necessary article of this nature is found in a cabin has been purchased with Sunday money. However injurious to the morals, it is certainly a blessing to the physical condition of the slave, to be permitted to break the Sabbath. Otherwise there would be no way to provide himself with any utensils, which seem to be indispensable to him who is compelled to be his own cook.

Solomon Northup, 1859, Twelve Years a Slave, *pp. 194–95.*

The softest couches in the world are not to be found in the log mansion of the slave. The one whereon I reclined year after year, was a plank twelve inches wide and ten feet long. My pillow was a stick of wood. The bedding was a coarse blanket, and not a rag or shred beside. Moss might be used, were it not that it directly breeds a swarm of fleas.

The cabin is constructed of logs, without floor or window. The latter is altogether unnecessary, the crevices between the logs admitting sufficient light. In stormy weather the rain drives through them, rendering it comfortless and extremely disagreeable. The rude door hangs on great wooden hinges. In one end is constructed an awkward fireplace.

Solomon Northup, 1859, Twelve Years a Slave, *pp. 170–71.*

The cabin was without glass windows; it had only openings in the side which let in the light, and also the cold, chilly air of winter. There was a door to the cabin—that is, something that was called a door—but the uncertain hinges by which it was hung, and the large cracks in it, to say nothing of the fact that it was too small, made the room a very uncomfortable one. In addition to these openings there was, in the lower right-hand corner of the room, the "cat-hole,"—a contrivance which almost every mansion or cabin in Virginia possessed during the ante-bellum period. The "cat-hole" was a square opening, about seven by eight inches, provided for the purpose of letting the cat pass in and out of the house at will during the night. In the case of our particular cabin I could never understand the necessity for this convenience, since there were at least a half-dozen other places in the cabin that would accommodate the cats. There was no wooden floor in our cabin, the naked earth being used as a floor. . . ,

Three children—John, my older brother, Amanda, my sister, and myself—had a pallet on the dirt floor, or, to be more correct, we slept in and on a bundle of filthy rags laid upon the dirt floor.

Booker T. Washington writing about his life ca. 1860, Up from Slavery, *pp. 2–3.*

I cannot remember a single instance during my childhood or early boyhood when our entire family sat down to the table together, and God's blessing was asked, and the family ate a meal in a civilized manner. On the plantation in Virginia, and even later, meals were gotten by the children very much as dumb animals get theirs. It was a piece of bread here and a scrap of meat there. It was a cup of milk at one time and some potatoes at another. Sometimes a portion of our family would eat out of the skillet or pot, while some one else would eat from a tin plate held on the knees, and often using nothing but the hands with which to hold the food. When I had grown to sufficient size, . . . I remember that at one time I saw two of my young mistresses and some lady visitors eating ginger-cakes, in the yard. At the time those cakes seemed to me to be absolutely the most tempting and desirable things that I had ever seen; and I then and there resolved that, if I ever got free, the height of my ambition would be reached if I could get to the point where I could secure and eat ginger-cakes in the way that I saw those ladies doing.

Booker T. Washington writing about his life ca. 1860, Up from Slavery, *pp. 6–7.*

As to your coming South, let me just here state, for all, that you wholly misapprehend the spirit of our people. We ask not one thing of the North which has not been secured to us by the Constitution and laws since they were established and enacted, and which has been granted to us until within a few years past. We demand no sacrifice nor the surrender of Northern rights and privileges. The party that elected Mr. Lincoln proclaimed uncompromising hostility to the institution of slavery—an institution which existed here, and has done so from the beginning, in its patriarchial character. We feel ourselves under the most solemn obligations to take care of, and to provide for, these people who cannot provide for themselves. Nearly every free-soil state has prohibited them from settling in their territory. Where are they to go?

Bishop Otey of the Episcopal Church in Tennessee writing to northern clergymen, May 17, 1861, in Caleb Perry Patterson, The Negro in Tennessee, 1790–1865, *p. 150.*

The Chaplain was called on frequently to visit and bury the "contrabands" whose poor little huts hung upon the edges of the camp and were scattered over the fields all the way to the city. After the Second Bull Run battle large numbers of blacks gathered about the Hospital and were kindly treated, the men being employed in policing and the women as laundresses, all receiving Government rations. So great, however, was the temptation afforded by their abject ignorance that they were at one time nearly starved by an acting commissary steward, who was summarily dealt with by the Surgeon in Charge and made to give up his evil-gotten gains. . . .

The huts about us, first homes of the wandering, sorrowful race, were strange patchwork; bits of shelter tents and blankets, ends of plank, barrel staves, logs and mud, but most of them were neatly whitewashed and with the likeness of a little, fenced garden behind, and near many and many, by the roadside, was a rough grave with a redwood cross at its head.

Jane Stuart Woolsey, nurse at a Union army hospital, Alexandria, Virginia, from fall 1863 until August 1865, Hospital Days, *pp. 55–56.*

The war, according to these negroes [of Wilmington, South Carolina], had, in some respects, made slavery harder for them than before. They were naturally trusted less, and watched more. Then, when provisions became scarce, their rations, on the large plantations, were reduced. On one, for example, the field hands got no meat at all, and their allowance consisted of a peck of unsifted corn-meal and a pint of molasses per week. On another, they got two pounds of meat, a peck of meal, and a quart of molasses per week. Before the war, they had double as much meat, and a peck and a-half of meal. Thus fed, they were expected to begin work in the fields at daybreak, and continue, with only the intermission of half an hour at noon, till dark.

Whitelaw Reid, journalist, 1866, After the War: A Southern Tour, May 1, 1865, to May 1, 1866, *p. 52.*

The doctor's health was a great calamity to us, for the estate and the slaves were to be sold and the proceeds divided among the heirs. The first sad announcement that the sale was to be; the knowledge that all ties of the past were to be sundered; the frantic terror at the idea of being sent "down south"; the almost certainty that one member of a family will be torn from another; the anxious scanning of purchasers' faces; the agony at parting, often for ever, with husband, wife, child—these must be seen and felt to be fully understood. Young as I was then, the iron entered into my soul. . . . The crowd collected round the stand, the huddling group of negroes, the examination of muscle, teeth, the exhibition of agility, the look of the auctioneer, the agony of my mother—I can shut my eyes and see them all.

Josiah Henson, who was born into slavery in 1789 in Charles County, Maryland, 1881, An Autobiography of the Rev. Josiah Henson ("Uncle Tom") from 1789 to 1881, *p. 17.*

In ordinary times we had two regular meals a day: breakfast at twelve o'clock, after labouring from daylight, and supper when the work of the remainder of the day was over. In harvest season we had three. Our dress was of tow-cloth; for the children, nothing but a shirt; for the older ones a pair of pantaloons or a gown in addition, according to the sex. Besides these, in the winter a round jacket or overcoat, a wool-hat once in two or three years, for the males, and a pair of coarse shoes once a year.

We lodged in log huts, and on the bare ground. Wooden floors were an unknown luxury. In a single room were huddled, like cattle, ten or a dozen persons, men,

women, and children. All ideas of refinement and decency were, of course, out of the question. We had neither bedsteads, nor furniture of any description. Our beds were collections of straw and old rags, thrown down in the corners and boxed in with boards; a single blanket the only covering. Our favourite way of sleeping, however, was on a plank, our heads raised on an old jacket and our feet toasting before a smouldering fire. The wind whistled and the rain and snow blew in through the cracks, and the damp earth soaked in the moisture till the floor was miry as a pig-sty. Such were our houses. In these wretched hovels were we penned at night, and fed by day: here were the children born and the sick—neglected.

Josiah Henson, 1881, An Autobiography of the Rev. Josiah Henson ("Uncle Tom") from 1789 to 1881, *pp. 19–20.*

Let me briefly state our food allowance so that you may judge how we lived. Some may think it plenty, but if they had been in our situation, working as hard as we did, I think they would have speedily changed their mind. A full grown man was allowed one and a half pecks of cornmeal a week; a half grown boy, a gallon and from that down to a quart. The meat allowed was two and a half pounds a week and graded less according to age and size, while some did not receive any. If you should raise a hog yourself, you would be entitled to one half of it and your master the other. We also had a half dozen herrings a week, and if we got any more, it was because we knew where they were kept and helped ourselves when night's dark mantle was charitably thrown around us.

I have known my family allowance to give out two days before the rations were distributed and then I had to go out on a still hunt to feed the babies and wife. We would generally after that have a plump chicken for Sunday dinner, over which grace was pronounced with great unction. My wife was a dining room waiter and would bring crumbs and scraps from what was left after the rest were through. Many a night towards the end of the week, we having been perhaps a little improvident and eaten up everything, I would have to sally out as a self-appointed commisary department in quest of forage, having to sacrifice many sleeping hours to keep my wife and wee ones from feeling the pangs of hunger.

Isaac D. Williams, 1885, Sunshine and Shadow of Slave Life, *pp. 58–59.*

There was a section of the plantation known as "the quarters," where were situated the cabins of the slaves. These cabins were built of rough logs, and daubed with the red clay or mud of the region. No attempt was made to give them a neat appearance—they were not even whitewashed. Each cabin was about fourteen feet square, containing but one room, and was covered with oak boards, three feet in length, split out of logs by hand. These boards were not nailed on, but held in their places by what were termed weight-poles laid across them at right angles. There were in each room two windows, a door and a large, rude fire-place. The door and window frames, or facings, were held in their places by wooden pins, nails being used only in putting the doors together. The interior of the cabins had nothing more attractive than the outside—there was no plastering and only a dirt floor. The furniture consisted of one bed, a plain board table and some benches made by the slaves themselves. Sometimes a cabin was occupied by two or more families, in which case the number of beds was increased proportionately. For light a grease lamp was used, which was made of iron, bowl shaped, by a blacksmith. The bowl was filled with grease and a rag or wick placed in it, one end resting on the edge for lighting. These lamps gave a good light, and were in general use among the slaves. Tallow candles were a luxury, never seen except in the "great houses" of the planters. The only light for outdoors used by the slaves was a torch made by binding together a bundle of small sticks or splinters.

Louis Hughes, 1897, Thirty Years a Slave, *pp. 25–26.*

One woman did the weaving and it was her task to weave from nine to ten yards a day. Aunt Liza was our weaver and she was taught the work by the madam. . . .

Each piece of cloth contained forty yards, and this cloth was used in making clothes for the servants. About half of the whole amount required was thus made at home; the remainder was bought, and as it was heavier it was used for winter clothing. Each man was allowed for summer two pairs of pants and two shirts, but no coat. The women had two dresses and two chemises each for summer. For winter the men had each two pairs of pants, one coat, one hat and one pair of coarse shoes. These shoes before being worn had to be greased with tallow, with a little tar in it. It was always a happy time when the men got these winter goods—it brought many a smile to their faces, though the supply was meager and the articles of the cheapest. The women's dresses for winter were made of the heavier wool-cloth used for the men. They also had one pair of shoes each and a turban. The women who could utilize old clothes, made for themselves what were called pantalets. They had no stockings or undergarments to protect their limbs—these were never given them. The pantalets were made like a pant-leg, came just above the knee, and were caught and tied. Sometimes they looked well and comfortable. The men's old pant-legs were sometimes used.

Louis Hughes, 1897, Thirty Years a Slave, *pp. 41–42.*

CHAPTER FOUR

Charity Reconsidered
1865-1900

Because it was formed just weeks before the South surrendered, the Freedmen's Bureau did most of its work in the uneasy early months of peace. Its agents distributed food, clothing, and medical care; opened schools for African-American children and adults that were staffed largely by white northern missionaries and charity workers; and attempted to secure employment for African Americans or resettle them on confiscated land.

The Civil War, the costliest American war in terms of destruction of property and loss of human life, was particularly disastrous for the South. Nearly every battle had been fought in the Confederate states, and the landscape was devastated. Sections of Richmond, Atlanta, Mobile, and other cities were in ruins. Throughout the countryside, conquering Union forces had gutted plantation houses, burned barns and bridges, pulled up railroad tracks, slaughtered livestock, interrupted planting, and seized or laid waste to crops. Whereas one in five Union soldiers had died of disease or battlefield wounds, one in four Confederate soldiers had lost his life in the war. Deprived of significant numbers of white male laborers and beasts of burden in addition to its enslaved workforce, the South struggled to feed itself and failed. "I've never heard such a cry for bread in my life," wrote one Jacksonville, Florida, Democrat to Governor Lewis E. Parsons in 1865. "If any thing can be done, for God's sake do it quickly. This is no panic but real great hunger that punishes people."[1]

Under the direction of General Oliver O. Howard, a West Point graduate who had lost an arm in the Peninsular Campaign, the Freedmen's Bureau distributed 13 million rations in the first 13 weeks after the war ended. (A ration consisted of flour, cornmeal, sugar, and other foodstuffs sufficient to sustain an adult for one week.) Bureau agents gave about two-thirds of these rations to former slaves; the remainder went to poor and displaced whites, because hunger and destitution afflicted Southerners regardless of race, and the bureau aided all refugees. In 1867 Congress authorized the use of federal funds to aid anyone left destitute in the South regardless of wartime loyalty, and by spring 1869, the Freedmen's Bureau had distributed 21 million rations, including 6 million to whites. In fact, in Alabama there was never a time when the Freedmen's Bureau assisted more blacks than whites.

75

An agent of the Freedmen's Bureau promotes peaceful coexistence between southern whites and blacks in the aftermath of the Civil War. *(Library of Congress, Prints and Photographs Division, LC-USZ62-105555)*

The bureau fed and educated thousands of people, and its hospitals cared for many sick and needy former slaves, but it was chronically short of funds and supplies, and it never had more than 900 agents to administer its services to millions of refugees. These agents also tried to prevent racially motivated violence and filed monthly reports on "outrages committed by whites against freedmen" and "outrages committed by freedmen against whites," as one agent said.[2] Most of the "outrages" were directed toward African Americans, though.

A series of constitutional amendments was intended to safeguard the freedom of African Americans. The Thirteenth Amendment, ratified December 6, 1865, abolished slavery in the United States. The Fourteenth Amendment, ratified July 9, 1868, conferred citizenship on the former slaves. The Fifteenth Amendment, ratified February 3, 1870, protected the rights to vote, to own property, and to life and liberty, regardless of race or color. Millions of African Americans exercised their new freedom by moving from one state to another. Some moved simply because they could, to discover how it felt. Others wanted to distance themselves from their old masters and any possibility of reenslavement—despite the protection guaranteed by the Constitution. Couples legalized marriages entered into under slavery, and men and women advertised in newspapers, hoping to find loved ones from whom bondage had separated them.

While the former slaves flexed their newly free muscles and agents of the Freedmen's Bureau and other northerners worked to rebuild the southern economy on a foundation of free labor, white southerners sought ways to keep blacks poor, out of competition for jobs, and under control. Threats and violence were powerful inhibitors, and the postwar years saw the formation of the Ku Klux Klan, Knights of the White Camellia, Shiloh Encampment, Brotherhood, and other terrorist groups founded on white supremacy. African Americans who displayed too much independence had their homes and barns burned and their crops destroyed, and they sometimes lost their lives.

In November 1865 Mississippi became the first southern state to pass a Black Code, a set of laws similar to the old Slave Codes, which was designed to restrict African Americans' rights and mobility. Black Codes varied from one state to another, but they generally limited African Americans' rights of free speech and free expression. To keep African Americans working on plantations the codes generally permitted them to rent property only in rural areas. In Mississippi and elsewhere, the state claimed the right to indenture African-American children. Strict vagrancy laws required African Americans to work under contract or risk imprisonment, thereby forcing them to labor with terms favorable to the employer, who was likely to be a plantation owner.

Typically a male field hand earned between nine and 15 dollars a month, and a female received between five and 10 dollars a month. Many became sharecroppers, agreeing to work the employer's land in return for a share of the crop, typically one-fourth to one-half the cotton or corn produced. The landlord extended credit to the sharecropper at the start of the growing season and deducted what was to be repaid from the profit at harvest. Sharecropping seemed to offer security to impoverished and uneducated African Americans, but because of high interest rates, careless accounting, and dishonesty, many sharecroppers realized scant return on their labor.

The Poor White Farmer

Despite the abuses, the sharecropping system also employed poor whites, some of whom had been small independent farmers before losing their land because they were unable to pay taxes.

Poverty inspired many southern whites to migrate from one state to another in search of a livelihood. Tens of thousands flocked to the South's rising industrial centers, such as Birmingham, Alabama, to find jobs in iron, steel, and textile mills. Timber and coal-mining companies established themselves in Appalachia, where people increasingly relied on seasonal wages to supplement their earnings from farming. By 1880 the average Appalachian farm was worth just three-fourths of its 1850 value, even though a greater percentage of its acreage had been improved. The principal reason for this decline is thought to be a drop in the productive value of the land caused by slash and burn agriculture, in which natural vegetation is cut away and the remaining stubble burned. This method of clearing fields leaves the land vulnerable to erosion. (It should be noted that most American farmers felt economic strain in the 1870s, even those with fertile, productive soil, because overproduction drove down prices. Agricultural output increased 53 percent while land in farms increased 31 percent and the population grew just 26 percent, from 39,819,449 to 50,256,000.)

"THE NEZ PERCES' STATE CARRIAGE."

BATTLE OF CAÑON CREEK.

THE NEZ PERCES DRIVING PONIES.

THE NEZ PERCES WAR.—FROM SKETCHES BY AN ARMY OFFICER.—[SEE PAGE 842.]

General Oliver O. Howard (left), commissioner of the Freedmen's Bureau from 1865 through 1874, conducted campaigns against the Nez Perce of the Northwest in 1877. *(Library of Congress, Prints and Photographs Division, LC-USZ62-130186)*

It might seem logical to ask why poor and struggling farmers did not move west, especially after the Homestead Act of 1862 granted 160 acres of western land to any head of household or person over 21 who was an American citizen or had applied for citizenship. The reason is that land was just one of the requirements for successful western settlement. Starting over in the West cost money. Pioneers had to pay to transport themselves, their families, and their equipment. They needed capital to erect a house, outbuildings, and fences; to stock the farm; and to support the family for the two years often required until the farm could feed them. Another two years might then have to pass before the farm yielded a surplus that could be sold. It was possible for a poor man to go west if he traveled alone and signed on as a hand with a family making the journey, and if after reaching his destination he were willing to labor for a railroad or a mining or timber company. A poor woman could support herself in the West as a teacher, domestic servant, or prostitute. The majority of western migrants, however, were from the prosperous middle class: successful farmers, merchants, lawyers, and the like.

Containing the Indians

In 1869, the Union Pacific and Central Pacific Railroad lines met in Utah, linking the West and East. The era of the frontier was coming to an end, and federal policy toward Native peoples had shifted from removal to containment on reservations. It was impossible to push the Indians farther west because there no longer were vast regions for them to occupy beyond the edge of settlement. It seemed more practical now to force assimilation and make the Indians take up traditional American farming—on their own land.

To say that the western tribal nations resisted U.S. attempts to herd them onto reservations would be an understatement. Their opposition took the form of 30 years of war with the United States and caused General William Tecumseh Sherman to declare ominously, "All who cling to their old hunting grounds are hostile and will remain so till killed off."[3]

Yet the U.S. government had demonstrated that treaties were made to be broken and land granted in perpetuity could be reclaimed, and now settlers were encroaching on Indian land for homesteading, planting, and grazing, and sometimes for obtaining mineral wealth, and the government was providing no protection. In 1874, for example, the army confirmed the presence of gold on Indian land in the Black Hills of South Dakota, and in 1875 the government opened the region to prospectors and settlers. In South Dakota and elsewhere in the West the government moved Indians to new reservations that were less desirable whenever white settlers craved what was theirs.

In the war to maintain their traditional ways of life and lands, the Native Americans won important battles over the years, most famously on June 25, 1876, near the Little Bighorn River in present-day Montana. On that day between 2,500 and 4,000 Cheyenne and Sioux (Lakota, Dakota, Nakota) warriors wiped out a column of the 7th Cavalry led by General George Armstrong Custer. Still, the army's grand strategy, described by one officer as "permitting the Indians no rest and rendering every hiding place insecure," eventually wore the Indians down.[4] The Indian Wars ended on December 29, 1890, when soldiers of the 7th Cavalry massacred hundreds of Lakota men, women, and children at Wounded Knee, South Dakota.

In the segregated environment of the reservation the Indians' religious practices and norms of family and community life were to be replaced by Christianity and non-Indian ideals of individual autonomy and private property. To further the government's goal of assimilation and promote the concept of individual rather than group ownership of land, the General Allotment Act of 1887, sponsored by Senator Henry L. Dawes of Massachusetts, gave the president the power—but not the obligation—to assign up to 160 acres of Indian land to a resident of the reservation who was a head of household and a fraction of an allotment to a single person or orphan. Exempted were lands occupied by the Cherokee, Creek, Choctaw, Seminole, Osage, Miami, Peoria, Sac, and Fox in the Indian Territory (present-day Oklahoma); the Seneca reservations in New York State; and one section of Nebraska. The government was to hold the allotted land in trust for 25 years, during which it could be neither taxed nor sold. The government had the right to negotiate for and open for non-Indian settlement any "surplus" land remaining after all allotments were accepted. Thus Native Americans saw their holdings fall from 155,632,312 acres in 1881 to 104,314,349 acres in 1890. By 1900 Indians held just 77,865,373 acres.

Only a minority of Indians became successful farmers. Most were unable to make a living from their barren, unproductive fields and lived in poverty as wards—not citizens—of the United States, dependent on financial support and rations from Washington to clothe and feed themselves. They looked on helplessly as their children were taken away to boarding schools to be educated in traditional Protestant American customs and values. Far from home at places such as the Carlisle Indian School in Pennsylvania, children forced to give up their traditional dress and language and adopt new names languished and frequently fell ill and died. Those who survived to graduate discovered that they fit in neither on the reservation where they had been born nor among the whites who had trained them.

Apache farmers deliver hay to Fort Apache, Arizona, in 1893. *(National Archives)*

Rapid Immigration

The Naturalization Act of 1870 restricted the extension of citizenship to "white persons and persons of African descent."[5] This meant that Native Americans and another group—Asians—were barred from becoming naturalized citizens of the United States. Predominantly in the West, Chinese immigrants had been laboring on farms, working as domestic servants, and, since 1866, helping to build railroad lines. In 1881, 11,890 Chinese immigrated to the United States; the following year Chinese immigration more than tripled, rising to 39,579. The Chinese were so different from the majority of Americans in terms of customs, language, and religion that many people believed they would never be part of the mainstream. The Chinese Exclusion Act of 1882, the first significant law to restrict immigration, barred Chinese laborers from entering the United States for a period of 10 years. In 1891 the federal government established control of immigration with the formation of the Department of Immigration and Naturalization (later the Immigration and Naturalization Service). The act that established the bureau also restricted immigration by barring from entry individuals likely to become public charges, including persons suffering from a contagious disease, felons, and those whose passage had been paid by others. In 1892 the Chinese Exclusion Act was extended for another 10 years.

More than 2 million Chinese had entered the United States since 1868, constituting a fraction of the 13 million immigrants to arrive between the end of the Civil War and the start of the 20th century. Throughout most of the 19th century the majority of immigrants were from northern and western Europe, mostly from Great Britain, Ireland, Germany, and the Scandinavian countries. Many were Protestant, as were most Americans, and many spoke English. After 1880, however, immigrants increasingly were Catholics and Jews from southern and eastern Europe, from Italy, Austria-Hungary, Russia, and Greece, who had left regions of overpopulation and poverty. Jewish immigrants often had fled oppression and overt persecution in eastern Europe.

The new immigrants tended not to speak English. They lacked employable skills and rarely had enough money to travel beyond ports of entry or industrial centers or to acquire land and take up farming. Most Chinese entered the United States on the West Coast, but the Europeans passed through eastern ports. European immigrants clustered in tenements in New York, Buffalo, Baltimore, Pittsburgh, Chicago, and other cities and took low-paying jobs in factories and steel mills. In many tenement neighborhoods, one impoverished immigrant group replaced another that had arrived earlier. This happened, for example, in New York City's Five Points. In 1855, 66 percent of the adult residents of Five Points had been born in Ireland, and 3 percent had been born in Italy. In 1880 just 31 percent had been born in Ireland, and 23 percent had been born in Italy. Many of the 22 percent born in the United States, however, were the sons and daughters of Irish-born parents. By 1890 Italians made up 49 percent and Irish 10 percent of the population of Five Points, and a new group, Jews, accounted for 18 percent, according to a census conducted by the city police department. Native-born Americans feared that these new immigrants and their descendants would remain in poverty and harm the economy; that they espoused anarchy and other dangerous political beliefs; and that they had ties to organized crime.

A Further Decline in Outdoor Aid

While immigration was soaring, public outdoor aid was gradually being abolished. The reasons for municipal governments' withdrawal of outdoor relief were both philosophical and practical. On one hand, the old concern remained that giving the poor something for nothing contributed to pauperism. On the other hand, outdoor relief was becoming too costly for the middle-class property owners whose taxes supported public works. Taxpayers understood the need for such services as a police force, fire department, and sanitation bureau, but public assistance for the needy in their homes seemed dispensable.

The poor hoping to avoid the almshouse relied increasingly on the kindness of their relatives and neighbors, including their landlord, the local grocer, and the corner saloonkeeper, who might provide an occasional loan or free meal. They turned as well to churches, trade unions, and the mutual-aid and ethnic societies that were being formed in U.S. cities. Private charities were proliferating (some even receiving subsidies from the same city governments that had abolished outdoor relief), and they, too, remained ready to lend a helping hand. Philadelphia alone had 800 charitable groups by 1878.

Private charity proved essential when the prosperity Americans had enjoyed in the years after the Civil War gave way to the economic depression known as the Panic of 1873. This severe international economic downturn announced itself in the United States with the collapse of Jay Cooke and Company, the Philadelphia firm that had financed the Great Northern Railroad and handled most of the government's war loans. The shock wave generated by the Cooke failure caused most of the major railroads to fold, closed banks and factories throughout the nation, and put thousands out of work. The New York Association for Improving the Condition of the Poor estimated that between 75,000 and 105,000 members of New York City's working population of 375,000 were unemployed. The association saw its yearly expenses rise from $50,189 in 1873 to $96,430 in 1874. Private citizens, churches, and community groups also aided the destitute as they had in years past by operating soup kitchens and breadlines and dispensing food, clothing, fuel, and cash—the very outdoor aid that local governments were withholding.

Perceiving that these vast and complicated networks of charity required oversight, states formed boards of charity to take on this task. By 1886, 12 boards were in operation, conducting studies to determine whether private charities were operating efficiently, advising the legislature on public support for private institutions, and preparing annual reports. Board members also brought to light corruption in the management of public institutions for the poor. In 1870, for example, an investigator reported that the president of the board of supervisors of the Chicago Almshouse had profited from bribery when awarding construction contracts for a shelter for the insane that was to be built on the poor-farm grounds. The president's dishonesty had cost Cook County $6,000 and delayed construction for several months. This matter prompted a member of the Illinois Board of State Charities to comment that "as a class, the public charities of Cook County appear to have been instituted for the benefit of the officers managing them."[6]

In the late 19th century some Americans went so far as to ask whether society or the poor benefited at all from charity or whether almsgiving might actually impede social and economic progress and weaken the human race. "[T]he need supplied by outdoor public relief is in fact, created by it," said Josephine Shaw Lowell, the first woman commissioner of the New York Board of Charities.[7] It was an era of acquisition and competitiveness, when business was poorly regulated and grasping, compassionless men amassed fortunes in steel, oil, railroads, and other industries by crushing smaller firms. It was the era of Social Darwinism, when only the strongest seemed worthy of survival.

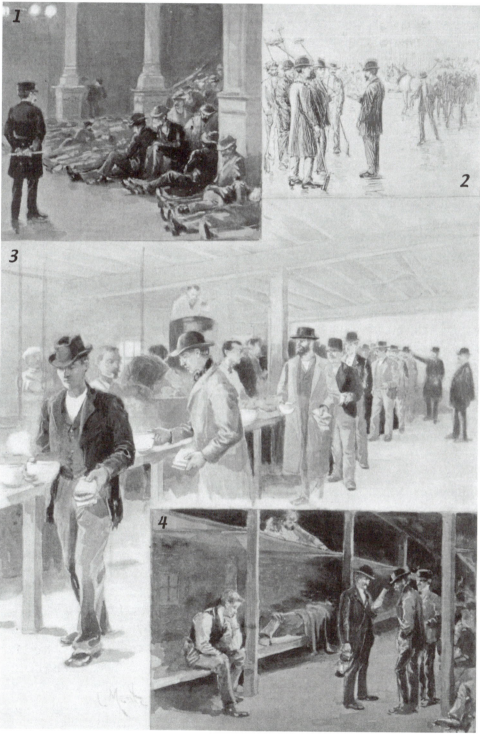

Scenes among the unemployed of Chicago are depicted in 1894: bedding down in a City Hall corridor (1); three hours of street sweeping (2); dinner at the Lakeside Kitchen, a charity soup kitchen (3); a bed for the night in a lodging house (4). *(Library of Congress, Prints and Photographs Division, LC-USZ62-109366)*

The most prominent expounder of this philosophy was the British civil engineer Herbert Spencer, who famously asserted, "If we do not like the survival of the fittest, we have only one possible alternative, and that is the survival of the unfittest. The former is the law of civilization, the latter is the law of uncivilization."[8] Only by winnowing the superior specimens from the worthless would the human race advance, according to Spencer's philosophy. Charitable impulses impeded social progress, he said; therefore governing bodies must refrain from aiding the poor and ministering to public health except to prevent epidemics. Even such government actions as operating schools and delivering mail countered progress by helping the weak survive and proliferate. Although Spencer's treatise *Social Statics* was published in 1851, eight years before Darwin's *Origin of the Species*, his line of thinking came to be called Social Darwinism because it seemed to many to apply Darwin's theory of natural selection to society.

Social Darwinism inspired the charity organization movement, which began in London in 1869. Professing that indiscriminate almsgiving encouraged the pauper class to multiply and thus impeded social progress, proponents of charity organization took a "scientific" approach to aiding the poor, attempting to diagnose the causes of poverty in individual cases. They worked to reduce waste, duplication, and fraud in the dispensing of relief and teach the poor to be self-supporting. The first American Charity Organization Society was founded in 1877 in Buffalo, New York, by Stephen Humphreys Gurteen. A graduate of Cambridge University who had traveled to the United States to study international law, Gurteen had stepped ashore in New York just in time to witness the draft riot of 1863, a frightening event that he believed was rooted in poverty.

By 1875, his career in law apparently forgotten, Gurteen was an ordained Episcopal minister serving at St. Paul's Church in Buffalo, a city suffering through the economic depression that had begun in 1873. Destitution was everywhere, and local charities were overwhelmed. Conditions deteriorated further in July 1877, when a nationwide railroad strike led to rioting in Baltimore, Pittsburgh, Chicago, San Francisco, and other cities, and in small towns from West Virginia to Upstate New York. In Buffalo, an important railroad hub, strikers did whatever they could to halt the movement of passengers and freight. They greased tracks, uncoupled trains, sabotaged switching equipment, and threatened strikebreakers. Hoping to extend the strike to other industries, they moved into factories, coal yards, and stone yards. Buffalonians feared what might happen, and the Reverend Stephen Humphreys Gurteen expected a riot like the one he had seen in Manhattan. Mayor Philip Becker called up a volunteer force of 300 to assist the city police, state militia, and Civil War veterans in putting down the revolt. The strike ended in Buffalo a week later, with eight strikers dead and eight soldiers wounded.

Violence could erupt again, though. Responding to the perceived crisis, to the need for the good people of Buffalo to defend themselves against what he called "the Frankenstein of Pauperism," in December Gurteen assembled local dignitaries to form the Charity Organization Society of Buffalo, a nonsectarian agency that acted as a clearinghouse for charities and was modeled on the London society.[9] Agents of Gurteen's group dispensed no relief. Instead they kept a file on applicants for alms, investigated their cases, weeded out the undeserving and those able to work, and directed the worthy poor to the most appropriate sources of aid. The society's "friendly visitors" called on the poor at home to offer suggestions for self-help, much as representatives of the New-York Association for Improving the Condition of the Poor had earlier in the century. The approach seemed new enough to interest civic leaders in other municipalities, though, and by 1883 there were charity organization societies in 25 U.S. cities; by 1900 the number of cities with charity organization societies had grown to 138.

Settlement Houses Empower the Poor

Charity organization was tied to the tradition of outdoor relief. Settlement houses, in contrast, removed themselves from charity altogether and instead offered "a new type of philanthropy," working to improve neighborhoods from within.[10] Settlement-house staff members, who tended to be young people trained in theology or the emerging field of social work, lived as neighbors of the people they wanted to help. To the extent that it was possible they lived under the same social conditions that affected the poor and remained alert for "the unsought information which tells the story of a neighborhood."[11] A settlement house was both a residence and a community center, offering employment counseling, child care, health services, recreation,

The backyard playground of the Henry Street Settlement, New York City, was photographed by Jacob Riis, ca. 1890. *(Library of Congress, Prints and Photographs Division, LC-USZ62-34696)*

and clubs and classes that promoted cultural and intellectual growth. Because so many community residents were immigrants, settlement workers gave instruction in English and citizenship and generally helped the local population assimilate into American life. They also saw it as their task to empower people to improve their surroundings, to campaign for safer tenements and improved sanitation.

As had charity organizations, the settlement-house movement began in England. The first settlement house in the United States, the Neighborhood Guild (later called the University Settlement), was founded in New York City in 1886 by Stanton Coit, who is also remembered as a proponent of Ethical Culture. Coit believed that every person helped by a settlement house would in turn influence his or her family, friends, and neighbors, so that the benefits of the movement extended far beyond the population directly assisted.

There were 74 settlement houses in the United States in 1897 and more than 100 in 1900, most in the Northeast and Midwest. The majority served impoverished urban immigrant neighborhoods. The most famous U.S. settlement, Hull-House, was founded on the West Side of Chicago by two Rockford College graduates, Jane Addams and Ellen Gates Starr, in 1886. Boston's Andover House (soon renamed South End House) was established in 1891 by the Reverend William J. Tucker, a Congregational minister who had lived at Toynbee Hall, the first social settlement in London, and staffed by college students. At the close of the 19th century, Boston's South End was a working-poor and lower-middle-class neighborhood of lodging houses and tenements. Sixty percent of tenement-house residents were Irish, and 20 percent were Jewish. Believing that social conditions in the South End mirrored those in all U.S. cities, some of the students spent their residency producing scholarly research. Most, however, preferred to work directly with the people of the community.

Continued Dependence on the Poorhouse

While pioneering settlement-house workers addressed the social conditions that they believed contributed to poverty, city and county governments continued treating the poor as victims of those social conditions or of their own character flaws and sheltering them in poorhouses. Orphan asylums had proliferated largely as an alternative form of institutional care for needy children, but in the second half of the 19th century thousands of youngsters remained behind almshouse walls. On April 24, 1875, New York outlawed the placement of children in poorhouses, and soon Indiana, Ohio, Pennsylvania, and other states passed similar laws. Enforcement was lax, however, and by 1880 approximately 8,000 American children between the ages of three and 16 remained poorhouse residents.

Records of the Onondaga County, New York, poorhouse from 1877 list the causes of dependency for 362 adult residents. The largest number, 127, were vagrants. Sixty-four were intemperate, and 53 were simply destitute. Forty-two were insane, and 30 were dependent on county care as a result of illness. Ten or fewer were institutionalized for each of the following reasons: debauchery, old age, bastardy, lameness, idiocy, and blindness. Medical reports from the Cook County, Illinois, poorhouse indicate that the old, ill, and insane accounted for larger segments of the inmate population as the 19th century progressed, a finding that is in keeping with the national trend for almshouses to reject younger, able-bodied applicants. Nationwide by 1886 the aged constituted 37 percent of people in poorhouses.

William G. Broad was keeper of the Onondaga County, New York, poorhouse from 1893 through 1907. *(Photo Courtesy of Town of Onondaga Historical Society)*

Challenges Persist for African Americans

After the Freedmen's Bureau was disbanded in 1872, the great majority of African Americans liberated by the Civil War were left to find their own way to live in freedom. People helped themselves and one another. By the late 19th century, fraternal orders, mutual-aid societies, and women's clubs had been formed in many African-American communities, ensuring that members' medical and burial expenses would be met if necessary in exchange for low monthly dues.

From the end of the Civil War through the close of the 19th century, some African Americans left the South to seek economic security in the North. Among the first to do so were newly freed slaves sent to Boston by the Freedmen's Bureau immediately after the war to ease the burden in crowded, economically strained areas of the Upper South, such as the Tidewater region of Virginia. The steamers that weekly followed the coastline to Boston from Norfolk and Baltimore continued to carry people, with the result that between 1870 and 1900, one-third of the African Americans of Boston had been born in Virginia or were the children of Virginians. Many of the others were from Maryland, North Carolina, South Carolina, and the District of Columbia. Philadelphia and New York City also were popular destinations, as many people followed family members who had gone before. By 1900 more than half the African Americans living in New York City had been born in other states.

African Americans in the North competed for jobs against newly arrived European immigrants. They often lost the contest because many whites refused to work alongside blacks. In Boston and elsewhere, charity organization societies tried to find jobs for African-American applicants and blamed their failure on discrimination. Most African Americans in the North lived in predominantly black neighborhoods such as San Juan Hill and the Tenderloin in New York, but some lived in mixed blocks, in the same tenement buildings as whites. Landlords generally denied African Americans apartments in new tenement buildings and charged high rents for the rundown housing made available to them. In 1899 this situation caused a Reverend Tompkins, an African-American minister in New York City, to complain, "The colored people of our city have either been entirely forgotten or neglected."[12]

The African Americans who moved north tended to be former slaves, but they represented a minority. Most southern blacks lived in rural areas and were illiterate, but many of the migrants were from cities or large towns and had some ability to read and write. The majority had left states of the Upper South; it was not until 1890, when boll weevils infested the cotton fields, that African Americans began to leave the Deep South in appreciable numbers.

For those who remained in the South, life grew harsher. For one thing, the lynching of African Americans became almost commonplace. Nearly all the victims of the more than 2,500 lynchings that occurred in the United States between 1894 and 1900 were African American. For another, beginning with Tennessee in 1875, the southern states passed their infamous "Jim Crow" laws, which were intended to keep blacks and whites apart in society. These laws barred blacks from patronizing hotels, restaurants, and theaters that catered to whites. They established separate schools for the two races and separate areas for blacks in trains, waiting rooms, and public libraries. The Supreme Court upheld this doctrine of "separate but equal" facilities in 1896, by letting stand a lower-court decision in the case of Homer Plessy, a 30-year-old shoemaker of mixed racial heritage who was jailed for sitting in a "white" car of the East Louisiana Railroad. Reading the majority opinion, Supreme Court Justice Henry Brown said that separation "has no tendency to destroy the legal equality of the two races."[13]

For African Americans the years between the Civil War and the start of the 20th century began with hope and ended with a Supreme Court decision confirming that, for most, equality would remain out of reach. Events occurring at this time set the stage for poverty in the 20th century not just among African Americans but also among Native Americans and the residents of Appalachia. White America attempted to resolve the problems of the urban poor scientifically, by observing them in their environment, diagnosing the causes of poverty, and prescribing solutions. The long-held belief that poverty was rooted in character flaws was at the heart of the charity organization movement, but settlement-house workers focused instead on social conditions and empowerment. Meanwhile, county poorhouses continued to fill an immediate need.

Chronicle of Events

1865

- *November:* Mississippi becomes the first state to enact a Black Code.
- *December 6:* The Thirteenth Amendment to the Constitution is ratified, formally abolishing slavery in the United States.

1866

- Chinese laborers are first hired to construct western railroads.

1867

- Congress authorizes the use of federal funds to aid all destitute persons in the South regardless of wartime loyalty.

1868

- *July 9:* The Fourteenth Amendment to the Constitution is ratified, granting citizenship to the former slaves.

1869

- The charity organization movement begins in London.
- *May 10:* The Central Pacific and Union Pacific Railroads meet at Promontory Summit, Utah.
- *Spring:* The Freedmen's Bureau has distributed 21 million rations, including 6 million given to whites.

1870s

- Agricultural output increases 53 percent during this decade. Land devoted to farming increases 31 percent, and the population grows 26 percent, from 39,819,449 to 50,256,000.

1870

- The Naturalization Act restricts citizenship to whites and African Americans.
- The president of the board of supervisors of the Chicago Almshouse is reported to have taken a bribe.
- *February 3:* The Fifteenth Amendment to the Constitution is ratified, protecting the rights of all citizens to own property and to vote, and the right to life and liberty.

1870–1900

- One-third of Boston's African Americans were born in Virginia or are the children of Virginians.

1872

- The Freedmen's Bureau is disbanded.

1873

- The United States enters a period of economic depression known as the Panic of 1873.

1874

- The army confirms the presence of gold on an Indian reservation in the Black Hills of South Dakota.

1875

- The U.S. government opens the Black Hills to non-Indian settlement.
- Tennessee becomes the first southern state to enact Jim Crow laws.
- *April 24:* New York is the first state to outlaw the placement of children in poorhouses.

1876

- *June 25:* Near the Little Bighorn River in present-day Montana, Cheyenne and Sioux (Lakota, Dakota, Nakota) warriors wipe out a column of the 7th Cavalry led by General George Armstrong Custer.

Well-dressed children of affluence point curious fingers at poor youngsters seeking warmth from a steam grate in this illustration from 1876. *(Library of Congress, Prints and Photographs Division, LC-USZ62-106379)*

1877

- Vagrancy, intemperance, and destitution are the principal causes of dependency among adult residents of the Onondaga County, New York, poorhouse.
- *July:* A nationwide railroad strike leads to violence in San Francisco, Pittsburgh, and other cities.
- *December:* The Reverend Stephen Humphreys Gurteen establishes the first American charity organization society in Buffalo, New York.

1878

- Eight hundred charitable groups are active in Philadelphia.

1880

- The average Appalachian farm is worth three-fourths its 1850 value.
- Immigrants increasingly arrive from southern and eastern Europe.
- Thirty-one percent of residents of Five Points were born in Ireland, and 23 percent were born in Italy.
- Approximately 8,000 children age three to 16 remain in U.S. poorhouses.

1881

- Native Americans hold 155,632,312 acres.
- Chinese immigrants number 11,890.

1882

- Chinese immigration totals 39,579 for the year.
- The Chinese Exclusion Act bars Chinese laborers from entering the United States for a 10-year period.

1883

- Charity organization societies have been formed in 25 U.S. cities.

This image shows a busy corner of the shoemakers' room in the Philadelphia Almshouse, 1889. *(Library of Congress, Prints and Photographs Division, LC-USZ62-73409)*

1886

- Twelve states have formed boards of charity.
- Stanton Coit founds the first settlement house in the United States, the Neighborhood Guild (later the University Settlement) in New York City.
- Jane Addams and Ellen Gates Starr found Hull-House in Chicago.
- Thirty-seven percent of poorhouse residents nationwide are elderly.

1887

- Congress passes the General Allotment Act, giving the president the power to assign up to 160 acres of reservation land to individual Indians. The act permits surplus land to be sold.

1890

- Native Americans hold 104,314,349 acres.
- Forty-nine percent of residents of Five Points were born in Italy, and 10 percent were born in Ireland; 18 percent are Jewish immigrants.
- An infestation of boll weevils affects the cotton-growing Deep South; African Americans begin to migrate from the region.
- *December 29:* The 7th Cavalry massacres hundreds of Lakota at Wounded Knee, South Dakota, and the Indian Wars end.

1891

- The Department of Immigration and Naturalization (later the Immigration and Naturalization Service) is established.

- The Reverend William J. Tucker founds Andover House (later South End House), a social settlement in Boston.

1892

- The Chinese Exclusion Act is extended for another 10 years; more than 2 million Chinese have entered the United States since 1868.

1894–1900

- More than 2,500 lynchings occur in the United States.

1896

- In the case *Plessy v. Ferguson* the U.S. Supreme Court upholds the constitutionality of legalized racial segregation in the South.

1897

- Settlement houses have been organized in 74 U.S. cities.

1900

- Native Americans hold 77,865,373 acres.
- Thirteen million immigrants have entered the United States since 1865.
- Charity organization societies are operating in 138 U.S. cities.
- There are more than 100 settlement houses in the United States.
- More than half the African Americans in New York City were born outside the state.

Eyewitness Testimony

One sees, at first, very little in the mere external appearance of Wilmington [South Carolina] to indicate the sufferings of war. The city is finely built (for the South); the streets are lined with noble avenues of trees; many of the residences are surrounded with elegant shrubbery; there is a bewildering wealth of flowers; the streets are full, and many of the stores are open. Sutlers [traders who sold provisions to military troops], however, have taken the places of the old dealers, and many of the inhabitants are inconceivably helpless and destitute. While I was riding over the city with Captain Myers, a young Ohio artillerist, a formerly wealthy citizen approached him to beg the favor of some means of taking his family three or four miles into the country. The officer could only offer the broken "Southron" a pair of mules and an army wagon; and this shabby outfit, which four years ago he would not have permitted his body servant to use, he gratefully accepted for his wife and daughter!

Struggling through the waste of sand which constitutes the streets, could be seen other and more striking illustrations of the workings of the war: a crazy cart, with wheels on the eve of a general secession, drawn generally by a single horse, to which a good meal of oats must have been unknown for months, loaded with tables, chairs, a bedstead, a stove and some frying-pans, and driven by a sallow, lank, long-haired, wiry-bearded representative of the poor white trash, who had probably perched a sun-bonneted, toothless wife, and a brace of tow-head children among the furniture; or a group, too poor even for a cart, clothed in rags, bearing bundles of rags, and, possibly, driving a half-starved cow. These were refugees from the late theater of military operations. They seemed hopeless, and, in some cases, scarcely knew where they wanted to go.

Whitelaw Reid, journalist, 1866, After the War: A Southern Tour, *May 1, 1865, to May 1, 1866, pp. 48–49.*

The loss of life has been frightful. Half the families are in mourning. I hear of a Danville regiment, twelve hundred strong, of whom less than fifty survive. Not less than eighty thousand arms-bearing men of the State are believed to have been killed or disabled. This, and the disorganization of the labor system, have naturally left thousands of families through the State utterly destitute. Mr. Pennington, the editor of the Raleigh *Progress,* predicts great distress next winter. In fact, the Government is already issuing rations to thousands of destitute whites.

Whitelaw Reid, journalist, 1866, After the War: A Southern Tour, *May 1, 1865, to May 1, 1866, p. 53.*

As I was passing Castle Thunder [Prison, Richmond], I observed, besieging the doors of the United States Commissary, on the opposite side of the street, a hungry-looking, haggard crowd,—sickly-faced women, jaundiced old men, and children in rags; with here and there a seedy gentleman who had seen better days, or a stately female in faded apparel, which, like her refined manners, betrayed the aristocratic lady whom the war had reduced to want.

These were the destitute of the city, thronging to receive alms from the government. The regular rations, issued at a counter to which each was admitted in his or her turn, consisted of salt-fish and hard-tack; but I noticed that to some tea and sugar were dealt out. All were provided with tickets previously issued to them by the Relief Commission. One tall, sallow woman requested me to read her ticket, and tell her if it was a "No. 2."

"They tell me it was, whar I got it, but I like to be shore."

I assured her that it was truly a "No. 2," and asked why it was preferable to another.

"This is the kind they ishy to sick folks; it allows tea and sugar," she replied, wrapping it around her skinny finger.

Colored people were not permitted to draw "destitute rations" for themselves at the same place with the whites. There were a good many colored servants in the crowd, however, drawing for their mistresses, who remained at home, too ill or too proud to come in person and present their tickets.

J. T. Trowbridge, New England writer, 1866, The South: A Tour of Its Battle-Fields and Ruined Cities, *p. 161.*

The most hopeful sign for the Negro was his anxiety to have his children educated. The two or three hundred boys and girls whom I used to see around the Bureau schoolhouse—attired with a decency which had strained to the utmost the slender parental purse, ill spared from the hard labor necessary to support their families, gleeful and noisy over their luncheons of cold roasted sweet potato—were proofs that the race has a chance in the future. Many a sorely pinched woman, a widow or deserted by her husband, would not let her boy go out to service, "bekase I wants him to have some schoolin'."

John William De Forest, who was assigned to the Freedmen's Bureau at Greensville, South Carolina, on October 2, 1866, A Union Officer in the Reconstruction, *pp. 116–17.*

The cabin consisted of one large room, with a fireplace, two doorways, and two windows. As in all dwellings of the people of this class, the windows were merely square openings, without glass or sashes, and closed by board shutters. The logs of the walls were unhewn, and on two sides the chinking of mud had entirely fallen out, leaving some fifty long slits, averaging two inches in width, through which the wind drove the inclemencies of winter. The moisture which came through these hencoop sides and through the porous roof drained off through the rotten and shattered floor. No furniture was visible beyond two broken chairs, two or three cooking utensils, and a pile of filthy rags which seemed to be bedding . . . .

The family consisted of the mother, two daughters named Susie and Rachel, a son of about five, and a grandson of two, named Johnnie. No man; the father had died years ago; the husband of Susie had fallen "in one of the first battles." Johnnie, flaxen-headed, smiling with health and content, as dirty as a boy could desire to be, squatted most of the time in the ashes, warming himself by a miserable fire of green sticks. His mother, Susie, sat in a broken chair in one corner of the chimney, her eyes bloodshot and cheeks flushed with fever. When I uttered a word or two of pity—it seemed such a horrible place to be sick in!—a few tears started down her cheeks.

"What makes me sick," she said, "is going bar'foot in the winter. I an't used to't. I had a husband once, and no call to go bar'foot."

"Oh, mam!" she presently groaned, addressing her mother, "this is an awful house!"

When I asked her how old she was she confessed ignorance. To the same question the other girl answered with a sheepish smile, "You are too hard for me."

The mother, after some reflection, gave their ages as nineteen and thirteen; but, looking in their worn faces, it seemed impossible that they could be so young. . . .

Such is the destitute class of the South, familiar to us by name as the "poor-white trash," but better known in Greenville as the "low-down people."

John William De Forest, who was assigned to the Freedmen's
Bureau at Greensville, South Carolina, on October 2, 1866,
A Union Officer in the Reconstruction, *pp. 51–52.*

The extreme value of land in the city makes tenement-houses a necessity. Usually they occupy a lot twenty-five by one hundred feet, six stories high, with apartments for four families on each floor. These houses resemble barracks more than dwellings for families. One standing on a lot fifty by two hundred and fifty feet has apartments for one hundred and twenty-six families. Nearly all the apartments are so situated that the sun can never touch the windows. In a cloudy day it is impossible to have sunlight enough to read or see. A narrow room and

bedroom comprise an apartment. Families keep boarders in these narrow quarters. Two or three families live in one apartment frequently. Not one of the one hundred and twenty-six rooms can be properly ventilated. The vaults and water-closets are disgusting and shameful. They are accessible not only to the five or six hundred occupants of the building, but to all who choose to go in from the street. The water-closets are without doors, and privacy is impossible. Into these vaults every imaginable abomination is poured. The doors from the cellar open in the vault, and the whole house is impregnated with a stench that would poison cattle.

Matthew Hale Smith, Universalist minister and writer, 1869,
Sunshine and Shadow in New York, *pp. 365–66.*

The repeated occurrence of . . . contagious diseases must be expected while such large liberty of communication with the city is allowed, and I earnestly recommend that special provision be made for the isolation and care of such cases. The present quarantine is not available for such purposes. It only serves as a house of temporary detention, to give time to examine the children and see that they are not the subjects of contagious disease. If it happens that they are suffering from such disease, they must be transferred at once to the general wards of the hospital, and as soon as this is done the danger of contamination of the other inmates commences.

A former epidemic of scarlet fever in this Institution, I am informed, destroyed *sixty* lives, and it is a wise and humane precaution to guard against such disastrous occurrences.

A physician visiting the nursery and nursery hospital of the
New York City Almshouse, December 31, 1869, in William P.
Letchworth, Extract from the Ninth Annual Report of
the State Board of Charities of the State of
New York Relating to Pauper Children in
New York County, *p. 21.*

Some portions of the city of New York present as dismal moral deserts as can be found on the entire globe. A portion of the Fourth Ward, with its narrow, crooked, filthy streets and dilapidated buildings, filled with a motley population collected from all countries, packed at the rate of 290,000 to the square mile, has long been noted as one of the principal "nests" for fever, cholera, and other deadly malaria on the island. But the moral aspect of this locality is even worse than the sanitary. Nearly every second door is a rum-shop, dance-house, or sailors' lodging, where thieves and villains of both sexes and of every degree assemble, presenting a concentration of all the most appalling vices of which fallen humanity is capable. . . .

New York has become the almshouse for the poor of all nations, and the Fourth Ward . . . is the very concentration of all evil and the head-quarters of the most desperate and degraded representatives of many nations. It swarms with poor little helpless victims, who are born in sin and shame, nursed in misery, want, and woe, and carefully trained in all manner of degradation, vice, and crime. The *packing* of these poor creatures is *incredible*. In this Ward there are less than two dwelling houses for each low rum hole, gambling house and den of infamy.

J. F. Richmond, New York City missionary, 1871, New York and Its Institutions, *pp. 488–89.*

That a city like ours, young, opulent, with a population considerably less than a million; the Metropolis too of a territory, but thinly peopled, with abundant natural resources, and seeking ever for new currents of immigration; should be weighted with such an incubus of pauperism in its very worst form, is a circumstance, not less remarkable than important. Nay, it is more than this, it is serious. When we remember that our laws and public institutions are incompetent to remedy the evil, when we recollect that if the hand of private charity were for one day to be withheld, a cry for food would rise up in our midst from tens of thousands of starving men, women, and children; we must recognize the depth of the precipice upon whose brink we stand.

It would be dangerous to ignore it. Those who have not cared to turn their eyes in that direction, may tell us that they cannot see it. But it is there, nevertheless. Any one may see it, who chooses. The sight may not be agreeable. It may not be flattering to our vanity; but still it is there. If any one does not care to visit the dens it has become our duty to describe, he may form some idea of the misery that surround him, by merely going with the eyes of observation through the streets at night. Let him learn the history and circumstances of the unhappy venders of corn and other trifles; of the many importunate beggars, whom he will meet in any number; of the women and children, who, with death-like faces and skeleton hands, solicit alms; of the wearied sleepers, who are to be found on door-steps, or among the lumber that is bestrewed upon the wharves; and he will learn lessons, that too many of us perhaps would prefer not to know.

Gustav Lening, writer, 1873, The Dark Side of New York Life and Its Criminal Classes from Fifth Avenue Down to the Five Points, *p. 15.*

If we now look for the dark sides of tenement-house life, we will find them to be very many. Even the best regulated of them have their dark sides, and the larger and more densely populated the tenement-houses are, the more prominently will these dark sides stand forth.

First among them are the dangers to life and health. Light and air, these two essential elements of human life, are dealt out to the people living in these places very sparingly. In building these houses, the chief object has been to crowd as many dwellings as possible into the available space. The sanitary regulations, which are just the very least that could be required, are observed only so far as is absolutely necessary, or as the dangers of the situation may dictate. The most prominent point, however, has been overlooked in the sanitary regulations, viz: that of the number of persons to the size of a house. A house that can be safely tenanted by ten families, becomes a breeder of disease if twenty families are crowded into it. Generally the proprietors of these dens care for nothing but the prompt payment of the rent. The tenants have perfect liberty to receive as many boarders, lodgers, etc., as they please, as long as they pay their rent promptly. Thus it is that sometimes the number of inhabitants of such places is double that which it ought to be.

In such close quarters cleanliness in every direction should be one of the first conditions. But a look into one of these houses will show us the greatest carelessness in this respect. In the hallway, in the court, and on the stairs, dirt and filth meet the eye everywhere, not to speak of the privies, which are noticed by the faculty of smell long before they are seen by the eye. The dwellings themselves are not much better; among them clean and tidy ones are like oases in the desert. But even local cleanliness is not able to keep the poisonous air, which fills the whole house, away from a single lodging.

Gustav Lening, writer, 1873, The Dark Side of New York Life and Its Criminal Classes from Fifth Avenue Down to the Five Points, *p. 590.*

Cholera, small-pox, typhoid fever, etc., generally originate in the filthiest and most densely populated quarters, and there again in the filthy and overcrowded tenement-houses. There it is where these diseases assume such a malignant form that they mock all means employed to prevent their further spread. It has even been discovered that a new and, although not fatal, yet very serious disease, the so-called "relapsing fever," has been brooded out in the tenement dens of the Five Points. Consumption, diseases of the lungs, blood and skin humors, and all forms of malignant fevers, seem to be at home in the tenement-houses at all times. Under these circumstances, it needs no further explanation that the mortality among the children in these dens is very great.

Gustav Lening, writer, 1873, The Dark Side of New York Life and Its Criminal Classes from Fifth Avenue Down to the Five Points, *p. 593.*

One of the most fruitful sources of infection is the imperfect laundry work. The hospital clothing is kept separate from that of other departments, but all infected garments are washed together, no matter what the disease may have been, and used in common for all hospital children. The pretense of washing through which they go only facilitates the spread of contamination through all the garments. The supply of towels is usually insufficient. There is great carelessness in keeping the sponges and cloths used for ophthalmic patients apart from those used by the other children, and even if conveniences were supplied, the nurses and helpers are too ignorant and careless to use them properly. It can be readily understood that the children brought in for the cure of trifling and temporary ailments contract loathsome maladies, entailing upon them life-long suffering, and unfitting them for the homes into which they might be received.

State Charities Association reporting on conditions in the nursery hospital of the New York City Almshouse, 1875, in William P. Letchworth, Extract from the Ninth Annual Report of the State Board of Charities of the State of New York Relating to Pauper Children in New York County, *pp. 20–21.*

The Indians were the original occupants of the lands we now possess. They have been driven from place to place. The purchase money paid to them in some cases for what they called their own has still left them poor. In many instances, when they had settled down upon lands assigned to them by compact and begun to support themselves by their own labor, they were rudely jostled off and thrust into the wilderness again. Many, if not most, of our Indian wars have had their origin in broken promises and acts of injustice on our part.

President Rutherford B. Hayes, 1877, in Foster Rhea Dulles, The United States since 1865, *p. 41.*

It must be borne in mind, that by far the larger percentage of all the confirmed paupers in the country have hung for a time on this very border-line of involuntary poverty, and only by the sheer neglect, or still oftener through the misdirected charity of benevolent people, have they been dragged down to the lowest depths of confirmed pauperism. If, therefore, pauperism as an institution, a profession, is ever to be broken up, it can only be done by restoring the involuntary poor to a position of self-support, self-respect, and honorable ambition. If left to themselves and no kind hand is held out to assist, they will inevitably sink lower and lower, till perchance they end their course in suicide or felony. If, on the other hand, our charity is not tempered by judgment, they will as inevitably learn to be *dependent*, till at last, though by degrees, every vestige of manliness and ambition will have been destroyed, and they will come back as skilled beggars, to torment and curse the very people whose so-called charity has made them what they are.

Stephen Humphreys Gurteen, founder of the Charity Organization Society of Buffalo, New York, 1878, Phases of Charity, *pp. 19–20.*

The [Charity Organization] Society holds that there is such a thing as making a pauper—a confirmed and willing beggar of an honest man; that there is such a thing as undermining his manhood, robbing him of his self-esteem, destroying his independence of character and leaving him a moral wreck without a will to work or ambition to seek it. It holds that in unwise alms-giving there is infinitely more at stake than wasting one's own money. Yes, that it is disastrous to the poor—that it is often ruin to the poor. Take the case of a poor woman, a widow; a case that is constantly coming to the notice of the benevolent. What has usually been our action in such a case? Instead of once for all considering how much she could do for her own and her children's support, and deliberately uniting our forces to relieve her of that part of the cost which she could not possibly meet, we have allowed her to come to our houses whenever she could not fulfill her engagements, and we have given her, when her story or tears moved us, a few dollars. We eased our own feelings by doing this, but what besides did we accomplish? Did we fortify *her* for the battle of life? Did we cultivate in her the habit of frugality—of deliberate arrangement as to the best expenditure of her scanty means. No! We did our best to teach her how easy it was if she got into debt to go round to one house after another and solicit a few dollars from each, and having met the difficulty for the moment to begin involving herself in another. Now look at her a few years later. The sincere grief of the widowed mother degraded into a means of begging! The ready tears coming at call! The sacred grief paraded for every one to see in hopes that some one may alleviate it with half a dollar! The sense of a right to be helped has been fostered, the sense of her own duty has been diminished. The easily-begged money has been easily spent; the powers of endurance, the habits of industry, are gone, and grief has become her stock in trade. Perhaps she has discovered too, that professions of piety are rewarded with cash. We are shocked at her hypocrisy; we say we were only too glad to help her when she was an honest woman, and while her grief was strong and sincere, but now it is different.

And what, we ask, has made her different? What? but our own unwise alms-giving?

Stephen Humphreys Gurteen, founder of the Charity Organization Society of Buffalo, New York, 1879, Provident Schemes, *pp. 8–9.*

Those who have never given any earnest thought to the subject can scarcely appreciate the lasting good that might be accomplished if every woman of education and household experience would devote a small part of her spare time (it is all we ask) to the cultivation of the friendship of one poor family—to the bridging of the chasm between rich and poor . . . to treat the poor in all of her intercourse with the same delicacy of feeling and kind consideration which she would wish to have shown to herself. . . .

And what would be the natural result of such a system thoroughly organized and put into active operation?

Once let the visitor become the acknowledged friend of a poor family (not the doler out of charity), she would be a power in that home. In a very short time the house would be clean and kept clean for her reception. Her advice would be sought voluntarily upon matters of household economy. . . . If a crisis should arrive in the family when a son is to leave home or a daughter to go out to service she would be looked to for advice and kindly suggestion. In a word, all avoidable pauperism would soon be a thing of the past, and an age of good will would be ushered in when the poor would regard the rich as their natural friends and not as now fair objects for their deceit and imposition.

Stephen Humphreys Gurteen, founder of the Charity Organization Society of Buffalo, New York, 1879, Provident Schemes, *pp. 77–78.*

It is well-known to those familiar with the criminal classes, that certain appetites or habits, if indulged abnormally and excessively through two or more generations, come to have an almost irresistible force, and, no doubt, modify the brain so as to constitute almost an insane condition. This is especially true of the appetite for liquor and of the sexual passion, and sometimes of the peculiar weakness, dependence, and laziness which make confirmed paupers.

The writer knows of an instance in an almshouse in Western New York, where four generations of females were paupers and prostitutes. Almost every reader who is familiar with village life will recall poor families which have had dissolute or criminal members beyond the memory of the oldest inhabitant, and who still continue to breed such characters. I have known a child of nine or ten years, given up, apparently beyond control, to licentious habits and desires, and who in all different circumstances seemed to show the same tendencies; her mother had been of similar character, and quite likely her grandmother. The "gemmules," or latent tendencies, or forces, or cells of her immediate ancestors were in her system, and working in her blood, producing irresistible effects on her brain, nerves, and mental emotions, and finally, not being met early enough by other moral, mental, and physical influences, they have modified her organization, until her will is scarcely able to control them and she gives herself up to them.

Charles Loring Brace, founder of the Children's Aid Society, 1880, The Dangerous Classes of New York, and Twenty Years' Work among Them, *pp. 42–44.*

If a female child be born and brought up in a room of one of these tenement-houses, she loses very early the modesty which is the great shield of purity. Personal delicacy becomes almost unknown to her. Living, sleeping, and doing her work in the same apartment with men and boys of various ages, it is well-nigh impossible for her to retain any feminine reserve, and she passes almost unconsciously the line of purity at a very early age.

In these dens of crowded humanity, too, other and more unnatural crimes are committed among those of the same blood and family.

Here, too, congregate some of the worst of the destitute population of the city—vagrants, beggars, nondescript thieves, broken-down drunken vagabonds, who manage as yet to keep out of the station-houses, and the lowest and most bungling of the "sharpers." Naturally, the boys growing up in such places become, as by a law of nature, petty thieves, pick-pockets, street-rovers, beggars, and burglars. Their only salvation is, that these dens become so filthy and haunted with vermin, that the lads themselves leave them in disgust, preferring the barges on the breezy docks, or the boxes on the side-walk.

Charles Loring Brace, founder of the Children's Aid Society, 1880, The Dangerous Classes of New York, and Twenty Years' Work among Them, *pp. 55–56.*

Almsgiving and dolegiving are hurtful even to those who do not receive them, because they help to keep down wages by enabling those who do receive them to work for less than fair pay.

Almsgiving and dolegiving are hurtful to those who receive them, because they lead men to remit their own exertions and depend on others, upon whom they have no real claim, for all the necessaries of life, *which they do not receive after all.*

In this last fact lies one secret of the injury done—false hopes are excited, the unhappy recipients of alms become dependent, lose their energy, are rendered incapable of self-support, and what they receive in turn for their lost character is quite inadequate to supply their needs; thus they are kept on the verge of almost death by the very persons who think they are relieving them, by the kindly souls who are benevolent, but who will not take the trouble to be beneficent, too.

Josephine Shaw Lowell, first woman member of the New York State Board of Charities, 1884, Public Relief and Private Charity, *p. 90.*

In the late 19th century well-to-do sightseers toured slums in order to view the poor with their own eyes. In this illustration from 1885, an affluent trio has ventured into the Five Points section of New York City—with police protection. *(Library of Congress, Prints and Photographs Division, LC-USZ62-122660)*

[W]hile the acknowledgment is made that every person born into a civilized community has the right to live, yet the community has the right to say that incompetent and dangerous persons shall not, so far as can be helped, be born to acquire this right to live upon others. To prevent a constant and alarming increase of these two classes of persons, the only way is for the community to refuse to support any except those whom it can control—that is, except those who will submit themselves to discipline and education.

Josephine Shaw Lowell, first woman member of the New York State Board of Charities, 1884, Public Relief and Private Charity, *p. 68.*

I have not the slightest doubt that it is a *wrong*, and a great wrong, to give help to the family of a drunkard or an immoral man who will not support them. Unless the woman will remove her children from his influence, it should be understood that no public or private charity, and no charitable individual, has the right to help perpetuate and maintain such families as are brought forth by drunkards and vicious men and women.

Josephine Shaw Lowell, first woman member of the New York State Board of Charities, 1884, Public Relief and Private Charity, *p. 105.*

In all my previous life I had seen but few actual beggars. The outstretched palms were new to me. Little children have followed and crossed me in the streets, and crossed themselves, and mumbled about bread and sick mothers and little sisters. Strong men have sat on the street corners and begged "a few pennies, lady, in the name of heaven," never intimating why "in the name of heaven" they didn't do something to earn them. I one day helped an old crippled woman on crutches into an omnibus (our elegant streets had not then been mutilated by car tracks.) . . . I gave her some money and went afterwards to see her a long way off. I found the same crippled old woman, destitution, squalor, two or three young grown daughters, out of work, of course, and out of everything else but pitiful stories of want and trouble. I helped and visited them, tried to advise; they were as old as I in years, in many respects much older.

I looked into their way of living and doing. The extravagance and mismanagement practiced by them, exercised in the same proportion to means, would have beggared the richest family in town.

I tried finding work, giving work, to learn trades, always giving food and money, and in one way or another I had this family on my hands for years. Such work is ac-

cumulative. I had many other families and individuals in charge. Even through the war years I tried to carry them on in the little intervals of time between battles when I could be at home a few days. But as I grew older I began to reflect and to question my own course. What came of it? What was I doing for all these people? Under my treatment they grew "nothing better, but something worse." I was puzzled, confounded. I seemed to be creating the very condition of things I was striving so hard to put away. I began to doubt as well as to question. . . .

Little by little it dawned upon me that if the giving of money and of individual charity as such, in civilized communities, where the ordinary avocations of life were pursued and labor attainable, was not only needless, but a wrong and a sin; and not only a moral but a political sin; not only an individual but a national sin, requiring to be repressed and forbidden by law, if need be, like any other harmful indulgence.

It was difficult to find some one to do an honest and acceptable day's work, if you chanced to need one; and it was dangerous to leave your home unwatched while you went to search for help, for the prowling beggars who hung about it.

Who has created this state of things? Ourselves. How had we done it? By individual unquestioned and promiscuous alms-giving; and dear knows I have done my share. I realized that this course of procedure must come to an end, and it came to an end in my case with the prompt speed of enlightened conscience.

Clara Barton, founder of the American Red Cross, speaking at the Thirteenth National Conference of Charities and Corrections, July 15, 1886, in Charity Organization Society of the District of Columbia, Third Annual Report, *p. 16.*

The investigation reveals a state of affairs, than which nothing more horrible can be imagined, and which, although perhaps equaled, can certainly not be surpassed in any European city. The condition of some houses is one of which no adequate conception can be formed without a personal visit. And let it be understood that the following facts are not selected cases or in any way exaggerated; they are absolutely true, and taken at random from among the many hundreds of instances. Indeed, the worst facts will not be given at all, for no respectable printer would print, and no daily paper admit, even the barest statement of the horrors and infamies that may be discovered by any one on a personal visit. To get into pestilential human rookeries you have to penetrate courts and alleys reeking with poisonous and malodorous gases, arising from accumulations of sewage and refuse scattered in all directions, and often flowing beneath your feet. You have to ascend rotten staircases, which threaten to give way beneath every step, and which in some places have already broken down, leaving gaps that imperil the limbs and lives of the unwary. You have to grope your way along dark and filthy passages swarming with vermin. Then, if you are not driven back by the intolerable stench, you may gain admittance to the dens in which thousands of human beings herd together. Walls and ceilings are black with the accretions of filth, which have gathered upon them through long years of neglect. It is exuding through cracks in the boards overhead; it is running down the walls; it is everywhere. What goes by the name of a window is half stuffed with rags or covered by boards to keep out wind and rain; the rest is so begrimed and obscured that scarcely any light can enter or anything be seen from the outside. Should you ascend to the attic, where at least some approach to fresh air might

be expected from open or broken windows, you look out upon the roofs and ledges of lower tenements and discover that the sickly air which finds its way into the room has to pass over the putrefying carcasses of dead cats or birds, or viler abomination still.

Description of a New York City tenement from a report by the Sanitary Aid Society, 1887, in Marcus T. Reynolds, The Housing of the Poor in American Cities, *p. 15.*

Rows of old women, some smoking stumpy, black clay-pipes, others knitting or idling, all grumbling, sit or stand under the trees that hedge in the [New York City] alms-house, or limp about in the sunshine, leaning on crutches or bean-pole staffs. . . . They grumble and growl from sunrise to sunset, at the weather, the breakfast, the dinner, the supper; at pork and beans as at the corned beef and cabbage; at their Thanksgiving dinner as at the half rations of the sick ward; at the past that had no joy, at the present whose comforts they deny, and at the future without promise. . . .

When it is known that many of these old people have been sent to the almshouse to die by their heartless children, for whom they had worked faithfully as long as they were able, their growling and discontent is not hard to understand.

Jacob Riis, social reformer, 1890, How the Other Half Lives, *pp. 229–30.*

"The almshouse," wrote a good missionary, "affords a sad illustration of St. Paul's description of the 'last days.' The class from which comes our poorhouse population is to a large extent 'without natural affection.'" I was reminded by his words of what my friend, the doctor, had said to me a little while before: "Many a mother has told me at her child's death-bed, 'I cannot afford to lose it. It costs too much to bury it.' And when the little one did die there was no time for the mother's grief. The question crowded on at once, 'where shall the money come from?' Natural feelings and affections are smothered in the tenements."

Jacob Riis, social reformer, 1890, How the Other Half Lives, *p. 230.*

Of all the evils which are due to the tenement-house system, the one that concerns the public most directly is the danger, which at all times threatens the community, from the presence in the tenement district of contagious and infectious diseases.

That thousands of dwellings in all of our cities are in a more or less unsanitary condition, while their occupants

Jacob Riis documented the living conditions of the poor in New York City in the late 19th century. *(Library of Congress, Prints and Photographs Division, LC-USZ62-57745)*

lead lives conducive to the birth of disease, is too well known to need more than the mention.

The working people, who spend the night in such dirty and disease-breeding places, disperse in the morning, and by the nature of their occupations, find their way to all portions of the city, and are thrown in contact with all classes of society. It is not too much to say that there is not a home which is not entered daily by at least one person, who has his home in a dwelling occupied exclusively by the working classes.

Much of the clothing offered for sale by the best dry-good stores and tailors has passed through the hands of like persons, while no small portion has been made in their dwellings. Clothes sent out to be washed are usually carried to the homes of the working people.

Though we might prevent the actual entrance into our homes of persons carrying about with them the germs of disease, it is quite impossible to prevent contact in the street, or elsewhere, with such persons.

Marcus T. Reynolds, architect, 1892, The Housing of the Poor in American Cities, *pp. 34–35.*

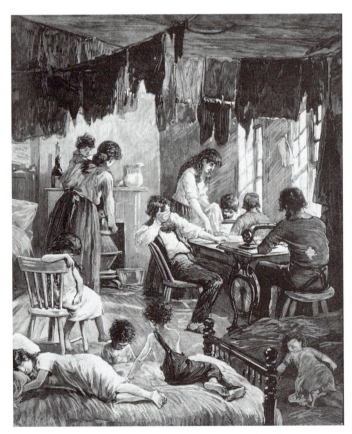

A crowded tenement was both home and workshop for many urban poor in 19th-century America. *(Library of Congress, Prints and Photographs Division, LC-USZ62-75197)*

While the public is indirectly affected by the misfortunes of its component parts, it is also directly affected in more than one way by the over-crowded tenement. One danger, which grows more and more apparent every year, is the danger of a social revolution. What manner of men and women must these millions of paupers be, if they can see without resentment the complacent exhibition of opulence and ease, which is forever flaunted in their faces, within a few hundred yards of the noisome courts and alleys. The cry of distress is as yet almost inarticulate, but it will not always remain so. It would be strange, indeed, if the striking contrast between the luxury of the rich and the misery of the poor, jostling one another upon every street corner, did not provoke bitter remonstrance, and even active revolt, on the part of the less fortunate members of our body politic.

Marcus T. Reynolds, architect, 1892, The Housing of the Poor in American Cities, *p. 43.*

A bed in the street, in an odd box or corner, is good enough for the ragamuffin who thinks the latitude of his tenement unhealthy, when the weather is warm. It is cooler there, too, and it costs nothing, if one can keep out of reach of the policeman. It is no new experience to the boy. Half the tenement population, men, women, and children, sleep out of doors, in streets and yards, on the roof, or on the fire-escape, from May to October.

Jacob Riis, social reformer, 1892, The Children of the Poor, *p. 260.*

[I]t is not to be forgotten that the Charity Organization Society does not exist for the purpose of giving aid or distributing alms. But it does intend to benefit the needy, not merely to save the pockets of the rich. And it is the bringing together and organizing for more effective work of societies that exist simply for the purpose of ministering in one way or another to the wants of the poor.

If those charities are doing useful work separately, there is no reason why they should not do better work in conjunction. If there be any radical mistake in the individual relief-agencies that vitiates their efforts, *that* will be likely to show itself only more plainly when they are organized. Or . . . if there be a lack of full recognition of the real and necessary relations that exist between men as men, whether poor or rich, on the part of the various constituents out of which the Associated Charities is formed, that association will not accomplish the task before it of "promoting the general welfare of the poor" unless it rises to a higher and truer conception and lifts up its component parts with it.

James O. S. Huntington, Anglican priest, 1893, "Philanthropy—Its Success and Failure," in Philanthropy and Social Progress, pp. 118–19.

What do you suppose becomes of the poor, the really penniless and helpless poor, in the intervals between the visits of the paid agent of the charitable society or the volunteer parish-worker? Here is a widow, with two or three young children, down sick with pneumonia. The visitor calls on Monday, and finds coal and food almost gone: she sends round a small quantity of the necessaries of life, enough to last, perhaps a day and a half. The "case" slips her mind, or she goes out of town to see a friend, and it is Saturday before she calls again. Has the poor woman frozen and starved meanwhile? Oh, no; she finds her in just about the same condition, but with still sufficient to live on. Has any other philanthropist been there? Quite possibly not; only "the woman upstairs she came in and brought us some dinner yesterday, and the baker next door gave my little girl a stale loaf, and when I was so sick Wednesday night that girl that works in the tailor's shop across the entry came and sat up with me. Some of the neighbors do talk about her, but she was real good, and she says she had a little sister that looked just like my Minnie, but she died last winter the time the work was slack; and the grocer across the way said he'd trust me with a hodful of coals: so we did get along. Ma'am; we poor folks have to help each other; but if you can do something for us we'd be very grateful."

Wretchedly unorganized, you see; and yet what a saving of self-respect, and consequently of strength for future effort, lies in that "we poor folks must help each other." And may there not be more real philanthropy in such commonplace, unmeasured, unrecorded acts than in the doles of a bureau supported by cheques written out in half-contemptuous compliance with the wheedling request of some "society leaders," who have taken to slumming for a diversion?

James O. S. Huntington, Anglican priest, 1893, "Philanthropy—Its Success and Failure," in Philanthropy and Social Progress, pp. 141–42.

To *prevent pauperism* is to go before the processes which lead to it, and to anticipate the causes which, if not counteracted, tend by successive steps to make the productive and independent worker lapse into indigence, and the indigent to descend into dependence. Preventive measures are therefore better than any and all means that are merely repressive or remedial.

The work of prevention is so imperfect in most communities, while the processes for the propagation of pauperism are so successful in many countries of Europe, that there is imposed on public authorities in the United States, the duty of exclusion or expulsion of all emigrants who may be infected with this vice or disease. This proscriptive duty devolves on charity administration in the State of New York more than elsewhere in America, for the reason that its territory includes the principal port of entry, and therefore naturally retains the worst elements, while most of the able-bodied and the right-minded pass into the interior States, where they become worthy and valuable citizens of the Republic.

Oscar Craig, president of the New York State Board of Charities, July 1893, "The Prevention of Pauperism," p. 122.

[T]he habitual and hardened pauper, as well as the congenital or confirmed criminal, should be restrained in his tendency to evil, and to the extent of his ability constrained to labor for the support of himself and his family, if any, dependent on him; and indefinitely continued in such discipline, with all needful instruction, recreation, and influence to recovery, under indeterminate sentence of confinement; and thus sequestered from society until he reforms or dies. This is the law for remedial, not retributive, and preventive, not punitive, relief; and is thus the law of kindness to the criminous or unworthy delinquents or dependents, and of safety to the virtuous workers and the honest poor, and therefore of justice. Such equity, rather than mere mercy, is the best expression of charity in public relations, and the true reconciliation of the scientific as well as the economical objections to the intervention of the State for the sake of humanity. Such relief would be within the practical reach, as well as the political right, of the State to-day, were the public conscience properly informed of the facts relating to the prevention of pauperism.

Oscar Craig, President of the New York State Board of Charities, July 1893, "The Prevention of Pauperism," p. 128.

The seriousness of the problem of poverty to-day is not that there are greater numbers of poor, relative to the total population, than ever before, but that greater numbers are constantly on the verge of poverty. The fluctuations of modern industries, the panics and crises and industrial depressions throughout the world, are constantly shoving armies of men over the poverty line. And even in our best of times there are more men to work than places to work. . . . Involuntary idleness and irregular employment are the antichrist of to-day that drives men and women into crime, intemperance, and shame.

John R. Commons, economist, 1894, Social Reform and the Church, *pp. 37–38.*

My calls were by no means of the nature of a perquisition, but they left very little unknown to me, I fancy, of the way the poor live, so frank and simple in their life. . . . The friend who went with me on my calls led me across the usual surface tracks, under the usual elevated tracks, and suddenly dodged before me into an alleyway about two feet wide. This crept under houses fronting on the squalid street we had left and gave into a sort of court some ten or twelve feet wide by thirty or forty feet long. The buildings surrounding it were low and very old. One of them was a stable, which contributed its stench to the odors that rose from the reeking pavement and from the closets filling an end of the court, with a corner left beside them for the hydrant that supplied the water of the whole inclosure. It is from this court that the inmates of the tenements have their sole chance of sun and air. What the place must be in summer I had not the heart to think, and on the wintry day of my visit I could not feel the fury of the skies which my guide said would have been evident to me if I had seen it in August. I could better fancy this when I climbed the rickety stairs within one of the houses and found myself in a typical New York tenement. Then I almost choked at the thought of what a hot day, what a hot night, must be in such a place, with the two small windows inhaling the putrid breath of the court and transmitting it, twice fouled by the passage through the living-room, to the black hole in the rear, where the whole family lay on the heaps of rags that passed for a bed.

William Dean Howells, novelist, 1896, Impressions and Experiences, *pp. 130–31.*

A community might be justified in viewing with equanimity the mere dependency of a portion of its population, if such dependency did not lead to worse conditions. The man who falls from independence to dependency invariably loses the desire for higher things, otherwise his ambition. The desires of the impoverished diminish, as his vitality is weakened by advancing years. This means, first, neglect of education; second, loss of the property sense and of the desire to accumulate property; third, disregard of parental duties; fourth, contentment with poor dwellings, meager and improperly prepared food, and insufficient clothing; fifth, the loss even of the desire for cleanliness. These various steps in the degradation of the human being are accompanied by a progressive loss of pride, which fosters dishonesty and immorality.

Neglected education results in a useless if not a dangerous citizen, with uncontrollable passions, and the inability to make proper use of the franchise. Loss of the property sense develops the thief. Loss of the desire to accumulate property renders one indifferent to the welfare of society. Contentment with poor dwellings, poor food, and poor clothing becomes evident in shattered constitutions. Loss of habits of cleanliness breads [*sic*] disease. And loss of morality leads to crimes against the person, to the social evil with its accompanying illegitimacy, and to the drink habit with its attendant sapping of vitality.

Nathan S. Rosenau, manager of the United Hebrew Charities, New York City, 1897, "Organized Charity," in Proceedings of the Section on Organization of Charity of the National Conference of Charities and Correction, *p. 17.*

Every organism has a trace of dependency in its nature, and man is no exception. The natural history of the barnacle is the natural history of every creature which finds that it can obtain support without personal exertion. Therefore the help, individual or institutional, that does not regard the consequences is sure to produce, not reformation, but dependency.

Nathan S. Rosenau, manager of the United Hebrew Charities, New York City, 1897, "Organized Charity," in Proceedings of the Section on Organization of Charity of the National Conference of Charities and Correction, *p. 21.*

It seems incredible that a shrewd, careful man of affairs, who, in business, will not allow the escape of a single dollar without a definite detailed statement as to its destination and purpose, a signed written receipt of its delivery, and a prompt after account of its administration and use, will yet toss a dollar to a stranger, whose very appearance stamps him as a fraud, without a question or perhaps even a thought.

The motive is doubtless mixed. Some do it to save time. Some from pride, fearing a refusal will cause others to doubt their generosity; a few do it from a genuine desire to help; but the larger number, I fear, do it that their own hearts may fill with gratitude to themselves as unselfish philanthropists. The public, however, considers them mere peacock philanthropists, ornamental but useless.

Alfred O. Crozier, Grand Rapids, Michigan, chairman of the Section on Organization of Charity, 1897, in Proceedings of the Section on Organization of Charity of the National Conference of Charities and Correction, *p. 26.*

The personal responsibility for the effect of acts of intended charity is rarely considered. A young man calls at your door asking for alms. It is his first appeal. He knows he is doing wrong. He feels guilty and ashamed. But you are an easy mark. You give him "relief,"—perhaps only a meal of cold victuals. You have boasted that you never let anyone leave your door hungry. He is emboldened by his easy success. He reflects how much easier it was to beg that meal than to earn it. At the next place his story is smoother, his lie more plausible. This time he wants money to take his poor old mother to the hospital for an operation, necessary to save her life, or some other equally touching appeal. He gets it, of course. His inherited moral restraints are giving away under the pressure of the temptation carelessly afforded him by your money. He takes to drink, and everything else bad follows. As his appetites increase, his demand for money with which to gratify them becomes more imperative. He steals. Slyly at first,—only a sneak thief. But on he goes, encouraged at every step by society in the name of charity. He is now desperate. He realizes himself a criminal, suspected, watched, hunted. Society he considers his enemy, his prey. Appetite is now complete master. He meets a prominent citizen in the shadows at night. Weapon in hand, he demands his money. He has no desire to injure him. It is only money that he wants. But in the struggle which follows he shoots, and kills, and he is a fugitive and a murderer!

This is a social evolution.

Alfred O. Crozier, Grand Rapids, Michigan, chairman of the Section on Organization of Charity, 1897, in Proceedings of the Section on Organization Charity of the National Conference of Charities and Correction, *p. 27.*

Instead of finding employment for the poor woman who begs for temporary help, you give her alms. It is easier, and perhaps cheaper. But you have poisoned her soul. Her children are now taught lies by their mother and sent out under fictitious names to forage on the public. You have converted that once happy, though poor, home into a nest of paupers breeding like vipers, and multiplying their accursed species. You set in motion the original cause which produced this ultimate and inevitable effect. But you plead that the applicant was a cripple, was blind, or had but one leg or one arm. This does not alter the case or change the responsibility.

No human being should be allowed to deliberately and publicly use his festering sores or maimed condition as capital stock to excite human sympathy and extort alms as dividends. If in such a physical condition as to be helpless, a public or private institution should always be open to him, and afford a better home than the public street.

Alfred O. Crozier, Grand Rapids, Michigan, chairman of the Section on Organization of Charity, 1897, in Proceedings of the Section on Organization Charity of the National Conference of Charities and Correction, *p. 28.*

The husband, a not very competent workman, and an occasional drinker, is thrown out of employment by the stopping of the factory where he has been working. A child falls sick, owing to defective drainage, and this unusual expense causes him to allow his trades-union dues to lapse just before a period of general financial depression. Discouraged and tired of "looking for work" and his resources exhausted, he applies for charity. Is the "cause of distress" lack of employment, incompetency, intemperance, sickness, bad sanitation, trades-unionism, or "general social conditions" beyond the control of the individual?

A. M. Simons, editor of the International Socialist Review, March 1898, "A Statistical Study in Causes of Poverty," p. 614.

In Bayonne, N.J., 53.97 per cent. Of the poverty treated by the Charity Organization Society is found to be due to intemperance. We quote from a letter written by the head of this society: "The character of our population, the notoriously lax administration of the liquor laws, and the irregularity of employment doubtless account to a large extent for the high percentage. . . . The police make no effort to enforce the law which forbids the sale of liquor to minors, for example. . . . A large number of men are employed as day laborers on the coal docks, whose work is uncertain and probably does not average over four days a week. I regard this as a very important factor in the connection I mention. Another important factor which should not be overlooked is that for a number of years our school facilities have been inadequate, so that the enforcement of the truancy law has been impossible. The effect of this is far-reaching, as our records bear evidence." The Bayonne investigation appears also to have been conducted on somewhat unusual lines. For it is said that, "in assigning the abuse of liquor as a direct or indirect cause of the distress of a family, the determining consideration was not the question of actual drunkenness, but whether the amount of money habitually spent on liquor was sufficient to impoverish the family."

John Koren, researcher and statistician for the Committee of Fifty for the Study of the Liquor Problem, 1899, Economic Aspects of the Liquor Problem, *pp. 91–92.*

In work with individual poor families we are likely to forget that these are part of a neighborhood and community, and that we have no right to help them in a way that will work to harm the community. We are always inclined to think that the particular family in which we are interested is an "exceptional case," and the exceptional treatment lavished upon our exceptional case often rouses in a neighborhood hopes that it is impossible for us to fulfil. Then, too, occupied as we are with individuals, we are likely to exaggerate the importance of those causes of poverty that have their origin in the individual. We are likely to over emphasize the moral and mental lacks shown in bad personal habits, such as drunkenness and licentiousness, in thriftlessness, laziness, or inefficiency; and some of us are even rash enough to attribute all the ills of the poor to drink or laziness. On the other hand, those who are engaged in social service often exaggerate the causes of poverty that are external to the individual. Bad industrial conditions and defective legislation seem to them the causes of nearly all the distress around them. Settlement workers are likely to say that the sufferings of the poor are due to conditions over which the poor have no control.

The truth lies somewhere between these two extremes; the fact being that the personal and social causes of poverty act and react upon each other, changing places as cause and effect, until they form a tangle that no hasty, impatient jerking can unravel.

Mary E. Richmond, general secretary of the Charity Organization Society of Baltimore, 1899, Friendly Visiting among the Poor, *pp. 7–8.*

A large majority of those who are thrown upon charity through lack of employment are either incapable or are unfit for service through bad habits, bad temper, lack of references, ignorance of English, or through some physical defect. Experience has proven that a certain portion of these can be reinstated in the labor market if we are careful (1) not to make it too easy for them to live without work, (2) if we will use every personal endeavor to fit them for some kind of work, and (3) help them find and keep the work for which they are fitted. . . .

Those who are simply incapable, without bad habits or other defects, are often the victims of their parents' necessities or greed: they were put to work too early, and at work where there was no chance of education or promotion. Sometimes they have been willfully careless and lazy, but, more often, the fault was either with the parents or with an economic condition that denied them proper training.

Mary E. Richmond, general secretary of the Charity Organization Society of Baltimore, 1899, Friendly Visiting among the Poor, *pp. 33–34.*

Many women in poor neighborhoods lead starved, sordid lives, and long for genuine friendliness and sympathy. A friend who would be helpful to them must exercise the same self-restraint that our friends exercise with us. The friends who encourage us to exaggerate our troubles and difficulties are not our best friends: theirs is a friendship that tends to weaken our moral fibre. But the sympathy that the poor need and all of us need is the sympathy that makes us feel stronger, the sympathy that is farthest removed from sentimentality. We should be willing to listen patiently to the homemaker's troubles, and should strive to see the world from her point of view, but at the same time we should help her to take a cheerful and courageous tone. One unfailing help, when our poor friends dwell too much upon their own troubles, is to tell them ours.

Mary E. Richmond, general secretary of the Charity Organization Society of Baltimore, 1899, Friendly Visiting among the Poor, *p. 71.*

CHAPTER FIVE

Social Research
and Recommendations
1900–1928

In 1904 a former Hull-House resident named Robert Hunter published a study titled *Poverty*, in which he asserted that at least 10 million Americans were poor. "I am largely guessing and there may be as many as fifteen or twenty million!" he wrote.[1] Hunter based his estimate on available figures, including the numbers of people who had applied for relief in New York City and Boston in recent years, numbers of evictions, percentages of burials in potter's fields, and unemployment statistics from the 1900 federal census.

Hunter found it incredible that the U.S. government had never taken a count of the nation's poor, because "to neglect even to inquire into our national distress is to be guilty of the grossest moral insensitiveness."[2] The majority of the poor lived in want through no fault of their own, he said. They were subject to social and economic forces beyond their control, such as seasonal demands for labor, periodic depressions, industrial accidents, and illness. Hunter also established an unofficial national poverty line, or minimal income necessary for sustenance. He set the line at $460 a year for a family of five in the North and at $300 a year for a family of the same size in the agricultural South.

According to this study and others, charity organization was ineffective in reducing the poor population. By 1907 even the Buffalo Charity Organization Society had reversed its purpose and was dispensing outdoor relief. In doing so the society filled a real need: This type of aid had become so unpopular among city officials that in 1900 Chicago was the only major U.S. city still providing aid to the poor in their homes. The others relied on poorhouses.

Agents appointed by the U.S. Census Bureau tallied the residents of all almshouses in the United States in 1910. The agents counted 84,198 inmates present in almshouses on January 1, 1910, and 88,313 admitted over the course of the year. That the number admitted exceeded the total almshouse population on a given date was explained by the fact that the inmates were "a rapidly shifting group."[3] During the year 17,486 died, and 59,110 were discharged. Poorhouse superintendents expected three-fourths of those discharged to be self-supporting, and released the rest into the care of relatives or friends. Half the almshouse population in 1880 had been under age 50; in 1910 the population was older. One-third of inmates were under 55, one-third were ages 55 to 69, and one-third were 70 or older. One in 60 U.S. residents age 80 or older lived in an almshouse. Additionally, the foreign born accounted for 42.6 percent of white paupers on January 1, 1910, and 41.1 percent of those admitted throughout the year.

The first decades of the 20th century also witnessed a shift in the administration of public relief from the local overseer of the poor to the municipal or county department of welfare. In 1910 Kansas City, Missouri, established a welfare department not only to attend to the needs of the poor but also to have responsibility for juvenile delinquents and other groups dependent on society for care. The Cook County, Illinois, Bureau of Welfare was established in 1913, just four years before reorganization of the Illinois state government resulted in the formation of a state department of welfare that served as a model for other states.

Attempts at Tenement-House Reform

Thousands of urban families with incomes at or above Hunter's poverty line consumed a monotonous, nutritionally marginal diet consisting largely of bread, potatoes, and bacon. They owned very little furniture and few possessions and rented

Mrs. Guadina, an Italian immigrant, photographed in her New York City tenement in 1912, struggles to complete piecework in order to be paid. The Guadinas had three children and were expecting a fourth, and the father was unemployed. On the day this picture was taken there was no food in the house. *(National Archives)*

tenement apartments of two or three rooms. In 1901 Hunter was a member of the City Homes Association, a citizens' group that inspected dwellings in three poor neighborhoods on the West Side of Chicago. Repeatedly the investigators observed poor families forced to live in unsanitary firetraps that were inadequately lit and ventilated. The hazard posed by substandard housing became clearer the following summer, when Chicago weathered a typhoid epidemic that was especially lethal in the crowded slums. Hull-House staff determined that the disease was being spread by houseflies that had visited uncovered privies, facilities that had been illegal since the late 19th century.

The social workers' efforts seemed to pay off in December 1902, when the city council passed an ordinance based on their recommendations. According to this ordinance new tenement houses of more than three stories had to be constructed of fire-resistant or fireproof materials and were required to have fire escapes. Also, by limiting the percentage of a building lot that a tenement could cover and requiring habitable rooms to have windows that let in air from outside, the council hoped to improve lighting and ventilation. In addition, the ordinance called for adequate toilet facilities and periodic whitewashing of inhabited rooms to aid sanitation.

When investigators returned to the West Side in 1905, however, they saw little change. They noted some improvements in sanitation, but most families continued to live in dark, dilapidated, badly ventilated buildings. Property owners had circumvented provisions of the 1902 ordinance for fire safety in new construction by building only three-story tenement houses. Because of corruption in city government, many property owners also evaded a 1908 ordinance requiring all new tenements to be inspected before occupancy. Although 6,000 or more tenements were built in Chicago each year between 1913 and 1916, the city issued only 910 occupancy permits during those years.

Americans became aware of settlement-house work as the prevailing attitude toward the urban poor shifted. At the very least, character defects offered "only a halfway explanation" for poverty, wrote the social worker Edward T. Devine in 1913, and they resulted "directly from conditions which society may largely control."[4] Although old prejudices lingered, the tenement house increasingly received blame for the miseries and dangers of slum life. As a result, citizens' groups investigated tenement conditions in cities large and small. In 1904 the Octavia Hill Association, a group named for a pioneering British reformer, surveyed tenements in three poor Philadelphia neighborhoods: the Italian quarter, the African-American section, and a district tenanted by eastern European and Irish immigrants as well as some "Americans." Of 65 tenement houses investigated, only nine had fire escapes. Everywhere the inspectors found overcrowding and appalling sanitation. Typical was the situation of a family of five living on the second story of a small tenement house. A single room served as their kitchen, dining room, and living area. They shared the lone outdoor privy with the other four families in the building and the staff of the bakery that operated in the cellar (and posed a fire hazard).

In Louisville, Kentucky, on February 16, 1909, Mayor James E. Grinstead appointed a committee to investigate and report on tenement conditions in his city. According to the 1900 U.S. Census, more than one-third of the 44,912 families in Louisville lived in tenements and apartment houses. Unlike tenements in such big cities as Chicago and Philadelphia, which were clustered in particular districts, those in Louisville were spread throughout the city. Many of the houses classified as tenements had been constructed to house one family but sheltered as many as eight. The commissioners also inspected alley houses, or one-story wooden shacks that opened on the city's back alleys and housed two, three, or four families.

Everywhere the commission saw dilapidation, an inadequate water supply, and overcrowding. The "Tin House," a two-story wooden building covered with corrugated tin that was located on Pearl Street, housed 31 black families in its 37 rooms. Twenty families lived in 21 rooms in the largest tenement occupied by whites, at the corner of Shelby and Main Streets. "A sink on the first story porch and another at the end of the second story porch supplied the entire tenement with water," the commissioners reported. "The privy was in such bad condition that it was difficult to get near enough to examine it without soiling one's garments or walking in filth."[5] In their report to the mayor and general council the commissioners proposed a law regulating tenement conditions that addressed the abuses that were observed.

By 1914, when the Minneapolis Civic and Commerce Association surveyed legislations regulating tenement and private dwellings in North America, such laws were on the books in 17 U.S. cities, including Chicago and Louisville; two Canadian cities, Calgary and Toronto; and nine U.S. states: California, Connecticut, Indiana, Kentucky, Massachusetts, New Jersey, New York, Pennsylvania, and Wisconsin.

This image shows slum conditions in Philadelphia at the start of the 20th century. Nearby tenants used this tumbledown structure as a washhouse. The pump in the foreground provided the neighborhood's only water supply. *(Library of Congress, General Collection)*

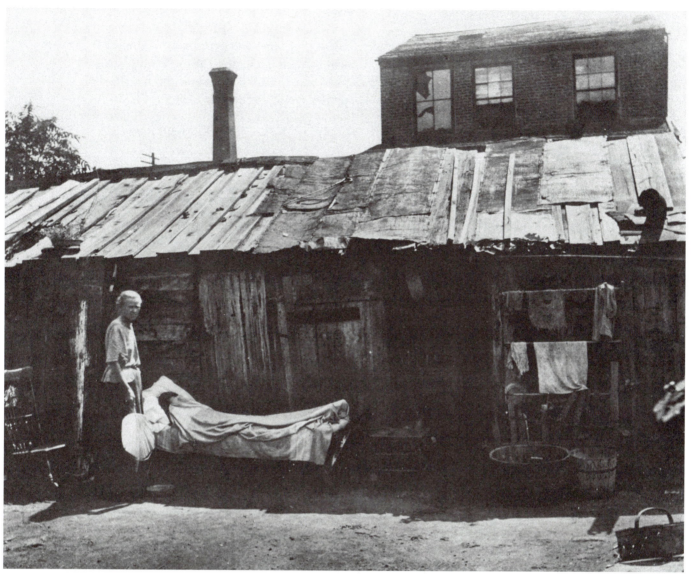

The tubercular tenant of an eight-room tenement in Louisville's Bug Alley is cared for outdoors in 1909. Each room houses a separate family. *(Library of Congress, General Collection)*

Many were based on a book-length model housing law developed in 1914 by the Russell Sage Foundation, a social-research group founded in 1907. The laws varied in detail from the model law and from one another, but they all contained provisions for fire safety, sanitation, adequate light and ventilation, and enforcement.

The new laws failed to generate real reform, though, often for reasons other than corruption. Sometimes opponents of the legislation succeeded in having it repealed, modified, or declared unconstitutional in the courts. In other cases municipalities simply lacked the initiative or the funds to hire enough inspectors or otherwise enforce the new provisions. There was concern, too, for the people living in illegal tenements. Was it in their best interest to order them to vacate? Where would they then live? According to a nationwide housing survey published in 1919, one-third of the people in the United States lived in substandard housing, and one-tenth lived in homes that posed an actual danger to health and well-being.

Limiting Immigration

As the 1904 Philadelphia housing survey indicated, many tenement-house residents were immigrants. The start of the 20th century had coincided with a substantial increase in immigration. Between 1906 and 1915, 9.4 million people entered the United States. Of those, 1.5 million arrived in a single, record year, 1907.

Old fears and prejudices lingered: Would poor and otherwise "undesirable" immigrants become a burden on society? Would the new arrivals assimilate, or would their foreign habits alter American culture for the worse? Federal legislation enacted on March 3, 1903, extended the list of groups barred from entry to include people with epilepsy, the insane, prostitutes, and anarchists. A 1907 law listed further exclusions and doubled the head tax on immigrants to four dollars. It was hoped that a higher head tax would act as a barrier to the needy.

Although the outbreak of World War I in Europe had caused immigration to decline sharply, an act that became law on February 5, 1917, was still more exclusionary. This law created more categories of unacceptable aliens based on physical and mental health, morals, and political beliefs. It also delineated an "Asiatic barred zone," stretching from the Arabian Peninsula to Indochina and Japan, from which immigration was prohibited. The 1917 law raised the head tax to eight dollars, and in its most controversial provision it imposed a literary test, requiring all aliens age 16 or older who were physically capable of reading to demonstrate literacy in English or another language.

In 1921 the government established a quota system, limiting immigration from any nation to 3 percent of the 1910 U.S. population of the same national origin. By 1924 the restrictions had been stiffened so that just 2 percent of the 1890 U.S. population of a given nationality might be admitted. "We were afraid of foreigners; we distrusted them; we didn't like them," said Emanuel Celler, a congressman from New York with a lifelong commitment to aiding immigrants. "Under this act only some one hundred and fifty odd thousands would be permitted to enter the United States. If you were of Anglo-Saxon origin, you could have over two-thirds of the quota numbers allotted to your people. If you were Japanese, you could not come in at all. . . . If you were southern or eastern European, you could dribble in and remain on sufferance."[6]

In all three years when Congress passed exclusionary immigration laws— 1917, 1921, and 1924—the agriculture, transportation, and mining industries successfully lobbied for the exemption of Mexicans. These were the industries that had come to rely most on Mexican labor. Mexicans entering the United States did have to pay an eight-dollar head tax and ten-dollar visa fee, however. In 1900 an estimated 100,000 people of Mexican descent lived in the United States; in 1930 there would be 1.5 million. Mexicans entered the United States seeking a secure political environment and good wages. Newly constructed Mexican railroads, which connected the cities of their homeland with U.S. border towns, facilitated the move north. Each year between 1910 and 1916, about 53,000 Mexicans entered the United States. In California they took over migratory agricultural work because white American growers perceived Mexicans to be more like them and therefore more acceptable than Asians. Immigration strengthened in 1917, when workers fleeing the Mexican Revolution replaced U.S. farmhands, railroad workers, and miners who were then serving in World War I. Employers in California and the Southwest, where the majority of Mexicans lived and worked, generally took advantage of their immigrant workforce by paying low wages and making available only substandard housing.

Meanwhile, faced with strict and exclusionary immigration laws, many people from China and other countries desiring to enter the United States did so illegally, through Mexico. Beginning in 1904 officers of the U.S. Immigration Service, operating out of El Paso, Texas, irregularly patrolled the southwestern border of the United States. The Labor Appropriation Act of 1924 established the U.S. Border Patrol, to collect taxes and visa fees from entering immigrants and secure the border between official inspection stations.

The Hazards of the Sweatshop

Many unskilled immigrant laborers found employment in urban sweatshops. In these rundown, unsafe factories they literally sweated out a meager living, working as hard and as fast as they could, producing clothing, artificial flowers, boxes, costume jewelry, and other items. Workers were often paid by the "piece": that is, they earned a set amount for each item, garment, or part of a garment completed. Piecework could also be done at home by everyone in the family, including the children.

Because the workplace was still largely unregulated and workers could be easily replaced from the pool of available labor, employers had little incentive to institute safety measures. Dangerous machinery, toxic chemicals, and airborne particles caused numerous work-related deaths, injuries, and chronic illnesses. In 1908 alone, 35,000 U.S. workers were killed in industrial accidents, and thousands more were disabled.

One of the worst industrial accidents in U.S. history occurred on March 25, 1911, when fire broke out in a ninth-story sweatshop operated by the Triangle Shirtwaist Company of New York City. The blaze quickly spread, fueled by the textiles on hand for clothing manufacture. Because their employer commonly locked the doors during working hours to discourage theft, the workers—nearly all of them young women—were trapped. As a result, 146 employees died in the fire or from jumping to the pavement.

American workers bettered job conditions by unionizing and presenting their demands as an organized body. The American Federation of Labor (AFL), an alliance of craft unions that had a membership of 500,000 at the start of the 20th century, claimed 2.5 million members in 1917 and 5 million at the close of World War I, in 1918. Beginning in 1905 unskilled workers could join the anticapitalist Industrial Workers of the World (IWW), which at its peak in 1917 was 100,000 strong. Labor leaders bargained with management on behalf of workers, and when their demands were rejected or ignored, they called strikes.

Between 1905 and 1915 American workers staged at least 150 strikes, demanding better pay, a shorter workday, and safer working conditions. Most strikes were peaceful, involving walkouts and picketing, but some grew violent. In 1912 the IWW led the largely immigrant workforce of Lawrence, Massachusetts, in a strike against the town's textile mills. The event that triggered the strike was a 3.5 percent pay cut that took effect January 1. Even such a small drop in wages was significant to families barely making ends meet. The strike began on January 12 and soon spread to mills in the neighboring towns of Fall River and Haverhill. Before the strike ended, riots erupted, the governor of Massachusetts declared martial law, one worker was killed in clashes with police, many more were injured, and two IWW leaders were arrested and charged with murder. Many strikes failed, but this one was a victory for the workers. On March 12, the American Woolen Company, the largest employer in Lawrence, agreed to a pay increase and higher wages for overtime work, and textile-mill employees throughout Massachusetts soon enjoyed similar gains.

In large part because of political lobbying by the AFL, in 1913 the government created the U.S. Department of Labor to improve working conditions, create job opportunities, and otherwise advance the interests of the working population. The Adamson Act of 1916 established an eight-hour workday for railroad workers, and by the end of World War I the eight-hour day and 48-hour week were the rule in most industries. The U.S. workforce also gradually received financial redress for injuries occurring on the job. In 1908 the federal government offered workers' compensation insurance to its employees for the first time. Several states adopted workers' compensation laws in 1911, and the others soon followed.

Making life better for unskilled laborers might even have been necessary for political stability. Many Americans viewed with alarm the spread of socialism within the proletariat of Europe and worried that an underpaid, resentful workforce provided a breeding ground for social unrest. "Public opinion is not really aroused to the serious character of this acute problem of modern civilization," stated a Congregational minister in 1915.[7] The Russian Revolution of 1917, which culminated on November 7, in assumption of power by the Bolshevik Party under Vladimir Lenin, reinforced this fear. The Bolsheviks' nationalization of land, industry, and transport was a chilling warning.

The Problem of Child Labor

By 1915 the federal government had begun collecting data on income levels and poverty. In that year the U.S. Commission on Industrial Relations concluded that an average family (one consisting of 5.6 people) needed an annual income of $700 to meet its expenses. At the time 79 percent of U.S. fathers earned less than $700 a year, an indication that many families relied on income from other sources. Poor working-class families commonly took in boarders, and millions of women and children held jobs. In 1910 approximately 1,600,000 children age 10 to 15 were gainfully employed, according to the U.S. Census Bureau. This figure excluded working children under age 10 and those paid off the books.

Child labor was not limited to urban factories. At the start of the 20th century 25,000 workers age 15 and younger operated machinery in southern textile mills, where children had replaced the enslaved workforce after the Civil War. Children shelled shrimp along the Gulf Coast, mined coal underground, harvested crops, and hawked newspapers and other goods on street corners. The risks were many: injury, including the loss of limbs or digits in mechanical accidents; contact with caustic substances; inhalation of airborne irritants; exposure to extremes of weather, crime, and the other hazards of the street; and even death. Working children suffered psychologically when they worried about being the next one maimed in an on-the-job accident; long hours and a lack of schooling hindered their physical and intellectual development.

In 1901 the Reverend Edgar Gardner Murphy, an Episcopal priest in Montgomery, Alabama, founded the Alabama Child Labor Committee to work for a comprehensive child-labor law in his state. Two years later, thanks to the efforts of his group, the state legislature barred children under 14 from factory work.

In 1904 Murphy was a founder of the National Child Labor Committee (NCLC), which sought to raise awareness of the problems inherent in child labor and to secure legislation nationwide at the state level. (Because the Constitution made no provision for federal control of child labor, this was a matter considered appropriately left to the states to regulate.) Public education was accomplished most effectively through the photography of Lewis Hine, whom the NCLC hired in 1907. From 1907 through 1918 Hine traveled the nation to create portraits of young miners with faces blackened by coal dust, barefoot children posing beside the textile machinery they operated for most of their waking hours, and exhausted youngsters leaving factories. In 1910 the NCLC drafted model state legislation that set a minimal age of 14 for factory work and 16 for mining. The model law barred anyone under 16 from night work and any child from work in a dangerous or unhealthy setting.

Thirty-nine states enacted legislation regulating child labor between 1911 and 1913. None was as comprehensive as the model law, and in some cases compliance was voluntary. The first national child-labor law was enacted on September 1, 1916; in 1918 the U.S. Supreme Court declared it unconstitutional. Congress then imposed a 10 percent tax on factories and mines employing children that had the effect of cutting in half the number of working children in the United States between April 25, 1919, when the law took effect, and May 15, 1922, when the Supreme Court declared it unconstitutional. The number of workers between the ages of 10 and 15 then began to rise; children would continue to help many families stay out of poverty.

A Hard Life for Indians in the West

Also on the rise in the early 20th century was the number of American Indians in the West who were adopting nontraditional occupations. Indians provided unskilled labor for the railroads; Apache men mixed concrete at construction sites; Zuni and Navajo (Dineh) workers operated steam drills as part of efforts to bring irrigation to their reservations. Some graduates of the Indian boarding schools had gone on to become civil engineers, physicians, college instructors, and other successful professionals. But most Native Americans in nontraditional occupations performed low-level jobs.

In June 1907 an article in a popular magazine reported optimistically that 90 percent of Indians were self-supporting, having been "weaned" from government rations, "this pauperizing source of supply."[8] The article portrayed the typical Indian man as a farmer raising corn and other vegetables on his own land, and the typical Indian woman as a contented farmer's wife making quilts and jam. Yet readers who went beyond the first few pages discovered that the true picture was far less rosy. In 1903 a federal-court decision gave the government the right to sell so-called surplus reservation land without the Indians' consent. The government held the receipts in trust, with the result that many Native Americans lacked the funds needed to develop their allotments into working farms while the U.S. Treasury held more than $35 million for about 53,000 Indians on reservations. Twenty-six percent of babies born on reservations died before one year of age, and 17 percent of those who survived their first year succumbed to disease by age five. In addition, tuberculosis was increasing among Indians of all ages at an alarming rate. It was true that conditions were improving slowly for Native Americans, but it was also true that three-fourths of the children on reservations were illiterate, and that most of those being educated attended boarding schools that aimed at assimilation.

Citizenship came slowly and belatedly to the American Indian population in the early 20th century. In a 1901 amendment to the Allotment Act of 1887, the government granted citizenship to all Native Americans living in Indian Territory, which in 1907 became the state of Oklahoma. Then, in 1919, Indian veterans of World War I gained the right to apply for citizenship. (Between 8,000 and 10,000 Native Americans served in the U.S. armed forces during the First World War.) Not until June 24, 1924, though, did Congress declare "that all non-citizen Indians born within the territorial limits of the United States be and they are hereby declared to be citizens of the United States."[9]

In 1923, concerned about alleged abuses, Secretary of the Interior Hubert Work initiated an investigation of the Bureau of Indian Affairs (BIA) by the Institute for Government Research (a forerunner of the Brookings Institute), a private organization that studied public policy at the national level. Lewis Meriam of the

"Lo, the Poor Indian," reads the caption to this 1913 cartoon. Carrying the broken shield of government neglect, the Indian walks a gloomy, downward path. *(Library of Congress, General Collection)*

institute headed the survey staff; their results, published in 1928 as *The Problem of Indian Administration,* came to be known as the Meriam Survey, or Meriam Report. The institute brought to light real poverty and appalling living conditions on Indian reservations. "The standard of living is often almost unbelievably low," the researchers stated. "Almost nothing is spent for shelter and firewood, and very little for clothing and food. Many homes were visited where there was almost no food on hand."[10] Tuberculosis and trachoma were widespread, and observation suggested that the overall death rate and infant mortality rates were high.

A little more than 70 percent of the Native Americans surveyed lived in jurisdictions where the annual per capita income was less than $200; 25 percent were from jurisdictions reporting an annual per capita income of $100 or less. Again and again the survey staff asked Indian Service field employees how the people eked out an existence. In their report they noted, "Several replied that it was hardly to be called an existence. Others said that they did not know the answer; that they had never been able to figure it out."[11]

African Americans Seek a Better Life

The fruits of citizenship also eluded many African Americans. In June 1905 a group of concerned blacks, led by the prominent intellectual W. E. B. DuBois, met in Niagara Falls, Canada, to discuss ways to protect African Americans' rights and end discrimination based on race. In May 1910 members of the so-called Niagara movement founded the National Association for the Advancement of Colored People (NAACP) to secure jobs in industry for African Americans in the North and safety and freedom from lynching for those in the South. The NAACP published a magazine, *Crisis,* which served as its mouthpiece. By 1921 more than 400 NAACP offices were active throughout the United States.

Another organization, founded in 1911, did more to help African Americans economically. The National League on Urban Conditions among Negroes (known after 1920 as the National Urban League) worked to gain job opportunities in industry for African Americans, and its members helped southern migrants adjust to life in northern cities.

On a smaller scale, African Americans opened boarding houses for single working women of their race. They also established settlement houses to serve their communities, such as the Frederick Douglass Center, which was founded in Chicago in 1905.

African Americans continued to leave the South in the first years of the 20th century; the rate of northward migration increased significantly in 1916, after World War I had stemmed the flow of immigrants into U.S. factories. More than 400,000 African Americans relocated from the South to the North between 1916 and 1918, and more than a million made the journey north in the decade that followed. This prodigious movement of people—one of the largest in U.S. history—became known as the Great Migration.

In 1915 and 1916 jobs were opening up in northern industries while flooding and boll weevils were making economic survival precarious for agricultural workers in the South. People therefore moved north to improve their financial prospects and to escape racial segregation and persecution. African Americans went to work in northern meatpacking plants, in iron and steel mills, and on automobile assembly lines. They labored for the railroads and in factories making ammunition—but nearly always in jobs at the lowest skill levels and with the least responsibility.

African Americans pour into a railroad station, eager to board trains for northern cities, in this painting by Jacob Lawrence, part of a series of works on the Great Migration. *(National Archives)*

White northerners enforced segregation by custom, if not by law. They used zoning ordinances and covenants to restrict African Americans to certain neighborhoods where rents generally were high and housing quality was poor. Banks and insurance agents discriminated against African Americans seeking to buy property through a practice called redlining. Either they withheld funds for purchases or denied insurance coverage in certain neighborhoods on the basis of the residents' race or income level, or they took advantage of African-American buyers by charging excessive fees and high interest rates. Studies conducted in New York City in the 1920s determined that blacks paid more for housing than whites did and received less acceptable housing. The same was true in other cities as well.

African-American migrants soon learned that living in the North offered no protection against racial violence. At least 48 people died and hundreds were injured in a race riot that erupted in East St. Louis, Illinois, on July 2, 1917. The African-American population of this industrial city had tripled between 1900 and 1914, and it continued to grow as the European war placed demands on U.S. factories. Many whites viewed this influx as an unwelcome invasion that threatened their community and their jobs. It was rumored that African Americans introduced crime to the city and that they were planning a race war.

In the industrial plants of East St. Louis as elsewhere in the North, blacks and whites worked in segregated labor gangs, used separate washrooms, and ate separately in the dining hall. Blacks did the dirtiest, most offensive tasks and earned the lowest pay. At a time when white workers in two of the city's largest plants were starting to unionize, management let it be known that any white unwilling to work under the established conditions would be replaced by a black laborer.

The incidents that touched off the riot happened on July 1. Twice whites fired shots into houses where blacks lived; blacks reacted by arming themselves and taking to the streets; when the police responded, two detectives were shot and killed. On July 2 a white mob began attacking and shooting blacks indiscriminately. People were pulled from streetcars and assaulted; a man was hanged from a telephone pole, and women had their faces and breasts beaten. The mob set the houses of African Americans on fire, and snipers fired at the residents as they ran from the flames. The mayor called up the Illinois National Guard, and the rioting slowed and ended. Thirty-nine blacks and nine whites were dead.

Riots occurred throughout the country during the "Red Summer" of 1919, when white soldiers returning from the war reacted against competition from blacks for jobs and housing. In July 1919 a riot erupted in Longview, Texas, after one of the town's African-American teachers reported on a lynching to the *Chicago Defender.* (At least 38 African Americans died in lynchings in 1919.) A week later Washington, D.C., endured four days of brutal street fighting when 400 whites, many of them soldiers and sailors home from overseas service, took out their frustration on the African-American population. Fueled by alcohol, difficulty finding jobs, and accusations that a black man had assaulted the wife of a white sailor, they armed themselves with guns, clubs, and lead pipes and overran an African-American section in the southwestern quadrant of the city. An estimated 30 people were beaten or shot to death. Rioting occurred that summer as well in Omaha, Nebraska; Charleston, South Carolina; Knoxville, Tennessee; and Chicago, where 38 people were killed and 537 injured in 13 days of violence.

Challenges for Rural Americans

In 1920 black and white southern tenant farmers and sharecroppers worked 50 acres, on average, and earned less than $200 a year. (Tenants and sharecroppers differed in that tenants rented their farms for cash or a portion of the crop and usually furnished their own stock and machinery, and sharecroppers contributed labor only.) Poverty had mastery of farmers in the South. Few owned tractors or other mechanized equipment, and the typical southern farmhouse lacked telephone service and electricity.

By 1920 the average U.S. farm encompassed 149 acres. Throughout most of the nation agriculture was becoming mechanized, and production of food by large farms for growing urban areas was replacing the old system of subsistence farming. The U.S. farm population was 32 million, including 925,000 African Americans. Many farmers relied on credit at low interest rates to cover their operating expenses from the start of the growing season until harvest, but the machinery, land, and supplies needed to enlarge their operations required working capital beyond most farmers' means. The solution for many was to mortgage their land. Logic told the individual farmer that to repay his mortgage and operating loan plus interest he needed to produce more. This strategy worked during World War I, when the government's need to feed its fighting force kept agricultural prices high, and in the years immediately following, when the United States aided its struggling European allies.

By summer 1920 Great Britain and France were once again feeding their people. Production continued to rise as domestic and international demand declined, with the result that prices fell sharply. The price of corn dropped 78 percent, and the price of wheat fell 64 percent. At the same time farmers were forced to pay high transportation charges to the railroads that carried their goods to consumers. The nation's farmers weathered an agricultural depression for the next three years and economic hardship throughout the 1920s. In 1921 net farm income fell from $9 billion to $3.3 billion, farm bankruptcies numbered 500,000, and farm tenancy moved into the Midwest as those who were foreclosed continued to work the same land as tenants.

In Appalachia people increasingly relied on the timber and mining industries for their livelihood, especially as the region responded to the great demand for coal to fuel the factories of World War I. Mining drew railroads into the mountains, but service remained poor as late as 1920, and in eastern Kentucky and elsewhere

Dr. J. N. McCormack demonstrates a sanitary privy at the 1913 Kentucky State Fair. Twelve thousand people saw the demonstration, and many built the privies on their property. *(Courtesy of the Rockefeller Archive Center)*

some counties were still without rail lines. Roads could be bad enough to allow a mule to sink shoulder deep in mud. Shut in by mountains with little or no access to transportation, thousands of residents of Appalachia lived isolated from the rest of the nation. "[F]ew of the men and women and children who lived in the recesses of the eastern hills had progressed far in habits of thought or life since their ancestors followed the Wilderness Trail into Kentucky, a century and a half ago," commented one social researcher in 1920.[12]

Although the United Mine Workers of America was founded in 1890, most coal miners worked without union representation until the 1930s. Instead of receiving a set wage, they were paid according to the amount of coal loaded. In 1920, when researchers averaged the daily earnings of 668 miners over a two-week period, they determined that 578 men earned less than eight dollars per day, on average. Of these 197 earned less than five dollars per day, and 14 earned less than three dollars per day, on average. Most miners returned nearly half their earnings to their employer to cover rent and fuel for company-owned housing, the cost of goods purchased with scrip in a company store, and other debts.

Serious public-health problems existed throughout the region. In a typical Appalachian county, Harlan County, Kentucky, 43 percent of residents whose blood was tested in 1913 by the Rockefeller Sanitary Commission, an organization founded in 1909 to cure and prevent hookworm, were found to be infected with this parasite. Hookworm is transmitted by direct contact with soil containing human feces and is easily treated with several medications and controlled through proper soil sanitation. In areas of infestation children who go barefoot and play in the dirt are at increased risk of infection. A mild hookworm infection causes diarrhea and abdominal cramps, but severe and chronic infection can lead to protein deficiency, anemia, and impaired physical and mental development. Of 278 homes inspected by the commission, 261 had no toilet facilities of any sort. (The commission failed to eliminate hookworm in the United States, but it did bring this parasite under control. Hookworm infection still occurs in Appalachia and in some mining towns.)

In 1915 the U.S. Public Health Service examined 816 children in 13 schools in Harlan County and determined that 2.3 percent had trachoma, a bacterial eye infection that leads to blindness. Because many parents kept sons and daughters with trachoma home from school, the incidence was thought to be much higher. According to the 1910 U.S. Census, just 68.2 percent of Harlan County children between the ages of six and 14 attended school, and 31.3 percent of county residents over age 10 were illiterate. Harlan County was not unique: Researchers from the U.S. Children's Bureau surveying homes in the North Carolina mountains in the early 20th century found overcrowding, poor light, and a lack of sanitary toilets in most homes. In addition, infant and maternal mortality rates were high.

A Beginning

As the 1920s came to a close, pioneering social researchers had made a good start at assembling a statistical portrait of the nation's poor, and the federal, state, and local governments had implemented some improvements based on their recommendations. The picture, however, was about to be altered significantly.

Chronicle of Events

1900

- Chicago is the only major city still providing outdoor relief.
- The American Federation of Labor (AFL) has 500,000 members.
- About 25,000 children age 15 or younger work in southern textile mills.
- An estimated 100,000 people of Mexican descent live in the United States.

1901

- The City Homes Association inspects tenements in three poor Chicago neighborhoods.
- The Reverend Edgar Gardner Murphy founds the Alabama Child Labor Committee.

- The federal government grants citizenship to all Native Americans living in Indian Territory (present-day Oklahoma).

1902

- *summer:* A typhoid epidemic in Chicago is tied to illegal, unsanitary toilet facilities.
- *December:* The Chicago City Council passes an ordinance regulating tenement-house construction based on recommendations from the City Homes Association.

1903

- Federal legislation bars certain groups of people, such as people with epilepsy, the insane, prostitutes, and anarchists, from entering the United States.
- A federal court gives the government the right to sell "surplus" land on Indian reservations.

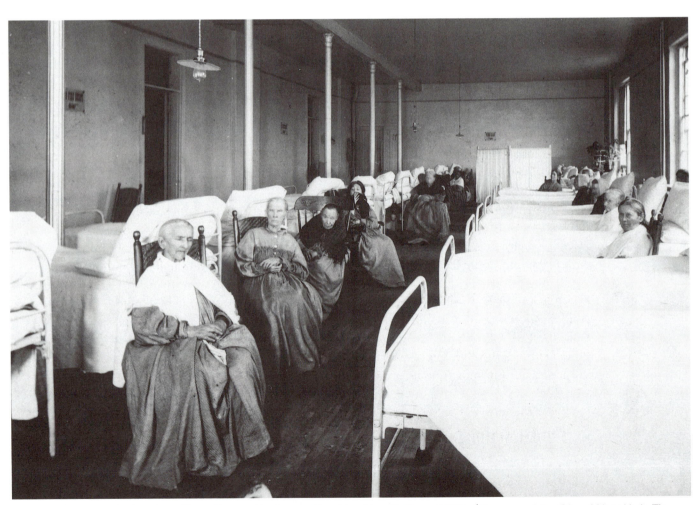

This was the women's dormitory, Kings County Almshouse, Brooklyn, New York, ca. 1900. *(Museum of the City of New York, The Byron Collection)*

1904

- Robert Hunter publishes *Poverty* and establishes the first unofficial poverty line in the United States, an annual income of $460 for a family of five in the North and of $300 for a family of equal size in the South.
- The Octavia Hill Association finds crowding, poor sanitation, and fire hazards to be common in the tenements of Philadelphia.
- The National Child Labor Committee (NCLC) is formed.
- Agents of the U.S. Immigration Service begin patrolling the southwestern border of the United States.

1905

- Investigators see little improvement in Chicago's tenements.
- The Industrial Workers of the World (IWW) is formed.
- The Frederick Douglass Center, a settlement house in an African-American neighborhood of Chicago, opens.
- *June:* Prominent African Americans meet in Niagara Falls, Canada, to discuss racial problems in the United States.

1905–1915

- American workers stage at least 150 strikes.

1906–1915

- About 9.4 million immigrants enter the United States.

1907

- The Buffalo Charity Organization Society is dispensing outdoor relief.
- The Russell Sage Foundation, a social-research organization, is founded.
- Some 1.5 million immigrants arrive in this record year.
- The government bars additional groups from entering the United States and sets the head tax at four dollars.

1907–1918

- Lewis Hine uses photography to document child labor for the NCLC.

1908

- A city ordinance requires all new tenements in Chicago to be inspected before occupancy.
- About 35,000 U.S. workers are killed in industrial accidents.
- The federal government first offers workers' compensation insurance to its employees.

1909

- The Rockefeller Sanitary Commission is formed to cure and prevent hookworm infection.
- *February 16:* Mayor James E. Grinstead of Louisville, Kentucky, appoints a committee to investigate tenement conditions.

1910

- Kansas City, Missouri, establishes a welfare department to attend to the poor, juvenile delinquents, and other dependent groups.
- Roughly 1,600,000 children ages 10 to 15 are employed.
- The NCLC drafts model child-labor legislation setting a minimal age of 14 for factory work and of 16 for mining. The law bars children under 16 from night work and all children from hazardous work environments.
- In Harlan County, Kentucky, 68.2 percent of children ages six to 14 attend school, according to U.S. Census figures; 31.3 percent of residents over age 10 are illiterate.
- *May:* The National Association for the Advancement of Colored People (NAACP) is founded.

1910–1916

- Each year, approximately 53,000 Mexicans enter the United States.

African-American field hands harvested cotton in 1907 much as people did during slavery. This photograph was taken near Dallas, Texas. *(Center for American History, The University of Texas at Austin, CN Number 01281)*

1911

- States begin to enact workers' compensation laws.
- The National League on Urban Conditions among Negroes (later the National Urban League) is formed.
- *March 25:* A fire at the Triangle Shirtwaist Company, New York City, leaves 146 workers dead.

1911–1913

- Thirty-nine states pass child-labor laws.

1912

- *January 12:* Under IWW leadership, a strike against the textile mills of Lawrence, Massachusetts, begins.
- *March 12:* The Lawrence strike ends in a victory for the workers.

1913

- The Cook County, Illinois, Welfare Bureau is established.
- The U.S. Department of Labor is formed.
- Forty-three percent of people examined by the Rockefeller Sanitary Commission in Harlan County, Kentucky, are infected with hookworm; 261 of 278 homes inspected have no toilet facilities.

1913–1916

- At least 6,000 tenements are constructed in Chicago each year, but only 910 occupancy permits are issued.

1914

- The Russell Sage Foundation develops a model housing law.
- Laws regulating tenement and private dwellings have been enacted in 17 U.S. cities, two Canadian cities, and nine U.S. states.

1915

- The U.S. Commission on Industrial Relations determines that $700 will support a family of 5.6 members for one year; 79 percent of fathers earn less than that amount.
- The U.S. Public Health Service determines that 2.3 percent of 816 schoolchildren examined in Harlan County, Kentucky, have trachoma.

1916

- The Adamson Act gives railroad workers an eight-hour day.
- *September 1:* Congress passes the first national child-labor law.

1916–1918

- As jobs in industry become available, more than 400,000 African Americans move from the rural South to the North.

1917

- Illinois forms a state department of welfare that serves as a model for other states.
- AFL membership reaches 2.5 million.
- Approximately 100,000 unskilled workers have joined the IWW.
- Illegal immigration from Mexico intensifies.
- *February 5:* A new federal immigration law creates more categories of unacceptable aliens, bars immigration from Asia, doubles the head tax to eight dollars, and imposes a literacy test for immigrants.
- *July 2:* Racial tension leads to a riot in East St. Louis, Illinois, that leaves 48 people dead.
- *November 7:* The Bolshevik Party assumes control of Russia.

1918

- AFL membership soars to 5 million.
- In most industries the eight-hour day and 48-hour week are the norm.
- The U.S. Supreme Court declares the federal child-labor legislation unconstitutional.

1919

- One-third of people in the United States live in substandard housing; one-tenth live in homes that threaten the health and well-being of residents, according to a housing survey published this year.
- Native American veterans of World War I may apply for citizenship.
- *April 25:* Congress imposes a 10 percent tax on factories and mines employing children; the number of working children is cut in half.
- *summer:* Race riots occur in towns and cities throughout the nation, including Longview, Texas; Washington, D.C.; Omaha, Nebraska; Charleston, South Carolina; Knoxville, Tennessee; and Chicago.

1920

- Some 32 million people, including 925,000 African Americans, live on U.S. farms; the average farm encompasses 149 acres.
- A three-year agricultural depression begins.
- Rail and road service remain substandard in Appalachia.
- Many Appalachian coal miners earn less than eight dollars a day, on average.
- *January 1:* The poorhouse population is 84,198. This population is aging and increasingly foreign born.

1921

- A federal law establishes immigration quotas based on nationality.
- There are more than 400 NAACP offices throughout the United States.
- Net farm income falls from $9 billion to $3.3 billion; 500,000 farmers declare bankruptcy.

1922

- *May 15:* The Supreme Court strikes down the 1919 tax on factories and mines employing children; the number of working children rises.

1923

- The Institute for Government Affairs investigates the Bureau of Indian Affairs.

1924

- A new law tightens the quotas on immigration; additionally, the Labor Appropriation Act passed by Congress this year creates the U.S. Border Patrol.
- *June 24:* Congress grants citizenship to all Indians born within the territorial United States.

1928

- The Institute for Government Affairs releases the Meriam Survey, which describes shocking social and economic conditions on Indian reservations.

Eyewitness Testimony

You are liable to arrest if you allow your stable to become filthy and a nuisance. The landlord may do pretty much what he pleases with his tenement. That is because you and I do not live near it, never smell it, and think it a man's own fault if he prefers to live in one. We do not realize that the people of the tenements pay really high rents, a large proportion of the daily wages, for inferior homes because they cannot get anything better and pay the grocer's bill.

Robert Alston Stevenson, a founder of the Allen-Stevenson School, a private elementary school for boys in New York City, 1901, "The Poor in Summer," p. 276.

[T]he problems with which American philanthropy has at present to deal have been largely imported along with the greatly increased volume of immigration that has come during the last fifty to sixty years. But the most important result of this immigration is in its permanent effect upon the character and composition of the race to which the destinies of this country are to be committed. The filling of the unskilled occupations by a squalid imported population has probably not increased the total of our population, but has checked the natural increase of the original stock to an extent probably equal to the whole volume of the immigration, the native American being unwilling to take the risk of his children falling into the lower caste which these importations have established. Our immigration, in short, has decided that the people who get born shall, to an increasing extent, be of the lower and peasant classes of Europe rather than of the native American stock.

Joseph Lee, social worker and philantropist, 1902,
Constructive and Preventive Philanthropy, *p. 8.*

To thousands and thousands of working-men the dread of public pauperism is the agony of their lives. The mass of working-men on the brink of poverty hate charity. Not only their words convey a knowledge of this fact, but their actions, when in distress, make it absolutely undeniable. When the poor face the necessity of becoming paupers, when they must apply for charity if they are to live at all, many desert their families and enter the ranks of vagrancy; others drink themselves insensible; some go insane; and still others commit suicide. . . .

These are the terrible alternatives which the working people in poverty accept in preference to pauperism, and yet it is a curious fact, which psychology alone explains, that the very men who will suffer almost anything rather than become paupers are often the very ones who never care to be anything else when once they have become dependent upon alms. When a family once become dependent, the mental agony which they formerly had disappears.

Robert Hunter, social worker and researcher, 1904,
Poverty, *pp. 2–3.*

[T]here are great districts of people who are up before dawn, who wash, dress, and eat breakfast, kiss wives and children, and hurry away to work or to seek work. The world rests upon their shoulders; it moves by their muscle; everything would stop if, for any reason, they should decide not to go into the fields and factories and mines. But the world is so organized that they gain enough to live upon only when they work; should they cease, they are in destitution and hunger. The more fortunate of the laborers are but a few weeks from actual distress when the machines are stopped. Upon the skilled masses want is constantly pressing. As soon as employment ceases, suffering stares them in the face. They are the actual producers of wealth, who have no home nor any bit of soil which they may call their own. They are the millions who possess no tools and can work only by permission of another.

Robert Hunter, social worker and researcher, 1904,
Poverty, *pp. 4–5.*

The selfishness which refuses to be its brother's keeper brings its punishment with especial swiftness in such a city as Philadelphia, where wretched, unhealthful alleys are found near the business streets or just back of the handsome residences, as well as in many of the so-called slums. The points of contact are many—the man or woman who jostles one in the street car may have come straight from the tenement or alley house concerning the disease-breeding condition of which the polite world prefers to be ignorant. Mere enlightened self-interest should furnish sufficient motive for effort to maintain in all parts of the city conditions required for decency and health. The contagion of disease and vice fostered in the neglected districts spreads to the remotest sections. . . .

The complacency which prevails here is dangerous; and the conditions are generally unknown. Those who discuss Philadelphia's housing problems are often met by the surprised exclamation, "I thought Philadelphia had no bad conditions; that it was a city of homes." Yet the intricate network of courts and alleys with which the interior of the blocks are covered is a conspicuous feature, and also the crowding together of the houses so closely that a large proportion have no open space at the rear or side, all light and air coming from the front windows opening on the narrow court, so that ventilation through the house is impossible. In many of the courts there is only surface drainage, slops are thrown out into a gutter, and if the alley is not properly paved and graded, as is frequently the case, the foul water remains in stagnant pools before the houses. Often there are stables among the dwellings and the tenants must go over or around the manure pits into which the refuse from these is thrown.

Emily W. Dinwiddie, secretary of the Tenement House Commission of the New York Charity Organization Society, 1904, Housing Conditions in Philadelphia, *pp. 1–2.*

One tenement visited was a three story house, without fire escapes, containing a grocery store, a fish stand and a meat shop on the first floor. Above in the seventeen living rooms of all kinds—kitchens, bed-rooms, and dining-rooms—were eight families, consisting of thirty-three persons. A goat was kept in the room back of the grocery and three dogs upstairs. The second story hall was filthy and strewn with accumulations of garbage and ashes. Two long hopper water closets in the hall were toilet accommodations for the eight families, an outdoor privy compartment serving for the stores. The closets and also the privy were extremely foul and in bad repair. The privy vault was in an archway under the upper part of the building and was the common well over which sixteen toilet rooms were built, one for the tenement, the others for the rows of rear houses beyond. The vault was also used as a cesspool, receiving the discharge from some of the waste pipes of the house. There was leakage into the cellar, which was damp, foul, and full of rubbish. The yard, a tiny passageway, extending from the grocery store to the toilet room, was in a filthy condition, being covered with fish, refuse and foul water from the first and third story sinks, which discharged on the surface of the ground. The waste pipe from the sink back of the grocery was a rubber hose. In the second story hall one trap served for the two closets and a sink. The odors in the building were very offensive.

Emily W. Dinwiddie describing a tenement dwelling inspected by the Octavia Hill Association, 1904, Housing Conditions in Philadelphia, *pp. 6–7.*

The state of the toilets belonging to many of the houses was beyond description. Frankly stated, it may be asserted that a fairly large part of the working classes is compelled to use toilet accommodations in a condition of which the rest of the world would be unwilling to hear in full.

Over half the accommodations were privies. The foul, malodorous vaults still exist in the crowded blocks, with butcher shops and bake shops, kitchens and sleeping rooms closely adjoining. Five privies were found enclosed within the walls of extensions built to the houses, and a number of others were under second story rooms.

Almost without exception the vaults beneath the three hundred and forty-two privy compartments were in offensive conditions; from forty-eight there was distinct evidence of leakage, and many others were probably in the same state, less manifestly, but still to an extent sufficient to contaminate the soil and pollute the cellar air, which is later drawn up into the living rooms. Five compartments were above the flowing vaults, and fifty over vaults full nearly to the top. The privy vaults belonging to thirty-eight houses were receiving waste drainage, thus serving as cesspools as well as vaults.

These open wells are a direct menace to the health of the community, and may with reason be held in part responsible for the high typhoid fever rate usual in Philadelphia.

Emily W. Dinwiddie writing on behalf of the Octavia Hill Association, 1904, Housing Conditions in Philadelphia, *p. 11.*

It must be remembered that before the Civil War few immigrants went to the South, because of slavery. Manufactures have sprung up as by magic, but only in recent years. The population is scattered over a wide area and families are isolated. The war left the white people poor and it destroyed many public institutions and arrested development of philanthropy. The public mind was devoted to politics and theological controversies and only recently has turned toward social amelioration. There were no large cities to force attention to the working class and their needs.

There is very much distress among the poor whites, and in the new industrial towns the miseries of child labor have appeared. There are few occupations open to poor women and the wages are low.

If we turn to the poorest class of all, the negroes, we must remember that they are excluded from many trades, although they are sought as farm laborers. Race feeling, fortified by the sentiments and habits of caste, has separated the whites from the blacks. Negroes generally assist each other as long as they have anything, and in the warmer regions their standard of life is very low, so that their poverty is not felt as wretchedness.

Charles Richmond Henderson, professor of sociology at the University of Chicago, 1904, Modern Methods of Charity, *p. 406.*

From the beginning, 1905 was a bad year for Pin Hook [Texas]. . . .

It was a year of sickness, of malaria, of swamp fever, of a rundown condition called "the dumb chills"—different from "the hard chills" of malaria. The blue quinine bottle was always on the table. There was almost always someone in bed. Men and women well enough to be up and around were called on to "set up" with the sick. Doctors were on the road day and night—one from Pin Hook, one from Woodland, two or three others from Blossom and Detroit.

It was a year of hard times. Corn planted did not come up. Corn saved for grinding at the mill had to be used for seed to plant over. Egg and chicken money went for doctors and medicine and the people had to make do or do without. They parched cornmeal and boiled it for coffee. In the spring they lived on hog jaw and poke "sallet," the greens of the poke weed. In summer they ate roasting ears and soft bread made from meal "gritted" on homemade graters. The man of the house made the grater by driving the side of a molasses bucket full of holes and nailing the edges to a board. He brought corn from the field when the kernels were hard enough to grit but not to grind. Children took turns at rubbing the ears up and down the gritter. It was the woman's job to turn the soft meal into bread.

William A. Owens recalling rural Texas in 1905, This Stubborn Soil, *pp. 3–4.*

The "noble red man" of Fenimore Cooper and of Caitlin, the fierce figure in warpaint and feathers, lost his romantic interest when he was confined to the reservation and fed on rations. He became of no more interest than any other stall-fed creature. Admiration of the untamed savage gave way to contempt for the dirty beggar in the streets and under the car windows. This period did not

The dining hall in New York City's Municipal Lodging House served as a shelter for homeless men. This photograph was taken January 2, 1908. Note the house rules posted in six languages. *(Library of Congress, Prints and Photographs Division, LC-USZ62-75781)*

have its picture-makers, yet the public got a vivid impression of it, nevertheless.

J. M. Oskison, Cherokee, writer and editor, June 1907,
"Making an Individual of the Indian," p. 723.

I take my allotment of land, 320 acres. I am without tools and money. I work on some job provided by the government until I can buy horses and a plow and materials to build some sort of house. Then I start my improvements. I get the house up, a garden planted, some pigs and chickens about my house, and—then I have to go back to work again to get money to buy food. The job and my allotment are many miles apart. If I leave my wife and my small child at home and go away to work, I am not sure that they will not be bothered by loafers. If I take them with me, then my garden grows up into weeds, cattle break into my crops, and my pigs and chickens are killed and stolen.

All the time in Washington lies a sum of money to the credit of my people. A little comes to us every year from the interest, but my share is hardly worth driving to the agency for. Now, if I could get my share, my wife's share, and my child's share of the tribal fund, I could afford to stay on my allotment and take care of it until I could make my living from the land.

Henry Leeds of the Lower Brule Lakota Sioux, June 1907, in
J. M. Oskison, "Making an Individual of the Indian,"
pp. 731–32.

To be able-bodied and willing to work and yet utterly unable to find it is hard; to have others quite helplessly dependent upon you in addition is so hard that it almost beggars description; but to be forced to stand in line with a basket for hours and then to be given, in the name of charity, a loaf of bread and a handful of withered vegetables, is a cruelty to which no human being should be subjected. None of the distributions improvised for dealing with this emergency have opened a door of real escape for the poor; all have led to no thoroughfare, but most of them have been well meant.

Philadelphia Society for Organizing Charity, "Thirtieth
Annual Report," August 1908, in Leah Hannah Feder,
Unemployment Relief in Periods of Depression,
p. 209.

To breathe bad air, laden with impurities from dirty yards and ill-kept and illegally maintained privy vaults, to live in sunless, unaired rooms and to be ceaselessly subjected to the nerve-fret of constant contact with the occupants of other crowded rooms—all this means a never-ending tax on the vitality of the tenement dweller. Energy, that expended in productive channels as working power would accomplish results beneficial alike to the individual and to the community, is needlessly and criminally wasted in the attempt to throw off the malaise and listlessness that are the least deadly effects of the disease-favoring surroundings under which we allow many of our citizens to live.

Janet E. Kemp, investigator employed by the Tenement House
Commission of Louisville, July 19, 1909, Report of the
Tenement House Commission of Louisville, under
the Ordinance of February 16, 1909, *pp. 18–19.*

The causes of friendless old age, of orphanage, of physical and mental disease and defect, are many and intricate. Some of it is due, no doubt, to defective personality, physical and moral. Much of it, certainly, is the direct result of remedial social conditions, maladjustments which can be corrected. Children are left fatherless and motherless by the premature death of their parents from preventable disease; people come to old age, frequently an early old age, disabled by overwork or work under bad conditions, having had little opportunity to make provision for age, or to bring up their children to a position in which they can care for their parents; much of the blindness is due to preventable causes; much of the feeble-mindedness to lack of custodial care for feeble-minded and epileptic women and men; some of the accidents to unguarded machinery; much of the illness to unsanitary conditions of home and factory and to a low standard of living imposed by a low rate of wages. Thus much of the misery which the institutional population reflects certainly represents a defective social economy.

Edward T. Devine, social worker and writer, 1913, Misery
and Its Causes, *p. 48.*

Economic conditions on a reservation is presented to us in no more bold relief than that of the Jicarilla [Apache] Reservation in northern New Mexico. These Indians live up in the mountains. The rock-ribbed, craggy mountains show their teeth at the inhabitants of the land and seem to flaunt defiance at any man who would try to eke out a living there. The stream that flows, through the Jicarilla country is so alkali horses will not drink it. The water in some of the lakes is bitter. Here the Jicarilla Apaches, seven hundred strong, are trying to keep body and soul together year after year. No one undertakes to farm, for their [*sic*] is no rain and no means of irrigation. No white people live in a land among whom they might hire out as farmhands. They own no cattle, but one or two own a few sheep and goats. They eat bread baked by the coals and drink black coffee for breakfast, bread and coffee at noon and the same at night. When the rigors of winter come on and the bread is gone they boil and eat the inner bark of the yellow pine on their reservation. In the days gone by the mothers, not having any milk for lack of proper nourishment, took their babies into the mountain caves, waiting in solitude and going home alone. The consumptives on this reservation, lacking that nutriment which plenty of healthful food gives to the blood to build up the waste tissues, die by the scores. Last winter, through hunger, cold, and disease, seventy of these Indians died. These Indians are flesh of our flesh, bone of our bone. I need not prophesy their future. Present conditions tell the future.

Henry Roe Cloud, Winnebago, 1913, "Some Social and Economic Aspects of the Reservation," p. 154.

If we are citizens of the United States of America we have a right to be protected as such and enjoy the privileges of the same. On the other hand, if we are wards of the Government of the United States we ought to be protected as such. We must have one status or the other. We tire of being hauled back and forth over this political fence. If this is kept up much longer there will be nothing left of us but a race of degenerates. The cry is, "Make laws to protect the Indian," but I fail to see wherein they are protected, as every year, through legislation, they are made poorer and still poorer, until soon we will see the Indian cast upon the world a miserable pauper. I tell you, the Indians need to be protected from the ones who have the making and unmaking of them and who make the laws governing the Indians as well as the surrounding whites.

We are not asking the officials to give us something for which they would have to dig into their own pockets, but we are asking for and working for justice due to every man and woman living in a Christian country, under the stars and stripes, emblem of Liberty, Peace and Justice.

Charles H. Kealear, Sioux, spring 1913, "Reservation Management," p. 161.

There are great bodies of people in country and in city who from birth have less than enough food, clothing, and shelter; who from childhood must toil long and hard to secure even that insufficient amount; who can benefit little from the world's advance in material comfort and in spiritual beauty because their bodies are under-nourished,

their minds are over-strained and their souls deadened by bitter struggle with want. These are the real poor of every community—the masses who, not lacking in industry and thrift, are yet never really able to earn enough for decent existence and who toil on in constant fear that bare necessities may fail.

Neither racial qualities not national characteristics account for the presence of such poverty. It persists as an accompaniment of modern economic life, in widely removed countries among ethnically different peoples. It cannot be identified with alien elements in native race stocks. Countries which have for generations been relatively free from foreign influx and have developed industrialism from within exhibit the same phenomenon of economic want. Wholesale immigration is likely to be attended by urban congestion and industrial exploitation, but these are supplementary phases of the problem of poverty. Even in the United States, where immigration has attained proportions unexampled in the world's history, there is no reason to believe that such influx—bearing in mind the part it has played in creating and enlarging industrial opportunity—has permanently affected the condition of poverty.

Jacob H. Hollander, professor of political economy, Johns Hopkins University, 1914, The Abolition of Poverty, *pp. 4–5.*

The problem of poverty is one that is destined to become more acute in this country with the passing of the years, unless society faces this problem and seeks its solution through economic and social changes. It is the persistence of poverty in modern society that sustains the propaganda of Socialism. The danger of the spread of Socialism lies in the fact that the well-to-do classes have neglected to study the causes which create poverty and to consider the remedies for its abolition. It is reasonable to believe that if the facts were known, the public would make a determined effort to remove poverty from modern society. Many are enjoying the fruits of industry who have given no thought to the costs in human life, toil, and social misery which they exact. Yet there are many signs today that those who control industry will be unwilling to profit by any system of distribution that flourishes at the expense of the efficiency and well being of the wage earners.

John Simpson Penman, Congregationalist minister, 1915, Poverty: The Challenge to the Church, *p. vii.*

[T]he problems of poverty have awakened a public interest and have become the burning questions of the twentieth century. Poverty is no longer an inevitable condition to be accepted and endured; it is a problem of economic and social life which demands solution. The industrial unrest which everywhere pervades the minds of the working classes in Western Civilization is a sign of the awakening of a new consciousness as to the value of the human element in industry. These workers are no longer satisfied to accept poverty as a permanent factor of civilization. They behold in poverty the evidence of maladjustments in economic and social life.

John Simpson Penman, Congregationalist minister, 1915,
Poverty: The Challenge to the Church, *p. 3.*

We have been so long accustomed to think of poverty as the result of personal defects of character rather than as the creation of economic and social conditions that we accept its existence as a necessity of the social order. Until the public mind is disabused of this point of view, there can be little hope that the facts of poverty will be seriously considered. The time has come when these problems must be faced; when some solution must be found to meet the demands which the social effects of poverty force upon society. And these effects are felt in proportion to the amount of poverty which exists in this country.

John Simpson Penman, Congregationalist minister, 1915,
Poverty: The Challenge to the Church, *p. 5.*

If poverty is of small dimensions, it can be left to the agencies of public and private relief. But if it exists on a large scale, it must be dealt with by means of economic and legislative changes.

The increasing amount of relief demanded by the poor, the growing wretchedness and misery of the many, the abundant wealth of the few, the industrial unrest of the wage earners, all are signs which point to the increase of poverty and to its deep rootage in the social organism. Behind all national legislation stands the deepening shadow of poverty. It is this which creates the social problem. It is the outstanding fact in all discussions of the social question.

John Simpson Penman, Congregationalist minister, 1915,
Poverty: The Challenge to the Church, *p. 6.*

It cannot be denied that "labor-saving" machinery does not save Labor so much as it helps Capital. In Lawrence and other factory towns of New England, the most ingenious labor-saving machinery is used. But it is impossible for a workman to support his family by his own efforts. Wages are so low that father, mother and children must all work in the mills, while a few rich mill-owners live in luxury. The serious strike in Lawrence a few years ago was one result of this un-Christian greed. And now they are building cotton-mills in the South and following New England methods. They are also employing child labor. There are now nearly two million child laborers in America. That's nothing to be proud of.

Now all this is caused by selfishness and greed. If we could put it in one word, we might call it Capitalism. Its tendency is to make the rich richer, and the poor poorer. No matter how much wealth is produced, no matter how rich we are, Capitalism will not share. There must always be a submerged tenth in the slums of Poverty.

Edwin Jennings, writer and lecturer, 1915, The Abolition of Poverty, *pp. 7–8.*

"Any man who really wants a job can get one of some kind." The implication is that every man in a breadline is aged, inform, deficient, or a shirker. There is complete disregard of the fact that many fields of work are highly specialized and the standards exacting. Why, it is asked, for instance, should not every man shovel snow, provided the snow is obliging enough to come at a critical time, and in sufficient quantity to warrant equipping all the waiting thousands with snow shovels? In the winter of 1913–14 one county superintendent of the poor in New York State, somewhat distrusting the old tradition that any man out of work should be able to do anything that could be called work, asked for a physical examination of thirty men who were detailed to go "out on the road." The physician that made the examination certified that twelve of the men were unfitted for the work in their present condition, and that six others were organically unfitted for that particular work at any time.

Frances A. Kellor, sociologist and reformer, 1915, Out of Work: A Study of Unemployment, *p. 3.*

"You can always get work on a farm." This popular theory ignores the seasonal and isolated nature of farm labor, the growth of manufacture, and the differences in wage rates. It minimizes the fact that it is often impossible for the laborer to pay for transportation to the places where farm work exists. It ignores the more obvious fact that there is no farm work in winter. The theory is as little tenable as the dictum "Anybody can raise chickens," the fallacy of which now perhaps needs no comment.

Frances A. Kellor, sociologist and reformer, 1915, Out of Work: A Study of Unemployment, *p. 4.*

From the beginning of this country's history the "mover on" from the Atlantic coast to the western frontier has been a dramatic figure. He is a manifestation of an eternal type, we are reminded, and is not a recent economic product. But it is not merely a spirit of adventure, not merely the impulsion of restless feet that drives many a steady workman "laid off" in a railroad shop or factory from one town to another, seeking an opening in another factory in his trade, in another railroad shop, or failing that, in allied industries such as machine shops or steel works. Meanwhile, as his entry into a town and an opening in his trade there usually fail to coincide, the only possible thing to do seems to be to move on; and move on he does until it becomes a habit and he is classed with the "drifters" of the earth. It is undoubtedly true that nowhere else in the world is there so much ground covered in the blind pursuit of work as there is in these United States.

Frances A. Kellor, sociologist and reformer, 1915, Out of Work: A Study of Unemployment, *p. 17.*

[W]here tenancy exists under such conditions as are prevalent in the Southwest, its increases can be regarded only as a menace to the Nation. . . .

The prevailing system of tenancy in the Southwest is shared tenancy, under which the tenant furnishes his own seed, tools, and teams and pays the landlord one-third of the grain and one-fourth of the cotton. There is, however, a constant tendency to increase the landlord's share through the payment either of cash bonuses or of a higher percentage of the product. Under this system tenants as a class earn only a bare living through the work of themselves and their entire families. Few of the tenants ever succeed in laying by a surplus. On the contrary, their experiences are so discouraging that they seldom remain on the same farm for more than a year, and they move from one farm to the next, in the constant hope of being able to better their condition. Without the labor of the entire family the tenant farmer is helpless. As a result, not only is his wife prematurely broken down, but the children remain uneducated and without the hope of any condition better than that of their parents. The tenants having no interest in the results beyond the crops of a single year, the soil is being rapidly exhausted and the conditions, therefore, tend to become steadily worse. Even at present a very large proportion of the tenants' families are insufficiently clothed, badly housed, and underfed. Practically all of the white tenants are native born. As a result of these conditions, however, they are deteriorating rapidly,

each generation being less efficient and more hopeless than the one proceeding [*sic*].

Industrial Relations: Final Report and Testimony Submitted to Congress by the Commission on Industrial Relations, *Vol. 1, 1916, pp. 86–87.*

In the great southwest, where a comparatively few years ago the "sturdy pioneer" homesteaded his hundred and sixty acres of land and had it deeded to him "free of all incumbrances," has developed a "problem," based on land tenantry that has assumed such stupendous proportions as to attract the attention of the entire country.

In Oklahoma 54 percent of the tillers of the soil live on rented farms, in Texas only 2 percent more own them there than in Oklahoma, while the percentage of tenants in the other states of the south and west is so large as to be almost unbelievable.

The tenant farmers of the southwest may be divided into two classes—those who possess their own farming implements, work animals, etc., constituting the larger, but rapidly decreasing class, while those who own nothing and are virtual serfs to the landlords and who constitute the smaller, but rapidly increasing class, the beginnings of a future "possessionless proletariat" of the soil. . . .

Nearly every newspaper in the southwest is crowded with notices of "Sheriff sales under mortgage foreclosures." This means that the one-time owner will now become a renter of the first class; a few years more and a "public auction" notice in the local paper will denote his entrance into the class of possessionless tenants.

W. W. Pannell, socialist and writer, January 1916, "Tenant Farming in the United States," p. 421.

The houses are usually unfinished and unpainted, the walls and ceilings sometimes being covered with old newspaper or cheap muslin. Into this habitation crowds the farmer and his family, which ranges all the way from the "lord of the manor" and his wife to a "force," using the parlance of the landlord, of from six to a dozen children. The renter with the largest "force" can usually secure the best farms and as a result the family of the average tenant farmer is larger than that of the average industrial worker.

In the renter's home modern furniture is conspicuous by its absence. A few rickety cane bottom chairs, bedsteads, according to the size of the family, and perhaps a bureau or "dresser" constitute the furnishings of the "front" room, while a common board table, cook stove and cupboard situated in the kitchen bring up the sum total of the renter's household belongings. Books and magazines, with the possible exception of a farm paper or two and a few old school books, are rarely ever found in a renter's abode.

W. W. Pannell, socialist and writer, January 1916, "Tenant Farming in the United States," pp. 421–22.

With the exception of two or three the houses are frame, and paint with them is a dim reminiscence. There is one rather modern seven-room flat building of stone front, the flats renting at $22.50 a month and offering the best in the way of accommodations to be found there. There is another makeshift flat building situated above a saloon and pool hall, consisting of six six-room flats, renting at $12 per month, but in a very poor condition of repair. Toilets and baths were found to be in no condition for use and the plumbing in such a state as to constantly menace health. Practically all of the houses have been so reconstructed as to serve as flats, accommodating two and sometimes three families. As a rule there are four, five, and sometimes six rooms in each flat, there being but five instances when there were more than six. It is often the

case that of these rooms not all can be used because of dampness, leaking roofs, or defective toilets overhead.

The owners are in most instances scarcely better off than their tenants and can ill afford to make repairs. One house in the rear of another on Federal Street near Twenty-seventh had every door off its hinges, water covering the floor from a defective sink, and windowpanes out. A cleaning of the house had been attempted, and the cleaners had torn loose what paper yielded readily and proceeded to whitewash over the adhering portion which constituted the majority of the paper. There were four such rooms and for them the family paid $7 a month.

Caswell W. Crews, University of Chicago student who in 1917 surveyed a neighborhood on the South Side of Chicago that was one-third African American, in Chicago Commission on Race Relations, The Negro in Chicago, *pp. 185–86.*

The labor of women and children is supposed to increase the income. As a matter of fact, however, the labor of women and children is frequently a sign of inadequate income. It indicates either that the normal wage-earner is lacking, or else that he has an inadequate wage. Moreover,

This image shows the Mulberry Settlement House Library, New York City, October 1920. *(The New York Public Library Archives, The New York Public Library, Astor, Lenox and Tilden Foundations)*

when large numbers of women and children are engaged in labor, it usually means that men have either been displaced in industry, or that the competition of women and children has so reduced their wages that they no longer are adequate for the support of a family. Furthermore, the labor of women and children has a bad effect upon their physical fitness and ultimately affects their earning capacity and independence. Frequently it leads to sickness and at other times to fatigue, the precursor of incapacity. So far as it results in sickness it means increased expenditure.

John Lewis Gillin, sociologist, 1921, Poverty and Dependency, *p. 77.*

With the development of the country and the increase of population there has grown up almost everywhere, either on the county farm or upon a plot of ground near a large city, such an institution [a poorhouse]. This institution now is usually not merely a remodeled farmhouse, but is built for the special purpose of caring for the poor of the county. Very frequently it is architecturally a credit to the county. It is usually built perfectly symmetrical, the two wings being equal in size, in spite of the fact that there are usually not more than half as many female as male paupers. It is an institution to which the county board as well as the inhabitants of the county can "point with pride." Many times, because of this symmetry, it is impossible to house the male paupers properly without overcrowding, while the wing of the institution for females is not half filled.

Furthermore, the institutional type provides in a very inadequate way for the classification of the inmates of the poorhouse, and thus prevents that attention to the treatment of the paupers which a humane institution should give.

John Lewis Gillin, sociologist, 1921, Poverty and Dependency, *p. 168.*

Sickness and disease reap a frightful toll among the poorer classes of Mexicans. A study of the Ann Street District in the heart of the Mexican section showed that while tuberculosis caused 17.4 per cent of the total deaths of the entire city, it caused 39.2 per cent of the deaths in that district during the same period. Poor and insufficient food, overcrowding and lack of ventilation, lack of facilities for cleanliness, ignorance of personal hygiene coupled with low wages have contributed largely to the tuberculosis menace mentioned, and likewise have developed the high infant mortality rate prevailing among the Mexicans. The infant mortality rate is nearly three times as high among this people as in the city at large.

The result of bad housing, illiteracy, and disease is seen clearly in the records of the Los Angeles County Charities. The Mexican, representing but one-twentieth of the population, contributes nearly one-quarter of the poverty cases handled by the county.

G. Bromley Oxnam, pastor of the Church of All Nations, Los Angeles, January 1921, "The Mexican in Los Angeles from the Standpoint of the Religious Forces of the City," p. 131.

Here we are at the little home of Pedro Soto, the sugar-beet topper, in California. Our guide having called before, we are admitted at once. At first glance we wonder if this is an out-of-doors school—or an orphanage. Out under the spreading fig tree are ten children, the eldest but seventeen. Near the door sits a pale, listless boy. The glands of his neck are diseased and greatly swelled. Don Pedro explains that within the *senora* and two more children are very sick.

As we pass in, the once vigorous toiler from the great silver mines of central Mexico adds that he has not been able to work for five weeks because of his injured foot. The offending member is carelessly bound up in dirty rags which are soaked with blood and pus and surrounded with flies. The misfortune came from a runaway accident. We are told later that this was the result of some extra "weeskey" on pay day.

We find the poor little mother sitting on the rude, cold floor. There are no chairs, just two boxes. Her face is drawn with pain and from long suffering. She is still young, though she says she has borne fourteen children. She is not too ill to brush away from the fevered little cheeks and lips of the two very sick children at either side of her the clouds of lazy flies which are bred by thousands in a pile of refuse from the horse stall just outside the unscreened windows. The mother tells us that the expected fifteenth child will demand another visit by the *medico* which will cost twenty dollars. We understand better why Don Pedro's injured foot is not "surgically safe" when he relates that it costs three dollars cash in advance for each visit of the doctor.

Vernon Monroe McCombs, superintendent of the Latin American Mission of the Methodist Episcopal Church, 1925, From over the Border, *pp. 13–14.*

Every reason which calls for the exclusion of the most wretched, ignorant, dirty, diseased, and degraded people of Europe or Asia demands that the illiterate, unclean, peonized masses moving this way from Mexico be stopped at the border. . . .

The admission of a large and increasing number of Mexican people to engage in all kinds of work is at variance with the American purpose to protect the wages of its working people and maintain their standard of living. Mexican labor is not free; it is not well paid; its standard of living is low. The yearly admission of several scores of thousands from just across the Mexican border tends constantly to lower the wages and conditions of men and women of America who labor with their hands in industry, in transportation, and in agriculture. One who has been in Mexico or in Mexican sections of cities and towns of the southwestern United States enough to make general observation needs no evidence or argument to convince him of the truth of the statement that Mexican peon labor is poorly paid and lives miserably in the midst of want, dirt, and disease.

In industry and transportation they displace great numbers of Americans who are left without employment and drift into poverty, even vagrancy, unable to maintain families or to sustain American communities. . . .

Congressman John Box of Texas, 1928, in "Mexican American Voices," p. 2.

[C]hildren of apparent equality in intelligence, and of similar physical equipment, may face life's circumstances so different as to render one of them a handicap throughout his career. Here is a chap with a good home; a sterling mother who knows how and what to feed her children; a father who furnishes ample support and provides opportunities for education. His little friend in the next street is born into a poor home. His father carries a dinner bucket, and gets work only when the factory is busy. His mother is an ill-trained, dull-witted slattern who prefers to fry the potatoes and buys soft white bread and feeds it to the children. Seeing that these little fellows in their helplessness are not masters of their own destiny, it must be admitted that they are unequal because their circumstances are so unequal. The problems of dependency cannot be thought through without much cogitation of these facts about declared social equality on the one hand and demonstrated natural inequality on the other. Man is never a free-willing individual. The best he can do is to avoid an overbearing, outspoken tyranny from other men.

Robert W. Kelso, social worker, 1928, The Science of Public Welfare, *pp. 143–44.*

Why should the public take over the burden of relieving young persons in want; of succoring the abandoned infant, the hungry and the sick? Why should it maintain almshouses for the destitute and aid hundreds of thousands of persons in their own homes? The persons who pay the bills, directly or indirectly, are the workmen, the householders, the individuals, mostly of moderate means, who are themselves spared dependency only by the fact that they are still able to carry on at the job.

It not infrequently happens that a hard-working artisan returning each evening to his wife and little ones must sit on his front stoop and listen to the quarreling and brawling of a drunkard next door. These neighbors may very likely be receiving an equal income; the worker from his toil, the ne'er-do-well from the poor funds. And as the money paid to the dependent family is raised by taxation, it is, by a well-known principle of political economy, levied directly on the property owner, who passes it along to the workingman in the price of the food, fuel and clothing he buys. As he sits on his front stoop smoking his pipe, therefore, he may reflect that his hard-earned pay is going to help buy food for his worthless neighbor, to supply him even with the tobacco he smokes.

Robert W. Kelso, social worker, 1928, The Science of Public Welfare, *p. 151.*

One of the oldest and perhaps the noblest of human aspirations has been the abolition of poverty. By poverty I mean the grinding by undernourishment, cold, and ignorance, and fear of old age of those who have the will to work. We in America today are nearer to the final triumph over poverty than ever before in the history of any land. The poorhouse is vanishing from among us. We have not yet reached the goal, but, given a chance to go forward with the policies of the last eight years, we shall soon with the help of God be in sight of the day when poverty will be banished from this nation. There is no guarantee against poverty equal to a job for every man. That is the primary purpose of the economic policies we advocate.

Herbert Hoover accepting nomination by the Republican Party to the presidency of the United States, August 11, 1928, The New Day, *p. 16.*

CHAPTER SIX

The Poor Take
Center Stage
1929-1941

In spring 1929 Americans had an ominous warning that the economy was not as healthy as they liked to think it was. In 120 cities warmer temperatures failed to usher in the usual springtime decline in public and private relief expenditures. This meant that seasonal workers were not finding their customary summer employment.

There were other danger signs as well. The 1920s had been a time of relative prosperity, when people bought automobiles, appliances, and other products of modern industry, often on the installment plan. Now factories continued to produce, but wages had lagged behind the rate of production, and consumers were buying less. With reduced demand, wholesale prices had dropped.

Widespread speculation and the practice of buying stocks on credit, in anticipation of gains (called buying on margin), had dangerously inflated the stock market, and by midyear stock prices started to fall. This decline resulted in a flurry of selling, as experienced investors and novices alike tried to minimize their losses and perhaps even escape with a profit. The selling triggered a further drop in prices and another rush to sell. Prices fell precipitously in October, following a surge in sales, and by Wednesday, October 23, losses added up to an estimated $5 billion. The next day true panic set in. On "Black Thursday" desperate investors rid themselves of a record 12,894,650 shares on the New York Stock Exchange. They broke their record the following Tuesday, when more than 16 million shares were traded and as much as $74 billion lost. The market reached its lowest point on November 13.

Now it was impossible to deny that the United States, as was much of the world, was entering a period of economic depression. Americans had weathered panics and recessions throughout their history, but none was as long or severe as the Great Depression of the 1930s would prove to be. Nearly 5,000 banks closed in the first few years of the depression, wiping out the savings and financial security of many thousands of people. Approximately 26,000 businesses folded in 1930 alone. There were no official government measurements of unemployment in the 1920s and 1930s, but estimates of the National Research League, the American

This breadline formed at the McCauley Water Street Mission in Lower Manhattan, ca. 1930–1934. *(Library of Congress, Prints and Photographs Division, LC-USZ62-91536)*

Federation of Labor, and other organizations indicate that joblessness affected 1.6 million workers in 1929. Unemployment rose to 4.5 million, affecting almost 9 percent of the workforce, in 1930.

In 1931, 8 million people, representing 16 percent of the workforce, were unemployed; 28,000 businesses closed; 200,000 families lost their homes or farms through foreclosure; and 20,000 despairing people committed suicide. Members of the newly poor middle class tried to help themselves: Families economized on groceries, sold their cars, and postponed purchases for better times. As the lines demarking economic status blurred, men in business suits stood on street corners selling apples for five cents apiece. Many who had been made homeless and destitute huddled on the edges of cities in collections of makeshift shanties called Hoovervilles, after President Herbert Hoover.

Private charities and churches pitched in, as they had in the past: Breadlines stretched around city blocks, and volunteers dished out watery soup. In 1930 private agencies spent 50 percent more on poor relief than they did in 1929. By spring 1930 many agencies had exceeded their budget for the year and had been forced to borrow money or draw on reserve funds. States spent twice as much on public relief in 1930 as in the previous year, and in 1931 both private and public agencies spent three times their 1930 expenditures. Poorhouses, poor farms, and orphan asylums were unequipped to house the large numbers of people seeking shelter and board. The almshouse in Jefferson County, Alabama, which had been built to hold 220 inmates, housed 500 in 1932. Throughout the country, resources were being exhausted, and no one, including Hoover, knew what to do.

Echoing his advisers in government and industry, the president assured the public that the emergency was temporary, and that the economy would correct itself in time if left alone. Nevertheless, on January 22, 1932, he signed a bill

A man reads to fellow residents in a shelter for homeless men operated by the U.S. Resettlement Administration, in December 1936. *(Library of Congress, Prints and Photographs Division, LC-USF33-011130-M1)*

establishing the Reconstruction Finance Corporation (RFC), a government agency that would lend money to banks and business and in that way foster expansion and spur an upturn. The $1.5 billion allocated to the RFC was too little to bring about real change, however, and the public perceived that most loans went to powerful corporations friendly to the White House.

Inmates sit on the porch of the Parker County Poor Farm, Weatherford, Texas, on a Sunday afternoon, ca. 1930. *(Texas Historical Commission)*

With factory production cut in half, 250,000 additional foreclosures, and wages just 40 percent of what they were in 1929, 1932 was the worst year of the depression. About 14 million workers (nearly 24 percent of the workforce) were unemployed, and 40 million Americans were experiencing poverty, many for the first time. In Birmingham, Alabama, more than 12,000 out-of-work men applied for nonexistent municipal jobs, and the American Red Cross reported that between 6,000 and 8,000 city residents lacked food, housing, or fuel. Ashamed of their changed status, the newly poor hid behind curtains and closed doors. Social workers expressed alarm at the psychological depression and mental deterioration they observed. Couples fought, and families broke apart.

One-fifth of African-American factory workers had already been let go by October 1929. Generally poorer than whites before 1929, blacks were more severely

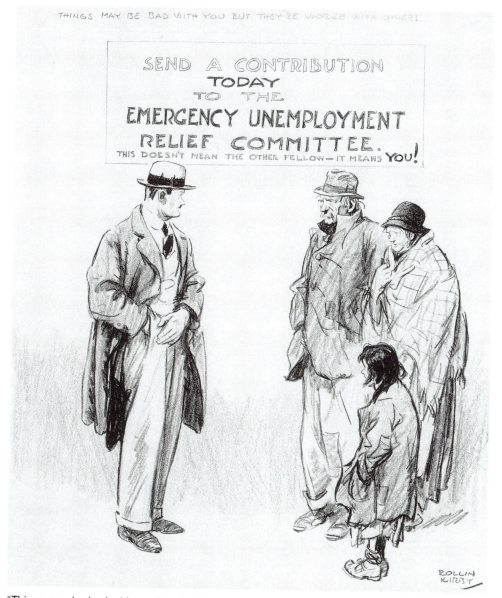

"Things may be bad with you but they're worse with others." This 1932 poster by Rollin Kirby and others like it reminded people to contribute to local charities in the absence of government relief. *(Library of Congress, Prints and Photographs Division, LC-USZ62-35858)*

affected by the economy's collapse. Throughout the depression, unemployment disproportionately affected blacks, who tended to be the first fired and who all too often saw their jobs given to whites. In 1931 the National Urban League surveyed 106 U.S. cities and found unemployment to be 30 percent to 60 percent higher among blacks than among whites. By 1935 one-fourth of domestic workers, a predominantly African-American group, were receiving some kind of relief. Their white employers had dismissed them in an effort to economize.

Many religious and charitable groups denied food and financial relief to African Americans. In some Texas towns, the people handing out emergency relief told African Americans and Mexican Americans to look elsewhere. Blacks fortunate enough to be hired to labor on work-relief projects usually earned less than the whites toiling beside them.

Hard Times on the Farm

The depression intensified hardship for most of the nation's farmers, who had been making the best of low crop and livestock prices since the 1920s. In 1930 the farm population totaled 30.5 million, and there were 6.2 million farms, averaging 157 acres. Farmers had ignored advice that they hold back on production. They continued to raise cotton, for example, although approximately 26 million surplus bales had accumulated by 1931. They saw the price of raw cotton fall from 20 cents a pound in 1928 to 6.4 cents a pound in 1932. Prices paid for most farm products had reached a point at which it was unprofitable to harvest crops and transport them to market.

A Louisiana sharecropper carries water to his home in 1939. *(Library of Congress, Prints and Photographs Division, LC-USF34-031943-D)*

Moving day in Arkansas cotton country, 1936: A sharecropping family hopes for better luck with the next landlord. *(Library of Congress, Prints and Photographs Division, LC-USF34-009753-E)*

At the start of the depression decade, close to 70 percent of cotton farmers were sharecroppers or tenant farmers, as were nearly 50 percent of tobacco growers and 40 percent of wheat and corn farmers. One-fourth of the southern population in 1930, or 8.5 million people (including 3 million African Americans), lived in sharecropping or tenant-farming families. Home for them was a rundown, unpainted cabin of two or three rooms with a roof of galvanized sheet iron, built of inferior lumber and resting on stones or concrete blocks. These tumbledown houses lacked such basics as indoor plumbing, electricity, window glass, screens to keep out mosquitoes, and safe drinking water. The people who lived in them cooked over an open hearth because they had no stove, and they possessed very little. One in five had never owned a mattress.

Tenants and sharecroppers consumed a monotonous, inadequate diet limited to salt pork, cornmeal, wheat flour, molasses, and beans. Landlords discouraged or forbade tenants from planting a vegetable patch because it would take land away from the cash crop. As the depression worsened living conditions, starving sharecroppers were known to eat feed intended for livestock. Tenants and sharecroppers dressed in shabby clothes and suffered from chronic, debilitating health problems that included malaria, typhoid, hookworm, tuberculosis, sexually transmitted diseases, and the deficiency diseases associated with malnutrition, such as rickets and pellagra. Without access to medical care, people relied on homemade poultices and medicinal teas and other folk remedies based on tradition and superstition. Rural schools for blacks and whites were substandard throughout the South, and illiteracy among sharecroppers and tenant farmers was above the national average. Their birth rate was the highest in the nation.

Average annual per capita income in the southern states in 1929 ranged from $270 in South Carolina to $521 in Florida, compared to $703 for the nation as a whole. In 1932 the average per capita income was $126 in Mississippi, $314 in Florida, and $401 nationally, yet in that year many southern tenant and sharecropping families had no income whatsoever. Among those who did earn money, the average annual income was $105.43. Because the verbal contracts under which they worked typically bound them for one year, up to one-third of tenant farmers moved in a given year in the hope of finding a "better house and better way of being treated," as one woman from a Mississippi sharecropping family put it.[1] Increasingly in the 1930s, tenants found themselves "tractored out" when landlords mechanized operations and no longer required their labor. Tenants therefore had little incentive to practice soil conservation.

Conditions were not much better for the many southern farmers who owned their land but risked slipping into tenancy because their soil had been depleted or eroded, or their farms were too small to be profitable. Poorer still than tenants and sharecroppers, though, were the day laborers who worked on southern plantations irregularly throughout the growing season. They lived in shacks on the farms where they had been hired and fed themselves on their paltry earnings. Men received between 40 cents and 60 cents a day, and women were paid between 30 cents and 50 cents a day. Southern poverty also reached from rural areas into the industrial centers. For textile workers in the mill-town slums of North and South Carolina, to be without sufficient food and clothing was a fact of everyday life, and rickets and pellagra were commonplace.

The United States was the only industrialized nation without unemployment insurance or social-security protection for its citizens, but Hoover remained opposed to direct federal aid to individuals and families. In his opinion legislation could not cure the nation's ills, and nothing the president might say or do would solve people's problems.

The Nation's Veterans Protest

Veterans of World War I were a particularly frustrated group. In 1945 they were to receive cash bonuses from the government, adjusted for length of service, but many among them were angry about waiting 13 years for money they desperately needed. In June 1932 veterans and their families began traveling to Washington, D.C., to lobby Congress for passage of a bill that would give them their bonuses immediately. They squatted in unused government buildings or camped alongside the Anacostia River in what became the nation's largest Hooverville.

The Patman Bonus Bill passed in the House of Representatives on June 15, but it was defeated in the Senate two days later. Twenty thousand veterans showed their disappointment by staging a three-day "Death March" on Pennsylvania Avenue. Many veterans then left Washington, but thousands lingered in the shacks of the

The shanties of the Anacostia Flats burn in sight of the U.S. Capitol on July 28, 1932. *(National Archives)*

Anacostia Flats until a July 28 confrontation in which police shot and killed two veterans convinced Hoover that the Bonus Army was a threat to public safety. He ordered the military to evict the marchers from the nation's capital.

Commanded by Army Chief of Staff General Douglas MacArthur, U.S. troops cleared downtown Washington of people and set fire to huts that marchers had erected alongside city streets. Although Hoover had ordered MacArthur to stay out of the Anacostia Flats, soldiers entered the settlement, forced out the remaining veterans and their families, and burned their makeshift homes to the ground. Two infants suffocated by tear gas were the only fatalities. By the next night all of the marchers had gone home, but the public remembered the violence and blamed the president.

Franklin Delano Roosevelt and the New Deal

Hoover, a Republican, lost the presidential election of 1932 to the Democratic candidate, Franklin Delano Roosevelt. On March 4, 1933, Roosevelt assumed leadership of "a stricken nation in the midst of a stricken world."[2] One-fourth of the workforce was unemployed, and those fortunate enough to be working were earning less than they had in 1929. Hourly wages had dropped 60 percent since the start of the depression, and white-collar salaries were down 40 percent.

Believing it imperative to act quickly and decisively, Roosevelt declared a bank holiday from Monday, March 6, through Thursday, March 9, to prevent fearful depositors from needlessly withdrawing funds. On March 9, Congress passed the Emergency Banking Act, which authorized the Treasury to print more money. The Roosevelt administration also drafted several pieces of legislation known collectively as the New Deal, which were intended to stabilize financial institutions and put the unemployed to work. New Deal legislation created the Federal Deposit Insurance Corporation to safeguard bank accounts and the Securities and Exchange Commission to regulate the stock market.

An early piece of New Deal legislation established the Federal Emergency Relief Administration (FERA), a welfare program that funded relief at the state level. (Alabama, for example, used FERA money to establish the state Department of Public Welfare and close its 65 poorhouses.) Roosevelt's federal relief administrator, Harry L. Hopkins, was convinced that improved purchasing power was fundamental to recovery but that the public would be more receptive to jobs programs than to cash "handouts." The tradition of discriminating between the "deserving" and "undeserving" poor persisted in the reluctance of many Americans to apply for relief or be "on the dole." Therefore, although the agency made available welfare payments to a record 28 million people in February 1934, the FERA offered work

Young men in Arizona learn to be automobile mechanics in a class sponsored by the National Youth Administration in 1936. *(Franklin D. Roosevelt Presidential Library)*

relief to between 1.4 million and 2.4 million people each month between 1933 and 1935 through the Civil Works Administration (CWA). CWA employees made needed repairs and improvements to roads, schools, playgrounds, and parks. They also worked to control insect pests and erosion.

The government gave preference in hiring to unemployed white-collar workers and white industrial working men; women accounted for about one-eighth of those employed on CWA projects. The wages paid to work-relief participants varied according to sex and race: Women, blacks, and Hispanics received less than white men. This discrimination led the economist Nancy E. Rose to conclude in 1989 that "the new 'deserving poor' appeared to be white men and white-collar workers of both genders."[3]

Ironically, recipients of government aid whose poverty was of long duration were better off on relief than they had ever been. They enjoyed an improved standard of living, a better diet, and a newfound sense of financial security. In November 1934, 30 to 60 percent of people in the mountain counties of Kentucky were receiving relief; many had never before had an adequate standard of living. Similarly, relief significantly improved life for people in the Ozark Mountains of Arkansas, who rarely handled more than 25 dollars in cash each year and subsisted on four or five foods.

Americans worried about the multitude of young men leaving school and unable to enter the working world. With no hope and believing themselves to be a drain on limited family resources, many were joining the large number of transients who hitched rides on freight trains and moved from town to town seeking handouts. A number of people, including the first lady, were concerned that the disillusioned young might be receptive to revolutionary political ideas. "I live in real terror when I think we may be losing this generation," said Eleanor Roosevelt. "We have got to bring these young people into the active life of the community and make them feel that they are necessary."[4]

The Civilian Conservation Corps (CCC), established April 5, 1933, employed males between the ages of 18 and 25 (later 17 and 28) on conservation and restoration projects. Young men were eligible for the CCC if they were unemployed and were members of families receiving relief. Most spent six to nine months with the corps and sent most of their 30-dollar monthly pay to their families. Living in military-style camps, often in wilderness areas, CCC crews built bridges and mountain roads and raised miles of telephone lines and fences. They planted trees to prevent soil erosion, fought forest fires, and restored historic sites, including Colonial Williamsburg in Virginia. Ten percent of the 2.5 million young men employed by the CCC between 1933 and 1942, the year it was disbanded, were African American. African-American representation therefore matched that of the overall population if not of the unemployed.

Young women waited two years for a federal jobs program to help them. Roosevelt established the National Youth Administration (NYA) by executive order on June 26, 1935, for three groups: women between the ages of 16 and 25, young men unable to perform hard physical labor, and students needing money to continue their education. The NYA paid six dollars a month to high-school students, 15 dollars a month to college students, and 20 dollars a month to graduate students to work part-time, usually in clerical or maintenance jobs. Full-time NYA workers who were not in school received between 10 and 20 dollars a month to help build community centers, courthouses, and schools and to lay out playgrounds and parks.

The Agricultural Adjustment Act (AAA), which Roosevelt signed into law on May 12, 1933, restricted agricultural production through subsidies. The government paid farmers not to grow staple crops or livestock or produce milk, with the goal of raising prices and encouraging diversification. In summer 1933 farmers plowed under countless acres of crops, including 10 million acres of cotton, and slaughtered millions of head of livestock. Yet the federal program proved most attractive to relatively prosperous farmers, who had large crops and surplus hogs, and it failed to improve prices significantly.

The National Industrial Recovery Act (NRA), signed into law on June 16, 1933, set a voluntary minimum wage and maximum working hours for 500 industries. It was the first federal legislation to guarantee workers' right to union membership and collective bargaining, and it established a minimal age of 16 for most industries and 18 for mining and logging, resulting in the loss of 150,000 youthful workers in the mining and logging industries.

The Public Works Administration (PWA), founded to stimulate the construction industry, was another provision of the NRA. With a budget of $6 billion, it employed 500,000 people a year on public-works projects. Most notably PWA workers built dams, including Boulder Dam (now Hoover Dam) on the Colorado River and the Bonneville Dam on the Columbia River, and New York City's Triborough Bridge and Lincoln Tunnel. The PWA built highways and airports throughout the country as well as military ships and aircraft. It directly aided the poor through slum-clearance projects and the construction of 25,000 public-housing units.

A New Deal for American Indians

Some New Deal legislation was intended to benefit Native Americans. Because the Meriam Survey had identified changes needed in the way the government administered its programs for Indians, in 1933 Roosevelt appointed as commissioner of Indian affairs John Collier, a social worker with 25 years of experience who had worked among the Pueblo Indians in New Mexico. Collier proposed a new government policy that involved ending land allotments, placing most tribal land under federal supervision, and permitting Indians to manage their own affairs through tribal governments.

Under the Allotment system established in 1887, Indians had fallen prey to embezzlers, forgers, and dishonest lawyers and judges, with the result that their holdings had dwindled to about 49 million acres by 1933. Also, not only had government efforts to assimilate the Native population failed, but federal agricultural policy had impoverished many Indians. Collier's aim was to help the Indians retain communally, rather than individually, the land they still held and become self-supporting in ways that were in keeping with their culture and values. "Under such a policy, the ideal end result will be the ultimate disappearance of any need for government aid or supervision," Collier said.[5] His recommendations became provisions of the 1934 Indian Reorganization Act.

One impediment to agricultural and economic progress on reservations was overgrazing of rangeland. In 1933 the Papago (now known as Tohono O'odham) of Arizona, for example, grazed 60,000 horses and cattle on land capable of supporting 12,000 head of cattle. Acreage denuded by livestock was subject to erosion, and animals raised under these adverse conditions were substandard. Although in the long run Indians stood to gain economically from livestock reduction, many measured social standing in animals, and giving up sheep, cattle, horses, or goats, even those that were diseased, old, or malnourished, would mean a loss of status. Several Indian nations, especially the Navajo (Dineh), thought that expanding the reservations was a better solution. (In fact, between 1934 and 1940 the federal government added 7 million acres to Indian holdings through purchases and the termination of leases. Some members of Congress from western states opposed enlarging reservations, however.)

Under the Indian Reorganization Act the government successfully reduced the number and improved the health of animals grazing on tribal land. The plan called for reductions across the board; as a result, Indians who owned large herds, who were able to cull inferior animals, weathered the change in policy with minimal discomfort while some with small herds sacrificed healthy, productive animals and suffered hardship as a consequence.

A program known officially as Indian Energy Conservation Work and popularly as the Indian CCC hired Native American men to conserve soil and restore rangeland on reservations. The Indian CCC was most active in Arizona, Montana, New Mexico, Oklahoma, South Dakota, and Washington State, where poverty and need seemed greatest. The men in its employ seeded wind-eroded range with grasses, put up fences to permit the rotation of grazing land, exterminated rodents that competed with livestock for forage, and channeled drinking water for the stock.

The Johnson-O'Malley Act of 1934 allocated federal funds to states and territories for educational, medical, and social services for Indians living off reservations. Schools for Indian children constructed with federal funds were located near enough for children to attend while living at home.

Indian Civilian Conservation Corps (CCC) workers lay the foundation for a garage at the Carson Agency of the U.S. Bureau of Indian Affairs in Nevada, 1937. *(National Archives, Pacific Region)*

Drought and Dust

A severe drought compounded economic misery for millions of people on the Plains, where careless farming and overgrazing had left the topsoil vulnerable to erosion. Some areas had no measurable rainfall in 1934 and again in 1936. As crops withered and animals starved, winds picked up the dry, dusty soil and lifted it high into the air, forming enormous dark clouds that looked like "rolling black smoke,"[6] according to one Texas observer. After traveling on air currents, sometimes for hundreds of miles, the dirt rained down, burying small farms in the Texas panhandle and elsewhere. Massive dust storms halted daily life in places like Clayton, New Mexico, where on May 21, 1937, visibility was reduced to zero for a full 30 minutes. Fine silt worked its way into the most tightly sealed rooms during this memorable storm, and even dust masks could not protect some people from suffocation.

Thousands of drought-stricken families toughed it out, but thousands of others abandoned the land. According to the Department of Agriculture, nearly 20 percent of farmers in the Midwest and central and southern Plains lost their farms to foreclosure between 1930 and 1935. With no work to be had in the towns and states where they lived, many joined the army of dispossessed tenants and sharecroppers who had taken to the highways, convinced that life must be better someplace else. The majority wandered into a neighboring state, but hundreds of thousands packed what little they owned into old, rusted automobiles and trucks and headed for the West Coast. Some 2.5 million people left the Plains states during the 1930s. More than 440,000 fled Oklahoma, and 227,000 moved out of Kansas.

Children fill their can from the only water supply in a camp for migrant cotton pickers in the San Joaquin Valley of California, November 1936. *(Library of Congress, Prints and Photographs Division, LC-USF34-016002-E)*

About 460,000 were absorbed into the Pacific Northwest, where men found work on government projects, including the Bonneville and Grand Coulee Dams. Other men learned to be lumberjacks, and whole families became transient agricultural workers and harvested hops and sugar beets.

The fertile soil and sunshine of California drew 306,000, most from the southwestern Plains region of Oklahoma, east Texas, Arkansas, Colorado, and New Mexico—the "dust bowl." Some of these migrants relied on the generosity of relatives in Los Angeles and other cities, but more than 100,000 joined the state's already large population of wandering farm labor. Work, if they were lucky enough to find it, was seasonal, and wages were far too low to feed and shelter a family. Desperate and distrustful of unions, some became strikebreakers, or "scabs," replacing striking agricultural workers in the fields of Salinas and other towns.

Broke and homeless dust bowl refugees camped in "Little Oklahomas," the Hooverville-style assemblages of thrown-together shelters that grew up outside Bakersville, Fresno, and other agricultural centers. Many native Californians resented the presence of "Okies" and "Arkies," who they feared might spread the flaws they still associated with poverty, namely alcoholism, laziness, and disease. They resorted to threats, harassment, and name-calling, but the squatters sent their children to local schools and, if they were eligible, collected state relief. Yet there remained many wretched, displaced people without money for food who slept beside roads and drank from irrigation ditches, whose children were sick, starving, and even dying.

The federal government tried to remedy the migrant-labor surplus in California by deporting Mexicans unable to show proof of legal residency. More than 415,000 Mexicans were deported between 1929 and 1935, and thousands more elected to return to Mexico.

A Second New Deal

Under Roosevelt the federal government had taken unprecedented steps into the realm of public welfare. Many Americans believed it had overstepped and legislated on matters that according to the Constitution were the responsibility of the individual states. A majority of the justices on the Supreme Court agreed. In 1935 and 1936 the Supreme Court struck down nine significant pieces of New Deal legislation, including the NRA and AAA. Immediately, any economic and social gains that had resulted from these programs began to be reversed. For example, the number of working children rose 150 percent in the year after the May 27, 1935, court decision on the NRA.

Roosevelt responded to the Supreme Court's rejection of his legislative program with a failed attempt to appoint to the court additional justices who were liberal in their thinking and supportive of his goals. Starting in 1935, he also responded with more laws. Although the legislation of the "second New Deal" was as radical and controversial as that of the first, it was less likely to be declared unconstitutional because in his second term Roosevelt appointed five justices to the Supreme Court after the retirement of four sitting justices and the death of a fifth.

The second New Deal most significantly included the Social Security Act of August 14, 1935, which gave direct federal financial aid to citizens. The Social Security Act established a retirement pension financed through mandatory contributions from workers and employers, and unemployment insurance funded through federal and state taxes. It authorized direct payment of government funds to men and women of retirement age who were ineligible for Social Security pensions, the blind and physically disabled, and dependent mothers and children.

The Works Progress Administration (later Work Projects Administration; the WPA) which came into existence on May 6, 1935, gave work to millions of people. The WPA built approximately 100,000 bridges and viaducts and more than 100,000 public buildings, including schools, libraries, post offices, and hospitals. Its efforts resulted in sewage systems and 500,000 miles of roads. The WPA also gave work to thousands of artists, writers, and musicians who were struggling through the depression as everyone else was. Artists on the WPA payroll painted posters and post-office murals, photographed historic buildings, and taught community art classes. Writers compiled oral histories, wrote guidebooks to the 48 states, and organized historical records. Musicians performed for the public in the bands, choral groups, chamber ensembles, and 155 orchestras founded by the WPA. Some musicians on the WPA payroll gave lessons, and others researched folk music.

The Fair Labor Standards Act (FLSA) of 1938 aimed to raise low wages without contributing significantly to unemployment. By setting a minimum wage of 25 cents an hour that would rise to 40 cents an hour seven years later, it reduced the wage discrepancy that existed between the South and the North. The FLSA outlawed most remaining forms of child labor primarily to get children out of the job market and open up positions for adults. The National Labor Relations Act of July 5, 1935, known as the Wagner Act because it was sponsored by Senator Robert F. Wagner of New York, once again gave workers the right to form unions and bargain collectively with management. It prohibited employers from firing anyone because of union activity, and it barred them from engaging in such unfair labor practices as requiring employees to join company-controlled unions. The act also established the National Labor Relations Board to enforce its provisions.

Many of the poorest farmers and farm workers, a group excluded from coverage under the Wagner Act, benefited from programs offered by the Farm Security Administration (FSA), a federal agency established in 1935. The FSA took 10 million inferior acres out of production and resettled the people who had farmed them on more fertile plots. It also made loans to tenants, to enable them to buy farms, and to struggling farmers, to help them keep theirs. In 1935 the FSA began to build migrant camps, first on the West Coast and later on the East Coast, to house the transient agricultural labor force. These were places such as the Arvin Federal Government Camp, located outside Bakersfield, California, which was made famous by John Steinbeck's classic depression novel *The Grapes of Wrath*. By 1936, 26 stationary camps were either operating or under construction, and there were a number of temporary mobile camps that moved their tents and trailers along with the workforce. The first camps on the East Coast were a pair of segregated camps at Belle Glade, Florida, that opened in spring 1940.

A family could call a government camp home in exchange for weekly rent of a dollar or two hours of maintenance work. For this they received shelter, food, and medical care as well as lessons in how to escape poverty by altering their behavior. As had 19th-century reformers, camp staff instructed residents in thrift, child care, health, and hygiene. Stationary camps offered cabins and tents for housing; an assembly building for meetings, church services, and entertainment; a clinic; a school; a nursery; and laundry facilities. Although some migrants remained wary of the government camps and chose to live elsewhere, many welcomed the chance to join a community and save a little money.

A Changed Policy

The Great Depression altered forever the way Americans cared for economically dependent members of society. Now that people had seen family members, neighbors, and friends thrown into a state of need, it was difficult to attribute poverty to character flaws—although prejudice against the poor would never disappear. Social Security, along with other forms of public welfare, enabled many of the poor to remain at home and out of institutions. Those almshouses that survived the strain of the depression housed a declining population of aged men and women.

New Deal programs helped millions of Americans and boosted morale, but ultimately they failed to lift the nation out of the depression. At the end of 1938 between 10 million and 11 million American workers were unemployed; in 1940, 8 million people, or nearly 15 percent of the labor force, remained jobless. It would take the gearing up of the defense industries in preparation for World War II to put the nation back to work. The New Deal also failed to boost agricultural prices significantly; it would take World War II to do that as well. Although many New Deal initiatives outlived their usefulness and were terminated, some continue to function, including the Federal Deposit Insurance Corporation, Security and Exchange Commission, National Labor Relations Board, and Social Security Administration. Thus the federal government took on, and retained, a significant role in economic and public welfare. As Franklin Delano Roosevelt told Congress in 1938, "Government has a final responsibility for the well-being of its citizenship."[7]

Chronicle of Events

1929
- Unemployment reaches 1.6 million.
- Average annual per capita income is $703 nationwide, $521 in Florida, and $270 in South Carolina.
- *spring:* Public and private relief expenditures remain at high winter levels in 120 cities.
- *October:* One-fifth of African-American factory workers have been fired.
- *October 23:* Investors lose an estimated $5 billion in the stock market.
- *October 24:* Stock prices continue to fall as investors sell 12,894,650 shares on the New York Stock Exchange.
- *October 29:* More than 16 million shares of stock are traded and $74 billion lost.
- *November 13:* The stock market reaches its lowest point.

1929–1935
- The federal government deports more than 415,000 Mexicans.

1930
- Approximately 26,000 businesses close.
- Unemployment affects 4.5 million people, or nearly 9 percent of the workforce.
- Relief expenditures for private agencies are up 50 percent from the year before; those for public agencies have doubled.
- Some 30.5 million people live on 6.2 million farms.
- One-fourth of southerners (8.5 million people) live in tenant-farming or sharecropping households. This total includes 3 million African Americans.

1930–1935
- Almost 20 percent of farmers in the Midwest and central and southern Plains lose their farms to foreclosure.

1930–1939
- About 2.5 million people leave the Plains states; more than 440,000 move from Oklahoma; 227,000 leave Kansas.
- Some 306,000 southwesterners go to California.

1931
- Eight million people, or 16 percent of workers, are unemployed.
- Unemployment is 30 to 60 percent higher for blacks than whites in 106 cities surveyed by the National Urban League.
- Public and private relief agencies spend three times as much as they did in 1930.
- The cotton surplus totals 26 million bales.

1932
- There are 250,000 foreclosures.
- Wages are 40 percent of what they were in 1929.
- Fourteen million Americans are unemployed, and 40 million are living in poverty.
- The Jefferson County, Alabama, almshouse, built to shelter 220 people, houses 500.
- Cotton, which sold for 20 cents a pound in 1928, now sells at 6.4 cents a pound.
- Average annual per capita income is $401 nationally, $314 in Florida, and $126 in Mississippi.
- *June 17:* The U.S. Senate defeats the Patman Bonus Bill, which would have paid an immediate cash bonus to veterans of World War I; veterans begin a three-day protest march in Washington, D.C.
- *July 28:* Two World War I veterans die in a confrontation with police in the national capital; acting on orders from President Herbert Hoover, the army routs the "Bonus Army" protesters from the city.

1933
- *March 4:* Franklin Delano Roosevelt is sworn in as president of the United States.
- *March 6–9:* An executive order temporarily closes the nation's banks.
- *March 9:* Congress passes the Emergency Banking Act, authorizing the Treasury to print more money.
- *April 5:* Congress establishes the Civilian Conservation Corps (CCC) to employ young men in families who are receiving relief.
- *May 12:* Roosevelt signs into law the Agricultural Adjustment Act to restrict agricultural production and raise prices through subsidies.
- *June 16:* The National Industrial Recovery Act sets voluntary minimum wages and maximum working hours for 500 industries, guarantees workers' right to unionization and collective bargaining, and establishes a minimal age of 16 for working in most industries and 18 for mining.
- *summer:* Farmers plow under millions of acres of crops and slaughter millions of hogs and other livestock.

1933–1935

• The Federal Emergency Relief Administration (FERA) employs 1.4 million to 2.4 million people each month through the Civil Works Administration.

1933–1942

• The CCC employs 2.5 million young men, of whom 10 percent are African American.

1934

• The Indian Reorganization Act ends land allotments on reservations, places Indian lands under federal supervision, permits the establishment of tribal governments, and reduces the size of Indians' herds.

• The Johnson-O'Malley Act makes federal funds available for services to Native Americans living off reservations.

• Some sections of the Great Plains have no measurable rainfall.

• *February:* The FERA funds relief to a record 28 million people.

• *November:* Thirty percent to 60 percent of people in the mountain counties of Kentucky are on relief.

1934–1940

• The federal government adds 7 million acres to Indian reservations.

Federal Emergency Relief Administration workers construct a terrace and retaining wall at the John B. Allen School, Seattle. *(University of Washington Libraries, Special Collections, UW20777z)*

African-American and Mexican migrant cotton pickers break for lunch in Robstown, Texas, in 1936. *(Library of Congress, Prints and Photographs Division, LC-USF34-009819-E)*

1935

- One-fourth of domestic workers receive public or private relief.
- The Farm Security Administration takes 10 million acres of substandard farmland out of production, makes loans to farmers, and begins building camps for migrant farm laborers.
- *May 6:* The Works Projects Administration is established to create public-works jobs.

- *June 26:* Roosevelt issues an executive order creating the National Youth Administration to employ young women, young men unable to perform hard physical labor, and students.
- *July 5:* The National Labor Relations Act restores workers' right to participate in unions and establishes the National Labor Relations Board.
- *August 14:* The Social Security Act becomes law, providing retirement pensions, unemployment insurance, and aid to the elderly, the disabled, and dependent mothers and children.

1935–1936

- The Supreme Court finds nine pieces of New Deal legislation unconstitutional.

1936

- Again some sections of the Great Plains have no measurable rainfall.
- Twenty-six stationary camps for migrant laborers are operating or under construction.

1937

- *May 21:* A severe dust storm strikes Clayton, New Mexico, and claims several lives.

1938

- The Fair Labor Standards Act sets a minimum wage and outlaws most forms of child labor.
- Between 10 million and 11 million workers are unemployed.

1940

- The first East Coast migrant-labor camps open at Belle Glade, Florida.
- About 8 million people (nearly 15 percent of the workforce) remain unemployed.

Eyewitness Testimony

I visited the Department of Public Welfare in the City Hall. Huddled in corridors of the new annex of the public mansion, the destitute of Philadelphia, who for the winter months were flooding its doors, waited their turn at the application desk. The charity organizations of the town, borne down by the weight of older social ills, could not handle the load of unemployment. Hence those who have lost their jobs and can find no others, turn up at the City Hall. Dozens of men and women came in during the morning I was there, but I heard the stories of only two. A strong young Italian day laborer said he had walked the streets for two months looking for work, that his baby was dying of mastoiditis, was too sick to be removed to the city hospital, and that very day the milk company had stopped delivering milk. A colored widow, sole support of her five children, came in half dazed with destitution. She had been evicted a week before. A neighbor had taken them in when they were no longer on the street, but she could shelter them no longer. The mother said she had not eaten for two days, although her children had been fed until that morning. Her name was put on file, and she was referred to a bureau that would help her get her marriage license for a mother's pension. I was alarmed at such a delay as seemed implied, but I was soothed. "Maybe she isn't even married," said the civil officer, comfortingly. "Maybe she won't get any pension at all. Of course she has eaten. If you believed all they told you you would go crazy. There isn't anyone here who hasn't eaten. Sure they all eat."

Clinch Calkins, pseudonym of Marion Merrell, writer and settlement-house worker, 1930, Some Folks Won't Work, *pp. 9–10.*

The criticism leveled at the idle because "they do not try" arises from ignorance of what the idle are up against. Bread-lines at the missions, overcrowded police-stations and city barges where the homeless are allowed to sleep, have strengthened in the critic the conviction that man was born into such a distaste for working that he prefers anything, even this, to a job. But the lines of men standing all night in the frozen fields outside automobile factories, the treadmill herds that mill in front of the employment offices, postured in the slumped curves of discouragement, shuffling their feet before the chalked boards where occasionally appear the miraculous words Help Wanted—these should enable the accuser to withdraw his accusation.

Clinch Calkins, pseudonym of Marion Merrell, writer and settlement-house worker, 1930, Some Folks Won't Work, *p. 73.*

The game of makeshifts is very much like chess. The better the defensive, the slower the game.

The chronology of moves may differ from tale to tale, but all of the moves are there. The family seeks smaller quarters. The mother goes to work. She works in a mill. She goes out to do domestic service by the day. She scrubs offices at night. She comes home and washes, cooks, and sews for her children. She takes in boarders. Small articles go to the pawnshop. The furniture is taken away in a van. The insurance is forfeited. The house is lost. If the children are old enough, they are taken out of school and put to work. If not, they stay out of school for lack of clothes, and wearing cotton dresses with no underwear. They play on draughty floors of unheated rooms. At dark the whole family goes to bed for lack of any sort of lamplight. They go without milk. They go without meat. Finally they go without food.

Which reduction they make first depends on the climate, on their social standard, and on their financial history. Ordinarily they make first the sacrifice of personal possessions in preference to imperiling the security for

An impoverished woman in North Carolina was photographed by Doris Ulmann in 1930. *(Library of Congress, Prints and Photographs Division, LC-USZ62-26633)*

coming years embodied in life insurance and real estate. Cash savings dissolve. Wedding rings and watches go. The parlor set returns to the store, which is demanding payments. If their housing standard has been carefully arrived at, the family spars for a time, willing to make first every other concession to society rather than to lose the painfully established place among their fellows which is indicated by their residence.

Clinch Calkins, pseudonym of Marion Merrell, writer and settlement-house worker, 1930, Some Folks Won't Work, *pp. 97–98.*

The thing used to be simple. You sowed cotton in rows, chopped it out later, bestowed reasonable attention on it for ninety days from planting, and then you sat down until it was ready for the pickers. The pests of Nature hadn't come. But during the past seven years (in this section), Mr. Boll Weevil has added his unpleasant note and just about turned things upside down. He can and will put a whole crop to the bad in almost the twinkling of an eye. There seems to be no real sure-fire antidote for him. He doesn't always come, but like the stork, nobody quite knows when he will show up. About the sweetest anthem the cotton farmers could hear over their radios would be the swan song of Mr. Boll Weevil. At the present he is singing in good strong tones, "I'm King for a Day" and fishing for an encore. Yet I heard it said that the coming of the boll weevil (from Mexico) has been a blessing in a way. Without him there would have been a staggering overproduction of cotton and a tumbling market. That is all rather confusing, one of those economic puzzles that sounds well but doesn't make consumers rich, or farmers either. As for the farmer who is hoping for two bales to an acre and gets only one half a bale, there is only one answer. He is operating at a loss and chaos looms up at the end of the season. And here is one reason why so many of the farming class have let go of the plow handles and rushed to the loom and spindles. Let George do it! There are better things at the end of the rusty, muddy road in the country. The cotton mills. There is, he feels, a job there, a house better than he has ever lived in, with rent next to nothing, electric lights, schools, movies, athletic buildings, and, last but not least, churches. He doesn't hesitate long. Into a wagon go family, furniture, dog, and what have you—and away he goes to try his luck in the mill.

Harry Shumway, writer and social researcher, 1930, I Go South: An Unprejudiced Visit to a Group of Cotton Mills, *pp. 20–21.*

—We squeeze each ounce of worth out of a carcass or a tree; we draw each stir of power from a ton of coal; but we fail to devise plans by which such desirable efficiencies and skills, such tangible bundles of productive energy as unemployed men and women have to offer, can be marketed without losses such as no business could stand without going bankrupt.

—We dovetail the wage-earner into a vast mechanism of production, beginning with his foreman and the bench at which he works, and ranging through huge contrivances of machines, power plants, shipping offices, banking and commercial ramifications. But as an unemployed man, we leave him with his bare hands and shoe-leather.

—We count it corporate forethought when a great industry lays by reserves in good times in order to stabilize the dividends it wishes to pay its stockholders in bad times; but only a handful of establishments have tried out employment reserves to stabilize the incomes of their employees.

—We insure every risk from a plate-glass window to the education of our grandchildren, but balk at the idea when it comes to any share of the unwritten payroll of the unemployed.

—We have instalment buying, and all manner of new credit schemes by which, as consumers, wage-earning householders may mortgage their incomes for months ahead, but nothing commensurate to give them any security in that income.

Paul U. Kellogg, editor of The Survey, *1931, "Introduction," in Unemployment Committee of the National Federation of Settlements,* Case Studies of Unemployment, *p. xv.*

We like to feel that no neighbor knocks in vain at the settlement door, but when Mrs. McNary comes saying, "Could you find me office work? My husband's been laid off three months now," we feel almost as helpless as Mrs. McNary. To her kind, office work means scrubbing floors at night, but there are so many of her kind. These knockings reach a crescendo in years of business depression such as this winter and last; none the less, the winter before last and the winter before that, years of apparent prosperity, they were insistent—and the responses we have made to them all along have raised questions in our minds that are still unanswered. We know that the milk we may be able to supply for the babies, and the loans we make now and again, are pitiful makeshifts when what the breadwinner of the family needs is a job. In our neighborhood speech, when a family gets behind in rent, the constable is "put on them." We try to hold him off while we call up employers, only to be met with the reply, "We're turning people off, not taking them on." We try private employment agencies, the public ones failing to help, generally to be told that a deposit must be made first and that there is such a long waiting list there's very little hope, anyway. I have in mind a household of fourteen, where at one time four grown men were out of work and the only ones to bring anything in were the mother, who scrubbed offices, and one young boy, who ran errands.

Helen Hall, committee chair, 1931, Unemployment Committee of the National Federation of Settlements, Case Studies of Unemployment, *pp. xxvi–xxvii.*

And as the assault on everyday living presses more and more inexorably, the families dig themselves in deeper. As Mrs. Cardani in New York put it to Mrs. Nelson, "You know what we do? If we pay the rent and there isn't enough left, you know what we do. If we're going to live honest, you know what we do." "We eat little—that's what we do," broke in her little girl, thinking her mother had not made herself clear. The Tiorsis of Boston "pulled in their belts." The Giaimos of Madison fed their children all the time on potatoes and bread, with beans for meat. The Monterey children in New Orleans picked up scraps of meat and vegetables cast aside in the market. One winter the Bertleys of Atlanta with their four children managed on less than $5 a week for groceries. This meant that the family ate only two meals a day consisting of corn bread, salt meat and dried beans. When Mrs. Bertley had several fainting spells, they finally got her to a doctor who said that she was not getting enough to eat.

Helen Hall, committee chair, 1931, Unemployment Committee of the National Federation of Settlements, Case Studies of Unemployment, *p. xlvii.*

The children cannot pass through all this untouched. The psychologist and psychiatrist help us to understand what a background of strain and bad feeling can do to the growing child. Like adults, children react differently to family tension. In some the spirit is not strong enough to throw it off, but most children unconsciously elude as best they can the pressure of trouble in their home. I have in mind a little friend of ours called Aggie, who took her small person out of her home as soon as she waked in the morning and was often picked up from neighboring doorsteps at night. She spent every possible moment in the settlement, and when in the evenings there were no activities for very little girls, she would find some reason to go to the dispen-

Children of migrant farmworkers pose for this 1935 photograph. *(Library of Congress, Prints and Photographs Division, LC-USZ62-85034)*

sary. It was warm and light and friendly, and she would sit waiting her turn. Once when told that the dentist couldn't see her, she was not to be put aside. "All right," she said, "I'll stay and see the doctor for me warts."

Helen Hall, committee chair, 1931, Unemployment Committee of the National Federation of Settlements, Case Studies of Unemployment, *p. xxxiv.*

In the summer of 1930 I was making a study of economic conditions in Europe. In early September, I was returning home. As we were passing through South Bend on a fast express train from New York to Chicago, the train came to a violent stop—jerked sickeningly, and stopped again. We soon got the story. An eyewitness related that a few minutes before the train arrived a young and slender girl had been walking up and down the track, apparently waiting for the train. When it approached, she flung herself in front of the engine and was killed instantly.

The coroner's investigation revealed that the satchel the girl carried was almost empty. In her purse was not even one cent piece.

The passengers were saddened for the rest of the journey. But this was not entirely due to the suicide of this girl. To those of us who were familiar with economic conditions, her death brought home the unwelcome truth that although America at that time had more money, more food, and more clothing than ever before, yet at the same time hundreds of thousands, perhaps millions, of our citizens were without money. Unemployed, undernourished, and so discouraged and despondent that some of them preferred death to life under such conditions. To make the situation worse it was realized these unemployed citizens were honest, self-respecting people who really wanted work.

In addition, to those of us who, like myself, had just come fresh from an observation of conditions as they existed in Europe, the tragedy was yet more significant. It seemed to me the suicide of this girl was symbolic not only of the world-wide depression at that time existing, but it was a protest, a mute yet powerful appeal for the abolition of poverty in America.

Harrison E. Fryberger, 1931, The Abolition of Poverty, *pp. 1–2.*

The evidence of our ability to solve great problems outside of government action and the degree of moral strength with which we emerge from this period will be determined by whether the individuals and the local communities continue to meet their responsibilities.

Throughout this depression I have insisted upon organization of these forces through industry, through local government and through charity, that they should meet this crisis by their own initiative, by the assumption of their own responsibilities. The Federal Government has sought to do its part by example in the expansion of employment, by affording credit to drought sufferers for rehabilitation, and by cooperation with the community, and thus to avoid the opiates of government charity and the stifling of our national spirit of self-help.

President Herbert Hoover, February 11, 1931, in Josephine Chapin Brown, Public Relief, 1929–1939, *p. 73.*

The family of John Mooney, 321 S. Sycamore St., was quarantined for scarlet fever four weeks and they were furnished with $9.65 worth of groceries, and when released the Welfare Board gave them one five-cent loaf of bread, small sack of stale cookies, (donated by bakery), one pound of sugar, half pound of lard, two pounds of beans, half pound of pork, one bar of soap, and they were notified not to come back before Saturday. Today Mr. Mooney applied again and was given one loaf of bread and a half pound of lard, this with what they got last Wednesday is supposed to last them a week. I believe this is a sample of the relief that is being given to several hundred families.

The County Commissioners are distressed as their poor fund is $11,000 overdrawn and the Welfare Board is out of funds.

Ottawa, Kansas, Chamber of Commerce, October 15, 1932, in Harry L. Hopkins, Spending to Save: The Complete Story of Relief, *p. 94.*

I am tired of reading unemployment reports which repeat over and over again the terrible situation in this and that place, about miners in various counties who will probably never earn a living again. Here is the chance of a lifetime to do something about some of these things if we have any brains at all. I am for experimenting with [federal emergency relief funds] in various parts of the country, trying out schemes which are supported by reasonable people and see if they work. If they do not work, the world will not come to an end. . . .

We have these great armies of government . . . all marching hand in hand under the direction of the President. Anybody tied up in Washington is part and parcel of the administration. In a united attack under the President's direction we are doing the work. I believe firmly that we are going to win. That is why I am not too worried about relief. Surely we cannot go on having four million families being handed grocery orders and tickets for clothing. Three hundred people in a city in the United States worked full time and averaged $3.50 per week during the last week in May, and every one of them received relief. The Federal Relief Administration does not intend to subsidize miserably low wages. We do not intend to permit anybody to use relief funds to reduce the standard of living lower than it is now. We are not going to allow relief agencies to starve people slowly to death with our money.

I think we are in a winning fight. We want to do a good job. Our job is to see that the unemployed get relief, not to develop a great social-work organization throughout the United States. Our business is to see that the people who need relief get it, and we intend to do it.

Harry L. Hopkins, head of the Federal Emergency Relief Administration, 1933, in Josephine Chapin Brown, Public Relief, 1929–1939, *pp. 152–53.*

We are now dealing with people of all classes. It is no longer a matter of unemployables and chronic dependents, but of your friends and mine who are involved in this. Every one of us knows some family of our friends which is or should be getting relief. The whole picture comes closer home than ever before. It seems to me that the intent of [the Federal Emergency Relief Act] is that relief should be given to the heads of families who are out of work and whose dependency arises from the fact that they are out of work; single men and women who are out of work, and to transient families, as well as the transient men and women roaming about the country. Those are the persons for whom relief is intended.

Harry L. Hopkins, head of the Federal Emergency Relief Administration, 1933, in Josephine Chapin Brown, Public Relief, 1929–1939, *pp. 153–54.*

One question of immediate interest concerns the place of made-work in a relief program. Although used in Philadelphia on a large scale in the winter of 1930–31, made-work was not repeated the next winter. The chief reason was the expensiveness of made-work as compared to direct relief. The average cost of made-work was $11.57 per week as compared with $5.01 for relief. The latter is given to the family on the basis of absolute minimum needs and is therefore adjusted to the lowest possible level, while made-work is paid on a wage basis which, although indirectly related to need, is not regularly and meticulously adjusted to it.

On behalf of made-work it can be urged that, although it is more expensive, it is much more satisfactory in that it preserves the self-respect of families in a way that direct relief does not. If well managed, it can be administered in such a way that the worker will regard it as a real job rather than as charitable relief. . . .

Many of these workers did not distinguish between made-work and a regular job. Some of them would have refused straight relief. The advantage of preserving the self-respect of the worker may in the long run more than counterbalance the extra expense involved in made-work.

Ewan Clague, director of research for the Community Council of Philadelphia, 1933, Ten Thousand out of Work, *pp. 88–89.*

[Y]ou will be interested to know that the whole [Indian CCC] camp idea is spreading. It is coming from all sides. The Indians are asking for it. I attended a protest meeting at Tuba City [Arizona] in which some twenty-five Indians wanted to know why they could not have a camp like the others on that reservation. The idea is firmly established with the superintendents that the camp suggestion is valuable. As a climax, I find that it is very strongly recommended by the medical examiners. There is a great deal of malnutrition with tendencies toward scurvy and

rickets. In fact, some men have collapsed on the work and have had to be removed to the hospital, with absolutely nothing the matter with them but poorly selected foods. I have just gotten out a bulletin to the superintendents on this matter, urging the placing of brown rice, whole wheat flour, tomatoes and dried fruit in the menu. We are planning, because of this situation, to establish eight or ten more camps on Southern Navajo [Reservation} at once.

Jay B. Nash, director, Indian Emergency Conservation Work, 1933, "Camps Fight Malnutrition," p. 6.

There are vast grazing lands belonging to the tribes, on which the dominant situation of erosion has become acute and is rapidly getting worse. Erosion is one of the major menaces to the country as a whole. To get the erosion situation in hand, Indians must not merely apply engineering devices. They must diversify their agriculture; they must diversify their industries; they must voluntarily control their own ranges; they must, to some extent, reorganize their individual and tribal existences. . . .

The country, in recent years, was brought to the verge of wreckage by planless individualism. The Indians, for more than a generation, have been suffering under a policy and a set of laws (particularly but not solely the allotment system) designed to force them into an individualism which has proved to be planless.

Planned community living and community development, planned cooperative use of the land and its resources, are for the Indian more absolutely needed than for most of the white populations of the country.

Indian success, in meeting the distress and the genuine crises of Indian life, unquestionably will blaze the way on many tracks for that vaster experiment and readjustment, now being started, which is intended to bring about a rebirth of the American people—a rebirth in spirit, even more than the rebirth of a more fairly distributed prosperity.

The Indians and their lands can become laboratories and pioneers (not the only laboratories and pioneers) in this supreme new American adventure now being tried under the leadership of the President.

John Collier, commissioner of Indian Affairs, September 15, 1933, "At the Close of Ten Weeks," pp. 2–3.

The Emergency Conservation Work now being done on the Eastern Cherokee Reservation is a greater benefit than anything that has been attempted here before.

Our Reservation, being situated in the heart of the Smoky Mountains, is naturally very rough. Our farms are small and a great deal of the livelihood of our people is derived from our mountain forests.

Our mountains are very beautiful and the Emergency Conservation appropriation made it possible to protect our forests from fire, which is the most destructive thing with which we must contend. The roads and trails which are being built will make it possible to transport men to a fire very quickly and it also makes some of the highest mountains accessible by automobile.

Due to the depression, our Indians have suffered some the last two years. As I have said before, our farms are small, though very productive, and with lots of work they provide us with enough to eat. But there are some things which we have to have that we cannot grow. And the Emergency Conservation Work has made it possible for our people to obtain these things.

Jarrett Blythe, chief of the Eastern Band of Cherokees, September 15, 1933 in "Tribal Leaders Voice Their Opinion," p. 28.

You think of a farmer with 640 acres of land as being rich. These fellows are "land poor." A 640-acre farm at $10 an acre—which is about what land is worth hereabouts these days—means only $6,400 worth of land. Most of them have a lot of stock, 30 or 40 head of cattle, 12 or 16 horses, some sheep and hogs. Their stock, thin and rangy, is trying to find a few mouthsful of food on land so bare that the winds pick up the top soil and blow it about like sand. Their cows have gone dry for lack of food. Their hens are not laying. Much of their livestock will die this winter. And their livestock and their land are in most cases mortgaged up to the very limit. They are all away behind on their taxes, of course. Some of them five years!

Lorena Hickok reporting on conditions in Dickinson, North Dakota, October 30, 1933, in Richard Lowitt and Maurine Beasley, eds., One Third of a Nation, p. 56.

Yesterday I visited one of the "better-off" families on relief. In what was once a house I found two small boys, about two and four years old, running about without a stitch on save some ragged overalls. No stockings or shoes. Their feet were purple with cold.

You could see light under the door in that house. The kitchen floor was so patched up—with pieces of tin, can covers, a wash boiler cover, old automobile license plates—that you couldn't tell what it might have looked like originally. Plaster falling off the walls. Newspapers stuffed in the cracks around the windows.

The mother of those children—bare-legged, although she wore some sneakers on her feet—is going to have another baby in January. IN THE HOUSE. When she diffidently asked the investigator who was with me for assurance that a doctor would be on hand to see her through her confinement, I could hardly bear it.

Lorena Hickok reporting on conditions in Bottineau County, North Dakota, November 3, 1933, in Richard Lowitt and Maurine Beasley, eds., One Third of a Nation, p. 68.

An old couple at the dinner meal sat on the front porch eating beans out of a rusty pan with their bread crumbled up in a bucket top. The bread was of corn meal and had been cooked several days. It was cold, as were the beans which they were eating. The wife was drinking milk along with her portion. They were slowly eating with their fingers. "We buy 'bout a peck of meal and it costs 40 cents a peck. I buys a dime's worth of sugar 'bout once a week." Other food habits were such as the following:

We country people have to eat rough food. They won't even let us have fertilizer. We ought to have oatmeal, grits, and things like that to eat but we can't get it.

The baby have to eat what we have and that ain't much. I got one old rooster. I wanted to kill him but I ain't got no grease to cook him wid. . . .

If the rations give out 'fore Saturday we just don't eat nothing 'till Saturday evening. Mostly we use is white meat and bread and white lard. I ain't got no taste for it 'cause I was raised on plenty vegetables. Sometimes we have peas. If it don't rain these people ain't going to have nothing to eat.

Charles S. Johnson reporting on the diet of Alabama sharecroppers, 1934, The Shadow of the Plantation, p. 101.

Fairly typical, for Western Tennessee, I gather, was a district I visited yesterday. Table land. Thin soil. Terrible housing. Illiteracy. Evidences of prolonged under-nourishment. No knowledge of how to live decently or farm profitably even if they had decent land. "Five years is about as long as you can get any crop on this land," one farmer told me. "Then it's gone and you have to clear some more and start over again." Crops grown on it are stunted. . . . Eastern Tennessee is worse of course. There you see constant evidence of what happens when you cut timber off mountain sides and plant crops there. . . . And all over the state, in the rural areas, the story is the same—an illiterate, wretched people, under-nourished, with standards of living so low that, once on relief, they are quite willing to stay there the rest of their lives. It's a mess.

Lorena Hickok investigating for the Federal Emergency Relief Administration, June 6, 1934, in Paul E. Mertz, New Deal Policy and Southern Rural Poverty, *p. 4.*

Among the important measures of government, both in the present Administration and the last, are a large number devoted to the relief of distress, both personal and institutional; the expansion of public works; revisions of the older laws regulating business; the reinforcement of State regulation by Federal acts; and the support of cooperative action among the citizens by temporary use of Federal credit. Many of the additional measures undertaken in these directions during the past months are admirable if properly administered.

Proper action in relief of distress is inherent in the social vision of the true American system. No American should go hungry or cold if he is willing to work. Under our system relief is first the obligation of the individual to his neighbors, then of institutions, then of local communities, and then of the State governments. The moment the need exceeds the honest capacities of the local agencies, then they must have support of the Federal Government as the final reservoir of national strength.

This includes an indirect relief through public works, direct relief when all other measures have failed, and proper support to financial institutions when failures will reduce large numbers to destitution. We may not approve the current methods of applying relief. We may feel that some of these methods undermine state and local responsibility; that they are wasteful or futile or alive with corruption. We may fear that they may be misused, by subversion of the electorate through partisan organization, to create future artillery against the walls of liberty. But even so, these are correctable abuses and lesser questions, evanescent in the long view of national life.

Former president Herbert Hoover, September 15, 1934, "Consequences to Liberty of Regimentation," *pp. 5–6.*

About the unemployed themselves: this picture is so grim that whatever words I use will seem hysterical and exaggerated. And I find them all in the same shape—fear, fear driving them into a state of semi-collapse; cracking nerves; and an overpowering terror of the future. . . . I haven't been in one home that hasn't offered me the spectacle of a human being being driven beyond his or

her powers of endurance and sanity. . . . They can't pay rent and are evicted. They . . . are watching their children grow thinner and thinner; fearing the cold for children who have neither coats nor shoes; wondering about coal.

Martha Gellhorn investigating in Massachusetts for the Federal Emergency Relief Administration, December 10, 1934, in James T. Patterson, America's Struggle against Poverty in the Twentieth Century, *p. 37.*

It is very hard to face bearing a baby we cannot afford to have, and the fact that it is due to arrive soon, and still there is no money for the hospital or clothing, does not make it any easier. I Have decided to stay home, keeping my 7 year old daughter from school to help with the smaller children when my husband has work. The oldest little girl is sick now, and has never been strong, so I would not depend on her. The 7 year old one is a good willing little worker and somehow we must manage—but without charity.

Mrs. H. E. C. of Troy, New York, writing to Eleanor Roosevelt, January 2, 1935, in Robert S. McElvaine, Down and Out in the Great Depression: Letters from the "Forgotten Man," *p. 63.*

Oh how I wish you could come to my home today & see what I have to keep house with we have an 8 room bunglelow that we paid $950 for it & it is going to ruin if we can't fix it up there is no roof on it & the sheeting is wearing out on account of the roof being so bad & the wood work inside is bad because the varnish is wore off I have nothing for on the floors except you might say rags left of the linoleum & we have no mattresses for our beds only things laid together for a bed. my dishes are nearly all broken. we have 4 boys. I am a Diabetic patient I am feeling pretty good but I do not have the money to get the medicine I should have no one knows what these hard times mean to one unless you have once gone through it with our family seems broken up the kiddies are not happy because they do not have one toy to play with & I have laid many a night & cried my self to sleep & there are no factory of an kind to get work from.

Mrs. C. C., Summerville, Pennsylvania, writing to Eleanor Roosevelt, April 1935, in Robert S. McElvaine, Down and out in the Great Depression: Letters from the "Forgotten Man," *pp. 70–71.*

The administration of relief and the researches we have made into standards of living of the American family have uncovered for the public gaze a volume of chronic poverty, unsuspected except by a few students and by those who have always experienced it. We might well ask where these people have been all our lives, if we did not already know the answer. The poorest have in large numbers been kept alive by the slightly less poor. Besides his wife and family, the American worker, more often than not, has had various invisible dependents in the offing with whom he has shared what he had. Add to this the fact that the American working family frequently demands the combined earnings of several earners to keep it solvent, and the situation becomes clear. Long before the worker loses his job, he had been cleaned of his surpluses by those of his friends and family whose unemployment antedated his own. It is our experience that men exhaust private patience and resources before they resort to relief.

Harry L. Hopkins, 1936, Spending to Save: The Complete Story of Relief, *p. 111.*

The [Bakersfield, California] school authorities stated that children of the migratory families often came to school hungry. In fact, one of the school clerks reported that two or three families each week complained that it was impossible to send the children to school as they had no food. At the time of the Survey visit to the County School Department, two men in ragged clothing came in. The spokesman of the two was dressed in denim trousers faded from much scrubbing on the washboard, and a coat with holes at the elbows and frayed edges carefully mended with white thread. He stated that he did not have a state residence and the public relief agencies had refused aid. His children were too hungry to go to school and he could not send them until he had food. The clerk explained the law of compulsory attendance and quoted the attendance officer as saying that the children were as well off in school as at home, even though they were hungry. At school at least they were warm. The man argued a little, but not in anger. The clerk explained the legal aspect and the man left.

The school teachers out of personal funds furnished assistance in the form of clothing and milk for many of the migratory children.

State Relief Administration of California, 1936, Transients in California, *p. 56.*

[J]ust outside the [Bakersfield, California] city limits along the bank of the Kern River and on the state highway, two camps, one called Hoovertown and the other Hollywood, had become established shack towns. They were separated by a winding dirt road which had been made by driving autos back and forth. Hollywood was considered the better of the two camps as the houses were a little farther apart, the autos and camping equipment not quite so dilapidated as was the case in Hoovertown. The area had never been cleaned of brush or levelled. There was no running water. Drinking water had to be purchased at a store located on the state highway, or dipped from the river. During the year a few toilets for men and women had been constructed. Houses had been built of canvas tents, odd pieces of wood, gasoline cans, sheets of canvas, and cardboard. Tree branches or tent posts had been used for upright pieces. The canvas tents were stained, the torn places mended with strips of carpet or cardboard. A few tents had wooden floors made of pieces of packing boxes but these were the exception.

State Relief Administration of California, 1936, Transients in California, *p. 56.*

On an afternoon in February a Survey worker strolled though the numerous groups of family camps and shack villages located along the east edge of [El Centro, California]. Old tents, gunny sacks, drygoods boxes, and scrap tin had been the principal building materials used in the construction of these villages. The families living here were almost all seasonal laborers, though a few of the camps showed signs of having been occupied for several years. The worker talked to people in five of the shacks. Three of them were homes of colored families and two of itinerant white laborers. One Negro woman with six small children told the worker that her "men folks" were unable to get work in the lettuce because colored men were not allowed to do that kind of work. It was done by Mexicans and white men. Her shack had no floor in it and the roof of scrap tin leaked when it rained. The six children were thinly clad and barefooted. On an outside fire, she was boiling a large pot of carrots. The shack and its surroundings were very dirty and flies swarmed in clouds. There were no sanitary facilities in evidence and the back yard had been used as a toilet. Behind the tent ran an irrigation ditch half full of muddy water. The woman said she used this water for all purposes unless the canal was dry, in which case "they" had to carry water half a mile from the big canal.

State Relief Administration of California, 1936, Transients in California, *p. 64.*

One woman wrote to a [Chicago] relief station as follows: "I am without food for myself and child. I only got $6.26 to last me from the tenth to the twenty-fifth. That order is out and I haven't anything to eat. We go to bed hungry. Please give us something to eat. I cannot stand to see my child hungry."

Another woman requesting rent wrote: "I must have rent for my flat. I am not strong enough to fight for anything so if I don't get attention in my desperate situation I just can't survive any more. It isn't worth it."

"Survey of Immediate Relief Situation in Illinois," July 31, 1936, in James T. Patterson, America's Struggle against Poverty in the Twentieth Century, p. 38.

Sharecropping has deprived millions of persons of what the rest of America considers the necessities of life.

It deprives children of adequate education because many of them have to work either part of the school year or all of it on their fathers' farms so that enough cotton can be raised to pay rent and buy fertilizer and to get food and clothing. It forces families to live in buildings that are detrimental to health, and it forces them to exist on food that is insufficient. Worse still, it continues in operation year after year, wringing dry the bodies and souls of men, women, and children; dragging down to its own level from higher economic planes new members to take the places of those crushed and thrown aside; breeding families of eight, ten, twelve, fourteen, sixteen, and more, in order to furnish an ever-increasing number of persons necessary to supply the rent-cotton for the landlord.

It is foolish to ask a tenant farmer why he remains where he is. He does move from farm to farm from time to time, but only rarely can he improve his status. Such a question is usually asked with the purpose of covering up an inability to suggest what the farmer could do to lift himself from the hole he stands in. There is cotton to be raised, and he has trained himself to raise it. That is his specialty. It is his life and, if sharecropping continues as an institution, it will become his death.

Erskine Caldwell, novelist, and Margaret Bourke-White, photographer and photojournalist, 1937, You Have Seen Their Faces, pp. 30–31.

Many children make a poor start in life because of unhappiness in the home. It may be because of ever present financial worry, or the personal incompatibility of parents or of brothers and sisters. Continual scolding may drive to the unfortunate influences of the street a child who might otherwise be a cooperative member of the household. Families may be too large, mothers anxious and worried, and the food supply meager or uncertain. Sleep may be interfered with by the necessity of having several children sleep in the same room or even in the same bed. There may be no source of comfort or beauty either within the home or in the slum which surrounds it. Wherever such conditions make the daily environment, or wherever irritability and belligerent attitudes are the rule, children start life under a heavy handicap. In such circumstances there is little hope of their developing the physical strength and energy or the cooperative attitudes essential in adult years for continuous and profitable employment.

The seeds of adult poverty thus are often planted in childhood years, for those who have known no other life. The habit of parasitism may even be learned from parental example. Such conditions are still found in American cities.

Though many families in poverty or upon relief succeed in "keeping their heads up" and maintaining surprisingly high standards in spite of their predicament, a high percentage of children in homes of the poor suffer in some degree from conditions of the sort which have just been described. To these must be added desertion—which is the poor man's divorce—and illegitimacy, each of which appears frequently in case records of dependent families. Although desertion may be fortunate where there is utter incompatibility, it causes dependency in families where there are young children, or else neglect because of the absence of the mother during the working hours of the day.

James Ford, professor of social ethics at Harvard University, and Katherine Morrow Ford, sociologist and writer, 1937, The Abolition of Poverty, pp. 106–7.

With 28 percent of the Nation's population, [the South] has only 16 percent of the tangible assets, including factories, machines, and the tools with which people make their living. With more than half the country's farmers, the South has less than a fifth of the farm implements. Despite its coal, oil, gas, and water power, the region uses only 15 percent of the Nation's factory horsepower. Its potentialities have been neglected and its opportunities unrealized.

The paradox of the South is that while it is blessed by Nature with immense wealth, its people as a whole are the poorest in the country. Lacking industries of its own, the South has been forced to trade the richness of its soil, its minerals and forests, and the labor of its people for goods manufactured elsewhere. If the South received such goods in sufficient quantity to meet its needs, it might consider itself adequately paid.

U.S. National Emergency Council, 1938, Report on Economic Conditions of the South, pp. 7–8.

For years evidence has been piling up that food, clothing, and housing influence not only the sickness rate and death rate but even the height and weight of school children. In the South, where family incomes are exceptionally low, the sickness and death rates are unusually high. Wage differentials become in fact differentials in health and life: poor health, in turn, affects wages.

The low-income belt of the South is a belt of sickness, misery, and unnecessary death. Its large proportion of low-income citizens are more subject to disease than the people of any similar area. The climate cannot be blamed—the South is as healthful as any section for those who have the necessary care, diet, and freedom from occupational disease.

> *U.S. National Emergency Council, 1938,* Report on Economic Conditions of the South, *p. 29.*

Truly rural slums are worse than city slums. Homes are, almost without exception, old frame farm or camp buildings on shallow foundations. They are heated by wood-burning stoves. In the past few years wood has become scarce and almost as costly as coal. Families from five to seven members have been obliged to move beds into kitchen and crowd up the best way possible to sleep and keep from freezing. . . . Hardly without exception, roofs leak, plastering is off walls and ceilings, and cracks let in cold air to add to the cold, damp mildewed air of the unheated rooms.

> *Report on Sullivan County, New York, in "Survey of Current Relief Situation," March 21, 1938, in James T. Patterson,* America's Struggle against Poverty in the Twentieth Century, *p. 37.*

The exploitation of farm labor in California, which is one of the ugliest chapters in the history of American industry, is as old as the system of landownership of which it is part. Time has merely tightened the system of ownership and control and furthered the degradation of farm labor. As far as the vast army of workers who operate these great tracts are concerned, their plight is nearly as wretched today as it was thirty years ago.

This photograph shows slum houses in Omaha, Nebraska, November 1938. *(Library of Congress, Prints and Photographs Division, LC-USF33-TO1-001301-M4)*

In all America it would be difficult to find a parallel for this strange army in tatters. It numbers 200,000 workers and a more motley crew was never assembled in this country by a great industry. Sources of cheap labor in China, Japan, the Philippine Islands, Puerto Rico, Mexico, the Deep South, and Europe have been generously tapped to recruit its ever-expanding ranks. As one contingent of recruits after the other has been exhausted, or has mutinied, others have been assembled to take their places. Although the army has been made up of different races, as conditions have changed and new circumstances arisen, it has always functioned as an army. It is an army that marches from crop to crop. Its equipment is negligible, a few pots and pans, and its quarters unenviable. It is supported by a vast horde of camp followers, mostly pregnant women, diseased children, and fleabitten dogs. Its transport consists of a fleet of ancient and battered Model T Fords and similar equipage. No one has ever been able to fathom the mystery of how this army supports itself or how it has continued to survive. It has had many savage encounters, with drought and flood and disease; and, occasionally, it has fought in engagements that can hardly be called sham battles, as its casualties have been heavy. Today the army has many new faces as recruits have swarmed in from the dust-bowl area eager to enlist for the duration of the crops at starvation wages. But, in substance, it is the same army that has followed the crops since 1870.

Carey McWilliams, journalist, 1939, Factories in the Field, *pp. 7–8.*

When the chief breadwinner loses his job no amount of initiative can turn up new resources which make the customary plane of living completely possible over an extended period. That means curtailment, and sometimes drastic curtailment, of expenditures. Where does this effort take hold most thoroughly? . . .

Five adjustments stand out as the major alternatives: economizing on clothing, recreational and community activities, food, insurance, and living quarters. . . .

These declared adjustments are indicative of the fact that management of the domestic economy without customary earnings is no easy task.

E. Wight Bakke, management theorist and professor, Yale University Labor and Management Center, 1940, The Unemployed Worker: A Study of the Task of Making a Living without a Job, *p. 264.*

What *personal expenses* are necessary for self-respect? . . . Haircuts in some shops are 25 c. That is the minimum.

The men go to the barber about once in every two or three months. How about shaving soap, razor blades, shaving brushes? Many mothers cut the younger children's hair, but it sometimes happens that an adolescent who is causing difficulty in the home reminds us that the father cannot cut his hair correctly and that he is not going to stand for it. When I have seen the scissors I have realized why the children's hair looks so unkempt.

How about toothbrushes? We advise cleaning teeth with salt, and frequently advise using a clean cotton cloth, but I question the practicability of the latter, especially for school children. Most of the families had the toothbrush habit before we ever knew them.

How about emergency first aids? Mercurochrome, vaseline, adhesive, cotton, particularly where there are children? Once one could borrow from neighbors, but today even the neighbor's cupboard is bare. Laxatives are needed in many families.

Cosmetics are taboo, but really, some items make the younger women feel better as they look better with a little powder, or a few bobby pins to hold their hair in place.

What do families do for combs? For handkerchiefs? For pins? All these items are carefully evaded. We just never discuss them.

E. Wight Bakke, management theorist and professor, Yale University Labor and Management Center, 1940, The Unemployed Worker: A Study of the Task of Making a Living without a Job, *pp. 335–36.*

Southern schooling remains a vexatious and difficult challenge. The schools of the cotton country are preponderantly rural, and country schools throughout the United States are deplorable. But schools of the cotton states are below average. In terms of juvenile literacy, school attendance, grades completed, length of school term, teacher's salary, funds expended per pupil, and value of buildings they are at the very bottom of the national list.

Public education in the South is fronted with incessant barriers. The worst of all is a smug, careless apathy on the part of the majority population. There is also the perennial race prejudice which requires separation of schools on a purely racial basis. Further, the actual planting, tilling, and harvesting of cotton keep tens of thousands of school children away from schools. Tenancy causes families to make frequent moves during the school year. And it keeps the majority population so abjectly poor that the majority population ceases to give a damn.

Charles Morrow Wilson, writer, 1940, Corn Bread and Creek Water, *pp. 189–90.*

Sixty-eight years ago we Navajos came back to the reservation. Then we were just a small band with only a small band of sheep and stock. Now we grow to 50,000 people and our stock must grow with us.

Then we had plenty of grass for our herds. A man could almost see the grass sprouting right after the rains. After it rained you could walk on the new grass and it would sound like you were walking in the snow—cracking under your feet.

But now the ground is like rock. The only thing a person hears cracking are his knee joints. Now after rains you hear the roar of water down these gullies. Every time we herd our sheep we have a small dust storm following our flock. . . . Our mother Earth is slowly dying. What of coming Navajos who must take our place?

Sam Gray, Navajo, 1940, in Charles Morrow Wilson, Corn Bread and Creek Water, *pp. 107–8.*

Yes, there's some purty hard cases about. There's Jim, there, up the creek holler—livin' in a' old leaky smokehouse. Jim's got three young'uns rangin' from three to fourteen year old. Ain't nary a bite to eat in the whole place. Been livin' for a month out'n a mound of hold-up turnips and a couple or three slabs of salt pork. Can't get no work to do nowhere. But, mister, if you was askin' me does that Jim need charity, I'd say, No, he shore don't!"

A small-town mayor, Arkansas, 1940, in Charles Morrow Wilson, Corn Bread and Creek Water, *p. 210.*

The bare dirt is more damp in the tempering shade; and damp, tender with rottenness, the ragged wood of the porch, that is so heavily littered with lard buckets, scraps of iron, bent wire, torn rope, old odors, those no longer useful things which on a farm are never thrown away. The trees: draft on their stalks their clouds of heavy season; the barn: shines on the perfect air; in the bare yard a twelve-foot flowering bush: in shroud of blown bloom slumbers, and within: naked, naked side by side those brothers and sisters, those most beautiful children; and the crazy, clownish, foxy father; and the mother; and the two old daughters; crammed on their stinking beds, are resting the night.

James Agee, writer, and Walker Evans, photographer, describing a Hale County, Alabama, tenant farmer's home, 1941, Let Us Now Praise Famous Men, *p. 76.*

Woods and Ricketts are tenants. . . .

From March through June, while the cotton is being cultivated, they live on the rations money.

From July through to late August, while the cotton is making, they live however they can.

From late August through October or into November, during the picking and ginning season, they live on the money from their share of the cottonseed.

From then on until March, they live on whatever they have earned in the year; or however they can.

During six to seven months of each year, then—that is, during exactly such time as their labor with the cotton is of absolute necessity to the landlord—they can be sure of whatever living is possible in rations advances and in cottonseed money.

During five to six months of the year, of which three are the hardest months of any year, with the worst of weather, the least adequacy of shelter, the worst and least of food, the worst of health, quite normal and inevitable, they can count on nothing except that they may hope least of all for any help from their landlords.

James Agee, writer, and Walker Evans, photographer, describing the lives of Hale County, Alabama, tenant farmers, 1941, Let Us Now Praise Famous Men, *pp. 116–17.*

The living conditions of migratory workers in the Yakima Valley [of Washington] have long been regarded as about the worst to be found in the entire West. One of the four richest agricultural counties in the United States, Yakima has had one of the highest typhoid-fever rates of any county in America. It is not uncommon to see mountain streams in the valley, crystal clear above a hop pickers' camp, muddy with filth and debris a few miles downstream. Other areas in the Northwest have long provided private labor camps; but Yakima has had the reputation of not providing camps. Camps near the orchards, according to the growers, would provide workers with too good an opportunity to steal fruit.

Carey McWilliams, journalist, 1941, Ill Fares the Land, *p. 62.*

Migrant farm families in Arizona live in four types of settlements: grower camps; cheap auto and trailer camps; squatter camps; and in the shacktowns of Phoenix and Tucson. . . .

The worst camps are, of course, the squatter camps, in which about 10 per cent of the migrants live. They are located on ditch banks, along the roadside, and on the open desert. Sometimes as many as fifty families collect in these improvised camps, usually located near a highway intersection or where some type of water supply is available. In the squatter camps, the FSA found "numerous cases where no shelter other than automobiles" existed. It is scarcely necessary to point out that it can be extremely hot and also extremely cold in Arizona during the cotton-picking season, which lasts through December and into January. Many of the squatter camps have come into existence as a result of a policy, followed by the growers, of not admitting to a grower-camp a family having less than three pickers. The effect of the policy is, of course, to force the smaller families to camp in the desert. "One squatter camp of twelve units was found on the outskirts of Glendale, Arizona, in which an old sedan body was being used as a make-shift privy." Garbage is thrown on the desert, filth and refuse litter the ground.

Carey McWilliams, journalist, 1941, Ill Fares the Land,
pp. 86–87.

CHAPTER SEVEN

The Invisible Mass
1940–1962

As the 1940s dawned, government spending for defense became the federal jobs program that finally ended the depression. In June and July 1940 Congress authorized $12 billion for defense, an amount significantly higher than ever was allotted for New Deal relief initiatives in a single year. Dust bowl migrants, refugees from Appalachia, African Americans who had left the Deep South—many who had endured poverty during the depression—found jobs on the West Coast, in the Midwest, and in other industrial centers producing 50,000 planes and 100,000 machine guns each year as well as tanks, jeeps, aircraft carriers, destroyers, and other vehicles and vessels. In addition, with 16 million Americans serving in the military during World War II, the armed forces also significantly reduced joblessness. For the first time in U.S. history, full employment seemed attainable, and people seriously considered a new concept, universal diffusion of income: Soon it might be possible for every American to have a means of support and for poverty to be eliminated.

The employment picture was not entirely rosy, however. More than 110,000 Japanese Americans from the West Coast spent the war years imprisoned in remote regions of the West, forced to give up their livelihood, their possessions, and their freedom. Also, blacks had gained the right to work beside whites in defense plants only after a struggle. At first North American Aviation and other firms with defense contracts would only hire African Americans for janitorial or other low-level jobs. It took a threat by the African-American labor leader A. Philip Randolph to lead 100,000 black marchers to Washington, D.C., to induce President Roosevelt to issue Executive Order 8802 on June 25, 1941. This document required the federal government and defense contractors to hire people without regard to race, religion, or national origin. Opportunities improved for African Americans, but workplace discrimination never disappeared, and some whites responded to the presence of blacks in the workplace with strikes and violence.

The poor became less visible during the years of World War II, and the number of Americans receiving relief declined, but poverty persisted. In July 1943 about 5 million people received public assistance. Many more—although it is not known how many—would have met eligibility requirements had they lived in communities with assistance programs or adequate funding.

J. C. Myers, a resident of the Shenandoah Valley, was only intermittently employed in 1941 and therefore a potential defense-plant worker. *(Library of Congress, Prints and Photographs Division, LC-USE6-D-000260)*

World events had given rise to some new, albeit temporary, groups of needy Americans. These included children in families destroyed by the disruption of war, who had lost a parent through death or desertion or who suffered from neglect. Men disabled by war either physically or mentally formed another subset of the new poor, and WPA workers who were unemployed at the termination of their program formed another. (In some communities in the 1930s, the WPA had been the principal employer.) Also, for many households induction into the military of a husband, father, son, or other male breadwinner resulted in lost income and privation.

Importing Mexican Labor

World War II created a demand for labor on U.S. farms, as growers sought to replace workers who were in uniform or who had taken jobs in defense plants. On August 4, 1942, the United States and Mexico signed an agreement establishing the Labor Importation Program to meet the need by issuing temporary work permits to Mexicans. The project was known in the West as the bracero program. The term *bracero*, a corruption of the Spanish word *braza*, meaning "arm," referred to manual labor.

Growers participating in the program entered into contracts with these workers under Farm Security Administration (FSA) supervision. They also signed performance bonds to ensure that they would fulfill their contract obligations: to pay a minimum wage of 30 cents per hour or the prevailing wage, whichever was higher; to offer at least 30 days of work; and to pay workers for 75 percent of the period specified in the contract if bad weather or some other unforeseen occurrence cut short the need for labor. Workers, growers, and the U.S. government shared transportation costs, and the laborers were to return to Mexico at the end of their fixed term of work.

Transportation of workers under the new agreement began on September 29, 1942, when a train carried the first 1,500 Mexican workers to California. By February 1943 the government had transported 4,000 Mexicans to fields in California and Arizona. In 1943, 52,098 Mexicans participated in the bracero program, and in 1944, 62,170 took part. FSA officials also moved 6,800 U.S. workers to places throughout the country. Most relocated American workers were from regions with a high percentage of underemployed farmers and sharecroppers, such as portions of Missouri and the area surrounding Memphis, Tennessee. The Labor Importation Program enabled them to supplement their incomes and aid the country in wartime.

Texas growers refused to employ laborers through the bracero program during its first five years of operation, preferring to hire directly Mexican workers who had entered the United States illegally. (More than half the Mexicans who entered the United States during the years of the bracero program did so illegally.) Also, under pressure from the agricultural industry, in April 1943 Congress stripped from U.S. farm workers the contract protections extended to foreigners under the Labor Importation Program and required them to obtain written permission from a county agricultural extension agent before being transported to a new locale. Because local agents almost never gave such permission, domestic agricultural workers had to find their own transportation. Congress also turned over the Labor Importation Program to the War Food Administration, the agency responsible for all agricultural production during the war. By late 1943 the program was importing

7,000 Mexicans per month and was placing West Indians and European prisoners of war on farms, especially in the South.

During the 1950s an estimated 300,000 Mexican workers entered the United States each year under the bracero program. The ready supply of labor caused Texans to reverse their stance and elect to participate, and by the late 1950s a significant percentage of the imported Mexicans went to Texas. Most of the 4.5 million Mexicans who entered the United States as part of the bracero program between 1943 and 1964, when the program was terminated, never returned to Mexico. Many gained legal residency through approved channels, but many others settled in the United States illegally.

It was thought that illegal immigration from Mexico furnished cheap labor that displaced U.S.-born farm workers, that it encouraged growers to violate laws that had been put in place to protect laborers, and that the impoverished workforce introduced crime, illiteracy, and disease. Certainly, undocumented Mexican workers suffered. In areas of the Southwest where they picked cotton, they might pick 200 to 250 pounds a day and receive 50 cents for every hundred pounds. When even $1.25 or $1.50 per hundred pounds was considered a low rate of pay. Some of these workers and their families lived in burrows carved into the sides of embankments or in holes covered with tentlike canvas roofs. For others home was an irrigation ditch or a stand of trees. Here and there homemade crosses marked the graves of loved ones who had succumbed to hardship or disease and for whom medical care quite possibly had been unaffordable. The children raised in these conditions suffered from malnutrition, chronic diarrhea, parasitic illnesses, and other health problems. With nowhere to turn for help, undocumented workers were at the mercy of everyone with whom they dealt, including Spanish-speaking people residing legally in the United States, who were not above charging them exorbitant prices and rents.

Covered holes in the ground were the homes of undocumented Mexicans on a farm adjacent to the Rio Grande in Texas. *(Courtesy, Texas AFL-CIO Collection, The University of Texas at Arlington Libraries, Arlington, Texas)*

Many Mexicans working in the United States under the bracero program also lived in deplorable conditions, despite contract provisions and government oversight. Thousands were housed in shacks, abandoned chicken coops, and railroad cars without adequate plumbing or toilet facilities. In 1954 the nation reacted with Operation Wetback, a combined effort of the Immigration and Naturalization Service (INS), the U.S. Border Patrol, municipal and state authorities, and the military to "repatriate," or return to Mexico, undocumented Mexicans found living in the United States. The slang term *wetback* (in Spanish *mojado*) was applied to undocumented Mexican immigrants because they allegedly swam or waded across the Rio Grande, which forms most of the border between Texas and Mexico.

On July 14, 1954, the first day Operation Wetback was in force, its agents apprehended 4,800 people, most in the lower Rio Grande valley of Texas. The search area was gradually expanded to the west, east, and north. Beginning September 18, 1954, the Air Transport Arm of the U.S. Border Patrol flew 11,459 undocumented Mexicans from Chicago to Brownsville, Texas, on the Gulf of Mexico. From there the captives were put on ships bound for Mexican ports. According to the INS 1.3 million Mexicans were repatriated as a result of Operation Wetback, either through seizure by authorities or voluntary surrender, and in March 1955 Commissioner of Immigration Joseph Swing told a congressional subcommittee that the flow of illegal immigration from Mexico had been stemmed for the first time since World War II. He said that the number of undocumented Mexicans apprehended by authorities had dropped from 3,000 a day to 300.

The INS total is probably inflated, however. During Operation Wetback agents rounded up 84,278 undocumented Mexicans in California and 80,127 in San Antonio, Texas, two major areas of concentration. The INS claimed that at least 500,000 people returned voluntarily to Mexico from each of those regions, but there is no evidence to support this assertion. Observers at ports of entry in Texas counted only 60,000 people returning, and there were no reports from Mexico of a large movement of people into border towns.

Operation Wetback may have removed thousands of poor people from the United States, but its focus on one ethnic group engendered ill will toward the U.S. government among Mexicans and Mexican Americans. Also, the many people who went to Mexican border towns, whether they were deported or left willingly, were ideally placed to reenter the United States when the hunt for illegal immigrants had lost momentum. Operation Wetback, then, may only have yielded temporary results.

A Shifting Policy toward Native Americans

A number of tribal nations had refused to participate in John Collier's plan for reorganization, and the government was too impatient—in Collier's view—to wait for it to bear fruit. Congressional opposition to reorganization increased during the war, and funding for the Bureau of Indian Affairs decreased. On January 19, 1945, Collier resigned in frustration.

At war's end American Indian farmers needed more land and training in modern agricultural methods such as using irrigation systems, applying chemicals, and breeding selectively in order to succeed. Many lacked the capital and access to credit necessary if they were to keep up with scientific and technological advances and compete with white farmers. On Arizona reservations the water supply was

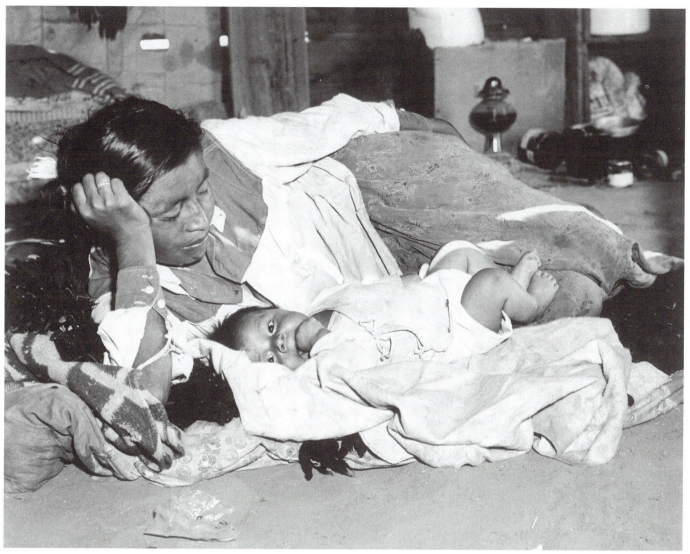

A young Navajo (Dineh) mother watches over her baby near Many Farms, Arizona. As do many Navajo in 1952, she has active tuberculosis that is untreated. *(Library of Congress, Prints and Photographs Division, LC-USZ62-133877)*

inadequate to support an irrigation system; most Navajo (Dineh) ranchers owned fewer than the 250 head needed to sustain a family economically, because overgrazing and erosion had depleted their rangeland. Some had never recovered from the forced livestock reduction of the 1930s.

In 1947 Congress appropriated $350,000 to increase Indians' land holdings, but this was too little to produce any real improvement. In that year the average Indian family earned $918 from agriculture, an amount that accounted for more than half the yearly income of two-thirds of families on reservations. By 1949 the average annual income from agriculture for Indians had fallen to $500, while that of the average white farmer was $2,500. The Direct Employment Assistance Program, established in 1951, encouraged unemployed Native Americans to leave reservations and move to Los Angeles, Seattle, Denver, and other cities, but most of those who relocated lacked the education and job skills necessary to compete in the urban market, and many remained out of work.

With industry eager to exploit the timber, minerals, and other resources on Indian land, the government adopted a new policy, one of "Termination." On August
1, 1953, with House Concurrent Resolution 108, Congress took a step toward terminating the Indians' status as wards of the United States. The resolution targeted
13 groups of Indians who would be expected to assume all the duties of citizenship.
Responsibility for their education, welfare, and health needs and for law enforcement on reservations would be transferred to the individual states. No longer did the
federal government recognize the sovereignty of tribes subject to termination.

These houses in rural West Virginia were photographed in the early 1960s. *(Photograph © Milton Rogovin 1952–2002, The Rogovin Collection, LLC)*

At the time few among the Dakota people on the Fort Totten Reservation in North Dakota could afford to cultivate more than 40 acres, although a farm of 160 acres was needed to yield a salable crop. Over generations the title to some allotted land had become unclear, and white ranchers grazed their stock on reservation land without paying anyone. At the same time some Dakota were so hungry and poor that they butchered breeding cattle, meeting an immediate need at the cost of long-term profit. Conditions on the Fort Totten Reservation were typical. In the 1950s, 66 percent of the Rosebud Reservation in South Dakota, 80 percent of the Crow Reservation in Montana, and large sections of reservations in the Pacific Northwest were leased to whites. The Blackfeet of Montana depended on nonagricultural employment for 77 percent of their income, and most lived in poverty.

Just 3 percent of American Indians, or 13,263 people, had their federal support withdrawn before the government abandoned the Termination policy in 1961, during the presidency of John F. Kennedy. Three tribal nations, the Klamath of Oregon, Menominee of Wisconsin, and Mixed-blood Ute of Utah, had lost the most land. Stewart Udall, secretary of the interior under Kennedy and his successor, Lyndon B. Johnson, favored a gradual reduction of federal responsibility for Native peoples through economic development.

A Broader Picture of Low-Income America

Buoyed by their recent military victories, the majority of Americans in the postwar years felt invincible. Poverty became a challenge to be met and conquered, much as defeating the Germans or Japanese had been. "The unfilled wants of American families now living on inadequate incomes constitute a great underdeveloped economic frontier—a new and expansible market for the products of American industry," concluded a congressional subcommittee that issued a report on low-income families in 1950.[1] The subcommittee studied urban families with an annual income of less than $2,000, and farm families with an annual income of less than $1,000. The researchers settled on these amounts, acknowledging that the cost of living varied from one region of the country to another, because according to the Bureau of the Census nearly 10 million families had incomes below $2,000 in 1948, and most of these families lived in cities. As in the past, living was cheaper in the country.

The study revealed several trends among low-income Americans. First, more than one-fourth of nonfarm families with incomes below $2,000 were headed by persons over age 65. In 1950, 12.3 million Americans were 65 or older, according to the U.S. Census Bureau. Improvements in health care were improving longevity, and the number of older Americans with low incomes was expected to increase. Second, low-income city dwellers were likely to be unskilled or semiskilled laborers or service workers who faced obsolescence as industry became increasingly mechanized. Construction firms that had invested in excavating machinery, for example, no longer hired crews to wield picks and shovels. Low-income Americans tended to be nonwhite and to have had little education. Only 6 percent of adults studied had attended high school. Low-income households were disproportionately headed by women who had been widowed, divorced, or deserted. Also, many in this income group were disabled. A major contributing factor to low income in farm families was the size of the farm. In 1945 the average farm measured 180 acres in the North, 131 acres in the South, and 639 acres in the West. The average low-income farm, in contrast, covered less than 50 acres.

Low-income families spent most of their budget on food. Their diet had improved during the war, possibly because wartime rationing made the distribution of some foods more equitable then in the past, and in 1948 they consumed more meat, fish, milk, eggs, and sugar and other sweets than in 1942. Yet even so, they still consumed less of these foods and more bread and flour than the average American family. In addition, nearly 15 percent of urban low-income families lived in dwellings needing major repairs. Nonwhites especially had homes that were in poor condition because they were restricted to undesirable neighborhoods.

Congress terminated the WPA and other New Deal programs that had outlived their usefulness, but the federal government had assumed a permanent role in public welfare during the depression, and it continued to aid the disadvantaged in the postwar years. The National School Lunch Program of 1946 subsidized

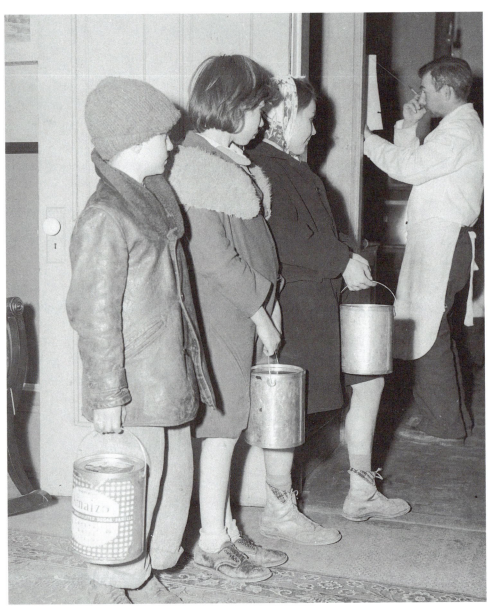

Children wait in line for soup at a Dubuque, Iowa, mission financed by the Community Chest. *(Library of Congress, Prints and Photographs Division, LC-USF34-060600-D)*

states for equipment purchases and food purchase and preparation costs to make a nutritious lunch an integral part of children's day; similarly, 1954's School Milk Program provided subsidies for milk. The Full Employment Act of 1946 reaffirmed the government's responsibility to promote employment, production, purchasing power, and investment. It authorized federal spending to create jobs, established the Council of Economic Advisers, and required the president to submit an annual economic report.

In 1950 Congress expanded the Social Security program by issuing grants to mothers of dependent children, thereby converting Aid to Dependent Children (ADC) to Aid to Families with Dependent Children (AFDC). The year 1953 marked the creation of the Department of Health, Education, and Welfare, a cabinet-level department charged with improving the administration of U.S. government social programs. In 1956 disability insurance became a provision of Social Security, and soon afterward Social Security retirement benefits were extended to farm workers and the self-employed, two groups that had been excluded.

Americans continued to aid their less-advantaged neighbors, often through contributions to the Community Chest, which gained popularity in the late 1940s. The Community Chest raised funds for distribution to local agencies, including hospitals, clinics, youth organizations, family agencies, and nursing homes. In 1949 Community Chests in 800 cities and towns raised $165 million.

It was easy to give and forget. The public was anxious to leave behind the hardships of the depression years and look toward a prosperous future. People largely ignored the poor, who lived in out-of-the-way places such as Appalachian towns and inner-city ghettos and had no way to make themselves heard. With the nation engaged in the cold war against the Soviet Union, to many people it seemed disloyal to criticize the American system. Was it not more patriotic—and reassuring—to put one's faith in prosperity and the power of corporate America? After all, the United States had the highest standard of living in the world.

In 1958 a leading economist, John Kenneth Galbraith, published *The Affluent Society*, a best-selling book in which he stated that the "great and quite unprecedented affluence" of the United States contrasted with economic conditions in most of the nations that had existed throughout history.[2] Yet Americans were hanging onto concepts forged not in a nation of wealth but in a world of poverty. "Our economic attitudes are rooted in the poverty, inequality, and economic peril of the past," Galbraith wrote.[3] The idea that only those who worked were entitled to a share of the collective wealth made sense where resources were scarce, but not in the United States. He dismissed the notions that unearned income in the form of relief or welfare payments corrupted, and hunger and privation built character. It was essential to share this great affluence, if only to prevent poverty from perpetuating itself. Galbraith advocated targeting the young by furnishing them with good schools, nutritious school meals and snacks, health services, access to higher education, and adequate police protection.

Updating the concepts of deserving and undeserving poor, Galbraith divided the nation's needy into two groups, the "case" poor and the "insular" poor. Case poverty could be found in every community, however prosperous. It was related to some characteristic of the individual case, perhaps alcohol abuse, a large number of children, low educational attainment, or failure to adapt to economic reality. Insular poverty afflicted whole communities, if the environment prevented people from prospering. This was the poverty of Appalachia and urban slums.

This is an Aid to Dependent Children (ADC) poster child from the early 1940s. *(Library of Congress, Prints and Photographs Division, LC-USE62-D-OA-000053)*

At the time Galbraith published his book, an estimated 20 percent of the population, or 40 million people, lived in poverty, and most got by with little or no public assistance. Nevertheless, lengthening welfare rolls in northern and western cities were difficult to ignore. Beginning in the 1940s and continuing into the 1960s, rapid growth in applications for relief accompanied the migration to cities of blacks from the South, whites from Appalachia, Mexican Americans, Native Americans, and another group, Puerto Ricans. Many were farm workers who had been displaced by mechanization in agriculture. The mechanical cotton picker, introduced in 1943, replaced 2.3 million people. About 25 percent of these workers found other employment locally, but the rest gravitated to urban ghettos and, lacking skills to offer employers, applied for public assistance.

From 1935 through the early 1950s, most federal and state relief went to older Americans. By 1960, however, the majority of welfare recipients were younger families collecting benefits from AFDC. In 1945 some 701,000 families collected benefits from ADC; in 1960 there were 3.1 million families receiving assistance from AFDC. Although federal funds supported AFDC, the individual states administered the program. States were permitted to add to the federal payments and to adopt eligibility requirements. Many states also set up their own welfare programs for needy residents who failed to qualify for federal assistance.

Whereas in the 1930s and 1940s ADC funds typically had gone to white widowed mothers, more and more recipients were unmarried black mothers. Illegitimate births had increased alarmingly between 1940, when they accounted for 7.1 per 1,000 live births, and 1962, when they accounted for 21.5 per 1,000 live births. Among African Americans the rate had risen from 35.6 to 90.1 per 1,000 live births over the same time span. The number of households headed by women had also grown. In 1940 white women headed 3 percent and black women headed 7 percent of U.S. households. In 1960 white women headed 6 percent and black women headed 20 percent of households.

Rejecting the view proposed by Galbraith, states and municipalities enacted restrictions with the hope of reducing the number of recipients, eliminating suspected fraud, and controlling expenditures and of encouraging the dependent population to work. For example, they instituted residency requirements to discourage out-of-state migrants. Some states, such as Texas, attempted to control through legislation the morals of the population on welfare. In Texas, women had to agree in writing to have no male callers and not to behave in ways that would shame their children.

Some jurisdictions also established a "man-in-the-house" rule, stating that the presence of an adult male in her household made a woman ineligible for AFDC benefits. In theory the man should have been capable of supporting the woman and her children. This rule generated criticism because it appeared to encourage people to break up their families in order to meet eligibility requirements. In 1961, in an effort to preserve families, the federal government extended AFDC to disadvantaged two-parent families if the head of the household was out of a job and had run through his or her unemployment benefits.

In 1960, the federal, state, and local government distributed $3.1 billion in relief funds in the United States. The majority of the poor—55 percent—lived in cities; 30 percent lived in small towns, and the remaining 15 percent lived on farms. More than one-third of the poor were children, and three-fifths were either under 18 or over 65. (The number of people over age 65 had reached 16.7 million.) Also in 1960, 20 percent of poor families were headed by white males who were working full-time. These figures are generally accepted, although estimates of poverty varied according to the level of income that determined the poverty line. In 1962 the Social Security Administration (SSA) set the poverty line at $3,089 for a family of four, and $1,519 for a single adult. SSA calculated its poverty line by determining the cost of a basic, nutritious diet and then tripling this amount. This method was based on findings of a 1955 study, which found that the poor spent one-third of their income on food. Many economists thought the SSA figures were too low, however.

Although thousands of middle-class Americans held a mental image of welfare "chiselers" living well at society's expense, life on welfare was hardly comfortable. Twenty-eight percent of families receiving AFDC support in 1960 lived in homes that lacked toilets and hot water, and 17 percent had no running water, hot or cold. The amount of money paid to welfare recipients varied according to location; for the nation as a whole, monthly payments averaged $30 per person and $115 per family.

States and municipalities based welfare payments on sample budgets worked out by the U.S. Department of Agriculture, state welfare departments, home economists working in academia, and private agencies such as the Visiting Nurses Association. These budgets took into account the costs of food, rent, utilities, clothing, household supplies, and personal-care items. In January 1961 the Michigan State Department of Welfare calculated that a 35-year-old woman with three children would need $223.05 per month, or $2,676.60 per year, to support her family at subsistence level. Social-service agencies in New York City set a nearly identical subsistence-level budget for a family of four, $2,660 per year, in 1960. This budget allowed for rental of a five-room apartment with linoleum floors but no carpeting; a living room with two chairs and a bed doubling as a couch; one or two lamps; and a table for dining and two straight-backed chairs. It allowed for an electric iron, one hour of radio each day (to control the cost of electricity), and no television. The food budget excluded frozen foods, beer, and tobacco, and the clothing budget permitted a woman to buy a coat every five years.

The major limiting factor was the public's attitude. Most Americans thought that giving welfare recipients more than basic necessities robbed them of the incentive to work and provide for their families. As in the days of the poorhouse, public agencies wanted to prevent the people they supported from becoming too comfortable.

In general, though, people living below the poverty line had a higher standard of living than the poor of earlier decades. In Harlan County, Kentucky, where in 1913 nearly all of the homes inspected by the Rockefeller Sanitary Commission lacked any kind of toilet facility, two-thirds of homes remained substandard in 1960, and one-fourth lacked running water. Yet 67 percent of families had television sets, 59 percent owned cars, and 42 percent had telephone service.

Appalachia: Some Hard Facts

In all of Appalachia, 60.8 percent of the population in 1960 lived in housing reported to be in sound condition and having modern indoor plumbing (hot and cold running water, a flush toilet, and a bathtub or shower) for the exclusive use of the occupants. For the rest of the nation, 75.2 percent of housing met these criteria. Appalachia is predominantly rural, and rural housing tends to be substandard, but the housing in Appalachian cities was generally in poorer condition than that in other metropolitan areas.

The average per capita annual income was 25 percent lower for Appalachia than the nation as a whole in 1959, according to the 1960 census. The national average was $1,889, and the Appalachian average was $1,423. Appalachia differed from the rest of the nation in other factors associated with poverty. For one thing, the population was less educated: 23.3 percent of 16- and 17-year-olds were not in school in Appalachia compared to 19 percent in the rest of the country. For another, unemployment affected 7.1 percent of the labor force in Appalachia and 5 percent elsewhere. These statistics are somewhat deceiving, because many adults in Appalachia had removed themselves from the job market, reasoning that if no jobs existed in the region, then it made no sense to look for one. The government omitted so-called discouraged workers from official unemployment totals, but discouragement in employment has been linked to several indicators of chronic psychological stress, including dissatisfaction with life, low self-esteem, and powerlessness, and to stress-related illness.

Many of those who were employed worked in industries that had a declining workforce, namely, agriculture, coal mining, forestry, and railroads. From 1950 to 1960, when job opportunities were opening elsewhere in other industries, Appalachia lost 643,000 jobs in agriculture and mining.

The Nation's Wake-Up Call

As the 20th century entered its seventh decade, articles on welfare abuse sold magazines, but most Americans remained ignorant of the extent of poverty in their affluent country. The suburban middle class rarely visited Indian reservations, inner cities, the fields where migrant laborers worked, or Harlan County, Kentucky. Then, in 1962, a socialist writer named Michael Harrington published *The Other America*, the best-selling book that opened the nation's eyes and made poverty impossible to ignore. For countless readers, Harrington described a different world, "the economic underworld of American life,"[4] populated by 50 million poor people who were "increasingly slipping out of the very experience and consciousness of the nation."[5]

The "new" poor had become invisible, Harrington explained, because they lived in segregated, out-of-the-way places. They were invisible because mass production enabled them to afford passable clothing and cover their hunger and depressed income in a costume. They were also invisible because many were very old or very young, either over age 65 or under 18. Harrington identified the population groups in which poverty was prevalent, including African Americans, Hispanics, Native Americans, the unemployed or underemployed, and those living in "economically obsolete" regions, such as Appalachia.[6]

Harrington challenged traditional ways of viewing the poor. "Disease, alcoholism, low IQ's, these express a whole way of life. They are, in the main, the effects of an environment, not the biographies of unlucky individuals," he wrote. "If there is to be a lasting assault on the shame of the other America, it must seek to root out of this society an entire environment, and not just the relief of individuals."[7]

Chronicle of Events

1940s–1960s
• Migration of the rural poor to northern and western cities yields significant growth in applications for public assistance.

1940
• Births to unmarried women account for 7.1 of every 1,000 live births; among African Americans the rate is 35.6 per 1,000 live births.
• Three percent of households are headed by white women; 7 percent of households are headed by black women.
• *June and July:* Congress authorizes $12 billion for defense manufacturing.

1941
• *June 25:* President Roosevelt issues Executive Order 8802, requiring the federal government and defense contractors to hire without regard to race, religion, or national origin.

1942
• *August 4:* The United States and Mexico agree to the Labor Importation Program, which becomes known in the West as the bracero program.
• *September 29:* The first 1,500 Mexican workers to participate in the bracero program arrive in California.

1943
• In this year 52,098 Mexicans enter the United States through the bracero program.

The "Hotel Pahokee" housed African-American migrant vegetable pickers in Pahokee, Florida, during World War II. *(Marion Post Walcott, Library of Congress, Prints and Photographs Division, LC-USF34-057221-D)*

- The mechanical cotton picker is introduced; it will replace 2.3 million laborers.
- *April:* U.S. farm workers lose the federal protections given to Mexicans working under the bracero program.
- *July:* Roughly 5 million people in the United States receive public assistance.

1943–1964
- Approximately 4.5 million Mexicans enter the United States through the bracero program.

1944
- Another 62,170 Mexicans take part in the bracero program.

1945
- About 701,000 families collect benefits from ADC.
- *January 19:* John Collier resigns as commissioner of Indian affairs.

1946
- The National School Lunch Program subsidizes states for equipment purchases and food purchases and preparation for school-lunch programs.
- With the Full Employment Act, the federal government reaffirms its commitment to furthering employment, production, purchasing power, and investment.

1947
- Congress makes available $350,000 to purchase land for Native Americans.
- The average American Indian family earns $918 from agriculture; two-thirds of families on reservations earn more than half their income from farming.

1948
- Almost 10 million U.S. families have an annual income below $2,000.
- The diet of low-income Americans has improved since World War II.

1949
- Community Chests in 800 cities and towns raise $165 million.

1950s
- About 300,000 Mexicans enter the United States each year under the bracero program.

- Sixty-six percent of the Rosebud Reservation in South Dakota, 80 percent of the Crow Reservation in Montana, and large percentages of other reservations are leased to whites.

1950
- Some 12.3 million Americans are 65 or older.
- Congress expands the Social Security program by issuing grants to mothers of dependent children; Aid to Dependent Children (ADC) becomes Aid to Families with Dependent Children (AFDC).

1950–1960
- Appalachia loses 643,000 jobs in agriculture and mining.

1951
- The Direct Employment Assistance Program is begun, to encourage unemployed Native Americans to seek jobs in cities.

1953
- The U.S. Department of Health, Education, and Welfare is created.
- *August 1:* With House Concurrent Resolution 108, Congress resolves to terminate the Indians' status as wards of the U.S. government.

1954
- The U.S. Immigration and Naturalization Service, U.S. Border Patrol, and state and municipal authorities in the West conduct Operation Wetback to round up undocumented Mexicans in the United States and return them to Mexico.
- The School Milk Program makes federal funds available to buy milk for schoolchildren.
- *July 14:* Government agents apprehend 4,800 people on the first day of Operation Wetback.
- *September 18:* The air transport arm of the U.S. Border Patrol flies the first of 11,459 undocumented Mexicans from Chicago to Brownsville, Texas.

1955
- *March:* The commissioner of immigration tells Congress that the illegal immigration from Mexico has been halted.

1956
- Disability insurance becomes a provision of the Social Security program.

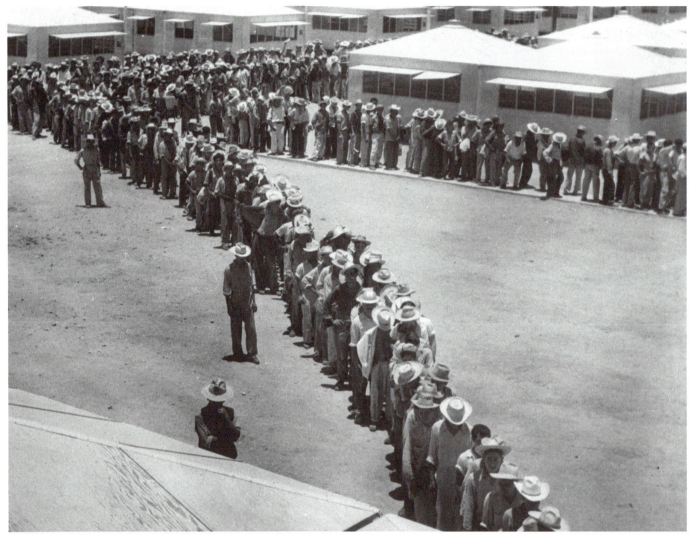

The Immigration and Naturalization Service processed as many as a thousand undocumented Mexicans per day in 1954. *(Courtesy, Texas AFL-CIO Collection, The University of Texas at Arlington Libraries, Arlington, Texas)*

1958

• John Kenneth Galbraith publishes *The Affluent Society,* urging Americans to discard old attitudes toward poverty and reclassifying the nation's poor as case poor and insular poor.

1959

• The average per capita annual income for the nation is $1,889; for Appalachia it is $1,423.

• In Appalachia 23.3 percent of 16- and 17-year-olds are not in school; in the rest of the United States 19 percent of people in this age group are not in school.

• Unemployment affects 7.1 percent of workers in Appalachia and 5 percent of workers in other parts of the United States.

1960

• Most welfare recipients, roughly 3.1 million families, collect benefits from AFDC.

• Six percent of households are headed by white women; 20 percent of households are headed by black women.

• Relief funds distributed in the United States total $3.1 billion.

• White males working full-time head 20 percent of poor families.

• Twenty-eight percent of families receiving support from AFDC live in homes lacking toilets and hot water; 17 percent have no running water.

• Nationwide, monthly welfare payments average $30 per person and $115 per family.

- New York City social service agencies set a $2,660 yearly subsistence-level budget for a family of four.
- In Harlan County, Kentucky, two-thirds of homes are substandard and one-fourth lack running water, but 67 percent of families have televisions, 59 percent own cars, and 42 percent have telephones.
- In Appalachia 60.8 percent of the population lives in homes that are in sound condition and have modern indoor plumbing; 75.2 percent of people outside Appalachia live in similar housing.

1961

- The federal government extends AFDC to needy two-parent families if the head of the household is unemployed and has exhausted unemployment benefits.
- The government abandons its policy of Termination toward Native Americans in favor of lessening federal responsibility through economic development.

- *January:* The Michigan Department of Welfare considers $223.05 per month, or $2,676.60 per year, adequate to support a family of four at subsistence level.

1962

- Births to unmarried women account for 21.5 of every 1,000 live births; among African Americans the rate is 90.1 per 1,000 live births.
- The Social Security Administration sets the poverty line at $3,089 annual income for a family of four and $1,519 for a single adult.
- Michael Harrington publishes *The Other America*, alerting many Americans to the severity of poverty in the United States.

Eyewitness Testimony

America is a wealthy nation enjoying unprecedented levels of comfort and leisure, of course, when contrasted with other countries, or when contrasted with its own past. But these things are relative. We are still incredibly poor and shamefully backward when measured by the yardstick of our unexploited possibilities. The areas we have conquered in the matter of living standards and general improvement are pathetically small when compared with the uncharted spaces still to be conquered. The American people are well off from the vantage point of any European or Asiatic people. I submit, however, that they are far from well off from the vantage point of what we could produce and could consume. . . .

We do not need statistics to confirm what our own eyes witness: Slums, substandard homes and diets, children deprived of the minimal conditions of civilized living, a thousand and one proofs that there is unlimited room for economic improvement. . . .

I certainly do not wish to join the ranks of those who focus attention only on shortcomings. But I do believe that we must correct them. As long as there are millions of American families existing on substandard levels, there are tasks to challenge our full energies as a nation. Not only must our whole population be brought above this subsistence line but the standards themselves must be raised. That, I say, is a challenge as grim as any war. We have what it takes to meet it.

Eric Johnston, president of the U.S. Chamber of Commerce, 1944, America Unlimited, *pp. 116–18.*

[I]t is a dangerous fact that millions of Americans are shabbily sheltered and living in filthy, malignant slum areas that are growing both in size and in their threat to the physical and political health of our country. Any slum-clearance legislation passed by Congress would have to be followed up by action in states and cities, and by continuous Congressional action.

We Americans like to think of the typical home as a vine-clad cottage, with roses growing on trellises, and trees and grass in the yard; and with all this we associate the pleasing and lively sounds of healthy children at play. It is one of the glories of America that so many of our homes are of that kind—or, at least, equally attractive.

But it is one of our moral, political, and economic responsibilities to do something to lift more homes at least to the minimum level for satisfactory living. The 15,000,000 or more Americans who live in the blighted areas are not inferior to the rest of us. They are only less fortunate. Imagine how you would feel if you and your family were housed as they are. Trouble does not come from men who live agreeable lives. It breeds among men who are frustrated, ashamed and envious.

Paul H. Douglas, U.S. senator from Illinois, July 9, 1949, "Democracy Can't Live in These Houses," p. 22.

Some of you may imagine that because you live in nice small towns where the refreshing air of heaven circulates freely, the cleansing rays of the sun penetrate every room and yard, and rats do not congregate nightly around garbage cans and outside privies, you are immune to the threat of blighted areas. I beg you, if you imagine you are safe, to stop and think. If, because of depression in some future decade, we should have dangerous unrest, the consequences would not be confined to the areas where the unrest is most likely to develop first. If some dreadful disease should begin in one area, it might spread anywhere.

Responsibility to do something to clear the blighted living areas is not limited to morality or to national pride. National internal security demands that something effective be done. National health demands it. Protection of your own health and protection of you and your family from crime require it.

Paul H. Douglas, U.S. senator from Illinois, July 9, 1949, "Democracy Can't Live in These Houses," p. 50.

Several weeks ago a commercial retail-credit agency in Detroit, while investigating instances of fraud and chiseling practiced by certain recipients of direct relief, along with alleged inefficiency and mismanagement of the city's Department of Public Welfare, had occasion to telephone a woman relief client to make some inquiries. An estimated 22 percent of all relief recipients in Detroit who own or rent their homes, it might be pointed out, have telephones listed in their own names.

Anyway, a woman who answered the credit man's call told him that the party he was seeking had gone downtown for the day. When the credit-firm representative suggested to the woman on the wire that she might be able to give him the information he wanted, she replied, "Oh, no; I wouldn't be able to do that. I'm just the maid."

Now, it is peculiar that a person receiving public charity—which is what general assistance, or relief, actually is—could afford the services of a maid.

Rufus Jarman, writer, December 10, 1949, "Detroit Cracks Down on Relief Chiselers," p. 17.

Not long ago the case was brought to light of one John E. O'Connor, father of fourteen, whom newspapers have called Detroit's "Welfare King." He went on relief when a department was officially opened for that purpose in 1929, and since then he has cost the taxpayers more than $70,000 in relief money by failing to support himself and his family.

O'Connor was released from prison recently, after serving a thirty-month term for nonsupport. During the thirty months, Mrs. O'Connor drew $3750 in relief, although O'Connor said in court that he found her with another man after his release from prison, and although only three of the fourteen children now live at home. Five are in the care of the city's juvenile home, five are with private charity homes, and the oldest son has married and gone on relief on his own. Since going on relief twenty years ago, O'Connor has been arrested seventeen times and convicted eight times on charges ranging from nonsupport to assault and battery.

Rufus Jarman, writer, December 10, 1949, "Detroit Cracks Down on Relief Chiselers," p. 19.

Miss L was 74 years of age when she was interviewed in the fall of 1946. She had been employed as a secretary in a legal office for some 36 years, and had quit working at the age of 70 upon the advice of her physician. She was awarded monthly benefits of $26.59—$319 a year—and this, together with $100 a year for her services as an administratrix of an estate, and $38 a year interest on her savings account, constituted her retirement income. For many years she had occupied an apartment for which she paid $35 a month rent. In order to economize Miss L had rented one room for $24 a month. Her income did not cover her expenses and she had withdrawn $750 from her savings. Miss L had $1,500 left at the end of the year, enough for probably two more years. She commented to the interviewer that she hoped she would die before her savings were exhausted. . . .

After working 33 years for the same company as a marble worker, Mr. N at age 65 quit his job because of failing health and became entitled to monthly benefits of $10.93. The company had no retirement pay plan. The beneficiary, who is a widower, lives alone in an attic apartment for which he pays $10 a month rent. His only son, who is single, paid a $72 electric bill for the beneficiary. During the survey year, he received $229 from public assistance and the payment of a $10 doctor bill by a lodge. He stated he needs more medical attention, but hesitates to ask for more as he feels that he is getting enough from

public assistance. The beneficiary's only asset is a $200 bank account, and a life insurance policy with a face value of $250, on which he is still paying premiums. . . .

Mr. O was awarded a monthly insurance benefit of $28.05, on an average monthly wage of $117. He had been forced to quit working in 1942 because of a serious heart condition. At the time of the interview in 1946 Mr. O was bedridden; he was living in a boarding house and paying his entire insurance check for his board and room. He had withdrawn $100 of his savings to pay doctor bills, but this had not been enough, and at the end of the year he owed the doctor $45. He had only $100 of his savings left. The landlady was objecting to the care of a bedridden roomer, and told the interviewer she could not continue the arrangement much longer. Mr. O was gloomily anticipating being moved to the city hospital.

Cases "L," "N," and "O" in Staff of the Subcommittee on Low-Income Families, Joint [Congressional] Committee on the Economic Report, 1950, Low-Income Families and Economic Stability, p. 104.

The frustration which results from overcrowding, conflict between the desires and needs of various members of the family, fatigue due to the performance of household duties under unfavorable conditions—these are health menaces quite as serious as (if less obvious than) poorly heated rooms or stairs without railing. The sense of inferiority due to living in a substandard home is a far more serious menace to the health of our children than all the unsanitary plumbing in the United States.

Committee on the Hygiene of Housing, American Public Health Association, 1950, in "Dirt, Disease, Degradation, and Despair," p. 9.

I was touring Washington in a police scout car. Suddenly it turned off one of the large open streets, nosed into an alleyway. We bumped over rough red bricks and mudholes, hugging the sides of buildings, grazing board fences and barbed wire. "Like going through a rathole, eh?" one officer joked.

My eyes darted over rows of filthy tumbledown shacks, with people swarming in and out of them; unpainted gray boards and sagging walls; a litter of garbage and bones, with scavenging dogs and cats and buzzing clouds of flies.

It was the center of a city block, hollowed out to make a slum. You could walk around that block for days, on the open streets, and never dream such a rotten inner core existed.

"But I had no idea Washington had slums like these," I said.

"Nobody does—they're hidden," replied the policeman.

The marble carpet had rolled back. I had my first view of the filth that has been swept beneath it. I had no idea just how much that marble carpet is hiding.

Howard Whitman, writer, February 1950, "Washington— Disgrace to the Nation," p. 34.

Would you expect to find outhouses in Washington, D.C.—within sight of the capitol dome?

The courts and alleys are full of them—rows of ramshackle privies, some with slats broken out and doors that don't close, sitting in the garbage-cluttered back yards, emitting a horrible stench. They have flush toilets in them, usually filthy and broken, one toilet to three or four families.

The slum dwellings, occupied by Negroes mostly, have neither steam heat nor running water. Kerosene lamps and candles provide light; coal stoves provide heat—for those who can afford to buy coal.

Howard Whitman, writer, February 1950, "Washington— Disgrace to the Nation," p. 45.

[B]ehind the ten million neediest cases, the misfits and the unproductive workers, lies the basic fact of scarcity. For what we are stricken with—at the lower levels of our economic structure—is the same disease that is eating all the world: a shortage of productive apparatus. We Americans—the most prodigious capital-builders the world has ever known—still lack the wealth—the real, hard, physical wealth, not the stocks and bonds—to make us all productive. And because the capital we have is unevenly spread from trade to trade, some sectors of the nation are badly undeveloped. Three-quarters of America has grown to an impressive stature: it can not only sustain itself in style but help the outside world as well. A laggard fourth remains. And in that fourth are not just those whose plight is age or weakness or ill health. There are also those for whom there is insufficient steel or electricity or education or managerial skill to raise them to the level of the rest.

Robert L. Heilbroner, economist, June 1950, "Who Are the American Poor?" p. 31.

We can face up to the problem of indigent old age by ladling out purchasing power with Old-Age Benefits and we can buy options on the future with old-age pension schemes. All that is well and good; at least it prevents the

bottom from dropping out of the market as our population reaches sixty-five.

But can we do nothing better than give the old a helping taken from the plates of others? We are not as young a nation as we were and the curve of average age is moving up: there is a limit to what we can afford. Already in Louisiana four-fifths of all the aged depend on Old-Age Benefits to get along; humanitarian considerations aside these folk are little more than economic parasites.

Robert L. Heilbroner, economist, June 1950, "Who Are the American Poor?" p. 32.

The Nelsons, for example, had been on relief for fifteen years. That's not their real name, but it will do. During those fifteen years, ten children were born, all of them destined to be supported by the city. The result was obvious. One of the youngsters became a petty thief, which was how I got to know about the family. The others, as they reached school age, became truants. I did a little quick figuring, which may not be accurate to the last penny, and discovered that this ne'er-do-well family had cost the taxpayers—Federal, state and city—some $35,000. The case hit me so hard that I wrote an opinion that pretty well sums up my views on relief.

"There is a school of thought," I wrote, "that to ask a person what he does with the relief money given him is to do something that will undermine his dignity and self-respect and his sense of security and self-reliance. There are people who feel demeaned because they are dependent on the community, but when it becomes a continuing situation, there is no dignity or self-respect or self-reliance or independence left to be destroyed.

"Cases come before me in which youngsters under twenty-one get married on home relief, and then for fifteen years they continue to be on home relief and to bring children into the world who are doomed to become unemployable. No person who has lost respect for himself can inspire respect in his children. No person who has become unemployable by reason of continuous dependence on the public can inspire dignity and self-reliance in his children. Indeed, the effect and the result are to the contrary."

Jacob Panken, justice of the Domestic Relations Court, New York City, September 30, 1950, "I Say Relief Is Ruining Families," p. 112.

These are the wetbacks—carrying all their possessions on their backs, ready to bed down at night in whatever shelter comes to hand—or without shelter; able to exist on a

Migrant farmworkers undergo customs inspection at the Mexican border in 1955. *(U.S. Citizenship and Immigration Services)*

few beans and a little flour for tortillas; spending only the few cents a day such meager fare requires; and saving the rest of their earnings for their return to Mexico.

These are the wetbacks—forced by circumstances and the avarice of employers to use a hole in a canal bank as "home," and to sleep amidst a swarm of flies which alternate between nearby filth and the napping children.

These are the wetbacks—illegally in this country and thus at the mercy of employers who can—and will—turn them over to the Border Patrol if they complain about working conditions or wages, living under the constant threat of apprehension and deportation, yet knowing that, even if deported, they will undoubtedly make the return trip across the river the next day or the day after.

These are the wetbacks—unfortunate human beings whose ignorance, poverty, illegal status, and willingness to accept indescribable hardships places them at the mercy of unscrupulous employers.

These are the wetbacks—hundreds of thousands of them pushing across the Rio Grande day after day, pushing their blood brothers, American citizens of Mexican descent, out of jobs in the border country and into competition farther north, pushing wages down, down, down.

These are the wetbacks—sad-eyed and sick, desperate beings unaware that their illegal entry and existence bring with them to the areas they infest soaring statistics on syphilis, tuberculosis, infantile diarrhea and other diseases, along with a host of crime and other socio-economic problems. . . .

Yes, these are the wetbacks—as we pity them, as we see them, as we know them, and, as we fear them from the standpoint of health, national security, welfare and economy.

American G.I. Forum, 1953, What Price Wetbacks? *p. 5.*

Within the major migratory labor areas, the aggregate movement may seem to resemble a pattern, but it is a mistake to assume that the lives of the majority are patterned on anything except harsh uncertainty. . . .

This uncertainty is a double one: (1) There is the hazard of whether there will be a crop on which to work. (2) There is always doubt whether the migrant will get the work he expects even if there is a good crop. In consequence, a hopeful trek of hundreds of miles may end with the crushing discovery that the crop is late or has failed or that other migrants have arrived earlier and have filled up the available housing and that there is no work to be had. The whole system of migratory labor is so chaotic and unsystematic that a comfortable balance of labor supply and demand is rare and unusual. Either surpluses or shortages are more normal.

Varden Fuller, agricultural economist, 1955, No Work Today! The Plight of America's Migrants, *p. 7.*

Migrants do not work at individual jobs like tending a machine, or occupying a station on an assembly line, or driving a truck. A hundredweight of cotton or a hamper of beans is the same whether picked by a child or by an adult and earns the same wage. Since farm employers and labor contractors seldom exclude women and frequently allow children as well, and since the family frequently needs the earnings, the entire family often works as a unit. Moreover, except in the rare instances of child-care facilities being provided, it is easier and safer for children to work along with parents than to be left behind in camp or in a locked automobile. Children as young as seven and eight years of age are often found at work in the fields, and child-labor laws, even where they do exist, have proved difficult to enforce.

Varden Fuller, agricultural economist, 1955, No Work Today! The Plight of America's Migrants, *p. 8.*

Here is a paradox. When we begin to consider the needs of those who are now excluded from the economic system by accident, inadequacy, or misfortune—we find that the normal remedy is to make them or their children productive citizens. This means that they add to the total output of goods. We see once again that even by its *own terms* the present preoccupation with material as opposed to human investment is inefficient. . . .

But increased output of goods is not the main point. . . . The main point lies elsewhere. Poverty—grim, degrading, and ineluctable—is not remarkable in India. For few the fate is otherwise. But in the United States the survival of poverty is remarkable. We ignore it because we share with all societies at all times the capacity for not seeing what we do not wish to see. Anciently this has enabled the nobleman to enjoy his dinner while remaining oblivious to the beggars around his door. In our own day it enables us to travel in comfort through south Chicago or the South. But while our failure to notice can be explained, it cannot be excused.

Economist and writer John Kenneth Galbraith, 1958, The Affluent Society, *pp. 332–33.*

Many central areas in big cities have changed their ethnic character several times in the past five or six decades, as the children of earlier immigrants have grown up and moved elsewhere and new national groups have come in. Recent years, however, have seen perplexing changes in the extent and tempo of movement though the central areas and in the types of people who move out and in.

Many of the longer-established families from which a neighborhood drew its leaders have moved their homes and interests to the suburbs. Their places frequently are taken by Spanish speaking newcomers from Puerto Rico and Mexico and by both Negro and white families from southern fields and mountains.

The amazing capacity of American communities to assimilate newcomers has been slowed down, even blocked in some places, by the evident and lasting characteristic of brown skin. Unlike the earlier immigrants, these families may find themselves trapped in a city's worst housing, paying exorbitant rentals, even when they have the means to move to better quarters.

Professor Wilbur J. Cohen of the University of Michigan, November 1958, in "Fighting Poverty," p. 43.

Ask any man in the street about "the welfare" and nine chances out of ten you will evoke a grimace or a derogatory remark about the sub-standard kind of human beings who are assumed to live on its bounty.

But if you ask the penniless old person who is obliged to depend on public assistance for survival—

or his grown children who are required by most state laws to contribute to his support, you will hear that "the welfare" is niggardly, snooping, unfair about small possessions, and expects decent people to manage on an impossible pittance.

Ask the economist and he will tell you that people have to have income in a money economy; ask the sociologist and he will say the family cannot always do the whole job in today's complex society. Public welfare underpins on both counts.

But ask the law-maker or other governmental official about public welfare policy and he will groan, thinking of heavy costs and the seemingly irreconcilable views that surround it.

Elizabeth Wickenden, public policy analyst, and Winifred Bell, professor of social work, Cleveland State University, 1961, Public Welfare: Time for a Change, *p. 11.*

"It's almost incredible that in one of the largest cities in the richest country in the world hundreds of people are literally starving." That was the statement Friday of Arthur K. Atkinson, chairman of the St. Louis Advisory Board of the Salvation Army. He said that, since January 26, the Salvation Army—the last resort for those who need help immediately—has had to turn down 315 of 631 families who need food.

The 1961 breadline at the Salvation Army headquarters in the Fullerton building at Seventh and Pine Streets has upward of 100 people waiting most of the time, Mr. Atkinson said. In the recent bad weather, many of them were soaked to the skin, wet and cold and literally famished, Mr. Atkinson said. One woman in the last few days fainted as she waited in line, he added. She was taken to City Hospital, where she was diagnosed as suffering from malnutrition. The Salvation Army sent workers to her home, found five small children there—and they too were suffering from malnutrition. All six wound up in City Hospital.

St. Louis, Missouri, Globe Democrat, *February 11, 1961, in Elizabeth Wickenden and Winifred Bell,* Public Welfare: Time for a Change, *p. viii.*

The great depression was a traumatic experience from which since the war we have made a complete economic recovery. But have we made a psychological and intellectual recovery? Or does the scar left by the depression delude us into thinking, whenever a public problem arises, that our society is paralyzed and only the federal government can cope? Among the dangers of this syndrome is that we will ignore, and by ignoring destroy, the actual sources of our ability to meet the future.

"The Public Business," March 1961, p. 102.

The Appalachian Mountains lack the ruggedness of the Rockies or the ultimate cruelty of the Andes, but they contain some tough country—tough topographically and tougher in terms of the human condition. Enter this region, say from Lexington, Kentucky, and the landscape at first has a deceptively pleasing mien. This is the Bluegrass, large estates, for the most part, with neat white fences, and behind the fences grazing cattle or grazing horses whose owners and guests will drink bourbon juleps on Derby Day. Farther on, however, the road begins to climb through the western spurs of the Appalachians, and the farms are pressed into the narrow bottom lands. Here, if a man owns a precious allotment for tobacco, he may do pretty well—eking out perhaps as much as $1,000 from a single acre. But up the "hollows" are many less fortunate, earning a precarious $400 or $500 per year in cash from hillsides so titled that as the moonshiners say, "The only way you can get corn down from those hills is in quart jars." Eastern Kentucky and much of Appalachia is full of this kind of subsistence farming where men are "underemployed" as surely as they are in many parts of the deeper South. Says one who knows the region well: "The people in these low-income farms don't come within the province of organized labor, which would dramatize the situation. If you have 5,000 unemployed in Dayton the uproar is terrific. But 50,000 underemployed on the farms and no one cares about it."

John Davenport, assistant editor, Fortune, *March 1961, "In the Midst of Plenty," p. 108.*

Many [caseworkers] believe that welfare largess is defeating its own goals and that the hour for reappraisal is at hand. Listen to two Washington, D.C., caseworkers—one a young white girl, the other a Negro woman with 24 years' experience in social work—who were picked at random for interviews.

"The pendulum has swung too far," said the veteran Negro caseworker. "We're raising a second generation of ADC children on relief. It's too easy. People are human. They'll take advantage."

"Something must be done," said the white caseworker, after three years on the job. "We're now raising children on ADC whose mothers were also raised on relief. They know nothing else. We must weed out the hangers-on and close the loopholes, but above all, we must build a decent rehabilitation program."

One worker described a typical case. A 40-year-old mother lives with three daughters, one son and two grandchildren, all illegitimate. The family receives $221 a month in ADC payments, including $64 rent for a low-cost-housing unit. One 15-year-old daughter's illegitimate child is three years old. The 14-year-old daughter's illegitimate child is almost two.

"The girls take their pregnancies as a matter of course," said the caseworker. "The home is like Grand Central Terminal. Members vanish, stay away five days at a time. All the girls should have been put in homes, away from their mother, but the program had no place to put them. It's a vicious circle."

In another case, a mother and father with nine children draw a total of $410 in relief payments. He quits one job after another, contending all are beneath his talents. A private charity wants to place the children in foster homes, but the mother and father and the child-welfare service think the family should remain together. The relief goes on—with nothing solved.

Fletcher Knebel, Look *magazine Washington Bureau, November 7, 1961, "Welfare: Has It Become a Scandal?" p. 33.*

Relief is gradually becoming an honorable career in America. It is a pretty fair life, if you have neither conscience nor pride. The politicians will weep over you. The state will give a mother a bonus for her illegitimate children, and if she neglects them sufficiently she can save enough of her ADC payments to keep herself and her boy friend in wine and gin. Nothing is your fault. And when the city fathers of a harassed community like Newburgh [New York] suggest that able-bodied welfare clients might sweep the streets the "liberal" editorialists arise as one man and denounce them for their medieval cruelty. I don't know how long Americans can stand this erosion of principle.

Jenkin Lloyd Jones, editor of the Tulsa Tribune, *addressing the Inland Daily Press Association, November 24, 1961, in Edgar May,* The Wasted Americans, *p. 7.*

Poverty is often off the beaten track. It always has been. The ordinary tourist never left the main highway, and today he rides interstate turnpikes. He does not go into the valleys of Pennsylvania where the towns look like movie sets of Wales in the thirties. He does not see the company houses in rows, the rutted roads (the poor always have bad

Boys play amid trash in a New York City lot, 1962. *(Library of Congress, Prints and Photographs Division, LC-USZ62-122639)*

roads whether they live in the city, in towns, or on farms), and everything is black and dirty. And even if he were to pass through such a place by accident, the tourist would not meet the unemployed men in the bar or the women coming home from a runaway [illegal] sweatshop.

Then, too, beauty and myths are perennial masks of poverty. The traveler comes to the Appalachians in the lovely season. He sees the hills, the streams, the foliage—but not the poor. Or perhaps he looks at a run-down mountain house and, remembering Rousseau rather than

seeing with his eyes, decides that "those people" are truly fortunate to be living the way they are and that they are lucky to be exempt from the strains and tensions of the middle class. The only problem is that "those people," the quaint inhabitants of those hills, are undereducated, underprivileged, lack medical care, and are in the process of being forced from the land into a life in the cities, where they are misfits.

Writer Michael Harrington, 1962, The Other America, *pp. 3–4.*

CHAPTER EIGHT

The War on Poverty and Its Aftermath

1962–1980

Michael Harrington's book *The Other America* persuaded President John F. Kennedy of the need to aid the nation's poor through legislation. "Poverty in the midst of plenty," wrote Kennedy on April 10, 1963, "is a paradox that must not go unchallenged."[1] Kennedy enlisted the Council of Economic Advisers to develop a plan for the needy, and the project continued under the direction of President Lyndon B. Johnson after Kennedy's assassination. Johnson's goals were far-reaching: On January 8, 1964, delivering his first State of the Union address, he asked Congress to declare "all-out war on human poverty and unemployment in these United States."[2] "Our aim," he said, "is not only to relieve the symptom of poverty, but to cure it and, above all, to prevent it."[3]

Johnson's major weapon in this war was an ambitious piece of legislation, the Economic Opportunity Act, signed into law on August 20, 1964, which attacked poverty from several directions. Title I of this act took aim at youth unemployment by creating Job Corps, a program to offer education, vocational training, and work experience to young people aged 16 to 21 who had dropped out of school. Instruction took place in training centers and conservation camps reminiscent of the Civilian Conservation Corps (CCC) of the 1930s. An additional work-training program for young women and men secured full- or part-time employment through state and local governments and nonprofit organizations. Its participants continued their education as they increased their employability and were discouraged from dropping out of school. Also, work-study program financed by the Department of Health, Education, and Welfare enabled college students in low-income families to help finance their education.

Title II of the Economic Opportunity Act sought to alleviate poverty through community-action programs in depressed areas. These included Operation Head Start, which prepared preschoolers for kindergarten; Upward Bound, which was intended to encourage young people to attend college; and day-care centers, neighborhood clinics, and recreation centers.

May 7, 1964: President Lyndon B. Johnson listens to the concerns of the poor while touring Appalachia. *(LBJ Library, Photo by Cecil Stoughton)*

The Economic Opportunity Act also provided loans and grants to families and businesses in low-income areas, and it funded Volunteers in Service to America (VISTA), sometimes called the "domestic peace corps," which supplied volunteer labor to federal, state, and local antipoverty initiatives. A VISTA volunteer might teach in a Job Corps training center or work on an Indian reservation or on a community-action project.

In addition, the act created the Office of Economic Opportunity (OEO), whose director was to be the president's "personal chief of staff for the war against poverty," Johnson said.[4] The director was to coordinate with existing government agencies to implement the provisions of the Economic Opportunity Act.

An Ambitious Legislative Agenda

Legislation enacted during Johnson's administration to aid disadvantaged Americans nearly rivaled that of the depression years. Johnson envisioned a "Great Society" and through his legislative agenda sought to raise the nation's quality of life. One of the most significant laws passed during his presidency was the Civil Rights Act of July 2, 1964, which empowered the attorney general to ensure citizens of equal access and opportunity in voting booths, schools, and public facilities. It outlawed discrimination in restaurants, hotels, and other establishments serving the public, and perhaps most important for the minority poor, it created the Equal

Employment Opportunity Commission (EEOC), the agency that enforces federal laws against discrimination in employment.

Thanks to the Food Stamp Act, passed August 31, 1964, qualifying families could afford to feed themselves adequately by purchasing at a discount stamps to use in place of cash in grocery stores. A family of four, for example, might purchase $78 in food stamps for $44. The Elementary and Secondary Education Act, signed into law on April 11, 1965, was the first federal law to give general financial aid to schools. It made available $1 billion to improve schools offering kindergarten through grade 12 classes in slums and depressed rural areas. The Higher Education Act, which became law on November 8, 1965, funded college loans and adult education programs.

On July 30, 1965, Johnson signed legislation making Medicare, a federal health insurance program for the aged, a provision of Social Security. The number of people in the United States age 65 and older had reached 17.5 million in 1963, accounting for 9.4 percent of the population. Not only was the population of older Americans growing, but hospital costs were rising faster than the cost of living, and private health insurance was becoming too costly for many older Americans. Another provision enacted on the same day created Medicaid, a health-insurance

Preschoolers gain improved nutrition and academic preparedness through a Head Start program in Buffalo, New York. This photograph was taken between 1965 and 1973. *(Photograph © Milton Rogovin 1952–2002, The Rogovin Collection, LLC)*

program for people with low incomes. Originally Medicaid served people who qualified for public assistance or had incomes just above the qualifying level but was limited to those who were 65 or older, blind, or disabled, as well as families with dependent children. Congress later extended coverage to children and pregnant women living in poverty, refugees, and children in state care.

The Appalachian Redevelopment Act of March 1965 was intended to improve the physical features of the region with the ultimate aim of stimulating economic development. It therefore allocated money where the potential for economic growth was greatest rather than where need was most severe. The heaviest investment— $840 million—was in highway construction, because access to all parts of the region was fundamental to the success of other endeavors. The act also sought to repair damage done by industries that had exploited Appalachia's natural resources and to improve human resources. These goals were addressed through land stabilization and conservation projects, erosion control, opening of vocational-education facilities and regional health centers, and other initiatives. Finally, the act created the Appalachian Regional Commission to administer federal programs and coordinate them with state and local agencies.

Outside Looking In

The government took these great steps although very little research on poverty in the United States had been carried out. This was about to change, however. In the mid-1960s public and private agencies and academics studied and theorized about the nation's poor.

On January 11, 1966, Johnson issued Executive Order 11306, establishing the National Advisory Commission on Rural Poverty and charging it with studying economic situations and trends in rural America. The 26 members of the commission, who included college presidents, members of the clergy, labor leaders, and the president of ABC Television, held public hearings and gathered information in regions where rural poverty was most acute, such as Appalachia, the Ozark Mountains, the U.S.-Texas border, Indian reservations, and the Delta and hill country of Mississippi. The commission also initiated 45 studies of various aspects of rural life.

In its 1967 report the commission noted that the rural poor had lost their sense of community. Most lived apart from the market economy and had enjoyed little benefit from postwar economic growth. "They are on the outside looking in, and they need help," the commission wrote.[5] Not only were average family incomes low in regions of rural poverty, but also the proportions of young and old who depended for support on the working-age population were higher than in other parts of the country. Making life more difficult in Appalachia, the region's working-age population was less likely to be in the job market than that of other regions. More than 70 percent of families in all the poverty areas studied had annual incomes below $2,000, "and one family in four exists, somehow, on less than $1,000 a year," the report stated.[6]

Unemployment and underemployment were widespread, of course, but even when all adult household members were working, some families could not get by, and some made so little money that their children literally were starving. Rural poverty was most severe among African Americans, American Indians, and Mexican Americans. Also, low average family incomes corresponded with low educational attainment and living in dilapidated housing.

The migration of many thousands of people from agricultural regions to blighted inner cities was a symptom of the severity of rural poverty, the commission concluded. The United States therefore never would alleviate urban poverty until it had solved the problem of rural poverty. The commission called for a national policy to give rural Americans the same access that other Americans enjoyed to jobs, medical care, housing, education, welfare, and other public services. It recommended legislation and appropriations to create jobs in rural areas and a manpower program to combat unemployment and underemployment. Additionally, it advocated changes in public-assistance programs to ensure a decent standard of living for the rural poor and free food stamps for the poorest families. Regions of rural poverty needed health centers and health professionals to staff them; residents also needed family-planning programs. Better housing and rent supplements were recommended, as were appropriations for housing on Indian reservations. Finally, the commission urged that the poor be involved in community affairs, both locally and regionally. It was a tall order.

Anthropologist Oscar Lewis, who studied impoverished communities in Puerto Rico, Mexico, and the United States, identified a "culture of poverty," which he described as a "way of life that is passed down from generation to generation along family lines."[7] The culture of poverty seemed to flourish wherever conditions were right for it, in regions separated geographically from mainstream society, in urban slums and rural pockets, and among different nationalities. The conditions for a culture of poverty included an economy in which people worked for wages and goods were produced for profit; chronically high unemployment or underemployment among unskilled laborers; low wages; a lack of social, political, and economic organization in the low-income population; and a prevailing belief that poverty results from personal shortcomings. Lewis identified about 70 interrelated social, economic, and psychological traits that characterized the population of this subculture. Chief among them was a lack of participation in the major institutions of the larger society. Members of this subculture were likely to have low levels of literacy and education and to live in substandard housing, in crowded conditions, and in communities that lacked organization.

Public-opinion polls conducted at this time found that many Americans were more likely to disapprove of the poor than to try to understand them. Thirty-three percent of respondents to a 1964 Gallup Poll said that poverty most often resulted from lack of effort, 29 percent said that economic and social factors were its major cause, and 32 percent said that individual shortcomings and outside circumstances contributed equally. (Six percent had no opinion.) In a January 1965 poll measuring attitudes toward welfare recipients, 84 percent of respondents said that able-bodied recipients should be required to take any available job that paid the going wage; 73 percent favored distribution of food and clothing instead of cash benefits; 69 percent wanted out-of-state migrants applying for welfare to offer proof that they had moved to the area in response to a firm job offer; 58 percent wanted 60-day residency requirements; 50 percent favored denying public support to single mothers receiving benefits who bore more children; and 20 percent wanted to see welfare mothers sterilized.

Ironically, a survey conducted in the mid-1960s by the Department of Health, Education, and Welfare found that nearly half of families receiving support from AFDC could not always afford milk; 17 percent of children in these families occasionally missed school because they had no clothes to wear. AFDC households commonly had too few beds and chairs, and 24 percent lacked running water. Eleven percent of families shared a kitchen.

In 1965, under the direction of Secretary of Labor Daniel P. Moynihan, the U.S. Department of Labor published *The Negro Family*, a study of social and economic conditions among African Americans that linked rising unemployment and low incomes in this population with a breakdown in the two-parent family structure. Nationwide, 25 percent of African-American marriages failed, 25 percent of African-American births were to single women, and 25 percent of African-American families were headed by women. All these factors led to an alarming dependence on public welfare. Using the District of Columbia as an example, the researchers found that 29.2 percent of African Americans were unemployed for at least part of the prosperous year 1963. In that year the illegitimacy rate in census tracts with median annual incomes exceeding $8,000 was one-third that of tracts with median incomes below $4,000.

"As with the population as a whole, there is much evidence that children are being born most rapidly in those Negro families with the least financial resources," the researchers wrote. "A cycle is at work; too many children too early make it most difficult for the parents to finish school. . . . Low education levels in turn produce low income levels, which deprive children of many opportunities, and so the cycle repeats itself."[8]

The Department of Labor report generated controversy because it also linked female-headed families among African Americans with slavery, claiming that slavery had weakened family bonds among African Americans and implying that family instability was a cultural trait. Critics challenging this assertion made the point that most African-American families were headed by two parents from the aftermath of the Civil War until fairly recently. Twentieth-century economic conditions and discrimination, they insisted, had strained African-American households. Furthermore, births to single women had increased among all races and ethnic groups in the 1950s as a result of changing sexual mores, and the illegitimacy rate among African Americans had stabilized in 1958.

The Poor Protest

Academic disputes were one thing; day-to-day living was another. On August 11, 1965, rage over crowding, rundown housing, and unemployment sparked a week of looting, fires, and violence in Watts, California, a low-income Los Angeles community. Houses and stores burned to the ground because the rioting blocked fire engines from moving along streets; 34 people died and 1,032 were injured in clashes with police before the California National Guard restored order, and property damage was estimated at $40 million.

As riots erupted in urban ghettos throughout the United States in the summers of 1966 and 1967, it became clear to many people that the legal victories against segregation achieved by the civil rights movement had made little difference in the lives of poor African Americans. Younger, emerging African-American leaders were rejecting the gradual, nonviolent approach of Martin Luther King, Jr.

King, meanwhile, had turned his attention to the poor. He criticized U.S. involvement in Vietnam, believing the war drew money away from social programs. His organization, the Southern Christian Leadership Conference (SCLC), formed an economic branch called Operation Breadbasket that provided people with food and worked to achieve employment of African Americans proportional to their presence in the community. By early 1968 King was planning his Poor People's Campaign, an effort to lead poor Americans of all races and ethnicities to Washington, D.C., to place their problems before lawmakers and the public and gain for them needed assistance. He hoped to shame the nation into ensuring that every person in the United States had enough to eat and a decent home, and that a job paying a fair wage was available to every man and woman seeking work.

On the day of his assassination, April 4, 1968, King was in Memphis, Tennessee, lending support to striking sanitation workers who sought a wage that would permit them to support their families, workers' compensation, and the right to organize. It fell to King's successor, the Reverend Ralph Abernathy, to oversee the Poor People's Campaign.

Police drag a youth in front of a looted store during the rioting in the Watts section of Los Angeles, California, August 12, 1965. *(Library of Congress, Prints and Photographs Division, LC-USZ62-113636)*

Resurrection City, USA: Rain turned the earth to mud, and plumbing was inadequate. *(Special Collections & Archives, George Mason University)*

Blacks, whites, Native Americans, and Hispanics from all parts of the country traveled to Washington by bus, car, and train. Some from the South journeyed part of the way by mule train, symbolically adopting a traditional means of transportation employed by the rural poor. The first participants arrived in the nation's capital on May 14, 1968, and set up camp near the Lincoln Memorial, where 600 plywood shelters had been erected. "Resurrection City, U.S.A.," their home for the next six weeks, was to be a model community where people of all backgrounds lived harmoniously and had their needs met. It had its own city hall, cultural and educational centers, dining hall, and dispensary, and even its own zip code. Residents marched daily to the Departments of Labor and Agriculture to publicize their need for jobs and food, while the press focused on the negative aspects of the campaign, such as the rain that fell for 28 of the 42 days of encampment and turned the grassy parkland to mud.

The population of Resurrection City fluctuated between 2,600 and 3,000. It swelled to 50,000 on June 19, which had been designated Solidarity Day and set aside for speeches at the Lincoln Memorial. After this culmination, only about 300 people lingered in the makeshift city, where repeated disturbances drew the police, with dogs, tear gas, and arrests. After the police closed the settlement on June 24, the remaining poor and their leaders left Washington, having failed to secure significant antipoverty legislation.

Robert Kennedy's Legacy

The assassination of Robert Kennedy on June 6, 1968, while he was campaigning in California for the Democratic nomination for president, had been especially discouraging for the people of Resurrection City, because Kennedy had demonstrated a strong commitment to the disadvantaged. As a U.S. senator from New York, he had worked hard to improve conditions in the Bedford-Stuyvesant neighborhood of Brooklyn. Some 300,000 people lived in the rundown brownstone houses of Bedford-Stuyvesant, making it one of the largest African-American ghettos in the country. Thirty percent of residents had incomes below $3,000 a year; infant-mortality and school-dropout rates were well above average, and drug abuse was a visible problem. In 1966 Kennedy called together community leaders and residents to form the Bedford-Stuyvesant Restoration Corporation, which assessed and prioritized needs, and he enlisted executives from IBM, CBS, and other firms to participate in

Senator Robert F. Kennedy meets the poor of the Mississippi Delta in April 1967. *(Photo No. PX81-32:351 in the John F. Kennedy Presidential Library)*

the Bedford-Stuyvesant Development and Services Corporation, which raised funds and offered guidance. By 1968 these efforts had borne some fruit. More than 300 brownstones had been renovated, and condemned residential blocks were being converted into parks and recreation areas. IBM was building a plant that would employ residents, and 80 financial institutions had agreed to offer conventional mortgages at competitive rates to people who wanted to buy homes in Bedford-Stuyvesant.

In April 1967, while in Jackson, Mississippi, with the Senate Subcommittee on Employment, Manpower, and Poverty, Kennedy and Senator Joseph Clark of Pennsylvania toured the severely impoverished Delta region and spoke to people living there. The sight of starving children, the most disturbing victims of the area's widespread hunger and malnutrition, caught the senators unprepared. It was all too obvious that federal food-assistance programs had failed to reach these painfully hungry youngsters.

Publicity surrounding the senators' tour led to a more thorough investigation in 1967 by a group of physicians that was sponsored by the Southern Regional Council, an organization formed in 1919 to promote racial justice and democratic rights in the South. In six Mississippi counties, the physicians encountered "literally penniless rural families who are often enough removed from any of the services that even the poor in America can usually take for granted."[9] The physicians explained that "these families are denied medical care, adequate sanitation, welfare or relief payments of any kind, unemployment compensation, protection of the minimum wage law, coverage under Social Security, and even recourse to the various food programs administered by the federal and local governments."[10] Among the children in these families, severe and chronic medical problems associated with starvation, environmental conditions, and lack of access to health care were the norm. In 1968 a widely viewed CBS News documentary, *Hunger in America*, sent images of the poor in Mississippi, on Indian reservations, in migrant-labor camps, and elsewhere into comfortable American homes. As one result of the increased public and government awareness generated by such programming and reports, the U.S. Department of Agriculture supplied surplus food to people in the 1,000 poorest counties in the United States.

As a presidential candidate Kennedy drew attention to poverty among American Indians, the most deprived minority group in the United States regardless of the measure employed: median income, nutritional level, educational attainment, or mortality rate. The average income of Native Americans was 75 percent below that of the nation. They experienced unemployment at 10 times the national rate and suffered disproportionately from tuberculosis and other preventable diseases. Indian youth had low levels of school achievement and high dropout and suicide rates. In 1967 the average age at death for Native Americans was 46, or about 20 years younger than for white Americans.

In 1966 the Fund for the Republic, a think tank founded in 1952, commissioned a study of the status of American Indians. The researchers reported that the people most affected by the Termination policy of the 1950s, the Klamath, Menominee, and Ute, were faring worse economically than they were before federal assistance was terminated. The commission urged a return to the policies of the Indian Reorganization Act—which had never been repealed. Not only did the tribal governments established under John Collier's stewardship continue to function, but they also had become adept at administering the economic development programs of the War on Poverty.

Nevertheless, in 1970 the U.S. Census Bureau classified one-third of Indians as poor. (In 1970 the Social Security Administration set the poverty line at $3,968 for a family of four living in a city and $3,385 for a family of the same size living on a farm.) The median income for Indians—$5,832—was 57 percent of the median income for whites. Thirty-six percent of Indian households were receiving public assistance and 20 percent were headed by single women. In 1970 almost half the Indian population lived in cities, and one-fifth claimed no tribal identity.

On January 2, 1975, Congress created the American Indian Policy Review Commission, with three senators, three representatives, and five Native Americans as its members. This commission was to study federal Indian policy and submit to the House and Senate a report modeled on the Meriam Survey of 1928. In its final report, presented to Congress in May 1977, the commission recommended replacement of the Bureau of Indian Affairs with an independent agency directed by Indians. It also recommended that the government contract directly with Indians for services provided by the bureau. The effectiveness of these recommendations cannot be evaluated, because they were never implemented.

Farm Workers Organize

Migrant farm laborers made some economic gains in the 1960s. In 1962 Cesar Chavez, a community activist and former migrant laborer, founded the National Farm Workers Association (NFWA), with the goal of unionizing California grape pickers as a first step toward organizing agricultural workers nationwide. As other migrants harvesting crops did, the grape pickers worked 12-hour days in the early 1960s, often for the poverty wage of $1.10 an hour. The federal laws that protected most American workers excluded them, although the Migrant Health Act, passed in September 1962, established health clinics for seasonal workers and their families. Migrants were treated badly by the permanent populations of the communities where they worked. In Delano, California, for example, migrant workers were subject to arrest even if they had broken no laws, if the police suspected that they might cause trouble.

On September 16, 1966, the NFWA voted to join a strike by the United Farm Workers Organizing Committee, a group affiliated with the American Federation of Labor–Congress of Industrial Organizations (AFL-CIO), whose members refused to pick grapes for less than $1.40 an hour. The combined union, the United Farm Workers of America, struck first against California vineyards and then against the growers of table grapes. Nationwide people who supported the strikers boycotted California grapes, cutting sales in half. In 1970, after four years of striking and boycotting, the union reached an agreement with 26 growers. Conditions improved for the migrant laborers, but poverty among them persisted.

Stalemate

The War on Poverty had proved difficult to win, at least as Lyndon Johnson had chosen to fight it. In 1968, 7.5 million people in the United States were receiving public assistance of all types, and about 4 million of these were in families who were receiving support from AFDC. In 1969 the AFDC caseload was twice that of 1963, although the years between were a period of high employment when the caseload had been predicted to fall.

A migrant laborer and his son are photographed in 1972. *(National Archives)*

Many critics thought that the War on Poverty had amounted to too little, too late; that the amounts allotted for job training and other initiatives had been inadequate or, on the local level, used to hire administrators or otherwise enrich bureaucrats rather than aid the needy. Some echoed the Reverend Martin Luther King's concern that the costly war in Vietnam was being fought at the expense of the well-being of millions of Americans.

Others—and their number was growing—felt that Johnson's approach was altogether wrong. One such person was Ronald Reagan, who was elected governor of California in 1966. In his 1967 inaugural address Reagan assured the people of California, "We are not going to perpetuate poverty by substituting a permanent dole for a paycheck."[11]

As Congress adjusted social programs for inflation, raising federal benefits 7 percent in 1965 and 13 percent in 1967, taxpayers felt the pinch. Also in 1967, in a move that inspired angry debate, Congress placed a freeze on the percentage of children in any state receiving AFDC because a parent was absent from the home. The freeze targeted families headed by single women, because it exempted children whose fathers had died or whose parents were unemployed. Daniel P. Moynihan called the freeze "the first purposively punitive welfare legislation in the history of the American national government." Moynihan wrote, "Inasmuch as no effort was made to conceal the fact that these provisions were designed to halt the rise in *Negro*

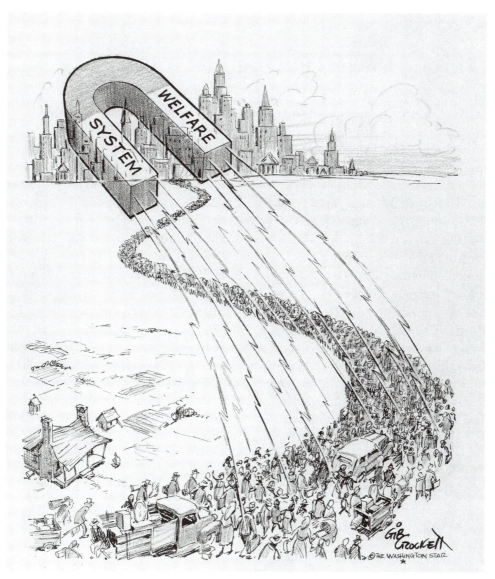

Public welfare is depicted as a magnet drawing the poor to a major city in this cartoon by Gib Crockett from 1967. *(Library of Congress, Prints and Photographs Division, LC-USZ62-135723)*

dependence on the AFDC program, the House action might also be considered the first deliberate anti–civil rights measure of the present era."[12] Congress lifted the controversial freeze in 1969.

Another Social Security measure launched in 1967, the Work Incentive Program (WIP; later WIN), required states to establish training and employment programs for adult welfare recipients who had no preschool children or special responsibilities requiring them to be at home. At first participation was voluntary, but in 1971 the federal government made it mandatory. Yet the program received inadequate federal funding, less than $250 per client, and state and local agencies hesitated to put additional money into it when it was cheaper and easier to issue monthly support checks. In many places WIN registration became merely a formality for welfare applicants.

Federal support of social services at the state and community levels was contrary to the political beliefs of President Richard M. Nixon, who was elected in 1968. After being reelected in 1972 by a wide margin, Nixon trimmed a number of Great Society programs. He also abolished the OEO in 1974.

Looking toward the Future

In 1966 economist Robert J. Lampman used two methods to predict the number of families in the United States that would be poor in 1975. His first method was to assume that the incidence of poverty would remain constant in every demographic group and that family incomes would rise 2.5 percent each year. According to this method, 8 million people, or 14 percent of families, would be poor in 1975. The second method was to project the average annual postwar decrease in poverty. Poverty had affected 32 percent of families in 1947 and 19 percent of families in 1963. This method told Lampman that 10 percent of families would be poor in 1975.

Lampman made his predictions without foreknowledge of the weak economic growth and high unemployment that would characterize the 1970s or the mounting inflation that would reach 13.5 percent in 1980. These economic conditions had an insignificant effect on the poverty rate, which was 12.3 percent in 1975, but they did erode optimism about conquering poverty, even among experts. By the late 1970s social scientists were describing an emergent "underclass" of people whose lives were defined by violence and despair, who were completely removed from the political and social life of the country, and who lacked the will and the means to protest or revolt. These were the passive poor: lifelong welfare recipients, drug abusers, gang members, street criminals, the homeless, and the mentally ill. It was suggested that even unprecedented economic growth would never alleviate this kind of poverty, that it would be necessary somehow for government to address the impediments to full participation of the underclass in the economy. This line of thinking ran contrary to the economic philosophy of Ronald Reagan, who was elected president in 1980.

Chronicle of Events

1962

- In California, Cesar Chavez founds the National Farm Workers Association (NFWA) as a first step in organizing the nation's migrant farm labor force.
- *September:* The Migrant Health Act provides for health clinics for migrant laborers and their families.

1963

- Some 17.5 million people, accounting for 9.4 percent of the population, are age 65 or older.
- In the District of Columbia, 29.2 percent of African Americans are unemployed for at least part of the year, and a low median income corresponds with a high rate of illegitimacy.

1964

- Respondents to a Gallup poll are evenly divided on whether poverty results from personal shortcomings, economic and social factors, or a combination of personal and social causes.
- *January 8:* Addressing Congress and the nation, President Lyndon B. Johnson declares war on poverty.
- *July 2:* The Civil Rights Act of 1964 is passed, giving the attorney general the power to enforce citizens' civil rights, outlawing discrimination in establishments open to the public, and creating the Equal Employment Opportunity Commission.
- *August 20:* The Economic Opportunity Act of 1964 becomes law, laying the groundwork for a broad range of social programs to aid the poor and establishing the Office of Economic Opportunity (OEO).
- *August 31:* The Food Stamp Act of 1964 is passed, enabling qualified people to purchase negotiable food stamps at a discount.

1965

- The Department of Labor publishes a controversial report, *The Negro Family,* in which it links the number of African-American households headed by women to slavery.
- Congress adjusts federal benefits 7 percent for inflation.
- *January:* The majority of Americans responding to a poll state that able-bodied welfare recipients should be required to work.

- *March:* The Appalachian Redevelopment Act, intended to spur economic growth in Appalachia, becomes federal law.
- *April 11:* Johnson signs into law the Elementary and Secondary Education Act, providing funds to schools in depressed areas.
- *July 30:* Medicare and Medicaid, health-insurance programs for older Americans and the poor, respectively, become provisions of Social Security.
- *August 11:* A week of rioting begins in the impoverished African-American community of Watts, California.
- *November 8:* The Higher Education Act, which funds college loans and adult education, becomes law.

1966

- Robert Kennedy oversees formation of the Bedford-Stuyvesant Restoration Corporation and the Bedford-Stuyvesant Development and Services Corporation, both dedicated to revitalizing the blighted Brooklyn community.
- A study of Native Americans commissioned by the Fund for the Republic concludes that the government's Termination policy increased economic hardship for the Indians most affected.
- Economist Robert J. Lampman predicts that 10 to 14 percent of U.S. families will be poor in 1975.
- *January 11:* Johnson issues Executive Order 11306, creating the National Advisory Commission on Rural Poverty to study economic trends and situations in rural America.
- *September 16:* NFWA joins the United Farm Workers Organizing Committee in a strike against California vineyards and growers of table grapes; public support of the strike leads to a boycott of California grapes.

1966–1967

- Summertime riots erupt in African-American urban ghettos.

1967

- In its report, the National Advisory Commission on Rural Poverty asserts that the nation cannot solve the growing problem of urban poverty until it addresses rural poverty, the major contributing factor.
- Ronald Reagan is inaugurated governor of California.
- The average age at death for American Indians is 46, or about 20 years lower than for white Americans.
- Congress adjusts federal benefits 13 percent for inflation and places a freeze on the percentage of children

receiving Aid to Families with Dependent Children (AFDC) support.

- The Work Incentive Program is launched, funding voluntary training and employment assistance for adult welfare recipients.
- *April:* Senators Robert Kennedy and Joseph Clark tour the impoverished Delta region of Mississippi; the resulting publicity leads to a more detailed study by physicians for the Southern Regional Council.

1968

- In Bedford-Stuyvesant, Brooklyn, more than 300 brownstones have been renovated, parks and recreation areas are being created, and jobs and investment money are introduced into the region.
- CBS News airs the widely watched documentary *Hunger in America.*
- The average income of Native Americans is 75 percent below that of the nation; unemployment among Native Americans is 10 times the national rate; Indians suffer disproportionately from tuberculosis and other diseases; Indian youth have low levels of school achievement and high dropout and suicide rates.
- About 7.5 million people are receiving public assistance; 4 million receive support from AFDC.
- Richard M. Nixon is elected president of the United States.
- *April 4:* The Reverend Martin Luther King, Jr., is assassinated in Memphis, Tennessee.
- *May 14:* The first participants in the Poor People's Campaign arrive in Resurrection City, the camp established in Washington, D.C., by the Southern Christian Leadership Conference.
- *June 6:* Robert Kennedy is assassinated while campaigning in California.
- *June 19:* Fifty thousand people gather at the Lincoln Memorial to hear Solidarity Day speeches.
- *June 24:* Police in Washington, D.C., close Resurrection City.

1969

- The AFDC caseload has doubled since 1963.
- Congress lifts the freeze on the percentage of children receiving AFDC support.

1970

- The Social Security Administration sets the poverty line for a family of four at $3,968 for urban areas and $3,385 for farm areas.

A scene in Rand, West Virginia, in 1973: Much of the population lives in poverty, substandard houses line unpaved roads, and junked cars litter the community. *(National Archives)*

- The U.S. Census Bureau classifies half of Indians as poor; 36 percent of Indian households receive public assistance, and 20 percent are headed by single women; 48 percent of Native Americans live in cities, and 20 percent claim no tribal identity.
- Striking California farmworkers reach an agreement with 26 growers.

1971

- The Work Incentive Program becomes mandatory.

1972

- Nixon wins reelection.

1974
• Nixon abolishes the Office of Economic Opportunity (OEO).

1975
• Poverty affects 12.3 percent of the population.
• *January 2:* Congress establishes the American Indian Policy Review Commission.

1977
• The American Indian Policy Review Commission recommends that Congress replace the Bureau of Indian Affairs with an Indian-run agency; this recommendation is not followed.

1980
• The rate of inflation reaches 13.5 percent.

Eyewitness Testimony

We live in a time of rapid change. The wonders of science and technology applied to a generous endowment of natural resources have wrought a way of life our grandfathers never knew. Creature comforts once the hallmark of luxury have descended to the realm of the commonplace, and the marvels of modern industry find their way into the home of the American worker as well as that of his boss. Yet there is an underlying disquietude reflected in our current social literature, an uncomfortable realization that an expanding economy has not brought gains to all in equal measure. It is reflected in the preoccupation with counting the poor—do they number 30 million, 40 million, or 50 million? Is it still, as in the 1930's, one-third of a nation that is ill-fed, ill-clothed, and ill-housed, or is it now only a fourth or fifth? Shall one point with pride or view with alarm?

Mollie Orshansky of the Division of Research and Statistics,
Social Security Administration, July 1963,
"Children of the Poor," p. 3.

If it be true that the children of the poor today are themselves destined to be the impoverished parents of tomorrow, then some social intervention is needed to break the cycle, to interrupt the circuits of hunger and hopelessness that link generation to generation. For the common benefit of all we must assure the security and well-being of all our children—at the same time the Nation's most precious and most perishable resource.

Mollie Orshansky of the Division of Research and Statistics,
Social Security Administration, July 1963,
"Children of the Poor," p. 13.

Out of the door came a tall, scrawny Negro woman. The porch boards gave a little under her step. She had grey kinky hair, her upper teeth were mostly eroded away, and she looked me straight in the eye. Driving at random, guided only by the impulse to get off the beaten path, I met Rebecca Franklin. It was, it so happened, her birthday. . . .

Her husband died from injuries in an automobile accident six years ago and left her with twelve children, ages six to twenty-seven. The youngest eight are still at home. Because she is a widow with dependent children whose husband was under Social Security she gets $70 a month in Federal survivors insurance. She earns about $100 a month cleaning and cooking for white families in town. Her older married children outside the state send her about $100 in cash a year. For a family of nine, $2200 a year is poverty.

Because she cooks for others, Mrs. Franklin assumes that her own food costs nothing. She spends $30 a week for the children's food, or 70 per cent of her income. At times she has enough for the 25 cents a day the children need for a hot lunch at their school but usually they are limited to 3 cents a day for milk. If there have been "extra" expenses during the month, on the last few days before the check they eat only bread, salt pork and cane syrup. The children have never been to a doctor or a dentist. They have no television set. In the evening they cut wood for the kitchen stove and if, after that and homework there is still time, they go to a neighbor's house to watch some TV. There is no running water in the house.

Ben H. Bagdikian, journalist, describing conditions for a poor
family near Columbia, South Carolina, 1964, In the Midst
of Plenty, pp. 2–3.

It is clear that today the public welfare department is no longer just a short-term government finance agency. It is the social seismograph of every community. It records the tremors of a faulty school system, the closing of a plant, the layoffs caused by automation, and the distinctions that are made between a face that is black and one that is white. Its difficulties are internal and external and their sum has made the big relief question both repetitious and louder:

What are we going to do about the welfare mess?

Edgar May, journalist, 1964, The Wasted Americans,
p. 190.

I have had so many men, honest men I have known all of my life, come into me in my office and make the statement that they wouldn't let their children starve if they had to steal. Some actually are stealing food; some are making moonshine. And some men are even going into the mines and cutting wire down, hot wire with juice in it, and stealing copper and going off and selling it to provide for their families. . . . I have passed along the garbage dumps where stores throw their garbage out and I have seen little kids eating discarded apples and stuff from the garbage dumps. And it is heartbreaking to see these things. . . .

I have people coming into my office day after day with small children. They can't send them to school. They have nothing to go on. They don't have any clothes or shoes to wear. They don't have any food in the house. . . . And just as I said before, people in my county are proud.

They are honest people and good people and they don't want a handout from the government. They don't want a handout from anyone. They want an honest living; they want something to do, to work and make an honest living. And how we can do that, God only knows.

A sheriff from West Virginia testifying before a U.S. Senate committee, 1964, in Hubert H. Humphrey, War on Poverty, *p. 11.*

A man came into the office not too long ago and he said, "Lady, I am not disabled, and I don't want assistance. But," he said, "look at these hands. Have they been used to an easy life? Aren't they toil-worn?" They were, gentlemen. There were calluses all over his hands. He said, "I am forty-five years of age; I have two children in high school. The rest of my children are in the grades and they can't go to school because they are unable to have shoes."

Another day a woman came in. She said, "Lady, my husband was ashamed to come into the office. He has never been without work. But," she said, "when I left home this morning there were five children who were hungry and I can't go home." It was then a few minutes before five o'clock. "I can't go home without some kind of food."

A welfare worker testifying before a U.S. Senate committee, 1964, in Hubert H. Humphrey, War on Poverty, *p. 12.*

Contemporary poverty's two faces are equally ugly. There are the traditional reasons for poverty: prejudice, ignorance, ill health, the thousand and one accidents which can change a life of comfort to iron-bound hardship. Remedies for these conditions are as many as there are causes and only a fearful lack of courage, determination, and wisdom in our society can prevent us from discovering and applying them. . . .

The other face of poverty is less familiar—and more dangerous. Because of automation and our increasingly complex civilization, a large part of the poor are trapped below, and increasingly apart from, the majority of our population. While those above a certain point in the income scale are included in that mass of society which allows for upward movement, those below the poverty level not only do not participate in the movement but are being forced into a position where they cannot. We may find ourselves in a society with hardened class lines—a society which America has never experienced.

Hubert H. Humphrey, vice president of the United States, 1964, War on Poverty, *pp. 188–89.*

There are millions of Americans—one fifth of our people—who have not shared in the abundance which has been granted to most of us, and on whom the gates of opportunity have been closed.

What does this poverty mean to those who endure it?

It means a daily struggle to secure the necessities for even a meager existence. It means that the abundance, the comforts, the opportunities they see all around them are beyond their grasp.

Worst of all, it means hopelessness for the young.

The young man or woman who grows up without a decent education, in a broken home, in a hostile and squalid environment, in ill health or in the face of racial injustice—that young man or woman is often trapped in a life of poverty.

He does not have the skills demanded by a complex society. He does not know how to acquire those skills. He faces a mounting sense of despair which drains initiative and ambition and energy. . . .

The war on poverty is not a struggle simply to support people, to make them dependent on the generosity of others.

It is a struggle to give people a chance.

It is an effort to allow them to develop and use their capacities, as we have been allowed to develop and use ours, so that they can share, as others share, in the promise of this Nation.

President Lyndon B. Johnson, "Message to the Congress of the United States on the Economic Opportunity Act of 1964," March 16, 1964, in Herman P. Miller, ed., Poverty American Style, *p. 212.*

We in the United States in the 1960's have reached a new stage in mankind's concern about poverty over the centuries. Due to our unparalleled productive capacities and the need to use them more fully, the abolition of poverty has passed from a "dream" or "possibility" or mere "practicality" to a veritable necessity. In this country, for the first time in human history anywhere—and sharply distinguishable from conditions among a large majority of mankind even today—massive poverty has now become *intolerable* because it is no longer *unavoidable*.

Within a decade, we can virtually eradicate the poverty which now engulfs more than 34 million Americans. And this war against poverty should be viewed not as a somber obligation, but rather as a shining opportunity to achieve what will benefit all. Victory in this war will necessarily involve success in all of the other undertakings which now engage us: the restoration and maintenance of maximum employment and high economic growth; the wiping-out of fundamental causes of racial tensions; the provision of full educational opportunities, adequate health services, and satisfactory housing for all people; the renewal of our cities and the improvement of rural living; the conservation and replenishment of our natural resources; the solution of the thorny financial problems which now bear down on governments at all levels. At that time in future when we celebrate the conquest of poverty in the United States, we shall have created a society so abundant, so just, and so meaningful that our people will have gained practical release from the "economic problem" which has burdened them throughout the ages, and be free to devote themselves to the higher purposes of human development.

Leon H. Keyserling, president of the Conference on Economic Progress, December 1964, Progress or Poverty, *p. 1.*

Definitions of poverty change and our attitudes toward the poor are altered accordingly. In the thirties you were not stigmatized for being poor. Poverty was blamed on the times and the system. Today, poverty and failure are blamed on the individual. Poor farmers are told to get off the farm; residents of depressed areas are advised to move elsewhere; the uneducated and the untrained are sent back to school. During the depression the poor were helped by giving them more money. Today, we want to make them "better people." Why the change?

Herman P. Miller, U.S. Census Bureau economist, 1965, "The Dimensions of Poverty," in Ben B. Seligman, ed., Poverty as a Public Issue, *p. 20.*

[W]e have been very resourceful in inventing new jobs for middle-class people. We have been unresourceful in inventing new jobs for poor people. But I think that there are new jobs to invent for poor people and that we are beginning now to understand this. We can, for example, simplify jobs right here and now, without waiting for the great society. We have done it with metermaids and auxiliary policewomen. That is to say, a metermaid is part of a policeman who doesn't have to have all the attributes of a policeman, because all she has to do is collect the coins from the meters and give out parking tickets. And an auxiliary policewoman standing outside a school, helping the children across the street, is also part of a policeman. In Chicago, Travelers Aid has hired women from Appalachia to help attend the desk in the bus depot, working with social workers. These women from Appalachia have very little education, but they

have one important attribute—they can talk to people from Appalachia.

Writer Michael Harrington, 1965, "A Social Reformer's View," in Margaret S. Gordon, ed., Poverty in America, *p. 35.*

Many of the poor have essentially zero productivity now. They lack skills, education, motivation, and sometimes even literacy. This is why there is so much emphasis on training and education in [Office of Economic Opportunity] programs, and this is why there is so much concern with youth. An elderly unemployed or retired person can usually be helped only by some form of income transfer; a dead-end 18-year-old high school dropout can become a charge on society and a probable crime statistic, or he can become a productive citizen for half a century. For society as well as for the individual, the option is incredibly important. Here lies the tremendous appeal of the Job Corps and the other job training parts of the program, for their success will mean, not only turning the young men and women into better adjusted people, but a real and continuing increase in the size of the GNP. The poor will be generating themselves the resources which will help eliminate poverty, not only this year, but for all those years to come.

Joseph A. Kershaw, economist, 1965, "The Attack on Poverty," in Margaret S. Gordon, ed., Poverty in America, *p. 57.*

The place was Watts, Los Angeles; the young men who ignited it were typical of ghetto youth across the country. . . . They were jobless and lacked salable skills and the opportunities to get them; they had been rejected and labeled as social problems by the police, the schools, the employment and welfare agencies; they were victims of the new camouflaged racism. For in addition to discrimination based on race, they were now rejected by "social profile." Detached from the broader white society, even largely from the seemingly complacent working Blacks around them, they drank, gambled, fought a little, but mostly just generally "hung out."

But suddenly something snapped. All the frustration and resentment burst out in a drama that will have a permanent place in Black history. . . .

And although I had only begun to know Watts—as I was a newcomer to the Red Rooster, the Parking Lot, and the many local stores—I sensed that this explosion was something different. For one thing, the Black-white confrontation characteristic of past race riots was absent:

here, young Blacks set fire to buildings in their own community, dramatically chanting, "Burn, baby, burn!" For another, the first feelings of charged anger were soon replaced by a lightness and exhilaration, almost a party-time mood. This then settled into the quiet determination and actions of justification that motivated the second stage of Operation Burn, Baby, Burn. The young men of the community were joined by many other neighborhood residents in seizing household goods from burning stores. There was a new unity among the generations and the classes. The slogan "Burn, baby, burn!" had become not just the chant of the young but a silently repeated rhythm emanating from the hearts of large numbers of Blacks, many of whom would not let themselves go out in the streets.

Douglas G. Glasgow, social researcher, remembering the August 1965 riot in Watts, California, The Black Underclass, *pp. 1–2.*

Living in an affluent society, we are especially aware that the proportionate share of the low income classes in our total national product is still small, remaining at about the level of the Depression years of the 1930's. They have benefited only in a token way from the general improvement in living styles; some, being outside the economy almost entirely, have not benefited at all.

Today's low-income Americans include a disproportionate number from certain demographic groups. We are developing a new type of poverty—the poverty of "underdog" or "pariah" classes versus the mass poverty characteristic of our economy during the Depression decade of the 1930's.

Non-whites, female heads of families, rural families, the very young, the aged, families with more than six children under 18 years of age, all have a much greater likelihood of being poor than other members of the population. Individuals who live alone also have a greater likelihood of being poor than those who live with their families.

Where families and individuals have not merely one but two or more of these characteristics the probability of their being poor is much greater. A large number of those living at or below "minimum subsistence" have more than one of these attributes.

In general these groups with a great likelihood of being poor had a slightly greater likelihood of poverty in 1960 than in 1947.

The groups with a great likelihood of being poor are also most likely to be unemployed, underemployed, or ill-paid. . . .

The "underendowment" in personal assets of the contemporary poor—their generally low levels of skill, education, and health—the result of cultural deprivation, is one of the most important aspects of their poverty.

Oscar Ornati, economist, 1966, Poverty amid Affluence, *pp. 132–33.*

Middle-class people—this would certainly include most social scientists—tend to concentrate on the negative aspects of the culture of poverty. They attach a minus sign to such traits as present-time orientation and readiness to indulge impulses. I do not intend to idealize or romanticize the culture of poverty—"it is easier to praise poverty than to live it." Yet the positive aspects of these traits must not be overlooked. Living in the present may develop a capacity for spontaneity, for the enjoyment of the sensual, which is often blunted in the middle-class, future-oriented man. Indeed, I am often struck by the analogies that can be drawn between the mores of the very rich—of the "jet set" and "café society"—and the culture of the very poor. Yet it is, on the whole, a comparatively superficial culture. There is in it much pathos, suffering and emptiness. It does not provide much support or satisfaction; its pervading mistrust magnifies individual helplessness and isolation. Indeed, poverty of culture is one of the crucial traits of the culture of poverty.

Oscar Lewis, anthropologist, October 1966, "The Culture of Poverty," *p. 25.*

Once the culture of poverty has come into existence it tends to perpetuate itself. By the time slum children are six or seven they have usually absorbed the basic attitudes and values of their subculture. Thereafter they are psychologically unready to take full advantage of changing conditions or improving opportunities that may develop in their lifetime.

Oscar Lewis, anthropologist, October 1966, "The Culture of Poverty," *p. 21.*

Many of these undeveloped people have developed a culture of poverty. . . . The poor think differently; they have a different sense of values. . . . Take the concept of education: To the middle class it stands for the road to better things for one's children and one's self. To the poor it is an obstacle course to be surmounted until the children can go to work. . . .

The poor tend to be fatalistic and pessimistic because for them there is no future; everything is today. They do not postpone satisfactions. When pleasure is available, they tend to take it immediately. They do not save, because for them there is no tomorrow.

The smug theories of the middle class would probably deplore this as showing a lack of traditional American virtues. Actually it is the logical and natural reaction of a people living without hope, without a future.

The Reverend A. J. McKnight of Louisiana describing rural poverty, 1967, in U.S. National Advisory Commission on Rural Poverty, The People Left Behind, *p. 8.*

In Delta counties (such as Humphreys and Leflore) recently visited by us and elsewhere in [Mississippi] (such as Clarke, Wayne, Neshoba, and Greene Counties, also visited by us) we saw children whose nutritional and medical condition we can only describe as shocking—even to a group of physicians whose work involves daily confrontation with disease and suffering. In child after child we saw: evidence of vitamin and mineral deficiencies; serious, untreated skin infections and ulcerations; eye and ear diseases, also unattended bone diseases secondary to poor food intake; the prevalence of bacterial and parasitic disease, as well as severe anemia, with resulting loss of energy and ability to live a normally active life; diseases of the heart and the lungs—requiring surgery—which have gone undiagnosed and untreated; epileptic and other neurological disorders; severe kidney ailments, that in other children would warrant immediate hospitalization; and finally, in boys and girls in every county we visited, obvious evidence of severe malnutrition, with injury to the body's tissues—its muscles, bones, and skin, as well as an associated psychological state of fatigue, listlessness, and exhaustion.

We saw children afflicted with chronic diarrhea, chronic sores, chronic leg and arm (untreated) injuries and deformities. We saw homes without running water, without electricity, without screens, in which children drink contaminated water and live with germ-bearing mosquitoes and flies everywhere around. We saw homes with children who are lucky to eat one meal a day—and that one inadequate so far as vitamins, minerals, or protein is concerned. We saw children who don't get to drink milk, don't get to eat fruit, green vegetables, or meat. They live on starches—grits, bread, flavored water. Their parents may be declared ineligible for commodities, ineligible for the food stamp program, even though they have literally nothing.

Southern Regional Council, 1967, Hungry Children, *pp. 4–5.*

A truly circular process helps to make many Negroes members of a disadvantaged class. The Supreme Court's 1954 school-segregation decision, if it did nothing else, pointed up the inferiority of the education available to the Negro, an education that left him less qualified for employment than the average white.

Now the sons of these disadvantaged Negroes are taking their seats in school. Educators are concerned with giving them a chance in life by providing a good primary and secondary education. But this first chance for the children may only raise false hopes if their parents are not given a second chance to gain the skills they need to secure worthwhile jobs in our society. Otherwise the adults may stay in the lost generation of the disadvantaged, thus making it more likely that their children will be unable to break free of the old pattern.

Albert A. Blum, economist, and Charles T. Schmidt, Jr., labor researcher, 1967, "Job Training through Adult Education: A Second Chance for the Negro and the Community," in Arthur M. Ross and Herbert Hill, eds., Employment, Race, and Poverty, *p. 460.*

Harlem needs immediate relief from the dreadful overcrowding maintained by the steady northward migration. It needs relief from rent costs that are, although lower than many rentals in white areas, still not commensurate with the lower incomes of Negroes. It needs a greater money influx, and more Negro-operated businesses and services to keep that money circulating longer in the Negro community; for, as matters now stand, dollars brought into Harlem flow straight back out into the white community through the predominantly white business establishments. Harlem needs more and better police protection, for its residents are no less fearful than white people of crime and violence, whether committed by Negroes or by whites. And Harlem needs jobs—new jobs for its unwanted men, and steadier jobs for those frequently unemployed.

For its children Harlem needs better schools, appropriately adapted curricula, more nursery schools, more teachers, and facilities for special tutoring to help overcome the educational gap. It desperately needs a vast increase in summer camp facilities—Federally financed, if city funds and private philanthropy cannot carry the burden—to take more children off the teeming streets during the long summer months. It needs better health services. It needs more public recreation facilities, because with the discriminatory differential in earning power and family income, Harlem families cannot afford to purchase for recreation what many white neighborhoods and families easily provide for themselves.

For its youth Harlem needs educational, social, and economic opportunities at least vaguely approximating those available to young people across the ghetto border, in white man's territory.

William F. Soskin, 1967, research psychologist, "Riots, Ghettos, and the 'Negro Revolt,'" in Arthur M. Ross and Herbert Hill, eds., Employment, Race, and Poverty, *p. 226.*

Most members of the National Indian Youth Council can remember when we were children and spent many hours at the feet of our grandfathers listening to stories of the time when the Indians were a great people, when we were free, when we were rich, when we lived the good life. At the same time we heard stories of droughts, famines and pestilence. It was only recently that we realized that there was surely great material deprivation in those days, but that our old people felt rich because they were free. They were rich in things of the spirit, but if there is one thing that characterizes Indian life today it is poverty of the spirit. We still have human passions and depth of feeling (which may be something rare in these days), but we are poor in spirit because we are not free—free in the most basic sense of the word. We are not allowed to make those basic human choices and decisions about our most personal life and about the destiny of our communities which is the mark of free mature people. We sit on our front porches or in our yards, and the world and our lives in it pass us by without our desires or aspirations having any effect.

We are not free. We do not make choices. Our choices are made for us; we are the poor. For those of us who live on reservations these choices and decisions are made by federal administrators, bureaucrats, and their "yes men," euphemistically called tribal governments. Those of us who live in non-reservation areas have our lives controlled by local white power elites. We have many rulers. They are called social workers, "cops," school teachers, churches, etc., and now OEO [Office of Economic Opportunity] employees. They call us into meetings to tell us what is good for us and how they've programmed us, or they come into our homes to instruct us and their manners are not always what one would call polite by Indian standards or perhaps by any standards. We are rarely accorded respect as fellow human beings. Our children come home from school to us with shame in their hearts and a sneer on their lips for their home and parents. We

are the "poverty problem" and that is true; and perhaps it is also true that our lack of reasonable choices, our lack of freedoms, our poverty of spirit is not unconnected with our material poverty.

Clyde Warrior, Ponca activist, testifying before the National Advisory Commission on Rural Poverty, February 2, 1967, "We Are Not Free," p. 1.

The marvelous products of modern technology—plumbing, electricity, cars, telephones, TV, plastics—have undoubtedly brightened the lives of all Americans, poorer as well as richer. But the society's total commitment to them has made them virtual necessities. They are almost compulsory improvements in the quality of life; poor or rich, we have little choice but to accept them and pay for them. In some degree this is the result of emulative pressures heightened by the new technology itself. For example, the children of the poor have to conform to social norms in clothing, in TV watching, and in consuming TV-advertised products. But there are more direct compulsions, too. Legal and social norms make it quite properly difficult for occupants of urban housing to avoid the costs of modern sanitation, central heating and electricity. In an automobile society public transportation declines in quality, availability and economy. When the whole society is geared to communication by telephone, it is more than inconvenient to be without one.

James Tobin, Nobel Prize-winning economist, June 3, 1967, "It Can Be Done!" p. 15.

When asked what they did about running out of money, two-thirds said they borrowed, either from relatives and friends or storekeepers, and one-third said they just "stayed run out." "Stay run out" is the theme of their lives—and for those who borrow too, because the loan must be paid back, and each month they sink a little deeper. Besides borrowing and staying run out, some found other ways to cope with the continuing crisis: One "lets the bills go." (Where does this end?) One cashes in bottles and borrows food. One cried in shame: "The lady downstairs gives us food." One said, "If the children get sick, I call the police to take them to the Receiving Hospital."

One has been "borrowing" secretly from the funds of a Ladies' Club of which she is treasurer. The club is her one meaningful adult social contact. There is soon to be an election for new club officers and she will be exposed. Her children ask: "Mama, why are you always so sad?" Half crazy with worry, she feels sick; at Receiving Hospital they have referred her to the psychiatrist. . . .

One said bitterly: "A woman could always get $10 if she had to. I prefer not to resort to this."

Consider our affluent society: in an economy generating wealth sufficient to supply every family of four with nearly $10,000 per year income, we reduce a family to cashing in pop bottles to get food, we push a woman to thoughts of prostitution to feed her children, we force an honest woman into theft and then provide her with $25 an hour psychiatric treatment.

Charles Lebeaux, professor, Wayne State University School of Social Work, writing about Detroit women supporting their families on AFDC funds, 1968,
"Life on A.D.C.: Budgets of Despair," p. 527.

There must be a commitment by the nation to the proposition that every child has the right to an adequate diet. What do we mean by a "commitment"? We mean more than a statement by the president, or the preamble of a law. We mean that there be an organized set of laws and executive policies framed to achieve this objective. What is our model? It is not the federal anti-poverty program, which has been a great and valuable force but has never represented an actual commitment to eradicate poverty. Our model, instead is a commitment such as we made to industrial and farm production during World War II; to explore space and place a man on the moon; or to build a gigantic interstate highway system. In contrast, there has not been in this century a comparable commitment to a social or humane end. With a realistic and sincere sense of resolve, we must say that all our children shall eat well.

Citizens' Board of Inquiry into Hunger and Malnutrition in the United States, 1968, Hunger, U.S.A., *p. 85.*

Once [the culture of poverty] comes into existence, it tends to perpetuate itself from generation to generation because of its effects on children. By the time slum children are age six or seven, they have usually absorbed the basic values and attitudes of their subculture and are not psychologically geared to take full advantage of changing conditions or increased opportunities which may occur in their lifetime.

Oscar Lewis, anthropologist, 1968, La Vida, *p. 50.*

One of the paradoxes of affluence is that it permits a society, as it does an individual, to indulge in practices that are both expensive and ultimately harmful, but which appear pleasant or convenient in the short run. The United States economy has reached the point where it can sustain a full-scale land war in Asia with no significant cutback in domestic spending, and, yet, no increase in taxes. To

such a behemoth, the cost of an annual increment in the number of welfare mothers is insignificant.

Daniel P. Moynihan, scholar and statesman, winter 1968,
"The Crises in Welfare," p. 7.

I do not see any grounds for believing that this country is now threatened by a mass of "new poor" whose objective situations, especially their opportunities to rise out of poverty, are much worse than those of earlier generations. The real changes I see are generally encouraging, or at least mixed. Some families are worse off today because they can't reap the benefits of child labor; but in the long run, presumably, their children are better off.

I think that one can be clear-headed about what is happening without being complacent about the *status quo.* I have never understood why so many Americans believe that to assert things are bad, you must insist that they are getting worse. I would argue that they could well be getting a little better—the situation of the poor in America is, on the whole—and still be intolerably bad. A little less unemployment can still be too damned much unemployment, in a culture where people have become civilized enough to understand that recurrent unemployment is due not to the will of God but to the inaction of man.

Stephan Thernstrom, historian, January–February 1968,
"Is There Really a New Poor?" p. 64.

Participants in the Poor People's Campaign march along Connecticut Avenue in Washington, D.C., demanding economic opportunity. *(Library of Congress, Prints and Photographs Division, LC-U9-19271-33A)*

I'm here because when I was a child, I got taken out of school and put to work on the farm helping my family. . . .

They didn't pay us in money, but in food, in the crops so we could eat.

Then I got married and had kids, and my husband worked in the cotton fields in season and fixing cars and trucks and stuff. But he got sick and don't work much no more and there ain't hardly no cotton to get picked by hand anyway. . . .

If people in the churches and these civil rights organizations didn't help us by giving us clothes, food and a little money from time to time, I don't know what we'd do. . . .

So I came here with the Campaign to tell people that we got to be treated like human beings—that we have a right to live because we've earned the right but we've yet to be paid.

Henrietta Franklin of Marks, Mississippi, participant in the Poor People's Campaign, May 24, 1968, in "What Brings the Poor People to the Capital?" p. A14.

It hurts me to hear people say people is poor because they don't want to work. My husband and I done worked hard all our lives. I don't believe white people would have worked as hard as we have for the little we got to show for it.

We just can't get noplace because things are against us, like my husband just got old and can't get no job. . . .

We sacrificed all our lives and we're sacrificing by being here. But we came because we hope we can change things, because for the first time someone gave us a chance to do something other than try to keep hardly alive till we die.

May Powell of Eutaw, Alabama, participant in the Poor People's Campaign, May 24, 1968, in "What Brings the Poor People to the Capital?" p. A14.

People in Sunflower [Mississippi] asked my friends was I sick 'cause they hadn't seen me. Then they saw me on TV in Washington and said I'd better head back before the first or they'd cut off my welfare check. Bur that's OK. I had to come. When S.C.L.C. chose me from [Senator James D.] Eastland's County, he met his match. I've seen so much. I've seen 'em selling food stamps and they tell you if you don't buy, they cut off your welfare check. And that stuff they sell there don't count—milk, tobacco, and washing powder. Well, how you gonna keep clean? All the welfare people know is what *they* need. I ain't raising no more white babies for them. Ain't goin' that road no more. I drug my own children through the cotton fields, now they talkin' 'bout not lettin' us go to Congress. Well,

I'll stand on Eastland's toes. People from 12 months to 12 months without work. People with no money. Where the hell the money at? I say to myself, I'll go to Washington and find out. Talking about using it to build clinics. Then they make people pay so much at the clinics they get turned away. What the people getting ain't enough to say grace over. I done wrote to Washington so much they don't have to ask my name.

Mrs. Brooks, participant in the Poor People's Campaign, spring 1968, in Charlayne A. Hunter, "On the Case in Resurrection City," p. 12.

The abolition of poverty will require money. But money must be accompanied by far-reaching, penetrating approaches, by bold and coordinated public and private programs that provide interrelated opportunities for the poor. For those who are able to work, greater emphasis must be placed on jobs, education, and training. For those who cannot or should not be expected to work, improvements must be made in the social security program, which, combined with private benefit plans, constitutes the most effective institution for income maintenance. It cannot, of course, do the whole job. The present welfare system must be drastically overhauled to adequately serve those whose needs are not met by other programs. Concomitant with improvements in existing programs, the search must continue for new and imaginative programs that will meet the needs of the decade ahead.

Setting the elimination of poverty as a national goal is a huge and complex undertaking. The Nation has the economic capacity, the technological capability, and the intellectual resources to accomplish this goal before the end of the next decade. But the most difficult task will be sustaining the determined commitment of the Nation to the American promise: Full and equal opportunity for all to share in the good life that can be offered by a dynamic, prosperous, democratic society.

Wilbur J. Cohen, secretary of Health, Education, and Welfare, December 1968, "A Ten-Point Program to Abolish Poverty," p. 13.

The baby was sick, but the young Public Health Service doctor could not find the cause. At 18 months, the infant's weight was a normal 21 pounds, yet her hands and feet were swollen, and she cried pitifully on the examining table.

"She cries all the time," her mother reported.

"What does she eat?" asked the doctor.

"Tea, soda water, and beans," the woman replied.

"How about milk?"

"No," the Navajo Indian mother answered, "We haven't had milk in a long time, and no meat, either."

In Tuba City, Arizona, Dr. Charles B. Wolf made a startling diagnosis. The infant suffered from "kwashiorkor," a disease caused by severe protein deficiency, and characterized by a distended belly, bulging eyes, loss of hair, and, if untreated, eventual death. The illness, known as the "starvation disease," is widespread among the most primitive nations of the world, but it rarely had been reported in 20th-century America. Dr. Wolf discovered two more cases of kwashiorkor and countless cases of malnutrition, including marasmus (severe calorie malnutrition).

That was in 1961. Dr. Wolf published his findings and attempted to improve the nutrition of the Navajos who live on the vast reservation that spreads across four southwestern states. The young physician left Tuba City confident that authorities would respond to his reports.

Eight years later, Dr. Jean VanDusen, a physician at the same Public Health Service Hospital told Congress that in 1969 she had treated 44 cases of kwashiorkor and marasmus among Indians on the reservation. For the Navajos, starvation is a continuing fact of life.

Nick Kotz, journalist, 1969, Let Them Eat Promises: The Politics of Hunger in America, *pp. 31–32.*

Located on South Carolina's lower coast, Beaufort County represents the kind of paradox so common today for much of our nation. It has extreme wealth and extreme poverty. The first shack we visited housed fifteen Negroes. It had no electricity, no heat, no running water, no bath, and no toilet, inside or out. It was typical of thousands of hovels occupied by millions of the very poor in this country.

The house had no steps and the cracks in the wall were covered by old copies of the *Savannah Morning News.* The entire store of food consisted of a slab of fatback, a half-filled jar of locally harvested oysters, and a stick of margarine. The only heat came from a worn wood-burning cooking stove. The entire family huddled in the kitchen area.

One man in the house was diagnosed by Dr. Aycock [who accompanied Hollings] as suffering from pellagra, a disease supposedly common only to poor natives of nondeveloped countries. He said one of the children had rickets and another had scurvy. They were all dressed in rags.

Ernest F. Hollings, U.S. senator from South Carolina, who surveyed poverty in his state, 1970, The Case against Hunger, *p. 36.*

We met Mattie Simmons on the porch of her home on Pulaski Street. The South Carolina capitol could be seen above the tarpaper and tin roofs of the neighboring houses. She paid $25 a month for rent and a fine of $1.50 each day it was late. The place had three rooms.

"They're all rotten," she said, looking around the room. It was true. She pointed to several holes in the floor where the boards had collapsed beneath her weight. There were no panes in the windows and she had pushed cardboard into the openings to keep out some of the chilly February wind. "I nearly freeze to death," she said, and we could believe it.

Mrs. Simmons was on welfare, but did not know how much she received. She could not read and someone cashed her check for her.

Ernest F. Hollings, U.S. senator from South Carolina, who surveyed poverty in his state, 1970, The Case against Hunger, *p. 38.*

I'm trying to make my children into good children, that's what. I'm trying to make them believe in God, and listen to Him and obey His Commandments. I'm trying to have them pay me attention, and my husband, their daddy, pay him attention, and I'd like for all of them to know what they can, and grow into good people, yes, and be a credit to their daddy and me. I knows it's going to be hard for them, real bad at times, it gets. I tell them that, and I tell them not to be too set on things, not to expect that life is going to be easy. . . . And I tell them it used to be we never saw any money at all, and they'd send you up in those small trucks, but now they'll pay you some, and we most often have a car—we lose it, yes sir, when there's no work for a few weeks and then we're really in trouble—and we have more clothes now than we ever before had, much more, because most of my children, they have their shoes now, and clothes good enough for church, most of the time. So you can't just feel sorry about things, because if you do, you'll just be sitting there and not doing anything—and crying, I guess. Sometimes I do; I'll wake up and I'll find my eyes are all filled up with tears, and I can't figure out why, no sir. I'll be getting up, and I'll have to wipe away my eyes, and try to stop it, so the children don't think something is wrong, and then, you know, they'll start in, too.

A migrant farm worker, 1971, in Robert Coles, Migrants, Sharecroppers, and Mountaineers, *pp. 79–81.*

Common arguments for proposing a work requirement [for welfare recipients] are that work is psychologically valuable for welfare mothers and provides a model for their children. The data indicate that even long-term welfare mothers and their teen-age sons, though the sons have spent virtually their entire lives on welfare, continue to have a strong work ethic and do not need to be taught the importance of work. To encourage welfare mothers to enter the work force, it is necessary to present them with a chance to experience success in jobs that will support them. But, realistically, what are the chances of training large numbers of welfare mothers so they can support their families above the poverty level?

Leonard Goodwin, sociologist, 1972,
Do the Poor Want to Work? p. 113.

The plight of the poor cannot be blamed on their having deviant goals or a deviant psychology. The ways in which the poor do differ from the affluent can reasonably be attributed to their different experiences of success and failure in the world. There is ample evidence to suggest that children who are born poor face discriminatory barriers to advancement in the educational and occupational worlds, which thrust them into failure much more consistently than their middle-class counterparts. Appropriate policies would enable more poor people to experience success. While success cannot be guaranteed, the probability of its attainment for large numbers of the poor might be increased in two ways. The first is to lessen the risk of failure by removing discriminatory barriers so that, for example, more poor people become eligible for better jobs; the second, to reduce the cost of failure, when it does occur, by providing a guaranteed income at least a small margin above the poverty level. Poor families should be given enough economic security and low-risk opportunity to rise in status, according to their desire and ability, without being overwhelmed by failure induced by inequities in the social system.

Leonard Goodwin, sociologist, 1972,
Do the Poor Want to Work? p. 118.

The needs of families living at bare subsistence are so large compared to their average daily income that it is impossible for families to provide independently for fixed expenses and daily needs. Lacking any surplus funds, they are forced to use most of their resources for major monthly bills: rent, utilities, and food. After a family pays these bills they are penniless.

The poor adopt a variety of tactics in order to survive. They immerse themselves in a domestic circle of kinfolk who will help them. To maintain a stable number of people who share reciprocal obligations, at appropriate stages in the life cycle people establish socially recognized kin ties. Mothers may actively seek out their children's father's kin, consciously expanding the number of people who are intimately obligated to care for one another.

Carol B. Stack, anthropologist, 1974, All Our Kin:
Strategies for Survival in a Black Community, p. 29.

Two necessary requirements for ascent from poverty into the middle class are the ability to form a nuclear family pattern, and the ability to obtain an equity. Close examination of the welfare laws and policies relating to public assistance show that these programs systematically tend to reduce the possibility of social mobility. Attempts by those on welfare to formulate nuclear families are efficiently discouraged by welfare policy. In fact, welfare policy encourages the maintenance of non-coresidential cooperative domestic networks. It is impossible for potentially mobile persons to draw all of their kin into the middle class. Likewise, the welfare law conspires against the ability of the poor to build up an equity. Welfare policy effectively prevents the poor from inheriting even a pitifully small amount of cash, or from acquiring capital investments typical for the middle class, such as home ownership.

It is clear that mere reform of existing programs can never be expected to eliminate an impoverished class in America.

Carol B. Stack, anthroplogist, 1974, All Our Kin:
Strategies for Survival in a Black Community, p. 127.

The "war on poverty" that began in 1964 has been won. The growth of jobs and income in the private economy, combined with an explosive increase in government spending for welfare and income transfer programs, has virtually eliminated poverty in the United States. Any Americans who truly cannot care for themselves are now eligible for generous government aid in the form of cash, medical benefits, food stamps, housing and other services.

Martin Anderson, economic policy specialist, 1978, Welfare,
p. 15.

[This] is the story of a band of "illegal aliens" who eventually sought help—because they had no food—from a San Dieguito, California, Catholic priest. The priest, Frank Sierra, went with an illegal Mexican national who had come from the hills seeking his help to see things for himself. It was January 1978, one of the wettest seasons in the state's history, breaking a two-year drought. The Volkswagen van driving Padre Sierra to the illegals' camp where he was to say mass plowed through six to twelve inches of mud in the canyons of the Encinitas foothills where there once were firm dirt roads. After a long and difficult ride, the car stopped to meet a group of men who escorted the priest two miles in the rain across fields and over fences to a place near their camp where they had put together an altar made from some old and water-logged crates. The priest celebrated mass and promised to return with food and clothes. What he had seen touched him: "As large a group as fifty men had not eaten in three of four days [except for] some vegetables found in the fields, mostly discard. As far as he was able to provide for himself, that was his day's allowance. Some were so weak they couldn't get off the ground."

The priest returned every five days or so to that camp and to others like it with sacks of flour and beans, and clothing donated by his parish. The trips continued until the rains let up in March. "It hardly mattered what road I took," he told a local reporter, "places [of need] opened up daily."

Why didn't the men, in their hunger, return to their homes in Mexico? The border was less than one hundred miles south. They stayed on in the rain and the mud and, later, the floods because when the rains ended, they could return to work in the fields. And besides, their lives on the other side of the border would hardly be different—except there would be no hope of work when the rains ended.

Sasha G. Lewis, writer and sociologist, 1979, Slave Trade Today: American Exploitation of Illegal Aliens, *p. 115.*

Work requirements are particularly futile, because they focus on women with small children, the official welfare clients, rather than on the unlisted beneficiaries—the men who subsist on the system without joining it, who live off welfare mothers without marrying them. These men are not necessarily fathers of the particular children they happen to be living among. They are just men who live for a while with a welfare mother, before moving on to another one. These men are the key beneficiaries—and victims—of the system. Because the system exists, they are not forced to marry or remain married or learn the disciplines of upward mobility.

There are hundreds of thousands of these men. Their legion is the inevitable counterpart of the mass of welfare mothers who preoccupy all the social workers and reformers. Yet the mothers in general cannot lift their families out of poverty, nor can the social workers. Making the mothers work confers few social benefits of any sort and contributes almost nothing to the fight against poverty. Only the men can usually fight poverty by working, and all the antipoverty programs—to the extent they make the mother's situation better—tend to make the father's situation worse; they tend to reduce his redemptive need to pursue the longer horizons of career.

These unlisted welfare men form a group almost completely distinct from the "able-bodied men" actually listed on the rolls—aging winos, over-the-hill street males, wearied ex-convicts, all the halt-and-lame founderers of the world—who receive money under the general assistance category and are harassed mercilessly during every crackdown. The real able-bodied welfare fathers are almost universally contemptuous of welfare and wouldn't go near a welfare office.

George F. Gilder, writer and pundit, 1981, Wealth and Poverty, *p. 116.*

CHAPTER NINE

The Years of
Welfare Reform
1981–1996

Ronald Reagan began his presidency in January 1981, facing what he called "the worst economic mess since the Great Depression."[1] Unemployment was on the rise, and inflation was continuing its sharp climb. In contrast to Franklin Delano Roosevelt, who addressed the economic woes of the 1930s with an ambitious legislative agenda, Reagan sought to improve the economy by cutting federal spending on social programs and lowering taxes to stimulate private-sector growth. He was convinced that Lyndon Johnson's Great Society legislation had helped to create the underclass by making welfare appealing to the poor. "In this present crisis, government is not the solution to our problem," he said in his Inaugural Address.[2] Reagan expressed confidence that if corporate America prospered, then financial good fortune would "trickle down" to society's lowest economic levels.

One of Reagan's first accomplishments as president therefore was passage of the Omnibus Budget Reconciliation Act of 1981 (OBRA), which became law on August 13 and authorized reductions totaling $135 billion in spending for such programs as AFDC, food stamps, school lunches and other nutrition plans, housing subsidies, and health services. One major federal initiative, grants for job training given to the states under the Comprehensive Employment and Training Act (CETA) of 1973, was abolished. Thousands of families lost their cushion of support as a result of this legislation, but their president insisted it was for their own good, that only by being forced to rely on their own resources would the dependent learn independence. Responsibility for those truly unable to work and care for themselves belonged to the states, according to Reagan's political philosophy, and to churches, charities, and other private organizations. OBRA also significantly increased defense spending, however.

Reagan initiated large tax cuts that were in keeping with his belief in the benefits of lower taxes and smaller government. The changes made to the tax code might be said to have favored the wealthy and big business, because the top marginal tax rate on individual income was reduced from 70 percent to 28 percent, and the corporate tax rate was dropped from 48 percent to 34 percent. Yet it also benefited most of the poor by exempting them from paying personal income tax.

The president's free-market economic approach, dubbed Reaganomics, was controversial in the 1980s, and economists continue to debate its pluses and minuses today. The unemployment rate fell from 7 percent in 1980 to 5.4 percent in 1988, and the inflation rate declined from 10.4 percent to 4.2 percent over the same period—two pluses. Reagan's approach failed to offer real help to low-income Americans, though. The poverty rate reached 15.3 percent in 1983; this meant that 35.3 million people in the United States lived below the poverty line. Nevertheless, the actual number of poor may have been higher; many economists claimed the poverty line was an inadequate measure. They pointed out that families spent a larger share of their income on housing in the 1980s than in 1955, when the formula for calculating the poverty line was devised, and that the cost of living varied from one part of the country to another. In cities such as New York, San Francisco, and Washington, D.C., people whose incomes placed them just above the poverty line often could not afford life's basic necessities. Suggested alternative formulas factored in all kinds of income, including food stamps, and a broad range of expenses, from food, clothing, and shelter to utilities, child care, child support, and medical bills.

The number of working poor, which had fallen in the 1960s and 1970s, also rose in the early 1980s and accounted for 7.3 percent of workers in 1985. Two million of these people worked full time, and 1.2 million were heads of households.

This photograph shows a slum scene in Washington, D.C., May 1988. *(John Reef)*

President Ronald Reagan delivers his first Inaugural Address at the U.S. Capitol on January 20, 1981. In this speech Reagan asserted that the United States was at its lowest point economically since the Great Depression. *(Ronald Reagan Presidential Library)*

More than half the working poor lived outside cities. The working poor tended to be less educated than other workers and to have fewer skills to offer employers. They were also more likely to be physically disabled or functionally illiterate. There were exceptions, of course. Some were capable of filling jobs paying better wages and requiring higher levels of skill but were prevented from finding these positions by discrimination or a lack of higher paying jobs within commuting distance: Even in a growing economy, not every willing worker can be accommodated. Faced with these social realities, Reagan made it one of the first acts of his second term, which began in 1985, to sign into law a bill making available $5 billion to extend unemployment benefits in 27 economically depressed states and $4.6 billion to create between 300,000 and 600,000 public-service jobs.

Critics of Reaganomics, including Michael Harrington, thought the government needed to do much more to aid the poor. It was a mistake to blame increases in poverty on the availability of public assistance, Harrington and others said. After all, many families receiving public assistance continued to live below the poverty line. In a recent month, March 1984, the average AFDC payment ranged from $232 per person and $585 per family in Alaska to $31 per person and $91 per family in Mississippi. According to the critics, the fault lay partly in the abolition of social programs and closing of institutions, which put dependent people out on the street. (In fact, by removing patients from mental hospitals and not providing care or support in the community, the government made homelessness a visible problem.)

The New Poverty

In his 1984 book, *The New American Poverty*, Harrington identified larger socioeconomic changes that were also responsible for increased poverty, such as the movement of people and industries to the Sun Belt of the South and Southwest, which resulted in plant closings, unemployment, and economic decline in northern manufacturing centers. Also, a growing population of undocumented foreign workers labored illegally in sweatshop conditions. "Two decades after the President of the United States declared an 'unconditional' war on poverty, poverty does not simply continue to exist," Harrington wrote. Conditions had become worse, because the nation now had to deal with "a new poverty much more tenacious than the old."[3] The poor of earlier generations had lived in an expanding economy that offered jobs even to workers with little schooling. They had been optimistic in the face of adversity, believing that they or their children would escape destitution. The new poor, in contrast, saw little or no opportunity for economic advancement. They and their offspring were trapped in poverty. The loss of manufacturing jobs, whether through relocation or automation, was helping to create an economy of extremes, a society of rich and poor. "The contrast between the electric engineer and the dishwasher and the disappearance of so many in-between jobs is a fact of life in every advanced country. It is also an important aspect of the new poverty," Harrington observed.[4]

The Physicians' Task Force on Hunger in America, a team of prominent medical doctors, conducted field investigations throughout the United States and reported in 1987 that an estimated 15 million Americans lived below the poverty line without food stamps or other nutritional assistance. In one state after another, they saw hungry people overwhelming the resources of churches and soup kitchens. Commenting on the investigation, Victor W. Sidel, M.D., president of the American Public Health Association, said that "behind statistics are the tears of children and the frail bodies of the elderly."[5]

Public welfare programs, including AFDC and Medicaid, consumed less than 2 percent of the federal budget but accounted for as much as 20 percent of states' total expenditures. By 1987, state lawmakers and the citizens who elected them had lost patience with the traditional welfare system, and some 40 states had instituted "workfare," or welfare-to-work, programs. The provisions of these programs varied by state, but they all required recipients to work in return for public assistance and, it was hoped, achieve self-sufficiency. Their purpose was not only to help the needy, but also to lower taxes, reduce expenditures, and trim the welfare rolls.

On October 13, 1988, as his presidency drew toward its close, Reagan signed the Family Support Act, which was national workfare legislation scheduled to begin taking effect in October 1990 and to be implemented fully over the next six years. The major provision of this act, the Job Opportunities and Basic Skills Training Program (JOBS), required single parents on welfare whose children were older than three to work in exchange for their assistance. (States had the option of lowering the qualifying child's age to one.) Any adult unable to find employment was obligated to enroll in school or job training at government expense. The law made funds available for child care, transportation, and other expenses related to participation, and it extended Medicaid coverage for one year for those who became self-supporting. It also required states to make welfare payments to two-parent families who otherwise qualified, and it strengthened states' power to collect child-support payments.

In 1985 only half of single mothers who were entitled to child support received the full amount that had been awarded. One-fourth received partial payment, and the other fourth received nothing at all. It was important for women to collect this money because in many cases child support, coupled with a custodial parent's income, enabled AFDC families to become financially independent.

The JOBS program made sense to millions of Americans, yet it proved ineffective at reducing poverty. States were reluctant to devote resources to its implementation at a time when their budgets were already stretched by a deepening recession, and during the presidency of Reagan's successor, George H. W. Bush, poverty rose. Poverty afflicted 12.8 percent of the population, or 31.8 million people, in 1989, according to the Census Bureau, and 14.2 percent of the population, or 35.7 million people, in 1991. Counting all the poor is impossible, however. The Census Bureau estimated that it missed 5.3 million poor in its 1990 population survey. Those not counted were largely immigrants, the homeless, and people living in remote rural regions or inner-city neighborhoods.

Along with poverty came increases in all the modern-day "vices" of the poor, including homelessness, crime, domestic violence, and substance abuse. In 1991 an estimated 50,000 people in New York City were homeless, 27,000 others were living in temporary shelters, and 100,000 were sharing crowded quarters with relatives. Other cities faced similar problems. The Republican Bush, who had been vice president under Reagan, adhered to an economic policy similar to that of his predecessor and encouraged reliance on a "thousand points of light," or the charitable and religious groups throughout the nation that each sent out a small beacon of hope.[7]

Clinton Imposes Limits

Voters dissatisfied with the economic state of their nation chose Bill Clinton over the incumbent George Bush in the 1992 presidential election. Clinton, who labeled himself a "new Democrat," entered office vowing to "end welfare as we know it."[8] True to his word, in August 1996 he signed the Personal Responsibility and Work Opportunity Reconciliation Act (PRWORA), which radically altered the federal public-assistance policy that had been in place since 1935 by abolishing AFDC. The act replaced these monthly payments with Temporary Assistance for Needy Families (TANF), a series of grants to the states to be used for public assistance that were scheduled to diminish by $54.5 billion over six years.

Although PRWORA was intended to lessen dependency on welfare rather than reduce poverty, government planners hoped that expansion of the federal Earned Income Tax Credit, a combination of tax refunds and cash supplements that since 1975 had augmented the earnings of those with low incomes, would help many people making the transition from welfare to work keep their families out of poverty. Critics warned, however, that the new law would have negative effects, perhaps causing women to remain in abusive relationships and adding a million children to the poor. There was worry, too, that an economic recession would leave many people unemployed and without a government safety net.

States retained the right to make their own rules for welfare eligibility, but they were required to end recipients' benefits at the end of two years. Also, there now was a lifetime limit of five years of assistance for every recipient. Welfare had officially become a temporary help while people looked for another means of support, and it would be terminated whether or not a recipient found work. In this way the act addressed public concerns about longtime dependency on welfare, although the majority of women who collected welfare did so for two years or less. Additionally, the act made teenage mothers, convicted drug felons, immigrants, and those unwilling to work ineligible for welfare benefits. It also barred legal immigrants who were not citizens from receiving food stamps and permitted states to deny Medicaid to legal immigrants.

Waivers from the federal government permitted many states to experiment with ways to administer aid. Some states followed the lead of New Jersey, which in 1993 instituted a family cap, or a limit on the amount of aid a family received. Under the family-cap system, having more children would not increase benefits to a family already on the welfare rolls. By 1996, 15 states had implemented family caps.

This photograph presents a portrait of poverty: Lyburn, West Virginia, in the early 1980s. *(Photograph © Milton Rogovin 1952–2002, The Rogovin Collection, LLC)*

In 1996, when PRWORA became the law of the land, the West fell behind the South, becoming the poorest section of the country for the first time, largely because of its high populations of Hispanics and recent immigrants. For the years 1994 to 1996, New Mexico had the highest average poverty rate, 24 percent; Louisiana was next, at 22 percent; and Mississippi was third, at 21.3 percent. In all of these states, the population was predominantly rural and included many members of racial and ethnic minorities. Also in 1996, 14.4 million people, or 39.5 percent of the nation's poor, lived on incomes that were less than half the poverty line. Social scientists called this deeply impoverished group the poor-poor.

Poverty Persists among Minorities

Several population subgroups remained chronically poor, and these included American Indians. In 1981, according to U.S. Census figures, 60 percent of Indians lived below the federally established poverty line, which was $9,287 for a family of four. Many Indians living on or near reservations inhabited homes lacking indoor plumbing and electricity. Of an Indian population of 1.965 million, though, 1.1 million lived in urban communities.

The economic picture for Indians was not any brighter several years later. Unemployment reached 40 percent among Native Americans in 1989, when it was close to 7 percent for the nation as a whole. Nationwide, 31 percent of Indian households received public assistance, and 22 percent of households on reservations had incomes below $5,000 per year. (Six percent of all U.S. households had annual incomes below $5,000.) In 1991, 63.1 percent of people on the Pine Ridge Reservation in South Dakota lived below the poverty line.

In the 1980s and early 1990s African Americans also continued to bear disproportionate burdens of unemployment and poverty. Unemployment tended to be twice as high for African Americans as for the nation as a whole. In 1995, for example, when the national unemployment rate was 5.6 percent, the rate for African Americans was 10.4 percent. African Americans also figured prominently among the population of discouraged workers, those men and women who had stopped looking for jobs because the search was futile. African Americans represented roughly 10 percent of the U.S. population, but they accounted for 20 percent of the unemployed and 40 percent of discouraged workers.

Increasingly since the civil rights era, African Americans had made gains in education and the professions and had been elected to public office, yet in 1989, 8.9 million African Americans lived below the poverty line. A study conducted in 1984 determined that black men between the ages of 25 and 34 earned 80 percent, on average, of what white men of the same age and educational level earned. At every age, though, blacks were worse off economically than whites, with those 75 and older suffering the greatest deprivation.

The number of African Americans living in impoverished city neighborhoods nearly doubled in the 1980s, increasing from 5.6 million in 1980 to 10.4 million in 1990 and renewing discussion of the underclass. Although most of the nation's poor were white and most lived outside cities, inner-city blacks endured worsening social isolation. In 1987 William Julius Wilson described an urban work environment in which the demand for low-skilled labor had dried up as a result of the movement of employers to suburbs or more distant locations. This trend had proved most harmful to the large number of African-American men who lacked the education or specialized training to be hired as white-collar or clerical workers and who could not afford transportation to suburban worksites. Envisioning no future for themselves in the working world, an alarming number of young men turned to gang membership, drug use, and crime: In 1990 nearly one-fourth of African-American men in their 20s spent time behind bars, on parole, or on probation. This, according to Wilson, reduced the number of marriageable African-American males in central cities and thereby contributed to births to single mothers. At the same time, middle-class African Americans, who could afford suburban homes, moved out of inner cities, thus removing themselves as successful role models for the young people left behind.

Not every social scientist accepted the concept of the underclass. Some saw it merely as another term for the idle or undeserving poor and a means to identify those unworthy of public support. Whether or not a measurable underclass existed, poverty and fatalism eroded ghetto family life. By the mid-1980s nearly half of African-American families were headed by women, and more than half of African-American babies were born to single mothers. By 1993, 66 percent of African-American children had single parents; in some inner-city neighborhoods, 80 percent of African-American children were born to single women.

In the 1980s demographers began to measure poverty among Asian Americans, a rapidly growing population group. The portion of the population identified as Asian had grown from 0.7 percent in 1970 to 3 percent in 1990, largely because of immigration. The Asian-American population was—and remains—largely foreign-born: In 1994 just 35 percent of Asian heads of households in the United States were U.S. citizens by birth. In 1990, according to data from the U.S. Bureau of the Census, the poverty rate for Asians and Pacific Islanders was 12.2 percent; this was higher than the rate for non-Hispanic whites, which was 10.7 percent.

Most of the poverty among Asians was related to their pattern of immigration. Beginning in 1965, most Asians who immigrated to the United States obtained visas based on their professional or educational qualifications and pursued prosperous careers in their adopted homeland. Then, in the 1970s, the end of U.S. involvement in Indochina led to an influx of refugees from that part of the world. These newcomers tended to be poorly educated and lacking in employable skills. Many people with limited assets and skills also fled political repression in China. By the 1990s poverty was higher among immigrants from Laos, Cambodia, Vietnam, China, and Korea than among those from other parts of Asia.

Children, Women, and Poverty

In 1989 people younger than 18 accounted for 27 percent of the U.S. population but 40 percent of the poor. The U.S. Census Bureau illustrated the scope of child poverty by reporting that one in five of the nation's children lived below the poverty level. By 1996, the percentage of children in poverty was largely unchanged: 20.5 percent of children under 18, or 14.46 million young people, lived below the poverty line. Children of color—African American, Hispanic, and Native American—were disproportionately represented among the poor. In general these children were at increased risk for low birth weight, malnutrition, and exposure to lead from peeling paint. They benefited from few of the cultural and educational opportunities that children in financially stable families enjoyed.

More than half of impoverished children lived in families headed by single women, most of whom were divorced. In 1990 there were 20.9 divorces in the United States for every 1,000 married women age 15 and older. The most common form of custody in divorces involving children was sole custody for single mothers. Because traditionally women have worked in low-paying service jobs, the loss of a husband's support often proved disastrous. In 1988 the median income of single mothers between the ages of 25 and 34 was $11,161; for two-parent families it was $31,358. Although women have numbered significantly among the poor since the

This Buffalo, New York, mother was only 12 years old when photographed in August 1991. Having children at a very young age puts mothers and their offspring at risk of poverty. *(Photograph © Milton Rogovin 1952–2002, The Rogovin Collection, LLC)*

colonial period, in the late 20th century the high divorce rate, the large number of never-married women having children, and the low incomes of many working women led social scientists to identify the feminization of poverty as a trend.

Finding affordable housing became a huge challenge for single mothers in the 1980s, as the expenses of renting or owning a home rose at a higher rate than the costs of most other goods and services. By 1987 half of single-parent households were spending 58.4 percent of their income on rent. The number of impoverished families renting or wishing to rent a home increased by 300,000 between 1983 and 1987, reaching 7.5 million. At the same time, the nation lost almost a million housing units renting for $300 or less (generally an affordable rent for low-income families). Some of these units had been abandoned, demolished, or destroyed by arson, but others in up-and-coming neighborhoods had been converted to condominiums or luxury apartments. Boston lost 80 percent of its housing renting for $300 or less between 1982 and 1984, and the number of apartments renting for more than $600 doubled. The National Housing Law Project, an agency that works to advance housing rights for the poor, estimated in 1984 that the nation was losing 500,000 low-cost housing units every year. In addition, escalating housing costs were keeping many would-be home buyers in the rental market, where they competed for available space. In 1987 just 1 percent of low-income housing units in New York City were vacant. Yet during roughly the same period, from 1981 to 1987, federal funding for low-income housing declined dramatically, from $32 billion to $9 billion.

Because they were struggling to make ends meet or possibly had been evicted for nonpayment of rent, single mothers and their children moved frequently. Several factors made these moves particularly stressful: Families were often forced to relocate to substandard housing in crime-ridden neighborhoods; for those moving in with relatives or friends, crowding and the change in household composition required adjustment; and moving itself created financial strain. Additionally, those who exhausted their resources faced the specter of homelessness. The homeless population, which numbered 2 million in 1982 and 3 million in 1987, according to the U.S. Department of Health and Human Services, increasingly included women and children. Children and their parents made up three-fourths of the homeless population in Massachusetts in 1986; in 1988, of the 28,000 homeless people living in emergency shelters in New York City, 18,000 were parents—usually mothers—and children. (City officials estimated that another 40,000 people were living in abandoned buildings, on streets, or in public places such as train stations.)

The homeless population also included men and women without dependent children at varying stages of life. Poverty and the unavailability of affordable housing were the principal reasons for their homelessness, but there were underlying causes as well, such as physical or mental illness, drug or alcohol abuse, disability, unemployment, and low wages. For women there were additional causes, namely, domestic violence and separation, divorce, or widowhood. In many cases, homelessness was cyclical: that is, people moved in and out of housing as it became affordable or available.

Shelters for the homeless became fixtures in cities throughout the country in the 1980s. By 1988 churches, community groups, and other private organizations operated 90 percent of these shelters; most publicly run shelters were in the East and Midwest. The nation's largest shelter system was the publicly run network of facilities in New York City. Many shelters offered a variety of services to the homeless, including mail delivery, meals, social work, transportation, help in finding permanent housing, and storage.

New York City and other municipalities temporarily housed homeless families in hotels leased for this purpose, with costs shared by the city, state, and federal governments. By January 1988, 63 "welfare hotels" were operating in New York City. The Department of Welfare required residents to look for permanent housing, but almost nothing was available for the maximal monthly rent the department was willing to pay ($244 for a family of three, $270 for a family of four). Families spent 13 months, on average, in welfare hotels, with some staying two or three years.

One of these lodging places, the 17-story Hotel Martinique, faced Herald Square, where Broadway, Sixth Avenue, and 33rd Street converge in the heart of a busy shopping district. The hotel's once-elegant ballroom had become the distribution site for a hot-lunch program administered by the Coalition for the Homeless, an advocacy group. Four elevators provided unreliable service to the floors above the main level, where children with nowhere else to play raced along dark corridors.

Homelessness compounded the risks of poverty for children. It disrupted their education, and it exposed them to crime, violence, drug abuse, and the other hard realities of street life. A psychiatrist examining children at the Hotel Martinique in the late 1980s repeatedly saw symptoms of clinical depression and anxiety disorders. Homelessness was especially risky to the very young: The infant mortality rate in New York City's welfare hotels was 25 per 1,000 live births in the years 1982 through 1984—more than twice the national average.

A Cushion for Older Adults

As more and more children fell into poverty and homelessness, Medicare and Social Security benefits kept many older people's incomes above the poverty line. In 1984 the poverty rate for people age 65 and older was 10.4 percent, two percentage points below the rate for the entire nation.

Older women were at greater risk of poverty than older men because fewer women had been employed outside the home long enough to earn a pension and because women lived longer than men. In 1986, among those age 65 and older, 15.2 percent of women and 8.5 percent of men were poor. Widowhood contributed to poverty as it had before the nation was founded and, indeed, throughout U.S. history, but because of increased life expectancy it tended to occur at later ages than in the past. Whether widowhood pushed a woman into poverty depended to a great extent on the couple's economic status when her husband was alive, but his death might mean the loss of any income he had been earning, loss of or changes to his pension, and changes in Social Security benefits.

The Rural Poor

The Appalachian Regional Commission reported that the disparity between poverty in Appalachia and that in the rest of the country lessened in the 1980s, but not because Appalachia prospered. Rather, poverty increased in the rest of the nation while it remained constant in Appalachia. Poverty was greatest in central Appalachia, where people relied on a single, declining industry, coal mining, for employment. In central Appalachia, which was also more rural than the rest of the region, the poverty rate was close to 24 percent in 1989 and again in 1995—much higher than in adjoining areas. In southern Appalachia, the strong economies of Atlanta, Birmingham, and Winston-Salem kept the poverty rate at 13.6 percent in

1989, 15.1 percent in 1993, and 13.6 percent once again in 1995. Northern Appalachia, which had experienced a decline in its manufacturing base and a loss of the associated higher-paying jobs, saw its poverty rate increase from 12.5 percent in 1989 to 15 percent in 1993, and then fall to 13.6 percent in 1995.

Hardship persisted as well among migrant farm laborers, who continued to work for low wages and under unsafe conditions. Frequent moves interrupted their children's education, and the dropout rate among migrant youth remained high. Among East Coast field workers, poverty, inadequate nutrition, and substandard, crowded housing contributed to high rates of illness. In 1991 African-American migrant laborers in North Carolina were found to have a rate of active tuberculosis infection that was 300 times that of the nation. Few eastern growers provided shelter for their workforce, and migrants often had to settle for whatever housing they could afford. Many East Coast farmworkers lived in temporary camps built by the Farm Security Administration in the 1940s that were still in use.

The Immigrant Reform and Control Act of 1986 prohibited the hiring of undocumented immigrants and granted amnesty to those who had been in the United States continuously since 1982. At the time of its passage there were about 4 million undocumented workers in the United States, who constituted approximately 4 percent of the labor force. Roughly half were Mexican, and many of these found employment on western farms. The hiring of illegal immigrants would continue despite the ban, however.

Chronicle of Events

1981

- The U.S. Census Bureau determines that 60 percent of Native Americans live below the poverty line ($9,287 for a family of four).
- The federal government spends $32 billion for low-income housing.
- *January 20:* President Ronald Reagan is inaugurated.
- *August 13:* The Omnibus Budget Reconciliation Act of 1981 becomes law. This act significantly reduces government spending for social programs.

1982

- Two million people in the United States are homeless, according to the Department of Health and Human Services.

1982–1984

- In Boston, the number of housing units renting for less than $300 a month declines by 80 percent while the number renting for more than $600 a month increases 100 percent.
- In New York City, the infant mortality rate in welfare hotels (25 per 1,000 live births) is more than twice the national average.

1983

- Poverty affects 15.3 percent of the population, or 35.3 million people.
- Approximately 7.2 million poor families rent or wish to rent a home.

1984

- Michael Harrington publishes *The New American Poverty*, in which he identifies as the "new poor" such groups as industrial workers who lost their jobs because of plant closings and immigrants working in sweatshops. The new poor lack the optimism that characterized the poor of earlier decades.
- Black men age 25 to 34 earn 80 percent of what white men of the same age and educational level earn.
- The United States is losing 500,000 low-cost housing units a year, according to the National Housing Law Project.
- The poverty rate among people 65 and older is 10.4 percent.
- *March:* Average AFDC payments range from $232 per person and $585 per family in Alaska to $31 per person and $91 per family in Mississippi.

1985

- The working poor account for 7.3 percent of the U.S. workforce.
- Half of single mothers entitled to child support receive the full amount to which they are entitled; one-fourth receive partial payment.
- *January 20:* Reagan begins his second term as president.

1986

- Three-fourths of the homeless in Massachusetts are women and children.
- Among people 65 and older, 15.2 percent of women and 8.5 percent of men are poor.
- The Immigrant Reform and Control Act prohibits the hiring of undocumented immigrants and grants amnesty to those living continuously in the United States since 1982.
- The 4 million undocumented laborers in the United States represent 4 percent of the workforce.

1987

- The Physicians' Task Force on Hunger in America estimates that 15 million Americans are living below the poverty line without food stamps or other nutritional assistance.
- At least 40 states have instituted workfare programs.
- Half of single-parent families spend 58.4 percent of their income on rent.
- The number of poor families renting or wishing to rent a home is now 7.5 million.
- The federal government spends $9 billion for low-income housing.
- Three million people are homeless in the United States, according to the Department of Health and Human Services.

1988

- The unemployment rate is 5.4 percent, down from 7 percent in 1980; the inflation rate has also declined over the same period, falling from 10.4 percent to 4.2 percent.
- The median income is $11,161 for women age 25 to 34 and $31,158 for two-parent families.
- Of the 28,000 homeless in New York City emergency shelters, 18,000 are parents and children.
- *January:* New York City operates 63 welfare hotels.
- *October 13:* Reagan signs the Family Support Act, which requires single parents of children older than three to work or attend job training in exchange for welfare benefits.
- Churches and other private groups operate 90 percent of the nation's homeless shelters.

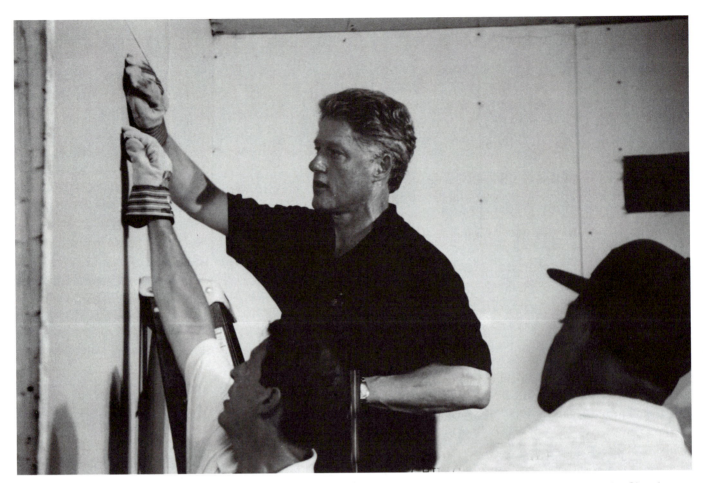

President Bill Clinton and Vice President Al Gore offer hands-on help during the rebuilding of Salem Missionary Baptist Church in rural Fruitland, Tennessee, after the original church was destroyed by arson in 1995. The church, which serves a poor African-American congregation, was one of hundreds of Baptist churches targeted by arsonists in the 1990s. *(William J. Clinton Presidential Library)*

1989

- The Census Bureau determines that 12.8 percent of the population, or 31.8 million people, live in poverty.
- The unemployment rate is 7 percent for the nation and 40 percent for Native Americans; 31 percent of Indian households receive public assistance.
- Six percent of U.S. households have annual incomes below $5,000; 22 percent of households on Indian reservations have incomes in this range.
- About 8.9 million African Americans live below the poverty line.
- Children under 18 make up 27 percent of the population but 40 percent of the poor.
- The poverty rate is approaching 24 percent in central Appalachia, 13.6 percent in southern Appalachia, and 12.5 percent in northern Appalachia.

1990

- In this year 10.4 million African Americans live in poor central-city neighborhoods, compared to 5.6 million in 1980.
- Nearly one-fourth of African-American men age 20 to 29 spend time incarcerated or on parole or probation.
- There are 20.9 divorces in the United States for every 1,000 married women age 15 and older.
- Nearly 3 percent of the U.S. population is of Asian heritage.
- Some 12.2 percent of Asian Americans and 10.7 percent of non-Hispanic white Americans live below the official poverty line.

1991

- Poverty affects 14.2 percent of the population, or 35.7 million people, according to the Census Bureau.

- Approximately 50,000 people in New York City are homeless; another 27,000 live in temporary shelters, and 100,000 live with relatives.
- On the Pine Ridge Reservation in South Dakota, 63.1 percent of people live below the poverty line.
- The rate of active tuberculosis infection among African-American migrant laborers in North Carolina is 300 times that of the nation.

1992

- Bill Clinton is elected president, promising to end the current welfare system.

1993

- New Jersey is the first state to place a family cap on welfare benefits, denying benefit increases to parents who have more children while receiving public assistance.
- Among African Americans, 66 percent of children have single mothers; the figure is higher (80 percent) in some inner-city neighborhoods.
- The poverty rate is 15.1 percent in southern Appalachia and 15 percent in northern Appalachia.

1994–1996

- New Mexico has the nation's highest average poverty rate (24 percent); Louisiana has the second-highest rate (22 percent); Mississippi has the third-highest rate (21.3 percent).

1994

- Thirty-five percent of Asian householders in the United States are U.S. citizens by birth.

1995

- The national unemployment rate is 5.6 percent; the rate for African Americans is 10.4 percent; African Americans make up 20 percent of the unemployed and 40 percent of discouraged workers.
- The poverty rate is nearly 24 percent in central Appalachia and 13.6 percent in northern and southern Appalachia.

1996

- For the first time, the West is the poorest section of the country.
- About 14.46 million children under 18 (20.5 percent of this age group) live in poverty.
- Some 14.4 million people (39.5 percent of the poor) live at less than half the poverty level.
- Fifteen states have implemented family caps on welfare payments.
- *August:* Clinton signs the Personal Responsibility and Work Opportunity Reconciliation Act, which places a five-year lifetime limit on welfare assistance and requires states to terminate support at the end of two years.

Eyewitness Testimony

In the sixties, the best people thought they were doing something for "them"—the blacks, the Appalachians, the truly *other* Americans. But now, more and more people are discovering that they, too, are "them." I do not mean to imply for a moment that the majority of Americans have become poor or will do so in the near future. I merely but emphatically insist that there is a growing sense of insecurity in the society, and for good reason. The very trends that have helped to create the new structure of misery for the poor are the ones that bewilder that famous middle of the American society, the traditional bastion of our complacency. And perhaps that middle will learn one of the basic lessons [I have] tried to impart: A new campaign for social decency is not simply good and moral, but is also a necessity if we are to solve the problems that bedevil not just the poor, but almost all of us.

Writer Michael Harrington, 1984,
The New American Poverty, *p. 255.*

That members of the underclass have little formal education, no employment, and few job skills is a serious indictment of the larger society. It is difficult enough to

This man is homeless and poor in Buffalo, New York, June 1985. *(Photograph © Milton Rogovin 1952–2002, The Rogovin Collection, LLC)*

be black in the United States and when this is combined with these factors, there appears to be little hope for these outcasts. There have been some attempts by the federal government to reach these citizens, but rather than declining, their numbers are increasing. And given the Reagan administration's proposed budget reductions for social and economic programs, one can only suspect that when the situation really becomes intolerable, there will be rebellions throughout the country. The members of the underclass have demonstrated on several occasions that they are capable of massive property destruction and of fighting a guerrilla war with the police for days.

Alphonso Pinkney, sociologist, 1984,
The Myth of Black Progress, p. 118.

The street culture of the underclass is largely an urban phenomenon. Some of the members have migrated from rural areas, and they land on the dreary streets of urban areas, streets with vacant lots, bars, liquor stores, pawnshops, and movie houses. In many places they select special places to spend their time together. Often it is a vacant lot or simply the street corner. In Watts it is the parking lot. And the parking lot culture is often both dull and turbulent, frequently requiring keen intelligence. The most enterprising in the group are frequently well dressed and own automobiles, although they do not hold legitimate jobs. Because the people are intelligent and articulate, they frequently serve as role models for the other members of the underclass.

Alphonso Pinkney, sociologist, 1984,
The Myth of Black Progress, p. 118.

Political expediency is clearly a factor in the assault on social-welfare programs. The Reagan administration does not depend on the poor for votes, and their lack of organizational resources makes effective resistance at the national level difficult. Further, the fragmentation of the American social-welfare programs has taken its toll in fragmentation and division among beneficiaries. But this overlooks a politically critical fact: the American poor are disproportionately women. With the revival of feminism in the late 1960s, women have developed a considerable organizational capacity, and a consciousness of common interests that cuts across class lines. As a result, the Reagan administration's policies are galvanizing a broad movement that joins together middle-class, working-class, and poor women.

Barbara Ehrenreich, journalist, and Frances Fox Piven,
political scientist and sociologist, spring 1984,
"The Feminization of Poverty," p. 169.

"The Sorcerer's Apprentice": In 1990 the political cartoonist Herblock lampooned President George H. W. Bush's inheritance of Ronald Reagan's economic policies. As a 1980 presidential hopeful, Bush had dismissed Reagan's strategy as "voodoo economics." *(from Herblock: A Cartoonist's Life, [Times Books, 1998], courtesy of the Herb Block Foundation)*

The Reagan administration still waves the banner of laissez-faire, but the banner is tattered and unconvincing. The public economy exists, in reality and in the understanding of most Americans. The central political question that has emerged is not whether government shall play a large role in American life, but who will pay for and who will gain from what government does. The significance of the steady stream of poll data showing women's strong disapproval of the Reagan policies is that women have been the first to recognize the question, and the first to offer the answer of resounding support for government policies promoting economic security and equality.

Barbara Ehrenreich, journalist, and Frances Fox Piven,
political scientist and sociologist, spring 1984,
"The Feminization of Poverty," p. 170.

Most Americans want to help. It makes us feel bad to think of neglected children and rat-infested slums, and we are happy to pay for the thought that people who are good at taking care of such things are out there. If the number of neglected children and the number of rats seem to be going up instead of down, it is understandable that we choose to focus on how much we put into the effort instead of what comes out. The tax checks we write buy us, for relatively little money and no effort at all, a quieted conscience. The more we pay, the more certain we can be that we have done our part. A solution—say, scrapping much of the modern welfare edifice—that would have us pay less, accomplish more, *and* acknowledge that some would go unhelped, is unacceptable.

As a result, the barrier to radical reform of social policy is not the pain that it would cause the intended beneficiaries of the present system, but the pain it would cause the donors. The real contest over the direction of social policy in America is not between people who want to cut budgets and people who want to help. When reforms finally do occur, they will happen not because stingy people have won but because generous people have stopped kidding themselves.

Charles Murray, writer and social researcher, autumn 1984,
"The War on Poverty," p. 136.

The progress of blacks must not be seen as a special case. The plight of blacks belongs within the context of the plight of all America's poor: black, Hispanic, and white. The agenda of blacks today must be part and parcel of an agenda for all Americans. It must include a national commitment to excellence in education, a renewed commitment to federal programs in vocational training, and a national industrial policy in which the government helps to fuel the growth of expanding industries, to ease the transition of workers displaced by a changing economy, and to develop a highly skilled work force able to compete in the international marketplace.

Bayard Rustin, civil rights activist, October 1984,
"Are Blacks Better Off Today?" p. 123.

The past three years haven't been kind to young Joe. He's traveled all over Ohio and even to California looking for work. Daily, he fills out applications. He's forgotten how many times he's stood in line with hundreds of other men for a chance at a job. It's hard to find employment when you're twenty-nine and have been trained to operate a machine that was obsolete in 1910.

Finally, he had to move back home. His $19,000 savings account has been reduced to a few hundred bucks. "The only thing keeping me here is that I don't have the money to drive around and look for work anymore. Without my parents," he says, "I'd probably be dead."

Now, Joe studies law enforcement at the university. He hopes to make it his new career. So far, all it's gotten him is a job as an undercover armed security guard for a few hours a week at a local grocery chain. Youngstown [Ohio] grocery stores never used to have armed guards. Now, the men with money fear the thousands who are penniless, and their worry has created some work for Joe.

Joe says he will not shoot anyone for stealing food. He'll let them take it.

Dale Maharidge, journalist, 1985, Journey to Nowhere,
p. 20.

Look at the big men aimlessly walking with their hands in their pockets down the downtown Federal Plaza, where numerous stores are closed. Their sad eyes tell you all you need to know.

Death is reflected in the neighborhoods. Homes are abandoned like so much trash. On Ford Avenue, near the university, over twenty homes are deserted and torn down in a two-year period because so many are fleeing Youngstown. There are few buyers for them. The empty homes are quickly vandalized, windows smashed, mysterious fires set.

Dale Maharidge, journalist, 1985, Journey to Nowhere,
p. 35.

Upon entering the hotel, one is greeted by a rush of noise, made in large part by the many small children living there. These children share accommodations with a considerable cockroach and rodent population. The nearly 400 families housed at the Martinique are assisted by just seven [Human Resource Administration] caseworkers, whose efforts to keep in contact with each family—at least once a month—often amount to no more than a note slipped under a door.

New York City Council's Select Committee on the Homeless
reporting on the Hotel Martinique, a shelter for homeless
families, 1986, in Jonathan Kozol,
"The Homeless and Their Children—1", p. 66.

It was one of those poignant scenes that talk shows thrive on. On September 17, 1986, Oprah Winfrey was hosting an hour on welfare. . . . But the action was in the audience. Two women were yelling, not at the host or the guest, but at each other. The women looked and even dressed similarly, but their antagonism was unmistakable. One said that even though she was working her tail off, trying to earn enough money to raise her family, she was hardly making it. But she certainly was not going to take any handouts. She deeply resented the mothers on welfare who were getting money, medical insurance, and food stamps while they were doing nothing. The other woman, who was on welfare, countered by saying that no lazy person could raise and clothe a family on the tiny amount that she was given for welfare and food stamps and that hers was a hard and often desperate struggle. Both women felt that they were trying hard. Both felt they weren't making it. And both hated the welfare system.

David T. Ellwood, political economist, describing a televised event occurring September 17, 1986, Poor Support, *p. 3.*

Today's ghetto neighborhoods are populated almost exclusively by the most disadvantaged segments of the black urban community, that heterogeneous grouping of families and individuals who are outside the mainstream of the American occupational system. Included in this group are individuals who lack training and skills and either experience long-term unemployment or are not members of the labor force, individuals who are engaged in street crime and other forms of aberrant behavior, and families that experience long-term spells of poverty and/or welfare dependency. These are the populations to which I refer when I speak of the *underclass.* I use this term to depict a reality not captured in the more standard designation *lower class.*

In my conception, the term *underclass* suggests that changes have taken place in ghetto neighborhoods, and the groups that have been left behind are collectively different from those that lived in these neighborhoods in earlier years. It is true that long-term welfare families and street criminals are distinct groups, but they live and interact in the same depressed community and they are part of the population that has, with the exodus of the more stable working- and middle-class segments, become increasingly isolated socially from mainstream patterns and norms of behavior.

William Julius Wilson, sociologist, 1987, The Truly Disadvantaged, *p. 8.*

[Pediatrician Debbie Frank] and I left to join other doctors at the nearby Fairhaven Soup Kitchen, an emergency feeding program attached to a local health center. Several hundred people were there for a warm meal. Debbie has a way with children and immediately hit it off with a child

she estimated to be about three years of age. For most people, judging a child's age is guesswork, but not for Debbie, who is a developmental specialist. . . .

But this time she had guessed wrong; the mother said her daughter was six. Thinking the mother had misunderstood her somehow, Debbie asked the child's age again and got the same response. Now incredulous, Debbie asked the child to open her mouth, knowing that the number of teeth would confirm her age. Her professional demeanor could hardly conceal the shock: the little girl was indeed six, but virtually all the teeth in her mouth were rotten. Bending over the little girl, Debbie's hands trembled as she tried to zip the child's jacket. "What does she eat?" she asked the mother. "We don't have much in the house. Sometimes I give her sugar water for the calories."

J. Larry Brown, M.D., chair of the Physicians' Task Force on Hunger in America, surveying hunger in New Haven, Connecticut, 1987, Living Hungry in America, *pp. 25–26.*

We're a middle-class family. I have four boys. My husband is hospitalized. We got no money and our food stamps last about two weeks each month. My sons are all in their teens, growing boys. The school serves no hot lunches and no breakfast. We have no car. The nearest soup kitchen is fourteen miles away. . . . The last food I bought was yesterday. I spent the money my fourteen-year-old made shoveling snow. There's nothing left.

Jacqueline Putnam of Sterling, Rhode Island, 1987, in J. Larry Brown and H. F. Pizer, Living Hungry in America, *p. 28.*

[A] generation ago, the most prevalent myth about welfare mothers and sex and babies probably was that the mothers had more babies to get higher welfare grants. Sometimes reality overcomes myths. The average AFDC family size—1.9 children per family—is essentially the same as the size of the average American family. If another child is born, almost invariably the additional grant is so small that it cannot support that child, much less improve the mother's standard of living. . . .

The extra-baby-for-profit myth has slowly dwindled, but the United States apparently cannot function without a myth that links welfare and sexuality. So we have a new myth—one that tells us that the availability of welfare is the cause of earlier teen sexuality and greater teen pregnancy, that welfare benefits and the financial independence they imply are such an attractive package that teenagers have babies, out of wedlock, in order to get assistance.

The new myth does not accord with logic or with the findings of studies in the field. It does not explain the earlier sexuality of middle-class girls for whom there is not the slightest expectation of going on welfare. It does not explain why a huge proportion of teen pregnancies are unintended.

Marian Wright Edelman, advocate for children and civil rights, 1987, Families in Peril, *pp. 70–71.*

If we begin with the premise that the poor respond to the same motivations and incentives as the rest of us, the potential conflicts between work and welfare become much more manageable. The issues then become economic, not behavioral. Poor Americans are no more likely to work than the rest of us when it is clear that their effort will leave them worse off than before. However, because work is so important to our self-esteem and our hopes for the future, economically and otherwise, the poor, like the rest of us, will work even under difficult circumstances and for marginal gains.

The similarities between poor and nonpoor in the United States argue for a broader perspective on the interrelation between work and welfare, and a broader restructuring of our policies to ensure adequate incomes for all members of society. There is a real link between welfare and work, but it is primarily a matter of dollars and cents, not of remedying some perceived pathology among the poor. Poor parents by and large are not those who have refused because of some character flaw to join the mainstream economic system; rather, they are people who have fallen or been pushed out of or never got a strong foothold in that system.

Marian Wright Edelman, advocate for children and civil rights, 1987, Families in Peril, *p. 76.*

[O]ur sense of community and the resultant desire for fairness is but one of our closely held values. Other attitudes, such as a belief in the importance of work, family, or self-reliance also color our thinking, and they do not always lead so clearly to charitable feelings. If the desire to help comes from one of these closely held values, then we ought to be conscious of this and other values when we consider and evaluate programs designed to help the poor. Programs that tap into and reinforce common values are likely to enjoy the support of the poor and the nonpoor alike. In contrast, programs that bring closely held values into conflict are sure to be politically volatile and controversial.

David T. Ellwood, political economist, 1988, Poor Support, *p. 15.*

If they'd just fix up some of these places, boarded buildings, they're all over—they are *every*place you go in New York City—I would love it. It doesn't need to have a back yard. It doesn't need to have no pretty floor. It doesn't even need to have a porch. It could be by dumpside city and it wouldn't bother me. I'd pay no mind if it had rats and broken windows just so long as it had heat. . . . Here in this building, I don't sleep. What's on my mind? I'm thinking, There's so many people, trash piled around. What if there's a fire on my floor? There's no fire escape outside this window. I'm on the fourteenth floor. To me it feels like prison.

A resident of the Hotel Martinique, a shelter for homeless families in New York City, January 25, 1988, in Jonathan Kozol, "The Homeless and Their Children—I," p. 75.

The children who live at the hotel dwell in rooms devoid of light and fresh air. Play is a part of education, but these children do not have much opportunity for play. Their room doors open onto a narrow corridor; their windows look out on a courtyard strewn with glass, or on the street, or on the wall of an adjacent wing of the hotel. . . . They are children who often have had no opportunity for Head Start, the federally supported preschool program. Many of them who are of school age will wait for months before they are assigned to a public school, because of the city's long delays in making school assignments for the homeless. Those who do get into school may find themselves embarrassed by the stigma that attaches to the "dirty baby," as the children of the homeless are described by hospital workers and sometimes regarded by their teachers. Whether they are so thought of or not, they *feel* dirty. Many, because of overflowing sewage in their bathrooms, *are* dirty, and bring the smell of destitution with them into class.

Jonathan Kozol, writer, January 25, 1988, "The Homeless and Their Children—I," p. 68.

When Americans talk about poverty, some things remain unsaid. Mainstream discourse about poverty, whether liberal or conservative, largely stays silent about politics, power, and equality. But poverty, after all, is about distribution; it results because some people receive a great deal less than others. Descriptions of the demography, behavior, or beliefs of subpopulations cannot explain the patterned inequalities evident in every era of American history. They result from styles of dominance, the way power is exercised, and the politics of distribution.

Poverty no longer is natural; it is a social product. As nations emerge from the tyranny of subsistence, gain control over the production of wealth, develop the ability to feed their citizens and generate surpluses, poverty becomes not the product of scarcity, but of political economy. Yet with few exceptions . . . this is not the way Americans have talked and written about poverty.

The question is, Why?

Michael B. Katz, historian, 1989, The Undeserving Poor, *p. 7.*

Given the rhetoric that surrounds it, debate about the utility of the term underclass remains more than a distracting and pedantic quibble. Aside from the moral judgment it implies, the term underclass focuses debate on a subset of the poor. It deflects attention from comprehensive social policies and encourages targeted approaches that historically have isolated their beneficiaries and reinforced the stigma attached to poverty and relief. Underclass also revives discredited notions of the culture of poverty by emphasizing the behavior of poor people rather than the sources of their poverty.

Michael B. Katz, historian, 1989, The Undeserving Poor, *p. 234.*

Welfare is not causing poverty, illegitimacy, and a flight from work. But overall poverty rates are as high now as they were in the late 1960s; illegitimacy is increasing; and the employment rate of some subgroups, particularly of young black men, lags far behind the general population. The homeless on the heating grates and seeking shelter in the subways and other public spaces have brought the plight of the "down and out" forcefully to the attention of most Americans. In the press and elsewhere, we are told that a serious poverty problem exists and that its character has changed. It is increasingly difficult to view poverty as a temporary economic reversal in the life cycle of families. Instead, the emerging image of poverty is one of permanent deprivation combined with serious social pathology; it is a vision of what has come to be called "the underclass."

Who is this underclass about which there is so much concern? As definitions vary, so do the estimates of how large the underclass might be. At the most inclusive end of the spectrum of meanings are families who could be described as persistently poor. On that definition, we are talking about as many as eight million Americans. But, "the persistently poor" is a very inclusive description of the underclass. At the more exclusive end of the

definition range, the underclass has been described as including only individuals living in areas of extreme poverty . . . who are either working-age males not regularly attached to the labor force or household heads receiving public assistance. If that is one's vision of the underclass, then about half a million Americans fall into the category.

Theodore R. Marmor, social policy analyst; Jerry L. Mashaw, researcher in social welfare and administrative law; and Philip L. Harvey, economist; 1990, America's Misunderstood Welfare State, *pp. 114–15.*

Welfare benefits have always been low, and their purchasing power has fallen steadily since the mid-1970s. Most people assume that low benefits just force recipients to live more frugally. But low benefits have another, more sinister effect that neither conservatives nor liberals like to acknowledge: they force most welfare recipients to lie and cheat in order to survive. Conservatives ignore this problem because admitting that welfare recipients cannot survive without cheating would weaken the case for cutting benefits. Liberals ignore the problem because admitting that welfare recipients cheat for any reason whatever reduces public sympathy for their plight.

In reality, however, welfare mothers operate on the same moral principles as most other Americans. They think their first obligation is to care for their children, and they assume this means providing food, shelter, heat, electricity, furniture, clothes, and an occasional treat. Since welfare seldom gives recipients who follow the rules enough money to pay for these necessities, they feel entitled to break the rules. Welfare recipients also think that working ought to make them better off. Since the welfare system does not allow them to keep what they earn if they report their earnings, they feel entitled to ignore the reporting requirement.

We have, in short, created a welfare system whose rules have no moral legitimacy in recipients' eyes. This feeling is not confined to second-generation welfare recipients in poor neighborhoods—the so-called "underclass." It is shared by "mainstream" recipients who have finished high school, held jobs, gotten married, had children, and ended up on welfare only when their husbands left them. It is a feeling bred by a system whose rules are incompatible with everyday American morality, not by the peculiar characteristics of welfare recipients.

Christopher Jencks, social policy analyst, and Kathryn Edin, sociologist, spring 1990, "The Real Welfare Problem," pp. 31–32.

[U]nderclass is a word that can be used by conservatives, liberals, and radicals alike. It is a fitting term for conservatives who wish to identify those people who are unable to care for themselves or their families or are prone to antisocial behavior. But underclass . . . is also a suitable concept for those who, like Karl Marx, want to identify a group shaped and dominated by a society's economic and political forces but who have no productive role. And underclass is acceptable to some liberals who somewhat ambiguously refuse to choose between these contrasting images but who nonetheless wish to distinguish between the mainstream of working-class and middle-class America and those who seem separate from or marginal to that society. But, above all, the concept has been called back into the social science lexicon because it offers an explanation for the paradox of poverty in an otherwise affluent society that seems to have made strenuous efforts to eradicate this problem.

Paul E. Peterson, director of the Center for American Political Studies, Harvard University, 1991, "The Urban Underclass and the Poverty Paradox," in Christopher Jencks and Paul E. Peterson, eds., The Urban Underclass, *pp. 3–4.*

—Working-age men should have a steady job. Those who violate this norm constitute the jobless underclass.

—Women should postpone childbearing until they are married. Those who violate this norm constitute what I call the "reproductive underclass."

—Everyone should refrain from violence. Those who violate this norm constitute what I call the "violent underclass."

Whether the underclass is growing depends on which of these ranking schemes one adopts.

Many Americans also think of the underclass as almost exclusively nonwhite. This perception may be partly due to racism, but it derives primarily from our habit of equating people's class position with their address. In most of the ranking schemes described above, the underclass includes considerably more whites than nonwhites. But the underclass constitutes only a small fraction of the white population, and American neighborhoods are only moderately segregated along economic lines. As a result, underclass whites are seldom a majority in any neighborhood. This means that if you equate membership in the underclass with living in an underclass neighborhood, not many whites will qualify.

Christopher Jencks, director of the Center for American Political Studies, Harvard University, 1991, "Is the American Underclass Growing?" in Christopher Jencks and Paul E. Peterson, eds., The Urban Underclass, *p. 30.*

A Chicago welfare recipient who wants an apartment within a year must apply to one of the big high-rise public housing projects, such as Cabrini Green or Robert Taylor Homes. The waiting lists for smaller, more desirable projects are much longer.

A Cook County welfare mother in subsidized housing might be able to survive on her check if she made her own clothes, fed her family a lot of beans and rice, never went anywhere beyond walking distance from the project, never smoked or drank, and entertained her children entirely with library books that she always returned on time. But a mother who could do all this would seldom be on welfare in the first place. If she were, she would most certainly supplement her welfare check rather than force her children to live in Cabrini Green or Robert Taylor Homes.

Christopher Jencks, social policy analyst, 1992, Rethinking Social Policy, *p. 219.*

When a great disaster, like a hurricane or an earthquake, strikes people in our country, the president often declares a state of emergency. This mobilizes resources; it cuts through red tape; and it focuses attention on the people who are in danger so they get the help they need—and get it right away. . . . Victims of floods and earthquakes didn't bring their misfortunes on themselves, and we give them help in rebuilding their lives. How can we deny poor children the chance to build theirs?

Albert Shanker, president of the American Federation of Teachers, 1992, in D. Stanley Eitzen and Maxine Baca Zinn, Social Problems, *p. 203.*

I think the main thing of being homeless is the loss of esteem, the loss of contributing to people, to the world, doing something constructive. You're treated like a piece of material that has to move to this line, to that line. I believe in rules and regulations. I spent eight years in the air force and I enjoyed rules and regulations. I know with a large group you have to do that. But I think when you're homeless, you can't do it. Because you have no identity. You're just, "You over here. You get up. You can eat now."

And it's sad to lay there at night. Last week there was a woman came, was a nurse, raised children. Unfortunately, she's on a pension, like myself, can't afford a place and she told me, "What am I going to do?" I said, "You'll have to ride it out. And maybe they'll get you into a boardinghouse or maybe your name will come up on a [subsidized housing] list or maybe you'll win Megabucks." And she went crazy the other night. She just couldn't control herself any more. Now, she's at the mental hospital and God knows if she'll be able to snap back.

"Caroline," a homeless woman, interviewed by Melissa Shook, July 7, 1988, in Padraig O'Malley, ed., Homelessness: New England and Beyond, *p. 186.*

American cityscapes today are eerily apocalyptic. The bleak vistas and visible poverty of inner-city Detroit, the nation's seventh largest city, offer a striking example of the social and economic devastation common to the former industrial centers of the Rustbelt. Empty hulks of abandoned factories loom over acres of rubble. Whole rows of storefronts are boarded up. Abandoned houses, falling down or burnt out, are surrounded by fields overgrown with prairie grass and ragweed. Sixty thousand vacant lots lay strewn throughout the city. Although the city still has a base of manufacturing employment and a substantial middle class, a large number of the city's residents live in poverty. Over a quarter of Detroit's population is unemployed and a third receives some form of public assistance. A visit to the city's hospitals, schools, and jails makes clear the terrible toll of the impoverishment of many of the city's residents.

Thomas J. Sugrue, historian and sociologist, 1993, "The Structures of Urban Poverty: The Reorganization of Space and Work in Three Periods of American History," in Michael B. Katz, ed., The "Underclass" Debate, *p. 85.*

For both popular and academic purposes, the term *underclass* is a convenient shorthand, but perhaps we should be a bit more troubled by its easy and immediate popular understanding and acceptance. The intuitive knowledge of who is meant by the term *underclass* in public perception, despite the imprecision of most academic definitions, has wider implications. The connection of the term to a large body of social and cultural thinking in the United States produced since the beginnings of social science study early in the century should not be overlooked. This thinking was centered on ideas of what was decent, modern, healthy, and respectable behavior within households and families.

The idea of an underclass implies the existence of an overclass that defines and sets ideological standards under which society in general is expected to live. In the United States, "having class" generally has not been an economic consideration in popular usage. Rather, it has been seen as a matter of behavior, social skills, aesthetics, manners, and morals. This moralistic and judgmental definition of class and its implications of good breeding, background,

and family play a significant role in both popular and academic views of people assigned to an underclass. They also connect to an American racial climate that has been all too willing to connect and elide race and class.

Andrew T. Miller, historical demographer, 1993, "Social Science, Social Policy, and the Heritage of African-American Families," in Michael B. Katz, ed., The "Underclass" Debate, *pp. 254–55.*

The [Mississippi] Delta is full of contradictions. For example, the Lower Mississippi Delta culture is rich and influential. Roots of blues, jazz, and rock 'n' roll music are found in the Delta. Yet to many of the region's citizens this music remains, in some respects, less accessible than to people in most other parts of the country. Similarly, some of the nation's most widely acclaimed authors— William Faulkner, Eudora Welty, [Richard] Wright, Maya Angelou, Anne Moody, Peter Taylor, Shelby Foote—are from the region yet the region has historically been home to a higher percentage of functionally illiterate people than any other comparably large region in the United States. Like the rest of the South it is also regarded as being politically and socially separate, resistant to progressive social change affecting the rest of the country, and therefore rather untypical of "real" America. At the same time, the high rate of southern participation in the armed services and the patriotic fervor that seems embedded in southern fundamentalism create an image of ultra-Americanism. Finally, the Delta seems remote and unconnected with mainstream American economic life, but in fact the conditions that characterize the region have been etched in large part by very real and specific cultural, political, and economic relationships with the rest of the country and the world.

Stanley Hyland, urban anthropologist, and Michael Timberlake, sociologist, 1993, "The Mississippi Delta: Change or Continued Trouble," in Thomas A. Lyson and William W. Falk, eds., Forgotten Places, *pp. 76–77.*

Thirty years ago, when we last awakened to the poverty problem and declared war against it, our motives (if not our thinking) appeared clearer than they do today. The Poverty Warriors of the 1960s truly believed that poverty could be eradicated, that enough money spent in just the right ways would inevitably solve the problem, that if we would only supply the opportunities, the poor would avail themselves of them. All this strikes us today as hopelessly naïve. The past three decades have made us more realistic and better informed about the dimensions and circumstances of the poverty problem than we have ever been before. But realism need not degenerate into cynicism, nor better information into a hard-bitten, uncaring mood. Being realistic about the poverty problem need not make us any less committed to finding appropriate, workable, humane solutions.

Joel A. Devine and James D. Wright, sociologists, 1993,
The Greatest of Evils, p. xx.

American society at the brink of the twenty-first century presents us with a troubling contradiction. On the one hand, we are a remarkably affluent society whose economic achievements and standard of living are the envy of the rest of the world. And yet we find ourselves saddled with a higher poverty rate, a higher crime rate, a higher infant mortality rate, more homelessness, more drug abuse, more violence, more hunger, than any other advanced Western democracy. Despite pious incantation, we are not "one nation, under God." Rather, we have become two nations: the first a nation of affluence, where material well-being is taken largely for granted, and the second a nation of poverty, where desperation, deprivation, and violence are the rule. Surely, this is not the example we want to set for the world or the legacy we wish to bequeath to our children.

Although no known present-day society has managed to eliminate poverty altogether, many have found the means and the political will to reduce the level of poverty well below the American standard. If other advanced industrial societies can do this, then so, surely, can we.

Joel A. Devine and James D. Wright, sociologists, 1993,
The Greatest of Evils, p. 189.

I eventually found my way up to the Roberto Clemente Housing Project in the Bronx and managed to gain entry to its basement, which was reserved exclusively for homeless families. You should understand that never in my life—a life grounded in the belief that the American system ensures, above all, the innocence of children and their right to pursue the boldest of dreams—have I encountered anything so shocking, so beyond comprehension. . . . The place was horrendous. The huge, dimly lit, stripped-down gymnasium contained about 400 cots grouped together in family sets along the floor. There were no lockers. Each family kept their possessions in plastic garbage bags beneath their cots. Needless to say, from the moment the shelter opened at five in the evening until its mandatory "close-out" at 10 the next morning, nobody strayed far from their designated area. Anyone who wished to leave, for whatever reason, was forced to check out with the one social worker on site—with their children and all their personal belongings—and then check back in upon their return. In our midst were a number of armed policemen who stood stiffly against the walls, stirring now and then to brush back an unruly child or bark instructions to a confused mother. Policemen also monitored the communal bathrooms, with young boys over the age of five required to use the "men's only" facilities under the watchful eye of a state trooper. This mass of dejected humanity was something I would never forget.

Leonard N. Stern, founder of Homes for the Homeless and the
Institute for Children and Poverty, Columbia University, 1994,
in Ralph Da Costa Nunez, Hopes, Dreams, and Promise,
pp. 3–4.

Most people lack the methodological skills of social scientists, and do not see the assumptions that underlie the approaches to underclass counting. Once word gets out that social scientists have identified some areas as underclass areas, however, these neighborhoods can easily be stigmatized, the population labeled accordingly and accused of whatever local meanings the term "underclass" may have acquired.

When areas become known as underclass areas, local governments and commercial enterprises obtain legitimation to withdraw or not provide facilities and services that could ameliorate the poverty of the area's inhabitants. Labeling areas as underclass can also encourage governments to choose them as locations for excess numbers of homeless shelters, drug treatment centers, and other facilities that serve the very poor and that are therefore rejected by other neighborhoods.

Herbert J. Gans, 1995, professor of sociology, Columbia
University, The War against the Poor, *p. 64.*

Eliminating "underclass" as a label will not eliminate its dangers, history having shown that if one label loses its appeal, another is likely to emerge sooner or later, new and old labels being merely new words for the undeserving poor. The more basic problem lies elsewhere: in the underlying idea of the undeserving poor. Behind that idea is the power of the stereotypes expressed in it, and even more important, the structural sources and reasons for that power, which are located in the larger society. The hatred aroused by the poor accused of being undeserving really has to do with more basic faults and social fault lines in America.

Why, for example, are politicians able to score symbolic triumphs by inveighing against alleged dangers from the imagined undeservingness of welfare recipients? What economic and moral problems in the country lead them to fall all over themselves to propose ending welfare or to invent new ways of making it ever more punitive? Why do some intellectuals feel that illegitimacy is a more serious American problem than violent crime, the failure of the economy to generate enough jobs, or the country's need to come to terms with worldwide wars and civil wars? Why does the country even need such scapegoats as the undeserving poor?

Herbert J. Gans, professor of sociology, Columbia University, 1995, The War against the Poor, *p. 74.*

And how do the poor see you and me, especially the most wretched of the poor who have never known either plenty or its prospect? I have found that these most damaged and undefended of our countrymen look at the rest of the United States, particularly the *official* United States, as an armed force attacking them. For them the cold war is already hot. "Every day I wake up, don't matter if it's in a shelter or under some bridge," a woman in Santa Monica told me, her chin cut and her straw hair matted but her eyes clear and doleful, "and it's like this cavalry's charging down on me, going to hoof me under good." Santa Monica, where I was born, was a town I'd always thought of as one of California's gentlest, its people mirrored in its ocean: pacific. Yet there and everywhere, members of the underclass have used terms from combat to describe the rest of America to me. The marines are coming to get them; they will be strafed; heavy artillery is being brought up against them; the infantry is advancing; the mayor called in an air strike on them when he closed the downtown shelter.

Peter Davis, writer and filmmaker, 1995,
If You Came This Way, *p. 6.*

Much of the underclass is still invisible, holed up in shelters, manacled to ghettos, hidden in rural hollows. But many of the underclass, or persistently poor, unlike the terrified millions staring into the abyss of poverty but still above it, are in your face. The man who lives on the subway steps, the two women who huddle together in the doorway of the dry cleaner's, the family that sleeps in the park just outside your children's playground. How often can you ride a subway, walk on a crowded street, leave a theater late at night, use a bathroom in a public park, or even walk in that same park after sundown, without being approached by someone who asks for and sometimes demands the money you worked for and he did not? You feel assaulted, first by the panhandler, next by guilt, finally by rage.

Peter Davis, writer and filmmaker, 1995, If You Came
This Way, *p. 7.*

The extreme poverty of ghetto neighborhoods notwithstanding, the popular and politically exploitable image of ghettos as places where everyone drops out of school, where no one works, and where everyone receives welfare is a gross distortion of reality. Many ghetto residents work, albeit at lower-skill occupations and for fewer hours and lower wages. Earnings account for about the same proportion of total income in the ghetto as elsewhere. Although households on public assistance are more common in the ghetto, most ghetto households receive no government assistance. Most ghetto teenagers are in school. Employed persons in ghettos work in the same industries as persons living in low-poverty neighborhoods and spend about the same time commuting to their jobs. . . . [T]he data do not suggest that the residents of ghettos constitute a separate "underclass," hopelessly at odds with mainstream culture.

Paul A. Jargowsky, professor of political economy, University of Texas at Dallas, 1 October–15 November 1996, "Beyond the Street Corner," p. 598.

CHAPTER TEN

Poverty Endures
1997-2006

Delivering the commencement address at Notre Dame University on May 20, 2001, President George W. Bush focused his remarks on aiding the nation's poor. Elected in 2000, Bush called himself a compassionate conservative. As a conservative he favored minimal government involvement in people's lives; as a compassionate leader he called on religious and charitable groups, corporations, and private citizens to aid the unfortunate. As had his Republican predecessors Ronald Reagan and George H. W. Bush, the president rejected the ambitious federal antipoverty effort of the 1960s. He called the "welfare entitlement" resulting from Lyndon Johnson's War on Poverty "an enemy of personal effort and responsibility, turning many recipients into dependents." He added that Johnson's initiatives had transformed caring citizens into "bystanders convinced that compassion had become the work of government alone."[1]

When Bush spoke at Notre Dame, the long-term effects of the Personal Responsibility and Work Opportunity Reconciliation Act (PRWORA) of 1996 were unknown, but some short-term results had been reported. In March 1999 welfare supported 7.3 million people, or less than 4 percent of the U.S. population. This was the lowest level of public assistance in the United States since the 1970s, and some states had achieved especially dramatic declines. Wisconsin, largely through vigorous job training and placement, had reduced its welfare roll 90 percent between 1996 and 2000. Governor Tommy Thompson boasted about his state's accomplishment, calling it "the most positive development in American social policy for about forty years."

In 1999, Wendell Primus, director of income security for the Center on Budget Policy Priorities, a nonpartisan research and policy institute, estimated that 700,000 families in the United States were worse off financially than their pre-PRWORA counterparts. These were families who had been forced off welfare rolls and therefore no longer received cash assistance. Many were headed by adults who were dependent on drugs or alcohol or had physical or mental disabilities that prevented them from working steadily. In other cases, a lack of transportation or child care was an obstacle to employment. Finally, some of these families lived in economically depressed areas, such as Appalachia or the Rust Belt, where jobs were hard to find. Another study, this one conducted by the Manpower Development Research Corporation, found that it was not parental employment but increased income that benefited children in measurable ways, such as improved school performance.

Nevertheless, results of welfare reform continued to make news. Minnesota measured a 13 percent decrease in its welfare roll between January 1997 and March 1999. Idaho supported 24,000 people on public assistance in 1996, but only 2,461 in March 2002. New York City's Hotel Martinique closed as a shelter for homeless families and reopened in 1998 as a Holiday Inn.

States were able to put greater resources into job training and related services because as the number of recipients declined, the amount available to spend per client increased. In every state, the federal grant per recipient rose at least 20 percent between 1994 and 1998. (The average monthly cash payment to a mother and two children rose only 5 percent nationwide between 1995 and 1998, however.) Sharing credit with the 1996 law for the drop in welfare dependency were independent economic factors, such as an increase in the minimum wage and a generally healthy economy that was adding jobs, although most of these were low-paying positions in service as waiters, cashiers, janitors, and the like.

The majority of people who left welfare and started to work were women who held low-paying jobs that kept their families in poverty. More than one-fourth worked at night, when it is difficult to find child care. Some of these people worked under deplorable conditions. For example, in 1997 workfare participants employed by the New York City Departments of Transportation and Sanitation filed a class-action suit against the city, claiming they were denied protective gear, water, and access to bathrooms and otherwise exposed to hazards on the job. "Because I have no dust mask or eye protection, I suffer from the dust that blows up in my face while I am sweeping," testified a 44-year-old man assigned to a street-sweeping crew.[2] "There is nowhere to wash your hands before lunch, and my hands are often dirty from picking up garbage," said a 57-year-old female sanitation worker.[3] In August 1997 the New York State Supreme Court ruled that the city was required to improve working conditions for 5,000 workfare participants.

In some states, "family caps" continued to generate controversy. In 2001, in a review of research on state-imposed limits on monthly welfare payments to parents who have additional children while receiving public assistance, the U.S. General Accounting Office found no evidence that family caps reduced the number of births to single mothers or Temporary Assistance for Needy Families (TANF) caseloads. In 2002, heeding the concerns of physicians and family-policy experts that restrictive welfare legislation might harm children, Maryland became the first of several states to repeal its family-cap provision. Then in 2003, in a move criticized by welfare-rights and women's advocates, Minnesota imposed a family cap as part of its effort to reduce a $4.5 billion budget deficit. By April 2005, however, the state legislature was considering a bill that would repeal the cap.

The Gap between Rich and Poor

As the 1990s drew to a close, the unemployment rate was low, just 4 percent, but the income gap was widening. In 1998 the fifth of households that were the richest took in almost half the money earned in the United States—49.1 percent. The richest 20th earned almost half of that, or 22.2 percent. The poorest fifth received just 5.1 percent of the nation's earnings. The gap, which reflected several social and economic trends, including the growing number of single parents and the difference in wages paid to skilled, educated workers and the unskilled, varied from one place to another. A study based on 1999 income conducted by the D.C. Fiscal Policy Institute identified the District of Columbia, Atlanta, and Miami as the major U.S. cities with the greatest income gaps. By 2000, though, families in the bottom 20 percent of income distribution showed gains. Their average income, measured in 2000 dollars, rose from $12,625 in 1990 to $15,232 in 2000.

Millions of people still faced material and economic hardship. In 1997 the U.S. Department of Agriculture calculated that roughly 11 million Americans, including 4 million children, lived in households where hunger was moderate or severe. A balanced, nutritious diet was beyond the budget of 8 million households, and 4 million families went hungry for at least part of the year. Food banks aided 26 million Americans, and emergency requests to these resources had increased 16 percent from 1996. In 1998, 2.8 million workers were employed full-time, year-round, but lived below the poverty level, and the U.S. Department of Housing and Urban Development estimated that 5.3 million families, or 12.5 million people, were at risk of homelessness because rent consumed half or more of their income. Never before had this number been so high.

In 1999 the poverty rate dropped to 11.8 percent, the lowest it had been since 1979. This meant that 2.2 million fewer people were poor in 1999 than in 1998, according to official counts. The Census Bureau measured declines in poverty in every racial, ethnic, and age group. The poverty rate of African Americans was the lowest ever measured for that group, 23.6 percent. The poverty rate of Hispanics was slightly lower, 22.8 percent, and that of Asians and Pacific Islanders was 10.7 percent. For the first time the Census Bureau released poverty data on Native Americans and Native Alaskans and stated that the poverty rate in this group averaged 25.9 percent from 1997 through 1999.

By 2000, 11.3 percent of the population (31.1 million people) lived in poverty, according to the official measure, and 4.4 percent were poor-poor. Just 5.7 million people were receiving income through TANF, an indication that the population on welfare represented a small fraction of the impoverished.

Poverty among people age 65 and older reached a low of 9.7 percent in 1999. Women in this age group still faced a greater likelihood of poverty than men, and older people who lived alone were at increased risk, especially if they lived in a rooming house or shared quarters with people to whom they were unrelated. Credit for keeping the poverty rate low in the older population went to government support, especially Social Security. Without government aid, poverty would have affected 41 percent of people 65 and older and 56 percent of those 75 and older, according to one estimate.

In 2000, more than half the poor population was female. The poverty rate was 12.5 percent among females and 9.9 percent among males. Families headed by single women were six times more likely than two-parent families to be poor, although 79 percent of single mothers were in the workforce. Many remained poor because they earned low wages. It therefore follows that children younger than six in families headed by women continued to be vulnerable as well. Experiencing poverty at the rate of 50.3 percent in 1999, these children were more than five times as likely to be poor as children of the same age in two-parent families. The poverty rate for all children was 16.2 percent in 2000.

Poverty has also continued to afflict farm laborers, both those who migrate and those who are permanent community residents. In 2004 more than 60 percent of farm workers were poor, and the percentage was increasing. Agricultural laborers who were U.S. citizens, were permanent residents, or possessed other authorization to work earned between $5,000 and $10,000 a year, and undocumented workers earned far less, between $2,500 and $5,000 a year. Despite their poverty, thousands of farm workers and their families were excluded from key federal social programs, such as food stamps and Medicaid. They also often went without needed medical care because of a lack of money or transportation, limited clinic hours, and an inability to communicate with non-Spanish-speaking health care professionals. (Approximately 84 percent of agricultural workers were native speakers of Spanish.)

Field work is now considered one of the most hazardous occupations in the United States because workers are exposed to chemicals that cause dermatitis and other health problems. These workers are also at risk for heat exhaustion and heat stroke, and they have higher-than-average rates of influenza, pneumonia, urinary tract infections, and tuberculosis. Infant-mortality rates are higher among migrants as well, and their children suffer disproportionately from parasitic infections, malnutrition, and dental decay.

Many agricultural workers were among the 28.4 million people of foreign birth in the United States in 2000. Immigration from Asia, Latin America, and other parts of the world was responsible for a third of U.S. population growth in the final decades of the 20th century. Most of these immigrants settled in New York, Florida, Texas, New Mexico, Arizona, California, or a large city. The poverty rate for foreign-born people in the United States was 17 percent in 2000, higher than that of the general population, but poverty was most prevalent among new arrivals. It declined with length of time in the United States, as people were assimilated into the economy.

What It Means to Be Poor

Statistics and percentages clarify how many members of society are poor as well as their ages, ethnicity, family status, and location, but they paint an incomplete picture of people's lives. To be poor in the United States at the start of the 21st century is to worry about having enough food and to know the sensation of hunger. Supermarkets in low-income urban neighborhoods and poor towns charge high prices and stock inferior produce, because the people living nearby often lack transportation to competitors' stores and therefore have no choice of places to shop. Also, buying in bulk and stocking up during a sale—both money-saving measures—require outlays of cash that the poor usually do not have. Many of the poor lack the resources to maintain even a small bank account and rely on check-cashing establishments that charge high fees. If they need a loan they commonly turn to one of the pawnshops that are so prevalent in low-income communities and that impose high interest rates.

Paying rent and utility bills is a monthly struggle. In the rundown housing of the poor, roofs leak, broken windows let in rain and cold, heating and plumbing may not work, rats and roaches scurry into holes in walls, and exposed wires and peeling paint pose hazards to children. People live with these maintenance problems because fixing them would cost money or because they have little clout with landlords responsible for such repairs.

Many of the rural poor find living in manufactured, or mobile, homes affordable, but these structures place residents at increased risk of injury or death from severe winds. A review of storm data by National Oceanic and Atmospheric Administration (NOAA) researchers revealed that one-third of the people killed by tornadoes between 1975 and 1997 in the United States were in mobile homes. During this period approximately 6 percent of the population lived in manufactured homes. In addition, scientists at Kent State University in Ohio reported in December 2002 that mobile-home occupants accounted for 45 percent of tornado deaths in 2002. The scientists stated that a relatively weak tornado, one with winds of 110 miles per hour, could destroy a typical mobile home; the most violent tornadoes have wind speeds in excess of 250 miles per hour.

Most poor families have the use of a refrigerator and stove, and many own microwave ovens, but they are less likely than other Americans to have regular use of a telephone, washing machine, dryer, or air conditioner, although material conditions are improving. Computers and the Internet remain beyond the reach of most, however. Meanwhile, their local scene is one of abandoned buildings, accumulated trash, public drinking and drug use, vandalism, and crime that makes residents wish they could escape. In 2003 the poverty rate was 17.5 percent in central cities, 14.2 percent in rural areas, and 9.1 percent in suburbs. Most large cities are segregated economically, with the poor restricted to certain neighborhoods as a result of housing affordability and prejudice.

In 2005 poor residents in suburbs outnumbered those in inner cities for the first time. The poverty rate remained higher in inner cities than in suburbs (18.8 percent v. 9.4 percent), but the number of poor people in the suburbs was greater. The Brookings Institution named Cleveland as the city with the highest poverty rate in 2005 (32.4 percent) and San Jose, California, as the city with the lowest rate (9.7 percent). McAllen, Texas, on the Mexican border, was the suburb with the highest poverty rate (43.9 percent), and the communities surrounding Des Moines, Iowa, had the lowest suburban rate (3.7 percent).

The concept of a culture of poverty has fallen out of favor, but one study suggests that as much as one-fourth of poverty in the United States results from having poor parents. The books, periodicals, and educational toys that stimulate the minds of youngsters growing up in middle-class or affluent homes are beyond the budget of most poor mothers and fathers. The strain of daily life drains so much of these parents' energy that they are often too tired and stressed to give their children the nurturing, supervision, and instruction they need. Low-income parents are twice as likely as other parents in the United States to exhibit violent behavior and signs of mental illness, and in 1997 reports of child abuse and neglect were an astonishing seven times higher for poor children than for other youngsters. Also, poor children are twice as likely as others their age to live in families that have been scarred by violent crime.

Infants born into poverty are more likely than others to weigh less than 2,500 grams at birth, a condition that puts them at risk for developmental disorders. Prenatal care for low-income women is often inadequate, and their babies are exposed in the womb to conditions that put them at risk, such as maternal hypertension, diabetes, human immunodeficiency virus (HIV) infection, drug or alcohol abuse, or malnutrition.

Mortality rates for infants and children remain higher among the poor. Also, poor children traditionally have been less likely than other children to be fully immunized or to see a doctor when they are sick, although by 1997 their medical care was improving. Unbalanced meals and environmental hazards contribute to the increased incidences of diabetes, asthma, and dangerous levels of lead in the blood found in children raised in poverty. As a result of deprivation, poor children are twice as likely to be in the lowest five percentiles for height for their age group, and an unhealthy diet certainly contributes to the obesity that is twice as common in poor white adolescents as in other teens.

Children in poor communities attend schools that are inadequately staffed and equipped and that are falling into disrepair as a result of limited funding. Educational achievement is lower than average, and more developmental problems are diagnosed in these schools than in schools serving the middle class and affluent. Poor children are more likely than others to perform below grade level, to repeat a grade, and to score below average on tests of cognitive skills. As these children mature, the stresses of poverty can erupt in adolescence as a serious emotional disorder, such as depression, or as antisocial behavior. Poor teens participate less in extracurricular activities, and they have a greater probability of being expelled or dropping out of high school before graduation. They are twice as likely as others their age to be out of school and unemployed. Younger children, too, exhibit signs of low self-esteem and depression and act out. The more years a child spends in poverty, the greater his or her chance of psychological problems.

Schools are inferior in rural pockets of poverty just as they are in poor inner-city neighborhoods. High rates of joblessness and low wages characterize the employment situation in places such as Appalachia, the Mississippi Delta, the Indian reservations of the West, and the Lower Rio Grande valley of Texas. These are places where educational attainment is low and men and women have few skills to offer employers. Rural poverty is not simply a matter of low earnings, though. The poor in these isolated areas are less likely to receive welfare or food stamps or to have access to social services, libraries, hospitals, and other community resources. Roads remain substandard, and public transportation may not exist. As a result of inadequate or deteriorating infrastructure, water may be unsafe to drink.

The Public Weighs In

In 2001, after surveying attitudes toward poverty in the United States, researchers from National Public Radio, the Kaiser Family Foundation, and the John F. Kennedy School of Government at Harvard University concluded that "Americans aren't thinking a lot about the poor these days."[4] Just one in 10 people surveyed mentioned poverty, welfare, or a related issue as one of the top two problems for government to address. When asked specifically about poverty, though, most people said it was a serious problem. The majority also considered the federal poverty line ($17,029 for a family of four) to be too low. Sixty-four percent said that a family of four earning $20,000 was poor, and 42 percent said that a family of the same size earning $25,000 was poor. Yet people with incomes at twice the poverty level still reported difficulty covering the cost of food, rent, utilities, transportation, and medical care.

Respondents' views differed on the causes and possible remedies of poverty; about half stated that the poor were doing too little to raise themselves out of poverty and half stated that circumstances beyond their control made people poor. Those earning less than twice the federal poverty level (roughly $34,000 for a family of four) were more likely than other respondents to attribute poverty to circumstantial causes, such as medical bills and a lack of jobs. Many of the poorest respondents thought drug abuse contributed significantly to poverty.

Americans were also evenly divided in their responses to questions about whether welfare recipients could get along without benefits if they tried and whether government assistance permitted the poor to live easy lives, although those with higher incomes were more likely than others to say that welfare was expendable and made life easy. People who knew about PRWORA thought the legislation was working well because it required the poor to work rather than be idle. The researchers noted, "Americans appear to value work so strongly that they support welfare reform even if it leads to jobs that keep people in poverty."[5]

Living on the Edge

Americans may not have thought much about the poor in 2001, but they did after Hurricane Katrina made landfall along the Gulf Coast as a category-four storm on August 29, 2005. Levees holding back Lake Pontchartrain gave way, and water poured into New Orleans. Many residents had heeded Mayor C. Ray Nagin's mandatory evacuation order, but many others remained in this city below sea level, mostly because they lacked the cash, credit cards, and automobiles needed to leave. Televised news reports showed 30,000 of the city's poor—who were predominantly African American—taking shelter in the Superdome with enough food to last 36 hours. Three thousand more gathered in the city's convention center without food or water.

Residents of St. Bernard Parish, Louisiana, an area flooded by Hurricane Katrina, continue to live in Federal Emergency Management Administration (FEMA) trailers in January 2006, while their homes are gutted and rebuilt. *(Federal Emergency Management Administration)*

Floodwaters rose to cover school buses that could have carried people to safety and forced stranded residents into attics or onto roofs. Days passed as the refugees in the convention center and Superdome waited in deteriorating conditions for local, state, and federal authorities to go to their aid. "A 2-year-old girl slept in a pool of urine. Crack vials littered a restroom. Blood stained the walls next to vending machines smashed by teenagers," wrote a reporter for the *Los Angeles Times* on September 1, 2005. "At least two people, including a child, have been raped. At least three people have died, including one man who jumped 50 feet to his death, saying he had nothing left to live for. There is no sanitation. The stench is overwhelming."[6] Eventually, helicopters and buses removed most victims from the flood zone, and federal authorities arranged to house thousands of evacuees in Baton Rouge, Houston, and other cities as Americans donated money, goods, and time to relief efforts.

By December 2005 tens of thousands of displaced adults and children remained in hotel rooms paid for with taxpayer funds, trying to find jobs and rebuild their lives. The 12,000 who remained in Georgia alone had cost the public $300 million. The Federal Emergency Management Agency (FEMA) warned the refugees that they had to vacate all hotel rooms by January 7, 2006, when federal support was to be terminated.

The nation's experience of Hurricane Katrina demonstrated that the poor are among the most vulnerable in times of emergency. Said the 2004 vice-presidential candidate John Edwards, who now directs the Center on Poverty, Work and Opportunity at the University of North Carolina at Chapel Hill, "They live on the razor's edge."[7]

During the week when Hurricane Katrina did its terrible damage, the Census Bureau reported that the number of Americans living in poverty increased 1.1 million in 2004; this meant that 37 million people were poor nationwide. Poverty affected 12.7 percent of the population after this fourth straight year of increase. In New Orleans 27 percent of residents lived below the federal poverty level, which was $16,090 for a family of three and $19,350 for a family of four. They lived in neighborhoods with high rates of HIV infection and teen pregnancy, inferior schools, and low rates of high school graduation.

The majority of Americans saw educational value in Hurricane Katrina and its impact on the poor, reported the Catholic Campaign for Human Development (CCHD), an organization that funds self-help programs for the poor, in January 2006. The same CCHD public-opinion survey found that 65 percent of Americans feared that poverty would increase in the United States in 2006, and almost as many, 63 percent, worried that they might be poor before the year was over.

The poor in some major cities had genuine cause for concern in 2006, when municipal governments cut back aid and services to reduce budget deficits. The New York City Housing Authority (NYCHA) announced in March 2006 that it would begin collecting fees from residents operating large electrical appliances and needing home repairs. The 400,000 people occupying public housing units would pay $5.75 per month to run a washing machine, $5 per month for a dishwasher, and $10 per month for a freezer. The NYCHA, the nation's largest public housing agency, maintained 181,000 apartments in close to 2,700 buildings.

Some 1.8 million city residents were poor in 2005 by federal standards, and another 1.6 million lived in households with incomes just above the official poverty line, according to the Community Service Society of New York, an independent nonprofit group that addresses the needs of the city's low-income population. In two-thirds of poor households, at least one person worked full time.

A month after NYCHA officials made their statement, Mayor Kwame Kilpatrick of Detroit proposed to eliminate bulk trash pickup and charge households $300 a year for trash collection. This added burden would weigh disproportionately on the poor, who accounted for 31.4 percent of the city's population in 2005. (Only one major U.S. city, Cleveland, had a higher poverty rate, 32 percent.)

The Detroit metropolitan area has been hurt economically by mass layoffs in the automobile industry. The loss of 27,000 factory jobs in suburban Macomb County, Michigan, between 2000 and 2005 affected 22 percent of the manufacturing workforce. In 2005 Michigan had a jobless rate of 6.7 percent, behind only Mississippi and Louisiana (both affected by Hurricane Katrina), Alaska, and South Carolina.

The federal poverty level in 2006 was $20,000 for a family of four, $16,600 for a family of three, and $13,200 for a family of two. The National Center for Children in Poverty at Columbia University pointed out that most families would need twice that amount to meet basic needs. Regional differences in the cost of living meant that a family of four would require $49,000 to meet basic expenses in Boston, $38,000 in Chicago, and $36,000 in Atlanta.

Researchers continue to add to what is known about poverty in the United States. In 2006 the Inter-American Development Bank reported that immigrants from Latin America often live on incomes that fall well below the federal poverty line. In that year the government considered a family of four living on a monthly income of roughly $1,600 to be poor, but the average Hispanic immigrant earned $900 a month. Hispanic newcomers' economic status improves more rapidly than does that of other poor U.S. residents, though, because of the immigrants' willingness to curb spending on rent, health care, and other living expenses. Latin American immigrants put 90 percent of their income back into the U.S. economy and invest the rest (an estimated $45 billion in 2006) in their home countries, often in real estate, thus reducing poverty there.

Like other recent immigrants, people from Latin America increasingly bypass the inner cities that were home to generations of newly arrived foreigners and move directly to suburbs, especially in the South and Midwest. In a study released on December 7, 2006, the Brookings Institution attributed the recent rise in suburban poverty in part to immigration patterns. They also identified job losses in the Midwest as a significant cause. The researchers noted that "the enduring social and fiscal challenges for cities that stem from high poverty are increasingly shared by their suburbs." These include deteriorating schools, rising crime rates, and the loss of high-paying employment. "Public and private efforts that give growing suburban poor populations access to economically integrated neighborhoods and [workplace] supports could enhance economic security and mobility for a significant number of Americans"[8]

Ten years had passed since President Bill Clinton signed the controversial welfare-reform legislation. In 2006 the Brookings Institution, a think tank in Washington, D.C., measured a decline of 60 percent in the nation's welfare rolls since 1996. This was the first sustained drop in the number of Americans receiving public assistance since Aid to Dependent Children (ADC) was enacted in 1935. The employment of single mothers heading families grew throughout the decade, and women and children living in these households consumed a more nutritious diet and lived in safer, more comfortable conditions in 2006 than in 1996. Ron Haskins, a senior fellow in economic studies with the Brookings Institution, concluded, "Welfare reform showed that work—even low-wage work—provides a more durable foundation for social policy than handouts."[9]

Chronicle of Events

1997

- Approximately 11 million Americans, including 4 million children, experience moderate to severe hunger, according to the U.S. Department of Agriculture.
- Eight million households cannot afford a balanced diet; 4 million families are hungry for at least part of the year.
- Food banks aid 26 million Americans and respond to 16 percent more emergency requests since 1996.
- Reports of child abuse and neglect are seven times higher for poor children than for others.
- Poor children are receiving better medical care than in the past, but they are still less likely than other children to be fully immunized or to see a doctor when sick.
- *August:* The New York State Supreme Court rules that the city of New York must improve working conditions for 5,000 workfare participants in its employ.

1997–1999

- The poverty rate for American Indians and Alaska Natives averages 25.9 percent.

1998

- Every state receives from the federal government at least 20 percent more funding per welfare recipient than in 1994.
- Nationwide the average monthly welfare payment to a mother and two children has increased 5 percent since 1995.
- The richest fifth of U.S. households earn 49.1 percent of all income in the United States, the richest 20th earn 22.2 percent of all income, and the poorest fifth earn just 5.1 percent.
- In this year 2.8 million full-time, year-round workers live below the poverty level.
- The U.S. Department of Housing and Urban Development estimates that 5.3 million families, or 12.5 million people, are at risk of homelessness because of inability to pay rent.

1999

- Wendell Primus of the Center on Budget Policy Priorities estimates that PRWORA has had a negative financial impact on 700,000 families.

- Washington, D.C.; Atlanta; and Miami are the major U.S. cities with the largest income gaps.
- The poverty rate reaches its lowest level since 1979, 11.8 percent; 2.2 million fewer people are poor than in 1998.
- The poverty rate for African Americans is 23.6 percent (the lowest ever measured for this group), and 22.8 percent for Hispanics and 10.7 percent for Asians and Pacific Islanders.
- The poverty rate among people age 65 and older reaches a low of 9.7 percent.
- The poverty rate for children under six in families headed by women is 50.3 percent; children under six in families headed by women are five times more likely to be poor than children under six in two-parent families.
- The poverty rate is 13.4 percent for nonmetropolitan areas and 10.8 percent for metropolitan areas.
- *March:* Welfare supports 7.3 million people, or less than 4 percent of the U.S. population.
- *March:* In Minnesota the welfare roll has decreased 13 percent since January 1997.

2000–2005

- Macomb County, Michigan, loses 27,000 factory jobs, and this affects 22 percent of the manufacturing workforce.

2000

- Wisconsin has reduced its welfare roll 90 percent since 1996.
- The average income of families in the lowest 20 percent of income distribution, measured in 2000 dollars, is $15,232, which is up from $12,625 in 1990.
- The government categorizes 11.3 percent of the population (31.1 million people) as poor and 4.4 percent as poor-poor.
- Roughly 5.7 million people receive income through Temporary Assistance for Needy Families (TANF).
- The poverty rate is 12.5 percent for females and 9.9 percent for males; more than half the poor population is female.
- The poverty rate for children is 16.2 percent.
- Some 28.4 million people of foreign birth live in the United States; the poverty rate for the foreign born is 17 percent.
- Families headed by single women are six times more likely than are two-parent families to be poor.

- Seventy-nine percent of single mothers are in the workforce.
- *November 7:* George W. Bush is elected president in one of the closest races in U.S. history.

2001

- A study by the U.S. General Accounting Office finds no evidence that family caps on welfare payments reduce either births to single mothers receiving public assistance or TANF caseloads.
- The majority of respondents to a survey conducted by National Public Radio, the Kaiser Family Foundation, and the John F. Kennedy School of Government at Harvard University consider the federal poverty line ($17,029 for a family of four) too low; respondents are evenly divided on whether personal shortcomings or outside circumstances cause poverty, and whether welfare is expendable and makes life easy.
- *May 20:* Speaking at Notre Dame University, President George W. Bush calls on citizens and private organizations to aid the poor.

2002

- Maryland becomes the first state to repeal its family-cap provision.
- *March:* Idaho supports 2,461 people on public assistance; in 1996 the number was close to 24,000.

In his commencement address at Notre Dame University on May 20, 2001, President George W. Bush calls on private citizens and corporations to aid the needy. *(Notre Dame Archives)*

2003

- Minnesota imposes a family cap on welfare payments.
- The poverty rate is 17.5 percent for central cities, 9.1 percent for suburbs, and 14.2 percent for rural communities.

2004

- New York City's Hotel Martinique, a former shelter for homeless families, reopens as a Holiday Inn.
- More than 60 percent of farm workers are poor.
- Approximately 84 percent of farm workers are native Spanish speakers.

2005

- Roughly 1.8 million New York City residents live below the federally established poverty line; another 1.6 million hover above that line.
- In Detroit, 31.4 percent of the population is poor. In Cleveland, the poor account for 32 percent of the population.
- Michigan has the nation's fifth-highest unemployment rate, 6.7 percent.
- The suburban poor outnumber the inner-city poor for the first time. The poverty rate is 18.8 percent in inner cities and 9.4 percent in suburbs.
- Among cities, Cleveland has the highest poverty rate (32.4 percent) and San Jose, California, has the lowest (9.7 percent). Among suburbs, McAllen, Texas, has the highest poverty rate (43.9 percent) and the communities surrounding Des Moines, Iowa, have the lowest (3.7 percent).
- *April:* The Minnesota legislature considers repealing the state's family cap.
- *August 29:* Hurricane Katrina, a category-four storm, causes flooding in New Orleans that displaces most of the city's poor.
- *September:* Thirty thousand people endure horrific living conditions in the New Orleans Superdome.
- *December:* Tens of thousands of displaced poor New Orleans residents live in hotel rooms in other cities at government expense.

2006

- The New York City Housing Authority (NYCHA) maintains 181,000 apartments in nearly 2,700 buildings.
- The federal poverty level is $20,000 for a family of four, $16,600 for a family of three, and $13,200 for a family of two.

Children evacuated from New Orleans show off their Christmas presents on December 25, 2005. These children are from the more than 600 families living in a Federal Emergency Management Administration (FEMA) trailer park in Baker, Louisiana, since Hurricane Katrina forced them to leave their homes. *(Federal Emergency Management Administration)*

- The Brookings Institution measures a 60 percent decline in the nation's welfare rolls since 1996.
- *January:* A survey conducted by the Catholic Campaign for Human Development (CCHD) finds that most Americans see educational value in Hurricane Katrina's impact on the poor; 65 percent of respondents fear that poverty will increase in 2006, and 63 percent worry about becoming poor themselves.
- *March:* The NYCHA announces a plan to charge fees for the use of major appliances in public housing units.

- *April:* Mayor Kwame Kilpatrick of Detroit makes public a plan to assess households $300 per year for trash collection.
- *October:* The Inter-American Development Bank reports that the average Hispanic immigrant worker earns $900 a month. The bank estimates that Hispanic immigrants will invest 10 percent of their yearly earnings (about $45 billion) in their Latin America homelands.
- *December 7:* The Brookings Institution releases a study linking the rise in suburban poverty to changing patterns of immigrant settlement.

Eyewitness Testimony

Instead of talking about the poor, we now talk about the underclass, which by common consensus includes only the undeserving poor: men who have no regular job, women who depend largely on welfare to survive, street criminals, winos, and addicts. The deserving poor, notably the elderly and two-parent families in which the man works steadily but cannot earn enough to feed all his children, are definitely not part of the underclass. The popularity of the term thus signals a political shift: instead of blaming poverty on society, as we did in the late 1960s, we are now more inclined to blame poverty on the poor. . . .

When the poor are doing all they can to better themselves, it is easy to argue that they deserve a helping hand. When people are too old, too sick, too deranged, or too retarded to help themselves, it is also easy to argue that compassion requires others to help. But when sane, healthy adults refuse to follow norms of behavior that most of society endorses, the claim that we should help them arouses intense controversy.

Those who favor compassion usually deny that the poor are undeserving. The poor are not poor, they maintain, because they have the wrong values or because they suffer from what philosophers call "weakness of the will." The poor behave as they do, according to the compassionate, only because they confront different choices from the rest of us—or because they have no choices at all. If they had our choices, they would act as we act. Compassionate liberals have therefore been hostile to those who write about the underclass, and especially those who see the underclass as having a "deviant" culture that approves (or at least fails to disapprove) of idleness, single parenthood, theft, and violence. This way of characterizing the poor is, they feel, a device for "blaming the victim."

Paul A. Jargowsky, professor of political economy, University of Texas at Dallas, 1997, Poverty and Place: Ghettos, Barrios, and the American City, *pp. 120–21.*

Where do poor people live? If you asked that question thirty years ago, most people would have mentioned rural America: the agricultural South or the isolated mining towns of Appalachia. If you ask that question today, many people will respond with images of urban ghetto poverty: high-rise public housing and abandoned buildings, with an ever-present threat of gang violence. Most Americans have become frighteningly familiar with this image of poverty in recent years, which has dominated media presentations.

Despite these images, relatively few among the poor live in poor urban ghettos. Most poor live in mixed-income city or suburban neighborhoods. In fact, there are few city neighborhoods, suburbs or midsized towns that do not have a substantial number of low-income families. The best answer to where the poor live: they live among us and with us.

Rebecca M. Blank, director of the Joint Center for Poverty Research, Northwestern University, 1997, It Takes a Nation: A New Agenda for Fighting Poverty, *p. 27.*

[N]onpoor citizens today expect minimum standards of civil behavior and responsible lifestyle decisions by those who receive public support. They are offended by dependency, teen out-of-wedlock births, homelessness, drug abuse and crime—all of which they see prevalent among the welfare recipient population.

While the images may be colored by stereotypes and prejudice (these problems are also concentrated in the African-American and Hispanic populations), to a large slice of nonpoor Americans, many of those in the bottom tail of the distribution today are there because of irresponsible choices they have made: the choice to bear children out of wedlock as a teen, the choice not to complete high school, the decision to refuse minimum wage employment when it is available, the decision to abuse drugs and sell them, the willingness to run in gangs and to engage in crime and violence, often against other poor people. After all, the poor did not used to be like this. And while many may be willing to admit that economic and social factors, urban schools, and the barriers created by racial prejudice may make these choices a rational response to the options available, they nevertheless seem to conclude that these socially costly and destructive outcomes are the result of choices encouraged by the welfare system.

Robert Haveman, economist, 1997, "Welfare Report—1996 Lifestyle," in Jon Neill, ed., Poverty and Inequality, *p. 10.*

Why, in a nation marked by prosperity unknown in most other societies, do we see an increasing number of people who work but are still poor? The labor market has shifted drastically in favor of the well-educated, leaving those who attend bad schools (or drop out of them) in trouble. Once upon a time, not so long ago, poorly educated jobseekers might have found refuge in high-wage work in the auto factories or the steel mills. Those days are history now. Where manufacturing retains a foothold, manual workers are now expected to gather statistical quality-control data, organize problem-solving groups to develop innovative solutions based upon their own research, and implement changes in the organization of assembly lines. The average high school dropout, and many an inner-city grad, cannot compete against more advantaged job-seekers when it comes to the written tests manufacturers now routinely employ to find people who can fit into the new, high-tech factory. And in many communities, manufacturing jobs hardly exist anymore anyway.

Katherine S. Newman, sociologist, 1999,
No Shame in My Game, *p. xiii.*

Secular forces and special circumstances have combined to make life particularly difficult for the working people of America's inner cities. Yet there is reason to believe that the efforts we make on the poverty policy frontier would have the greatest payoff if we focused attention on this large and growing population of poor workers. One of their greatest assets is the commitment they share with more affluent Americans to the importance of the work ethic. These are not people whose values need reengineering. They work hard at jobs the rest of us would not want because they believe in the dignity of work. In many instances they are not only better off, they are actually worse off from a financial perspective for having eschewed welfare and stayed on the job. It costs them—in child care, in transportation, in clothing costs—to remain in the labor force. But it also benefits them, as it benefits their middle-class counterparts, because working keeps them on the right side of American culture. Nonetheless, they are poor, and because of this unhappy truth, they are subjected to many of the same forces that the nonworking poor must contend with: decaying housing, poor diet, lack of medical attention, lousy schools, and persistent insecurity.

Katherine S. Newman, sociologist, 1999,
No Shame in My Game, *p. xv.*

Welfare programs have become known as "entitlements," implying that once enacted they are impossible to withdraw. But that connotation is now under a severe test, particularly in programs of welfare for the poor who lack political clout to protect their interests. One result is that the "conversation" going on in the country at this time is not about poverty, but about "welfare," who should conduct it, and who should pay for it. This quick turning of attention to "what to do" without a diagnosis of basic causes is very American. We are doers, and often seem to believe that all social problems are solvable.

This may be so, but what do we mean by "solving"? For some it means getting poverty off our radar screen.

Too often in the past we have "solved" social problems by moving them elsewhere and leaving them for others to handle. These are false prescriptions because they are based on inadequate knowledge. An adequate diagnosis must address both basic causes of poverty and the many institutional and cultural structures of our society which share in perpetuating poverty.

J. Gordon Chamberlin, Methodist minister and writer, 1999,
Upon Whom We Depend, *p. 19.*

I am a 24-year-old working mom of two kids, making a little over minimum wage. I am stressed. I don't eat, sleep, or have time for my kids anymore. Just because I thought that I would be self-sufficient. I went to these programs made to "help." I ended up with a low paying job with hope of making more in the future. My money can never be saved because I don't make enough to save. Bills consume my whole check. Just from the little money I make, I am no longer eligible for any kind of assistance.

Greed is what this system is all about. How can we as the working poor ever afford the necessities of life? The minute we get some money it is gone. That sounds like TRAPPED to me!

Nikkie Thompson, November 2000, in D. Stanley Eitzen and Kelly Eitzen Smith, Experiencing Poverty:
Voices from the Bottom, *p. 33.*

In the 1960s, the United States experienced a long period of sustained economic growth, rising real wages, and low unemployment. Although the fruits of this prosperity were widely visible in the period between the Korean and Vietnam Wars, a combination of academic writings and magazine articles focused attention on those who were not benefiting from economic growth. President Kennedy, concerned with the extent of the poverty he had seen during the 1960 campaign, asked his economic advisers to prepare proposals to address the problem. President Johnson would later endorse these proposals and declare the War on Poverty in his 1964 State of the Union address. Within a few years, numerous pieces of legislation were drafted and enacted into law. They dramatically transformed the federal budget and the scope of the nation's social welfare policies. Many new programs were introduced (for example, Medicare, Medicaid, Head Start), and benefit levels were increased in many others (Social Security, Aid to Families with Dependent Children).

Now, as the new millennium begins, the nation has again experienced a period of sustained prosperity. However, unlike the mid-1960s, the topics now occupying center stage include reducing taxes on large estates, granting income tax relief, especially to high-income taxpayers, enforcing work requirements for welfare recipients, and ensuring that retirement and medical benefits for the older population are maintained. Public and presidential concern for the nation's poverty problem has been minimal for years, despite the long-standing labor-market problems of less-skilled workers and the dramatic increase in income and wealth inequalities of the last quarter-century.

Sheldon H. Danziger, professor of public policy, the University of Michigan, and Robert H. Haveman, economist, 2001, Understanding Poverty, *p. 1.*

Karen, an African-American resident of Cleveland, had just left a $6-per-hour job assembling light fixtures when we first met her. Because the job's physical demands exacerbated long-standing health problems, Karen felt compelled to leave the job and return to welfare. Though she was committed to working, she wanted a job that was less taxing physically. She went to a temporary employment agency, whose staff informed her that her education and skills didn't qualify her for the desk jobs that she sought. After a six-month spell without work, Karen was assigned by the agency to another factory job, this time assembling vacuum cleaners, at a higher wage ($7.50 per hour). After half a year at that factory, Karen's health had deteriorated to the point where she was hospitalized. She followed her employer's advice and quit her job rather than being fired. Several weeks later . . . she had been diagnosed with multiple sclerosis. She had not yet reapplied for welfare but knew that she would have to do so unless she could find a job that didn't require her to be on her feet all day. She also wanted to find a day job, because, in her view, the evening-shift factory job had led to both children's being held back a grade in school. Additionally, her health problems mandated that she land a job with benefits. Given these barriers to work, Karen was unsure whether she could manage to sustain employment over the long term.

Denise F. Polit et al., 2001, Is Work Enough? *pp. 2–3.*

Welfare as we knew it has ended but poverty has not. When over 12 million children live below the poverty line, we are not a post-poverty America. Most states are seeing the first wave of welfare recipients who have reached the law's five-year time limit. The easy cases have already left the welfare rolls.

The hardest problems remain: People with far fewer skills and greater barriers to work. People with complex human problems like illiteracy and addiction, abuse and mental illness. We do not yet know what will happen to these men and women or to their children. But we cannot sit and watch, leaving them to their own struggles and their own fate.

This is a great deal at stake. In our attitudes and our actions we are determining the character of our country. When poverty is considered hopeless, America is condemned to permanent social division, becoming a nation of caste and class, divided by fences and gates and guards.

Our task is clear, and it's difficult. We must build our country's unity by extending our country's blessings. We make that commitment because we're Americans. Aspiration is the essence of our country. We believe in social mobility, not social Darwinism. We are the country of the second chance where failure is never final. And that dream has sometimes been deferred. It must never be abandoned. . . .

Much of today's poverty has more to do with troubled lives than a troubled economy. And often when a life is broken, it can only be restored by another caring, concerned human being.

The answer for an abandoned child is not a job requirement, it is the loving presence of a mentor. The answer to addiction is not a demand for self-sufficiency, it is the personal support on the hard road to recovery.

The hope we seek is found in safe havens for battered women and children, in homeless shelters and crisis pregnancy centers, in programs that tutor and conduct job training and help young people who happen to be on parole.

President George W. Bush, May 20, 2001, Commencement Address at Notre Dame University, p. 2.

The cabinet met with President Bill Clinton in the Roosevelt Room of the White House on a sultry day in the summer of 1996. Many of us recommended that he not sign the welfare bill that the Republican Congress had sent him (the third one it sent, only slightly less punitive than the first two, which he had vetoed). But an election was on the horizon, and the president's political advisers urged him to sign, lest Robert Dole use the president's timidity as a battering ram.

In the end, he did sign, of course, and since then he and many Democrats have celebrated the decline in America's welfare rolls without acknowledging that millions of people who are now at work but had been on welfare are not earning enough to support their families, that they are in dead-end jobs without a future, and that the greater harm will come when the economy slows and they will no longer be able to find work.

Robert B. Reich, secretary of labor under President Bill Clinton, 2002, "Introduction: Working Principles," in Robert Kuttner, ed., Making Work Pay, *p. vii.*

In 1999, when a magazine editor asked me to write about the progress of welfare reform in America, I called around to see which state was leading the way. I ended up in Wisconsin. Under the direction of Republican governor Tommy Thompson, Wisconsin had begun cutting its rolls earlier than most other states and had pared them far more sharply. During my visit there, almost everyone I met embraced the idea of welfare reform. Even longtime advocates for the poor said they had become convinced that too many people had become too dependent on welfare and that reform had given them a needed push.

But I also heard many complaints about how welfare reform was being carried out. Thousands of people who were unable to work were being pushed off the rolls; hunger and homelessness had increased. Even those who had found jobs were having trouble retaining them, and their average wage was falling. Welfare reform was getting many people off the dole, I was told; it was not getting them out of poverty.

Increasingly, this is the national story.

Michael Massing, journalist, 2002, "Ending Poverty as We Know It," in Robert Kuttner, ed., Making Work Pay, *p. 21.*

Since February 1997 I have been working on a crew that cleans the ramps and service roads near the highways. I cut weeds and grass all morning by swinging a long wooden stick with a flat metal blade. The tool is heavy and hurts my shoulders after a few minutes. I'm about five feet tall, and some of the grass is taller than I am.

While working, I see rats everywhere along the roads. They don't bite us, because we scream and run away. They are about eight inches long, with long, stringy tails. They are sometimes right next to us. There are also all sorts of plants, maybe poison ivy, that give me rashes. But the supervisors give us no work clothes, either in the winter or the summer. The only things we get for protection are an orange vest, a pair of cotton gloves, and a hard hat. The gloves and the hard hat are filthy, but I am not allowed to take anything home to wash it. They gave out boots for one week in February, but they were all size 12 and did not fit me.

Because there is no place to go to the bathroom, I do not drink water. This makes me feel like I am suffocating.

When I work I feel nauseated and lightheaded, and I get terrible headaches. . . .

My health and my spirit have been worn down by this program.

Mery Mejia, workfare participant employed by the city of New York, 2003, in Stanley Eitzen and Kelly Eitzen Smith, Experiencing Poverty: Voices from the Bottom, *pp. 122–23.*

The poverty line is an inadequate measure that relies on out-dated thresholds, such as food costs, and fails to account for societal changes, like the cost of housing as the major portion of families' budgets. While the debate will continue about how to measure poverty in America, the real discussion needs to be about new policies, not new measures of wealth and hardship.

America needs policies that allow everyone the opportunity to find a job that provides a dignified standard of living and a decent retirement. America needs quality healthcare for all and a guarantee that an illness will not wipe out the family bank account or threaten job security. America needs a public education system with enough resources to ensure that children can attain their fullest potential.

Center for Community Change, an advocacy group for low-income people, August 26, 2004, "Statement on U.S. Census Income and Poverty Data," p. 1.

"When I was 4, my dad left us," says Heidi, now an eighth grader at Avery Middle School in Newland, North Carolina. "He was supposed to come back to visit for my fifth birthday—but he never showed up. I called to ask why he didn't make it, but he'd disconnected his phone. I was so confused and upset."

Since no one was able to find Heidi's dad, her mom, Lisa, had to start supporting Heidi and her two younger brothers, Keith, now 12, and Kailan, now 10, by herself. Lisa worked as a full-time receptionist—but she made less than $5 an hour, so the family was in big trouble. After paying for rent, utilities, and gas for the beat-up station wagon they needed to get to school and work, Heidi's family barely had enough money left for the basics. "First my mom couldn't afford to buy us any more new clothes. Then she had to stop buying us birthday presents and birthday cakes. Then she couldn't even get us pencils for school," says Heidi. "But what scared me the most was that soon there was almost no food to eat."

Sarah Eisen Nanus, deputy editor of Seventeen, *September 2004, "My Mom Can't Feed Our Family," p. 172*

The press has been full of stories about the rich, the super-rich and the just absurdly rich, and it's certainly a scandal that families earning $80,000 a year may face higher average tax rates than those with $400,000. Yet much of the press anguish is about secondary problems. It's bad that the income of the median American family has risen by only a fifth over the past three decades, but at least it has been rising. Sharper ups and downs in middle-class income are troubling, but the middle-class could protect itself by saving a bit more.

Now, you want to hear something really bad? The poorest fifth of Americans has experienced a rise in incomes of just 3 percent over the past three decades. The real problem in America is not about the middle class. It's about the underclass: about Americans who lack the skills and habits to advance at all.

Sebastian Mallaby, Washington Post *columnist, June 13, 2005, "A Bridge for the Underclass," p. A19.*

A homeless man sleeps in the doorway of Philadelphia's 30th Street Station.   *(National Archives)*

God help the run-of-the-mill poor.

I'm not talking about the suddenly chich, in-vogue poor, such as destitute tsunami survivors or the displaced Gulf Coast residents whom Hurricane Katrina blew into every U.S. region—though goodness knows, they need every possible blessing.

I mean the poor represented by a man I saw Monday while driving with a friend on a busy Northwest Washington street. Filthy, his eyes rimmed fire-engine red, the man approached my car, stopped before my bumper and fell to his knees.

Although smack in the middle of an active lane of traffic, he bowed his head, genuflecting on the concrete as if in active worship.

I screamed. My friend, a longtime inner-city dweller who's seen hundreds of handout seekers, shook his heada and said, "So that's what run-of-the-mill poor people have to do to get out attention."

The *run-of-the-mill poor*. We see them—and refuse to see them—all the time.

Staring at us from "please give" posters. Milling on trash-strewn corners. Waiting on city lots, hoping to be picked up for pay-by-the-day labor.

Donna Britt, Washington Post *columnist, September 16, 2005, "Every Day, We Ignore the Poor," p. B1.*

Where I'm from is called "far northeast" [Washington, D.C.] for a reason. It's as far as possible from being what most people think of as the nation's capital. There are no museums, reflecting pools or cherry blossom trees on my block. Our monuments are boarded-up apartment buildings, homes with bedsheets blowing from glassless windows and the shells of abandoned stores strewn with graffiti. . . .

Growing up, everyone on my street was poor, though not as bad off as some people left destitute by Katrina. If the Katrina survivors' lives were washed into the gutter, the people in my neighborhood lived on the curb. Like many of my friends, I lived in a home with extended family because my parents couldn't afford a place of their own.

It wasn't always that way. We used to have our own apartment. . . . Then my mom got sick and my dad fell down some steps, injured his back and lost his job as a courier. That's when my parents, sister, brother and I moved in with my grandparents and uncle in a three-bedroom row house at the end of Foote Street, Northeast. . . .

My high school, Woodson Senior High, was five blocks from my grandparents' home. . . . Each day, on my walk to school, I would hopscotch past people straddling

the line between struggling and surviving. Men selling crack cocaine in the alley or stealing cars. Women selling their belongings or themselves on a corner. . . .

Ever since Hurricane Katrina forced America to stare into the face of the impoverished, there has been a lot of debate about the differences between Main Street and Foote Street. I believe the main one lies in that often unexplored variable of poverty: hope.

That's the real difference between my street and yours. Odds are hope lives on your street. It only occasionally visited mine.

Kayce T. Ataiyero, November 27, 2005, "Rising from Poverty," p. 3.

While many neighborhoods remain troubled, and many older inner-ring suburban neighborhoods are showing signs of distress, far fewer neighborhoods than in the recent past have the confluence of low levels of education, few men in the workforce, and large numbers of unmarried women raising children on welfare. Crime rates have fallen, teen pregnancy and birth rates are down, and the rising proportion of children born outside marriage has slowed or leveled off. Progress on this scale—a relatively rare occurrence in the arena of social problems—should be celebrated.

That said, it would be a grave mistake to complacently assume that these changes will continue or even be maintained. Without public policies that discourage crime and encourage education, work and delayed childbearing, as well as housing policies that facilitate spatial access to opportunity, these positive trends could easily reverse. The two groups most at risk are adolescents and low-income working families. These two groups need ladders into the middle class. For adolescents in distressed neighborhoods, this means smaller, more effective high schools, afterschool programs, and adult mentors or counselors. For low-income families, the success of welfare reform in moving many single mothers into the job market needs to be followed by efforts to keep them there with wage supplements, child care, health care and employer-based training programs. Without strong rungs on the bottom of the ladder, they—or more likely their children—could just as easily become tomorrow's underclass.

Paul A. Jargowsky, associate professor of political economy, University of Texas at Dallas, and Isabel V. Sawhill, senior fellow in economic studies, Brookings Institution, "The Decline of the Underclass," p. 4.

Powerful folk beliefs in the United States portray the poor as profligate, undisciplined consumers. In fact, those who have carefully studied the day-to-day purchases and economic behavior of the poor know better, and the poor know best of all how carefully their resources are managed, bartered, exchanged. Without access to the super-sized reservoirs of credit that the middle class can amass through both property and little plastic cards, the poor are often laid flat by large expenses: a refrigerator, a car, a hospital stay. Savings accounts, retirement funds, mad money—these are not options, not so much because the poor are incapable of thinking about these things, but because, as one anthropologist describes it, "there's a lot of month left at the end of the money."

Consider this: many poor children have never had the opportunity to purchase a gift for a loved one. Whatever conflicts the affluent might feel about rampant consumerism, it is worth wondering whether—and how—something so seemingly simple as being able to buy your mother a present for Mother's Day might also be a powerful moment of self-actualization. The power to buy is, in this society, inevitably and fundamentally, the power to be.

Elizabeth Chin, associate professor of critical theory and social justice, Occidental College, Los Angeles, March 1, 2006, "I Will Simply Survive," p. 3.

From July 15–17, PPEHRC [the Poor People's Economic Human Rights Campaign] held a National Truth Commission in Cleveland, Ohio to unveil the realities of poverty in the United States. This Truth Commission brought together hundreds of poor people and allies from throughout the country and world . . . .

While there, we heard stories of mothers in Maine who lost heat and had to huddle around kitchen stoves in the winter with their children. We heard about several families who were doing well and working hard until illness struck and left them bankrupt and unable to work. We heard about workers in Florida stuck making less than minimum wage and having no way out. We heard about low-income housing being torn down for new "mixed" income housing, leaving people on the street. This is happening all over our country. . . .

One story we've documented from Ithaca [New York], with the help of students from Cornell's Urban Studies Program . . . involves a grandmother and her three grandchildren. The story helps demonstrate the difficulties that poor people face every day, and that most middle and upper income people rarely have to think about.

Isabella is a 68-year-old African-American grandmother working two minimum wage jobs. She lives in public housing with her three grandchildren whom she loves very much. Isabella works hard at her two jobs, earning a meager $18,000/year, because she dreams of giving her grandchildren a better life than what she's lived. After eighth grade she dropped out of school to work and hasn't stopped since. Isabella dreams of sending her grandchildren to college so they can get good jobs and not depend on food pantries and soup kitchens like she has.

Jessica Brown, advocate for peace and social justice, July 31, 2006, "America's Poor Speak, but Who Will Listen?" pp. 1–2.

Appendix A
Documents

1. An Act for the Relief of the Poor, Pennsylvania, 1705

For the better relief of the poor of this province, Be it enacted by John Evans, Esquire, by the queen's royal approbation, lieutenant governor under William Penn, Esquire, absolute proprietary and governor in chief of the province of Pennsylvania and territories, by and with the advice and consent of the freemen of said province, in general assembly met, and by the authority of the same, That the justices of the peace of the respective counties of this province, or any three or more of them, shall on the five and twentieth day of March, yearly (unless that shall happen on the first day of the week) and then on the day following, meet at some convenient place within their county, and there nominate and appoint one, two or more (as the case may require) of substantial inhabitants of the respective townships, and where the townships are small and inhabitants few, two or more (as the justices shall think fit) may be joined together with their county, to be overseers of the poor of said townships for the year ensuing.

And be it further enacted by the authority aforesaid, That it shall and may be lawful for the overseer or overseers of the poor so nominated and appointed, to make or lay a rate or assessment after the rate of one penny per pound, clear value of the real and personal estates of all and every the freeholders and inhabitants within their respective townships, to be employed for the relief of poor, indigent and impotent persons inhabiting within the said townships, in such a manner as by this act is directed and appointed; and four shillings per head on all freemen not otherwise rated.

And be it further enacted by the authority aforesaid, That the said overseers, before they proceed to the collecting of the said rate, shall procure the same to be allowed by three or more justices of the peace of the county wherein the said tax is made. And if any person or persons so rated or assessed, shall refuse to pay the sum or sums on them charged, that it shall and may be lawful to and for the said overseer or overseers, having first obtained a warrant under the heads and seals of two justices of the peace of the county where the said assessment is made, who are hereby impowered to grant such warrant to levy the same on the goods and chattels of the person or persons so refusing; and in case such person shall not, within three days next after such distress made, pay the sum or sums on him assessed, together with the charge of such distress, that the said overseer or overseers may proceed to the sale of the goods distrained, rendering to the owner the overplus (if any) that shall remain on such sale; reasonable charges first deducted. And in case such person or persons have no goods or chattels, whereby they may be distrained, that then it shall be lawful for the said justices to commit the offenders to prison, there to remain without bail or mainprize until they have paid the same.

Provided always, That if any person or persons find themselves aggrieved with such rate or assessment, that then it shall be lawful for the justices of the peace, at their next general quarter sessions, upon petition of the party, to take such order therein as to them shall be thought convenient, and the same to conclude and bind all parties; and the overseer or overseers shall forbear such distress till the same be determined in the quarter sessions.

And be it further enacted by the authority aforesaid, That the said overseers shall lay the said rate according to the best of their skill and judgment, wherein they shall be guided by the county assessment on other occasions, having due regard to every man's estate without favor or affection to any.

And be it further enacted by the authority aforesaid, That the father and grand father, and the mother and grand mother and the children of every poor, old, blind, lame and impotent person or other poor person, not able to work, being of a sufficient ability, shall at their own charges, relieve and maintain every such poor person as the justices of the peace at their general quarter sessions shall order and direct on pain of forfeiting forty shillings for every month they fail therein.

And be it further enacted by the authority aforesaid, That it shall and may be lawful for the said overseers of the poor, by the approbation and consent of two or more justices of the peace, to set on work the children of all such whose parents shall not be by the said justices thought able to maintain them; and also to put such children out apprentices for such term, as they in their discretion shall see meet.

And be it further enacted by the authority aforesaid, That the justices of the peace of the said respective counties shall, at least ten days before the said twenty-fifth day of March yearly, issue out their warrants, directed to the overseers of the poor of the respective townships within their county, commanding the said overseers to appear before them on the said day and produce their accounts of what money they have received, and disbursed for the use of the poor, and also to return the names of one or two, or more (as the place may require) of the sufficient inhabitants of the respective townships, to succeed them in that office for the year ensuing: And in case the overseers shall neglect to bring in such their accounts, as also the names of such sufficient persons to succeed them in that office the year ensuing, such person or persons so neglecting shall serve in that office one year longer or otherwise forfeit any sum not exceeding fifty pounds, as the said justices shall think fit and direct. And in case the person or persons approved on and appointed by the said justices to be overseers of the poor of any township within the respective counties shall refuse to take upon him or them the said office, and to do his or their duty therein he or they shall forfeit the sum of five pounds each; which said forfeitures shall go and be to the use of the poor of the town or place where such neglect or refusal shall be made, and shall be levied by the constable, by warrant from any two justices of the peace of the said county, under their hands and seals, on the goods and chattels of such person or persons so neglecting or refusing, and by the constable sold within three days next after such distress made: And if there happen any overplus upon sale thereof, the same shall be paid to the person or person to whom the same shall belong; reasonable charges first deducted. And if such person or persons, so neglecting or refusing as aforesaid, shall not have goods or chattels, whereby he or they may be distrained as aforesaid, that then the said justices may commit the offender or offenders to prison, there to remain without bail or mainprize till the said forfeitures shall be by the fully satisfied and paid.

And be it further enacted by the authority aforesaid, That the mayor and aldermen of the city of Philadelphia shall have the same power and authority, by virtue of this act, within the limits and precincts of their jurisdiction, as well out of sessions, as at their sessions, as is herein limited, prescribed and appointed to the justices of the peace of the county.

2. Extracts from An Act for Supplying Some Defects in the Law for the Relief of the Poor, Pennsylvania, 1718

Whereas by a law of this province, intituled, *An act for the relief of the poor,* it is provided, that the overseers of the poor for the respective townships shall make rates or assessments for the relief of the poor, indigent and impotent persons inhabiting within the said townships, but it is not ascertained what settlements shall render one an inhabitant, relievable by the said act: Be it therefore enacted . . . That where any unmarried person, not having child or children is or shall be lawfully hired as a servant into any city, township or district, in this province and did or shall

continue and abide in the same service during the space of one whole year, such service shall be adjudged and deemed a good settlement therein. And if any person shall be bound an apprentice by indenture, and inhabit in any city or township in this province, such binding and inhabiting shall be adjudged a good settlement. And if any person, who hereafter shall come to inhabit in any of the said townships, or districts, shall, for himself, and on his own account, execute any public annual office or charge in the said township or district during one whole year, and shall be charged with and pay his share towards the county taxes or levies for the poor of the said township or district, then he shall be adjudged and deemed to have a legal settlement in the same. And that no other person or persons whatsoever, who shall come into any county, city, township or district, within this province shall be adjudged to have procured a legal settlement in such county, city, township or district, unless he or they shall really and bona fide take a lease of a tenement or plantation of the yearly value of five pounds, or unless he or they give sufficient security for the discharge of the said county, city, township or district, or be allowed by any two justices of the peace or magistrates of such county or city.

II. *Provided always,* That where any person or persons are come into any county, city, township or district, in this province, out of any other county, city, township or district, or out of any other place or province, and being likely to become chargeable to the place where they are so come to inhabit, have been or shall be by required the overseers of the poor to return from whence they came, or give security for the discharge of the county, township or place where they are come to inhabit, he, she or they refusing and neglecting so to do, shall not be deemed to have acquired a legal settlement by their continuance in the place or places where they are so come to inhabit, but that upon complaint made by the overseers of the poor of the proper township or district to any one or more of the justices of peace or magistrates of the proper county or city respectively, where any of the said persons (refusing or neglecting to give security, or coming to settle in any tenement or plantation under the said yearly value of five pounds, or not otherwise obtaining a lawful settlement, according to the true meaning of this act) shall reside or be found at the time of such complaint, it shall and may be lawful to and for any two justices of the peace of the county or city, where any of the said persons who are likely to be chargeable to the township or place where they reside, or shall come to inhabit, by their warrant to remove and convey such person or persons to the county, city, township or place, where he, she or they were last legally settled, either as native, householder, sojourner, apprentice or servant, unless he or they give sufficient security for the discharge of the said county, city or township; to be allowed by the said justices . . . .

VI. And to the end, that the monies raised only for the relief of such as are impotent and poor may not be misapplied and consumed by the idle, sturdy and disorderly beggars, *Be it further enacted by the authority aforesaid,* That every such person, as from the twenty-fourth day of June, in this present year, one thousand seven hundred and eighteen, shall be upon the collection, and receive relief of any county, city or place and the wife and children of any such person cohabiting in the same house (such child only excepted as shall be by the overseers of the poor permitted to live at home, in order to have the care of, and attend any impotent and helpless parent) shall, upon the shoulder of the right sleeve of the upper garment of every such person, in an open and visible manner, wear such badge or mark, as is herein after mentioned and expressed; that is to say, a large Roman (P.) together with the first letter of the name of the county, city or place, whereof such poor person is an inhabitant, cut either in red or blue cloth, as by the overseers of the poor it shall be directed and appointed.

VII. And if any such poor person shall at any time neglect or refuse to wear such badge or mark as aforesaid, and in manner aforesaid, it shall and may be lawful for any justice of the peace of that county, city or place where any such offence shall be committed, upon complaint to him for that purpose made, to punish every such offender for every such offence, either by ordering of his or her relief, or usual allowance on the collection to be abridged, suspended or withdrawn; or otherwise, by committing such offender to the house of correction, there to be whipped, and kept at hard labor for any number of days, not exceeding twenty-one, as to the said justice should seem meet.

3. Extracts from a Report on the Subject of Pauperism to the New-York Society for the Prevention of Pauperism, February 4, 1818

The Committee appointed to prepare a Constitution for the government of the Society, and a statement of the prevailing causes of pauperism, with suggestions relative to the most suitable and efficient remedies, Report,

That we entered upon the duties assigned us, under a strong conviction of the great importance of the subject of Pauperism. We were persuaded that on the judicious management of this subject depend, in high degree, the comfort, the tranquility, and the freedom of communities.

We were not insensible of the serious and alarming evils that have resulted, in various places, from misguided benevolence, and imprudent systems of relief. We knew that in Europe and America, where the greatest efforts have been made to provide for the sufferings of the poor, by high and even enormous taxation, those sufferings were increasing in a ratio much greater than the population, and were evidently augmented by the very means taken to subdue them.

We were fully prepared to believe, that without a radical change in the principles on which public alms have been usually distributed, helplessness and poverty would continue to multiply—demands for relief would become more and more importunate, the numerical difference between those who are able to bestow charity and those who sue for it, would gradually diminish, until the present system must fall under its own irresistible pressure, prostrating perhaps, in its ruin, some of the pillars of social order.

It might be long indeed before such a catastrophe would be extensively felt in this free and happy country. Yet it is really to be feared, as we apprehend, that it would not be long before some of the proximate evils of such a state of things would be perceived in our public cities, and in none, perhaps, sooner than in New-York. Although these consequences are but too apparent from the numerous facts which recent investigations have brought to light, particularly in Great Britain, and in some parts of the United States, yet we are very sensible of the difficulties attendant upon every attempt to provide an adequate remedy for poverty, and its concomitant wretchedness.

The evil lies deep in the foundation of our social and moral institutions; and we cannot but consider it as one of the most obscure and perplexing, and at the same time, interesting and imposing departments of political economy.

While there exists so great a disparity in the physical and intellectual capacities of men, there must be, in every government, where a division of property is recognized by law and usage, a wide difference in the means of support. Such, too, is the complication of human affairs, the numerous connexions, and close dependencies of one part upon another, it is scarcely to be presumed, and it would be extravagant to expect, that under the most moral, and the wisest civil regulation to which human society is susceptible of attaining, partial indigence and distress will not be experienced to an amount that will ever demand the exercise of Christian benevolence.

The great and leading principles, therefore, of every system of charity, ought to be, *First,* amply to relieve the unavoidable necessities of the poor; and, *Secondly,* to lay the powerful hand of moral and legal restriction upon every thing that contributes, directly and necessarily, to introduce an artificial extent of suffering; and to diminish, in any class of the community, a reliance upon its own powers of body and mind for an independent and virtuous support. That to the influence of those extraneous, debilitating causes, may be ascribed nine tenths of the poverty which actually prevails, we trust none will doubt, who are extensively acquainted with facts in relation to this subject.

The indirect causes of poverty are as numerous as the frailties and vices of men. They vary with constitution, with character, and with national and local habits. Some of them lie so deeply entrenched in the weakness and depravity of human nature, as to be altogether unassailable by mere political regulation. They can be reached in no other way, than by awakening the dormant and secret energies of moral feeling.

But with a view to bring the subject committed to our charge more definitely before the Society, we have thought it right, distinctly to enumerate the more prominent of those causes of poverty which prevail within this city; subjoining such remarks as may appear needful.

1st. Ignorance. Arising either from inherent dullness, or from want of opportunities for improvement. This operates as a restraint upon the physical powers, preventing the exercise and cultivation of the bodily faculties by which skill is obtained, and the means of support increased. The influence of this cause, it is believed, is particularly great among the foreign poor that annually accumulate in this city.

2d. Idleness. A tendency to this evil may be more or less inherent. It is greatly increased by other causes, and when it becomes habitual, it is the occasion of much suffering in families, and augments to a great amount the burden of the inductrious portions of society.

3d. Intemperance in drinking. This most prolific source of mischief and misery drags in its train almost every species of suffering which afflicts the poor. This evil, in relation to poverty and vice, may be emphatically styled the *Cause of Causes.* The box of Pandora is realized in each

of the kegs of ardent spirits that stand upon the counters of the 1600 licensed grocers of this city. At a moderate computation, the money spent in the purchase of spirituous liquors would be more than sufficient to keep the whole city constantly supplied with bread. Viewing the enormous devastations of this evil upon the minds and morals of the people, we cannot but regard it as the crying and increasing sin of the nation, and as loudly demanding the solemn deliberation of our legislative assemblies.

4th. Want of economy. Prodigality is comparative. Among the poor it prevails to a great extent, in inattention to those small but frequent savings when labour is plentiful, which may go to meet the privations of unfavourable seasons.

5th. Imprudent and hasty marriages. This, it is believed, is a fertile source of trial and poverty.

6th. Lotteries. The depraving nature and tendency of these allurements to hazard money, is generally admitted by those who have been most attentive to their effects. The time spent in inquiries relative to lotteries, in frequent attendance on lottery offices, the feverish anxiety which prevails relative to the success of tickets, the associations to which it leads, all contribute to divert the labourer from his employment, to weaken the tone of his morals, to consume his earnings, and consequently to increase his poverty. But objectionable and injurious to society as we believe lotteries to be, we regard as more destructive to morals, and ruinous to all character and comfort, the numerous self-erected lottery insurances, at which the young and old are invited to spend their money in such small pittances, as the poorest labourer is frequently able to command, under the delusive expectation of a gain, the chance of which is as low, perhaps, as it is possible to conceive. The poor are thus cheated out of their money and their time, and too often left a prey to the feelings of desperation: or, they are impelled by those feelings to seek a refuge in the temporary, but fatal oblivion of intoxication.

7th. Pawnbrokers. The establishment of these offices is considered as very unfavourable to the independence and welfare of the middling and inferior classes. The artifices which are often practised to deceive the expectation of those who are induced, through actual distress, or by positive allurement, to trust their goods at these places, not to mention the facilities which they afford to the commission of theft, and the encouragement they give to a dependence on stratagem and cunning, rather than on the profits of honest industry, fairly entitle them, in the opinion of the Committee, to a place among the *causes of Poverty.*

8th. Houses of ill fame. The direful effects of those sinks of iniquity upon the habits and morals of a numerous class of young men, especially of sailors and apprentices, are visible throughout the city. Open abandonment of character, vulgarity, profanity, &c. are among the inevitable consequences, as it respects our own sex, of those places of infamous resort. The effects upon the several thousands of females within this city, who are ingulphed in those abodes of all that is vile, and all that is shocking to virtuous thought, upon the miserable victims, many of them of decent families, who are here subjected to the most cruel tyranny of their inhuman masters—upon the females, who, hardened in crime, are nightly sent from those dens of corruption to roam through the city "seeking whom they may devour," we have not the inclination, nor is it our duty, to describe. Among the "causes of poverty," those houses, where all the base-born passions are engendered—where the vilest profligacy receives a forced culture, must hold an eminent rank.

9th. The numerous charitable institutions of the city. The Committee by no means intends to cast an indiscriminate censure upon these institutions, nor to implicate the motives, nor even to deny the usefulness, in a certain degree, of any of them. They have unquestionably had their foundation in motives of true philanthropy; they have contributed to cultivate the feelings of Christian charity, and to keep alive its salutary influence upon the minds of our fellow-citizens; and they have doubtless relieved thousands from the pressure of the most pinching want, from cold, from hunger, and probably, in many cases, from untimely death.

But, in relation to these societies, a question of no ordinary moment presents itself to the considerate and real philanthropist. Is not the partial and temporary good which they accomplish, how acute soever the miseries they relieve, and whatever number they may rescue from sufferings or death, more than counterbalanced, by the evils that flow from the expectations they necessarily excite; by the relaxation of industry, which such a display of benevolence tends to produce; by that reliance upon charitable aid in case of unfavourable times, which must unavoidably tend to diminish, in the minds of the labouring classes, that wholesome anxiety to provide for the wants of a distant day, which alone can save them from a state of absolute dependence, and from becoming a burden to the community?

In the opinion of your Committee, and in the opinion, we believe, of the greater number of the best writers, of the wisest economists, and of the most experienced philanthropists, which the interesting subject of pauperism has recently called into action; the balance of good and evil is unfavourable to the existence of societies for gratuitous relief:—that efforts of this nature, with whatever zeal they may be conducted, never can effect the removal of poverty, nor lessen its general amount; but that indigence and helplessness will multiply nearly in the ratio of those measures which are ostensibly taken to prevent them.

Such as the consequences of every avowal on the part of the public of a determination to support the indigent by the administration of alms. And in no cases are measures of this kind more prolific in evil, than where they are accompanied by the display of large funds for the purposes of charity; or where the poor are conscious of the existence of such funds, raised by taxation, and of course, as they will allege, drawn chiefly from the coffers of the rich.

How far these evils are remediable, without an entire dereliction of the great Christian duty of charity, is a problem of difficult solution. The principle of taxation is so interwoven with our habits and customs, it would, perhaps, in the present state of things, be impossible to dispense with. But while our poor continue to be thus supported, to prevent the misapplication and abuse of the public charity, demands the utmost vigilance, the wisest precaution, and the most elaborate system of inspection and oversight.

To what extent abuses upon our present system of alms are practised, and how far the evils which accompany it are susceptible of remedy, we should not at present feel warranted in attempting to state. The pauperism of the city is under the management of five Commissioners, who, we doubt not, are well qualified to fulfil the trust reposed in them, and altogether disposed to discharge it with fidelity. But we cannot withhold the opinion, that without a far more extended, minute, and energetic scheme of management than is possible for any five men to keep in constant operation, abuses will be practised, and to a great extent, upon the public bounty; taxes must be increased, and vice and suffering perpetuated.

Lastly. Your Committee would mention WAR, during its prevalence, as one of the most abundant sources of poverty and vice, which the list of human corruptions comprehends. But as this evil lies out of the immediate reach of local regulation, and as we are now happily blessed with a peace which we hope will be durable, it is deemed unnecessary further to notice it.

Such are the causes which are considered as the more prominent and operative in producing that amount of indigence and suffering, which awakens the charity of this city, and which has occasioned the erection of buildings for eleemosynary purposes, at an expense of half a million of dollars, and which calls for the annual distribution of 90,000 dollars more. But, if the payment of this sum were the only inconvenience to be endured—trifling, indeed, in comparison would be the evils which claim our attention. Of the mass of affliction and wretchedness actually sustained, how small a portion is thus relieved! Of the quantity of misery and vice, which the causes we have enumerated, with others we have not named, bring upon the city, how trifling the portion actually removed, by public or by private benevolence! Nor do we conceive it possible to remove this load of distress, by all the alms-doing of which the city is capable, while the causes remain in full and active operation.

Effectually to relieve the poor, is therefore a task far more comprehensive in its nature, than simply to clothe the naked and to feed the hungry. It is, to erect barriers against the encroachments of moral degeneracy;—it is to heal the diseases of the mind;—it is to furnish that ailment to the intellectual system which will tend to preserve it in healthful operation.

But can a task of this nature come within the reach of any public or any social regulation? We answer, that to a certain, and to a very valuable extent, we believe it can. When any measure for the promotion of public good, or the prevention of public evil, founded upon equitable principles, is supported by a sufficient weight of social authority, it may gradually pass into full and complete operation, and become established upon a basis as firm as a law of legislative enactment . . . .

To conclude, the committee has by no means intended, in the freedom with which it has thus examined the causes of pauperism, and suggested remedies, to encourage the expectation that the whole of these remedies can be speedily brought within the power and control of society. A work of so much importance to the public welfare cannot be the business of a day; but we nevertheless entertain the hope, that if the principles and design of this Society shall, upon mature examination and reflection, receive the approbation of the great body of our intelligent fellow-citizens, and the number of its members be augmented accordingly, it will be able gradually to bring within its operation all the important measures suggested in this report. By what particular mode these measures shall be encountered, whether through the agency of large and efficient Committees of this Society, or by

auxiliary societies, each established, for a specific purpose, under the patronage of the parent institution, and subordinate to its general principles, we leave to the wisdom and future decision of the Society.

On behalf of the Committee,
JOHN GRISCOM, *Chairman.*
New-York, Second month 4, 1818.

4. Extracts from the First Annual Report of the Managers of the Society for the Prevention of Pauperism in the City of New York, October 26, 1818

The Managers of the Society for the Prevention of Pauperism in the city of New York, report:

That their anticipation of the importance and difficulty of their duties has been fully realized. Their first efforts were necessarily directed to the development of the objects which they were appointed to consider. Though these objects were specified as far as practicable; though the nature of the duty allotted to the Board was pointed out; as well as the general aspect of the plan, such as the Managers should have in view, yet the basis only was laid, and it was their work to erect the superstructure. They were not at a loss for materials. These were more and more exhibited to them in the multifarious ramifications of their labours. But it was not an easy task to arrange them in proper order, and to dispose of them to advantage; it therefore required time, deliberation, and assiduity, to digest an effectual plan, and to take measures for rendering it subservient to the momentous purposes of the Society.

In order to investigate, and as far as possible to remove the various causes of mendacity; to devise plans for meliorating the condition of the poor and wretched, and to secure their successful operation, the Managers, immediately after their appointment, respectfully solicited the Corporation of this city to appoint five Managers from that body, agreeably to the 6th article of the constitution. The favourable result of this application warrants the Board to calculate upon municipal countenance and aid.

The 3rd article of the By-laws declares that "each attending Committee shall consist of as many members of the Society as the Board may think necessary. They shall make rules, or by-laws, to govern themselves; keep a book, wherein they shall enter their proceedings, and report to the Board at every stated meeting, a summary of their proceedings, with their opinions on the most adviseable course for the Board to pursue relative thereto."

Nine Standing Committees were accordingly appointed, to carry into effect the views of the Managers, as stated in the following extract from the minutes:—

Districting Committee

This Committee shall consist of as many members of this Board as there are wards in the city, who shall form a general plan of operations;—and as soon after as possible each person shall, in his respective ward, associate with as many members of the Society as may be thought adviseable, who shall divide the ward into as many districts as they may think proper. These sub-committees shall embrace in their operations the duties specified on the 12th and 13th pages of the printed Report on the subject of Pauperism.

Idleness and Sources of Employment

The object of this Committee shall be to devise means for the employment of the poor.

Intemperance

This Committee shall inform the Board as to the number of places where ardent spirits are retailed in small quantities;—what quantity is drunk, with an estimate of its cost, and the class of citizens most subject to the vice of intemperance.

The Committee shall give opinions at large on every thing connected with this subject, including the law, police regulations, officers, &c. &c.

Lotteries

This Committee shall report the number of lottery offices in the city; the amount of money annually expended; the probable waste of time occasioned by lotteries; the usual percent advance on tickets; the extent of the evil arising from the insuring of tickets, how far the restraining laws are enforced, &c. &c.

Houses of Ill Fame

This Committee shall report the probable number of houses of this description; families that live by prostitution; and in what particular the police regulations on the subject may be amended.

Pawn-brokers

This Committee shall report the number of pawn-brokers, their manner of doing business, and the best mode respectively adopted by them, in the distribution of charity to the poor.

Charitable Institutions

This Committee shall inform the Board as to the number in the city; the gross and annual amount of their funds, and the mode respectively adopted by them, in the distribution of charity to the poor.

Gambling

This Committee shall report the number and kinds of gambling houses, and their opinion as to the best mode of diminishing or suppressing them.

Ignorance

This Committee shall report the number of children who do not attend any school; the number of adults who cannot read; the number of families and individuals who do not attend public worship; and the causes which prevent . . . .

[T]he object of the New-York Society for Preventing Pauperism is such as cannot, in the nature of things, be speedily accomplished. Habits and vices, which take their rise from the worst habits and propensities of men, however deplorable in their effects upon individuals and society, will yield to no sudden remedies. They must be supplanted gradually by the influence of appropriate agencies, by the assiduities of patient and persevering labour, by the constant and meliorating operations of benevolence. The measures pointed out in [A Report on the Subject of Pauperism], are adapted ultimately to remove those evils which so much afflict society, and which the severest enactments of civil authority have been found unable to repress. Let the moral sense be awakened, and a moral influence be established in the minds of the improvident, the unfortunate, and the depraved; let them be approached with kindness and an ingenuous concern for their welfare; inspire them with self-respect, and encourage their industry and economy: in short, enlighten their minds, and teach them to care for themselves. These are the methods of doing them real and permanent good, and relieving the community from the pecuniary exactions, the multiplied embarrassments, and threatening dangers of which they are the authors. Happily, the object proposed by this institution is one which may be aided by every individual, whatever be his circumstances; though it prospectively demands the concurrence and patronage of all. The public is called upon not so much for pecuniary subscriptions and benefactions, as for friendly advice, for vigilant attention to the common good, for the adoption of wholesome opinions, and the exertion of a salutary influence. Those who experience the ill effects of pauperism and its attendant evils, are urged, not to make fresh sacrifices and incur additional embarrassments, but to act upon the defensive, to employ the means of prevention, to check an inundation which threatens to overwhelm them. They are invited to adopt measures which cannot possibly be hurtful in any instance; which seem along adapted to the end in view, which are required by the necessity of the case, and sanctioned by the results of experience.

The Managers consider the information which they have thus laid before the Society, of sufficient moment to encourage every member, and to stimulate the citizens generally, to give their utmost sanction and support to this truly benevolent institution, whose aim is to improve the temporal and moral condition of a considerable portion of this community.

Conscientiously engaged in so good a cause, let all rely on the blessing of that Almighty Father who "maketh his sun to rise on the evil and the good, and sendeth rain on the just and on the unjust."

MATTHEW CLARKSON, *President*
JOSEPH CURTIS, *Sec'y, pro tem.*
New-York, Oct. 26, 1818.

5. Extracts from a Report of the Secretary of State in 1824 on the Relief and Settlement of the Poor, February 9, 1824

STATE OF NEW-YORK—Secretary's Office
Albany, February 9, 1824.

SIR,

In obedience to concurrent resolutions of the honourable the Senate and Assembly, of the last session, I have the honor to transmit a report, together with a bill and other papers, prepared on the subject of the laws for the relief and settlement of the poor.

I remain, sir,

Very respectfully,
Your most obt. Servt.
J. V. N. YATES.

The Hon. Richard Goodell,
Speaker of the Assembly.

REPORT . . .

The poor of this state consist of two classes—the permanent poor, or those who are regularly supported, during the whole year, at the public expense; and the occasional, or temporary poor, or those who receive occasional relief, during a part of the year, chiefly in the autumn or winter.

Of the first class, according to the official reports and estimates received, there are, in this state, 6,896; and of the last, 15,215; making a grand total of 22,111 paupers. Among the permanent paupers, there are 446 idiots and lunatics; 287 persons who are blind; 928 who are extremely aged and infirm; 797 who are lame, or in such a confirmed state of ill health, as to be totally incapable of labor; 2604 children, under 14 years of age, and 1789 paupers of both sexes, all of whom, though not in the vigor of life, may yet be considered capable of earning their subsistence, if proper labor were assigned, and suitable means used to induce them to perform it, and whose labor might produce at least 150,000 dollars annually to the state. Of the whole number of permanent paupers, the returns and estimates will warrant the assertion, that at least 1585 male persons were reduced to that state by the excessive use of ardent spirits; and of consequence, that their families, (consisting of 989 wives, and 2167 children,) were reduced to the same penury and want; thus presenting strong evidence of the often asserted fact, that "Intemperance has produced more than two-thirds of all the permanent pauperism in the state:" and there is little hazard in adding, that to the same cause may be ascribed more than one half of the occasional pauperism. Of the whole number of both classes of paupers, 10,523 are males, and 11,588 females, (being an excess of 1065 female paupers:) 5883, including their children in that number, are either aliens or naturalised foreigners; and 16,228, including also their children, are native citizens.

There are 8753 children of both classes under 14 years of age, the greater number of whom is entirely destitute of education, and equally in want of that care and attention, which are so necessary to inculcate correct moral habits: It is feared that this mass of pauperism, will at no distant day form a fruitful nursery for crime, unless prevented by the watchful superintendance of the legislature . . . .

In the year 1815, according to the returns and estimates received, the whole pauper expense in this state, derived from taxation and the excise duties, amounted to 245,000 dollars. In the year 1819, it had increased to 368,645 dollars, and in 1822, to 470,000 . . . . 1796 paupers, among whom were more than 600 children and 320 women were removed (and many of them while sick and diseased,) during the year 1822, to different parts of the state, under orders or warrants of justices, at an expense far exceeding 25,000 dollars; a sum if it had been applied for their support instead of their removal, would have maintained 833 of those paupers for a whole year, being nearly half the number removed . . . .

With respect to the amount necessary for the support of a pauper in an alms house, it appears to be variously estimated, as much depends on the skill, fidelity, and management of the keeper, the number of paupers supported and able to work, the expense of fuel, the contiguity of the institution to a market town, the economy of the house, and the conveniences for agricultural labour, connected with it. It is believed that with proper care and attention, and under favorable circumstances, the average annual expense in an alms house, having a convenient farm attached to it, will not exceed from 20 to 35 dollars for the support of each pauper, exclusive of the amount of labour he may perform; while out of an alms house, it will not be less than from 33 to 65 dollars, and in many instances where the pauper is old and infirm, or diseased, from 80 to 100 dollars, and even more . . . .

The expenses for physicians and nurses, in attending paupers, in towns where there are no poor houses, form a very prominent article in the amount of taxation. Pauperism and disease, except in an alms house, are generally found associated together, and hence it is, that this item of expense is so much complained of in the towns just alluded to.

After a full examination of the pauper system, and its various provisions and results, two questions will probably arise for the consideration of the legislature.

The first is—Ought the whole system to be abolished, and the support of the poor left altogether to the voluntary contribution of the charitable and humane. Or,

Secondly. If the system ought not to be abolished, is it susceptible of improvement, and in what mode can it be best effected.

The affirmative of the first proposition, viz. That there ought to be no compulsory provision for the poor, has many powerful advocates. Men of great literary acquirements, and profound political research, have insisted, that distress and poverty multiply in proportion to the funds created to relieve them, and that the establishment of any poor rates is not only unnecessary, but hurtful . . . .

It is worthy of particular observation . . . that every state in the union, and many governments in Europe, have adopted a code of laws for the relief and maintenance of the poor; even in China, the laws of the empire have made provision for their support. All this is certainly no slight proof, that the total want of a pauper system, would be inconsistent with a humane, liberal, and enlightened policy. Indeed it can hardly be urged, that the idiot and lunatic, the sick, the aged, and the infant, (and few others, perhaps, should be made the objects of legal support,) ought to be placed in this precarious state for protection and subsistence; and still less will it be pretended, that no provision

ought to be made for the education of the children of the poor; and though it is true to a certain extent, that compulsory provision, for the relief of pauperism has a tendency to impair that anxiety for a livelihood which is almost instinctive, and thus to relax individual exertion by unnerving the arms of industry; yet the consequence by no means follows, that all provision of that nature should be abandoned, because individual cases of its abuse might, and perhaps necessarily, would exist. A similar objection could be urged against the adoption of any insolvent system, because it not only produces great improvidence and neglect in the ordinary concerns of life, but it is also frequently the parent of perjury and fraud. All then perhaps that can be done under such circumstances, is to prevent or check, in the best manner that human legislation can devise, those excrescences that cannot be eradicated from wholesome and necessary systems, without destroying the systems themselves.

Proceeding then upon the necessity and utility of having a pauper system, the remaining question is, "whether our present laws are susceptible of improvement, and if so, in what manner it can be best effected." Before we can apply a remedy with certainty and success, it is necessary to have a distinct view of the existing evils intended to be removed. That our poor laws are manifestly defective in principle, and mischievous in practice, and that under the imposing and charitable aspect of affording relief exclusively to the poor and infirm, they frequently invite the able bodied vagrant to partake of the same bounty, are propositions very generally admitted . . . .

The removal of so many human beings, like felons, for no other fault than poverty, seems inconsistent with the spirit of a system professing to be founded on principles of pure benevolence and humanity . . . .

In obedience . . . to the directions of the legislature, a bill has been prepared and submitted for revision to the Attorney General . . . . Without professing to believe that its adoption will remove altogether the evils alluded to, (for so long as human frailty and vice prevail, the hope would be vain,) it is presumed that it will remove or ameliorate many of them. And it is also confidently believed, that two prominent features of the proposed system, are entitled to much consideration, to wit: First,—It will relieve the poor with greater humanity, and emphatically with more economy, than under the existing poor laws: And, secondly,—It will provide employment for the idle, and compel them to labor, and of consequence put an end to the practice of street beggary. It is obvious, however, that vigilance, fidelity and intelligence, in the officers to whom the execution of this plan is entrusted, are indispensable to those favorable results.

The plan presented, proposes as improvements to the present pauper system

First—The establishment of one or more houses of employment, under proper regulations, in each of the counties of this state, with a farm of sufficient extent, to be connected with each institution. The paupers there to be maintained and employed at the expense of the respective counties, in some healthful labor, chiefly agricultural their children to be carefully instructed, and at suitable ages, to be put out to some useful business or trade.

Secondly—That each house of employment be connected with a work house or penitentiary, for the reception and discipline of sturdy beggars and vagrants. The discipline to consist either of confinement upon a rigid diet, hard labor, employment at the stepping mill, or some treatment equally efficacious in restraining their vicious appetites and pursuits.

Thirdly—That the excise duties be increased, and a tax be laid upon the owners of distilleries of whiskey, and other ardent spirits, to compose a fund for the relief and maintenance of the poor,

Fourthly—That one year's residence in a county shall constitute a settlement, (except in certain specified cases,) instead of the present difficult and perplexing requisites of a settlement, which are contained in our poor laws.

Fifthly—That all orders of removal, and consequently appeals, be abolished; persons who claim relief, shall receive it in the county where they become sick or infirm—the healthy vagrant shall be commanded to return to the county where he belongs; and upon refusal, shall be sent to the workhouse, and there treated according to his demerits. It is believed that no order of removal, under the present system, can be so effectual, and certainly none so economical, as the one here suggested.

Sixthly—That no male person in health, with the use of all his faculties, and being between the ages of 18 and 50 years, shall be placed upon the pauper list, or be maintained at the public expense.

Seventhly—That severe penalties be inflicted upon all those who bring to, or leave in, a county, paupers, not legally chargeable to it.

Eighthly—That street beggary be entirely prohibited—Beggars of this description, to be instantly sent to the work-house; and magistrates shall be subject to indictment and punishment, for any neglect of this duty; and grand juries shall be specially charged to inquire into such neglects, and to present the offenders.

Ninthly—That the expenses of erecting and completing each house of employment, be paid by the county, and raised by tax, in four equal annual instalments . . . .

It is confidently believed, that with such a mass of evidence before us, *there can be no hazard in adopting the poor-house system, in every county in the state.* If, however, there is any county, whose small population, in the opinion of the legislature, would not at present warrant the expense, suitable provision might be made, either for exempting it from the operations of the proposed bill, attaching it to some other county, or directing some small building with a farm to be hired as a temporary poor-house.

The next enquiry is, *what will be the probable amount of expense of supporting all the paupers in poor-houses, throughout the state.* The following comparative statements are respectfully submitted on this branch of enquiry.

The expense in 1822, of supporting the permanent paupers, was.	$344,800
And for relief to occasional paupers,	125,782
Total,	$470,582

Upon the proposed system of maintaining the poor in alms-houses, the expense is estimated as follows:

6,000 paupers at $30 each,	$180,000
Relief to occasional paupers,	52,500
Total,	$232,500

(Difference $238,082.)

Thus, a saving of more than one half, or of $238,082 in the support of paupers, would be effected in one year. But this saving would increase every year, by the gradual diminution of pauperism, and the increased experience of our public officers in the management and economy of this plan. Besides under the present system of poor laws, our taxes, for the support of the poor, double almost in every ten years; and it is fair then to take into view, also, the prospective benefits for a series of years, in a geometric ratio.

But to the above amount of $232,500, for the support of paupers, upon the proposed plan, is to be added *the expense of erecting and preparing the alms-houses, for the reception of paupers, &c. The estimate will then stand thus,*

Expense of supporting, &c. as above,	$232,500
Say 40 alms-houses, with farms, &c., at $5,000 each.	
(It is believed the amount is overrated.)	200,000
Total,	$432,500

Thus it is perceived that, even if the amount of expense in providing poor-houses, be added to the expense of supporting the poor, still the amount will be $38,000 less than the amount expended for the support of the poor, in the year 1822. But as the expense of erecting these houses, is not chargeable after they are once completed, the annual saving, by the proposed plan, still remains at more than *two hundred thousand dollars,* after making every liberal allowance for keeping those institutions in repair, &c.

6. Extracts from the Visitor's Manual of the New-York Association for the Improvement of the Condition of the Poor, 1845

With a view to promote uniformity of action, and to aid Visitors in the discharge of their responsible duties, the following series of Rules and Instructions, supplementary to those prescribed in the By-Laws, have been adopted by the Association, and are hereby earnestly recommended to the careful attention of all who may engage in carrying out its principles.

Article I

The first principle of this Association is founded in the admission, that the Alms of Benevolent Societies, and of private liberality, are often misapplied, and as often abused by those who receive them. As a visitor of this Association, therefore, be especially careful to do all that a cautious and discriminating judgment may suggest, to prevent every abuse of the charity you may dispense. But if, after suitable precaution on your part, to guard against the misapplication of charity, it should appear, that it has been bestowed on objects of pretended distress, or upon those who may be receiving adequate relief from other sources, it will be your immediate duty to report all such cases . . . , that the names of the undeserving applicants may be placed upon record at the General Office, and become known to every Visitor and member of the Association.

Article II

The persons who will address themselves to your sympathies, though differing in many particulars, may here be divided into three classes. *First,* those who have been reduced to indigence by infirmity, sickness, old age, and unavoidable misfortune; *Second,* those who have brought themselves to want and suffering by their improvidence and vices; and, *Third,* persons who are able but unwilling to labour, and are beggars and vagrants by profession. The well-being of these different classes evidently requires a mode of treatment adapted to each. And as this cannot be applied without a knowledge of their character and

circumstances, your first duty is, *to withhold all relief from unknown persons.* Let this rule be imperative and unalterable.

Article III

In all cases referred to you for aid, if the applicants reside in your section, remember they have claims upon your sympathies and kind offices which belong to no other Visitor of this Association, and if neglected by you, they may suffer unrelieved. Without delay, therefore, visit them at their homes; personally examine every case; ascertain their character and condition; and carefully inquire into the causes which have brought them into a state of destitution. You will become an important instrument of good to your suffering fellow-creatures, when you aid them to obtain this good from resources within themselves. To effect this, show them the true origin of their sufferings, when these sufferings are the result of imprudence, extravagance, idleness, intemperance, or other moral causes which are within their own control; and endeavour, by all appropriate means, to awaken their self-respect, to direct their exertions, and to strengthen their capacities for self-support. In your intercourse with them, avoid all appearance of harshness, and every manifestation of an obtrusive and a censorious spirit. Study to carry into your work a mind as discriminating and judicious as it is kindly disposed, and a heart ready to sympathize with the sick and the infirm, the widow and the orphan, the tempted and the vicious.—In short, if you would confer great and permanent good upon the needy, you first must distinctly understand in what that good consists; and as this knowledge can only be acquired by personal intercourse with them at their dwellings, the second rule becomes as absolute as the first, viz.—*Always to visit those for whom your benevolent services are required, before granting relief.* Having given these general instructions in relation to visitorial duties, it may be useful to present a few practical directions concerning each of the classes of the poor before named.

First. Those who have been reduced to indigence by unavoidable causes.

In your intercourse with this class, if you meet with industry, frugality, and self-respect, and a preference for self-denial to dependence upon alms, let not your charities become the means of undermining one right principle, or of enfeebling one well-directed impulse. Alms in such cases must often be given, and the temptation is to bestow freely; but let them be administered with great delicacy and caution. The most effectual encouragement for such persons is not *alms chiefly,* or any other form of charity as a substitute for alms, but that sympathizing counsel which re-enkindles hope, and that expression of respect for character which such individuals never fail to appreciate. A wise distribution of charity, connected with a deportment of this kind towards the deserving poor, will often save them from pauperism, when the absence of these may degrade them to habitual dependence on alms for subsistence.

Second. Individuals who have become mendicants through their own improvidence and vices.

The evils of improvidence can never be diminished, except by removing the cause; and this can only be done by elevating the moral character of the poor, and by teaching them to depend upon themselves. Many able-bodied persons apply for alms who earn enough for their own maintenance, but expend their earnings in improper indulgences, with the calculation of subsisting on charity when their own resources fail them, who might have obviated this necessity by proper self-denial and economy. In respect to these cases, if relief must be given,—and it sometimes must be,—it should never be of a kind, or to a degree, that will *make this dependence preferable to a life of labour.* And it should not be forgotten, that many would be economical and saving if they knew how to be. Let it be your endeavour, therefore, to instruct them; to encourage deposits in savings banks for rent, fuel, and winter supplies; and by all the motives which you can present, stimulate them to habits of thriftiness, industry, and foresight. The rule is, *that the willingly dependent upon alms should not live so comfortably with them as the humblest labourer without them.*

In this class is also included those who have been reduced to want by their vices. Among these, the vice of Intemperance is the most prolific source of pauperism and abject poverty. How to act wisely in reference to this class of applicants, is a most perplexing question, yet, as it will frequently occur, it must be met. As a general rule, *alms should, as far as possible, be withheld from the drunkard.* But here, perhaps, is the inebriate's family in actual want of the absolute necessaries of life. Still the rule is, that *relief should never be given to the families of the intemperate, beyond the demands of urgent necessity.* You should, if possible, become the instruments of their rescue; but any alms you can bestow may only perpetuate their misery. They may minister to the drunkard's recklessness, and induce him to feel he is relieved from the necessity, perhaps from the moral obligation of providing for his wife and children. Much must here be left to your discretion. Seek, however, by all the means of which you can avail yourself, to save the intemperate from ruin. Depraved though he be, shut not your heart against him. Though apparently lost, he is not beyond hope. Act on this principle, and you may be the instrument of his recovery. But whatever may be your success with the guilty, and perhaps incorrigible parent, never abandon your interest in the welfare of his children.

Third. To the third general class specified, viz., those who are able but unwilling to labour, and professional paupers, the Scriptural rule applies without qualification: "This we command you, that if any will not work, neither should he eat." If the entire community were to act on this principle, some of this class might be exposed to the risk of starvation. But as such unanimity is not likely to occur, this Association cannot, by bestowing alms on objects so undeserving, become a willing accessory in perpetuating the evils of vagrancy and pauperism.

Article IV

Another rule is, *where there are relatives of the indigent who are able to provide for them, alms should never be so given as to interfere with the duties of such relatives.* If those alms are evil which become substitutes for industry and economy, in a still higher sense are they evil because they offend against a higher law, when their tendency or result is to cancel just claims on kindred or consanguinity. Let it therefore be your endeavour so to awaken and strengthen the natural sympathy of relatives, that those who have the means of aiding their dependent connexions, may never suffer them to be cast upon the charity of the world.

Article V

Endeavour by a systematic attention to the education and religious instruction of the children of the poor, through the aid of the Public and Sunday Schools, to fit them for the proper pursuits of life; and as they arrive at suitable age, to assist those parents who of themselves are unable, to provide eligible situations for their children, in such useful occupations or trades as will qualify them in after life to obtain their own support, and to be introduced into society as industrious and useful citizens.

Article VI

In all your intercourse with the poor, endeavour to gain their respect and confidence. Be careful to encourage habits of cleanliness, both of houses and persons. Show them the absolute necessity of employment, and, as far as in your power, aid them in obtaining it. Be particularly attentive to the infirm, the sick, and the aged. Sympathize with the widow, have compassion on the fatherless, and endeavour to promote the good of all, by pointing out the advantages of education, the duty of religiously observing the Sabbath, the importance of attending a place of worship, and the value of the Sacred Scriptures.

Article VII

You will observe, that it is not the design of this Association to extend relief to the poor indiscriminately. Those who are accustomed to avail themselves of the public provision made them at the Alms House, and who leave it in summer to pass a few months in idleness, and return to it again when other means fail, are considered as undeserving our aid; but even persons of this class should not be wholly disregarded. You must advise and encourage them to change their habits of life; but until they manifest by their exertions to assist themselves a disposition to reform their course of conduct, they have no claims for relief on this Association. To the needy, however, who have no other resource, it will be your duty to extend a friendly hand in providing food, fuel, clothing, and shelter; and in your visits to the abodes of suffering and sorrow to provide, for the sick, medical aid, by means of the public dispensaries or otherwise, and such necessary comforts as their condition may require. And ever endeavour to evince a deep and permanent interest in the social and moral welfare of the persons whom your charities relieve.

Article VIII

As there are certain fundamental rules to be observed in the distribution of charity which cannot be too familiar to your minds. They will here be summarily stated. It is best, as far as possible,

First. To give the necessary articles, and what is immediately necessary.

Second. To give what is least susceptible of abuse.

Third. To give even necessary articles only in small quantities, in proportion to immediate need.

Fourth. To give assistance, both in quantity and in quality, inferior, except in cases of sickness, to what might be procured by labor.

Fifth. To give assistance at the right moment; and not to prolong it beyond the duration of the necessity which calls for it; but to extend, restrict and modify it with that necessity . . . .

Article X

Bear in mind that two prominent and serious evils exist in this city, in relation to pauperism. The one is, that the worst class among the poor stands the best chance of obtaining, and do in fact obtain, the greatest amount of charity. The other is, that of the best class of poor, including all who are more or less in want, and who are not vicious, some obtain much less, and others far more than they deserve. These evils are chiefly attributable to the injudicious mode of bestowing alms, which has too generally prevailed in this city. The benevolent, by acting independently of each other, have necessarily been ignorant of each other's doings, and the artful and designing have turned this ignorance to their own advantage, and to the injury of the deserving. Now, it is one object of this Association, by establishing a comprehensive, uniform, and systematic mode of distributing charity, and by an intelligent co-operation on the part of all who engage in the work, greatly to facilitate the detection of imposture. To this important reform, therefore, let your attention be vigilantly directed.

Article XI

Use every exertion in your power to advance the cause of temperance, by imparting judicious advice, and the circulation of tracts and other useful publications on the subject.

7. The First Circular of the Children's Aid Society, March 1853

This society has taken its origin in the deeply settled feelings of our citizens, that something must be done to meet the increasing crime and poverty among the destitute children of New York. Its object are to help this class by opening Sunday Meetings and Industrial Schools, and, gradually as means shall be furnished, by forming Lodging-houses and Reading-rooms for children, and by employing paid agents whose solo business shall be to care for them.

As Christian men, we cannot look upon this great multitude of unhappy, deserted, and degraded boys and girls without feeling our responsibility to God for them. We remember that they have the same capacities, the same kind and good influences, and the same Immortality as the little ones in our own homes. We bear in mind that One died for them, even as for the children of the rich and happy. Thus far, alms-houses and prisons have done little to affect the evil. But a small part of the vagrant population can be shut up in our asylums, and judges and magistrates are reluctant to convict children so young and ignorant that they hardly seem able to distinguish good and evil. The class increases. Immigration is pouring in its multitude of poor foreigners, who leave these young outcasts everywhere abandoned in our midst. For the most part, the boys grow up utterly by themselves. No one cares for them, and they care for no one. Some live by begging, by petty pilfering, by bold robbery; some earn an honest support by peddling matches, or apples, or newspapers; others gather bones and rags in the street to sell. They sleep on steps, in cellars, in old barns, and in markets, or they hire a bed in filthy and low lodging-houses. They cannot read; they do not go to school or attend a church. Many of them have never seen the Bible. Every cunning facility is intensely stimulated. They are shrewd and old in vice, when other children are in leading-strings. Few influences which are kind and good ever reach the vagrant boy. And, yet, among themselves they show generous and honest traits. Kindness can always touch them.

The girls, too often, grow up even more pitiable and deserted. Till of late no one has ever cared for them. They are the crosswalk sweepers, the little apple-peddlers, and candy-sellers of our city; or, by more questionable means, they earn their scanty bread. They traverse the low, vile streets alone, and live without mother or friends, or any share in what we should call a home. They also know little of God or Christ, except by name. They grow up passionate, ungoverned, with no love or kindness ever to soften the heart. We all know their short wild life—and the sad end.

These boys and girls, it should be remembered, will soon form the great lower class of our city; they will, assuredly, if unreclaimed, poison society all around them. They will help to form the great multitude of robbers, thieves, vagrants, and prostitutes who are now such a burden upon the law-respecting community.

In one ward alone of the city, the Eleventh, there were, in 1852, out of 12,000 children between the ages of five and sixteen, only 7,000 who attended school, and only 2,500 who went to Sabbath School; leaving 5,000 without the common privileges of education, and about 9,000 destitute of public religious influence.

In view of these evils we have formed an Association which shall devote itself entirely to this class of vagrant children. We do not propose in any way to conflict with existing asylums and institutions, but to render them a hearty co-operation, and, at the same time, to fill a gap, which, of necessity, they all have left. A large multitude of children live in the city who cannot be placed in asylums, and yet who are uncared-for and ignorant and vagrant. We propose to give these work, and to bring them under religious influence. As means shall come in, it is designed to district the city, so that hereafter every Ward may have its agent, who shall be a friend to the vagrant child. 'Boys' Sunday Meetings' have already been formed, which we hope to see extended until every quarter has its place of preaching to boys. With these we intend to connect "Industrial Schools," where the great temptations to this class arising from want of work may be removed, and

where they can learn an honest trade. Arrangements have been made with manufacturers, by which, if we have the requisite funds to begin, five hundred boys in different localities can be supplied with paying work. We hope, too, especially to be the means of draining the city of these children, by communicating with farmers, manufacturers, or families in the country, who may have need of such for employment. When homeless boys are found by our agents, we mean to get them homes in the families of respectable, needy persons in the city, and put them in the way of an honest living. We design, in a word, to bring humane and kindly influences to bear on this forsaken class—to preach in various modes the gospel of Christ to the vagrant children of New York.

Numbers of our citizens have long felt the evils we would remedy, but few have the leisure or the means to devote themselves personally to this work with the thoroughness which it requires. This society, as we propose, shall be a medium through which all can, in their measure, practically help the poor children of the city.

We call upon all who recognize that these are the little ones of Christ; all who believe that crime is best averted by sowing good influences in childhood; all who are the friends of the helpless, to aid us in our enterprise. We confidently hope this wide and practical movement will have its full share of Christian liberality. And we earnestly ask the contributions of those able to give, to help us in carrying forward the work.

8. Extracts from a South Carolina Plantation Overseer's Contract, 1857

RULES, & c.

The Proprietor, in the first place, wishes the Overseer MOST DISTINCTLY to understand that his first object is to be, under all circumstances, the care and well being of the negroes. The proprietor is always ready to excuse such errors as may proceed from want of judgment; but he never can or will excuse any cruelty, severity, or want of care towards the negroes. For the well being, however, of the negroes, it is absolutely necessary to maintain obedience, order, and discipline, to see that the tasks are punctually and carefully performed, and to conduct the business steadily and firmly, without weakness on the one hand, or harshness on the other. For such ends the following regulations have been instituted:

Lists, Tickets.—The names of all the men are to be called over every Sunday morning and evening, from which none are to be absent but those who are sick, or have tickets. When there is an evening Church, those who attend are to be excused from answering. At evening list, every negro must be clean and well washed. No one is to be absent from the place without a ticket, which is always to be given to such as ask for it, and have behaved well. All persons coming from the Proprietor's other places should shew their tickets to the Overseer, who should sign his name on the back; those going off the plantation should bring back their tickets signed. The Overseer is every now and then to go round at night and call at the houses, so as to ascertain whether their inmates are at home.

Allowance, Food.—Great care should be taken that the negroes should never have less than their regular allowance; in all cases of doubt, it should be given in favor of the largest quantity. The measures should not be struck, but rather heaped up over. None but provisions of the best quality should be used. If any is discovered to be damaged, the Proprietor, if at hand, is to be immediately informed: if absent, the damaged article is to be destroyed. The corn should be carefully winnowed before grinding. The small rice is apt to become sour: as soon as this is perceived it should be given every meal until finished, or until it becomes too sour to use, when it should be destroyed.

Allowances are to be given out according to the following schedule. None of the allowances given out in the big pot are to be taken from the cook until after they are cooked, nor to be taken home by the people.

SCHEDULE OF ALLOWANCES

Daily, (Sundays Excepted)

During Potato-time.

To each person doing any work............................ 4 qts.
To each child at the negro-houses........................ 2 qts.

During Grits-time.

To the cook for the public-pot, for every person
doing any work.. 1 qt.
To the child's cook, for each child at the
negro-houses... 1 pt.
Salt to cook for the public-pot.............................. pt.
Salt to child's cook... pt.

On every Tuesday and Friday throughout the year.

To cook for public-pot, for whole gang of workers, trades, drivers, &c., Meat.. lbs.
To child's-cook for all the children, Meat............... lbs.

On every Tuesday and Friday from April 1st to October 1st.

To the plantation cook for each person doing any work, instead of the pint of grits, Small Rice................. 1 pt.
To the child's-cook for each child instead of the ½ pt. of grits, Small Rice...................................... ½ pt.
To plantation cook for the whole gang of workers, tradesmen, drivers, &c., Peas.............................. qts.

Every Thursday throughout the year.

To the child's-cook, for all the children, Molasses.. qts.

Weekly Allowance throughout the year—to be given out Every Saturday Afternoon.

To each person doing any work, Flour.................. 3 qts.
To each child at negro-houses............................. 3 pts.
To each person who has behaved well, and has not been sick during the week, 2 Fish or 1 pt. Molasses.
To each nurse................. 4 Fish or 1½ pt. Molasses.
To head-carpenter; to head-miller;
To head-cooper; to head ploughman;   2 Fish or
To watchman; to trunk minder;   1½ pt. Molasses
To drivers; to mule minder;   each.
To hog-minder; to cattle-minder; and
To every superannuated person,

Monthly Allowance—On the 1st of Every Month

To each person doing any work, and each superannuated person ....Salt, 1 qt.
Do [Ditto]..Tobacco 1 hand.

Christmas Allowance.

To each person doing any work,
And each superannuated person

Fresh Meat,	3 lbs.
Salt do	3 lbs.
Molasses	1 qt.
Small Rice	4 qts.
Salt	½ bushel.

To each child at negro-houses

Fresh Meat	1½ lbs.
Salt Meat	1½ lbs.
Molasses	1 pt.
Small Rice,	2 qts.

Additional Allowance.

Every day when rice is sown or harvested, to the cook, for the whole gang in the field

Meat	lbs.
Peas	lbs.

No allowances or presents, besides the above, are on any consideration to be made—except for sick people. . . .

Nourishing food is to be provided for those who are getting better. The Overseer will keep an account of the articles he purchases for this purpose, during the Proprietor's absence, which he will settle for as soon as he returns . . . .

Great care must be taken to prevent persons from lying up when there is nothing or little the matter with them. Such persons must be turned out immediately; and those somewhat sick can do lighter work, which encourages industry. Nothing is so subversive of discipline, or so unjust, as to allow people to sham, for this causes the well-disposed to do the work of the lazy . . . .

MISCELLANEOUS OBSERVATIONS

The Proprietor wishes particularly to impress on the Overseer the criterions by which he will judge of his usefulness and capacity. *First*—by the general well being of the negroes; their cleanly appearance, respectful manners, active and vigorous obedience; their completion of their tasks well and early; the small amount of punishment; the excess or births over deaths; the small number of persons in hospitals, and the health of the children. Secondly—the condition and fatness of the cattle and mules; the good repair of all the fences and buildings, harness, boats, flats, and ploughs . . . .

Finally.—The Proprietor hopes the Overseer will remember that a system of strict justice is necessary to good management. No person should ever be allowed to break a law without being punished, or any person punished who has not broken a well known law. Every person should be made perfectly to understand what they are punished for, and should be made to perceive that they are not punished in anger, or through caprice. All abusive language or violence of demeanor should be avoided; they reduce the man who uses them to a level with the negro, and are hardly ever forgotten by those to whom they are addressed.

9. Extract from the Superintendent's Journal, Five Points House of Industry, April 17–May 8, 1857

April 17th, 1857.—E., seven years old, goes to-day with Mr. and Mrs. ——, who live at F., some thirty miles from the city. She is a fine little girl, and those who have taken her, are, from appearance and the highest recommendations, in every way suited for the charge, and will doubtless give her an excellent home, in all respects the reverse of that from which she as taken.

April 18th.—Visited a sick woman in West-Broadway, who has a fine little girl, six years old, in the Institution; and

a more perfect picture of wretchedness and the effects of intemperance and its kindred vices cannot well be drawn.

A low and most filthy garret, an old dirty heap answering for a bed, and sundry persons of the lowest grade of both sexes met the eye, as the home of this sick woman was reached by an almost impassible stairway; and every thing but quiet, good, and comfort, seemed to find a place in that sick-room, where, to all human appearance, death will soon perform his work.

No desire to learn the way of salvation was discoverable; but the main object of our visit, to obtain the consent of the mother to send her daughter to a good home which offered for her in the country, was by much persuasion accomplished; and in a few days the child will be enjoying her new home, a striking contrast to the one in which her wretched parent is dragging out the few remaining days of her wasted existence.

April 21st.—Visited a sick woman in "Cow-bay." She was a Catholic, with no comforts of life, and only filth and wretchedness as her portion; but death will soon remove her from physical suffering. Nine adults, eight of whom are women, victims of rum and prostitution, occupy the same room with the sick woman.

April 27th.—Visited twenty-four families this afternoon, consisting of one hundred and four persons, congregated in three cellars, two garrets, and seven rooms on the first and second floors. Found two widows, one woman whose husband is in Wisconsin, one widower, twenty-one husbands and wives, two single men, and seven single women. Two women were entirely blind, and two were confined with children a few days old; saw also one person distressingly sick of erysipelas [a bacterial skin infection], and two sick children. Of the seventy-one children, but few were older than ten years. Sixty-three attended no school, and eight attended Catholic schools. Thirty-nine are too young to attend anywhere. Fourteen are engaged in selling wood, picking rags, and similar occupations. Four will not go to school, and six have promised to come to ours.

Found one Protestant family, and there the room was neat and comfortable, while in no other place was there any appearance of neatness or comfort, and in two instances not even a necessary of life. One child, eight years old, who had eaten nothing during the day, was brought home, and after satisfying its hunger and passing through the process of bathing and dressing, could scarcely be recognized as the same child.

April 29th.—Visited ten families, consisting of seventy-one persons, all destitute of the comforts of life, and three with none of its necessaries. In a mean, low garret, with but three small, dirty panes of glass to admit the light, on a filthy pile of rags a poor emaciated little boy, some eighteen months old, lay sleeping, the only being in the room. Upon inquiry, I found the father in the streets laboring under the effects of intoxicating drinks, and learned that the mother had just been taken on a cart to the Tombs [jail]. The father had reason enough remaining to wish to have his son cared for, and brought him to our house, where we have cleaned, clothed, and fed him, and a very interesting, happy little fellow he seems.

In an adjacent room we heard the cries of an infant, and on visiting the place, an indescribably miserable apartment, the mother was found lying upon an old dirty mattress in a state of intoxication, and sleeping heavily. The child, which was some five or six months old, lay by her side without a single article of covering, while in the corner of the room stood a bright-eyed little girl four years old, who had shrunk timidly away. The children were both taken to the Institution, and after a few hours the mother had so far recovered as to be able to come after them, but has finally concluded to let them remain.

About three weeks ago, a boy, some nine years old, was found crying at our door at midnight. He was brought in, and his half-starved, cold, and filthy condition deeply excited our sympathy. He said his parents had moved that day, and that he had got separated from them and lost, and knew not where to find them. We thought his loss was gain, and therefore made no effort to find his home. When the little girl of four came into the school-room, a smile of joy passed over his countenance; and running to her, he exclaimed: "My sister, my dear little sister!" He indeed is the child of the drunken woman of Cow-bay; but she must not have him, nor the little ones either, if it can be prevented, till a very decisive change takes place in her character and conduct.

May 4th.—Visited four families in Mott Street. Of the thirteen children four attend our school, nine attend none, but four of these have promised to come to ours. Two of the families are Catholic, one attends no church, and one attends the Baptist church, when they have clothes to go. They seemed very poor; still an air of neatness was manifest. The parents have both been ill, the mother so severely as to have been in the Hospital. They are both now better and seem in a fair way to become comfortable.

A clean cloth was on the table, and food enough to about half satisfy their appetites, but the morsel was eaten with thankfulness, with apparent confidence that He who had commanded them to ask for daily bread would not fail to supply their returning wants. A promise that four of their five children should be at school to-morrow was readily given.

May 5th.—Visited twenty-three families to-day at the upper end of Mission-row, "Cow-bay." One hundred and seventy-nine inmates congregated in fifteen rooms. But one room presented, even in a small degree, any air of neatness or comfort, and, in nearly all, the most common necessaries were wanting, while in their place vice, filth, and extreme wretchedness were on all sides depicted. In five instances, intoxicating drinks were vended in the rooms where these miserable people live, and on nearly all adult years the marks of this soul-destroyer were plainly and painfully evident. Almost all call themselves Catholics; some say, "bad Catholics."

But seventeen of the more than fifty children that are of suitable age attend school.

May 8th.—Visited eighteen families living in eleven rooms. In nearly one half of these rooms intoxicating drinks are sold and in all were freely used by the greater portion of the inmates.

A less number of children were found in this section than in any previously visited. But nine of the usual school-going age who do not attend were found, and two of these are to be in or school on Monday, if their parents fulfill their promise. The remaining seven, I think, are being trained for thieves, and will, in all probability, receive the young thief's portion. In one garret two colored men and eleven abandoned white women resided. Rum and prostitution seemed to have full sway, bringing in their train destitution and wretchedness in the extreme. According to their own admission several of these victims have brought themselves to that state where life itself is but a burden and a curse, endured only because of the dark eternity beyond.

10. The Emancipation Proclamation, January 1, 1863

By the President of the United States of America: A Proclamation

Whereas on the 22nd day of September, A.D. 1862 a proclamation was issued by the president of the United States, containing, among other things, the following, to wit:

"That on this 1st day if January, A.D. 1863, all persons held as slaves within any State or designated part of a State the people whereof shall then be in rebellion against the United States shall be then, thenceforward, and forever free; and the executive government of the United States, including the military and naval authority thereof, will recognize and maintain the freedom of such persons and will do no act or acts to repress such persons, or any of them, in any efforts they may make for their actual freedom.

"That the executive will on the 1st day of January aforesaid, by proclamation, designate the States and parts of States, if any, in which the people thereof, respectively, shall then be in rebellion against the United States; and the fact that any State or the people thereof shall on that day be in good faith represented in the Congress of the United States by members chosen thereto at elections wherein a majority of the qualified voters of such States shall, in the absence of strong countervailing testimony, be deemed conclusive evidence that such State and the people thereof are not then in rebellion against the United States."

Now, therefore, I, Abraham Lincoln, President of the United States, by virtue of the power vested in me as Commander-in-Chief of the Army and Navy of the United States in time of actual armed rebellion against the authority and government of the United States, and as a fit and necessary war measure for suppressing said rebellion, do, on this 1st day of January, A.D. 1863, and in accordance with my purpose so to do, publicly proclaimed for the full period of one hundred days from the first day above mentioned, order and designate as the States and parts of States wherein the people thereof, respectively, are this day in rebellion against the United States the following, to wit:

Arkansas, Texas, Louisiana (except the parishes of St. Bernard, Plaquemines, Jefferson, St. John, St. Charles, St. James, Ascension, Assumption, Terrebonne, Lafourche, St. Mary, St. Martin, and Orleans, including the city of New Orleans), Mississippi, Alabama, Florida, Georgia, South Carolina, North Carolina, and Virginia (except the forty-eight counties designated as West Virginia, and also the counties of Berkeley, Accomac, Northhampton, Elizabeth City, York, Princess Anne. And Norfolk, including the cities of Norfolk and Portsmouth), and which excepted parts are for the present left precisely as in this proclamation were not issued.

And by virtue of the power and for the purpose aforesaid, I do order and declare that all persons held as slaves within said designated States and parts of States are, and henceforward shall be, free; and that the Executive Government of the United States, including the military and

naval authorities thereof, will recognize and maintain the freedom of said persons.

And I hereby enjoin upon the people so declared to be free to abstain from all violence, unless in necessary self-defense; and I recommend to them that, in all cases when allowed, they labor faithfully for reasonable wages.

And I further declare and make known that such persons of suitable condition will be received into the armed service of the United States to garrison forts, positions, stations, and other places, and to man vessels of all sorts in said service.

And upon this act, sincerely believed to be an act of justice, warranted by the Constitution upon military necessity, I invoke the considerate judgment of mankind and the gracious favor of Almighty God.

11. Extracts from the Mississippi Black Code, November 1865

I. Apprentice Law

Section 1. *Be it enacted by the legislature of the state of Mississippi,* that it shall be the duty of all sheriffs, justices of the peace, and other civil officers of the several counties in this state to report to the Probate courts of their respective counties semiannually, at the January and July terms of said courts, all freedmen, free Negroes, and mulattoes under the age of eighteen within their respective counties, beats, or districts who are orphans, or whose parent or parents have not the means, or who refuse to provide for and support said minors; and thereupon it shall be the duty of said Probate Court to order the clerk of said court to apprentice said minors to some competent and suitable person, on such terms as the court may direct, having a particular care to the interest of said minors:
Provided, that the former owner of said minors shall have the preference when, in the opinion of the court, he or she shall be a Suitable person for that purpose.

Section 2. *Be it further enacted,* that the said court shall be fully satisfied that the person or persons to whom said minor shall be apprenticed shall be a suitable person to have the charge and care of said minor and fully to protect the interest of said minor. The said court shall require the said master or mistress to execute bond and security, payable to the state of Mississippi, conditioned that he or she shall furnish said minor with sufficient food and clothing; to treat said minor humanely; furnish medical attention in case of sickness; teach or cause to be taught him or her to read and write, if under fifteen years old; and will conform to any law that may be hereafter passed for the regulation of the duties and relation of master and apprentice:

Provided, that said apprentice shall be bound by indenture, in case of males, until they are twenty-one years old, and in case of females until they are eighteen years old.

Section 3. *Be it further enacted,* that in the management and control of said apprentices, said master or mistress shall have the power to inflict such moderate corporeal chastisement as a father or guardian is allowed to inflict on his or her child or ward at common law:

Provided, that in no case shall cruel or inhuman punishment be inflicted . . . .

Section 10. *Be it further enacted,* that in all cases where the age of the freedman, free Negro, or mulatto cannot be ascertained by record testimony, the judge of the county court shall fix the age.

II. Vagrancy Law

Section 1. *Be it enacted by the legislature of the state of Mississippi,* that all rogues and vagabonds, idle and dissipated persons, beggars, jugglers, or persons practising unlawful games or plays, runaways, common drunkards, common nightwalkers, pilferers, lewd, wanton, or lascivious persons, in speech or behavior, common railers and brawlers, persons who neglect their calling or employment, misspend what they earn, or do not provide for the support of themselves or their families or dependents, and all other idle and disorderly persons, including all who neglect all lawful business, or habitually misspend their time by frequenting houses of ill-fame, gaming houses, or tippling shops, shall be deemed and considered vagrants under the provisions of this act; and, on conviction thereof shall be fined not exceeding $100, with all accruing costs, and be imprisoned at the discretion of the court not exceeding ten days.

Section 2. *Be it further enacted,* that all freedmen, free Negroes, and mulattoes in this state over the age of eighteen years found on the second Monday in January 1866, or thereafter, with no lawful employment or business, or found unlawfully assembling themselves together either in the day or nighttime, and all white persons assembling with freedmen, free Negroes, or mulattoes, or usually associating with freedmen, free Negroes, or mulattoes on terms of equality, or living in adultery or fornication with a freedwoman, free Negro, or mulatto, shall be deemed vagrants; and, on conviction thereof, shall be fined in the sum of not exceeding, in the case of a freedman, free Negro or mulatto, $150, and a white man, $200, and imprisoned at the discretion of the court, the free Negro

not exceeding ten days, and the white man not exceeding six months. . . .

Section 5. *Be it further enacted,* that all fines and forfeitures collected under the provisions of this act shall be paid into the county treasury for general county purposes; and in case any freedman, free Negro, or mulatto shall fail for five days after the imposition of any fine or forfeiture upon him or her for violation of any of the provisions of this act to pay the same, that it shall be, and is hereby made, the duty of the sheriff of the proper county to hire out said freedman, free Negro, or mulatto to any person who will, for the shortest period of service, pay said fine or forfeiture and all costs:

Provided, a preference shall be given to the employer, if there be one, in which case the employer shall be entitled to deduct and retain the amount so paid from the wages of such freedman, free Negro, or mulatto then due or to become due; and in case such freedman, free Negro, or mulatto cannot be hired out, he or she may be dealt with as a pauper.

Section 6. *Be it further enacted,* that the same duties and liabilities existing among white persons of this state shall attach to freedmen, free Negroes, and mulattoes to support their indigent families and all colored paupers; and that, in order to secure a support for such indigent freedmen, free Negroes, and mulattoes, it shall be lawful, and it is hereby made the duty of the boards of county police of each county in this state, to levy a poll or capitation tax on each and every freedman, free Negro, or mulatto, between the ages of eighteen and sixty years, not to exceed the sum of $1 annually, to each person so taxed, which tax, when collected, shall be paid into the county treasurer's hands and constitute a fund to be called the Freedman's Pauper Fund, which shall be applied by the commissioners of the poor for the maintenance of the poor of the freedmen, free Negroes, and mulattoes of this state, under such regulations as may be established by the boards of county police, in the respective counties of this state.

Section 7. *Be it further enacted,* that if any freedman, free Negro, or mulatto shall fail or refuse to pay any tax levied according to the provisions of the 6th Section of this act, it shall be prima facie evidence of vagrancy, and it shall be the duty of the sheriff to arrest such freedman, free Negro, or mulatto, or such person refusing or neglecting to pay such tax, and proceed at once to hire, for the shortest time, such delinquent taxpayer to anyone who will pay the said tax, with accruing costs, giving preference to the employer, if there be one . . . .

III. Civil Rights of Freedmen

Section 1. *Be it enacted by the legislature of the state of Mississippi,* that all freedmen, free Negroes, and mulattoes may sue and be sued, implead and be impleaded in all the courts of law and equity of this state, and may acquire personal property and choses in action, by descent or purchase, and may dispose of the same in the same manner and to the same extent that white persons may:

Provided, that the provisions of this section shall not be construed as to allow any freedman, free Negro, or mulatto to rent or lease any lands or tenements, except in incorporated towns or cities, in which places the corporate authorities shall control the same.

Section 2. *Be it further enacted,* that all freedmen, free Negroes, and mulattoes may intermarry with each other, in the same manner and under the same regulations that are provided by law for white persons: Provided, that the clerk of probate shall keep separate records of the same.

Section 3. *Be it further enacted,* that all freedmen, free Negroes, and mulattoes who do now and have heretofore lived and cohabited together as husband and wife shall be taken and held in law as legally married, and the issue shall be taken and held as legitimate for all purposes. That it shall not be lawful for any freedman, free Negro, or mulatto to intermarry with any white person; nor for any white person to intermarry with any freedman, free Negro, or mulatto; and any person who shall so intermarry shall be deemed guilty of felony and, on conviction thereof, shall be confined in the state penitentiary for life . . . .

Section 5. *Be it further enacted,* that every freedman, free Negro, and mulatto shall, on the second Monday of January 1866, and annually thereafter, have a lawful home or employment, and shall have a written evidence thereof . . . .

Section 6. *Be it further enacted,* that all contracts for labor made with freedmen, free Negroes, and mulattoes for a longer period than one month shall be in writing and in duplicate, attested and read to said freedman, free Negro, or mulatto by a beat, city, or county officer, or two disinterested white persons of the county in which the labor is to be performed, of which each party shall have one; and said contracts shall be taken and held as entire contracts; and if the laborer shall quit the service of the employer before expiration of his term of service without good cause, he shall forfeit his wages for that year, up to the time of quitting.

Section 7. *Be it further enacted,* that every civil officer shall, and every person may, arrest and carry back to his or her legal employer any freedman, free Negro, or mulatto who shall have quit the service of his or her employer before the expiration of his or her term of service without good cause, and said officer and person shall be entitled to receive for arresting and carrying back every deserting employee aforesaid the sum of $5, and 10 cents per mile from the place of arrest to the place of delivery, and the same shall be paid by the employer, and held as a setoff for so much against the wages of said deserting employee . . . .

IV. Penal Code

Section 1. *Be it enacted by the legislature of the state of Mississippi,* that no freedman, free Negro, or mulatto not in the military service of the United States government, and not licensed so to do by the board of police of his or her county, shall keep or carry firearms of any kind, or any ammunition, dirk, or Bowie knife; and, on conviction thereof in the county court, shall be punished by fine, not exceeding $10, and pay the costs of such proceedings, and all such arms and ammunition shall be forfeited to the informer; and it shall be the duty of every civil and military officer to arrest any freedman, free Negro, or mulatto found with any such arms or ammunition, and cause him or her to be committed for trial in default of bail.

Section 2. *Be it further enacted,* that any freedman, free Negro, or mulatto committing riots, routs, affrays, trespasses, malicious mischief, cruel treatment to animals, seditious speeches, insulting gestures, language, or acts, or assaults on any person, disturbance of the peace, exercising the function of a minister of the Gospel without a license from some regularly organized church, vending spirituous or intoxicating liquors, or committing any other misdemeanor the punishment of which is not specifically provided for by law shall, upon conviction thereof in the county court, be fined not less than $10 and not more than $100, and may be imprisoned, at the discretion of the court, not exceeding thirty days.

12. Extracts from the Second Biennial Report of the State Commissioners of Public Charities of the State of Illinois Presented to the Governor, December 1872

The almshouses of Illinois are of several distinct types.

The most common ideal is that of a county farmhouse, corresponding in its general style to the average farmhouses of the district in which it is situated, with, perhaps, a tendency to be a little below average, in respect of convenience and comfort. In the larger counties, there is ordinarily to be found upon the county farm a group of houses, and this is often the case in the smaller counties as well—one house, better than the rest, for the family of the keeper, and the others for the use of male and female paupers and the insane, to each of whom separate buildings when the number is sufficient to justify classification, are allotted. The life, in an almshouse of this description, is that of a family in the country, rather poorly clothed and fed, and bearing the marks of a listless poverty.

Another type of almshouse is the hospital, of which St. Clair County probably affords the best illustration. The St. Clair County almshouse, only a mile distant from the courthouse at Belleville, and almost on the outskirts of the town, differs from all ordinary almshouses in this respect. The whole air of the establishment, the internal arrangements, the management and discipline resemble those of a well-kept hospital proper, in which are collected not only the temporarily sick or disabled but the permanently helpless and infirm, and no others. A flower garden blooms in front of the premises; a pesthouse has been erected at some distance in the rear; and a thoroughly well-planned, well-built, and every way comfortable receptacle for the insane has been provided. The county judges visit the place daily, and it exhibits, in its entire aspect, the marks of thorough oversight and intelligent care. It is a credit to the county and to the state.

A third type is modeled after the idea of the state or public institution, with a large brick building or buildings, divided into center and wings, and approximating more or less nearly (generally less) in its plan of organization to the commonly received notion of what an institution should be. A very favorable instance of this style of almshouse is to be seen in Knox County, at Knoxville. It was built after plans of which Dr. McFarland, of Jacksonville, furnished the preliminary sketches, and although not yet completed, one wing having only been erected, it is ably and satisfactorily presided over by a lady superintendent, Mrs. Cleveland, who has been in charge for a number of years. In this institution also, proper provision has been made for the care of the hopelessly insane, in an "l" at the extremity of the wing . . . .

The first fault in the management of the majority of county farms that strikes a visitor is the excessive quantity of land commonly contained in them. The objections to large farms are the loss of interest on the original investment, the impossibility of working them profitably with pauper labor, and the diversion of the attention of the keeper from the care and oversight of the paupers to the care of the farm. There are few instances in which forty acres are not amply sufficient for all practical purposes, and oftentimes ten or twenty would be enough. Yet it is not uncommon for a county to own a poor farm (and poor farms the most of them are, in fact) of three or four hundred acres. In several of the counties visited by us, we have been informed that the original purchase was a speculation, on the part of some prominent and influential citizen, who wished to dispose of comparatively worthless land for a price far in excess of its actual value.

A second fault is often observable in the nature of the selection of a keeper, and in the nature of the contract made with him. Many of the counties appear indifferent as to the character and capacity of the keeper employed, and only anxious to secure the cheapest man who will do, whether really competent or not. Some of the almshouse keepers in this state are only a degree above the paupers under their charge, in point of efficiency or intelligence. When the care of the paupers is let to the lowest bidder, this must ordinarily be so. The contracts made with the men employed are often loosely drawn, so as not to guard the interests either of the county or of the unfortunate inmates. The worst of all contracts is that in which an individual agrees to take all the paupers that are sent to him, and furnish everything, medicines and medical attendance included, at his own cost, for a stipulated sum per annum. This is simply an attempt on the part of county officials to throw off all responsibility for the care of the poor, by hiring a proxy to do their duty for them. Under such a system, it is the interest of the keeper to mistreat his victims, for the sake of personal profit. If complaint is made to him, he alleges that he cannot afford to keep them better at the price allowed him by the county. If complaint is made to the county authorities, they wash their hands of all responsibility in the matter; they have made their contract; they feel no personal interest in paupers; and they presume the contractor keeps them well enough. Very little better are the contracts in which the same agreement is made for a stipulated sum per capita. The true method of caring for paupers in almshouses is for the county to employ the best man and wife that can be had for the price, especial pains being taken to secure a kind but efficient woman, as head of the domestic department, and to pay them a fixed salary; to require an account to be kept of the production and consumption of supplies on the farm, and insist upon the farm being made to yield as much for the support of the paupers as possible; and all purchases should be made by authority of the county at county expense, the bills to be carefully audited before being paid. This is the usual practice, and it is altogether the best and most satisfactory. The farm should be worked in the interest of the county and not of the keeper—the object not being to make money, but to secure proper attention to the paupers.

A very important point in the management of almshouses is the selection of a physician, who should be possessed of fair ability and attainments, and should be required to visit the establishment not simply when sent for but at stated intervals. Stated visits of inspection by a physician have the effect of improving the general management, and often prevent the rise and spread of epidemics, or arrest individual cases of sickness by securing medical attention at the right moment. Of course the physician should be required to make visits as frequently as necessary, in sickness . . . .

Great care ought to be taken in the admission of inmates, not to exclude any who are actually in need of assistance, not on the other hand to allow lazy and vicious persons to become pensioners upon public bounty. Thoroughness in the discipline and employment at hard labor, in proportion to their strength, will present serious imposition because able-bodied beggars will not submit to it. Those who do, and whose misfortunes are irremediable, are entitled to sympathy, and should not be permitted to suffer, because they are poor and unfortunate. They should be made thoroughly comfortable, and the small expense necessary to accomplish this ought not to be grudgingly bestowed . . . .

Another point that needs attention is the care of the hopelessly insane, of whom a greater or less number are to be found in all our almshouses. They are the victims of disease, they suffer greatly, and no pains should be spared to make them as comfortable as circumstances will admit. When receptacles are built for them they should be well lighted, well warmed, well ventilated, provided with suitable bedding and other conveniences, protected against peril from fire, so arranged as to protect the insane from each other, in case of violent excitement, and under no circumstances should they be allowed to degenerate into the living tombs that they too often are. The horrors that we have seen in some of the county almshouses are too shocking to repeat—nakedness, filth, starvation, vice, and utter wretchedness, which a very slight exercise of common sense and of humanity might have entirely prevented.

The improvement of our almshouse system must be a work of time. It would be greatly facilitated were these abodes of misery more often visited by the better class of citizens in each county. A voluntary association for the relief of pauperism and crime, by regular and methodical inspection of the county almshouses and jails at least as often as once in every month, might be organized in Illinois, with a branch or auxiliary society in each county, and might accomplish a world of good.

The almshouses can be made self-sustaining only to a very limited extent. Pauper labor is worth little, and what labor is expended will be more effective if directed to the production of supplies for home consumption than for the market.

The presence of children in such places is the saddest feature. What can be more dreary than the future prospects of a pauper child? All such should be provided with homes, if possible, and, at the almshouse, should be given every facility for obtaining the rudiments of an education, in the hope of lifting them out of their forlorn condition.

Closely connected with the question we have been discussing is that of outdoor relief, or assistance granted outside the almshouses. We find, in different counties directly opposite principles and practices, in this particular, prevailing. In some of the counties, the authorities grant outdoor relief to an extent that is appalling—multitudes of persons receiving aid, to whom aid is a positive injury, inasmuch as it fosters a spirit of dependence which undermines all energy and personal effort to obtain a livelihood. One case was reported to us of an able-bodied man who received aid from the county in which he lived to support his wife, living at home with him in his own house. Other counties, to avoid this drain upon the treasury, go to the opposite extreme, and refuse relief to anyone who will not first give his consent to become an inmate of the county house. This policy is as cruel and shortsighted as the other is unwise, since it has a tendency to convert temporary misfortune into permanent poverty, for it is difficult for one who has once been forced to seek admission to an almshouse ever to fully regain his self-respect. On the other hand judicious temporary assistance often enables a man struggling with adversity to regain his feet. Wisdom seems to dictate a medium course, namely, the reduction of outdoor relief to a minimum, in order to prevent the growth of pauperism by undue indulgence, but the granting of temporary aid, at home, whenever the suffering is so great that it ought to be relieved, and it is probable that only temporary relief will be necessary. The great problem of all charity, public or private, is how to diminish suffering without increasing, by the very act, the number of paupers; how to grant aid, in case of need, without obliterating the principle of self-reliance and self-help. To accomplish this, a mixture of the two systems appears to be essential.

13. Extracts from the Ninth Annual Report of the State Board of Charities of the State of New York Relating to Pauper Children in New York County, December 27, 1875

To the State Board of Charities:

GENTLEMEN—.... The establishments of New York for the care of pauper children, are located on Randall's Island, and practically constitute the children's department of the alms-house of that city. During the past year I have made several visitations to these establishments, accompanied on one occasion by Commissioner [Theodore] Roosevelt . . . . The report is based upon the information gathered during these visitations . . . .

Building "B"—Reception House and Department for Small Girls

On entering the building we found the little girls just passing from the play-room into the dining-room. The table was set with crockery plates and mugs, with spoons, knives and forks. The meal for each child consisted of a plate of soup, with an ample supply of potatoes and meat, also a large slice of bread. A work-housewoman dressed in blue jean, the common dress of this class here, was serving the food to the children.

The dresses of all the children were of blue gingham with white linen aprons. Cotton stockings and shoes were worn. The winter dress was stated to be a woolen or flannel underskirt, and a cotton chemise. In summer a canton-flannel underskirt and a cotton chemise are worn. Only such cases as are directed by the attending physician, wear shoes and stockings in the summer. Sometimes these are furnished by parents. Children on leaving are dressed in the same clothing they wore when admitted. It was observed that the dresses were, many of them, ludicrously out of proportion; some too short, others much too long; some too large and loosely gathered, others looking as though the children had out-grown their clothes. This was unavoidable where so many were coming in and going out, and wearing clothes not made for them.

The matron in charge, in reply to our inquiries said: "We keep the children here but a short time after their arrival. We dress and wash them, and after the doctor has examined them, they are transferred to their proper places. We keep here smaller girls. We can accommodate eighty by putting two in a bed. To-day we have seventy-one; their ages ranging from four to eight years."

In the dormitories we saw double bedsteads of iron, three feet six inches wide. Straw beds and pillows were in use. The straw was said to be changed as often as the matron considered necessary. Each bed had two sheets and a double pair of blankets.

The floors of the room were clean, and connected with each was a bath-tub and a night-closet, the air of the apartment, however, did not seem sweet and wholesome. In this building six adult persons including matron, were employed. Two were work-house women, and one was from the alms-house.

Building "C"—Dining-room and Dormitories for Large Boys

Here the dinner was being served for about two hundred and fifty boys. It consisted of meat, potatoes, pudding and gravy. Each boy had two pieces of bread. The bread is baked in the Blackwell's Island department of the alms-house. The meal seemed ample. The boys marched across the yard and into the dining-room, in companies of about twenty-five. They beat time with the right foot, marched in close column with the lock step, and in the same manner as the convicts march across the yards at Auburn and Sing Sing. The drill-master said he had "forbidden the use of this step, but the boys seemed to prefer it, and would use it when they could." This feature of the institution is doubtless owing to the association of the children with the convict class. Each company had a boy at its head who was termed a non-commissioned officer. He has a blue uniform. The best behaved boys, we were told, were selected as officers, and the effect was said to be good. The boys all stood at the table except ten or twelve who were crippled. The boys were mostly dressed in jackets and pants of gray cassimere. Forty of them have a blue uniform . . . .

Administrative Force

The eight nursery buildings, and the affairs connected with them, excepting the school department, are under the charge of a warden. He is assisted by a drill-master, clerk, head matron, and three assistant matrons. There were also attached to the establishment thirteen nurses and paid domestics, and a large force of male and female "helpers" who had been sent up from the alms-house and work-house . . . . The paid domestics receive $10 per month. Quite a number of these had formerly been inmates of the alms-house . . . .

Mental and Physical Condition

701 of the children were regarded as being of average mental capacity—some of them "very bright"—48 below the average, 17 feeble minded, and 3 idiotic.

Of the 599 children in the nursery proper, 551 were considered healthy.

The physical condition of the remaining number, 48, appeared to be as follows: Four were suffering from temporary sickness, six from general feebleness of body, six from some form of skin disease, three from sore eyes, three from blindness, ten from loss of sight in one eye, and sixteen from being deformed or crippled.

Among the cases of disease and affliction in the hospital there appeared to be the following. Some of the children suffering from more than one disease at the same time:

Diseased scalp	29
Itch	19
Other diseases of the skin	25
Diseased eyes	57
Blindness	7
Loss of sight in one eye	3

It is sad to state, that the inquiry at the Hospital closed with the belief in the mind of the examiner, that five of the children who were placed in the Hospital in consequence of some temporary sickness, had, by coming in contact with other children suffering from sore eyes, been inoculated with the virus producing disease of the eye and, it was thought, would become blind, and that in two cases out of the five the calamity was certain . . . .

Adult Female Helpers

Seventy-four adult females were employed in the Nursery and Nursery Hospital; 50 in the former, and 24 in the latter . . . .

The habits of 7 were temperate; 13 were moderate drinkers; 35 were periodical drinkers, and 19 were constant drinkers.

Twenty-three of these females belonged to the pauper class, and 51 to the work-house class that had been sent up from Blackwell's Island. Of the former, 1 was a pauper in consequence of a permanent disabling disease; 2 from destitution; 4 by abandonment of husband; 8 by death of husband; 7 were self-committed, and 1 was placed in the Nursery when a child.

Of the 51 that belonged to the criminal class, 13 had been committed as vagrants, 2 for disorderly conduct, and 36 for drunkenness and disorderly conduct . . . .

There were 40 adult males registered on the books of the Nursery and Nursery hospital, 24 in former, and 16 in the latter. They were employed in the performance of various duties, under the direction of the warden or superintendent.

Twenty-two of these men were self-committed to the poor-house, 17 had been committed to the work-house for drunkenness, and one for assault and battery . . . .

Placing Children Out

The manner in which children are disposed of at the Nursery is, according to the statement of the Warden, substantially as follows: Applications are made to the central office. If the applicant obtains an order for a child, he comes to the Nursery and makes his own selection. He has four months to try the child. If he is satisfied, the child is then indentured to him. There is a greater demand for girls than for boys. The boys are hard to dispose of . . . . Further, it was understood that there is no systematic plan for visiting the children, after they have been placed out, to ascertain if they are properly educated or humanely treated, nor does it appear that any attempt is made to maintain a correspondence with the children, or to place them under disinterested benevolent surveillance. As stated, any person taking a child is at liberty to return it at the end of four months, if not satisfied. It is believed that this privilege is not unfrequently availed of by parties who merely desire to obtain the services of a child during pressure of work . . . .

One of the great evils in every poor-house system, and that of New York cannot be regarded as an exception, has been found to be the facility with which children may repeatedly be admitted to and discharged from the alms-house. After going in and coming out a few times a don't-care feeling takes hold of the child, and it loses whatever self-reliance of character it may have possessed . . . .

Home Life

The absence of any thing like home-life, or the best orphan asylum life, in the nursery is painful. The unfitting dresses of the little ones, giving them a grotesque appearance; the habit of standing in great rooms to eat; the bare floors and walls without a picture or article of furniture to suggest home-life; the moving to and fro in great masses, destroying, as it does, all individuality; are among the conditions which should awaken sympathy for this tender class . . . .

Conclusion

After a patient and impartial examination of this subject, the conclusion seems to be inevitable, that the whole Randall's Island nursery system should be set aside agreeably to the statute, and that the children should be placed in asylums suited to their various needs under the charge of those devoted to the interests of the young, or into good families where they may be trained and educated to useful and respectable citizenship . . . .

It is believed that whatever may be done to improve this system, it will still have the same general characteristics, and retain about it the indolent atmosphere peculiar to all institutions having the care of the pauper classes, and that all attempts in this direction will only serve to gild over or cover up a radical evil without effecting a cure . . . .

The proper mental and moral improvement of so large a number of children as are inmates of the Nursery is not a question of immediate cost of keeping only, but it involves the future well-being of society. It is believed that the attempt to afford to these children the best possible advantages, at whatever cost, will be found in the end to be true economy. Every child preserved from a life of pauperism and crime, adds so much to the productive forces of society, and, at the same time, lessens greatly the public burdens . . . .

Since writing the foregoing, and before closing this report, it is gratifying to be able to state that the Commissioners of Public Charities and Corrections, have declined to receive children over three years of age, excepting idiots, epileptics, paralytics and those otherwise diseased; have notified such parents and guardians as have children in the Nursery, to remove them, and have taken other action looking to the closing up of that institution . . . .

That jealous and almost affectionate care with which the State now enfolds its dependent children, and preserves them from the stigma of pauperism, enables its citizens virtually to say, with a just pride, that in no county within her borders does there exist a system, under legal sanction, that brands the orphan or homeless child, a "pauper."

Respectfully submitted,
WILLIAM P. LETCHWORTH
Commissioner Eight Judicial District.
ALBANY, *December 27, 1875*

14. Extract from the Third Annual Report of the Charity Organization Society of the District of Columbia, 1886

Central Office, Room 8, Gunton Building, cor. 9th and Pa. Ave. N.W.

THIRD ANNUAL MEETING
IN
Spencerian college halls and parlors,
Thursday Evening, October 21, 1886, at 8 o'clock.

A large audience, representing the District Government, the leading churches, benevolent organizations, and individual philanthropists of the National Capital, assembled at an early hour.

Mrs. Harriette H. Mills, contralto of the St. Cecilia Quartette, sang exquisitely "The New Kingdom," and being encored, sang "Many Happy Returns."

The President of the Society, Mr. A. S. Pratt, said:

Less than three years ago, December 15, 1883, the Charity Organization Society of the District of Columbia was organized and chartered for twenty years under the general law of Congress. As members and friends of this Society you have assembled to participate in its Third Annual Meeting and learn how the trusts committed to us have been fulfilled. We welcome you here to-night, and trust when you leave this meeting the principles of "Charity Organization" will be better understood, and will claim from you hearty and continued support. I am convinced that an intelligent conception of our plans and work would secure to us the adherence and aid of all fair-minded citizens.

I must draw from the wisdom and experience of those abler than myself and longer engaged in this work in the few thoughts I shall now submit to you.

Our Society is based on the broad principle of love to our fellow-man—a love that looks far beyond transient gratification of selfish impulses; that seeks to lift the pauper, the tramp, the idle, the criminal to self-support, to self-respect, and the confidence of the community. We welcome all to this labor of love, without regard to creed, politics, or nationality. Upon this ground Jew and Gentile, Catholic and Protestant, Democrat and Republican, Caucasian and African, can work together, and are now working together in the charity organization societies of this country for the elevation of the race.

Rev. Howard Crosby describes this organization (now in practical operation in some sixty cities of the United States) as "a society for getting the community out of bad habits," and gives the following illustration:

"I had a dear friend who used to give regularly ten cents every day to a poor blind beggar that stood at the corner of Second avenue. Every day that she passed the ten cents went in. I admired her benevolence, her sympathy, and her generosity, but I had a little suspicion that she was wrong, and concluded I would find out the history of the poor blind man. So I engaged a very excellent fellow I knew well to follow him up, and see if he could find out something of his history. My young friend followed him up. At six o'clock in the evening a woman came and took the blind man in tow from Second avenue and Eleventh street, and led him to Forty-ninth street and Tenth avenue, and there two stout young men, who kept a little gambling den, received the blind man most graciously, and he counted out the money he had received for that day's blindness, and it was fourteen dollars; and those two young men kindly kept the blind man, gave him food and lodging, and the blind man paid them for the kindness fourteen dollars, which the kind ladies, like my friend, managed to give him."

To protect our community from similar imposition we furnish to our members and to citizens who will use it a card in calendar form, with a package of green tickets attached, one to be given to each applicant for relief who is personally unknown, instead of alms. The giver of the green ticket should write upon it his own name and address that the Society may report to him the result of their investigation of the case. A faithful use of these cards by our citizens, instead of the ready nickle or dime, would soon clear our streets of professional beggars and tramps. The idle will be compelled to work if he cannot obtain alms, and the really helpless will be cared for by the proper agencies, *i.e.*, the Church, the Society, the friendly neighbor who, at the request of our Society, undertakes the case.

In the city of London, some seventeen years ago, the parent Society of this and kindred bodies was organized, and "Charity Organization" was the term chosen as best fitted to describe the work proposed, viz., to organize existing charities—not to create another alms-giving society. All institutions, societies, churches, benevolent individuals were to be drawn together for one common purpose—the effective relief of the poor, permanent improvement in their condition, and the protection of the benevolent from imposition. No city in the world needed such a society more. Parliament was quick to sanction and further this work.

In true charity organization there is no interference with the work, plans, individuality, or funds of any properly constituted benevolent organization. It supplants the work of no church or society by giving direct relief. It asks to know who are the persons seeking or obtaining relief in all available directions, and where they live, that it may promptly notify the benevolent, when they are hurting where they mean to help, and also where their kind service is really needed. This aggregation of information in one file bureau makes of the central office of a charity organization society a

"CLEARING-HOUSE"

of information for the charities of a great city.

Our system of card registration contemplates a faithful, reliable record of every person in the District asking or receiving alms, including every case of real distress reported to us and placed in proper hands by our Society.

We desire to acknowledge the moral support and co-operation of our District Commissioners, our Chief of Police and his force, the superintendents of all Government institutions, and many private charities and churches.

We need the co-operation of every church, institution, and benevolent society to make our records complete. We need also a much larger supply of money, for the intelligent labor required to carry on so vast a work must be unintermitting, and, therefore, paid labor.

The work accomplished yields ten-fold, in revealing imposture, for the chronic pauper and fraud element carry off the bulk of all public and private charity.

We also need the labor of the printing-press and the use of the U.S. mails to a far greater extent than we have been able to secure them. Our publications should be in the hands of every citizen, for enlightenment and education upon the foundation principles of true charity.

We need not only a central office, but branch offices. We need at least five good agents for different sections of the city. We need telephone service.

Which is the wiser—to give money for alms, or to use it to lift thousands out of the need of receiving alms?

One of our hardest tasks is to convince citizens that this is not only not an alms-giving society, but that its better purpose is the suppression of pauperism.

A few of our members (less than half a dozen, I am glad to say, or less than 3 per cent.) have withdrawn from us because some pet mendicant protégé of their own was not promptly fed and clothed by our Society. In each of these cases we had ascertained that the individual sent was a smooth-tongued fraud, who was drawing "relief" from various sources, yet forever in distress. We do not take the ground that no relief should ever be given to families or individuals in distress; but we maintain that proper agencies already exist to save a worthy family from immediate suffering, and also from public mendicancy.

How We Save from Real Suffering

As an illustration: A lady reported to us a family in great need. She had done for them all she could. They would not beg, and were averse to having their condition known. The father, a mechanic, was prostrated by sickness, probably fatal. I asked if they attended any church. Was told they did, but the minister had not been informed of the circumstances. This we lost no time in doing, and the response came quickly, "yes, the family belong to my congregation. They are worthy people, and as soon as I learned from you of their sickness and need I obtained from our society all that it could spare; but our church is poor, and more help will be needed." Did our Charity Organization Society then take this case in hand and directly appropriate for its relief? No. At once a wealthy and benevolent lady of the same communion was made acquainted with the facts, and was asked to put into that minister's hands what might be needed for the family, which she cheerfully did. Were not all of these persons—the family, the minister, the church, the benevolent woman—benefited far more by performing their own duty to each other than they could have been by our shouldering their responsibilities? And especially was it not less humiliating to the sensitive family to be aided by their own household of faith than by strangers? They only knew in the matter their own minister and church in the time of distress.

As to the repressive work of this Society in the detection of fraud, its reformatory work in the correction of social abuses, its preventive work in inculcating habits of self-dependence and thrift among the poor—all this is only begun, and needs your earnest sympathy, approval, and co-operation. Friends, we need you to help us, not only with your means, but by giving yourselves to this work of redemption.

Above and beyond paid workers, whom we must have, we want a friendly visitor for every side of every square in this city—men and women with warm hearts and strong common sense—who will enter this wide field of benevolent labor and strengthen the hands and encourage the hearts of the few over-worked toilers who have hitherto wrought alone, and much to oppose and dismay, and little to cheer, except the consciousness of improving the condition of fellow-beings.

Secretary's Report

Mr. J. C. Pratt, the General Secretary, reported as follows:

The records of our Society show that during the past year substantial progress has been made toward the accomplishment of the great aims of this Society, to wit, the organization of the charities of the city—the churches, benevolent societies, and individuals—for mutual protection against impostors, and prompt and judicious relief of emergency cases among the deserving poor. This progress is indicated, not by the increased number of applicants for relief, for in proportion as honesty, industry, and thrift prevail in a community, the number of persons needing relief will diminish, but by the larger number of pastors of churches, officers of societies, and benevolent citizens who apply for information to our office before administering relief, and report to us when they do administer it.

We were especially encouraged to believe that the true value of our Central Office as a clearing-house of information was coming to be properly understood and appreciated when the Chief of Police, Major Dye, after counsel with the Commissioners, instructed his force to enquire by telephone at our Central Office concerning the record of persons applying for relief at the several stations, and if the person was unknown to us or to them, to await our friendly examination of the case. Under these circumstances, there was no occasion for complaint of the funds falling short. What is saved by the exposure of fraud is sufficient to meet genuine cases of distress among the worthy.

Letters received from officials, from pastors of churches, and from philanthropic citizens express warm appreciation of the advantages they have derived from co-operation with this Society, while our own members are continually declaring that they find themselves largely protected from the importunities, interruptions, and annoyances of street and door beggars by their very membership in our organization. The regular Washington beggar or tramp knowing he is on record at our office, avoids our members, assured that he will not obtain "relief" from them, and may get into the workhouse, as we promise on our charter to "prosecute imposters," while those who do not and will not beg, and may be suffering and neglected, are sure to be promptly provided for by the proper person when the case is referred to us.

15. Extracts from the General Allotment Act (Dawes Act), February 8, 1887

Be it enacted . . . That in all cases where any tribe or band of Indians has been, or shall hereafter be, located upon any reservation created for their use, either by treaty stipulation or by virtue of an act of Congress or executive order setting apart the same for their use, the President of the United States be, and hereby is, authorized, whenever in his opinion any reservation or any part thereof of such Indians is advantageous for agricultural and grazing purposes, to cause said reservation, or any part thereof, to be surveyed, or resurveyed if necessary, and to allot the lands in said reservation in severalty to any Indian located thereon in quantities as follows:

To each head of a family, one-quarter of a section;

To each single person over eighteen years of age, one-eighth of a section;

To each orphan child under eighteen years of age, one-eighth of a section; and

To each other single person under eighteen years now living, or who may be born prior to the date of the order of the President directing an allotment of the lands embraced in any reservation, one-sixteenth of a section: *Provided,* That in case there is not sufficient land in any of said reservations to allot lands to each individual of the classes above named in quantities as above provided, the lands embraced in such reservation or reservations shall be allotted to each individual of each of said classes pro rata in accordance with the provisions of this act: And provided further, That where the treaty or act of Congress setting apart such reservation provides for the allotment of lands in severalty in quantities in excess of those herein provided, the President, in making allotments upon such reservation, shall allot the lands to each individual Indian belonging thereon in quantity as specified in such treaty or act: *And provided further,* That when the lands allotted are only valuable for grazing purposes, an additional allotment of such grazing lands, in quantities as above provided, shall be made to each individual.

Sec. 2. That all allotments set apart under the provisions of this act shall be selected by the Indians, heads of families selecting for their minor children, and the agents shall select for each orphan child, and in such manner as to embrace the improvements of the Indians making the selection . . . Provided, That if any one entitled to an allotment shall fail to make a selection within four years after the President shall direct that allotments may be made on a particular reservation, the Secretary of the Interior may direct the agent of such tribe or band, if such there be, and if there be no agent, then a special agent appointed for that purpose, to make a selection for such Indian, which selection shall be allotted as in cases where selections are made by the Indians, and patents shall issue in like manner. . . .

Sec. 5. That upon the approval of the allotments provided for in this act by the Secretary of the Interior, he shall cause patents to issue therefor in the name of the allottees, which patents shall be of the legal effect, and declare that the United States does and will hold the land thus allotted, for the period of twenty-five years, in trust for the sole use and benefit of the Indian to whom such allotment shall have been made, or, in case of his decease, of his heirs according to the laws of the State or Territory where such land is located, and that at the expiration of said period the United States will convey the same by patent to said Indian, or his heirs aforesaid, in fee, discharged of said trust and free of all charge or incumbrance whatsoever: Provided, That the President of the United States may in any case in his discretion extend the period. . . . And provided further, That at any time after lands have been allotted to all the Indians of any tribe as herein provided, or sooner if in the opinion of the President it shall be for the best interests of said tribe, it shall be lawful for the Secretary of the Interior to negotiate with such Indian tribe for the purchase and release by said tribe, in conformity with the treaty or statute under which such reservation is held, of such portions of its reservation not allotted as such tribe shall, from time to time, consent to sell, on such terms and conditions as shall be considered just and equitable between the Unite States and said tribe of Indians, which purchase shall not be complete until ratified by Congress, and the form and manner of executing such release shall also be prescribed by Congress: Provided however, That all lands adapted to agriculture, with or without irrigation so sold or released to the United States by any Indian tribe shall be held by the United States for the sole purpose of securing homes to actual settlers and shall be disposed of by the United States to actual and bona fide settlers only in tracts not exceeding one hundred and sixty acres to any one person, on such terms as Congress shall prescribe . . . .

Sec. 8. That the provision of this act shall not extend to the territory occupied by the Cherokees, Creeks, Chickasaws, Seminoles, and Osage, Miamies and Peorias, and Sacs and Foxes, in the Indian Territory, nor to any of the reservations of the Seneca Nation of New York Indians in the State of New York, nor to that strip of territory in the State of Nebraska adjoining the Sioux Nation on the south added by executive order.

16. Extract from The Problem of Indian Administration (Meriam Survey), 1928

The Conditions Among the Indians

An overwhelming majority of the Indians are poor, even extremely poor, and they are not adjusted to the economic and social system of the dominant white civilization.

The poverty of the Indians and their lack of adjustment to the dominant economic and social systems produce the vicious circle ordinarily found among any people under such circumstances. Because of interrelationships, causes cannot be differentiated from effects. The only course is to state briefly the conditions found that are part of this vicious circle of poverty and maladjustment.

Health. The health of the Indians as compared with that of the general population is bad. Although accurate mortality and morbidity statistics are commonly lacking, the existing evidence warrants the statement that both the general death rate and the infant mortality rate are high. Tuberculosis is extremely prevalent. Trachoma, a communicable disease which produces blindness, is a major problem because of its great prevalence and the danger of its spreading among both the Indians and the whites.

Living Conditions. The prevailing living conditions among the great majority of the Indians are conducive to the development and spread of disease. With comparatively few exceptions the diet of the Indians is bad. It is generally insufficient in quantity, lacking in variety, and poorly prepared. The two great preventive elements in diet, milk, and fruits and green vegetables, are notably absent. Most tribes use fruits and vegetables in season, but even then the supply is ordinarily insufficient. The use of milk is rare, and it is generally not available even for infants. Babies, when weaned, are ordinarily put on the same diet as older children and adults, a diet consisting of meats and starches.

The housing conditions are likewise conducive to bad health. Both in the primitive dwellings and in the majority of more or less permanent homes which in some cases have replaced them, there is great overcrowding, so that all members of the family are exposed to any disease that develops, and it is virtually impossible in any way even partially to isolate a person suffering from a communicable disease. In certain jurisdictions, notably the Osage and the Kiowa, the government has stimulated the building of modern homes, bungalows, or even more pretentious dwellings, but most of the permanent houses that have replaced primitive dwellings are small shacks with few rooms and with inadequate provision for ventilation. Education in housekeeping and sanitation has not proceeded far enough so that the Indians living in these more or less permanent shacks practice ventilation and domestic cleanliness. From the standpoint of health it is probably true that the temporary, primitive dwellings that were not fairly air-tight and were frequently abandoned were more sanitary than the permanent homes that have replaced them. The furnishing of the primitive dwellings and of the shacks is limited. Although many of them still have very primitive arrangements for cooking and heating, the use of modern cook stoves and utensils is far more general than the use of beds, and the use of beds in turn is far more common than the use of any kind of easily washable bed covering.

Sanitary facilities are generally lacking. Except among the relatively few well-to-do Indians the houses seldom have a private water supply or any toilet facilities whatever. Even privies are exceptional. Water is ordinarily carried considerable distances from natural springs or streams, or occasionally from wells. In many sections the supply is inadequate, although in some jurisdictions, notably in the desert country of the Southwest, the government has materially improved the situation, an activity that is appreciated by the Indians.

Economic Conditions. The income of the typical Indian family is low and the earned income is extremely low. From the standpoint of the white man the typical Indian is not industrious, nor is he an effective worker when he does work. Much of his activity is expended in lines which produce relatively small return either in goods or money. He generally ekes out an existence through unearned income from leases of his land, the sale of land, per capita payments from tribal funds, or in exceptional cases through rations given him by the government. The number of Indians who are supporting themselves through their own efforts, according to what a white man would regard as the minimum standard of health and decency, is extremely small. What little they secure from their own efforts or from other sources is rarely effectively used.

The main occupations of the men are some outdoor work, mostly of an agricultural nature, but the number of real farmers is comparatively small. A considerable proportion engage more or less casually in unskilled labor. By many Indians several different kinds of activity are followed spasmodically, a little agriculture, a little fishing, hunting, trapping, wood cutting, or gathering of native products, occasional labor and hauling, and a great deal of just idling. Very seldom do Indians work about their homes as the typical white man does. Although the permanent structures in which they live after they give up primitive dwellings are simple and such as they might easily build and develop for themselves, little evidence of such activity was seen. Even where more advanced Indians occupied structures similar to those occupied by neighboring whites it was almost always possible to tell the Indian homes from the white by the fact that the white man did much more than the Indian in keeping his house in condition.

In justice to the Indians it should be said that many of them are living on lands from which a trained and experienced white man could scarcely wrest a reasonable living. In some instances the land originally set apart for the Indians was of little value for agricultural operations other than grazing. In other instances part of the land was excellent but the Indians did not appreciate its value. Often when individual allotments were made, they chose for themselves the poorer parts, because those parts were near a domestic water supply or a source of firewood, or because they furnished some native product important to the Indians in their primitive life. Frequently the better sections of the land originally set apart for the Indians have fallen into the hands of the whites, and the Indians have retreated to the poorer lands remote from markets.

In many places crops can be raised only by the practice of irrigation. Many Indians on the Southwest are successful in a small way with their own primitive systems of irrigation. When modern highly developed irrigation systems have been supplied by governmental activities, the Indians have rarely been ready to make effective use of the land and water. If the modern irrigation enterprise has been successful from an economic standpoint, the tendency has been for whites to gain possession of the land either by purchase or by leases. If the enterprise has not been economically a success, the Indians generally retain possession of the land, but they do not know how to use it effectively and get much less out of it than a white man would.

The remoteness of their homes often prevents them from easily securing opportunities for wage earning, nor do they have many contacts with persons dwelling in urban communities where they might find employment. Even the boys and girls graduating from government schools have comparatively little vocational guidance or aid in finding profitable employment.

When all these factors are taken into consideration it is not surprising to find low incomes, low standards of living, and poor health.

Suffering and Discontent. Some people assert that the Indians prefer to live as they do; that they are happier in their idleness and irresponsibility. The question may be raised whether these persons do not mistake for happiness and content an almost oriental fatalism and resignation. The survey staff found altogether too much evidence of real suffering and discontent to subscribe to the belief that the Indians are reasonably satisfied with their condition. The amount of serious illness and real poverty is too great to permit of real contentment. The Indian is like the white man in his affection for his children and he feels keenly the sickness and the loss of his offspring.

The Causes of Poverty. The economic basis of the primitive culture of the Indians has been largely destroyed by the encroachment of white civilization. The Indians can no longer make a living as they did in the past by hunting, fishing, gathering wild products, and the extremely limited practice of primitive agriculture. The social system that evolved from their past economic life is ill suited to the conditions that now confront them, notably in the matter of the division of labor between the men and the women. They are by no means yet adjusted to the new economic and social conditions that confront them.

Several past policies adopted by the government in dealing with the Indians have been of a type which, if long continued, would tend to pauperize any race. Most notable was the practice of issuing rations to able-bodied Indians. Having moved the Indians from their ancestral lands to restricted reservations as a war measure, the government undertook to feed them and to perform certain services for them which a normal people do for themselves. The Indians at the outset had to accept this aid as a matter of necessity, but promptly they came to regard it as a matter of right, as indeed it was at the time and under the conditions of the inauguration of the ration system. They felt, and many of them still feel, that the government owes them a living, having taken their lands from them, and that they are under no obligation to support themselves. They have thus inevitably developed a pauper point of view.

When the government adopted the policy of individual ownership of the mand on the reservations, the expectation was that the Indians would become farmers. Part of the plan was to instruct and aid them in agriculture, but this vital part was not pressed with vigor and intelligence. It almost seems as if the government assumed that some magic in individual ownership of property would in itself prove an educational civilizing factor, but unfortunately this policy has for the most part operated in the opposite direction. Individual ownership has in many instances permitted Indians to sell their allotments and to live for a time on the unearned income resulting from the sale. Individual ownership brought promptly all the details of inheritance, and frequently the sale of property of the deceased Indians to whites so that the estate could be divided among the heirs. To the heirs the sale brought further unearned income, thereby lessening the necessity for self support. Many Indians were not ready to make effective use of their individual allotments. Some of the allotments were of such a character that they could not be effectively used by anyone in small units. The solution was to permit the Indians through the government to lease their lands to the whites. In some instances government officers encouraged leasing, as the whites were anxious for the use of the land and it was far easier to administer property leased to whites than to educate and stimulate Indians to use their own property. The lease money, though generally small in amount, gave the Indians further unearned income to permit the continuance of a life of idleness.

Surplus land remaining after allotments were made was often sold and the proceeds placed in a tribal fund. Natural resources, such as timber and oil, were sold and the money paid either into tribal funds or to individual Indians if the land had been allotted. From time to time per capita payments were made to the individual Indians from tribal funds. These policies all added to the unearned income of the Indian and postponed the day when it would be necessary for him to work to support himself.

Since the Indians were ignorant of money and its use, had little or no sense of values, and fell an easy victim to any white man who wanted to take away their property, the government, through its Indian Service employees, often took the easiest course of managing all the Indians' property for them. The government kept the Indians' money for them at the agency. When the Indians wanted something they would go to the government agent, as a child would go to his parents, and ask for it. The government agent would make all the decisions, and in many instances would either buy the thing requested or give the Indians a store order for it. Although money was sometimes given the Indians, the general belief was that the Indians could not be trusted to spend the money for the purpose agreed upon with the agent, and therefore they must not be given opportunity to misapply it. At some agencies this practice still exists, although it gives the Indians no education in the use of money, is irritating to them, and tends to decrease responsibility and increase the pauper attitude.

The typical Indian, however, has not yet advanced to the point where he has the knowledge of money and values, and of business methods that will permit him to control his own property without aid, advice, and some restrictions; nor is he ready to work consistently and regularly at more or less routine labor.

17. Extracts from the Wheeler-Howard Act (Indian Reorganization Act), June 18, 1934

Be it enacted . . . That hereafter no land of any Indian reservation, created or set apart by treaty or agreement with the Indians, Act of Congress, Executive order, purchase, or otherwise, shall be allotted in severalty to any Indian.

Sec. 2. The existing periods of trust placed upon any Indian lands and any restriction on alienation thereof are hereby extended and continued until otherwise directed by Congress.

Sec. 3. The Secretary of the Interior, if he shall find it to be in the public interest, is hereby authorized to restore to tribal ownership the remaining surplus lands of any Indian reservation heretofore opened, or authorized to be opened, to sale, or any other form of disposal by Presidential proclamation, or by any of the public land laws of the United States: *Provided, however,* That valid rights or claims of any persons to any lands so withdrawn existing on the date of the withdrawal shall not be affected by this Act . . . .

Sec. 4. Except as herein provided, no sale, devise, gift, exchange or other transfer of restricted Indian lands or of shares in the assets of any Indian tribe or corporation organized hereunder, shall be made or approved: *Provided, however,* That such lands or interests may, with the approval of the Secretary of the Interior, be sold, devised, or otherwise transferred to the Indian tribe in which the lands or shares are located or from which the shares were derived or to a successor corporation; and in all instances such lands or interests shall descend or be devised, in accordance with the then existing laws of the State, or Federal laws where applicable, in which said lands are located or in which the subject matter of the corporation is located, to any member of such tribe or of such corporation or any heirs of such member: Provided further, That the Secretary of the Interior may authorize voluntary exchanges of lands of equal value and the voluntary exchange of shares of equal value whenever such exchange, in his judgment, is expedient and beneficial for or compatible with the proper consolidation of Indian lands and for the benefit of cooperative organizations . . . .

Sec. 16. Any Indian tribe, or tribes, residing on the same reservation, shall have the right to organize for its common welfare, and may adopt an appropriate constitution and bylaws, which shall become effective when ratified by a majority vote of the adult members of the tribe, or of the adult Indians residing on such reservation, as the case may be, at a special election authorized and called by the Secretary of the Interior under such rules and regulations as he may prescribe. Such constitution and bylaws when ratified as aforesaid and approved by the Secretary of the Interior shall be revocable by an election open to the same voters and conducted in the same manner as hereinabove provided. Amendments to the constitution and bylaws may be ratified and approved by the Secretary in the same manner as the original constitution and bylaws.

In addition to all powers vested in any Indian tribe or tribal council by existing law, the constitution adopted by said tribe shall also vest in such tribe or its tribal council the following rights and powers: To employ legal counsel, the choice of counsel and fixing of fees to be subject to the approval of the Secretary of the Interior; to prevent the sale, disposition, lease, or encumbrance of tribal lands, interests in lands, or other tribal assets without the consent of the tribe; and to negotiate with the Federal, State, and local Governments. The Secretary of the Interior shall advise such tribe or its tribal council of all appropriation estimates of Federal projects for the benefit of the tribe prior to the submission of such estimates to the Bureau of the Budget and the Congress.

18. Extracts from the Social Security Act, August 14, 1935

An Act

To provide for the general welfare by establishing a system of Federal old-age benefits, and by enabling the several States to make more adequate provision for aged persons, blind persons, dependent and crippled children, maternal and child welfare, public health, and the administration of their unemployment compensation laws; to establish a Social Security Board; to raise revenue; and for other purposes. . . .

Title II—Federal Old-age Benefits Old-age Reserve Account

Section 201. (a) There is hereby created an account in the treasury of the United States to be known as the "Old-Age Reserve Account" herinafter in this title called the "Account." There is hereby authorized to be appropriated to the Account for each fiscal year, beginning with the fiscal year ending June 30, 1937, an amount sufficient as an

annual premium to provide for the payments required under this title, such amount to be determined on a reserve basis in accordance with accepted actuarial principles, and based upon such tables of mortality as the Secretary of the Treasury shall from time to time adopt, and upon an interest rate of 3 per centum per annum compounded annually. The Secretary of the Treasury shall submit annually to the Bureau of the Budget an estimate of the appropriations to be made to the Account . . . .

Old-age Benefit Payments

Sec. 202. (a) Every qualified individual (as defined in section 210) shall be entitled to receive, with respect to the period beginning on the date he attains the age of sixty-five, or on January 1, 1942, whichever is the later, and ending on the date of his death, an old-age benefit (payable as nearly as practicable in equal monthly installments) as follows:

(1) If the total wages (as defined in section 210) determined by the Board to have been paid to him, with respect to employment (as defined in section 210) after December 31, 1936, and before he attained the age of sixty-five, were not more than $3,000, the old-age benefit shall be at a monthly rate of one-half of 1 per centum of such total wages;

(2) If such total wages were more than $3,000, the old-age benefit shall be at a monthly rate equal to the sum of the following:

(A) One-half of 1 per centum of $3,000; plus

(B) One-twelfth of 1 per centum of the amount by which such total wages exceeded $3,000 and did not exceed $45,000; plus

(C) One-twenty-fourth of 1 per centum of the amount by which such total wages exceeded $45,000.

(b) In no case shall the monthly rate compounded under subsection (a) exceed $85.

(c) If the Board finds at any time that more or less than the correct amount has theretofore been paid to any individual under this section, then, under regulations made by the Board, proper adjustments shall be made in connection with subsequent payments under this section to the same individual.

(d) Whenever the Board finds that any qualified individual has received wages with respect to regular employment after he attained the age of sixty-five, the old-age benefit payable to such individual shall be reduced, for each calendar month in any part of which such regular employment occurred, by an amount equal to one month's benefit. Such reduction shall be made, under regulations prescribed by the Board, by deductions from one or more payments of old-age benefit to such individual.

Payments Upon Death

Sec. 203. (a) If any individual dies before attaining the age of sixty-five, there shall be paid to his estate an amount equal to 3 ½ per centum of the total wages determined by the Board to have been paid him, with respect to employment after December 31, 1936.

(b) If the Board finds that the correct amount of the old-age benefit payable to a qualified individual during his life under section 202 was less than 3 ½ per centum of the total wages by which such old-age benefit was measurable, then there shall be paid to his estate a sum equal to the amount, if any, by which such 3 ½ per centum exceeds the amount (whether more or less than the correct amount) paid to him during his life as old-age benefit.

(c) If the Board finds that the total amount paid to a qualified individual under an old-age benefit during his life was less than the correct amount to which he was entitled under section 202, and that the correct amount of such old-age benefit was 3 ½ per centum or more of the total wages by which such old-age benefit was measurable, then there shall be paid to his estate a sum equal to the amount, if any, by which the correct amount of the old-age benefit exceeds the amount which was paid to him during his life.

Payments to Aged Individuals Not Qualified for Benefits

Sec. 204. (a) There shall be paid in a lump sum to any individual who, upon attaining the age of sixty-five, is not a qualified individual, an amount equal to 3 ½ per centum of the total wages determined by the Board to have been paid to him, with respect to employment after December 31, 1936, and before he attained the age of sixty-five.

(b) After any individual becomes entitled to any payment under subsection (a), no other payment shall be made under this title in any manner measured by wages paid to him, except that any part of any payment under subsection (a) which is not paid to him before his death shall be paid to his estate . . . .

Definitions

Sec. 210. When used in this title—

(a) The term "wages" means all remuneration for employment, including the cash value of all remuneration paid in any medium other than cash; except that such term shall not include that part of the remuneration which, after remuneration equal to $3,000 has been paid to an individual by an employer with respect to employment during any calendar year, is paid to such individual by such employer with respect to employment during such calendar year.

(b) The term "employment" means any service, of whatever nature, performed within the United States by an employee for his employer, except—

(1) Agricultural labor;
(2) Domestic service in a private home;
(3) Casual labor not in the course of the employer's trade or business;
(4) Service performed as an officer or member of the crew of a vessel documented under the laws of the United States or of any foreign country;
(5) Service performed in the employ of the United States Government or of an instrumentality of the United States;
(6) Service performed in the employ of a State, a political subdivision thereof, or an instrumentality of one or more States or political subdivisions;
(7) Service performed in the employ of a corporation, community chest, fund, or foundation, organized and operated exclusively for religious, charitable, scientific, literary, or educational purposes, or for the prevention of cruelty to children or animals, no part of the net earnings of which inures to the benefit of any private shareholder or individual.

(c) The term "qualified individual" means any individual with respect to whom it appears to the satisfaction of the Board that—

(1) He is at least sixty-five years of age; and
(2) The total amount of wages paid to him, with respect to employment after December 31, 1936, and before he attained the age of sixty-five, was not less than $2,000; and
(3) Wages were paid to him, with respect to employment after December 31, 1936, and before he attained the age of sixty-five, each day being in a different calendar year . . . .

Title IV—Grants to States for Aid to Dependent Children Appropriation

Section 401. For the purpose of enabling each State to furnish financial assistance, as far as practicable under the conditions in such State, to needy dependent children, there is hereby authorized to be appropriated for the fiscal year ending June 30, 1936, the sum of $24,750,000, and there is hereby authorized to be appropriated for each fiscal year thereafter a sum sufficient to carry out the purposes of this title. The sums made available under this section shall be used for making payments to States which have submitted, and had approved by the Board, State plans for aid to dependent children.

State Plans for Aid to Dependent Children

Sec. 402. (a) A State plan for aid to dependent children must (1) provide that it shall be in effect in all political subdivisions of the State, and, if administered by them, be mandatory upon them; (2) provide for financial participation by the State; (3) either provide for the establishment or designation of a single State agency to supervise the administration of the plan; (4) provide for granting to any individual, whose claim with respect to aid to a dependent child is denied, an opportunity for a fair hearing before such State agency; (5) provide such methods of administration (other than those relating to selection, tenure of office, and compensation of personnel) as are found by the Board to be necessary for the efficient operation of the plan; and (6) provide that the State agency will make such reports, in such form and containing such information, as the Board may from time to time require, and comply with such provisions as the Board may from time to time find necessary to assure the correctness and verification of such reports.

(b) The Board shall approve any plan which fulfills the conditions specified in subsection (a), except that it shall not approve any plan which imposes as a condition of eligibility for aid to dependent children, a residence requirement which denies aid with respect to any child residing in the State (1) who has resided in the State for one year immediately preceding the application for such aid, or (2) who was born within the State within one year immediately preceding the application, if its mother has resided in the State for one year immediately preceding the birth . . . .

Definitions

Sec. 406. When used in this Title—
(a) The term "dependent child" means a child under the age of sixteen who has been deprived of parental support or care by reason of the death, continued absence from the home, or physical or mental incapacity of a parent, and who is living with his father, mother, grandfather, grandmother, brother, sister, stepfather,

stepmother, uncle, or aunt, in a place of residence maintained by one or more of such relatives in his or their own home;
(b) The term "aid to dependent children" means money payments with respect to a dependent child or dependent children.

19. Extracts from the Economic Opportunity Act, August 20, 1964

AN ACT
To mobilize the human and financial resources of the Nation to combat poverty in the United States. . . .

Findings and Declaration of Purpose

Sec. 2. Although the economic well-being and prosperity of the United States have progressed to a level surpassing any achieved in world history, and although these benefits are widely shared throughout the Nation, poverty continues to be the lot of a substantial number of our people. The United States can achieve its full economic and social potential as a nation only if every individual has the opportunity to contribute to the full extent of his capabilities and to participate in the workings of our society. It is, therefore, the policy of the United States to eliminate the paradox of poverty in the midst of plenty in this Nation by opening to everyone the opportunity for education and training, the opportunity to work, and the opportunity to live in decency and dignity. It is the purpose of this Act to strengthen, supplement, and coordinate efforts in furtherance of this policy.

Title I—Youth Programs
Part A—Job Corps Statement of Purpose

Sec. 101. The purpose of this part is to prepare for the responsibilities of citizenship and to increase the employability of young men and young women aged sixteen through twenty-one by providing them in rural and urban residential centers with education, vocational training, useful work experience, including work directed toward the conservation of natural resources, and other appropriate activities . . . .

Part B—Work-Training Programs Statement of Purpose

Sec 111. The purpose of this part is to provide useful work experience opportunities for unemployed young men and young women, through participation in State and community work-training programs, so that their employability may be increased or their education resumed or continued and so that public agencies and private nonprofit organizations (other than political parties) will be enabled to carry out programs which will permit or contribute to an undertaking or service in the public interest that would not otherwise be provided, or will contribute to the conservation and development of natural resources and recreational areas . . . .

Part C—Work-Study Programs Statement of Purpose

Sec. 121. The purpose of this part is to stimulate and promote the part-time employment of students in institutions of higher education who are from low-income families and are in need of the earnings from such employment to pursue courses of study at such institutions . . . .

Title II—Urban and Rural Community Action Programs

Part A—General Community Action Programs Statement of Purpose

Sec. 201. The purpose of this part is to provide stimulation and incentive for urban and rural communities to mobilize their resources to combat poverty through community action programs.

Community Action Programs

Sec. 202. (a) The term "community action program" means a program—

(1) which mobilizes and utilizes resources, public or private, of any urban or rural, or combined urban and rural, geographical area (referred to in this part as a "community"), including but not limited to a State, metropolitan area, county, city, town, multicity unit, or multicounty unit in an attack on poverty;

(2) which provides services, assistance, and other activities of sufficient scope and size to give promise of progress toward elimination of poverty or a cause or causes of poverty through developing employment opportunities, improving human performance, motivation, and productivity, or bettering the conditions under which people live, learn, and work;

(3) which is developed, conducted, and administered with the maximum feasible participation of residents of the areas and members of the groups served; and

(4) which is conducted, administered, or coordinated by a public or private nonprofit agency (other than a political party), or a combination thereof . . . .

Title III—Special Programs to Combat Poverty in Rural Area Statement of Purpose

Sec. 301. It is the purpose of this title to meet some of the special problems of rural poverty and thereby to raise and maintain the income and living standards of low-income rural families and migrant agricultural employees and their families.

Part A—Authority to Make Grants and Loans

Sec. 302. (a) The Director is authorized to make—

(1) loans having a maximum maturity of 15 years and in amounts not exceeding $2,500 in the aggregate to any low income rural family where, in the judgment of the Director, such loans have a reasonable possibility of affecting a permanent increase in the income of such families by assisting or permitting them to—

(A) acquire or improve real estate or reduce encumbrances or erect improvements thereon,

(B) operate or improve the operation of farms not larger than family sized, including but not limited to the purchase of feed, seed, fertilizer, livestock, poultry, and equipment, or

(C) participate in cooperative associations; and/or to finance nonagricultural enterprises which will enable such families to supplement their income.

(b) Loans under this section shall be made only if the family is not qualified to obtain such funds by loan or under other Federal programs . . . .

Title V—Work Experience Programs . . . . Volunteers in Service to America

Sec. 603. (a) The Director is authorized to recruit, select, train, and—

(1) upon request of State or local agencies or private nonprofit organizations, refer volunteers to perform duties in furtherance of programs combating poverty at a State or local level; and

(2) in cooperation with other Federal, State, or local agencies involved, assign volunteers to work (A) in meeting the health, education, welfare, or related needs of Indians living on reservations, of migratory workers and their families, or of residents of the District of Columbia, the Commonwealth of Puerto Rico, Guam, American Samoa, the Virgin Islands, or the Trust Territory of the Pacific Islands; (B) in the care and rehabilitation of the mentally ill or mentally retarded under treatment at nonprofit mental health or mental retardation facilities assisted in their construction or operation by Federal funds;

and (C) in furtherance of programs or activities authorized or supported under title I or II of this Act.

20. U.S. National Advisory Commission on Rural Poverty, Statement of Beliefs, 1967

The National Advisory Commission on Rural Poverty has made its recommendations on the basis of specific beliefs to which all members of the Commission subscribe. These beliefs are as follows:

1. The United States today has the economic and technical means to generate adequate food, clothing, shelter, health services, and education to every citizen of the Nation.
2. Involuntary tragedy is a tragedy under any circumstances and poverty in the midst of plenty is both a tragedy and a social evil.
3. The rural poor are not a faceless mass. They are individual human beings. All programs designed to eliminate poverty must therefore give paramount consideration to the rights and dignity of the individual.
4. Every citizen of the United States must have equal access to opportunities for economic and social advancement without discrimination because of race, religion, national origin, or place of residence.
5. Because rural Americans have been denied a fair share of America's opportunities and benefits they have migrated by the millions to the cities in search of jobs and places to live. This migration is continuing. It is therefore impossible to obliterate urban poverty without removing its rural causes. Accordingly, both reason and justice compel the allotment of a more equitable share of our national resources for improving the conditions of rural life.
6. All levels of government—local, State, and Federal—must accept responsibility for public measures to eliminate poverty and must be aware of the effect that any of their activities have on the poor.
7. Inasmuch as the consent of the governed is a basic tenet of American government, the rural poor must be given a voice in the planning and administration of public programs designed to eliminate poverty.
8. We can no longer evade the fact that far too high a proportion of our rural population is unemployed and that the national policy of full employment is not

effective. We believe it to be an obligation of private enterprise and of government working together to provide employment at adequate wages for all persons able and willing to work.
9. The cost to the Nation of rural poverty is much too high to permit its continuance. We believe the time for action against rural poverty has arrived.

21. Extracts from the Personal Responsibility and Work Opportunity Reconciliation Act, 1996

Title I—Block Grants for Temporary Assistance for Needy Families

Sec. 101. Findings

The Congress makes the following findings:

(1) Marriage is the foundation of a successful society.
(2) Marriage is an essential institution of a successful society which promotes the interests of children.
(3) Promotion of responsible fatherhood and motherhood is integral to successful child rearing and the well-being of children.
(4) In 1992, only 54 percent of single-parent families with children had a child support order established and, of that 54 percent, only about one-half received the full amount due. Of the cases enforced through the public child support enforcement system, only 18 percent of the caseload has a collection.
(5) The number of individuals receiving aid to families with dependent children (in this section referred to as "AFDC") has more than tripled since 1965. More than two-thirds of these recipients are children. Eighty-nine percent of children receiving AFDC benefits now live in homes in which no father is present.
   (A) (i) The average monthly number of children receiving AFDC benefits—
      (I) was 3,300,000 in 1965;
      (II) was 6,200,000 in 1970;
      (III) was 7,400,000 in 1980; and
      (IV) was 9,300,000 in 1992.
   (ii) While the number of children receiving AFDC benefits increased nearly threefold between 1965 and 1992, the total number of children in the United States aged 0 to 18 has declined by 5.5 percent.

(B) The Department of Health and Human Services has estimated that 12,000,000 children will receive AFDC benefits within 10 years.

(C) The increase in the number of children receiving public assistance is closely related to the increase in births to unmarried women. Between 1970 and 1991, the percentage of live births to unmarried women increased nearly threefold, from 10.7 percent to 29.5 percent.

(6) The increase in out-of-wedlock pregnancies and births is well documented as follows:

(A) It is estimated that the rate of nonmarital teen pregnancy rose 23 percent from 54 pregnancies per 1,000 unmarried teenagers in 1976 to 66.7 pregnancies in 1991. The overall rate of nonmarital pregnancy rose 14 percent from 90.8 pregnancies per 1,000 unmarried women in 1980 to 103 in both 1991 and 1992. In contrast, the overall pregnancy rate for married couples decreased 7.3 percent between 1980 and 1991, from 126.9 pregnancies per 1,000 married women to 117.6 pregnancies in 1991.

(B) The total of all out-of-wedlock births between 1970 and 1991 has risen from 10.7 percent to 29.5 percent and if the current trend continues, 50 percent of all births by the year 2015 will be out-of-wedlock.

(7) An effective strategy to combat teenage pregnancy must address the issue of male responsibility, including statutory rape culpability and prevention. The increase of teenage pregnancies among the youngest girls is particularly severe and is linked to predatory sexual practices by men who are significantly older.

(A) It is estimated that in the late 1980's, the rate for girls age 14 and under giving birth increased 26 percent.

(B) Data indicates that at least half of the children born to teenage mothers are fathered by adult men. Available data suggests that almost 70 percent of births to teenage girls are fathered by men over age 20.

(C) Surveys of teen mothers have revealed that a majority of such mothers have histories of sexual and physical abuse, primarily with older adult men.

(8) The negative consequences of an out-of-wedlock birth on the mother, the child, the family, and society are well documented as follows:

(A) Young women 17 and under who give birth outside of marriage are more likely to go on public assistance and to spend more years on welfare once enrolled. These combined effects of "younger and longer" increase total AFDC costs per household by 25 percent to 30 percent for 17-year-olds.

(B) Children born out-of-wedlock have a substantially higher risk of being born at a very low or moderately low birth weight.

(C) Children born out-of-wedlock are more likely to experience low verbal cognitive attainment, as well as more child abuse, and neglect.

(D) Children born out-of-wedlock were more likely to have low cognitive scores, lower educational aspirations, and a greater likelihood of becoming teenage parents themselves.

(E) Being born out-of-wedlock significantly reduces the chances of the child growing up to have an intact marriage.

(F) Children born out-of-wedlock are 3 times more likely to be on welfare when they grow up.

(9) Currently 35 percent of children in single-parent homes were born out-of-wedlock, nearly the same percentage as that of children in single-parent homes whose parents are divorced (37 percent). While many parents find themselves, through divorce or tragic circumstances beyond their control, facing the difficult task of raising children alone, nevertheless, the negative consequences of raising children in single-parent homes are well documented as follows:

(A) Only 9 percent of married-couple families with children under 18 years of age have income below the national poverty level. In contrast, 46 percent of female-headed households with children under 18 years of age are below the national poverty level.

(B) Among single-parent families, nearly 1/2 of the mothers who never married received AFDC while only 1/5 of divorced mothers received AFDC.

(C) Children born into families receiving welfare assistance are 3 times more likely to be on welfare when they reach adulthood than children not born into families receiving welfare.

(D) Mothers under 20 years of age are at the greatest risk of bearing low birth weight babies.

(E) The younger the single-parent mother, the less likely she is to finish high school.

(F) Young women who have children before finishing high school are more likely to receive welfare assistance for a longer period of time.

(G) Between 1985 and 1990, the public cost of births to teenage mothers under the aid to families with dependent children program, the food stamp program, and the medicaid program has been estimated at $120,000,000,000.

(H) The absence of a father in the life of a child has a negative effect on school performance and peer adjustment.

(I) Children of teenage single mothers have lower cognitive scores, lower educational aspirations, and a greater likelihood of becoming teenage parents themselves.

(J) Children of single-parent homes are 3 times more likely to fail and repeat a year in grade school than are children from intact 2-parent families.

(K) Children from single-parent homes are almost 4 times more likely to be expelled or suspended from school.

(L) Neighborhoods with larger percentages of youth aged 12 through 20 and areas with higher percentages of single-parent households have higher rates of violent crime.

(M) Of those youth held for criminal offenses within the State juvenile justice system, only 29.8 percent lived primarily in a home with both parents. In contrast to these incarcerated youth, 73.9 percent of the 62,800,000 children in the nation's resident population were living with both parents.

(10) Therefore, in light of this demonstration of the crisis in our Nation, it is the sense of the Congress that prevention of out-of-wedlock pregnancy and reduction in out-of-wedlock birth are very important Government interests and the policy contained in Part A of title IV of the Social Security Act (as amended by section 103(a) of this Act) is amended to address the crisis . . . .

Part A—Block Grants to States for Temporary Assistance for Needy Families
401 Sec. 401. PURPOSE

(a) In General.—The purpose of this part is to increase the flexibility of States in operating a program designed to—

(1) provide assistance to needy families so that children may be cared for in their own homes or in the homes of relatives;

(2) end the dependence of needy parents on government benefits by promoting job preparation, work, and marriage;

(3) prevent and reduce the incidence of out-of-wedlock pregnancies and establish annual numerical goals for preventing and reducing the incidence of these pregnancies; and

(4) encourage the formation and maintenance of two-parent families.

(b) No Individual Entitlement.—This part shall not be interpreted to entitle any individual or family to assistance under any State program funded under this part.

Appendix B
Biographies of Major Personalities

Abernathy, Ralph David (1926–1990) *civil rights leader, clergyman*

Abernathy served in the army in Europe in World War II and was ordained a Baptist minister in 1948. He attended Alabama State College on the G.I. bill and received a degree in mathematics in 1950. In 1951, he received a master of arts degree in sociology from Atlanta University and became pastor of the First Baptist Church in Montgomery, Alabama. He and the Reverend Martin Luther King, Jr., were founders of the Montgomery Improvement Association in 1955 and the Southern Christian Leadership Conference (SCLC) in 1957. Both organizations worked for nonviolent social change. Abernathy was King's closest associate in the civil rights movement and often worked behind the scenes to organize demonstrations. In 1961, he became pastor of the West Hunter Street Baptist Church in Atlanta, Georgia. He assumed the presidency of the SCLC upon King's death in 1968 and held that position until 1977. He continued work that King had begun, marching with striking sanitation workers in Memphis, Tennessee, on April 8, 1968, and leading the Poor People's Campaign in Washington, D.C., in May 1969. His controversial autobiography *And the Walls Came Tumbling Down* was published in 1989.

Addams, Jane (1860–1935) *social reformer, pacifist, Nobel laureate*

Addams was born in Illinois and educated at the Rockford Female Seminary (now Rockford College), graduating in 1881. While in Europe in 1887 and 1888, she was inspired by the social reform movement. In 1889 she and her college classmate Ellen Starr founded Hull-House, a social welfare center, or settlement house, in a poor immigrant neighborhood of Chicago. The Hull-House staff was active in child labor reform and education. The settlement provided the community with a day nursery and a gymnasium, among other services. Addams became chairperson of the Woman's Peace Party in 1915. That same year she also chaired the International Congress of Women at the Hague, Netherlands. She traveled in Europe at the start of World War I, urging peace through mediation. Her pacifism after U.S. entry into the war, however, earned her criticism at home. In 1931, she shared the Nobel Prize in peace with American educator Nicholas Murray Butler. Her 10 books include *Democracy and Social Ethics (1902), The Spirit of Youth and the City Streets (1909),* and *Twenty Years at Hull-House (1910).*

Brace, Charles Loring (1826–1890) *social reformer, child-welfare advocate*

Brace was born in Connecticut and educated at Yale College. A devout Christian, he entered Yale Divinity School in 1847 but soon decided he was unsuited for the traditional ministry. In 1848, he moved to New York City to continue his studies and work among the poor. In January 1853, Brace became the first secretary of the Children's Aid Society, a position he held for the rest of his life. He worked unceasingly to help New York's poor children and to find homes for destitute children in rural communities. A fervent abolitionist, Brace wrote many newspaper articles during the Civil War advocating emancipation. His books include *The Dangerous Classes of New York (1872) and Gesta Christi; or a History of Humane Progress under Christianity (1882),* a work influenced by the ideas of Charles Darwin.

Bush, George Herbert Walker (1924–) *41st president of the United States*

Bush was born in Milton, Massachusetts, and raised in Greenwich, Connecticut. He graduated from Phillips Academy in Andover, Massachusetts, on his 18th birthday, June 12, 1942. He enlisted in the navy on the same day, having decided to postpone college to serve in World War II. In June 1943, before he turned 19, Bush received his wings and an officer's commission. At the time he was the youngest pilot in the navy. Between August 1942 and September 1945 Bush flew 58 combat missions in the South Pacific. He was awarded the Distinguished Flying Cross and three Air Medals. After the war he enrolled in Yale University and in 1948 earned a degree in economics. He and his wife, Barbara, moved to Texas, where he worked for Dresser Industries, an oil-field supply company. In 1951 Bush was a founder of the Bush-Overby Oil Development Company. In 1953 he founded the Zapata Petroleum Corporation, and in 1954 he was a founder and president of Zapata Off-Shore, which pioneered off-shore oil drilling. In 1964 Bush became chairman of the Republican Party of Harris County, Texas, and ran unsuccessfully for the U.S. Senate. He had better luck in 1966, when he was elected to the U.S. House of Representatives. He was reelected in 1968 and in 1970 again ran unsuccessfully for the Senate. In the 1970s Presidents Richard M. Nixon and Gerald R. Ford appointed Bush to several positions of responsibility. In 1971 he was named U.S. ambassador to the United Nations. In 1973 he became chairman of the Republican National Committee. In 1974, when the United States was reestablishing ties with the People's Republic of China, he went to Beijing as chief of the U.S. Liaison Office. In 1976 he was appointed director of the Central Intelligence Agency. In 1980 Bush was elected vice president of the United States under President Ronald Reagan; the Reagan-Bush ticket was reelected in 1984. In 1988 Bush was elected president of the United States. He presided over Operation Desert Storm, the 1990 military campaign to remove Iraqi invaders from Kuwait. Bush lost his 1992 bid for reelection to Bill Clinton. He and Barbara Bush reside in Houston, Texas.

Bush, George Walker (1946–) *43rd president of the United States*

Bush was born in New Haven, Connecticut, and grew up in Midland and Houston, Texas, where his father, future president George H. W. Bush, was in the oil business. In 1968 he graduated from Yale University with a degree in history. He then served in the Texas Air National Guard, piloting an F-120 fighter jet. After receiving a master's degree in business administration from Harvard Business School in 1975, Bush returned to Texas and started his own oil business. In 1977 he ran unsuccessfully for the U.S. Congress as a Republican. In 1985, after his business was acquired by a Dallas firm, Bush became a paid adviser to his father's 1988 presidential campaign. The following year he assembled the investors who purchased the Texas Rangers baseball franchise. Bush was elected governor of Texas in 1994 and again in 1998, the first Texas governor elected to two consecutive four-year terms. In November 2000 he ran for president of the United States against Democrat Al Gore. The election, one of the closest in the nation's history, was the first to be decided in the U.S. Supreme Court. It was ultimately determined that Bush won, and he was sworn in to office on January 20, 2001. He achieved an easy victory in his bid for reelection in 2004. Bush has presided over military actions in Afghanistan and Iraq. His social agenda, labeled "compassionate conservatism," has stressed the need for private aid to the poor and has included a tax cut to stimulate the economy, which critics say favors the wealthy.

Carey, Mathew (1760–1839) *publisher, writer, bookseller*

Carey was born in Ireland, the son of a prosperous baker, and apprenticed at age 15 to a printer and bookseller. In 1777 he published his first writing, an argument against dueling. In 1779, after publishing a pamphlet critical of British rule in Ireland, he sailed for France to escape capture and prosecution. He was employed in the Paris printing office of Benjamin Franklin, then U.S. minister to France, before returning to Ireland after a year's absence. In 1783 he founded the *Volunteer's Journal*, a radical paper. The publication of an article attacking Parliament led to his arrest and imprisonment in London. Carey was released when Parliament was dissolved and then immigrated to the United States, reaching Philadelphia in 1784. In 1785, he used a monetary gift from the marquis de Lafayette to establish the *Pennsylvania Herald*. He published *American Museum*, a leading magazine of the late 18th century, from 1787 until 1792, and then devoted himself to printing and selling books. He wrote and published a number of controversial pamphlets and essays on economics and politics, most notably *The Olive Branch* (1814), an effort to unite rival factions during the War of 1812. He was a member of the Committee of Health during the 1793 yellow-fever epidemic in Philadelphia.

Celler, Emanuel (1888–1981) *U.S. representative from New York, immigrants' advocate*

Celler was born in Brooklyn, New York, on May 6, 1888. His father, Henry Celler, brewed and sold whiskey. After the whiskey business failed, Henry Celler sold wine door to door. Emanuel Celler graduated from public high school, and while he was enrolled in Columbia College (now Columbia University) his parents died within five months of each other. Celler took over the household and his father's wine route while continuing his studies. He graduated from Columbia in 1910 and Columbia Law School in 1912. Celler was admitted to the bar in 1912 and began practicing law in New York City. Many of his clients were immigrants who faced deportation for minor violations of the immigration law. During World War I Celler was an appeal agent for his local draft board. With the restoration of peace he built a highly successful law practice, organized two banks, and served on the boards of two others. He ran for Congress in 1922, becoming the first Democrat elected from his district. He was a member of the 68th and 24 succeeding Congresses, serving 49 years and 10 months, the second longest term in congressional history. He was chairman of the House Judiciary Committee in the 81st, 82nd, and 84th through 92nd Congresses. As a member of Congress Celler made it his calling to liberalize immigration laws and eliminate national origin as a basis for immigration. In 1948 his efforts resulted in passage of a bill permitting 339,000 displaced persons from Europe, many of them Jews, to enter the United States. He also supported a bill signed into law by President Lyndon B. Johnson in 1965 that did away with national origin as a basis for exclusion. Celler lost his bid for reelection in 1972 and was a member of the Commission on Revision of the Federal Appellate Court System from 1973 through 1975. He then resumed the practice of law and resided in Brooklyn, where he died on January 15, 1981. Celler's autobiography, *You Never Leave Brooklyn,* was published in 1953.

Channing, William Ellery (1780–1842) *Unitarian clergyman, writer*

Channing was born in Newport, Rhode Island, the second of nine children. He was 13 years old when his father died, leaving the family in financial hardship. Channing nevertheless continued his education and attended Harvard. During his senior year he decided on a career in the ministry. After graduating in 1798 he spent two years in Richmond, Virginia, as a private tutor. He returned to New England and in 1803, at age 23, was ordained minister of the Federal Street Congregational Church in Boston. He was to remain in this post for life. Among the most liberal Congregational ministers, Channing rejected Calvinist teachings. In 1819, speaking in Baltimore at the ordination of historian Jared Sparks, he delivered an important speech in the history of religion in the United States, in which he outlined the doctrines of Unitarianism. These include rejection of the concept of the Trinity, belief in human goodness, and subjection of theology to reason. In 1820, Channing organized the Berry Street Council of Ministers, which in 1825 formed the American Unitarian Association. An influential thinker and writer, Channing denounced slavery and war, and he wrote insightfully on social issues.

Chavez, Cesar Estrada (1927–1993) *leader of the United Farm Workers (UFW)*

Chavez was born in Yuma, Arizona, near his family's farm. The Chavezes were among the millions of American farmers who lost their farms during the Great Depression, and they migrated to California in search of work. Chavez was a migrant farm worker both before and after his naval service in the Pacific in the aftermath of World War II. Throughout the 1950s he worked with the Community Service Organization (CSO), a Latino civil rights group, first as a volunteer and later as a paid staff member, leading voter-registration drives and assisting Mexican farm laborers with immigration problems. In 1958 Chavez became general director of the CSO. He resigned from that position in 1962 to found the National Farm Workers Association and recruited 1,700 families by 1965. When an American Federation of Labor–Congress of Industrial Organizations (AFL-CIO)–affiliated farmworkers' union went on strike in September 1965, NFWA voted to join it. The unions combined to form the United Farm Workers (UFW), with Chavez as its leader. Later in 1965 Chavez organized a national boycott of California table grapes to combat the grape growers' practice of importing Mexican laborers and paying them a lower wage than union members were demanding. During the five years of the boycott U.S. grape consumption declined 20 percent. On April 1, 1970, two major grape producers signed a contract with the UFW granting a pay increase and health insurance to their workers. Other growers followed their example. In 1968 Chavez fasted for 25 days to affirm his commitment to nonviolent protest. He fasted again in 1972, and in 1988 he fasted for 36 days to draw attention to the problem of pesticide exposure among farm workers and their families. On March 31, 1994,

Chaves was posthumously awarded the Medal of Freedom, the nation's highest civilian honor.

Clark, Joseph Sill (1901–1990) *U.S. senator, mayor of Philadelphia*

Clark, whose father was an attorney, was born in Philadelphia. He had a private-school education and in 1919 graduated first in his class from the Middlesex School in Concord, Massachusetts. He graduated with honors from Harvard University in 1923 and entered the University of Pennsylvania Law School, where he edited the law review. After receiving his law degree in 1926 and being admitted to the bar, he joined his father's law firm. Clark had been born into a Republican family, but in 1928 he transferred his allegiance to the Democrats and supported Alfred E. Smith for president. With political ambitions of his own, he ran unsuccessfully for the Philadelphia City Council in 1933. The following year, he left his father's firm, which had lost many clients as a result of the Great Depression, to be deputy attorney general of Pennsylvania. In that position, he handled court cases resulting from the many bank closings that occurred in the early years of the depression. Clark returned to private law practice in 1935. During World War II, from 1941 to 1945, he served in the Army Air Corps and attained the rank of colonel. He earned the Bronze Star for service in the India-China-Burma theater of operations. In 1950, Clark was elected city controller of Philadelphia, and in 1952, he was elected mayor. As mayor he created career opportunities in city government for African Americans and increased funding for schools and cultural institutions. Clark was elected to the U.S. Senate in 1956 and again in 1962. In 1967, he and Senator Robert F. Kennedy of New York toured poverty-stricken communities in the Mississippi Delta. Clark lost the 1968 senatorial election. In 1969, he served as president of Temple University. From 1969 through 1971, he was president of World Federalists, U.S.A., an organization that lobbied for political action. In retirement he lived in Philadelphia.

Clinton, Bill (William Jefferson Clinton) (1946–) *42nd president of the United States*

Clinton was born William Jefferson Blythe IV in Hope, Arkansas, three months after his father, a traveling salesman, died in an automobile accident. When he was four his mother, Virginia, who was a nurse, married Roger Clinton of Hot Springs, Arkansas. Bill grew up in Hot Springs and as a teenager adopted his stepfather's name.

As a high school junior he participated in Boys Nation, a citizenship program conducted by the American Legion in Washington, D.C., and shook hands with President John F. Kennedy in the White House Rose Garden. The experience inspired Clinton to pursue a career in public service. He returned to Washington to attend college and in 1968 received a bachelor's degree in international affairs from Georgetown University. The same year he won a Rhodes scholarship to study in England at Oxford University. Then, after earning a law degree from Yale University in 1973, he taught at the University of Arkansas. In 1976 he was elected state attorney general, and in 1978 he was elected governor of Arkansas. Clinton, a Democrat, lost the 1980 gubernatorial election, but he won the governorship again in 1982. He served in that post until 1992, when he defeated the incumbent, George H. W. Bush, and the third-party candidate, Ross Perot, in the presidential election. Clinton was fortunate to be president in a time of peace and economic expansion. In 1993 he signed the Family and Medical Leave Act, which required employers of 50 or more people to permit their workers to take unpaid leave for family or medical emergencies. In 1996 he signed the Personal Responsibility and Work Opportunity Act, which limited lifetime eligibility for public assistance to five years. Clinton was reelected in 1996, and in 1998 he was the second president in U.S. history to be impeached. He was tried in the Senate on grounds of perjury and obstruction of justice relating to his romantic involvement with a White House intern and was found not guilty of the charges against him.

Cloud, Henry Roe (Wonah'ilayhunken) (1884–1950) *American Indian educator and activist, Indian Service employee*

The boy named Wonah'ilayhunken by his people was born on the Winnebago Indian Reservation in Nebraska. He was renamed Henry Clarence Cloud at the government boarding school in Genoa, Nebraska, to which he was sent. He subsequently attended the Santee Normal Training School on the nearby Santee Indian Reservation, where he learned printing and blacksmithing. There he also converted to Christianity. He studied at the Mount Hermon School, a college-preparatory academy in Northfield, Massachusetts, and in 1906 he enrolled in Yale University. A year later he befriended Mary and Walter Roe, missionaries who worked among the Indians of Oklahoma, and he adopted the middle name Roe. In 1910 Cloud became the first Native American to graduate from Yale, receiving a degree in psychology and philosophy. He furthered his education at Oberlin College in Ohio, Auburn Theological Seminary in New York, and Yale. He earned a master's degree in anthropology from Yale in 1912 and was ordained a Presbyterian minister in 1913. He also had begun to speak on American Indian issues. He was an early and active member of the Society of American Indians, and he worked for the 1913 liberation of Apache prisoners held at Fort Sill, Oklahoma. He helped establish the Roe Indian Institute (later the American Indian Institute) in Wichita, Kansas, in 1915, and was its director for 16 years. At the time the only Indian-run high school in the country, the institute prepared young Native American men for college. In 1914 and 1915 Cloud also investigated the Indian school system for the Phelps-Stokes Fund, a philanthropic group dedicated to improving minority education. In 1923 Secretary of the Interior Hubert Work selected him to join the Committee of 100, which advised the executive branch of the government on Indian affairs. In 1926 he became a principal investigator with the Meriam Survey, conducted by the Institute for Government Research. The survey findings, published in 1928 as *The Problem of Indian Administration,* influenced federal policy on American Indians. In 1931 Cloud became the first Native American field representative for the government's Indian Service. Commissioner of Indian Affairs John Collier appointed him superintendent of the Haskell Indian School in Lawrence, Kansas, in 1933, but soon called on him to travel throughout the West and elicit Indian support for the Indian Reorganization Act of 1934. In 1935 Cloud received the Indian Achievement Award from the Indian Council Fire, and in 1939 he took on the duties of superintendent of the Umatilla Agency in Oregon. In 1948 he was assigned to the Bureau of Indian Affairs office near Portland, Oregon. Cloud died of a heart attack in Siletz, Oregon, on February 9, 1950. In 1997 Haskell Indian Nations University in Lawrence, Kansas, named a residence hall in his honor.

Collier, John (1884–1968) *social worker, commissioner of Indian affairs*
Collier was born in Atlanta, Georgia. His father, Charles A. Collier, was a banker and, from 1897 to 1899, mayor of Atlanta. A diligent student, John Collier was valedictorian of his high school class. In 1897 his mother died, and in 1900 his father committed suicide. In 1902 Collier enrolled in Columbia University. Rather than pursue a

degree, he took a variety of courses with an emphasis on social concerns. His first attempt at social work was with New York City's immigrant population. In 1905 he became executive director of the newly formed Associated Charities of Atlanta. In 1906 he studied at the College de France in Paris under the renowned psychologist Pierre M. F. Janet. In 1908, upon returning to New York, he joined the staff of the People's Institute, an organization that worked among immigrants on the Lower East Side of Manhattan. He directed the institute's National Training School for Community Workers beginning in 1915. Collier moved to California in 1919 to work for the state government. He resigned within a year, however, and went to Taos, New Mexico, where he studied the history and culture of the Pueblo Indians. In 1922 he mobilized opposition to the Bursum Bill, which would have opened 60,000 acres of Pueblo land to non-Indian settlement. After the bill was defeated he helped establish the American Indian Defense Association, an organization of whites dedicated to protecting Indians' rights, and served as executive secretary. He also edited the association's magazine, *American Indian Life.* In 1933 Secretary of the Interior Harold Ickes appointed Collier commissioner of Indian affairs. In that post Collier secured passage in June 1934 of the Indian Reorganization Act, which reversed government efforts to assimilate the Native population and encouraged Indian self-government and cultural and economic independence. The act was less successful than Collier had anticipated, and, facing growing opposition to his objectives, he resigned in January 1945. Five months later he became president of the Institute of Ethnic Affairs in Washington, D.C., and in 1945 he attended the first session of the United Nations General Assembly in London. In 1947 he also began teaching sociology and anthropology at the City College of New York. He retired in 1954 but fulfilled teaching commitments at Columbia University; the Merrill-Palmer Institute, a school of child and family development in Detroit; and Knox College in Galesburg, Illinois, before settling in Taos. His books include *Indians of the Americas* (1947) and *From Every Zenith* (1963).

Dickens, Charles John Huffam (1812–1870) *English novelist whose writings often dealt with social issues*
Born in Portsmouth, England, Dickens spent most of his childhood in London and Kent. He left school and went to work when his father was imprisoned for debt in 1824. Although he soon returned to school, he was to be largely self-educated. He later worked as a legal clerk and

a court reporter. In 1833, he published a series of literary sketches of London life under the pseudonym Boz. His first novel, *The Pickwick Papers* (1836–37), was initially published in monthly installments, as were subsequent works. *American Notes* (1842) describes his experiences on a lecture tour of the United States, including his visits to factories, schools, and prisons. Among Dickens's major works are *Oliver Twist* (1837–39), the autobiographical novel *David Copperfield* (1849–50), *A Tale of Two Cities* (1859), and *Great Expectations* (1860–61).

Dix, Dorothea Lynde (1802–1887) *reformer, advocate for the mentally ill*

Dix was born in rural Hampden, Maine. As a child she stitched together the religious tracts that her father, an itinerant preacher, sold. At 12 she went to Boston to live with her grandmother, who supervised her education, and at 19 she opened a girls' school in Boston. She served as its headmistress for 15 years, until poor health forced her to close the school. (Dix would battle tuberculosis for the rest of her life.) She traveled to Europe to recuperate and in England met reformers who were working to improve prison conditions and the care of the mentally ill. Dix returned to Boston in 1838. Her grandmother had died and left her an income sufficient to live independently. In 1841, after touring the Cambridge, Massachusetts, jail, where the insane were kept in the cellar in appalling conditions, Dix embarked on a crusade to improve the care of the mentally ill in her state. She visited prisons and almshouses and in 1843 presented her findings to the Massachusetts legislature. She also lobbied for laws mandating better treatment. Dix then inspected institutions in other states and made recommendations to lawmakers there. Hospitals for the mentally ill would be established in 20 states, the District of Columbia, and Canada thanks to her effort. In the 1850s her work also took her to Great Britain, France, Greece, Russia, and Japan. In 1861, one week after the attack on Fort Sumter, Dix offered her services to the Union army. She was placed in charge of all female nurses working in army hospitals. She served in that position without pay for the duration of the war. With the return of peace, Dix resumed her crusade for the mentally ill. When her health gave out in 1881, she moved into a private apartment at the New Jersey State Hospital and wrote letters advocating reform.

Douglass, Frederick (Frederick Augustus Washington Bailey) (1817–1895) *abolitionist, orator, writer*

Frederick Augustus Washington Bailey was born into slavery in Tuckahoe, Maryland, and separated from his mother in infancy. He learned to read while working as a house servant in Baltimore. He escaped from slavery in 1838 and made his way to New Bedford, Massachusetts, where he changed his name to Frederick Douglass. In 1841 he was asked to speak about his life in slavery at an abolitionist meeting; his eloquence impressed members of the Massachusetts Anti-Slavery Society, and he became an agent of the organization. Douglass published his autobiography, *Narrative of the Life of Frederick Douglass*, in 1845. Because he had identified his former owner in the book, he embarked on a two-year speaking tour of Great Britain and Ireland to escape recapture. Between 1847 and 1860 Douglass lived in Rochester, New York, and published the North Star, an abolitionist newspaper. He actively supported the Union in the Civil War by advising President Abraham Lincoln and helping to raise two African-American regiments, the Massachusetts 54th and 55th. In later life he served the District of Columbia as U.S. marshal (1877–81) and recorder of deeds (1881–86). From 1889 until 1891 he was U.S. minister to Haiti. A revised version of Douglass's autobiography, *Life and Times of Frederick Douglass*, was published in 1882.

Edelman, Marian Wright (1939–) *lawyer, civil rights activist, founder of the Children's Defense Fund*

A native of Bennettsville, South Carolina, Edelman graduated from Spelman College in Atlanta in 1960 and the Yale University Law School in 1963. She worked on voter-registration drives in Mississippi before becoming a staff attorney for the Legal Defense and Educational Fund of the National Association for the Advancement of Colored People (NAACP). In 1964 Edelman was the first African-American woman admitted to the Mississippi bar. She headed the NAACP Legal Defense and Education Fund office in Jackson, Mississippi, from 1964 to 1968. She then moved to the nation's capital, where she founded the Washington Research Project, forerunner of the Children's Defense Fund, the advocacy group for children's rights established in 1973 of which she is the head. From 1971 to 1973 Edelman directed the Center for Law and Education at Harvard University. In 1996 she formed a second children's rights organization, Stand for Children. Edelman's many awards include the Albert

Schweitzer Humanitarian Prize, a MacArthur Foundation Fellowship, and the Presidential Medal of Freedom.

Franklin, Benjamin (1706–1790) *statesman, scientist, writer, printer*

Franklin was the 15th of 17 children born to a Boston chandler and soap maker. He attended school for two years before going to work for his father at age 10. Two years later, he was apprenticed to his older half brother, James, a printer. For the next five years he educated himself by reading, and he submitted anonymous essays to James Franklin's newspaper, the *New England Courant*. In 1723, after a quarrel with his half brother, Franklin moved to Philadelphia, where he planned to establish his own print shop. He traveled to London to buy equipment but was unable to transact business because he lacked the necessary letters of credit. He worked for two years as a printer in London to earn enough to return to Philadelphia, and by 1730 he was publishing the *Pennsylvania Gazette*, which he had purchased. From 1732 to 1757, Franklin published *Poor Richard's Almanac*, which contained many of his aphorisms. In 1848, he gave up printing to devote himself to scientific experiments. He is credited with inventing a stove that reduced chimney smoke, bifocals, and the lightning rod. He also participated in government, serving in the Pennsylvania Assembly for 14 years, beginning in 1750. As postmaster general of the colonies, from 1753 to 1774, he reduced inefficiency in the colonial postal system. In 1754, at an intercolonial conference held in Albany, New York, he advocated that the colonies unite against the French and Native Americans. His farsighted plan was accepted by the delegates but rejected by the colonial assemblies and British government. Three years later, Franklin went to England on behalf of the Pennsylvania Assembly to petition for the right to levy taxes on proprietary lands. He spent five years in Britain as a representative of the American colonies. He went again to England as an agent of Pennsylvania in 1764, to negotiate a new charter. During this stay he persuaded Parliament to repeal the Stamp Act. After returning to America in 1775, he was a member of the Second Continental Congress and helped to draft the Declaration of Independence. Throughout most of the American Revolution Franklin was in France, where he negotiated a commercial and defensive alliance. In 1778, he became the first U.S. minister to France, and in 1783 he helped to conclude the Treaty of Paris, the agreement ending the war between the United States and Great Britain. Franklin sailed home to Philadelphia in 1785 and was a member of the Constitutional Convention in 1787. His autobiography, published in 1791, continues to be widely read.

Galbraith, John Kenneth (1908–2006) *economist, professor*

Galbraith was born in Iona Station, Ontario, and in 1931 received a bachelor's degree in agricultural economics from Ontario Agricultural College. He continued his education at the University of California at Berkeley, earning a master's degree in 1933 and a doctorate in 1934. He assumed teaching duties at the University of California at Davis and Harvard University, and in 1937 he became a U.S. citizen. In the early 1940s, as deputy administrator of the Office of Price Administration, Galbraith oversaw the wartime system of price controls. He left government in 1943 to be an editor of *Fortune* magazine but returned in 1945 to direct the U.S. Strategic Bombing Survey. In 1948 he joined the Harvard faculty. In 1952 he published his first important book, *American Capitalism*, on the relative power of large corporations and labor unions. In 1952 and 1956 he worked in the presidential campaigns of Democrat Adlai Stevenson. In 1958 he published *The Affluent Society*, for which he received the Tamiment Book Award and the Sidney Hillman Award. In this examination of American consumerism he advocated grants and social programs to combat poverty in the United States. Galbraith was economic adviser to John F. Kennedy during the 1960 presidential campaign and ambassador to India from 1961 until 1963. He remained politically active, supporting the 1968 presidential bid of Eugene McCarthy and opposing the Vietnam War. Galbraith, who retired from Harvard in 1975, was elected to the American Academy of Arts and Letters in 1982 and served as president of the combined American Academy and Institute of American Arts and Letters from 1984 through 1987. His many awards include 45 honorary doctorates from universities throughout the world. On August 9, 2000, President Bill Clinton presented him with the Medal of Freedom in a ceremony at the White House. Galbraith's more than 30 books include *The Nature of Mass Poverty* (1979) and *The Voice of the Poor* (1983).

Greeley, Horace (1811–1872) *journalist, politician, antislavery activist*

Greeley was born in Amherst, New Hampshire, and apprenticed to a printer at age 14. At 18 he was an itinerant journeyman printer. In 1831 he moved to New York City, where he edited the *New Yorker,* the *Jeffersonian,* and then the *Log Cabin.* He also published political articles and promoted progressive government policies. In 1841 he founded the *New York Tribune,* and he was its editor in chief for 31 years. As the *Tribune's* editor he spoke out against the unequal distribution of wealth and the growth of monopolies. He advocated westward migration and the development of agriculture. Greeley opposed slavery prior to the Civil War, although he was not an abolitionist. He objected to the Mexican War and the Kansas-Nebraska Act, viewing both as means of extending slavery into the West. He criticized Lincoln for hesitating to free the slaves during the Civil War and angered many northerners after the war when he signed a bail bond for Jefferson Davis. In 1872 Greeley was the Democratic candidate for president, but he was defeated by the incumbent, Ulysses S. Grant.

Gurteen, Stephen Humphreys (1836–1908)
clergyman, proponent of charity organization

Gurteen was born in Canterbury, England. His father, the Reverend Stephen Gurteen, died when young Stephen was nine months old. The boy and his sister were placed under the guardianship of an uncle. Stephen H. Gurteen graduated from Cambridge University in 1863 and sailed for the United States, intending to study international law at Albany Law School. He enrolled in 1863, but how long he studied in Albany and whether he graduated are unknown. In fact, little is known about Gurteen's life between 1864 and 1874, although there is evidence to suggest that he visited England sometime during this decade. By 1874 Gurteen was in Geneva, New York, where he taught Latin at Hobart College for the 1874–75 academic year, and on February 21, 1875, he was ordained in the Episcopal Church. In November 1875 he moved to Buffalo, New York, to serve as associate rector at St. Paul's Church. He was made assistant rector in March 1877. In December 1877 Gurteen founded the Charity Organization Society of Buffalo, the first such society in the United States. In summer 1878 he went to Europe to observe poor-relief efforts in England and Paris. In the following months he helped establish charity organization societies in Boston, New York City, Philadelphia, and Baltimore, and he lectured on charity organization in Detroit and elsewhere. In 1879 he persuaded the New York City philanthropist Benjamin Fitch to endow the Fitch Creche, which has been called the first day care center in the United States, for the

children of poor working women in Buffalo. Gurteen's conservative liturgical teachings and practices conflicted with the beliefs of the more progressive bishop, and he was dismissed from his church post in 1880. He moved to Toledo, Ohio, as rector of Trinity parish, but there he was at odds with the congregants. In 1883 Gurteen went to Chicago to head a new charity organization society, but he withdrew at the end of one year. In 1884 he was named rector of St. Paul's Cathedral in Springfield, Illinois. This post was a comfortable one for Gurteen, but he held it for only a short time before ill health forced him to resign. At age 50 he moved with his wife to New York City, where he devoted himself to Old English scholarship, which had been a lifelong interest.

Harrington, Michael (Edward Michael Harrington) (1928–1989) *socialist, writer, professor*

Harrington was born in St. Louis. In 1947 he graduated from the College of the Holy Cross in Worcester, Massachusetts, and in 1949 he received a master's degree from the University of Chicago. As a young man he was attracted to the Catholic Workers, a movement devoted to Christian teaching, economic socialism, and pacifism. In 1951 and 1952, he edited its publication, the *Catholic Worker,* and in 1953 he served as organizational secretary of the Workers Defense League, which protects the legal rights of working people. A conscientious objector during the Korean War, Harrington in 1954 became a consultant to the Fund for the Republic, a think tank studying the effects of anticommunism, especially McCarthyism. From 1960 until 1968, he served on the national executive board of the Socialist Party. Harrington favored a democratically elected government and a planned economy, with public control of large corporations and banks. With his 1962 book, *The Other America,* he drew national attention to the prevalence of poverty in the postwar United States. The book persuaded Presidents John F. Kennedy and Lyndon B. Johnson to draft antipoverty legislation. In the 1960s, Harrington was a consultant to the government's War on Poverty and an adviser to the Reverend Martin Luther King, Jr. From 1968 through 1972, he chaired the Socialist Party. In 1972, he became a professor of political science at Queens College in Flushing, New York, and in 1981 he was a founder of the Democratic Socialists of America. After his death of cancer in 1989, Queens College founded the Michael Harrington Center to promote discussion of social issues and social change. Harrington wrote numerous books and articles on economic issues and socialism. Harrington's honors include the George

Polk Award (1963), Sidney Hillman Award (1963), Riordan Award of the Washington Newspaper Guild (1964), and Eugene V. Debs Award (1973).

Hartley, Robert Milham (1796–1881) *social reformer*

Hartley was born in Cockermouth, England, the son of a prosperous manufacturer. When he was three years old his family immigrated to the United States and settled in New England. Hartley worked in a woolen mill as a young man to prepare for a career in textile manufacturing, but he felt called to the ministry at age 24 and entered Fairfield Academy in Herkimer, New York, to study theology. Illness forced him to terminate his studies, however, and he moved to New York City and became a dry-goods merchant. He also was active in local Bible and tract societies. In 1829 he helped organize the New York City Temperance Society, and he later became its secretary. In his activities for this society he learned that tenement children were drinking milk from cows fed the waste products of whiskey distillation. Believing that milk thus tainted spread disease, he published in 1842 *An Historical, Scientific, and Practical Essay on Milk*, and in 1850 *The Cow and the Dairy*. In 1843 he was a founder of the New York Association for Improving the Condition of the Poor, a nonsectarian agency. He served as its general agent for more than 30 years. In that role Hartley promoted temperance, thrift, and education to counteract poverty. He lobbied for a compulsory school attendance act, which the New York legislature passed in 1874, and he worked for tenement reform. In 1863 he founded the Society for the Relief of the Ruptured and Crippled, which dispensed artificial limbs and free surgical care to the poor. Hartley retired from charitable work in 1876, at age 80; he died of pneumonia in New York City in 1881.

Hickok, Lorena Alice (1893–1968) *journalist, Federal Emergency Relief Administration investigator*

Hickok was born in East Troy, Wisconsin. She grew up in an abusive home, in a family that moved frequently, and she struck out on her own at age 14 and worked as a maid. She went to live with an aunt two years later and finished high school. She was enrolled in Lawrence College in Appleton, Wisconsin, in the 1912–13 academic year but left to work for the *Battle Creek News*. She soon became society editor for the *Milwaukee Sentinel* and then joined the staff of the *Minneapolis Tribune*. After a brief experiment in living in New York City she re-joined the *Tribune*. In 1928 the Associated Press hired Hickok as a feature writer, but she also covered national stories, including the Lindbergh baby kidnapping. She reported on Eleanor Roosevelt's activities during the 1932 presidential campaign and formed a close friendship with Roosevelt. In 1933 she became an employee of the Federal Emergency Relief Administration and reported to the government on living conditions throughout the United States and New Deal programs in action. She also served as an adviser and companion to First Lady Eleanor Roosevelt. In 1936 she returned to the private sector to work for a public-relations firm. From 1940 until 1945 Hickok was executive secretary of the Women's Division of the Democratic National Committee, and in 1947 she was employed by the New York State Democratic Committee. She retired in 1954 as a result of complications of diabetes and settled in Hyde Park, New York, near Roosevelt. Hickok and Roosevelt collaborated on *Ladies of Courage* (1954), a book about female political leaders. Hickok also wrote a biography of Roosevelt, *Reluctant First Lady* (1962), and several biographies for children.

Hine, Lewis Wickes (1874–1940) *pioneer of social documentary, photographer whose images of working children inspired support for child-labor legislation*

Hine attended the state normal school at Oshkosh, Wisconsin, and spent a year at the University of Chicago before being hired in 1901 to teach nature study and geography at the Ethical Culture School in New York City. In 1904 he began to photograph immigrants arriving at Ellis Island, becoming one of the first photographers to document American social history. During this period he also photographed immigrants and the poor in tenements and sweatshops. In 1907 the National Child Labor Committee hired Hines to photograph working children in a variety of settings: coal mines, farms, factories, canneries, and sweatshops. Hine spent 11 years at this task. In 1919 he documented Red Cross relief efforts in Europe in the aftermath of World War I. In the 1930s he focused his camera on the American worker. As part of this effort he made more than 1,000 photographs of the construction of the Empire State Building. He published *Men at Work*, a collection of his industrial photographs, in 1932.

Hoover, Herbert Clark (1874–1964) *31st president of the United States*

Hoover, who was born into a Quaker family in rural Ohio, studied geology and mining at Stanford University. He began his career managing mining properties in Western Australia and China. He performed relief work during World War I, arranging transportation home for 120,000 American tourists stranded in Europe and securing food for war-torn Belgium. After the war, he headed the American Relief Administration, which distributed food, clothing, and medical supplies in eastern Europe. Between 1921 and 1928, he was secretary of commerce under Presidents Warren G. Harding and Calvin Coolidge. Hoover, a Republican, was elected president in 1928. Although he took unprecedented steps to attempt to pull the nation out of the Great Depression, sanctioning government spending for public works and federal loans to businesses through the Reconstruction Finance Corporation, the public perceived him as insensitive to their distress. Franklin D. Roosevelt defeated him in the 1932 election. Hoover headed commissions under Presidents Harry S. Truman and Dwight D. Eisenhower to streamline the executive branch of the federal government. He was the author of *American Individualism* (1922), *Challenge to Liberty* (1934), and the three-volume *Memoirs*.

Hopkins, Harry Lloyd (1890–1946) *administrator of social programs, government official, presidential adviser*

Hopkins was born in Sioux City, Iowa. In 1912 he graduated from Grinnell College in Grinnell, Iowa, and began his career in social work at Christodora House, a settlement on the Lower East Side of Manhattan. In spring 1913 he was hired as a friendly visitor by the New York Association for Improving the Condition of the Poor; he also supervised the association's employment bureau. In 1915 New York City mayor John Purroy Mitchell named him executive secretary of the Bureau of Child Welfare. In 1917 Hopkins moved with his wife and young son to New Orleans, where he directed civilian relief for the Gulf Division of the American Red Cross. He was promoted to general manager and lived and worked in Atlanta after the Gulf Region merged with the Southwestern Division in 1921. The following year Hopkins returned to New York City to be general director of the New York Tuberculosis Association. He helped draft the charter of the American Association of Social Workers (AASW) and was elected AASW president in 1923. In 1931, with the nation struggling through the Great Depression, Governor Franklin Delano Roosevelt of New York chose Hopkins to head the Temporary Relief Administration, an agency that cre-

ated public-works jobs and gave aid to the needy of the state. In 1933, after being sworn in as president of the United States, Roosevelt appointed Hopkins to oversee the Federal Emergency Relief Administration, which made funds available at the state level to aid the unemployed and their families. In 1935 Hopkins headed the Works Progress Administration. Between 1938 and 1940 he served as secretary of commerce. In 1941 he administered the Lend-Lease program, which provided war materials to Britain and other nations resisting fascist aggression. During World War II he sat on the War Production Board and the Pacific War Council. He also accompanied Roosevelt to wartime conferences in Tehran in 1943 and Yalta in 1945. Under President Harry S. Truman he helped prepare for the 1945 Potsdam Conference, at which Truman discussed arrangements for postwar Europe with Soviet premier Joseph Stalin and British prime minister Winston Churchill. Hopkins died of cancer in 1946.

Howard, Oliver Otis (1830–1909) *army general, commissioner of the Freedmen's Bureau, founder and president of Howard University*

Howard was born in Leeds, Maine. He graduated in 1850 from Bowdoin College in Brunswick, Maine, and in 1854 from the United States Military Academy at West Point, New York. In 1857 he fought the Seminole Indians in Florida and then returned to West Point to teach mathematics. Howard resigned his regular army commission in 1861, at the start of the Civil War, to become a colonel with the 3rd Maine Volunteer Infantry Regiment. He commanded a brigade in the Battle of Bull Run, which was fought on July 21, 1861, and was promoted to brigadier general the following September. On June 1, 1862, while participating in the Peninsular Campaign under General George McClellan, Howard lost an arm in battle. He returned to active duty in August and took part in the Battle of Antietam, on September 17, 1862. In 1863, now a major general of volunteers, Howard commanded XI Corps of the Army of the Potomac in the Battles of Chancellorsville and Gettysburg. He was active in the Chattanooga Campaign in 1863, and after the death of General James B. McPherson in 1864 he was named commander of the Army of the Tennessee. He commanded the right wing of General William Tecumseh Sherman's 1864 march from Atlanta to Savannah. Howard served as commissioner of the Freedmen's Bureau from 1865 through 1874.

Committed to aiding African Americans, he helped in 1867 to found Howard University, the traditionally black university in Washington, D.C., that was named for him. He was the third president of the university, from 1869 until 1874. In 1872 Howard went to Arizona as a special commissioner to the Apache. He negotiated with the Chiricahua Apache leader Cochise, who had vowed never to make peace with the United States, and secured a reservation for the Chiricahua in southeastern Arizona. In 1877 Howard threatened a cavalry attack to persuade the Nez Perce leader Chief Joseph to move with his followers onto an Idaho reservation. (A raid by young Nez Perce warriors and the U.S. Army's retaliation later caused Chief Joseph to reverse his decision.) In 1878 Howard conducted capaigns against the Bannock and Paiute, and from 1880 to 1882 he was superintendent of West Point. Between 1882 and 1894, when he retired from active duty with the rank of major general, he commanded the Departments of the Platte, Pacific, and East. He was awarded the Medal of Honor in 1893 for valor in the Peninsular Campaign and in 1895 he founded Lincoln Memorial University in Harrogate, Tennessee. He died in his home in Burlington, Vermont, in 1909.

Howells, William Dean (1837–1920) *novelist, critic*
As a child in Ohio, Howells learned the printing trade from his father. He worked as a typesetter and later as a journalist. During the presidential campaign of 1860 he wrote a brief biography of candidate Abraham Lincoln. After the election Lincoln appointed Howells U.S. consul in Venice, Italy. In 1866 Howells returned to the United States and worked for the *Atlantic Monthly*. He was editor in chief from 1871 through 1881. In 1909, he became the first president of the American Academy of Arts and Letters; he held that position until his death. Howells was one of the most influential literary personages of his time. He wrote more than 30 novels, many of which offer insightful descriptions of American life. They include *A Modern Instance* (1882), *The Rise of Silas Lapham* (1885), *Annie Kilburn* (1888), *Through the Eye of the Needle* (1907), and *A Hazard of New Fortunes* (1890). Howells also published several volumes of literary criticism. He furthered the careers of such promising young American writers as Stephen Crane, Mark Twain, Henry James, and Paul Laurence Dunbar, and he introduced American readers to Leo Tolstoy, Emile Zola, Henrik Ibsen, and other European authors.

Humphrey, Hubert Horatio, Jr. (1911–1978) *U.S. senator, vice president of the United States*
Humphrey was born in Wallace, South Dakota, and attended public schools in Doland, South Dakota, where he grew up. In 1933 he graduated from the Capitol College of Pharmacy in Denver and became a registered pharmacist. He worked at a family-owned business, the Humphrey Drug Company in Huron, South Dakota, until 1937, when he resumed his education at the University of Minnesota, where he earned a bachelor of arts degree in 1939. In 1940 Humphrey received a master's degree in political science from Louisiana State University. He then returned to Minnesota and held a variety of jobs in government, academia, and broadcasting before being elected mayor of Minneapolis in 1945. At the 1948 Democratic National Convention Humphrey delivered a speech advocating a strong civil rights platform that gained him recognition beyond his own state. In November of that year the voters of Minnesota elected him to the U.S. Senate. As a senator he supported strong civil rights legislation, laws to improve social welfare, and tax breaks for low-income groups. He was the Senate majority whip from 1961 through 1964. In 1964 he was elected vice president on the ticket with Lyndon Johnson in a landslide victory. Four years later, as the Democratic candidate for president, Humphrey was narrowly defeated by Richard Nixon. He left Washington to teach at the University of Minnesota and Macalester College in St. Paul, Minnesota. On June 9, 1980, he was posthumously awarded the Medal of Freedom.

Hunter, Robert (Wiles Robert Hunter) (1874–1942) *social worker, researcher*
Hunter was born in Terre Haute, Indiana, the son of a carriage manufacturer. He graduated from Indiana University in 1896 and moved to Chicago, where he was organizing secretary of the Board of Charities. After meeting Jane Addams he became a resident of Hull-House. In 1899 he lived at the Toynbee Hall settlement in London and met some prominent socialists. Hunter returned to Chicago in 1901 and chaired the City Homes Commission, which investigated tenement conditions. In 1902 he moved to New York City to head the University Settlement House, and in 1903 he married Caroline Stokes, the sister of James Phelps Stokes, a millionaire socialist. In 1904 Hunter published *Poverty*, the first attempt to measure poverty in the United States

and establish a poverty line. He joined the American Socialist Party in 1905. His books include *Socialist at Work* (1908), *Violence in the Labor Movement* (1914), *Labor in Politics* (1915), *Inflation and Revolution* (1934), and *Revolution: Why, How, When?* (1940).

Johnson, Lyndon Baines (1908–1973) *36th president of the United States*
Johnson was born on a farm in Gillespie County, Texas. In 1913, he moved with his parents to Johnson City, a community that his forbears had helped to found. He graduated from Southwest Texas State Teachers College in 1930 and taught high school briefly before moving to Washington, D.C., in 1931, as secretary to Congressman Richard M. Kleberg. He also attended Georgetown University Law School in 1934. On November 17, 1934, Johnson married Claudia "Lady Bird" Taylor. The couple would have two daughters, Lynda Byrd (born 1944) and Luci Baines (born 1947). In 1937, President Franklin D. Roosevelt appointed Johnson to direct the National Youth Administration (NYA) in Texas. The NYA, a New Deal program, provided employment to teenagers and young adults. In 1937, Johnson was elected to Congress as a Democrat to fill the seat left vacant by the death of Representative James P. Buchanan. He was elected to five succeeding Congresses. In 1941, Johnson was the first member of Congress to enlist in World War II. He served in the navy as a lieutenant commander and earned a Silver Star in the South Pacific. He returned to government in 1942, when Roosevelt recalled members of Congress from active duty. Johnson was first elected to the U.S. Senate in 1948. He distinguished himself during 12 years in the Senate, serving as Democratic whip (1951–53), minority leader (1953–55), and majority leader (1955–61). In November 1960, he was elected vice president on the ticket with John F. Kennedy. He assumed the presidency on November 22, 1963, after Kennedy's assassination. President Johnson envisioned a "Great Society" and pursued economic and cultural initiatives toward that end. Declaring "War on Poverty," he signed into law the 1964 Economic Opportunity Act. Also, during his administration such social programs as Head Start, food stamps, Medicare, and Medicaid had their beginnings. Johnson was elected president in 1964 but faced with racial violence at home and deepening military involvement in Vietnam, he did not seek reelection in 1968. He retired to his ranch near Johnson City and died on January 22, 1973.

Keckley, Elizabeth Hobbs (1818–1907) *seamstress, writer*
Elizabeth Hobbs was born in Dinwiddie County, Virginia. Her parents, Agnes and George Hobbs, were slaves on plantations 100 miles apart. Elizabeth lived with her mother and saw her father only when he visited on Christmas and Easter until she was seven or eight years old. At that time her father's owner moved farther away and took George Hobbs with him. Elizabeth learned dressmaking from her mother, and soon she was sewing for the master's family and for paying clients. As a result of sexual abuse by a white man she became pregnant and gave birth to her son, George. In 1852 she married James Keckley, who presented himself as a free man, but she later learned that he was enslaved and drank heavily. In 1855 one of her clients lent Elizabeth Keckley $1,200 to purchase freedom for herself and her son. Five years later Keckley left her husband and settled first in Baltimore and then in Washington, D.C., where she made gowns for prominent women, including the wives of Jefferson Davis, Stephen Douglas, and Abraham Lincoln. Mary Todd Lincoln was so pleased with Keckley's work on her inaugural gown that she hired the former slave as her personal dressmaker. The two women became close friends. In August 1861 Keckley's son died as a soldier in the Union army. In 1862, when refugees from slavery were pouring into the national capital, Keckley founded the Contraband Relief Association, an organization of African Americans. The following year she established a school for African-American girls. Keckley published a book, *Behind the Scenes, or, Thirty Years a Slave and Four Years in the White House,* in 1868. In it she described her friendship with Mary Lincoln and revealed details of President Lincoln's assassination that his family had kept private. As a result Mary Lincoln ended the friendship, and her son, Robert Lincoln, had the book recalled and withdrawn from publication. From 1892 to 1898 Keckley taught sewing at Wilberforce University in Ohio. In 1893 she represented Wilberforce at the World's Columbian Exposition in Chicago. Her life ended at the Home for Destitute Women and Children in Washington, D.C., which she had helped establish.

Kennedy, John Fitzgerald (1917–1963) *35th president of the United States*
Kennedy graduated from Harvard University in 1940; his expanded senior thesis, *Why England Slept*, was published the same year. He served in the navy during World War II.

In August 1943, he was commanding a PT boat that was rammed and sunk by a Japanese destroyer off the Solomon Islands. Kennedy, severely injured, led the surviving crew members to safety. After the war, he entered politics. Massachusetts voters elected him to the U.S. House of Representatives as a Democrat in 1946 and to the Senate in 1952. Kennedy wrote *Profiles in Courage* (1956) while recovering from back surgery. In 1960, Kennedy was elected president. As president he took decisive steps internationally, sending the first U.S. military personnel to South Vietnam in December 1961 and responding to the installation of Soviet missiles in Cuba with a naval blockade of the island. He also attended to domestic issues and at the time of his death was preparing legislation to address poverty. Kennedy was assassinated in Dallas, Texas, on November 22, 1963.

Kennedy, Robert Francis (1925–1968) *U.S. attorney general, U.S. senator*

Kennedy earned a law degree from the University of Virginia in 1951. The same year, the U.S. Justice Department hired him as an attorney. He resigned in 1952 to manage the campaign of his brother, John F. Kennedy, who sought a U.S. Senate seat from Massachusetts. From 1955 through 1957, he was chief counsel to the Senate subcommittee investigating corruption in organized labor. In 1960, after John Kennedy's election as president, Robert Kennedy was appointed attorney general. He distinguished himself in that position by actively enforcing civil rights legislation. In 1964, he resigned from his cabinet post and was elected to the Senate from New York. He and Senator Joseph Clark of Pennsylvania attracted national attention in 1967, when they toured African-American homes in the Mississippi Delta to investigate poverty-related hunger. Kennedy was assassinated in June 1968, while campaigning for the Democratic nomination for president.

King, Martin Luther, Jr. (1929–1968) *civil rights leader, Nobel laureate, clergyman*

King was ordained a Baptist minister at 17 and graduated from Crozer Theological Seminary in 1951. He received a Ph.D. from Boston University in 1954. The same year, he became pastor of the Dexter Avenue Baptist Church in Montgomery, Alabama. He emerged as a national civil rights leader after directing the Montgomery bus boycott in 1955 and 1956. The boycott ended when the U.S. Supreme Court outlawed segregation on municipal transportation. He and other African-American ministers then formed the Southern Christian Leadership Conference (SCLC), an organization devoted to nonviolent change, with King as president. In 1959, King traveled to India to study the nonviolent protest methods of Mohandas K. Gandhi. He became copastor of the Ebenezer Baptist Church in Atlanta, Georgia, in 1960. King led civil rights demonstrations in Birmingham, Alabama, in 1963, and a voting-rights drive in Selma, Alabama, in 1965. He was arrested several times, and his home was bombed in 1956. In 1964, King was awarded the Nobel Prize in peace for his efforts in the civil rights movement. He broadened his concerns in the years that followed to address poverty and housing for African Americans in northern cities and to protest U.S. military involvement in Vietnam. He was assassinated in Memphis, Tennessee, where he was offering support to striking sanitation workers. King's writing include *Stride toward Freedom* (1958), about the Montgomery bus boycott; "Letter from a Birmingham Jail" (1963), an essay outlining the need for nonviolent civil disobedience; and *Why We Can't Wait* (1963), on civil rights issues.

Lampman, Robert James (1920–1997) *economist, educator*

Lampman was born in Plover, Wisconsin, where his father taught in the high school. After graduating from the University of Wisconsin in 1942, he enlisted in the U.S. Navy. He served as an air navigator in the South Pacific for the duration of World War II and attained the rank of lieutenant senior grade. Lampman was discharged from active duty in 1946 and returned to the University of Wisconsin, where he earned a doctorate in economics in 1950. Beginning in 1948, he taught economics at the University of Washington in Seattle for a decade before joining the economics faculty at the University of Wisconsin. He was a visiting professor at the American University of Beirut in 1951 and 1952, the University of the Philippines in 1966 and 1967, and Cornell University in 1973 and 1974. A specialist in income distribution, Lampman was a member of President John F. Kennedy's Council of Economic Advisers in 1962 and 1963. He wrote the chapter on poverty in President Lyndon B. Johnson's 1964 Economic Report; this piece of writing provided the ideological foundation for Johnson's antipoverty legislation. Lampman died of lung cancer in Madison, Wisconsin. His books include *The Low Income Population and Economic Growth* (1959), *The Share of Top Wealth-Holders in National Wealth, 1922–1956* (1962), and *Ends and Means of Reducing Income Poverty* (1971).

Lewis, Oscar (Oscar Lefkowitz) (1914–1970)
anthropologist
Lewis was born Oscar Lefkowitz in New York City. His parents were Jewish immigrants from the region that is now Belarus. Oscar spent most of his youth in Liberty, New York, where his family operated a summer hotel. Oscar also helped his family financially by working on nearby farms. In 1936 he graduated from the City College of New York with a degree in history. While a graduate student at Columbia University, he met and married Ruth Maslow, who would be his most important professional collaborator. In 1940 he earned a doctorate in anthropology from Columbia and legally changed his name to Oscar Lewis. During World War II Lewis worked for the U.S. Departments of Justice and the Interior. In 1943 Commissioner of Indian Affairs John Collier sent the Lewises to Mexico to conduct research. Their study, *Life in a Mexican Village: Tepoztlan Revisited,* was published in 1951. Meanwhile, Lewis had led an investigation of land use in Texas for the Department of Agriculture that resulted in the book *On the Edge of the Black Waxy* (1948). From 1946 through 1948 Lewis taught in the Department of Sociology and Anthropology at Washington University in St. Louis. In 1948 he joined the faculty of the University of Illinois, and in 1960 he founded that school's Department of Anthropology. He carried out research in places as diverse as Mexico, Spain, Puerto Rico, Cuba, India, and New York City. He also published a series of family studies that included *Five Families* (1959), *Children of Sanchez* (1961), and *La Vida* (1966), for which he received the National Book Award in nonfiction. In the October 1966 issue of *Scientific American* he explained the culture of poverty, his assertion that pockets of poverty displaying cultural similarities develop independently of one another in capitalist countries. In the late 1960s he served as a consultant to the federal government's Head Start program. The posthumously published *Living the Revolution: An Oral History of Contemporary Cuba* (1977–78) was based on research Lewis conducted in Cuba shortly before his death.

Lincoln, Abraham (1809–1865) *16th president of the United States, commander in chief during the Civil War, author of the Emancipation Proclamation*
Lincoln grew up in the Kentucky and Illinois wilderness and had little formal education. As a young man he worked as a postmaster, surveyor, and store clerk. He also served as a captain in the Black Hawk War of 1832. Lincoln studied law on his own and was admitted to the bar in 1836, having won a seat in the Illinois legislature in 1834. He became a local leader in the Whig Party and in 1846 was elected to the U.S. House of Representatives and served one term. In 1858 he was the Republican candidate for the Senate from Illinois, challenging the incumbent, Stephen A. Douglas. Lincoln spoke against slavery during the campaign and gained national recognition but lost the election. In 1860, as the Republican nominee for president, he defeated two Democrats and one candidate from the Constitutional Union Party. After the election seven southern states seceded from the Union. Four others would later secede as well. When Lincoln attempted to relieve forces stationed at Fort Sumter, South Carolina, in April 1861, the Confederates fired on the fort and thereby touched off the Civil War. On January 1, 1863, Lincoln's Emancipation Proclamation took effect, freeing slaves in regions held by the Confederates. He advocated passage of a constitutional amendment outlawing slavery; it was ratified December 6, 1865. Lincoln was reelected in November 1864 but was assassinated on April 14, 1865, days after the Confederate surrender.

Lowell, Josephine Shaw (1843–1905) *charity worker, reformer*
Josephine Shaw was born in West Roxbury, Massachusetts, into a prominent abolitionist family. In 1848, the Shaws moved to Staten Island, New York, and from 1851 until 1856 they lived in Italy and other European countries. Josephine attended private schools in Europe and New York. In 1863 she worked with the Women's Central Association of Relief, the predecessor of the U.S. Sanitary Commission, which provided care and comfort to Union soldiers during the Civil War. In July 1863, her brother, Colonel Robert Gould Shaw, the white commander of the 54th Massachusetts Colored Infantry, was killed in the assault on Fort Wagner, South Carolina. On October 31, 1863, Josephine Shaw married Colonel Charles Russell Lowell. Colonel Lowell was killed in the Battle of Cedar Creek, Virginia, on October 19, 1864. The couple's only child, a daughter, was born six weeks later. After the war Lowell hired teachers and inspected schools for former slaves in Virginia. She was also a member of the visiting committee of the Prison Association of New York, which worked to improve prisons and jails. In 1873 she joined the State Charities Aid Association and reported on conditions in county poorhouses. In 1876 Governor Samuel J. Tilden of New York appointed her to the State Board of Charities. As the first female board member Lowell took a special interest in girls and women, confined to

almshouses because they were mentally ill or had been arrested for prostitution or committing petty crimes, who were often abused by male inmates or staff members. She worked to remove these women from almshouses and place them in asylums and reformatories supervised by women. Her investigation of waste among New York City charities led in 1882 to the formation of the New York Charity Organization Society, which Lowell led for many years. In 1884 she published a book, *Public Relief and Private Charity*. In 1890 Lowell resigned from the State Board of Charities and founded the Consumer's League of New York to improve working conditions in stores and facilitate the formation of trade unions for women. In her final years she spoke out against American imperialism in the Caribbean and the Philippines.

Mather, Cotton (1663–1728) *Congregational minister, author*

Mather was born in Boston, the son of Increase Mather, pastor of Boston's North Church. Cotton Mather was educated at Harvard College (now Harvard University), and in 1685 he was formally ordained and joined his father in ministering to the North Church. Increase Mather continued to perform his ecclesiastical duties while serving as president of Harvard from 1685 until 1701, and until his death in 1723. Cotton Mather then served as the sole pastor of the North Church for the rest of his life. He was an influential author who wrote on theology, science, witchcraft, history, and biography. *Wonders of the Invisible World* (1693) recounted some of the cases leading to the Salem witch trials; *Magnalia Christi Americana* (1702) traced the history of Protestantism in New England and is considered one of the most significant scholarly works produced in colonial America; *Essays to Do Good* (1710) offered advice on charitable living; and *Ratio Disciplinae* (1726) dealt with governance of the Congregational Church. Between 1712 and 1724 Mather published his *Curiosa Americana*, dealing with natural phenomena in the New World. In 1713 he became the first American-born member of the Royal Society of London, Britain's national academy of science. In 1721 Mather advocated smallpox inoculation, which was new and controversial.

Moynihan, Daniel Patrick (1927–2003) *scholar, U.S. senator, ambassador to India, presidential adviser*

Moynihan was born on March 16, 1927, in Tulsa, Oklahoma, and grew up in New York City. He enrolled in the City College of New York in 1943 but interrupted his studies in 1944 to enlist in the U.S. Navy. After serving in World War II, he studied on the G.I. Bill at Tufts University in Medford, Massachusetts, graduating in 1948. He continued his academic work at the Fletcher School of Law and Diplomacy, at Tufts, and earned a master's degree in 1949 and a Ph.D. in 1961. In 1950 and 1951, he attended the London School of Economics and Political Science as a Fulbright Fellow. Moynihan married Elizabeth Brennan, an artist, on May 29, 1955. Also in 1955, he became assistant and secretary to Governor W. Averell Harriman of New York. In 1959, he was a member of the New York State Tenure Commission and joined the political science faculty at Syracuse University. From 1961 through 1965, Moynihan served as an assistant to the secretary of labor under Presidents Kennedy and Johnson. He gained national attention in 1963 with the publication of *Beyond the Melting Pot*, his book written with Nathan Glazer about the principal racial and ethnic minority groups in New York City. In 1965, the year he published *The Assault on Poverty*, he returned to academia. He spent a year at Wesleyan University in Middletown, Connecticut, before moving to the Joint Center for Urban Studies at Harvard University and the Massachusetts Institute of Technology. Moynihan remained active in government service as a member of the U.S. Commission on Civil Rights in 1967 and the President's Science Advisory Committee from 1971 through 1973. He chaired the Advisory Committee on Public Safety, Department of Health, Education, and Welfare, during the same years. In 1973, President Richard Nixon appointed him ambassador to India. From 1975 to 1976, he was the U.S. permanent representative to the United Nations. Moynihan ran successfully for the U.S. Senate as a Democrat from New York in 1976 and was reelected in 1982, 1988, and 1994. In the Senate he chaired the Committee on the Environment and Public Works from 1992 to 1993, and he was on the Committee on Finance from 1993 to 1995. In 1995, he published *Family and a Nation*, a compilation of lectures delivered at Harvard in which he explored the link between single-parent families and childhood poverty, especially among African Americans. Moynihan chose not to seek reelection in 2000. In 2001, he taught at the Maxwell School, the graduate school of social sciences at Syracuse University. From 2001 through 2003, he was a senior scholar at the Woodrow Wilson International Center for Scholars in Washington, D.C. He died of a ruptured appendix on March 26, 2003, and was buried at Arlington National Cemetery.

Murphy, Edgar Gardner (1869–1913) *clergyman, reformer*

Murphy entered the Episcopal priesthood in 1893. In 1900, while assigned to a parish in Montgomery, Alabama, he founded a church for African Americans, managed the construction of Young Men's and Young Women's Christian Association (YMCA and YWCA) buildings, and persuaded Andrew Carnegie to donate a public library to the city. Also in that year he organized a conference to discuss racial and social issues facing the South, including child labor. He founded the Alabama Child Labor Committee in 1901 and helped to create the National Child Labor Committee (NCLC) in 1904. Murphy left the priesthood in 1903 to continue his social activism outside the church. From 1903 to 1908 he was secretary of the Southern Education Board. He resigned from the NCLC in 1907 because of the committee's support of federal child-labor legislation, which he viewed as unconstitutional. In 1908 ill health forced Murphy to retire from reform work. Beginning in that year he studied and wrote about astronomy. His writings include *The Problems of the Present South* (1904) and *A Beginner's Star Book* (1912), the latter published under the pseudonym Kelvin McKready.

Nixon, Richard Milhous (1913–1994) *37th president of the United States*

Nixon was born to poor parents in Yorba Linda, California. He attended public schools and Whittier College in Whittier, California, from which he graduated second in his class in 1934. In 1937 he graduated third in his class from Duke University Law School in Durham, North Carolina. The same year he was admitted to the bar and began the practice of law in Whittier. Nixon was an attorney in the Office of Emergency Management in Washington, D.C., for several months before enlisting in the U.S. Navy in August 1942. He served as a supply officer in the South Pacific and was discharged in January 1946 as a lieutenant commander. In November 1946 he was elected to the U.S. House of Representatives as a Republican. Congressman Nixon gained a national reputation as a member of the House Committee on Un-American Activities in 1948 and 1949, when it investigated Alger Hiss, a former government official and accused communist spy. In 1950 Nixon was elected to the U.S. Senate, and in 1952 he was elected vice president of the United States on the ticket with Dwight David Eisenhower for the term beginning January 20, 1953. In 1960 he was the Republican nominee

for president but lost the election to John F. Kennedy. He returned to the practice of law in California and New York and in 1962 ran unsuccessfully for governor of California. Nixon was elected president of the United States in 1968 and reelected in 1972. As president he ordered the gradual withdrawal of 500,000 Americans from Vietnam. In 1970, however, he authorized military operations in Cambodia, and in 1972 he ordered the bombing of Hanoi and mining of Haiphong Harbor. He insisted that these actions persuaded North Vietnam to reach a negotiated settlement and release all known prisoners of war by March 1973. As president Nixon also established diplomatic relations with China. He resigned the presidency on August 9, 1974, after the House Judiciary Committee began impeachment proceedings against him for his alleged cover-up of the attempted burglary and wiretapping of the Democratic National Committee Headquarters at the Watergate Hotel in Washington. He accepted a pardon from his successor, President Gerald R. Ford, on September 8, 1974. After his resignation Nixon lived in New York City and then Park Ridge, New Jersey. He died in New York City on April 22, 1994, and was buried on the grounds of the Richard Nixon Library in Yorba Linda.

Paine, Thomas (1737–1809) *political philosopher, writer*

Paine was born in Thetford, Norfolk, England, the son of a Quaker. He became an excise officer but was dismissed in 1772 for leading a campaign for higher salaries. After receiving letters of introduction from Benjamin Franklin, who was in Britain representing the American colonies, Paine immigrated to Philadelphia in 1774. There he edited *Pennsylvania Magazine* and published other writings. On January 1, 1776, he issued the pamphlet *Common Sense*, in which he asserted that Great Britain was exploiting the colonies; for the colonies to gain their independence and establish themselves as a republic was a matter of common sense. The pamphlet was widely read and influenced the authors of the Declaration of Independence. During the American Revolution Paine wrote a series of 16 pamphlets to encourage patriotism that were titled collectively *The American Crisis*. General George Washington had them read to his troops to improve morale. In 1778 Congress appointed Paine secretary of the committee of foreign affairs. He also served as clerk of the Pennsylvania legislature before sailing for Great Britain in 1787. In 1791 and 1792 he published his defense of the French Revolution, *The*

Rights of Man, in two parts. Because this work advocated republican government in Europe, Great Britain indicted him for treason. Paine fled to France, where he became a deputy to the national convention. In France he spent 11 months in prison, however, for favoring the exile rather than the execution of Louis XVI, the former king. Paine published his book *The Age of Reason* in three parts, in 1794, 1795, and 1807. His criticism in this book of widely accepted religious views turned public opinion against him, and when he returned to the United States in 1802, he was shunned. In 1797 Paine had published *Agrarian Justice,* a pamphlet calling for government funds to be given to citizens to prevent poverty. Ironically, he died a poor man in New York City on June 8, 1809.

Poor, Salem (1747–unknown) *Revolutionary War soldier*

Poor grew up in slavery in Andover, Massachusetts. He purchased his freedom on July 22, 1769, at age 22. On April 24, 1775, at the start of the American Revolution, he enlisted in the 5th Massachusetts Regiment. On June 16, 1775, the regiment was put to work building a fortification on Breed's Hill, overlooking Boston Harbor. The following day the soldiers defended the site when British forces attacked both Breed's Hill and nearby Bunker Hill. The Americans put up a good defense, but after three assaults the British captured the heights. Poor has been credited with fatally shooting British lieutenant colonel James Abercrombie during the encounter, which is remembered as the Battle of Bunker Hill. Poor fought in the Battle of White Plains, on October 28, 1776, and spent the winter of 1777–78 with General George Washington at Valley Forge, Pennsylvania. Poor's service with the Continental army ended on March 20, 1780; how and where he spent the rest of his life are unknown.

Reagan, Ronald Wilson (1911–2004) *40th president of the United States*

Reagan was born in Tampico, Illinois. He worked his way through Eureka College in Eureka, Illinois, studying economics and sociology. In college he also played football and acted in dramatic productions. He worked as a radio announcer after graduation in 1932, until a screen test in 1937 led to a Hollywood contract. Reagan appeared in 53 films over the next two decades, including *Knute Rockne, All American* (1940) and *King's Row* (1942). In March 1947, he was elected president of the Screen Actors Guild. He was reelected for five more consecutive one-year terms. In 1954, Reagan hosted the television series *G. E. Theater.* He also toured the country to represent General Electric in radio broadcasts and public appearances. He was again elected president of the Screen Actors Guild in November 1959, but he resigned in July 1960. In 1965 and 1966, he hosted *Death Valley Days* on television. In 1966, Reagan was elected to the first of two terms as governor of California. He had held liberal views as a young adult, but his political philosophy had shifted toward conservatism. In 1980, he ran for president as a Republican, receiving 489 electoral votes and defeating President Jimmy Carter. Reagan survived an assassination attempt 69 days into his presidency. His economic agenda, which became known as Reaganomics, included cutting taxes, reducing government spending for social programs, and increasing defense expenditures. These policies resulted in low interest rates and inflation and a large budget deficit. Reagan was reelected in 1984. In 1994, he announced that he had been diagnosed with Alzheimer's disease.

Reid, Whitelaw (1837–1912) *journalist, politician, diplomat*

Reid was born into a devout Presbyterian farming family living near Xenia, Ohio. He attended Xenia Academy, where his uncle was principal, and at age 15 enrolled as a sophomore in Miami University in Oxford, Ohio. He graduated with scientific honors in 1856 and spent a year as a schoolmaster in South Charleston, Ohio. In 1857 Reid and his brother purchased the *Xenia News,* and he served as editor for nearly two years. A zealous member of the new Republican Party, Reid supported Abraham Lincoln in the 1860 presidential campaign. Beginning in 1861 he was a war correspondent for the *Cincinnati Gazette.* He covered the Battles of Shiloh and Gettysburg; the capture of Richmond, Virginia; and the funeral of Abraham Lincoln, all to widespread acclaim. He was also one of the first eastern correspondents for the Western Associated Press, a news-gathering agency founded in Detroit during the Civil War. In 1863, as a result of his Republican connections, Reid became librarian of the House of Representatives. He also was named clerk of the House Committee on Military Affairs during the third session of the 37th Congress. In May 1865 he accompanied Chief Justice Salmon P. Chase on an inspection tour of the war-ravaged South. In 1866 he published his observations in a book, *After the War.* In 1867 he tried raising cotton in the South but quickly gave it up. He returned to writing and in 1868 published *Ohio and the War.* In 1868, at age 31, Reid joined the staff of Horace Greeley's *New York Tribune,* and within a short time he became its editor. He was campaign manager when Greeley ran unsuccessfully for president against the incumbent, Ulysses S. Grant. Greeley died a month after the 1872 election, and with a loan from financier Jay Gould, Reid took control of the *Tribune.* As editor in chief he built the paper into a forum of national importance. In 1889 President Benjamin Harrison appointed Reid minister to France. Reid returned to the United States in 1892 to be Harrison's running mate in his bid for reelection. Harrison and Reid lost the race to Grover Cleveland, and Reid retired from public life until 1897, when President William McKinley sent him to Great Britain as special ambassador to the Queen's Jubilee. In 1898 Reid served on the U.S. commission that negotiated peace after the Spanish-American War, and in 1900 he published a book on colonialism, *Problems of Expansion.* President Theodore Roosevelt named Reid special ambassador to the coronation of King Edward VII in 1902 and ambassador to Great Britain in 1905. Reid died in London.

Riis, Jacob August (1849–1914) *social reformer, writer, photographer*
Riis immigrated to the United States from Denmark at age 21. He settled in New York City and in 1873 became a police reporter for the *New York Tribune,* assigned to cover the Lower East Side of Manhattan. In 1888, he was hired by the *New York Evening Sun.* Riis used flash photography to record the interiors of tenement buildings; the illustrations in his 1890 book on slum life, *How the Other Half Lives,* were based on these photographs. The deplorable conditions shown in this popular book shocked the public and caught the attention of New York Police Commissioner Theodore Roosevelt, who later worked with Riis on social reforms, such as improvements in tenement housing and schools and the creation of playgrounds and parks in urban neighborhoods. Riis's many books include *The Children of the Poor* (1892), *Out of Mulberry Street* (1896), and his autobiography, *The Making of an American* (1901).

Roosevelt, Franklin Delano (1882–1945) *32nd president of the United States*
The only child of wealthy parents, Roosevelt spent his early life in New York City and Hyde Park, New York. He graduated from Harvard University in 1904, and after studying law at Columbia University, he was admitted to the New York State bar in 1907. In 1905 he married a distant cousin, Eleanor Roosevelt. His political career began with his election to the New York State

Senate in 1910. President Woodrow Wilson appointed him secretary of the navy during World War I. In 1920, Roosevelt was the Democratic candidate for vice president, sharing the ticket with James M. Cox, but Cox lost the election to Warren G. Harding. Although an attack of poliomyelitis in 1921 left Roosevelt unable to walk, he was elected governor of New York in 1928. In 1932, he defeated the incumbent, Herbert Hoover, in the presidential election. He would be elected to an unprecedented four terms. During his first three months in office, Roosevelt prevailed on Congress to pass the laws known collectively as the New Deal, which were efforts to combat the economic instability and unemployment of the Great Depression. The depression was the first crisis of Roosevelt's presidency; the second was World War II. Roosevelt asked Congress to declare war after the December 7, 1941, Japanese attack on Pearl Harbor, Hawaii. He died in 1945, before the United States and its allies achieved victory.

Warrior, Clyde (1939–1968) *American Indian activist*
Warrior was born in eastern Oklahoma among the Ponca Indians, a tribal nation that had formerly occupied land around the Niobrara River in Nebraska. He was raised by his grandparents in a traditional Ponca setting and spoke Ponca as his first language. As a teenager he became an accomplished practitioner of traditional dance, and as a young man he committed to memory a great number of Ponca and traditional songs. Warrior's activism began while he was in college. He headed the National Indian Youth Council (NIYC), a civil rights organization he helped to found in Gallup, New Mexico, in 1961. In 1963 and 1964 he led the NIYC in demonstrations for Indian fishing rights in the Pacific Northwest. Warrior graduated from Northeastern State University in Tahlequah, Oklahoma, in 1966. In May and June 1968 the NIYC participated in the Poor People's Campaign in Washington, D.C. In July 1968 Warrior died of liver failure brought on by alcoholism.

Washington, Booker Taliaferro (1856–1915) *educator, founder of the Tuskegee Institute, spokesperson for African Americans*
Washington, who was born a slave in Franklin County, Virginia, moved with his family to Malden, West Virginia, after the Civil War. There, from the age of nine, Washington worked in a salt furnace and in coal mines. In 1872 he enrolled in the Hampton Normal and Agricultural Institute in Virginia. He taught for two years in Malden after

graduating in 1875 and then entered the Wayland Seminary in Washington, D.C. He returned to the Hampton Institute to teach in 1879. In 1881 the institute's director, Samuel Chapman Armstrong, chose Washington to head the recently established Tuskegee Institute, a trade school for African Americans in Alabama. Washington's advocacy of vocational training and temporary educational and professional inferiority for African Americans persuaded whites to recognize him as a spokesperson for his race. Although many black Americans accepted Washington's line of thinking, his opinions provoked criticism from other African-American leaders, most notably the scholar W. E. B. Du Bois. Washington's books include *The Future of the Negro* (1899); his autobiography, *Up from Slavery* (1901); Life of Frederick Douglass (1907); *The Story of the Negro* (1909); and *My Larger Education* (1911).

Wilson, William Julius (1935–) *sociologist, scholar*

Wilson was born in Derry Township, Pennsylvania, and raised in the working-class town of Blairsville, east of Pittsburgh. He was the oldest of six children born to Esco Wilson, a coal miner, and Pauline Williams, a homemaker. When William was 12 his father died of lung disease. The family received public assistance until Pauline Wilson found work as a housekeeper. William received a scholarship to attend historically black Wilberforce University in Ohio and earned a bachelor's degree in sociology in 1958. He went on to receive a master's degree in 1961 from Bowling Green State University in Ohio and a doctorate in 1966 from Washington State University. In 1965 he began his academic career as an assistant professor at the University of Massachusetts at Amherst. In 1970 he won the university's teacher of the year award. The following year Wilson joined the sociology faculty at the University of Chicago. There he moved ahead quickly: He was granted tenure in his first year and appointed full professor in 1975. In 1978 he assumed the chair of the Sociology Department. During these years Wilson published two influential books; *Power, Racism, and Privilege* (1973) examined race relations in the United States and South Africa. *The Declining Significance of Race* (1978) argued that economic factors and social class were greater determinants of African Americans' prospects than race. In 1987 Wilson published *The Truly Disadvantaged*, which detailed the effects of middle-class flight and the loss of industry on inner-city neighborhoods. In 1990 Wilson reached the pinnacle of academia when he was named a university professor, and in 1991 he was elected to the National Academy of Sciences. At the time his Urban Poverty and Family Life Study was under way. As part of this ambitious project Wilson's research team interviewed 2,500 poor Chicagoans and 190 local employers. With funding generated by this study Wilson established in 1993 the Center for the Study of Urban Inequality at the University of Chicago. In 1996 he published *When Work Disappears*, an exploration of the devastating effects on individual behavior when unemployment in a community becomes chronic and widespread. Also in 1996 he became Malcolm Wiener Professor of Social Policy at the John F. Kennedy School of Government at Harvard University. In 1997 he was part of a research team that undertook a long-term study of the impact of welfare reform on low-income residents of Boston, Chicago, and Baltimore.

Woodmason, Charles (unknown–unknown) *itinerant Anglican minister*

Woodmason was born in England, probably around 1720. Around 1752, he sailed to South Carolina, leaving behind a wife and son. Hoping to establish himself as a planter and merchant, he purchased 18 slaves and gradually acquired 2,150 acres of farmland. In 1757, he opened a store on Black Mingo Creek and also became a lieutenant in the Black River militia company. In 1758, he was appointed justice of the peace for Craven County, a vast area ranging from present-day Cherokee County southwest to Charleston County. Woodmason served as a constable in 1759 and as coroner and collector of the general tax in 1761. It is thought that he returned to England in 1762 to settle the estate of his wife, who had recently died. In his absence the provost marshal seized his land and sold it for debts. Woodmason was back in South Carolina by July 1763 and serving as justice of the peace in Charleston. On December 21, 1765, he sailed once more to England to be ordained in the Anglican Church. He was licensed to be an itinerant preacher in the Parish of St. Mark's, a thinly settled frontier region of South Carolina where people lived in relative poverty. Between 1766 and 1772, he traveled more than 3,000 miles a year and founded more than 30 congregations. Exactly when Woodmason left South Carolina is unknown, but in 1773 he moved to Maryland and preached at churches in Baltimore County and as far away as York County, Pennsylvania. In 1774, he refused to read aloud in church a plea for money to aid the poor of Boston, believing the funds would be spent on ammunition for fighting the British. Fearing for his safety, he sailed to England and preached there for two years before being lost to history.

Yates, John Van Ness (1779–1839) *secretary of the state of New York*

Yates was born in Albany, New York, and was a lifelong inhabitant of his childhood home. He was educated in the classics and became a clerk in a law office, where he learned the legal profession. In 1801 he was one of the first trustees of Albany's United Presbyterian Church, and in 1806 he was appointed captain of a light infantry company. In 1806 he was master in chancery, and from 1809 until 1816, with some interruption, he served as recorder of the city. From 1818 through 1826 Yates was secretary of the state of New York. In 1824 he surveyed poverty in New York for the legislature. His recommendations, including the construction of a poorhouse in every county, influenced public policy toward the poor in New York and other states. Yates authored several books on law and was known among Albany's lawyers as "The Walking Library" because of his vast knowledge of points of law.

Appendix C
Maps

1. Tenant Farms, 1920–1925
2. Percent of All People in Poverty, 1960
3. Poverty in America, 1970
4. Aid to Families with Dependent Children (AFDC) Payments, 1984
5. Poverty in Appalachia, 1989

Tenant Farms, 1920–1925

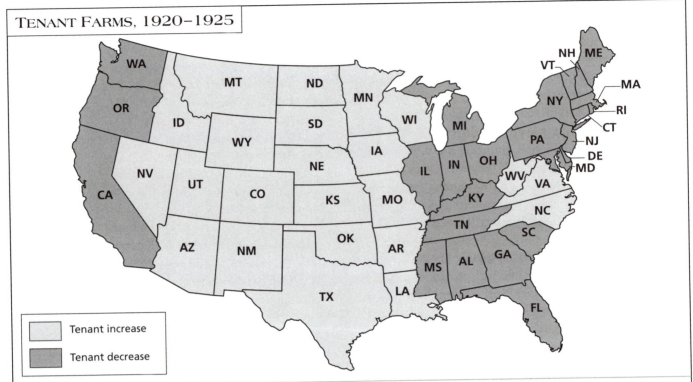

Tenant increase

Tenant decrease

State	Tenants, Increase or Decrease	Percent of Farms Operated by Tenants, 1920/1925	Owners (Incl. Managers), Increase or Decrease	State	Tenants, Increase or Decrease	Percent of Farms Operated by Tenants, 1920/1925	Owners (Incl. Managers), Increase or Decrease
Alabama	−4,071	57.9%/60.7%	−14,465	Nebraska	+5,869	42.9%/46.4%	−2,552
Arizona	+526	18.1%/21.6%	+297	Nevada	+10	9.4%/7.8%	+740
Arkansas	+6,678	51.3%/56.7%	−17,288	New Hampshire	−359	6.7%/4.8%	+901
California	−5,095	21.4%/14.7%	+23,834	New Jersey	−2,103	23.0%/15.9%	+2,072
Colorado	+4,160	23.0%/30.9%	−6,068	New Mexico	+1,771	12.2%/17.1%	+72
Connecticut	−431	8.5%/6.4%	+1,016	New York	−10,558	19.2%/14.1%	+6,117
Delaware	−318	39.3%/35.8%	+435	North Carolina	+10,795	43.5%/45.2%	+2,924
Florida	−1,068	25.3%/21.3%	+6,280	North Dakota	+6,178	25.6%/34.4%	−7,898
Georgia	−47,945	66.6%/63.8%	−13,685	Ohio	−13,348	29.5%/25.5%	+1,356
Idaho	+3,185	15.9%/24.4%	−4,698	Oklahoma	+17,662	51.0%/58.6%	−12,432
Illinois	−6,546	42.7%/42.0%	−5,034	Oregon	−21	18.8%/16.8%	+5,725
Indiana	−8,498	32.0%/29.2%	−842	Pennsylvania	−9,305	21.9%/17.4%	+7,498
Iowa	+6,332	41.7%/44.7%	−6,281	Rhode Island	−161	15.5%/12.1%	−11
Kansas	+3,300	40.4%/42.2%	−2,707	South Carolina	−11,801	64.5%/65.1%	−8,125
Kentucky	−7,532	33.4%/32.0%	−4,580	South Dakota	+7,005	34.9%/41.5%	−2,105
Louisiana	+2,180	57.1%/60.1%	−5,192	Tennessee	−166	41.1%/41.0%	+61
Maine	−305	4.2%/3.4%	+2,111	Texas	+48,913	53.3%/60.4%	−19,304
Maryland	−914	28.9%/26.4%	+2,007	Utah	+102	10.9%/11.1%	+235
Massachusetts	−682	7.1%/4.8%	+2,135	Vermont	−796	11.6%/9.3%	−493
Michigan	−5,603	17.7%/15.1%	+1,483	Virginia	+1,104	25.6%/25.2%	+6,377
Minnesota	+6,945	24.7%/27.1%	+2,808	Washington	−476	18.7%/16.3%	+7,455
Mississippi	−4,060	66.1%/68.3%	−10,813	West Virginia	+677	16.2%/16.3%	+2,414
Missouri	+9,303	28.8%/32.6%	−11,829	Wisconsin	+2,678	14.4%/15.5%	+1,182
Montana	+3,749	11.3%/21.9%	−14,520	Wyoming	+808	12.5%/17.9%	−1,044
United States	**+7,724**	**38.1%/38.6%**	**−84,450**				

Source: Truesdell, Leon E. *Journal of Farm Economics* 8, no. 4 (Oct. 1926), p. 445.

© Infobase Publishing

PERCENT OF ALL PEOPLE IN POVERTY, 1960

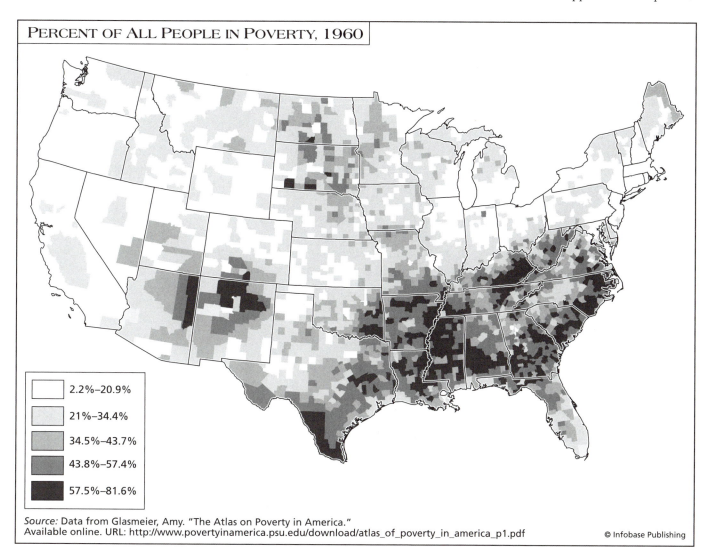

- 2.2%–20.9%
- 21%–34.4%
- 34.5%–43.7%
- 43.8%–57.4%
- 57.5%–81.6%

Source: Data from Glasmeier, Amy. "The Atlas on Poverty in America."
Available online. URL: http://www.povertyinamerica.psu.edu/download/atlas_of_poverty_in_america_p1.pdf

© Infobase Publishing

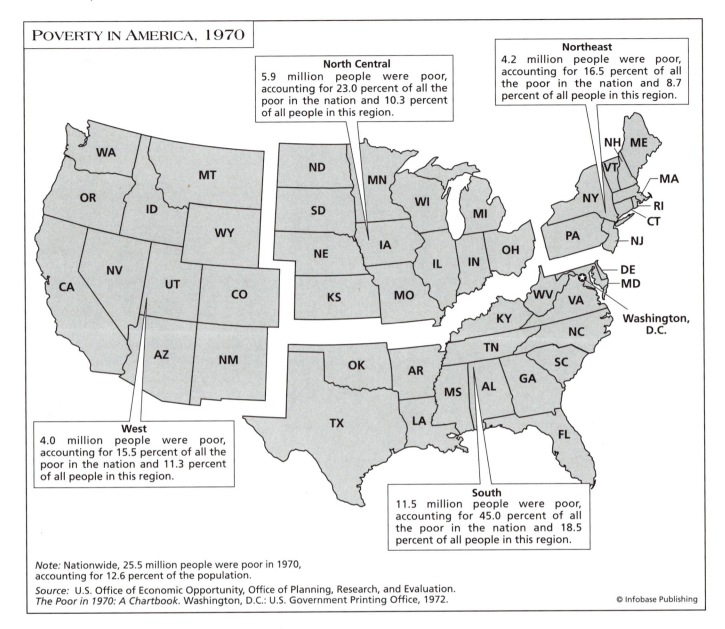

POVERTY IN AMERICA, 1970

North Central
5.9 million people were poor, accounting for 23.0 percent of all the poor in the nation and 10.3 percent of all people in this region.

Northeast
4.2 million people were poor, accounting for 16.5 percent of all the poor in the nation and 8.7 percent of all people in this region.

West
4.0 million people were poor, accounting for 15.5 percent of all the poor in the nation and 11.3 percent of all people in this region.

South
11.5 million people were poor, accounting for 45.0 percent of all the poor in the nation and 18.5 percent of all people in this region.

Washington, D.C.

Note: Nationwide, 25.5 million people were poor in 1970, accounting for 12.6 percent of the population.

Source: U.S. Office of Economic Opportunity, Office of Planning, Research, and Evaluation. *The Poor in 1970: A Chartbook.* Washington, D.C.: U.S. Government Printing Office, 1972.

© Infobase Publishing

AID TO FAMILIES WITH DEPENDENT CHILDREN (AFDC) PAYMENTS, 1984

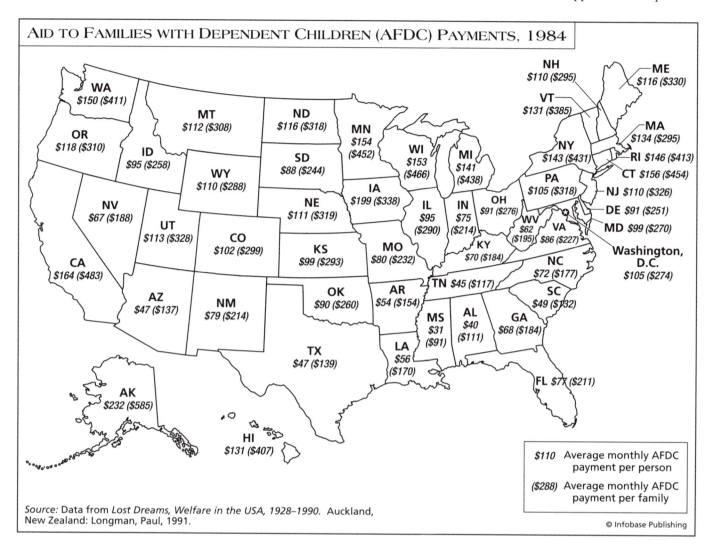

WA $150 ($411)

OR $118 ($310)

MT $112 ($308)

ND $116 ($318)

MN $154 ($452)

NH $110 ($295)

ME $116 ($330)

VT $131 ($385)

ID $95 ($258)

SD $88 ($244)

WI $153 ($466)

MI $141 ($438)

NY $143 ($431)

MA $134 ($295)

RI $146 ($413)

CT $156 ($454)

WY $110 ($288)

IA $199 ($338)

PA $105 ($318)

NJ $110 ($326)

NV $67 ($188)

NE $111 ($319)

IL $95 ($290)

IN $75 ($214)

OH $91 ($276)

WV $62 ($195)

VA $86 ($227)

DE $91 ($251)

MD $99 ($270)

UT $113 ($328)

CO $102 ($299)

KS $99 ($293)

MO $80 ($232)

KY $70 ($184)

NC $72 ($177)

Washington, D.C. $105 ($274)

CA $164 ($483)

AZ $47 ($137)

NM $79 ($214)

OK $90 ($260)

AR $54 ($154)

TN $45 ($117)

SC $49 ($132)

MS $31 ($91)

AL $40 ($111)

GA $68 ($184)

TX $47 ($139)

LA $56 ($170)

FL $77 ($211)

AK $232 ($585)

HI $131 ($407)

$110   Average monthly AFDC payment per person

($288)   Average monthly AFDC payment per family

Source: Data from *Lost Dreams, Welfare in the USA, 1928–1990.* Auckland, New Zealand: Longman, Paul, 1991.

© Infobase Publishing

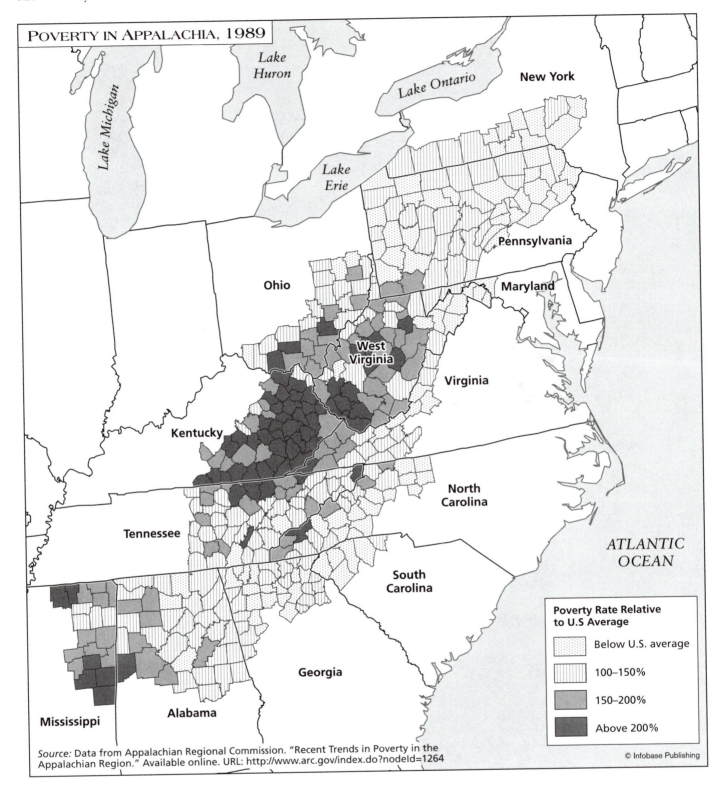

POVERTY IN APPALACHIA, 1989

Lake Huron

Lake Ontario

Lake Michigan

Lake Erie

New York

Ohio

Pennsylvania

Maryland

West Virginia

Virginia

Kentucky

North Carolina

Tennessee

South Carolina

ATLANTIC OCEAN

Georgia

Mississippi

Alabama

Poverty Rate Relative to U.S Average

- Below U.S. average
- 100–150%
- 150–200%
- Above 200%

Source: Data from Appalachian Regional Commission. "Recent Trends in Poverty in the Appalachian Region." Available online. URL: http://www.arc.gov/index.do?nodeId=1264

© Infobase Publishing

Appendix D
Graphs and Tables

Graphs

1. Habits of Poorhouse Inmates in New York State, by Sex, 1873
2. Poverty among Selected Groups, 1970
3. Number of People in Poverty, 1959–1985
4. Number in Poverty and Poverty Rate, 1959–2004
5. Poverty Rates by Age, 1959–2004
6. Three-Year Average Poverty Rate by State, 2002–2004

Tables

1. Ages at Time of Admission of Pauper Inmates of Poorhouses and Almshouses in New York State, 1873
2. Ages of Pauper Inmates of Poorhouses and Almshouses in New York State, 1873
3. Birthplaces of 12,614 Paupers in New York State, 1873
4. Principal Disabilities in Five Thousand Dependent Families in New York City, 1913
5. Weighted Average Poverty Thresholds for Families of Specified Size, 1959–2003
6. Percent of Families and Unrelated Individuals with Income below Specified Levels, 1963
7. People Sixty-five Years and over in Poverty, by Race and Spanish Origin, Selected Years, 1959–1985
8. Related Children under Eighteen in Poverty, by Race and Spanish Origin, Selected Years, 1960–1985
9. Percentage of Population in Poverty, 1964–1983
10. Number and Percentage of Population in Poverty, by Family Status and Race, Female-Headed Households, 1973–1985
11. Number and Percentage of Population in Poverty, by Family Status and Race, Total Population, 1973–1985
12. People and Families in Poverty by Selected Characteristics, 2003 and 2004

HABITS OF POORHOUSE INMATES IN NEW YORK STATE, BY SEX, 1873

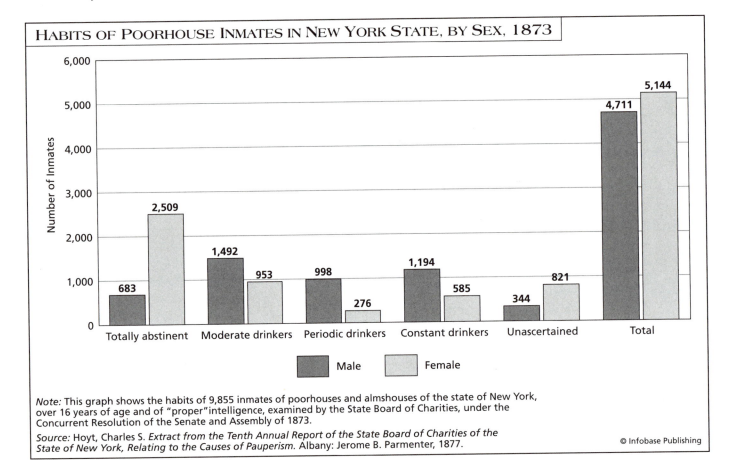

Note: This graph shows the habits of 9,855 inmates of poorhouses and almshouses of the state of New York, over 16 years of age and of "proper" intelligence, examined by the State Board of Charities, under the Concurrent Resolution of the Senate and Assembly of 1873.

Source: Hoyt, Charles S. *Extract from the Tenth Annual Report of the State Board of Charities of the State of New York, Relating to the Causes of Pauperism.* Albany: Jerome B. Parmenter, 1877.

© Infobase Publishing

POVERTY AMONG SELECTED GROUPS, 1970

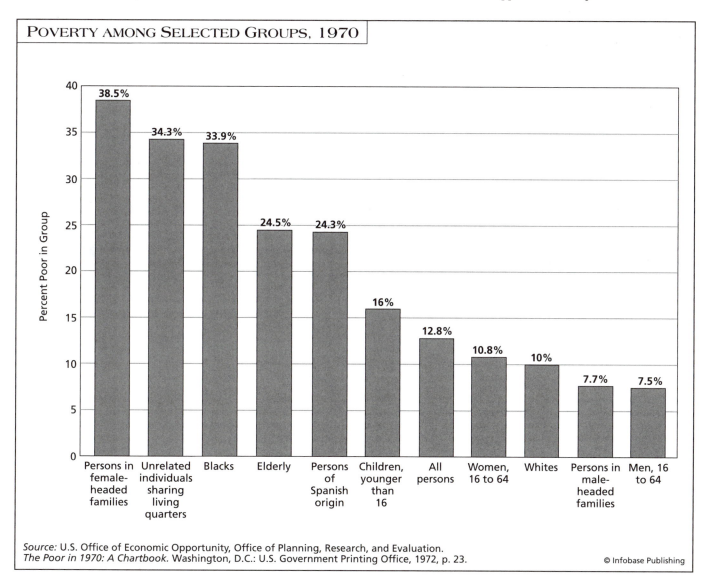

Source: U.S. Office of Economic Opportunity, Office of Planning, Research, and Evaluation.
The Poor in 1970: A Chartbook. Washington, D.C.: U.S. Government Printing Office, 1972, p. 23.

© Infobase Publishing

NUMBER OF PEOPLE IN POVERTY, 1959–1985

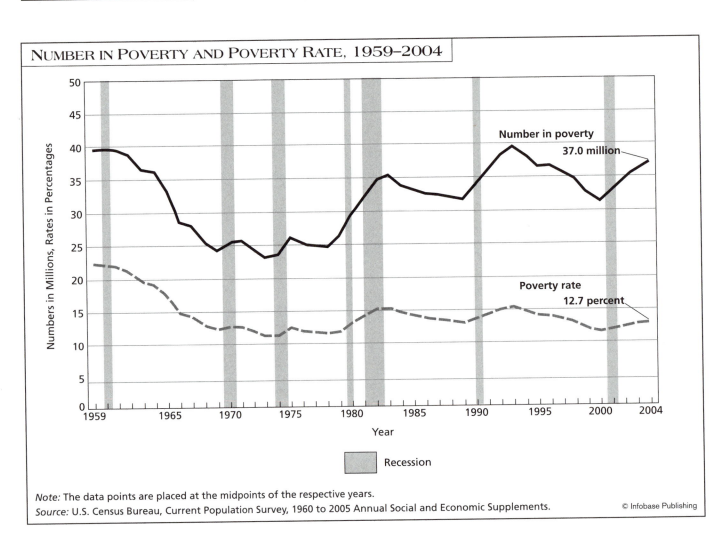

Note: Numbers are in thousands.

Source: Data from Axinn, June, and Mark J. Stern. *Dependency and Poverty.* Lexington, Mass.: Lexington Books,1988.

© Infobase Publishing

NUMBER IN POVERTY AND POVERTY RATE, 1959–2004

Number in poverty
37.0 million

Poverty rate
12.7 percent

Recession

Note: The data points are placed at the midpoints of the respective years.

Source: U.S. Census Bureau, Current Population Survey, 1960 to 2005 Annual Social and Economic Supplements.

© Infobase Publishing

POVERTY RATES BY AGE, 1959–2004

65 years and older

Under 18 years

17.8 percent

11.3 percent

18 to 64 years

9.8 percent

Rates in Percentages

Year

Recession

Note: The data points are placed at the midpoints of the respective years. Data for people 18 to 64 and people 65 and older are not available from 1960 to 1965.

Source: U.S. Census Bureau, Current Population Survey, 1960 to 2005 Annual Social and Economic Supplements.

© Infobase Publishing

THREE-YEAR AVERAGE POVERTY RATE BY STATE, 2002–2004

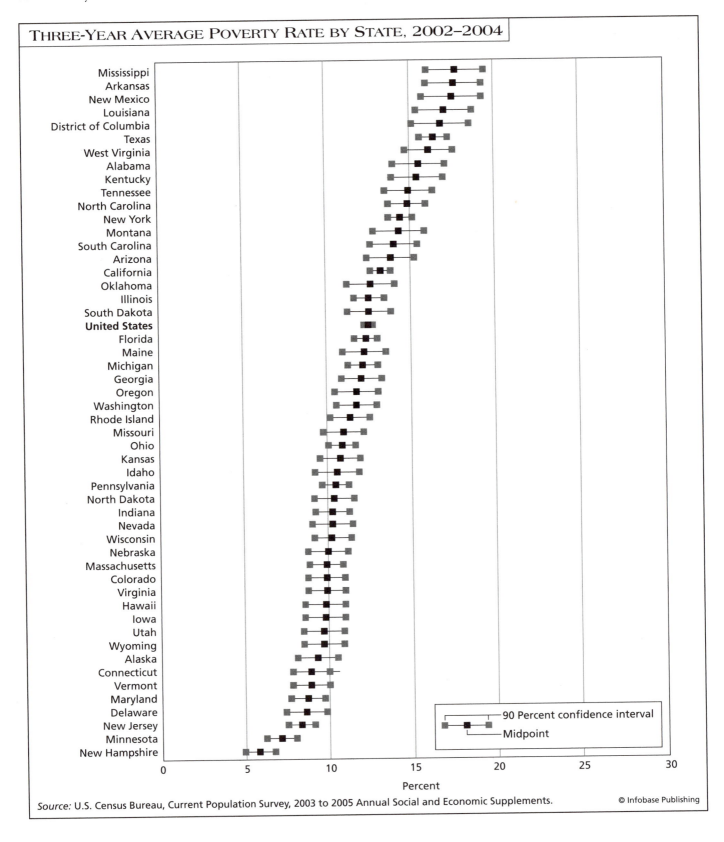

Source: U.S. Census Bureau, Current Population Survey, 2003 to 2005 Annual Social and Economic Supplements.

© Infobase Publishing

Ages at Time of Admission of Pauper Inmates of Poorhouses and Almshouses in New York State, 1873

Counties	Total	At Birth	Under Two Years	Two Years and under Five	Five Years and under Ten	Ten Years and under Twenty	Twenty Years and under Thirty	Twenty Years and under Forty	Forty Years and under Fifty	Fifty Years and under Sixty	Sixty Years and under Seventy	Seventy Years and under Eighty	Over Eighty Years
Albany	259	10	7	12	16	24	36	45	49	21	18	19	2
Allegany	63	2	–	3	2	9	14	7	2	7	10	3	4
Broome	78	3	1	–	5	12	8	8	8	13	10	8	2
Cattaraugus	91	2	–	1	2	6	11	24	13	10	11	7	4
Cayuga	84	5	–	–	–	5	15	9	14	15	12	7	2
Chatauqua	161	5	–	1	4	10	34	29	23	24	17	10	4
Chemung	36	1	–	–	–	6	10	2	3	5	3	3	3
Chenango	85	4	2	–	4	10	10	11	16	13	7	5	3
Clinton	52	1	1	–	1	8	7	7	8	4	12	1	2
Columbia	118	3	1	2	2	10	12	18	17	20	19	10	4
Cortland	70	2	1	4	3	6	9	5	13	11	9	6	1
Delaware	45	1	1	–	–	5	6	6	9	8	4	3	2
Dutchess	162	7	2	1	6	8	16	21	18	25	37	17	4
Erie	462	6	1	3	2	26	99	88	83	63	49	25	17
Essex	86	12	2	4	11	12	8	14	5	6	7	2	3
Franklin	43	3	–	–	–	6	5	8	2	3	7	5	4
Fulton	58	3	2	4	3	5	9	7	10	4	5	2	4
Genesee	71	4	2	–	1	8	11	7	12	6	10	6	4
Greene	104	10	5	3	5	9	10	13	7	17	11	10	4
Hamilton	–	–	–	–	–	–	–	–	–	–	–	–	–
Herkimer	77	3	1	–	3	3	11	11	9	7	17	7	5
Jefferson	148	8	4	4	3	14	26	27	18	15	15	11	3
Kings	1,870	28	26	96	174	138	358	343	273	209	148	58	19
Lewis	53	1	–	1	1	6	10	11	6	1	8	7	1
Livingston	106	8	–	5	5	4	16	12	12	16	12	8	8
Madison	89	2	–	1	–	9	17	8	15	14	12	8	3
Monroe	327	6	2	–	4	18	58	67	51	51	38	19	13
Montgomery	44	4	2	–	1	8	9	8	4	3	2	3	–
New York	4,698	115	132	224	514	384	824	912	612	449	331	158	43
Niagra	115	2	7	10	8	5	11	10	12	17	20	9	4
Oneida	312	8	2	7	5	25	68	54	43	35	36	18	11
Onondaga	212	4	–	–	1	6	42	46	41	31	23	14	4
Ontario	113	7	4	7	10	7	13	14	18	15	10	5	–
Orange	218	15	8	9	10	24	18	29	25	22	32	21	5
Orleans	58	3	1	2	2	3	5	7	10	11	9	4	1
Oswego	115	1	4	2	3	8	25	18	17	14	9	11	3
Otsego	82	10	5	5	3	9	12	5	8	10	6	7	2
Putnam	39	2	4	6	2	4	3	8	1	1	4	4	–
Queens	109	6	7	3	3	14	15	16	14	13	9	7	2
Rensselaer	156	16	9	4	3	7	26	26	15	24	14	12	–
Richmond	84	8	2	6	3	5	7	13	14	13	7	5	1
Rockland	50	3	–	7	4	2	3	7	5	8	6	4	1
St. Lawrence	104	5	2	6	3	12	10	8	19	13	9	12	5
Saratoga	114	3	1	4	3	7	9	18	16	22	16	10	5
Schenectady	56	–	–	1	–	3	4	10	7	15	9	5	2
Schoharie	50	7	–	1	3	5	3	4	8	3	6	10	–
Schuyler	–	–	–	–	–	–	–	–	–	–	–	–	–
Seneca	36	4	3	2	1	3	2	5	4	3	5	4	–
Steuben	87	6	2	3	3	9	12	7	18	7	12	8	–
Suffolk	130	8	2	1	1	11	13	17	16	19	23	13	6
Sullivan	76	5	1	2	1	6	10	10	12	8	14	5	2
Tioga	45	2	–	1	3	5	8	4	8	5	4	4	2
Tompkins	39	–	–	3	–	2	4	3	5	8	8	6	–
Ulster	153	8	2	8	14	12	20	20	23	18	20	6	2
Warren	57	2	–	2	4	7	12	5	8	7	7	3	–
Washington	108	8	3	–	4	14	13	18	14	17	12	5	–
Wayne	72	5	3	–	2	5	10	8	11	6	10	11	1
Westchester	188	11	6	13	15	8	23	21	25	29	23	8	6
Wyoming	63	1	2	1	–	5	7	16	10	4	5	8	4
Yates	32	3	1	–	3	4	3	2	4	5	4	2	1
Totals	12,614	422	276	485	889	1,006	2,070	2,157	1,743	1,443	1,213	669	241

Note: This data was collected by the State Board of Charities under the Concurrent Resolution of the Senate and Assembly of 1873.
Source: Hoyt, Charles S. Extract from the *Tenth Annual Report of the State Board of Charities of the State of New York, Relating to the Causes of Pauperism.* (Albany: Jerome B. Parmenter, 1877), pp. 212–213.

Ages of Pauper Inmates of Poorhouses and Almhouses in New York State, 1873

Counties	Total	Under Two Years	Two Years and under Five	Five Years and under Ten	Ten Years and under Sixteen	Sixteen Years and under Twenty	Twenty Years and under Thirty	Thirty Years and under Forty	Forty Years and under Fifty	Fifty Years and under Sixty	Sixty Years and under Seventy	Seventy Years and under Eighty	Over Eighty Years
Albany	259	7	12	19	13	11	24	34	53	31	23	30	2
Allegany	63	2	1	1	3	2	8	4	11	4	13	8	6
Broome	78	3	–	–	1	5	9	5	9	12	17	12	5
Cattaraugus	91	1	1	1	2	2	4	20	15	15	12	9	9
Cayuga	84	5	–	–	–	1	9	5	6	14	23	17	4
Chatauqua	161	2	1	3	1	4	20	27	29	25	22	16	11
Chemung	36	1	–	–	–	2	4	11	1	4	2	8	3
Chenango	85	2	–	2	4	4	9	11	8	17	16	7	5
Clinton	52	–	–	1	2	1	10	10	3	6	10	4	5
Columbia	118	2	1	1	–	3	12	17	15	18	24	15	10
Cortland	70	2	1	2	1	3	8	3	8	14	11	10	7
Delaware	45	1	1	–	–	–	8	5	8	4	10	5	3
Dutchess	162	2	3	4	3	3	12	15	15	19	36	40	10
Erie	462	6	1	–	4	10	79	83	80	83	55	48	13
Essex	86	2	6	8	9	9	4	12	9	9	8	6	4
Franklin	43	2	–	–	2	1	4	5	8	2	4	8	7
Fulton	58	4	2	4	3	3	5	6	4	9	9	3	5
Genesee	71	1	1	4	1	2	7	7	8	10	14	11	5
Greene	104	3	6	11	2	4	6	5	11	13	17	19	7
Hamilton	–	–	–	–	–	–	–	–	–	–	–	–	–
Herkimer	77	–	1	2	2	–	4	9	8	7	19	17	8
Jefferson	148	3	5	2	5	3	20	19	20	23	18	15	15
Kings	1,870	21	57	172	113	40	224	364	293	253	186	103	44
Lewis	53	–	–	3	–	2	5	5	10	9	8	10	1
Livingston	106	4	3	6	4	2	12	9	14	16	15	10	11
Madison	89	2	–	–	1	3	12	12	10	10	17	12	10
Monroe	327	7	–	2	1	9	30	55	56	57	63	32	15
Montgomery	44	2	2	1	2	2	7	6	7	6	3	6	–
New York	4,698	188	177	459	281	128	611	916	693	510	397	256	82
Niagra	115	2	9	9	6	3	8	6	7	16	22	20	7
Oneida	312	8	5	5	6	7	28	66	45	49	42	33	18
Onondaga	212	–	3	1	1	3	13	41	47	40	31	28	4
Ontario	113	2	4	11	6	4	6	14	13	14	20	13	6
Orange	218	6	16	10	8	12	17	20	27	17	29	41	15
Orleans	58	1	2	1	2	1	3	4	9	13	12	9	1
Oswego	115	2	1	3	2	3	12	20	18	16	18	12	8
Otsego	82	3	5	7	4	2	11	10	6	10	10	11	3
Putnam	39	2	5	5	4	–	–	5	3	4	3	7	1
Queens	109	1	5	7	5	3	6	16	24	15	13	10	4
Rensselaer	156	15	12	4	3	1	17	18	15	29	23	15	4
Richmond	84	2	4	11	1	1	5	10	12	16	9	10	3
Rockland	50	2	2	6	4	1	2	5	6	7	6	7	2
St. Lawrence	104	6	1	4	2	5	10	10	11	15	15	15	10
Saratoga	114	3	2	3	4	2	5	11	12	20	21	23	8
Schenectady	56	–	–	1	1	1	–	2	10	8	20	9	4
Schoharie	50	2	1	4	3	1	2	4	4	7	7	10	5
Schuyler	–	–	–	–	–	–	–	–	–	–	–	–	–
Seneca	36	1	1	4	1	–	1	5	6	3	6	5	3
Steuben	87	6	3	4	2	3	11	5	8	14	21	9	1
Suffolk	130	4	5	1	1	5	12	15	18	17	23	23	6
Sullivan	76	1	7	–	1	1	7	8	11	8	16	12	4
Tioga	46	1	1	2	2	1	3	5	8	6	8	7	2
Tompkins	39	–	2	–	–	1	2	3	1	6	7	16	1
Ulster	153	7	9	12	6	6	13	20	22	17	24	14	3
Warren	57	2	–	2	4	2	7	5	9	7	13	4	2
Washington	108	4	4	4	4	4	12	16	12	20	12	16	–
Wayne	72	3	–	2	1	1	9	10	10	4	16	12	4
Westchester	188	10	9	22	4	2	12	24	28	23	28	18	8
Wyoming	63	2	–	–	–	–	6	10	10	12	5	12	6
Yates	32	–	3	1	1	1	3	–	4	5	6	5	3
Totals	12,614	373	403	854	549	336	1,411	2,068	1,828	1,638	1,538	1,163	453

Note: This data was collected by the State Board of Charities under the Concurrent Resolution of the Senate and Assembly of 1873.
Source: Hoyt, Charles S. Extract from the *Tenth Annual Report of the State Board of Charities of the State of New York, Relating to the Causes of Pauperism.* (Albany: Jerome B. Parmenter, 1877), pp. 214–215.

Birthplaces of 12,614 paupers in New York State, 1873

Counties	Total	New York	Other States of the Union	Canada	Other British American Provinces	England	Ireland	Scotland	Wales	France	Germany	Other Countries of Europe	Other Countries	Unascertained
Albany	259	92	4	2	-	11	128	-	-	1	15	3-	-	3
Allegany	63	37	17	-	-	1	6	-	-	-	-	-	-	2
Broome	78	50	13	-	-	3	12	-	-	-	2	1	-	-
Cattaraugus	91	50	6	-	-	6	12	2	-	-	7	2	-	7
Cayuga	84	41	10	-	-	3	26	-	-	-	1	5	-	1
Chatauqua	161	84	35	23	-	4	14	-	4	-	10	-	-	3
Chemung	36	21	9	-	-	2	3	-	-	-	1	-	-	-
Chenango	85	61	10	-	-	1	5	-	-	1	1	-	-	6
Clinton	52	19	6	12	-	2	10	-	-	3	-	-	-	-
Columbia	118	69	4	-	-	4	32	1	-	-	6	-	-	2
Cortland	70	44	8	21	-	1	3	-	-	-	1	-	-	11
Delaware	45	31	1	-	-	2	7	2	-	-	2	3	-	-
Dutchess	162	91	15	1	-	2	41	2	-	1	6	14	1	-
Erie	462	92	35	13	2	18	147	4	1	3	117	-	-	15
Essex	86	522	8	15	-	1	5	1	-	2	-	-	-	2
Franklin	43	12	10	10	-	-	10	-	-	-	-	-	-	1
Fulton	58	47	5	-	1	1	4	-	-	-	-	1	-	-
Genesee	71	33	12	-	-	9	13	-	-	-	3	-	-	-
Greene	1	4	78	7	-	-	10	1	-	-	2	-	-	3
Hamilton	-	-	-	-	-	-	-	-	-	-	-	2	-	-
Herkimer	77	40	3	2	1	3	12	2	-	1	8	1	1	3
Jefferson	148	79	7	15	1	4	31	1	1	-	3	22	2	4
Kings	1,870	554	88	7	5	72	854	18	-	9	213	1	-	26
Lewis	53	29	2	1	-	-	4	-	1	4	7	-	1	4
Livingston	105	62	14	2	-	4	17	1	-	-	2	-	-	3
Madison	89	46	16	1	-	3	14	3	1	-	1	4	-	4
Monroe	327	90	15	11	-	17	138	9	1	1	41	-	-	-
Montgomery	44	33	2	-	-	-	6	-	-	-	2	91	13	1
New York	4,698	1,469	198	22	207	2,040	2,040	45	3	42	507	1	-	49
Niagra	115	47	9	6	-	8	29	2	-	4	9	1	-	-
Oneida	312	126	40	5	-	19	77	3	7	3	22	3	-	9
Onondaga	212	77	12	3	-	10	79	2	-	1	25	-	-	-
Ontario	113	56	13	-	-	4	35	-	-	-	4	-	-	1
Orange	218	145	5	-	-	10	36	1	-	2	13	-	-	6
Orleans	58	35	7	-	-	1	11	-	-	-	2	1	-	2
Oswego	115	51	7	6	-	9	34	-	-	1	3	3	-	3
Otsego	82	60	6	-	-	1	10	2	-	-	-	-	-	-
Putnam	39	33	-	-	-	-	4	-	-	-	2	-	-	-
Queens	109	56	9	1	-	1	30	1	-	-	7	1	-	4
Rensselaer	156	65	9	2	-	3	70	1	-	-	5	-	-	-
Richmond	84	36	8	1	-	2	29	2	-	1	5	-	-	-
Rockland	50	29	4	-	-	5	8	1	-	-	3	1	-	-
St. Lawrence	104	34	14	17	-	5	22	1	-	2	-	-	-	8
Saratoga	114	66	5	-	-	2	38	-	-	1	2	2	-	-
Schenectady	56	28	4	-	-	3	7	2	-	1	8	-	-	1
Schoharie	50	42	-	-	-	1	3	-	-	-	2	-	-	2
Schuyler	-	-	-	-	-	-	-	-	-	-	-	-	-	-
Seneca	36	24	3	-	-	-	7	-	-	-	1	1	-	1
Steuben	87	63	5	-	-	4	11	-	-	1	-	2	-	2
Suffolk	130	96	5	-	-	5	11	1	-	1	9	-	-	-
Sullivan	76	2	2	2	-	-	11	2	-	1	14	-	-	4
Tioga	46	32	6	1	-	-	5	-	-	-	-	-	-	2
Tompkins	39	21	7	-	-	2	4	-	-	-	1	1	-	3
Ulster	155	86	3	1	-	7	38	2	-	1	8	1	-	6
Warren	57	42	6	2	-	3	4	-	-	-	-	-	-	-
Washington	108	64	9	4	-	3	24	-	-	-	1	-	-	3
Wayne	72	44	10	-	-	3	8	-	-	-	5	2	-	-
Westchester	188	83	14	1	-	7	65	2	-	1	7	4	1	3
Wyoming	63	27	16	-	-	2	7	1	-	1	7	1	-	1
Yates	32	21	2	-	-	-	7	-	-	-	-	-	-	2
Totals	12,614	5,035	800	170	22	502	4,328	118	19	90	1,123	175	19	213

Note: This data was collected by the State Board of Charities under the Concurrent Resolution of the Senate and Assembly of 1873.
Source: Hoyt, Charles S. Extract from the *Tenth Annual Report of the State Board of Charities of the State of New York, Relating to the Causes of Pauperism.* (Albany: Jerome B. Parmenter, 1877), pp. 208–209.

Principal Disabilities in Five Thousand Dependent Families in New York City, 1913

Disabilities	Number of Individuals Affected	Families	
		Number	Percent
1. Unemployment	4424	3458	69.16
2. Overcrowding	—	2014	44.68[1]
3. Widowhood	—	1472	29.44
4. Chronic physical disability other than tuberculosis or rheumatism	1603	1365	27.30
5. Temporary physical disability other than accident or childbirth	1158	984	19.68
6. More than three children under fourteen	—	944	18.88
7. Intemperance	1000	833	16.66
8. Less than five years in New York City	—	814	16.28
9. Tuberculosis	675	619	12.38
10. Desertion and persistent non-support	—	606	12.12
11. Head of family sixty years old or more	—	599	11.98
12. Laziness, shiftlessness, etc.	667	588	11.76
13. Childbirth	363	363	7.26
14. Rheumatism	359	347	6.94
15. Immorality	337	256	5.12
16. Mental disease, defect, or deficiency	267	248	4.96
17. Cruelty, abuse, etc.	229	221	4.42
18. Accident	201	198	3.96
19. Untruthfulness, unreliability, etc.	210	194	388
20. Criminal record	161	151	3.02
21. Violent or irritable temper, etc.	148	140	2.80
22. Waywardness of children	160	129	2.58
23. Disposition to beg	134	117	2.34
24. Child labor (generally not illegal)	45	42	0.84
25. Gambling	22	22	0.44

[1] Based on the 4508 in which there was definite information on this point.
Source: Devine, Edward T. *Misery and Its Causes* (New York: Macmillan Co., 1913), p. 204.
Weighted Average Poverty Thresholds for Families of Specified Size, 1959–2003

Weighted Average Poverty Thresholds for Families of Specified Size, 1959–2003

Calendar Year	Unrelated Individuals			Two People		
	All Ages	Under Age 65	Aged 65 or Older	All Ages	Head of Household under Age 65	Head of Household under Age 65 or Older
1959	$1,467	$1,503	$1,397	$1,894	$1,952	$1,761
1960	1,490	1,526	1,418	1,924	1,982	1,788
1961	1,506	1,545	1,433	1,942	2,005	1,808
1962	1,519	1,562	1,451	1,962	2,027	1,828
1963	1,539	1,581	1,470	1,988	2,052	1,850
1964	1,558	1,601	1,488	2,015	2,079	1,875
1965	1,582	1,626	1,512	2,048	2,114	1,906
1966	1,628	1,674	1,556	2,107	2,175	1,961
1967	1,675	1,722	1,600	2,168	2,238	2,017
1968	1,748	1,797	1,667	2,262	2,333	2,102
1969	1,840	1,893	1,757	2,383	2,458	2,215
1970	1,954	2,010	1,861	2,525	2,604	2,348
1971	2,040	2,098	1,940	2,633	2,716	2,448
1972	2,109	2,168	2,005	2,724	2,808	2,530
1973	2,247	2,307	2,130	2,895	2,984	2,688
1974	2,495	2,562	2,364	3,211	3,312	2,982
1975	2,724	2,797	2,581	3,506	3,617	3,257
1976	2,884	2,959	2,730	3,711	3,826	3,445
1977	3,075	3,152	2,906	3,951	4,072	3,666
1978	3,311	3,392	3,127	4,249	4,383	3,944
1979	3,689	3,778	3,479	4,725	4,878	4,390
1980	4,190	4,290	3,949	5,363	5,537	4,983
1981	4,620	4,729	4,359	5,917	6,111	5,498
1982	4,901	5,019	4,626	6,281	6,487	5,836
1983	5,061	5,180	4,775	6,483	6,697	6,023
1984	5,278	5,400	4,979	6,762	6,983	6,282
1985	5,469	5,593	5,156	6,998	7,231	6,503
1986	5,572	5,701	5,255	7,138	7,372	6,630
1987	5,778	5,909	5,447	7,397	7,641	6,872
1988	6,022	6,155	5,674	7,704	7,958	7,157
1989	6,310	6,451	5,947	8,076	8,343	7,501
1990	6,652	6,800	6,268	8,509	8,794	7,905
1991	6,932	7,086	6,532	8,865	9,165	8,241
1992	7,143	7,299	6,729	9,137	9,443	8,487
1993	7,363	7,518	6,930	9,414	9,728	8,740
1994	7,547	1,710	7,108	9,661	9,976	8,967
1995	7,763	7,929	7,309	9,933	10,259	9,219
1996	7,995	8,163	7,525	10,233	10,564	9,491
1997	8,183	8,350	7,698	10,473	10,805	9,712
1998	8,316	8,480	7,818	10,634	10,972	9,862
1999 11/	8,499	8,667	7,990	10,864	11,213	10,075
2000 12/	8,791	8,959	8,259	11,235	11,589	10,418
2001	9,039	9,214	8,494	11,569	11,920	10,715
2002	9,183	9,359	8,628	11,756	12,110	10,885
2003	9,393	9,573	8,825	12,015	12,384	11,133

Families of Three People or More					
Calendar Year	Three People	Four People	Five People	Six People	Seven People or More
1959	$2,324	$2,973	$3,506	$3,944	$4,849
1960	2,359	3,022	3,560	4,002	4,921
1961	2,383	3,054	3,597	4,041	4,967
1962	2,412	3,089	3,639	4,088	5,032
1963	2,442	3,128	3,685	4,135	5,092
1964	2,473	3,169	3,732	4,193	5,156
1965	2,514	3,223	3,797	4,264	5,248
1966	2,588	3,317	3,908	4,388	5,395
1967	2,661	3,410	4,019	4,516	5,550
1968	2,774	3,553	4,188	4,706	5,789
1969	2,924	3,743	4,415	4,958	6,101
1970	3,099	3,968	4,680	5,260	6,468
1971	3,229	4,137	4,880	5,489	6,751
1972	3,339	4,275	5,044	5,673	6,983
1973	3,548	4,540	5,358	6,028	7,435
1974	3,936	5,038	5,950	6,699	8,253
1975	4,293	5,500	6,499	7,316	9,022
1976	4,540	5,815	6,876	7,760	9,588
1977	4,833	6,191	7,320	8,261	10,216
1978	5,201	6,662	7,880	8,891	11,002
1979	5,784	7,412	8,775	9,914	12,280
1980	6,565	8,414	9,966	11,269	13,955
1981	7,250	9,287	11,007	12,449	···
1982	7,693	9,862	11,684	13,207	···
1983	7,938	10,178	12,049	13,630	···
1984	8,277	10,609	12,566	14,207	···
1985	8,573	10,989	13,007	14,696	···
1986	8,737	11,203	13,259	14,986	···
1987	9,056	11,611	13,737	15,509	···
1988	9,435	12,092	14,304	16,146	···
1989	9,885	12,674	14,990	16,921	···
1990	10,419	13,359	15,792	17,839	···
1991	10,860	13,924	16,456	18,587	···
1992	11,186	14,335	16,952	19,137	···
1993	11,522	14,763	17,449	19,718	···
1994	11,821	15,141	17,900	20,235	···
1995	12,158	15,569	18,408	20,804	···
1996	12,516	16,036	18,952	21,389	···
1997	12,802	16,400	19,380	21,886	···
1998	13,003	16,660	19,680	22,228	···
1999 11/	13,289	17,030	20,128	22,730	···
2000 12/	13,740	17,604	20,815	23,533	···
2001	14,128	18,104	21,405	24,195	···
2002	14,348	18,392	21,744	24,576	···
2003	14,680	18,810	22,245	25,122	···

Calendar Year	Families of Three People or More			Annual Average CPI, All Items (1982–84=100) B/
	Seven People	Eight People	Nine People or More	
1959	...	...	...	29.2
1960	...	...	...	29.6
1961	...	...	...	29.9
1962	...	...	...	30.3
1963	...	...	...	30.6
1964	...	...	...	31.0
1965	...	...	...	31.5
1966	...	...	...	32.5
1967	...	...	...	33.4
1968	...	...	...	34.8
1969	...	...	...	36.7
1970	...	...	...	38.8
1971	...	...	...	40.5
1972	...	...	...	41.8
1973	...	...	...	44.4
1974	...	...	...	49.3
1975	...	...	...	53.8
1976	...	...	...	56.9
1977	...	...	...	60.6
1978	...	...	...	65.2
1979	...	...	...	72.6
1980	$12,761	$14,199	$16,896	82.4
1981	14,110	15,655	18,572	90.9
1982	15,036	16,719	19,698	96.5
1983	15,500	17,170	20,310	99.6
1984	16,096	17,961	21,247	103.9
1985	16,656	18,512	22,083	107.6
1986	17,049	18,791	22,497	109.6
1987	17,649	19,515	23,105	113.6
1988	18,232	20,253	24,129	118.3
1989	19,162	21,328	25,480	124.0
1990	20,241	22,582	26,848	130.7
1991	21,058	23,582	27,942	136.2
1992	21,594	24,053	28,745	140.3
1993	22,383	24,838	29,529	144.5
1994	22,923	25,427	30,300	148.2
1995	23,552	26,237	31,280	152.4
1996	24,268	27,091	31,971	156.9
1997	24,802	27,593	32,566	160.5
1998	25,257	28,166	33,339	163.0
1999 11/	25,918	28,970	34,436	166.6
2000 12/	26,750	29,701	35,150	172.2
2001	27,517	30,627	36,286	177.1
2002	28,001	30,907	37,062	181.7
2003	28,544	31,589	37,656	184.0

Percent of Families and Unrelated Individuals with Income below Specified Levels, 1963

Social Characteristics	All Families Percent with Incomes Below			All Unrelated Individuals Percent with Incomes Below		
	Total Number Thousands	Economy Level[a]	Low-Cost Level[b]	Total Number Thousands	Economy Level[a]	Low-Cost Level[b]
Race of head:						
white	42,663	12.0	19.3	9,719	41.8	48.0
nonwhite	4,773	42.5	55.6	1,463	57.6	61.8
Type of family:						
male head	42,554	12.3	20.0	4,275	33.7	39.4
female head	4,882	40.1	49.3	6,907	50.3	56.3
Work status of head:						
worked in 1963	40,753	11.3	18.2	6,729	26.4	30.8
did not work in 1963	6,683	38.3	51.9	4,453	70.4	78.5
ill or disabled	1,745	46.5	59.9	974	79.8	86.4
keeping house	1,063	49.7	57.8	2,076	71.5	79.8
could not find work	202	49.3	60.5	128	83.3	87.5
Number of earners:						
none	3,695	53.4	70.2	4,204	73.8	82.0
1	20,832	15.7	24.7	6,978	26.0	30.4
2	17,306	8.7	14.4	—	—	—
3 or more	5,603	7.4	12.3	—	—	—
Number of related children under age 18:	19,119	12.7	20.1	—	—	—
none	8,682	12.1	17.7	—	—	—
1	8,579	11.3	17.5	—	—	—
2	5,554	17.4	26.8	—	—	—
3	2,863	22.8	34.8	—	—	—
4	1,429	35.8	53.0	—	—	—
5	1,210	49.3	63.5	—	—	—
6 or more						
Total	47,463	15.1	23.0	11,182	43.9	49.8

Source: Mollie Orshansky, "Counting the Poor," *Social Security Bulletin* 28 (January 1965): 12.
[a]Incomes ranging from $1,580 for a single person under age 65 to $5,090 for a family of seven or more persons.
[b]Income ranging from $1,885 to $6,395.

People Sixty-five Years and over in Poverty, by Race and Spanish Origin, Selected Years, 1959–1985

(number in thousands)

Year	Total		White		Black		Spanish Origin	
	Number	Rate	Number	Rate	Number	Rate	Number	Rate
1959	5,481	35.2%	4,744	33.1%	711	62.5%	NA	NA
1966	5,144	28.5	4,357	26.4	722	55.1	NA	NA
1967	5,388	29.5	4,646	27.7	715	53.3	NA	NA
1968	4,632	25.0	3,939	23.1	655	47.7	NA	NA
1969	4,787	25.3	4,052	23.3	689	50.2	NA	NA
1970	4,709	24.5	3,984	22.5	683	48.0	NA	NA
1971	4,273	21.6	3,605	19.9	623	39.3	NA	NA
1972	3,738	18.6	3,072	16.8	640	39.9	NA	NA
1973	3,354	16.3	2,698	14.4	620	37.1	95	24.9%
1974	3,085	14.6	2,460	12.8	591	34.3	117	28.9
1975	3,317	15.3	2,634	13.4	652	36.3	137	32.6
1976	3,313	15.0	2,633	13.2	644	34.8	128	27.7
1977	3,177	14.1	2,426	11.9	701	36.3	113	21.9
1978	3,233	14.0	2,530	12.1	662	33.9	125	20.9
1979	3,682	15.2	2,911	13.3	740	36.2	154	26.8
1980	3,871	15.7	3,042	13.6	783	38.1	179	30.8
1981	3,853	15.3	2,978	13.1	820	39.0	146	25.7
1982	3,751	14.6	2,870	12.4	811	38.2	159	26.6
1983	3,625	13.8	2,776	11.7	791	36.0	173	22.1
1984	3,330	12.4	2,579	10.7	710	31.7	176	21.5
1985	3,456	12.6	2,698	11.0	717	31.5	219	23.9

Source: U.S. Bureau of the Census, *Money Income and Poverty Status of Families and Persons in the United States*, Current Population Reports, Series P-60 (Washington, D.C.: Government Printing Office, selected years).

Related Children under Eighteen, in Poverty, by Race and Spanish Origin, Selected Years, 1960–1985

(number in thousands)

Year	Total		White		Black		Spanish Origin	
	Number	Rate	Number	Rate	Number	Rate	Number	Rate
1960	17,288	26.5%	11,229	20.0%	NA	NA	NA	NA
1965	14,388	20.7	8,595	14.4	NA	NA	NA	NA
1966	12,146	17.4	7,204	12.1	4,774	50.6%	NA	NA
1967	11,427	16.3	6,729	11.3	4,558	47.4	NA	NA
1968	10,739	15.3	6,373	10.7	4,188	43.1	NA	NA
1969	9,501	13.8	5,667	9.7	3,677	39.6	NA	NA
1970	10,235	14.9	6,138	10.5	3,922	41.5	NA	NA
1971	10,344	15.1	6,341	10.9	3,836	40.7	NA	NA
1972	10,082	14.9	5,784	10.1	4,025	42.7	NA	NA
1973	9,453	14.2	5,462	9.7	3,822	40.6	1,364	27.8%
1974	9,967	15.1	6,079	11.0	3,713	39.6	1,414	28.6
1975	10,882	16.8	6,748	12.5	3,884	41.4	1,619	33.1
1976	10,081	15.8	6,034	11.3	3,758	40.4	1,424	30.1
1977	10,028	16.0	5,943	11.4	3,850	41.6	1,402	28.0
1978	9,772	15.7	5,674	11.0	3,781	41.2	1,354	27.2
1979[a]	9,993	16.0	5,909	11.4	3,745	40.8	1,505	27.7
1980	11,114	17.9	6,817	13.4	3,906	42.1	1,718	33.0
1981[a]	12,068	19.5	7,429	14.7	4,170	44.9	1,874	35.4
1982	13,139	21.3	8,282	16.5	4,388	47.3	2,117	38.9
1983	13,427	21.8	8,534	17.0	4,273	46.2	2,251	37.7
1984	12,929	21.0	8,086	16.1	4,320	46.2	2,317	38.7
1985	12,483	20.1	7,838	15.6	4,057	43.1	2,512	39.6

Source: U.S. Bureau of the Census, *Money Income and Poverty Status of Families and Persons in the United States,* Current Population Reports, Series P-60 (Washington, D.C., Government Printing Office, selected years).
[a]Revised.

Percentage of Population in Poverty, 1964–1983

Year	Official Measure	Pretransfer Poverty*
1964	19.0%	—
1965	17.3	21.3%
1966	14.7	—
1967	14.2	19.4
1968	12.8	18.2
1969	12.1	17.7
1970	12.6	18.8
1971	12.5	19.6
1972	11.9	19.2
1973	11.1	19.0
1974	11.2	20.3
1975	12.3	22.0
1976	11.8	21.0
1977	11.6	21.0
1978	11.4	20.2
1979	11.7	20.5
1980	13.0	21.9
1981	14.0	23.1
1982	15.0	24.0
1983	15.2	24.2

* An estimate of the percentage in poverty in the absence of all government cash transfers.
Source: Sheldon H. Danziger, Robert H. Haveman, and Robert D. Plotnick, "Antipoverty Policy: Effects on the Poor and the Nonpoor," in *Fighting Poverty: What Works and What Doesn't,* edited by Sheldon H. Danziger and Daniel H. Weinberg (Cambridge, Mass.: Harvard University Press, 1986), p. 54.

Number and Percentage of Population in Poverty, by Family Status and Race, Female-Headed Households, 1973–1985

(in thousands)

Group	1973			1985			Percentage Growth in		
	N	Poverty Rate	% of Poor	N	Poverty Rate	% of Poor	N	Poverty Rate	% of Total Increase
All races:									
All persons	11,357	34.9%	49.4%	16,365	33.5%	49.5%	44.1	-4.0%	49.6%
Householders	2,193	32.2	9.5	3,474	34.0	10.5	58.4	5.6	12.7
Children	5,171	52.1	22.5	6,716	53.6	20.3	29.9	2.9	15.3
Whites:									
All persons	6,642	27.9	28.9	9,778	27.3	29.6	47.2	-2.2	31.0
Householders	1,190	24.5	5.2	1,878	27.4	5.9	63.9	11.2	7.5
Children	2,461	42.1	10.7	3,372	45.2	10.2	37.0	7.3	9.0
Black:									
All persons	4,564	55.4	19.9	6,215	51.8	18.8	36.2	-6.5	16.4
Householders	974	52.7	4.2	1,452	50.5	4.4	49.1	-4.2	4.7
Children	2,635	67.2	11.5	3,181	66.9	9.6	20.7	-0.4	5.4

Source: Calculated from the U.S. Bureau of the Census, Current Population Reports, Series P-60, *Money Income and Poverty Status of Families and Persons in the United States* (Washington, D.C.: Government Printing Office, selected years.)

Number and Percentage of Population in Poverty, by Family Status and Race, Total Population, 1973–1985

(in thousands)

Group	1973			1985			Percentage Growth in		
	N	Poverty Rate	% of Poor	N	Poverty Rate	% of Poor	N	Poverty Rate	% of Total Increase
All races:									
All persons	22,973	11.1%	100.0%	33,064	14.0%	100.0%	43.9%	26.1%	100.0%
In families	18,299	9.9	79.7	25,798	12.6	77.8	43.9	26.1	73.6
Householders	4,828	8.8	21.0	7,223	11.4	21.8	49.6	29.5	23.7
Children < 18	9,453	14.2	41.1	12,483	20.1	37.8	32.0	41.5	30.0
Other family	4,018	5.9	17.4	6,032	7.7	18.2	50.1	30.5	20.0
Unrelated individuals	4,674	25.6	20.3	6,725	21.5	20.3	43.9	-16.0	20.3
Over 65	3,354	16.3	14.5	3,456	12.6	10.5	3.0	-22.7	1.0
Whites:									
All persons	15,142	8.4	65.9	22,860	11.4	69.1	51.0	35.7	76.4
In families	11,412	6.9	49.7	17,125	9.9	51.8	50.1	43.4	56.6
Householders	3,219	6.6	14.0	4,983	9.1	15.1	54.8	37.9	17.5
Children <18	5,462	9.7	23.8	7,838	15.6	23.7	44.4	60.8	23.5
Other family	2,731	4.5	11.9	4,304	6.4	13.0	57.6	42.2	15.6
Unrelated individuals	3,730	23.7	16.2	5,299	19.6	16.0	42.0	-17.3	15.5
Over 65	2,698	14.4	11.7	2,698	11.0	8.2	0	-23.6	0
Black:									
All persons	7,388	31.4	32.1	8,926	31.3	27.0	20.8	-2.4	15.2
In families	6,560	30.8	28.6	7,54	30.5	22.7	14.3	-0.1	9.3
Householders	1,527	28.6	6.6	1,983	28.7	6.0	29.9	0.3	4.5
Children <18	3,822	40.6	16.6	4,057	43.1	12.3	6.1	6.2	2.3
Other family	1,211	18.7	5.3	1,464	17.7	4.4	20.9	-5.3	2.5
Unrelated individuals	828	37.9	3.6	1,264	34.7	3.8	52.7	-8.4	4.3
Over 65	620	37.1	2.7	717	31.5	2.2	15.6	-15.1	1.0

Source: Calculated from the U.S. Bureau of the Census, Current Population Reports, Series P-60, *Money Income and Poverty Status of Families and Persons in the United States* (Washington, D.C.: Government Printing Office, selected years.)

People and Families in Poverty by Selected Characteristics, 2003 and 2004

(Numbers in thousands and percentages. People as of March of the following year)

Characteristic	2003 below Poverty		2004 below Poverty		Change in Poverty (2004 Less 2003)	
	Number	Percentage	Number	Percentage	Number	Percentage
PEOPLE						
Total	35,861	12.5	36,997	12.7	*1,136	*0.3
Family Status						
In Families	25,684	10.8	26,564	11.0	*879	*0.3
Householder	7,607	10.0	7,854	10.2	*247	0.2
Related children under 18	12,340	7.2	12,460	17.3	120	0.1
Related children under 6	4,654	19.8	4,737	19.9	84	0.1
In unrelated subfamilies	464	38.6	570	45.4	*106	6.8
Reference person	191	37.6	235	45.4	44	7.9
Children under 18	271	41.7	314	46.5	43	4.8
Unrelated individual	9,713	20.4	9,864	20.5	151	0.1
Male	4,154	18.0	4,284	18.3	130	0.3
Female	5,559	22.6	5,580	22.5	21	-0.1
Race[2] and Hispanic Origin						
White	24,272	10.5	25,301	10.8	*1,029	*0.4
White, not Hispanic	15,902	8.2	16,870	8.6	*968	*0.5
Black	8,781	24.4	9,000	24.7	219	0.3
Asian	1,401	11.8	1,209	9.8	*-192	*-2.0
Hispanic origin (any race)	9,051	22.5	9,132	21.9	81	-0.6
Age						
Under 18 years	12,866	17.6	13,027	17.8	161	0.2
18 to 64 years	19,443	10.8	20,514	11.3	*1,071	*0.5
65 years and older	3,552	10.2	3,457	9.8	-95	*-0.4
Nativity						
Native	29,965	11.8	30,991	12.1	*1,027	*0.3
Foreign born	5,897	17.2	6,006	17.1	109	-0.1
Naturalized citizen	1,309	10.0	1,328	9.8	19	-0.1
Not a citizen	4,588	21.7	4,678	21.6	91	-0.1
Region						
Northeast	6,052	11.3	6,233	11.6	181	0.3
Midwest	6,932	10.7	7,538	11.6	*606	*0.9
South	14,548	14.1	14,798	14.1	249	—
West	8,329	12.6	8,429	12.6	100	—
Work Experience						
All workers (16 years and older)	8,820	5.8	9,383	6.1	*563	*0.3
Worked full-time, year-round	2,636	2.6	2,896	2.8	*259	*0.2
Not full-time, year-round	6,183	12.2	6,487	12.8	304	*0.7
Did not work at least one week	15,446	21.5	15,845	21.7	400	0.2
Families						
Total	7,607	10.0	7,854	10.2	*247	0.2
Type of Family						
Married couple	3,115	5.4	3,222	5.5	107	0.1
Female householder, no husband present	3,856	28.0	3,973	28.4	117	0.4
Male householder, no wife present	636	13.5	658	13.5	22	—

Source: U.S. Census Bureau, Current Population Survey, 2004 and 2005 Annual Social and Economic Supplements.

- Represents zero or rounds to zero.

* Statistically different from zero at the 90-percent confidence level.

[1]Details may not sum to totals because of rounding.

[2]Federal surveys now give respondents the option of reporting more than one race. Therefore, two basic ways of defining a race group are possible. A group such as Asian may be defined as those who reported Asian and no other race (the race-alone or single-race concept) or as those who reported Asian regardless of whether they also reported another race (the race-alone-or-in combination concept). This table shows data using the first approach (race alone). The use of the single-race population does not imply that it is the preferred method of presenting or analyzing data. The Census Bureau uses a variety of approaches. Information on people who reported more than one race, such as White *and* American Indian and Alaska Native or Asian *and* Black or African American, is available from Census 2000 through American FactFinder. About 2.6 percent of people reported more than one race in Census 2000.

Glossary

absolute poverty   A level of poverty at which such fundamental needs as those for food, clothing, shelter, and medical care cannot be met.

Appalachia   A region that stretches from northeastern Mississippi north and east along the Appalachian mountain chain into southwestern New York. Appalachia encompasses all of West Virginia and portions of 12 other states: Mississippi, Alabama, Georgia, South Carolina, North Carolina, Tennessee, Kentucky, Virginia, Ohio, Maryland, Pennsylvania, and New York.

Black Codes   Sets of laws enacted in southern states during the Reconstruction period that were intended to restrict the freedom of African Americans and force them to remain agricultural laborers in the South.

board of charities   A state agency formed in the late 19th century to oversee the management of private charitable organizations and public institutions for the poor.

Bonus Army   World War I veterans who camped and protested in Washington, D.C., in June and July 1932 in an unsuccessful effort to persuade Congress to award them a cash bonus they were scheduled to receive in 1945.

bracero program   Popular name for the Labor Importation Program, an agreement between the United States and Mexico to permit Mexicans to work in U.S. agriculture on a temporary basis. The bracero program began in 1942 and was terminated in 1964.

case poverty   A term used by the economist John Kenneth Galbraith in the 1950s to describe poverty resulting from a personal shortcoming such as alcohol abuse or low educational attainment.

charity organization   A nonsectarian movement that began in London in 1869 and was imported to the United States in 1877 by the Reverend Stephen Humphreys Gurteen. Charity organization societies attempted to minimize waste and fraud in almsgiving by investigating applicants for relief and referring the worthy poor to the appropriate agency. The societies' "friendly visitors" called on the poor to encourage thrift, diligence, and sobriety.

Children's Aid Society   An organization founded in 1853 in New York City, with Charles Loring Brace as its first chief officer, to remove impoverished children from the streets of Manhattan and place them with rural families. The society also operated schools and lodging houses for poor and working children.

culture of poverty   Anthropologist Oscar Lewis's term for poverty as a way of life that is passed from one generation to the next. Conditions that support a culture of poverty include a market economy, high unemployment or underemployment, low wages, a lack of job skills, and community disorganization.

depression   A severe economic downturn characterized by high unemployment rate and inactivity in business and trade.

deserving poor   People who are poor as a result of circumstances beyond their control, such as illness or widowhood, and therefore deserving of society's help. The term *deserving poor* fell out of favor in the 20th century as attitudes toward poverty changed.

dust bowl   A large section of the southwestern United States that suffered from drought and wind erosion in the 1930s.

Emancipation Proclamation   The document issued by President Abraham Lincoln on January 1, 1863, during the Civil War, conferring freedom on slaves in any state or portion of a state in rebellion.

family cap   A state-imposed limit on a family's welfare benefits. Under the family-cap system, the benefit level established at the time a family began receiving public assistance would not be increased if additional children were born. New Jersey was the first state to impose a family cap, in 1993.

feminization of poverty   The disproportionate representation of women among the poor that began in the late 20th century.

Five Points   An infamous 19th-century New York City slum that was reputed to be a center of vice and crime. Today a new federal courthouse stands at Foley Square, on the site of the old Five Points neighborhood.

food stamps   Coupons purchased at a discount through a government agency by needy individuals and used to buy food.

Freedmen's Bureau   A federal agency formed on March 3, 1865, to help African Americans make the transition from slavery to freedom. The Freedmen's Bureau provided food and supplies, established schools, resettled people, and protected them in their efforts to find paying employment. The bureau was discontinued in 1869 and all of its programs were terminated by 1872.

Fugitive Slave Act of 1850   A federal law creating a force of commissioners to pursue and recapture fugitive slaves in the North and South. Private citizens were compelled to aid in the retrieval of escaped slaves and were subject to a fine or prison sentence of six months for abetting an escape. The law also barred suspected runaways from having a trial by jury or testifying in their own behalf.

Great Depression   A catastrophic worldwide economic decline lasting from 1929 roughly until the end of the 1930s that led to widespread unemployment and poverty.

Great Migration   The movement of African Americans from the rural South to the industrial North that occurred roughly between 1910 and 1940. As many as 1 million people relocated to find jobs and escape southern racism.

Hooverville   A collection of shacks and makeshift dwellings, named for President Herbert Hoover, that took shape on the outskirts of a city during the Great Depression to house the poor and homeless.

indenture   A contractual arrangement whereby one party labors for another for a specified term of years without pay, in return for room and board, in the 18th and early 19th centuries. Some immigrants were indentured to the individuals who paid their passage to North America; some poor and orphaned children were also indentured until they reached majority.

indoor relief   Care of the indigent in institutions such as poorhouses and orphanages.

insular poverty   John Kenneth Galbraith's term for poverty that afflicts entire communities.

Jim Crow laws   Laws enacted in the South in the late 19th century to separate the races socially. Jim Crow laws barred blacks from service in restaurants, hotels, and theaters patronized by whites and established separate facilities for blacks and whites, including separate schools, railroad cars, and waiting rooms.

Medicaid   The federal health-insurance program for the poor that became part of the Social Security program in 1965.

Medicare   The federal health-insurance program for the aged that, as did Medicaid, became a provision of Social Security in 1965.

Nat Turner's insurrection   A slave revolt that began on August 21, 1831, in Southampton, County, Virginia, led by Nat Turner. Turner and his followers murdered about 60 whites before being stopped by military force. The state of Virginia executed Turner and 54 others.

New Deal   A series of laws enacted under President Franklin Delano Roosevelt that were intended to revive the economy and boost morale. New Deal initiatives varied from the Civilian Conservation Corps, which employed young men on public-works projects, to the Federal Deposit Insurance Corporation, which insured bank deposits, to the Social Security Administration.

new poor; new poverty   A collective term for population groups that were increasingly represented among the poor in the late 20th century. These included women and workers who were unemployed because they had been replaced by technology or their jobs had moved to a suburb, a different region, or another country.

New York Association for Improving the Condition of the Poor   An organization founded in 1843 to instill in the poor qualities thought to uplift them morally and economically, including thrift and temperance. In 1855 the association opened the Workmen's Home, a model tenement for African Americans.

Operation Wetback   A 1954 effort by the U.S. Immigration and Naturalization Service (INS), the U.S. Border Patrol, and state and local authorities in the West to round up undocumented Mexicans and return them to Mexico. The INS claimed that the program resulted in the repatriation of 1.3 million people, but this figure has been disputed.

outdoor relief   Public or charitable aid provided to the poor in their own homes in the 18th and 19th centuries. Outdoor relief took the form of money, food, clothing, firewood, and other necessities.

Panic of 1819   An economic downturn that led to large-scale unemployment in U.S. cities and exposed poverty as a social problem. Economic depressions, or "panics," occurred cyclically in U.S. history, from the Panic of 1819 through the Great Depression of the 1930s.

piecework   Completing one part, or "piece," of a manufactured item, usually a garment. Piecework was common in the sweatshops of the late 19th and early 20th centuries. Workers were paid according to the number of pieces they had finished.

placing out   The 19th-century practice of entrusting needy urban children to the care of rural foster families.

poorhouse (almshouse)   A public institution to house paupers. There were poorhouses in North America from the colonial period through the 1930s, but they were most prevalent in the 1800s.

poor laws   Laws governing treatment of the poor in a colony, state, or territory during the colonial and early national periods. Poor laws established taxes to support the poor and created the position of overseer of the poor to collect those taxes and distribute aid. Colonial poor laws were based on British legislation, the Elizabethan Poor Law of 1601.

poor-poor   People living on incomes that fall below half the poverty line.

poverty line   An estimate of the minimal annual income required to provide the necessities of life.

Reaganomics   A nickname given to President Ronald Reagan's economic policy, which attempted to reduce inflation and increase economic growth by cutting taxes and spending for social programs, increasing defense spending, and deregulating domestic markets.

Reconstruction Finance Corporation (RFC)   An agency established in 1932 by President Herbert Hoover to make emergency loans to banks, railroads, and other businesses that were in danger of collapsing as the Great Depression worsened. The RFC disbursed $1.5 million in its first year.

redlining   Illegal discriminatory lending practices. Financial institutions practicing redlining refuse to do business in certain neighborhoods because of residents' race or income level or charge high interest rates to minority home buyers.

relative poverty   A measurement of poverty based on an income level that provides a low standard of living in relation to that of the rest of the population. People living in relative poverty may satisfy such basic needs as those for food, shelter, clothing, and health care but lack other goods and services that are generally available in the society.

Rust Belt   A heavily industrialized region characterized by the closing of old, unprofitable factories and high unemployment. The Rust Belt encompasses the lower peninsula of Michigan, northern Indiana and Ohio, most of Pennsylvania, and portions of West Virginia and New York.

settlement house   A community center, usually in a poor urban immigrant neighborhood, staffed by resident social workers. The first U.S. settlement houses were founded in 1886 and offered instruction in English, child care for working mothers, health services, classes, and cultural and recreational activities. Several hundred settlement houses continue to operate in the United States, although they no longer serve as residences for their personnel.

settlement laws   Colonial laws that established criteria for residency and eligibility for poor relief. Colonial settlement laws were modeled on a British law, the Settlement Act of 1662.

Slave Codes   Prior to 1865, laws enacted in the southern states to keep slaves subordinate and powerless. These codes denied slaves the right, for example, to assemble, to participate in the legal system, or to leave the bounds of the plantation.

Social Darwinism   According to this social philosophy, popular in the late 19th century, humanity progressed by weeding out its inferior specimens. The leading philosopher of Social Darwinism, Herbert Spencer, originated the phrase *survival of the fittest* to justify the self-interest he believed was essential to progress.

Stono Rebellion   The most significant slave uprising of the colonial years, which occurred near the Stono River in South Carolina in September 1739 and involved 60 to 100 rebels. This insurrection left more than 20 whites and 40 blacks dead.

Sun Belt   The southern and southwestern states, especially southern California and Nevada, Arizona, New Mexico, Texas, and Louisiana, that experienced demographic and economic growth beginning in the 1980s.

sweatshop   A factory where employees are pressured to work quickly and hard under conditions that are often unsafe and illegal. Sweatshops traditionally have employed immigrants. Although more prevalent a century ago, sweatshops still exist in the United States.

tenant farmer   A farmer who rents the land on which he or she works. A tenant who pays as rent a share of the crop is known as a sharecropper.

tenement   An urban housing structure offering the most basic amenities and housing large numbers of people in small rented apartments.

Termination   A policy toward Native Americans adopted by Congress on August 1, 1953, with House Concurrent Resolution 108. Congress took steps toward terminating government responsibility for the Indians and the reservation system. Three percent of Indians had their federal support withdrawn before 1956, when Congress reversed itself on Termination. Most affected were the Klamath, Menominee, and Mixed-blood Ute.

underclass   A term to describe the passively poor population existing apart from the political and social life of the nation, unwilling or unable to protest. Included are longtime welfare recipients, drug abusers, street criminals, and the homeless.

underemployment   Part-time or irregular employment of people who desire full-time jobs.

Underground Railroad   A 19th-century organized movement for transporting escaped slaves to freedom in the North and Canada that relied on a network of individuals (conductors), conveyances, and safe homes and stations.

vicious   Prior to the 20th century, the term *vicious* referred to a person who was addicted to vice and immorality.

War on Poverty   President Lyndon B. Johnson's effort to defeat poverty in the United States through legislation. The cornerstone of Johnson's legislative approach was the Economic Opportunity Act of 1964, which established an array of social programs, including Job Corps, to address youth unemployment; Head Start, to prepare preschoolers for kindergarten; and Volunteers in Service to America (VISTA), to recruit and train volunteer labor for federal initiatives to aid the poor.

welfare   Financial and other aid provided to people who qualify by being unemployed or having an income below a specified level, especially when this aid is provided through a government agency or program.

wetback   A derogatory term for an undocumented Mexican immigrant.

workers' compensation   Insurance required of employers that provides financial protection to workers who are injured or made ill on the job.

workfare   A system of public welfare that requires recipients to work in return for their support or that attempts to help them become self-supporting.

workhouse   A public institution of the 18th and 19th centuries in which the able-bodied poor were required to labor in return for their board. For a fee southern workhouses whipped disobedient African-American slaves.

Notes

Introduction

1. Edward Bellamy, *Looking Backward: 2000–1887* (Indianapolis: Cork Hill Press, 2003), pp. 83–84.
2. Ibid., p. 84.
3. Ibid., p. 86.
4. Charles Lebeaux, "Life on A.D.C.: Budgets of Despair," in Louis A. Ferman, Joyce L. Kornbluh, and Alan Haber, eds., *Poverty in America: A Book of Readings* (Ann Arbor: University of Michigan Press, 1968), p. 528.
5. Ibid., p. 529.
6. Billy G. Smith, "The Institutional Poor: The Almshouse Daily Occurrence Docket," in Billy G. Smith, ed., *Life in Early Philadelphia* (University Park: Pennsylvania State University Press, 1995), p. 30.
7. Michael B. Katz, "Underclass as Metaphor," in Michael B. Katz, ed., *The "Underclass" Debate: Views from History* (Princeton, N.J.: Princeton University Press, 1993), p. 9.
8. J. Wayne Flynt, *Dixie's Forgotten People: The South's Poor Whites* (Bloomington: Indiana University Press, 1979), p. 64.
9. Robert J. Lampman, "Population Change and Poverty Reduction, 1947–75," in Leo Fishman, ed., *Poverty amid Affluence* (New Haven: Yale University Press, 1966), p. 19.
10. U.S. National Advisory Commission on Rural Poverty, *The People Left Behind* (Washington, D.C.: U.S. Government Printing Office, 1967), p. 7.
11. Lampman, p. 32.
12. D. Stanley Eitzen and Maxine Baca Zinn, *Social Problems*, 8th ed. (Boston: Allyn and Bacon, 2000), p. 185.

1. The Deserving Poor in Colonial America: 1601–1775

1. Alan D. Watson, "Public Poor Relief in Colonial North Carolina," *North Carolina Historical Review* (October 1977): p. 358.

2. Walter I. Trattner, *From Poor Law to Welfare State: A History of Social Welfare in America*, 5th ed. (New York: Free Press, 1994), p. 23.
3. Marcus Wilson Jernigan, *Laboring and Dependent Classes in Colonial America, 1607–1783* (New York: Frederick Ungar, 1960), p. 206.
4. Gary B. Nash, "Up from the Bottom in Franklin's Philadelphia," *Past and Present* (November 1977): p. 71.
5. Peter R. Virgadamo, "Charity for a City in Crisis: Boston, 1740 to 1775," *Historical Journal of Massachusetts* (January 1982): p. 29.
6. Elizabeth Wisner, "The Puritan Background of the New England Poor Laws," *Social Service Review* (September 1945): p. 387.

2. Industrialization, Immigration, and Urban Poverty: 1790–1864

1. Samuel Reznek, "The Depression of 1819–1822, a Social History," *American Historical Review* (October 1933): p. 31.
2. Ibid.
3. Thomas Paine, *Agrarian Justice* (Johnstown: T. G. Ballard, 1797), p. 4.
4. Tyler Anbinder, *Five Points: The 19th-Century New York Neighborhood That Invented Tap Dance, Stole Elections, and Became the World's Most Notorious Slum* (New York: Free Press, 2001), p. 208.
5. Mathew Carey, *Miscellaneous Essays* (Philadelphia: Carey and Hart, 1830), p. 66.
6. New York Association for Improving the Condition of the Poor, *Thirteenth Annual Report* (New York: John F. Trow, 1856), p.46.
7. Douglas G. Carroll, Jr., and Blanche D. Coll, "The Baltimore Almshouse: *An Early History," Maryland Historical Magazine 66, no. 2* (summer 1971): p. 150.
8. Glenn C. Altschuler and Jan M. Saltzgaber, "Clearinghouse for Paupers: The Poorfarm of Seneca County, New York, 1830–1860," *Journal of Social History* (summer 1984): p. 580.

9. Dorothea Dix, *Memorial: To the Legislature of Massachusetts* (Boston: Munroe and Francis, 1843), p. 1.

10. June Axinn and Mark J. Stern, *Social Welfare: A History of the American Response to Need*, 5th ed. (Boston: Allyn and Bacon, 2001), p. 78.

11. James Brown, *The History of Public Assistance in Chicago, 1833 to 1893* (Chicago: University of Chicago Press, 1941), p. 20.

12. Washington City Orphan Asylum, *"1841 Annual Report,"* Hillcrest Children's Center Collection, Library of Congress, unnumbered page.

13. Ibid.

14. Charles Loring Brace, *The Best Method of Disposing of Our Pauper and Vagrant Children* (New York: Wynkoop, Hallenbeck and Thomas), 1859.

15. *Official Documents, Addresses, Etc., of George Opdyke, Mayor of the City of New York, During the Years 1862 and 1863* (New York: Hurd and Houghton, 1866), p. 271.

16. Horace Greeley, "Tenement Houses—Their Wrongs," *New York Tribune* 23 November 1864, p. 4.

3. "Who Can Describe Their Misery?": Poverty and American Slavery: 1619–1865

1. Booker T. Washington, *Up from Slavery* (New York: Signet Classic, 2000), p. 8.

2. Solomon Northup, *Twelve Years a Slave* (New York: C. M. Saxton, 1859), p. 170.

3. Frederick Douglass, *Narrative of the Life of Frederick Douglass* (New York: Signet Classic, 1997), p. 42.

4. Henry Bibb, *Narrative of the Life and Adventures of Henry Bibb, an American Slave* (New York: Author, 1850), p. 15.

4. Charity Reconsidered: 1865–1900

1. Wayne Flynt, *Poor but Proud: Alabama's Poor Whites* (Tuscaloosa: University of Alabama Press, 1989), p. 47.

2. John William De Forest, *A Union Officer in the Reconstruction* (Baton Rouge: Louisiana State University Press, 1997), p. 1.

3. Robert G. Athearn, *William Tecumseh Sherman and Settlement of the West* (Norman: University of Oklahoma Press, 1956), p. 223.

4. Richard White, *"It's Your Misfortune and None of My Own: A New History of the American West"* (Norman: University of Oklahoma Press, 1991), p. 107.

5. June Axinn and Herman Levin, *Social Welfare: A History of the American Response to Need*, 4th ed. (New York: Longman, 1982), p. 84.

6. James Brown, *The History of Public Assistance in Chicago: 1833 to 1893* (Chicago: University of Chicago Press, 1941), p. 24.

7. Barry J. Kaplan, "Reformers and Charity: The Abolition of Public Outdoor Relief in New York City, 1870–1898," *Social Service Review* (June 1978): p. 207.

8. Walter I. Trattner, *From Poor Law to Welfare State: A History of Social Welfare in America*, 6th ed. (New York: Free Press, 1999), p. 89.

9. Verl S. Lewis, "Stephen Humphreys Gurteen and the American Origins of Charity Organization," *Social Service Review* (June 1966): p. 196.

10. William Jewett Tucker, "The Work of the Andover House in Boston," *Scribner's Magazine*, March 1893, p. 360.

11. Ibid.

12. Alvin B. Kogut, "The Negro and the Charity Organization Society in the Progressive Era," *Social Service Review* (March 1970): 15.

13. "Plessy v. Ferguson (May 18, 1896)," *Swarthmore College* (URL: http://www.swarthmore.edu/Humanities/kjohnso1/plessy.html), p. 1.

5. Social Research and Recommendations: 1900–1928

1. Robert Hunter, *Poverty* (New York: Macmillan, 1904), p. 11.

2. Ibid.

3. U.S. Bureau of the Census, *Paupers in Almshouses, 1910* (Washington, D.C.: Government Printing Office, 1915), p. 9.

4. Edward T. Devine, *Misery and Its Causes* (New York: Macmillan Co., 1913), p. 11.

5. Janet E. Kemp, *Report of the Tenement House Commission of Louisville, Under the Ordinance of February 16, 1909* (N.p., July 19, 1909), p. 16.

6. "1917 Immigration Act," *Spartacus Educational* (URL: http://www.spartacus.schoolnet.co.uk/USAE1917A.htm), p. 4.

7. John Simpson Penman, *Poverty: The Challenge to the Church* (Boston: Pilgrim Press, 1915), p. 5.

8. J. M. Oskison, "Making an Individual of the Indian," *Everybody's Magazine*, June 1907, p. 724.

9. Laurence Armand French, *The Winds of Injustice: American Indians and the U.S. Government* (New York: Garland Publishing, 1994), p. 60.

10. Institute for Government Research, *The Problem of Indian Administration* (Baltimore: Johns Hopkins University Press, 1928), p. 448.

11. Ibid.

12. Mabel Brown Ellis, "Children of the Kentucky Coal Fields, *The American Child*, February 1920, p. 289.

6. The Poor Take Center Stage: 1929–1941

1. J. Wayne Flynt, *Dixie's Forgotten People: The South's Poor Whites* (Bloomington: Indiana University Press, 1979), p. 68.

2. "Inaugural Speech of Franklin Delano Roosevelt Given in Washington, D.C., March 4th, 1933," *History and Politics Out Loud* (URL: http://www.hpol.org/fdr/inaug/), p. 4.

3. Nancy E. Rose, "Work Relief in the 1930s and the Origins of the Social Security Act," *Social Service Review* (March 1989): p. 66.

4. "National Youth Administration," *The Eleanor Roosevelt Papers* (URL: http://www.gwu.edu/~erpapers/abouteleanor/q-and-a/glossary/nya.htm), p. 1.

5. "'We Took Away Their Best Lands, Broke Treaties': John Collier Promises to Reform Indian Policy," *History Matters* (URL: http://historymatters.gmu.edu/d/5058/), p. 2.

6. *Hard Times: The Thirties* (Alexandria, Va.: Time-Life Books, 1998), p. 53.

7. Roger Biles, "The Legacy of the New Deal," in *The 1930s*, edited by Louise I. Gerdes (San Diego, Calif.: Greenhaven Press, 2000), p. 325.

7. The Invisible Mass: 1941–1962

1. Staff of the Subcommittee on Low-Income Families, Joint Committee on the Economic Report, *Low-Income Families and Economic Stability* (Washington, D.C.: U.S. Government Printing Office, 1950), p. 1.

2. John Kenneth Galbraith, *The Affluent Society* (Boston: Houghton Mifflin, 1958), p. 1.

3. Ibid., p. 3.

4. Michael Harrington, *The Other America: Poverty in the United States* (New York: Macmillan Co., 1962), p. 2.

5. Ibid., p. 4.

6. Ibid., p. 11.

7. Ibid.

8. The War on Poverty and Its Aftermath: 1962–1980

1. Ben B. Bagdikian, *In the Midst of Plenty: The Poor in America* (Boston: Beacon Press, 1964), p. 192.

2. Lyndon B. Johnson, "Annual Message to the Congress on the State of the Union, January 8, 1964," *Lyndon Baines Johnson Library and Museum* (URL: http://www.lbjlib.utexas.edu/johnson/archives.hom/speeches.hom/640108.asp), p. 1.

3. Ibid., p. 3.

4. Lyndon B. Johnson, "Presidential Message on Poverty," in Herman P. Miller, *Poverty American Style* (Belmont, Calif.: Wadsworth Publishing, 1966), p. 216.

5. U.S. National Advisory Commission on Rural Poverty, *The People Left Behind* (Washington, D.C.: U.S. Government Printing Office, 1967), p. x.

6. Ibid., p. 5.

7. Oscar Lewis, "The Culture of Poverty," in Daniel P. Moynihan, ed., *On Understanding Poverty: Perspectives from the Social Sciences* (New York: Basic Books, 1969), p. 187.

8. U.S. Department of Labor, Office of Policy Planning and Research, *The Negro Family: The Case for National Action* (Washington, D.C.: U.S. Government Printing Office, 1965), p. 27.

9. Southern Regional Council, *Hungry Children* (Atlanta: Southern Regional Council, 1967), p. 2.

10. Ibid., p. 3.

11. Walter I. Trattner, *From Poor Law to Welfare State: A History of Social Welfare in America*, 6th ed. (New York: Free Press, 1999), p. 331.

12. Daniel P. Moynihan, "The Crises in Welfare," *Public Interest*, winter 1968, p. 3.

9. The Years of Welfare Reform: 1981–1996

1. Walter I. Trattner, *From Poor Law to Welfare State: A History of Social Welfare in America*, 6th ed. (New York: Free Press, 1999), p. 362.

2. "First Inaugural Address of Ronald Reagan," *Avalon Project at Yale Law School* (URL: http://www.yale.edu/lawweb/avalon/presiden/inaug/reagan1.htm), p. 2.

3. Michael Harrington, *The New American Poverty* (New York: Holt, Rinehart and Winston, 1984), p. 1.

4. Ibid., p. 11.

5. J. Larry Brown and H. F. Pizer, *Living Hungry in America* (New York: New American Library, 1987), p. 12.

6. Walter I. Trattner, *From Poor Law to Welfare State: A History of Social Welfare in America*, 6th ed. (New York: Free Press, 1999), p. 383.

7. Ibid., p. 396.

10. Poverty Endures: 1997–2006

1. George W. Bush, "Text of President Bush's Commencement Address at Notre Dame University on May 20, 2001 in Notre Dame, Indiana," *CNN.com* (URL: http://archives.cnn.com/2001/ALLPOLITICS/05/20/bush.speech.text/), p. 2.

2. D. Stanley Eitzen and Kelly Eitzen Smith, *Experiencing Poverty: Voices from the Bottom* (Belmont, Calif.: Thomson, Wadsworth, 2003), p. 122.

3. Ibid., p. 123.

4. "NPR/Kaiser/Kennedy School Poll on Poverty in America," *Kaiser Family Foundation* (URL: http://www.kff.org/kaiserpolls/loader.cfm?url=/commonspot/security/getfile.cfm&Page ID=13806), p. 1.

5. Ibid., p. 2.

6. "Katrina Timeline," *Think Progress* (URL: http://www.thinkprogress.org/katrina-timeline), p. 4.

7. Vincent T. Davis, "Edwards Urges War on Poverty," *San Antonio Express-News*, 30 November 2005, p. 5.B.

8. Alan Berube and Elizabeth Kneebone, "Two Steps Back: City and Suburban Poverty Trends 1999–2005," *Brookings Institution* (URL: http://www.brook.edu/metro/bubs/20061205_citysuburban.htm).

9. Ron Haskins, "Welfare Check," *Opinion Journal* (URL: http://www.opinionjournal.com/extra/3id-110008720), p. 2.

Bibliography

Abbott, Carl. "Neighborhoods of New York, 1760–1775." *New York History* 55, no. 1 (January 1974): 35–54.

Abbott, Edith. *The Tenements of Chicago, 1908–1935.* Chicago: University of Chicago Press, 1936.

Affleck, Thomas. "On the Hygiene of Cotton Plantations and the Management of Negro Slaves." *Southern Medical Reporter* 2, 1850, 429–36.

Agee, James, and Walker Evans. *Let Us Now Praise Famous Men.* Boston: Houghton Mifflin, 1960.

Altschuler, Glenn C., and Jan M. Saltzgaber. "Clearinghouse for Paupers: The Poorfarm of Seneca County, New York, 1830–1860." *Journal of Social History* 17, no. 4 (summer 1984): 573–600.

American G. I. Forum. *What Price Wetbacks?* Austin, Tex.: American G. I. Forum of Texas and Texas State Federation of Labor (AFL), 1953.

Anbinder, Tyler. *Five Points: The 19th-Century New York City Neighborhood That Invented Tap Dance, Stole Elections, and Became the World's Most Notorious Slum.* New York: Free Press, 2001.

Anderson, Martin. *Welfare: The Political Economy of Welfare Reform in the United States.* Stanford, Calif.: Hoover Institution Press, 1978.

Anderson, Terry L. *Sovereign Nations or Reservations: An Economic History of American Indians.* San Francisco: Pacific Research Institute for Public Policy, 1995.

Ataiyero, Kayce T. "Rising from Poverty." *Chicago Tribune,* 27 November 2005, p. 3.

Athearn, Robert G. *William Tecumseh Sherman and the Settlement of the West.* Norman: University of Oklahoma Press, 1956.

Axinn, June, and Mark J. Stern. *Social Welfare: A History of the American Response to Need.* 5th ed. Boston: Allyn & Bacon, 2001.

Bagdikian, Ben H. *In the Midst of Plenty: The Poor in America.* Boston: Beacon Press, 1964.

Bakke, E. Wight. *The Unemployed Worker: A Study of the Task of Making a Living without a Job.* New Haven, Conn.: Yale University Press, 1940.

Bartlett, William S. *The Frontier Missionary: A Memoir of the Life of the Rev. Jacob Bailey.* Boston: Ide and Dutton, 1853.

Bellamy, Edward. *Looking Backward: 2000–1887.* Indianapolis: Cork Hill Press, 2003.

Berube, Alan, and Elizabeth Kneebone. "Two Steps Back: City and Suburban Poverty Trends 1999–2005." *Brookings Institution.* URL: http://www.brook.edu/metro/bubs/ 20061205_citysuburban.htm. Downloaded on December 15, 2006.

Bibb, Henry. *Narrative of the Life and Adventures of Henry Bibb, an American Slave.* New York: Author, 1850.

Blank, Rebecca M. *It Takes a Nation: A New Agenda for Fighting Poverty.* New York: Russell Sage Foundation, 1997.

Blassingame, John W. *The Slave Community: Plantation Life in the Antebellum South.* New York: Oxford University Press, 1979.

Blevins, Brooks. *Hill Folks: A History of Arkansas Ozarkers and Their Image.* Chapel Hill: University of North Carolina Press, 2002.

Blythe, Jarrett. "Tribal Leaders Voice Their Opinion." *Indians at Work* 1, no. 3 (September 15, 1933): 28.

Boccaccio, Mary. "Ground Itch and Dew Poison: The Rockefeller Sanitary Commission, 1909–14." *Journal of the History of Medicine and Allied Sciences* 27, no. 1 (January 1972): 30–53.

Brace, Charles Loring. *The Best Method of Disposing of Our Pauper and Vagrant Children.* New York: Wynkoop, Hallenbeck and Thomas, 1859.

———. *The Dangerous Classes of New York, and Twenty Years' Work Among Them.* 3rd ed. New York: Wynkoop & Hallenbeck, 1880.

Bremner, Robert H. *The Discovery of Poverty in the United States.* New Brunswick, N.J.: Transaction, 1992.

Britt, Donna. "Every Day, We Ignore the Everyday Poor." *Washington Post,* September 16, 2005, pp. B1, B4.

Brown, J. Larry, and H. F. Pizer. *Living Hungry in America.* New York: New American Library, 1987.

Brown, James. *The History of Public Assistance in Chicago, 1833 to 1893.* Chicago: University of Chicago Press, 1941.

Brown, Jessica. "America's Poor Speak, but Who Will Listen?" *Ithaca Journal.* Available online. URL: http://www.theithacajournal.com/apps/pbcs/dll/article?AID=/20060731/OPINION02/607310312/1014. Downloaded on August 6, 2006.

Brown, John. *Slave Life in Georgia: A Narrative of the Life, Sufferings, and Escape of John Brown, a Fugitive Slave.* Savannah: Beehive Press, 1972.

Brown, Josephine Chapin. *Public Relief, 1929–1939.* New York: Henry Holt, 1940.

Burroughs, Charles. *A Discourse Delivered in the Chapel of the New Almshouse, in Portsmouth, N.H.* Portsmouth, N.H.: J. W. Foster, 1835.

Bush, George W. "Commencement Address at Notre Dame University, May 20, 2001." *CNN.com.* Available online. URL: http://archives.cnn.com/2001/ALLPOLITICS/05/20/bush.speech.text/. Downloaded on June 8, 2005.

Caldwell, Erskine, and Margaret Bourke-White. *You Have Seen Their Faces.* New York: Viking Press, 1937.

Calkins, Clinch. *Some Folks Won't Work.* New York: Harcourt, Brace, 1930.

Carey, Mathew. *Appeal to the Wealthy of the Land.* Philadelphia: J. Johnson, 1833.

———. *Essays on the Public Charities of Philadelphia.* Philadelphia: J. Clarke, 1829.

———. *A Plea for the Poor.* Philadelphia: L. R. Bailey, December 20, 1837.

Carroll Douglas G., Jr., and Blanche D. Coll. "The Baltimore Almshouse: An Early History." *Maryland Historical Magazine* 66, no. 2 (summer 1971): 135–52.

Centinel, Vincent. *Massachusetts in Agony: or, Important Hints to the Inhabitants of the Province.* Boston: D. Fowle, 1750.

Chamberlin, J. Gordon. *Upon Whom We Depend: The American Poverty System.* New York: Peter Land, 1999.

Champagne, Duane, ed. *The Native American Almanac.* 2nd ed. Detroit: Gale Group, 2001.

Channing, William Ellery. *A Discourse Delivered before the Benevolent Fraternity of Churches in Boston, on Their First Anniversary.* Boston: Russell, Odiorne, and Metcalf, 1835.

Charity Organization Society of the District of Columbia. *Third Annual Report.* Washington, D.C.: Thomas McGill and Co., 1886.

Chauncy, Charles. *The Idle-Poor Secluded from the Bread of Charity by the Christian Law.* Boston: Thomas Fleer, 1752.

Chicago Commission on Race Relations. *The Negro in Chicago: A Study of Race Relations and a Race Riot.* Chicago: University of Chicago Press, 1922.

Chin, Elizabeth. "I Will Simply Survive." *Grist Magazine.* Available online. URL: http://www.grist.org/comments/soapbox/2006/03/01/chin/. Downloaded on August 6, 2006.

Citizens' Board of Inquiry into Hunger and Malnutrition in the United States. *Hunger, U.S.A.* Washington, D.C.: New Community Press, 1968.

Clague, Ewen. *Ten Thousand Out of Work.* Philadelphia: University of Pennsylvania Press, 1933.

Clarke, Lewis. *Narrative of the Sufferings of Lewis Clarke.* Boston: David H. Ela, 1845.

Clifton, James M. *Life and Labor on Argyle Island: Letters and Documents of a Savannah River Rice Plantation, 1833–1867.* Savannah, Ga.: Beehive Press, 1978.

Cloud, Henry Roe. "Some Social and Economic Aspects of the Reservation." *Quarterly Journal of the Society of American Indians* 1, no. 2 (April–June 1913): 149–58.

Cobbett, William. *A Year's Residence in the United States of America.* London: Sherwood, Neely, and Jones, 1818.

Cohen, Wilbur J. "A Ten-Point Program to Abolish Poverty." *Social Security Bulletin* 31, no. 2 (December 1968): 3–13.

Coles, Robert. *Migrants, Sharecroppers, and Mountaineers.* Boston: Atlantic Monthly Press, 1971.

Collier, John. "At the Close of Ten Weeks." *Indians at Work* 1, no. 3 (September 15, 1933): 1–5.

Commons, John R. *Social Reform and the Church.* New York: Thomas Y. Crowell and Co., 1894.

Cooper, Samuel. *A Sermon Preached in Boston, New-England, before the Society for Encouraging Industry, and Employing the Poor; August 1753.* Boston: J. Draper, 1753.

Craig, Oscar. "The Prevention of Pauperism." *Scribner's Magazine,* July 1893, 121–28.

Da Costa Nunez, Ralph. *Hopes, Dreams and Promise: The Future of Homeless Children in America.* New York: Homes for the Homeless, 1994.

Danziger, Sheldon H., and Robert H. Haveman, eds. *Understanding Poverty.* New York: Russell Sage Foundation, 2001.

Davenport, John. "In the Midst of Plenty." *Fortune,* March 1961, 107–9, 236–40.

Davis, Peter. *If You Came This Way: A Journey through the Lives of the Underclass.* New York: John Wiley & Sons, 1995.

Davis, Vincent T. "Edwards Urges War on Poverty." *San Antonio Express-News,* 30 November 2005, p. 5.B.

De Crevecoeur, J. Hector St. John. *Letters from an American Farmer.* New York: E. P. Dutton and Co., 1912.

De Forest, John William. *A Union Officer in the Reconstruction.* Baton Rouge: Louisiana State University Press, 1997.

De Forest, Robert W., and Lawrence Veiller. *The Tenement House Problem.* Vol. 1. New York: Macmillan, 1903.

Devine, Edward T. *Misery and Its Causes.* New York: Macmillan Co., 1913.

Devine, Joel A., and James D. Wright. *The Greatest of Evils: Urban Poverty and the American Underclass.* New York: Aldine de Gruyter, 1993.

Dickens, Charles, *American Notes for General Circulation.* Paris: Baudry's European Library, 1842.

Dinwiddie, Emily W. *Housing Conditions in Philadelphia.* Philadelphia: n.p., 1904.

"Dirt, Disease, Degradation, and Despair." *American City* 66, no. 6 (June 1951): 9.

Dix, Dorothea L. *Memorial: To the Legislature of Massachusetts.* Boston: Munroe & Francis, 1843.

Dobyns, Henry. *Their Number Become Thinned: Native American Population Dynamics in Eastern North America.* Knoxville: University of Tennessee Press, 1983.

Douglas, Paul H. "Democracy Can't Live in These Houses." *Collier's,* July 9, 1949, 22–23, 50–51.

Douglass, Frederick. *Narrative of the Life of Frederick Douglass.* New York: Signet Classic, 1997.

Dulles, Foster Rhea. *The United States Since 1865.* Ann Arbor: University of Michigan Press, 1969.

Edelman, Marian Wright. *Families in Peril: An Agenda for Social Change.* Cambridge, Mass.: Harvard University Press, 1987.

Ehrenreich, Barbara, and Frances Fox Piven. "The Feminization of Poverty." *Dissent* 31, no. 2 (spring 1984): 162–70.

Eitzen, D. Stanley, and Kelly Eitzen Smith. *Experiencing Poverty: Voices from the Bottom.* Belmont, Calif.: Thomson, Wadsworth, 2003.

Eitzen, D. Stanley, and Maxine Baca Zinn. *Social Problems,* 8th ed. Boston: Allyn & Bacon, 2000.

Eldridge, Larry D., ed. *Women and Freedom in Early America.* New York: New York University Press, 1997.

Ellis, Mabel Brown. "Children of the Kentucky Coal Fields." *The American Child* 1, no. 4 (February 1920): 285–405.

Ellwood, David T. *Poor Support: Poverty in the American Family.* New York: Basic Books, 1988.

Ely, Ezra Styles. *Visits of Mercy; or the Journals of the Rev. Ezra Styles Ely, D.D.* Vol. 1. Philadelphia: Samuel F. Bradford, 1829.

Fay, Joseph Dewey. *Pauperism.* Philadelphia: Privately published, 1827.

Feder, Leah Hannah. *Unemployment Relief in Periods of Depression.* New York: Russell Sage Foundation, 1936.

Ferman, Louis A., Joyce L. Kornbluh, and Alan Haber, eds. *Poverty in America: A Book of Readings.* Ann Arbor: University of Michigan Press, 1968.

"Fighting Poverty." *Negro History Bulletin* 22, no. 2 (November 1958): 43.

Fishman, Leo, ed. *Poverty amid Affluence.* New Haven, Conn.: Yale University Press, 1966.

"The Five Points." *National Magazine,* February 1853, 169–73.

"The Five Points." *National Magazine,* March 1853, 267–71.

Fleishner, Jennifer. *Mrs. Lincoln and Mrs. Keckly.* New York: Broadway Books, 2003.

Flynt, J. Wayne. *Dixie's Forgotten People: The South's Poor Whites.* Bloomington: Indiana University Press, 1979.

Flynt, Wayne. *Poor but Proud: Alabama's Poor Whites.* Tuscaloosa: University of Alabama Press, 1989.

Fogel, Robert William, and Stanley L. Engerman. *Time on the Cross: The Economics of American Negro Slavery.* Lanham, Md.: University Press of America, 1984.

Ford, James, and Katherine Morrow Ford. *The Abolition of Poverty.* New York: Macmillan, 1937.

Foster, George G. *New York by Gas-Light and Other Urban Sketches.* Berkeley: University of California Press, 1990.

Franklin, Benjamin. "On the Price of Corn and Management of the Poor." In *The Autobiography of Benjamin Franklin and Selections from His Other Writings.* New York: Modern Library, 1950.

Franklin, John Hope, and Alfred A. Moss, Jr. *From Slavery to Freedom: The History of Negro Americans.* 6th ed. New York: McGraw Hill, 1988.

French, Laurence Armand. *The Winds of Injustice: American Indians and the U.S. Government.* New York: Garland, 1994.

Fryberger, Harrison E. *The Abolition of Poverty.* New York: Advance, 1931.

Fuller, Varden. *No Work Today! The Plight of America's Migrants.* New York: Public Affairs Committee, 1953.

Gans, Herbert J. *The War against the Poor: The Underclass and Antipoverty Policy.* New York: Basic Books, 1995.

Garcia, Juan Ramon. *Operation Wetback: The Mass Deportation of Mexican Undocumented Workers in 1954.* Westport, Conn.: Greenwood Press, 1980.

Genovese, Eugene D. *Roll, Jordan, Roll: The World the Slaves Made.* New York: Vintage Books, 1974.

Gerdes, Louise I., ed. *The 1930s.* San Diego, Calif.: Greenhaven Press, 2000.

Gilder, George F. *Wealth and Poverty.* New York: Basic Books, 1981.

Gilje, Paul A. *Rioting in America.* Bloomington: Indiana University Press, 1996.

Gillin, John Lewis. *Poverty and Dependency.* New York: Century, 1921.

Glasgow, Douglas G. *The Black Underclass: Poverty, Unemployment, and Entrapment of Ghetto Youth.* San Francisco: Jossey-Bass, 1980.

Golay, Michael. *Reconstruction and Reaction.* New York: Facts On File, 1996.

Goodwin, Leonard. *Do the Poor Want to Work? A Social-Psychological Study of Work Orientations.* Washington, D.C.: Brookings Institution, 1972.

Gordon, Margaret S., ed. *Poverty in America.* San Francisco: Chandler, 1965.

Grayson, William J. *The Hireling and the Slave, Chicora, and Other Poems.* Charleston, S.C.: McCarter, 1856.

Greeley, Horace. *Recollections of a Busy Life.* New York: J. B. Ford, 1868.

———. "Tenement Houses—Their Wrongs." *New York Tribune,* November 23, 1864, p. 4.

Griscom, John H. *The Sanitary Condition of the Laboring Classes of New York.* New York: Harper and Brothers, 1845.

Gurteen, Stephen Humphreys. *Phases of Charity.* 2nd ed. New York: Anson D. F. Randolph, 1878.

———. *Provident Schemes.* Buffalo, N.Y.: Courier Co., 1879.

Hahamovich, Cindy. *Fruits of Their Labor: Atlantic Coast Farmworkers and the Making of Modern Poverty, 1870–1945.* Chapel Hill: University of North Carolina Press, 1997.

Hall, Basil. *Travels in North America, in the Years 1827 and 1828.* Vols. 2 and 3. Edinburgh: Cadell and Co., 1829.

Hard Times: The Thirties. Alexandria, Va.: Time-Life Books, 1998.

Harrington, Michael. *The New American Poverty.* New York: Holt, Rinehart & Winston, 1984.

———. *The Other America: Poverty in the United States.* New York: Macmillan Co., 1962.

Haskins, Ron. "Welfare Check." *Opinion Journal.* Available online. URL: http://www.opinionjournal.com/extra/?id=110008720. Downloaded on August 8, 2006.

Heilbroner, Robert L. "Who Are the American Poor?" *Harper's Magazine,* June 1950, 27–33.

Henderson, Charles Richmond. *Modern Methods of Charity.* New York: Macmillan, 1904.

Henson, Josiah. *An Autobiography of the Rev. Josiah Henson ("Uncle Tom") from 1789 to 1881.* London, Ontario: Schuyler, Smith and Co., 1881.

Hilliard, Sam Bowers. *Hog Meat and Hoecake: Food Supply in the Old South, 1840–1860.* Carbondale: Southern Illinois University Press, 1972.

Hollander, Jacob H. *The Abolition of Poverty.* Boston: Houghton Mifflin, 1914.

Hollings, Ernest F. *The Case against Hunger: A Demand for a National Policy.* New York: Cowles Book Company, 1970.

Hooker, Richard J., ed. *The Carolina Backcountry on the Eve of the Revolution: The Journal and Other Writings of Charles Woodmason, Anglican Itinerant.* Chapel Hill: University of North Carolina Press, 1953.

Hoover, Herbert. "Consequences to Liberty of Regimentation." *Saturday Evening Post,* 15 September 1934, pp. 5–7, 85–89.

———. *The New Day: Campaign Speeches of Herbert Hoover, 1928.* Stanford, Calif.: Stanford University Press, 1928.

Hopkins, Harry L. *Spending to Save. The Complete Story of Relief.* New York: W. W. Norton and Co., 1936.

Housing Laws: A Summary of the More Important Provisions in City and State Codes. Minneapolis: Prepared for the Housing Committee of the Minneapolis Civic and Commerce Association, 1914.

Howells, William Dean. *Impressions and Experiences.* New York: Harper and Brothers, 1896.

Hughes, Louis. *Thirty Years a Slave.* New York: Negro Universities Press, 1969.

Humphrey, Hubert H. *War on Poverty.* Toronto: McGraw Hill, 1964.

Hunter, Charlayne A. "On the Case in Resurrection City," in August Meier, ed. *The Transformation of Activism.* n.p.: Aldine Publishing, 1970, 5–28.

Hunter, Robert. *Poverty.* New York: Macmillan, 1904.

Hurt, R. Douglas. *Indian Agriculture in America: Prehistory to the Present.* Lawrence: University of Kansas Press, 1987.

———. *Problems of Plenty: The American Farmer in the Twentieth Century.* Chicago: Ivan R. Dee, 2002.

"Inaugural Speech of Franklin Delano Roosevelt Given in Washington, D.C., March 4, 1933." *History and Politics out Loud.* Available online. URL: http://www.hpol.org/fdr/inaug/. Downloaded on February 16, 2005.

Industrial Relations: Final Report and Testimony Submitted to Congress by the Commission on Industrial Relations. Vol. 1. Washington, D.C.: Government Printing Office, 1916.

Ingersoll, C. J. *African Slavery in America.* Philadelphia: T. K. and P. G. Collins, 1856.

Institute for Government Research. *The Problem of Indian Administration.* Baltimore: Johns Hopkins University Press, 1928.

Jargowsky, Paul A. "Beyond the Street Corner: The Hidden Diversity of High-Poverty Neighborhoods." *Urban Geography* 17, no. 7 (1 October–15 November 1996): 579–603.

———. *Poverty and Place: Ghettos, Barrios, and the American City.* New York: Russell Sage Foundation, 1997.

———, and Isabel V. Sawhill. "The Decline of the Underclass." *The Brookings Institution.* Available online. URL: http://www.brookings.edu/es/research/projects/wrb/publications/pb/pb36/htm. Downloaded on October 31, 2006.

Jarman, Rufus. "Detroit Cracks Down on Relief Chiselers." *Saturday Evening Post,* 10 December 1949, 17–19, 122–26.

Jencks, Christopher. *Rethinking Social Policy.* Cambridge, Mass.: Harvard University Press, 1992.

Jencks, Christopher, and Kathryn Edin. "The Real Welfare Problem." *American Prospect* no. 1 (spring 1990): 31–50.

Jencks, Christopher, and Paul E. Peterson, eds. *The Urban Underclass.* Washington, D.C.: Brookings Institution, 1991.

Jennings, Edwin. *The Abolition of Poverty.* New York: Edwin Jennings, 1915.

Jernigan, Marcus Wilson. *Laboring and Dependent Classes in Colonial America, 1607–1783.* New York: Frederick Ungar, 1960.

Johnson, Charles S. *The Shadow of the Plantation.* Chicago: University of Chicago Press, 1934.

Johnston, Eric. *America Unlimited.* Garden City, N.Y.: Doubleday, Doran, 1944.

Kaplan, Barry J. "Reformers and Charity: The Abolition of Public Outdoor Relief in New York City, 1870–1898." *Social Service Review* 52, no. 2 (June 1978): 202–14.

"Katrina Timeline." *Think Progress.* Available online. URL: http://www.thinkprogress.org/katrina-timeline. Downloaded on December 13, 2005.

Katz, Michael B. *The Undeserving Poor: From the War on Poverty to the War on Welfare.* New York: Pantheon Books, 1989.

Katz, Michael B., ed. *The "Underclass" Debate: Views from History.* Princeton, N.J.: Princeton University Press, 1993.

Kealear, Charles H. "Reservation Management." *Quarterly Journal of the Society of American Indians* 1, no. 2 (April–June 1913): 158–65.

Kellor, Frances A. *Out of Work: A Study of Unemployment.* New York: G. P. Putnam's Sons, 1915.

Kelso, Robert W. *The Science of Public Welfare.* New York: Henry Holt and Co., 1928.

Kemp, Janet E. *Report of the Tenement House Commission of Louisville, under the Ordinance of February 16, 1909.* n.p., 1909.

Keyserling, Leon H. *Progress or Poverty.* Washington, D.C.: Conference on Economic Progress, 1964.

Knebel, Fletcher. "Welfare: Has It Become a Scandal?" *Look,* 7 November 1961, 31–33.

Kogut, Alvin B. "The Negro and the Charity Organization Society in the Progressive Era." *Social Service Review* 44, no. 1 (March 1970): 11–21.

Koren, John. *Economic Aspects of the Liquor Problem.* Boston: Houghton Mifflin, and Co., 1899.

Kotz, Nick. *Let Them Eat Promises: The Politics of Hunger in America.* Englewood Cliffs, N.J.: Prentice-Hall, 1969.

Kozol, Jonathan. "The Homeless and Their Children—I." *New Yorker,* January 25, 1988, 65–84.

Kuttner, Robert, ed. *Making Work Pay: America after Welfare.* New York: New Press, 2002.

Lee, Charles R. "Public Poor Relief and the Massachusetts Community, 1620–1715." *New England Quarterly* 55, no. 4 (December 1982): 564–85.

Lee, Joseph. *Constructive and Preventive Philanthropy.* New York: Macmillan Co., 1902.

Lee, Sharon M. "Poverty and the U.S. Asian Population." *Social Science Quarterly* 75, no. 3 (September 1994): 541–59.

Lening, Gustav. *The Dark Side of New York Life and Its Criminal Classes from Fifth Avenue Down to the Five Points.* New York: Frederick Gerhard, 1873.

Letchworth, William P. *Extract from the Ninth Annual Report of the State Board of Charities of the State of New York Relating to Pauper Children of New York County.* Albany, N.Y.: Weed, Parsons and Co., 1876.

Lewis, Oscar. "The Culture of Poverty" *Scientific American,* October 19–25, 1966.
———. *La Vida.* London: Panther Books, 1968.

Lewis, Sasha G. *Slave Trade Today: American Exploitation of Illegal Aliens.* Boston: Beacon Press, 1979.

Lewis, Verl S. "Stephen Humphreys Gurteen and the American Origins of Charity Organization." *Social Service Review* 40, no. 2 (June 1966): 190–201.

Lichter, Daniel T., and Martha L. Crowley. "Poverty in America: Beyond Welfare Reform." *Poverty Bulletin* 57, no. 2 (June 2002): 3–31.

Loewenberg, Frank M. "Federal Relief Programs in the 19th Century: A Reassessment." *Journal of Sociology and Social Welfare* 19, no. 3 (September 1992): 121–36.

Lowell, Josephine Shaw. *Public Relief and Private Charity.* New York: G. Putnam's Sons, 1884.

Lowitt, Richard, and Maurine Beasley, eds. *One Third of a Nation: Lorena Hickok Reports on the Great Depression.* Urbana: University of Illinois Press, 1981.

Lyson, Thomas A., and William W. Falk, eds. *Forgotten Places: Uneven Development in Rural America.* Lawrence: University Press of Kansas, 1993.

Mackey, Howard. "Social Welfare in Colonial Virginia. The Importance of the Old Poor Law." *Historical Magazine of the Protestant Episcopal Church* 36, no. 4 (December 1967), 359–82.

Maharidge, Dale. *Journey to Nowhere: The Saga of the New Underclass.* Garden City, N.Y.: Dial Press, 1985.

Mallaby, Sebastian. "A Bridge for the Underclass." *Washington Post,* 13 June 2005, p. A19.

Marmor, Theodore R., Jerry L. Mashaw, and Philip L. Harvey. *America's Misunderstood Welfare State: Persistent Myths, Enduring Realities.* New York: Basic Books, 1990.

Massachusetts General Court. Committee on Pauper Laws. *Report.* Boston: N.p: 1821.

Mather, Cotton. *Essays to Do Good, Addressed to All Christians, Whether in Public or Private Capacities.* Johnstown, N.Y.: Child and Clapp, 1815.

May, Edgar. *The Wasted Americans.* New York: Harper & Row, 1964.

McCombs, Vernon Monroe. *From over the Border: A Study of the Mexicans in the United States.* New York: Council of Women for Home Missions and Missionary Education Movement, 1925.

McElvaine, Robert S. *Down and out in the Great Depression: Letters from the "Forgotten Man."* Chapel Hill, N.C.: University of North Carolina Press, 1983.

McWilliams, Carey. *Factories in the Field: The Story of Migrant Farm Labor in California.* Boston: Little, Brown, 1939.

———. *Ill Fares the Land.* New York: Barnes & Noble, 1967.

Melville, Herman. *The Complete Shorter Fiction.* New York: Everyman's Library, 1997

Mertz, Paul E. *New Deal Policy and Southern Rural Poverty.* Baton Rouge: Louisiana State University Press, 1978.

"Mexican American Voices." *Digital History.* Available online. URL: http://www.digitalhistory.uh.edu/Mexican_voices/voices_display.cfm?id=92. Downloaded on March 10, 2005.

Miller, Herman P., ed. *Poverty American Style.* Belmont, Calif.: Wadsworth, 1966.

Mohl, Raymond A. *Poverty in New York, 1783–1825.* New York: Oxford University Press, 1971.

Moynihan, Daniel P. "The Crises in Welfare." *Public Interest* (winter 1968): 3–29.

———, ed. *On Understanding Poverty: Perspectives from the Social Sciences.* New York: Basic Books, 1969.

Murray, Charles. "The War on Poverty." *Wilson Quarterly* 8, no. 4 (autumn 1984): 94–136.

Nanus, Sarah Eisen. " 'My Mom Can't Feed Our Family." *Seventeen,* September 2004, p. 172.

Nash, Gary B. "Up from the Bottom in Franklin's Philadelphia." *Past and Present,* no. 77 (November 1977): 56–83.

Nash, Jay B. "Camps Fight Malnutrition." *Indians at Work* 1, no. 1, p. 6.

"National Youth Administration." *The Eleanor Roosevelt Papers: The Human Rights Years.* Available online. URL: http://www.gwu.edu/~erpapers/abouteleanor/q-and-a/glossary/nya.htm. Downloaded on February 20, 2005.

Neill, Jon, ed. *Poverty and Inequality: The Political Economy of Redistribution.* Kalamazoo, Mich.: W. E. Upjohn Institute for Employment Research, 1997.

Newman, Katherine S. *No Shame in My Game: The Working Poor in the Inner City.* New York: Alfred A. Knopf, 1999.

New-York Association for Improving the Condition of the Poor. *Eighth Annual Report.* New York: John F. Trow, 1851.

———. *Thirteenth Annual Report.* New York: John F. Trow, 1856.

New York Five Points House of Industry. Monthly Record 1, no. 1. New York: Published at the Institution, May 1857.

"1917 Immigration Act." *Spartacus Educational.* Available online. URL: http://www.spartacus.schoolnet.co.uk/USAE1917A.htm. Downloaded on January 22, 2005.

Northup, Solomon. *Twelve Years a Slave.* New York: C. M. Saxton, 1859.

"NPR/Kaiser/Kennedy School Poll on Poverty in America." *Kaiser Family Foundation.* Available online. URL: http://www.kff.org/kaiserpolls/loader.cfm?url=/commonspot/security/getfile.cfm&Page ID=13806. Downloaded on June 24, 2005.

Official Documents, Addresses, Etc., of George Opdyke, Mayor of the City of New York, During the Years 1862 and 1863. New York: Hurd and Houghton, 1866.

Olmsted, Frederick Law. *A Journey in the Back Country in the Winter of 1853–4.* Vol. 1. New York: G. P. Putnam's Sons, 1907.

O'Malley, Padraig, ed. *Homelessness: New England and Beyond.* Amherst, Mass.: John W. McCormack Institute of Public Affairs, 1992.

Ornati, Oscar. *Poverty amid Affluence: A Report on a Research Project Carried Out at the New School for Social Research.* New York: Twentieth Century Fund, 1966.

Orshansky, Mollie. "Children of the Poor." *Social Security Bulletin* 26, no. 7 (July 1963): 3–13.

Oskison, J. M. "Making an Individual of the Indian." *Everybody's Magazine,* June 1907, 723–33.

Osofsky, Gilbert. "The Enduring Ghetto." *Journal of American History* 55, no. 2 (September 1968): 243–55.

Owens, William A. *This Stubborn Soil: A Frontier Boyhood.* New York: Lyons Press, 1986.

Oxnam, G. Bromley. "The Mexican in Los Angeles from the Standpoint of the Religious Forces of the City." *Annals of the American Academy of Political and Social Science* 93, no. 1 (January 1921): 130–33.

Padelford, Philip, ed. *Colonial Panorama, 1775: Dr. Robert Honyman's Journal for March and April.* San Marino, Calif.: Huntington Library, 1939.

Paine, Thomas. *Agrarian Justice.* London: T. G. Ballard, 1797.

Panken, Jacob. "I Say Relief Is Ruining Families. *Saturday Evening Post,* 30 September 1950, pp. 25, 111–15.

Pannell, W. W. "Tenant Farming in the United States." *International Socialist Review* 16, no. 7 (January 1916): 421–22.

Patterson, Caleb Perry. *The Negro in Tennessee, 1790–1865.* New York: Negro Universities Press, 1968.

Patterson, James T. *America's Struggle against Poverty in the Twentieth Century.* Cambridge, Mass.: Harvard University Press, 2000.

Pencak, William. "The Social Structure of Revolutionary Boston: Evidence from the Great Fire of 1760." *Journal of Interdisciplinary History* 10, vol. 2 (autumn 1979): 267–78.

Penman, John Simpson. *Poverty: The Challenge to the Church.* Boston: Pilgrim Press, 1915.

Peterson, Arthur Everett. *New York as an Eighteenth Century Municipality, Prior to 1731.* New York: Columbia University, 1917.

Philanthropy and Social Progress. New York: Thomas Y. Crowell and Co., 1893.

Pinkney, Alphonso. *The Myth of Black Progress.* Cambridge: Cambridge University Press, 1984.

Pleck, Elizabeth. B*lack Migration and Poverty: Boston 1865–1900.* New York: Academic Press, 1979.

Polit, Denise F., et al. *Is Work Enough? The Experience of Current and Former Welfare Mothers Who Work.* New York: Manpower Demonstration Research Corporation, 2001.

Proceedings of the Section on Organization of Charity of the National Conference of Charities and Correction. St. Paul, Minn.: Pioneer Press, 1897.

"The Public Business." *Fortune,* March 1961, 101–2.

Quinby, G. W. *The Gallows, the Prison, and the Poor-House.* Cincinnati: G. W. Quinby, 1856.

Reid, Whitelaw. *After the War: A Southern Tour, May 1, 1865, to May 1, 1866.* Cincinnati and New York: Moore, Wilstach and Baldwin, 1866.

Report of the Committee of Merchants for the Relief of Colored People, Suffering from the Late Riots in the City of New York. New York: G. A. Whitehorne, 1863.

Reynolds, Marcus T. *The Housing of the Poor in American Cities.* College Park. Md.: McGrath Publishing Co., 1969.

Rezneck, Samuel. "The Depression of 1819–1822, a Social History." *American Historical Review* 39, no. 1 (October 1933): 28–47.

Richmond, J. F. *New York and Its Institutions, 1609–1871.* New York: E. B. Trent, 1871.

Richmond, Mary E. *Friendly Visiting among the Poor: A Handbook for Charity Workers.* New York: Macmillan Co., 1899.

Riis, Jacob. *The Children of the Poor.* New York: Garrett Press, 1970.

———. *How the Other Half Lives.* Boston: Bedford Books, 1996.

Rogovin, Milton. *Milton Rogovin: The Forgotten Ones.* New York: Quantuck Lane Press, 2003.

———. *Milton Rogovin: The Mining Photographs.* New York: J. Paul Getty Museum, 2005.

Rose, Nancy E. "Work Relief in the 1930s and the Origins of the Social Security Act." *Social Service Review* 63, no. 1 (March 1989): 61–91.

Ross, Arthur M., and Herbert Hill, eds. *Employment, Race, and Poverty.* New York: Harcourt, Brace & World, 1967.

Rothman, David J. *The Discovery of the Asylum.* New York: Aldine de Gruyter, 1990.

Rustin, Bayard. "Are Blacks Better Off Today?" *Atlantic,* October 1984, 121–23.

Salstrom, Paul. *Appalachia's Path to Dependency: Rethinking a Region's Economic History, 1730–1940.* Lexington: University of Kentucky Press, 1994.

Schneider, David M. *The History of Public Welfare in New York State,* 1609–1866. Chicago: University of Chicago Press, 1938.

———. "The Patchwork of Relief in Colonial New York, 1664–1775." *Social Service Review* 12, no. 3 (September 1938): 464–94.

Schultz, Ronald. *The Republic of Labor: Philadelphia Artisans and the Politics of Class, 1720–1830.* New York: Oxford University Press, 1993.

Seligman, Ben B., ed. *Poverty as a Public Issue.* New York: Free Press, 1965.

Shumway, Harry. *I Go South: An Unprejudiced Visit to a Group of Cotton Mills.* Boston: Houghton Mifflin, 1930.

Smith, Billy G., ed. *Down and out in Early America.* University Park: Pennsylvania State University Press, 2004.

———, ed. *Life in Early Philadelphia.* University Park: Pennsylvania State University Press, 1995.

Smith, Matthew Hale. *Sunshine and Shadow in New York.* Hartford, Conn.: J. B. Burr and Co., 1869.

Southern Regional Council. *Hungry Children.* Atlanta: Southern Regional Council, 1967.

Stack, Carol B. *All Our Kin: Strategies for Survival in a Black Community.* New York: Harper & Row, 1974.

Staff of the Subcommittee on Low-Income Families, Joint Committee on the Economic Report. *Low-Income Families and Economic Stability.* Washington, D.C.: Government Printing Office, 1950.

Stafford, Ward. *New Missionary Field: A Report to the Female Missionary Society for the Poor of the City of New-York and Its Vicinity, at Their Quarterly Prayer Meeting, March, 1817.* New York: Clayton and Kingsland, 1817.

State Relief Administration of California. *Transients in California.* San Francisco: n.p., 1936.

"Statement on U.S. Census Income and Poverty Data." *Center for Community Change.* Available online. URL: http://www.communitychange.org/press/releases/?page=082604. Downloaded on October 31, 20006.

A Statistical Inquiry into the Condition of the People of Colour of the City and Districts of Philadelphia. Philadelphia: Kite and Walton, 1848.

Stevenson, Robert Alston. "The Poor in Summer." *Scribner's Magazine,* September 1901, pp. 259–77.

Steward, Austin. *Twenty-two Years a Slave, and Forty Years a Freeman.* New York: Negro Universities Press, 1968.

Stuart, Paul. "United States Indian Policy: From the Dawes Act to the American Indian Policy Review Commission." *Social Service Review* 51, no. 3 (September 1977): 451–63.

Thernstrom, Stephan. "Is There Really a New Poor?" *Dissent* 15, no. 1 (January–February 1968): 59–64.

Tobin, James. "It Can Be Done! Conquering Poverty in the US by 1976." *New Republic,* 3 June 1967, 14–18.

Toulmin, Harry. *The Western Country in 1793: Reports on Kentucky and Virginia.* San Marino, Calif.: Henry E. Huntington Library and Art Gallery, 1948.

Tower, Philo. *Slavery Unmasked.* New York: Negro Universities Press, 1969.

Tracy, L. Jane. "The Onondaga Hill Poorhouse Story." *Town of Onondaga Historical Society.* Available online. URL: www.townononhist.org/poorhousenarr.htm. Downloaded on May 8, 2004.

Trattner, Walter I. *From Poor Law to Welfare State: A History of Social Welfare in America.* 5th ed. New York: Free Press, 1994.

Trowbridge, J. T. *The South: A Tour of Its Battle-Fields and Ruined Cities.* Hartford, Conn.: L. Stebbins, 1866.

Tucker, William Jewett. "The Work of the Andover House in Boston." *Scribner's Magazine,* March 1893, 357–72.

Unemployment Committee of the National Federation of Settlements. *Case Studies of Unemployment.* Philadelphia: University of Pennsylvania Press, 1931.

U.S. Bureau of the Census. *Paupers in Almshouses, 1910.* Washington, D.C.: Government Printing Office, 1915.

U.S. Department of Housing and Urban Development. *A Report on the 1988 National Survey of Shelters for the Homeless.* Washington, D.C.: U.S. Government Printing Office, 1989.

U.S. Department of Labor, Office of Policy Planning and Research. *The Negro Family: The Case for National Action.* Washington, D.C.: U.S. Government Printing Office, 1965.

U.S. National Advisory Commission on Rural Poverty. *The People Left Behind.* Washington, D.C.: U.S. Government Printing Office, 1967.

U.S. National Emergency Council. *Report on Economic Conditions of the South.* Washington, D.C.: U.S. Government Printing Office, 1938.

Virgadamo, Peter R. "Charity for a City in Crisis: Boston, 1740 to 1775." *Historical Journal of Massachusetts* 10, no. 1 (January 1982): 22–33.

Ware, Nathaniel A. *Notes on Political Economy as Applicable to the United States by a Southern Planter.* New York: Augustus M. Kelley, 1967.

Warrior, Clyde. "We Are Not Free." *American Journey Online.* Available online. URL: http://www.americanjourney.psmedia.com/cgi-bin/aj/ajpagescan.cgi?getdoc+aj+aj_na_txt. Downloaded on April 14, 2005.

Washington, Booker T. *Up from Slavery.* New York: Signet Classic, 2000.

Waterston, R. C. *An Address on Pauperism, Its Extent, Causes, and the Best Means of Prevention.* Boston: Charles C. Little and James Brown, 1844.

Watson, Alan D. "Public Poor Relief in Colonial North Carolina." *North Carolina Historical Review* 54, no. 4 (October 1977): 347–63.

Weld, Theodore Dwight. *American Slavery as It Is: Testimony of a Thousand Witnesses.* New York: American Anti-Slavery Society, 1839.

"'We Took Away Their Best Lands, Broke Treaties': John Collier Promises to Reform Indian Policy." *History Matters.* Available online. URL: http://historymatters.gmu.edu/d/5058. Downloaded on February 21, 2005.

"What Brings the Poor People to the Capital?" *Washington Post,* May 24, 1968, p. A14.

White, Richard. *"It's Your Misfortune and None of My Own": A New History of the American West.* Norman: University of Oklahoma Press, 1991.

Whitman, Howard. "Washington—Disgrace to the Nation." *Woman's Home Companion,* February 1950, pp. 34–35, 45–48.

Wickenden, Elizabeth, and Winifred Bell. *Public Welfare: Time for a Change.* Mount Vernon, N.Y.: Golden Eagle Press, 1961.

Willard, Samuel. *A Compleat Body of Divinity.* New York: Johnson Reprint Corp., 1969.

Williams, Isaac D. *Sunshine and Shadow of Slave Life.* East Saginaw, Mich.: Evening News Printing and Binding House, 1885.

Wilson, Charles Morrow. *Corn Bread and Creek Water.* New York: Henry Holt, 1940.

Wilson, Lisa. *Life after Death: Widows in Pennsylvania, 1750–1850.* Philadelphia: Temple University Press, 1992.

Wilson, William Julius. *The Truly Disadvantaged: The Inner City, the Underclass, and Public Policy.* Chicago: University of Chicago Press, 1987.

Wisner, Elizabeth. "The Puritan Background of the New England Poor Laws." *Social Service Review* 19, no. 3 (September 1945): 381–90.

Woolsey, Jane Stuart. *Hospital Days: Reminiscence of a Civil War Nurse.* Roseville, Minn.: Edinborough Press, 1996.

Yamin, Rebecca. "New York's Mythic Slum." *Archaeology* 50, no. 2 (March–April 1997): 44–53.

Index

Locators in *italic* indicate illustrations. Locators in **boldface** indicate main entries. Locators followed by *m* indicate maps. Locators followed by *t* indicate graphs and tables. Locators followed by *g* indicate glossary entries. Locators followed by *c* indicate chronology entries.